TOWARD A NEW PSYCHOLOGY
OF GENDER

Routledge
New York and London

TOWARD A NEW PSYCHOLOGY
OF GENDER

edited by

Mary M. Gergen and Sara N. Davis

Published in 1997 by
Routledge
29 West 35th Street
New York, NY 10001

Published in
Great Britain by
Routledge
11 New Fetter Lane
London EC4P 4EE

Copyright © 1997 by
Routledge
Printed in the United
States of America on acid–
free paper.

Library of Congress Cataloging-in-Publication Data

Toward a new psychology of gender : a reader / edited by Mary M.
   Gergen & Sara N. Davis.
      p.   cm.
   ISBN 0-415-91307-1 (c1). — ISBN 0-415-91308-X (pbk.)
   1. Sex differences (Psychology) 2. Feminist psychology. 3. Sex
role—Psychological aspects. 4. Gender identity. 5. Women-
-Psychology. I. Gergen, Mary M. II. Davis, Sara N.,
BF692.2.T68   1996
155.3′3—dc20   95-52893
                                             CIP

To all those with whom we have had enriching relationships,
especially to our husbands and children.

For Sara: Bill, and Eli and Rebecca

For Mary: Ken, and Laura, Lisa, Stan, and Michael, and their families

CONTENTS

ix

x

PREFACE

WHEN WE first came together to create this book, we had a fairly clear idea of what it should be and how we could put it together. It appeared to us that there was a particular place in the psychological literature that this book should fill, and we were confident the work would flow easily. (Perhaps most such partnerships start with these illusions of simplicity and focus.) The area of psychology in which we were most interested—the psychology of women or gender studies—had produced few books that introduced and applied a "social constructionist" perspective, especially in the United States. Thus, we envisioned a reader that would bring together from the far reaches of the world (Auckland, New Zealand to Capetown, South Africa, with intermittent stops in the Northern hemisphere) work that fell into the psychological bailiwick, broadly defined, as social constructionist.

Once we were underway we relished opportunities to read widely in psychology, and also in the neighboring disciplines of sociology, cultural studies, and philosophy. We paid particular attention to work that might be of interest to scholars who teach women's studies courses because we were aware that for various historical and disciplinary reasons, women's studies and psychology, two fields that should be intertwined, are rather distant cousins, at least at the level of curriculum requirements and syllabi. Dozens of manuscripts and many versions of the table of contents later, we finally settled on the following chapters. There are many more of our favorites that rustle in our cubby holes and closets, but we had to forego those that were not as available, affordable, or accessible to as many readers as other choices; we eliminated them, often with deep regrets. Throughout these critical discussions, we are happy to report, our friendship grew, and our anxiety levels remained quite bearable. (Having a son go to college and a daughter marry during the final days before submission proved to be serious distractions, however.)

One of the criteria we used in choosing these materials is that they spoke in some special way to topics that are familiar to teachers of gender courses. So you will see something within these pages of such issues as mother-daughter relations, therapeutic methods, eating disorders, gender identity, and sexual orientation, as well as more theoretical issues of critique, research, and applications within psychology. For reasons of scholarship and expertise in social constructionism, we also conscientiously strove to include many authors from the British Commonwealth. We thought it especially important to include non-Americans, in part, as an effort to compensate for the lack of cross-fertilization of scholarship between the United States and other English speaking countries, which is often the result of publishers' agreements that restrict book sales. (Fortunately, Routledge, our publisher, is established on both sides of the Atlantic.) A certain chauvinism is also at stake in this mutual ignorance, as each enclave of English speakers takes particular interest in the writings of their own authors to the exclusion of others. We also tried to include authors who spoke to issues of "otherness," in terms of physical ability, race, ethnicity, and religious heritage.

Another choice, which we considered deeply and from many perspectives, was whether or not to invite men into the round of authors. We did, and can now justify this decision with some ease. One of our reviewers pointed out that to exclude men was to "naturalize" them, to give them status as unconstructed humans; women were the socially constructed gender. So we decided that men should be included as subjects and as authors. This decision has brought to the book new and interesting realms of study. We discovered, of course, in rounding out our lists of authors, that it is not possible to "be fair" in terms of balancing various criteria for inclusion. Most important of our considerations was our dedication to provide our readers a vision of how a social constructionist approach could enhance gender studies. Despite inevitable compromises, to this aim we remained true.

One of the omissions that you may note is that no chapters directly concern the so-called biological substratum of behavior. As editors we took the liberty of advancing our own vision of how the psychology of women or gender should be taught, and we believe that there is often too much emphasis on the biological basis of gender difference in our field. Anatomy is not (necessarily) destiny; (nor is destiny necessarily Freudian). On the other side of this argument, a good thing about a social constructionist orientation is that while you never can claim that any particular orientation is ultimately true, you never have to say "goodbye" to any theoretical framework forever.

To continue with our story of the book's development, after we had become deeply involved with the contents, we began to see how it could provide the textual basis for a course in gender studies, either in psychology or in women's studies, as well as an intriguing auxiliary text. In psychology, we envisioned that each section of the book could be the "starter dough" for various class activities, discussions, and projects that would involve specific work in various other venues, for example, in the field, on the internet, with other library materials, or in video productions. Given the social constructionist framework, any special interests or theoretical perspectives of the instructor could be added harmoniously. While there is great diversity in the offerings within this book, they are all congenial to a social constructionist position; this arrangement allows for an important kind of coherence in terminology and outlook.

For a project of this magnitude, the talents of many have been committed for many months of cooperative endeavor. For their contributions, we thank:

Philip Rappaport, former Psychology editor at Routledge, for taking a chance, and then giving us the support we needed to succeed in producing this book.

Maura E. Burnett, our developmental editor, for answering all our questions, big and small, as well as the others on the Routledge staff who made this book a reality.

The thirty-three splendid authors who responded so quickly and kindly to our requests for permissions, for editorial consultations, and for biographies. They are the stars of this show.

The many anonymous and self-identified reviewers who so enthusiastically assisted us in the shaping of our book. We wish we could have accepted *all* their excellent ideas.

Our students at Rosemont College, Swarthmore College, and Pennsylvania State University who have given us their views on many of these topics, articles, and author's ideas, and thus helped us in our selections.

Each other for the wonderful opportunity to learn how joyful collaborating can be with the right person.

In addition, Sara gives thanks to Rosemont College for encouraging this effort by providing a variety of resources, to Sr. Frances Gospill, Ann Trotter and the library staff for their bibliographic help, to Carmella DiMartino for her cheerful secretarial assistance, and to Dani Butz, student assistant, for her invaluable support. And she especially thanks her husband Bill for his continuous interest and searching questions.

Mary wishes to thank the Delaware County Campus of the Pennsylvania State University for its financial and service support, Lisa Gebhart for her daughterly advice and manuscript assistance, and her always-interruptible husband, Ken for his wise and caring counsel and wicked editorial pen.

The East and West banks of the Crum Wald Creek, Pennsylvania
September, 1995

TOWARD A NEW PSYCHOLOGY OF GENDER
Opening Conversations

Sara N. Davis and Mary Gergen

"Language inevitably structures one's own experience of reality as well as the experience of those to whom one communicates."

Rachel Hare-Mustin & Jeanne Marecek[1]

THESE ARE exciting times for those who study gender relations. Feminist scholars, including many psychologists, now question what has heretofore been accepted as scientific truth about women and men. They have examined claims to knowledge with new questions and new philosophies about what it means to gain knowledge (Butler, 1990; Harding, 1986; Oliver, 1991). They are investigating issues of self-interest and power. They ask how established views have justified or made invisible the power of some and the oppression of many, and how knowledge has benefitted some people and harmed others (Flax, 1990; Grosz, 1994; Hare-Mustin & Marecek, 1990; Hekman, 1990). Central to the concerns of these gender scholars has been a focus on language. How have the terms used to describe differences between women and

[1]Hare-Mustin, Rachel & Marecek, Jeanne (Eds.) (1990). *Making a difference, Psychology and the construction of gender.* New Haven: Yale University Press, 25.

men been influenced by sexist biases? (Gergen, 1994). Their work has provoked strong reactions, both within and beyond the academic community, as it opened the way for new understandings of the world, and of ourselves as gendered beings.

Within this book, we have gathered together a collection of work that we believe lies at the cutting edge of feminist scholarship, work that challenges psychological traditions, but at the same time attempts to generate alternatives. Yet even as we commend this collection we recognize that its meanings are not sealed within the borders of these pages. What these words mean—what importance they have—depends upon the reader as their co-construer. As such, the book is both an invitation and a challenge to the reader, an invitation to enter this exciting world, to enjoy the prospects that these authors bring to gender studies. It is also a challenge to join this endeavor yourself, and with the support of these chapters, generate new perspectives of gendered relations and new practices within science and society. As Brenda Marshall[2] has said, "What is at stake in our readings, our interpretations? It's not just a game. Every interpretation is a political move." So too are your responses to these pages.

FEMINIST PSYCHOLOGY: A GLANCE BACKWARD

The basic commitment of feminist psychologists from many backgrounds has been to overcome the commonplace stereotypes of gender differences, and to eradicate the biases that suppress women in society. They have taken several different scientific paths to achieve this goal. Following the work of philosopher Sandra Harding (1986), we can describe three such paths in the field of gender studies in psychology today, and gain a better appreciation of the particular character of this book.

The traditional path, still predominant in much of psychology, is the empiricist one. Here the scientist sets out to study events in the world, to collect data in a reliable and valid manner, and to report these findings objectively. The empirical study of sex differences dates to the early part of the century, and already the feminist voice could be heard, often objecting to the practices of other researchers.

Two early feminist psychologists who attacked the traditional wisdoms of the field were Helen Thompson Woolley and Leta Hollingworth. Woolley criticized the sex difference research then practiced for being the codification of male biases against women. For example, psychologists, as well as other scholars, believed that too much intense brain activity, as required by higher education, would enfeeble the reproductive capacities of women, and thus

[2]Marshall, Brenda K. (1992). *Teaching the postmodern*, New York: Routledge, 192.

women were unsuitable candidates for professional degrees. Leta Holling-worth also challenged the prevailing wisdom; she argued that sex difference research was founded on few significant results, despite efforts by psychologists to emphasize differences, and this research tended to segregate the sexes into the categories of "well-adjusted males" and "maladjusted females" (Morawski, 1994).

Despite these critiques of early research efforts to define sex differences, the effort to find scientific evidence that differentiated the sexes continued unabated over the century. The earliest major summary of this work covering the first sixty years of the century in the United States was *The Psychology of Sex Differences* (Maccoby and Jacklin, 1974). In their conclusions, these editors, in agreement with Woolley and Hollingworth, found few well-documented differences between the sexes. Thereafter, more sophisticated quantitative methods, such meta-analysis, were developed; yet, despite the capacity to increase the scope and precision of the measurements, researchers discovered few significant differences in psychological variables between the sexes (Eagly, 1987; Hyde & Linn, 1986).

Although empirical studies are still the most prevalent form of inquiry within gender studies in psychology, limitations to this method of research have been noted. Most importantly, some have argued that empirical research disrupts the contextualized nature of subjects' lives. Ideally, from the empirical point of view, subjects are taken out of their normal environments and placed in a situation designed by the researcher. In order to maintain scientific rigor, the scientist controls as many aspects of the research situation as possible, and then manipulates significant variables in order to discover the causal relations among variables. Studying "real" people in their ordinary settings is not ideal for developing scientifically sophisticated results, from the empiricist viewpoint. Critics argue that this method of research interferes with the utility of the results (Curt, 1994; Fonow & Cook, 1991; Gergen, 1988); they are not about real people in their life circumstances, but are artifacts of scientific manipulations. Empirical research practices also discourage any relationship between the scientist and subject, thus people are objectified (as "things") for research purposes. Empirical researchers also believe that research methods should be value-neutral in order to avoid the danger of any politicized interest influencing the subjects within the experimental setting. Rather than trying to solve immediate practical problems, empirical scientists argue that they are testing scientific hypotheses drawn from theory, not exploring everyday life (Gergen, 1988). While there are many advantages to the empirical method, these limitations have encouraged some feminist psychologists to attempt other approaches to increasing knowledge within the field.

An important alternative to the empirical approach is identified as the

DAVIS AND GERGEN

3

Feminist Standpoint Position (Harding, 1986).[3] This position emphasizes the importance of knowledge-gathering as a personal activity, in which the researcher and the researched are recognized as in relation to one another. Both must take into account their own experiences, gained from their own perspectives, not from some universal standpoint, the so-called "God's eye view," which the objectivity-seeking empirical psychologists value (Haraway, 1988). In the United States, the most well-known exponents of the feminist standpoint position in psychology are psychologist, Carol Gilligan and her colleagues. Gilligan's classic book, *In a Different Voice*, emphasized the capacity of women to speak from their own experiences (1982). Many standpoint psychologists have studied individual experiences as a way to enrich the psychology of women, while also indirectly challenging the validity of traditional scientific methods. In rejecting the negativity of the traditional stereotypes of women, Feminist Standpoint researchers have often celebrated women's special natures, and thus, have emphasized rather than denied important differences between the sexes (Daly, 1978; Hartsock, 1983).

Empiricist psychologists have both benefitted from and criticized the views of standpoint psychologists. Many scientific psychologists have faulted the feminist standpoint researchers for the lack of scientific rigor and objectivity in their work. The standpoint theorists have also been criticized for their essentialist views of women, that is views that suggest that women are either born different from men, or inevitably must become so. Others question the feminist standpoint notion that personal narratives can serve as the final arbiter of "truth."

While many feminists have accepted women's differences from men, especially as they are celebrated in many standpoint theories, there is also a wariness among some feminist psychologists that widening the gaps between men and women in terms of basic human qualities may initiate stereotyped thinking and the rigidifying of social segregation. If, for example, women are found to be more nurturant than men, can they make difficult and important decisions? Should they be allowed to become police officers, attend military academies or run for President, who is Commander in Chief of all the Armed Services, if they are so nurturant?

With numerous doubts about past practices, many feminists have sought ways of working that would capitalize on the strengths of each of these positions, but at the same time alter our understanding of how they contribute to the field. In adding richness and dimension to feminist inquiry, this new posi-

---

[3]Of particular importance to feminist scholarship, in general, and European psychology, in particular, has been the influence of those who developed Marxist-based explanations of the oppression of women. These feminists can be found across the spectrum of epistemological positions described here; for a variety of historical reasons, they have generally had little impact on American psychology.

tion also links psychology to other feminist studies, thus giving it a voice in broader fields of inquiry. Compelled by the view of science and knowledge as human inventions, these scholars join many others in the sciences and humanities in a social constructionist orientation.

SOCIAL CONSTRUCTION IN THE FOREGROUND

"The danger of thinking you know it all is at no time greater than when it comes to grasping hold of definitions." Diane Elam[4]

As Diane Elam suggests in this quotation, it is always dangerous to define something. And although there are many differences and disagreements among feminist scholars who call themselves social constructionists, one theme provides a broad accord. This is the awareness of science as a communal achievement. To help you evaluate the contributions appearing in this volume, a description of the core features of social constructionism are set forth.

1. Central to the social constructionist position is the view that "facts" are dependent upon the language communities that have created and sustained them. Social constructionists argue that all forms of naming are socially constructed, including seemingly basic biological categories, such as the female—male sex distinction (Butler, 1990; 1993). The social constructionist stance is at odds with our everyday notions that sex is an essential biologically-based distinction. Talking about "the sexes" is an important way of making sense within our world, and it is not easy to imagine that this distinction is arbitrary or that we could eliminate it from our vocabularies (Fuss, 1989; Hekman, 1990). While on the surface it may seem absurd to argue against "the reality" of basic biological sex differences, recall that "women" have been ejected from the Olympics in recent years for lacking the proper chromosomal indicators proving that the athlete in question is actually female. This determination of sex, as provided by chromosome measurements, can result in a person being *declared* "male," despite all other indicators that the person *is* a woman. In terms of a psychology of gender, the findings concerning gender differences and the nature of women and men are intimately connected to the scientific communities that advance them. The social constructionist position does not imply that such facts are, therefore, useless or invalid; on the contrary, they are used by people to make sense of their lives (Kitzinger, 1987; Marecek, 1995).

2. People generate their truth from languages available to them. Thus, any "fact" about the world depends upon the language within which it is expressed. Things are known through their names. Words do not simply "map" or "copy" the world; they create how we perceive the world. The impact of

DAVIS AND GERGEN

5

---

[4]Diane Elam (1994) *Feminism and deconstruction Ms. en Abyme*. New York: Routledge. p. 4.

this view on a psychology of gender is that terms of understanding within the field are open to question and reconstruction. Some feminist social constructionists, for example, have challenged the ways in which the sexes have often been described as "opposites" (Butler, 1990; Hekman, 1990). Constructionists ask whether psychologists, for example, should accept the notion that the basic polarities of the discipline—man vs. woman; male vs. female; and masculine vs. feminine—are the most important distinctions to study? They ask: do we always, everywhere, or anywhere, want to accept these dichotomies? What are the social costs in doing so? At the same time as questions such as these should be asked, the social constructionist does not require questioning every choice in every situation. Sometimes one may emphasize sex differences, and sometimes one may minimize them (Gergen, 1993). For example, in cases of job equity, arguing gender differences may (or may not) be essential to the effort of ensuring the rights of women (Farganis, 1994).

Within the psychology of gender, and in other disciplines, women of color have objected to the manner in which non-colored women have claimed to speak for all women, without taking the differences among women into account. Social constructionist ideas have been liberating to those who struggle with the difficulties of being defined by others, without suggesting that there is only one proper way to be defined. As bell hooks has said, social constructionist "thought is useful for African Americans concerned with reformulating outmoded notions of identity. We have too long had imposed upon us from both the outside and the inside a narrow, constricting notion of blackness."[5] We are reminded that there are multiple ways of giving words to create worlds, and no one way is the only way.

3. The social constructionist position implies that any type of description of the nature of reality is dependent upon the historical and cultural location of that description. Every culture has its own notions of the "real." How ancient Greek or Roman philosophers described the members of a household was influenced by whether they had the status of free men or women and slaves, for example; their written passages are filled with distinctions between free men and women and slaves that do not "make sense" to us. In addition, within any subculture, even within the same historical and general cultural period, groups of people have different distinctions that are useful for them, but might not be sensible to outsiders. People who are heavily involved in body piercing and tattooing, for example, adhere to standards of fashion, physical beauty, and body boundaries that differ from people who are not involved in these practices. Because there are many such linguistic groups, even within one locale, the opportunities for different images of the good, the true, and the beautiful are great. The social constructionist position helps to over-

DAVIS AND GERGEN

6

[5]bell hooks, (1990). *Yearnings, race, gender, and cultural politics*. Boston: South End Press. 28.

come the conflicts that may occur when different versions of reality come into contention. From this position, it is possible to acknowledge the multiplicity of worldviews, and to work toward creating conditions wherein the separate parties can find opportunities for mutuality, tolerance, and compromise.

4. Social constructionists generally hold that there are no universal ethical principles, but that they are constituted within so-called "language games" and sustained by discrete social communities (Elam, 1994).[6] Thus, there is no single way to set ethical standards, but there may be many. In this sense a social constructionist position is congenial with the standpoint position represented by Gilligan, in that there is no hierarchy of universal moral principles that gives preference to justice considerations over caring. From the social constructionist approach, there are no answers to moral dilemmas that are independent of communities. Despite the inadmissibility of foundational principles, the social constructionist position has strong implications for moral inquiry and action (Gergen, 1995). A concern with the nature of values is intrinsic to a feminist social constructionist position, and when one evaluates a scientific explanation one can ask what are the ethical considerations that are embedded in the framing of the explanation, its origins, its classification system, and its consequences. One cannot ignore value considerations and claim that one is "merely reporting the facts." Because facts are socially constructed, they are always subject to questioning for their ethical implications. This is consistent with the political goals of feminism.

5. Social constructionists emphasize that any claims to reality can be viewed with skepticism. Unlike some scientific viewpoints that claim that we can know the facts about the world by merely looking (or smelling, tasting, touching, or listening), the social constructionist position emphasizes that our sensory experiences are mediated by our linguistic descriptions of our experiences (Burr, 1995). That is, we know our sensory worlds via language, just as we know the abstract world. The social constructionist position does not allow exceptions to this skeptical stance, even when one's private sensory experiences are at stake. We cannot know ourselves, free of cultural constraints, any more than we can know other parts of the world. We must always recognize ourselves as embedded in cultural communities. One can ask questions about the world, but cannot claim to have discovered the truth. The best one can expect is that a new interpretation, a different perspective, or an interesting slant can be created. In this sense social constructionism invites creativity, new interpretations, and an openness to other fields of knowledge. Whether a new interpretation becomes acceptable depends importantly upon others in the linguistic community.

7

---

[6]A term used by philosopher Ludwig Wittgenstein to refer to the coordinated ways we have of speaking together.

CONTEXTUALIZING SOCIAL CONSTRUCTIONISM: THE CASE OF "FAMILY VALUES"

Once words gain usage in the culture, it is often difficult to imagine that they create rather than reflect a given reality in the world. If we investigate the nature of a relatively new phrase, we can more easily see the constructed nature of a reality. Let us consider the phrase, "family values," a widely used political slogan that in the 90s has become a code word for a certain kind of family unit. By evaluating this phrase, one can gain a sense of how language works to shape our notions of reality.

"Family Values" is most often used today to suggest a general good. While once it may have been a phrase that would bring up a question as to what kinds of values a family might have, or a question of how much families were valued as a social unit, a shift has taken place such that "family values" has become defined more narrowly. Although never specifically defined, this slogan functions to suggest that good family values are found in a single kind of family: middle-class, with few children, a mother at home, engaged in childrearing and other "non-work" activity, and a strong father, who is the major wage-earner. The family is invested with Northern European cultural, social, and religious values. The use of this term in a persistent and strategic manner by conservative politicians, especially, has had the effect of denigrating anyone who does not fit this mold. Note that while apparently saying something good, which is designed to encompass all people, the phrase has evolved so as to belittle and exclude those who do not conform.

The deployment of this concept within our culture raises some serious concerns from a social constructionist position.[7] If our description above is an adequate framing of the phrase, (and some of those who use this term might argue about that), many important questions may be asked. How can a single model of family adequately serve a diverse, heterogeneous society? Who gains power by supporting this model for family life? Will those who do not fit this definition be considered sufficiently unworthy that valuable resources will be withheld from them? What opportunities does adherence to this model open or deny to women? What other ways of viewing the world become invisible?

Some answers are immediately apparent. Adherence to a single model denies the richness and diversity of the culture. If people have only one version of family life to follow they become limited in the vision of their lives. Women's ambitions to careers and men's desires to be primarily family-oriented are thwarted. One's failure to meet the standards of the correct family values may result in punishment, for example, being eliminated from welfare

DAVIS AND GERGEN

---

[7]We do not mean to imply that these questions could not be asked from a variety of other intellectual and value positions. Marxists, for example, could ask questions of a similar nature to some of these.

rolls, losing medical care benefits, and so forth. Politicians who favor this rhetoric can appear to be supporting positive social values and decrying the impact of "bad families" on society. The result of insinuating the universality of family values into the society produces a narrow and rigid version of families, in which diversity cannot be accommodated. The concept of family values functions in a way that attempts to unite people behind a single shared vision, in which traditional sex roles are legitimated and extended, at the cost of alternatives. For many people, both those squeezed within this one form of life, and those squeezed out of it, the results are negative. Yet, because of the repetitious rehearsal of this phrase within the public arena, this restricted notion of what is the good life slips into the vocabulary and becomes a part of our social reality.

In the arena of gender studies, terms such as "family values" become insinuated into forms of speech, and shape how men and women live together. Several chapters in the book illustrate how various forms of language have restricted people's lives.

CONSTRUCTIONIST EMPHASES IN THE PRESENT VOLUME

As editors of this book, our intentions are to bring to diverse audiences readings in which the authors have expanded the boundaries and potentials of psychology. We invite our readers to come together in this circle where different intellectual trends converge. Scholars from sociology, philosophy, education, anthropology, sexology, family therapy, and elsewhere have added a voice in this colloquy on gender issues. While they have come from many backgrounds, and many theoretical and feminist positions, they all have enriched a social constructionist form of work. While each of the chapters, briefly described below, is unique, the authors have related to their materials in ways that unite them. We think five qualities in particular give them a coherence with one another.

1. *Reflexivity in their approach to their subject matters*. Far from attempting to hide their own involvement in their projects, these authors frequently reflect on their own position with respect to the context of their work. They ask themselves: Who am I with respect to the respondents, how do I understand the social customs described here? What are the consequences to others if I present information in a particular fashion? This reflexivity enables them to participate with subjects in relationships with a high degree of openness, and to use these experiences to help organize their understandings with a sense of commitment to their values about gender relations.

The authors' reflexive forms of writing also provide an entry into the text for readers, allowing them to develop a questioning attitude toward the contents and conclusions the authors are advancing. Usually authors try to seal their texts against this type of intrusion. In this sense readers are encouraged to raise questions about the author's views, to develop their own syntheses of the materials, as well as to develop greater reflexivity about their own positions.

2. *Knowledge claims are seen as continually developing, never reaching a permanent endstate.* As evidence of this stance, several of our authors rethink the assumptions that guided earlier work and how they would now structure the text differently. They understand that a particular piece of research or theory grows out of a common intellectual understanding in a particular historical period. When a particular ethos changes, new ways of constructing materials develop, which may surpass the old in some fashion. In general, mainstream psychologists do not expect to scrutinize the linguistic conventions that govern their research and writing, the historical period in which they have collected data, or the political implications of their work. This type of reflection, if it happens at all, occurs outside of the research arena and separated from the research itself (Eagly, 1995). The emerging view, in contrast, is that work should be constantly under review from diverse political and social positions. One recognizes that every choice within the development of a research condition or form of reporting is open to critical evaluation and possible alteration.

3. *The authors continually affirm that they and all with whom they are working are identified with particular groups that influence their own formations.* Most particularly, the authors attend to the ways in which gender, class, ethnicity, sexual orientations, ableness, and other personal qualities combine to influence their own discourses. In many instances, an author claims a personal vantage point, and then grapples with its utility and its limitations for understanding others. At times authors may want to transcend their vantage points, but be unable to do so. Locating one's own social class boundaries, for example, may help to explain one's understanding of a particular issue and one's ways of relating to others.

4. *The search for new forms of cultural life is a central focus.* In everyday life we seldom question common sense language and its many uses. Each morning when the alarm clock goes off, we cannot spend several minutes considering Einstein's theory of relativity as it relates to time. Because the notion of clock-time is so deeply embedded in our daily lives, it is difficult to recognize its constructed nature. It has been the role of feminists to heighten our awareness of many of these common sense ideas, and especially to show the ways in which they can function in a subtle manner to oppress women, as well as men. In this vein, many common words and expressions,—the term *mankind*, for example—are unpacked to expose them for the multiple agendas they carry and the ways that they benefit some people over others. Equally important is the opportunity to create new linguistic forms that can reorganize, refresh, and alter existing ways of living (Lather, 1995). Within these readings illustrations of these efforts to create new ways of talking abound.

5. *Research endeavors should be contextualized so as to enhance their usefulness to*

10

DAVIS AND GERGEN

that psychologists adopt a discourse model in which one can analyze the many contradictory aspects of the person. In an example, she describes the repertoires apparent in the responses of undergraduates when questioned about their understandings of career, children, employment, and achievement. The method of discourse analysis reflected the many conflicting messages prevailing in our society that would not have been accessible to more conventional methods of analysis.

III. CHALLENGING DIFFERENCES: CULTURAL CONSTRAINTS AND NARRATIVES OF LIVES

The four articles presented in this section deal with the questions raised by the concept of gender difference itself. While acknowledging the fact that female/male exist powerfully as categories in our society, they question the utility and accuracy of seeing the world through this lens. A focus on gender differences frequently precludes looking at the ways in which the genders are alike. It also suppresses analyses that favor other categorical factors that may be equally important as organizing units: race, class, sexual orientation, ethnicity, ableness, and so forth. Gender has typically been described and utilized as a fundamental category. These articles deconstruct this approach.

The metaphor of "performance" is central to Valerie Walkerdine's description of women's struggles to fulfill socially prescribed, but oppositional positionings, in the academic arena. The difficulties of this stance are coupled with culturally-imposed notions of femininity. If our conceptions of gender require a splitting of roles, with rationality the domain of the man and emotionality that of the woman, a capable woman must be able to demonstrate both sets of attributes without threatening the underpinnings of patriarchy. Walkerdine deconstructs notions of difference that often pass as fact in our society. It has frequently been documented that people attribute inherent ability to boys, whether or not their performance warrants it but assume that girls achieve as a result of hard work, not ability. This bifurcation is especially prevalent with regard to mathematical performance. These apparent differences are necessitated in a society that requires that woman be constructed as the "other." Therefore, any effort to empirically demonstrate that women can perform equally well in math will miss the point that this attributed lack of rationality among women leaves men as the sole possessors of the ability to control the "calculable universe."

A similar stance is taken by Barrie Thorne when she questions the emphasis many place on gender difference. She notes that, typically, the gender researcher observing classes of young school children will select gendered groups and then describe the different ways in which boys and girls play. For someone interested in studying gender, the way boys and girls are organized in opposition becomes an obvious point of description. However, her observations reveal that this fixation leads one to neglect other meaningful config-

15

urations. She found that in the fourth/fifth grade classroom in which she observed, there were also many instances in which boys and girls mixed during the school day, including voluntarily during the play period. Although she observed a dominant male group that followed the pattern that has typically been attributed to boys, there were other boys who played in small dyadic and triadic groups that were more typical of girls' patterns. In some cases, ethnic links or situational factors proved to be more compelling for guiding the choice of playmates than gender. While acknowledging that our frameworks for studying adults have been expanded as a result of feminist theorizing, Thorne argues that we still continue to box children into static gender categories. This overemphasizes a single unit and shifts the gaze from the many other forms of social organization. To understand children's lives we need to include the range of interactions. We must look at how gender, class, race, and ethnicity interact and affect each other. Researchers can profit from looking at process instead of emphasizing static categorizations.

Mary Gergen is concerned with both form and content in the telling of life stories. She suggests that the traditional method of story telling and the narratives that are viewed as canonical are in fact male stories based on heroic myths. Men focus on the linear quest towards career success and unabashedly leave women and children as part of the background. Women tell a story of relationships, even in competition. Gergen's chapter poses questions regarding the layers of gendering that exist in our society. For example, if females and males are raised differently, then can we assume the differences that we observe are a product of these experiences? When women write a different story is it to be construed as a result of their own particular experiences, or is it because those are the stories made available to them by the patriarchal culture? Do women tell the story of relationship because it is expected that they will not appear openly competitive, or is that truly reflective of their lives? Gergen takes these narrative concepts further than merely describing them. In modelling a new form of story telling, she employs a nonlinear form of narrative. She allows many voices to be intermingled, creating a chorus rather than a solo voice.

Competing myths of masculinity are of interest to Michael Kimmel. He argues there are dominant myths to which men in our society aspire, yet the typical developmental trajectory makes these difficult to attain. As a result, men work to assume outward trappings of prowess and power with the hope that these will hide their more complex and vulnerable internal feelings. He believes that today the most prevalent myth is what he calls *Marketplace Manhood*, in which manhood is defined in terms of the accumulation of wealth, power, and status. This vision of manhood demands demonstrations of power that complement exclusionary attitudes as a way of bolstering one's self image. It creates the constant need to separate oneself by dominating the many "others": women, ethnic minorities, homosexuals, and so forth to insure that one sustains a dominant position. Living with the constant fear of being revealed as unmanly, today's man dissociates himself from what he believes are feminine attributes of emotion and weakness. In order to be viewed as tough, men exaggerate masculine shows of dominance that are "intimately interwoven with both sexism and racism."

IV. OPEN TO INTERPRETATION: MULTIPLE LENSES

The five articles in this section demonstrate the power of multiple interpretations on the construction of reality. Rather than locking oneself in a single perspective, one that produces a narrow view, many positions can be entertained. In many instances a single, unmarked point of view organizes interpretations for us. In three instances, authors Lama Abu Odeh, Nancy Datan, and Laura Brown, make clear how their own life positions led them to consider certain situations in particular ways. However, their openness to multiple interpretations enabled them, to see the difficulties in sustaining any single position. Mary Crawford demonstrates the power of multiple positionings by showing how a reader would form different views of a book, depending on what epistemological perspective guided the book review. Dafna Izraeli demonstrates that when a single vantage point controls the dissemination of a world view, we get a truncated picture.

Lama Abu Odeh, as a modern Arab woman, eschews wearing the veil herself, but recognizes how it might be a significant and positive act for other Arab women. Acknowledging her own position, she is open to investigating the multiple meanings carried by the veil within the Arab culture. In exploring these meanings she engages in a process of finding her similarities and differences from the women who have chosen the veil. She thus describes her work as "a personal journey of exploration and reflection." What is particularly noteworthy is that the adoption of the veil reflects fundamentalist shifts within Arab societies. On one level its purpose is to veil or hide the female body. However, paradoxically, it also represents a certain freedom for women who participate in the public world by shielding them from unwanted attentions. Furthermore, there is no simple dichotomy between the ideas of those who have chosen to adopt this mode of dress and those who continue to wear Western attire. What Odeh finds is that between the most radical positions are many shades of difference in which women are engaged in balancing many competing ideologies.

Dafna Izraeli anchors her description of *Beit Hatefusot*, a major Israeli museum, in ideas about the transmission of culture. This museum fills an important educational role in Israel—it is visited by most school children and is required viewing for soldiers in training. Izraeli believes that culture is transmitted to the ordinary people by specialists who have control over certain forms of the media. She rejects the idea that culture simply evolves from the lives of ordinary people. Therefore, she argues that the museum functions in a pre-

17

DAVIS AND GERGEN

scriptive manner and that the "reality" of Jewish life as it is presented in the exhibits will come to stand for Jewish history. In her description of the *Beit Hatefusot* museum she demonstrates how, as the museum traces the life of the average Jewish person, the role of women is strangely absent or marginalized. Thus, when portraits of men appear they tend to be of specific great and wise men. The few portraits of women tend to be of generic women only, e.g., "Jewess from Morocco." Izraeli concludes that when an influential museum presents a message that marginalizes women, the general perception of women is influenced. In contrast to the power of official messages like this, the evolving experience of women would be less influential.

Mary Crawford addresses the validity of two epistemological positions: feminist empiricism and the feminist standpoint view. She applies each perspective in the evaluation of a single highly influential book, *Women's Ways of Knowing*, by Belenky, Clinchy, Goldberger, & Tarule. Based on in-depth and freely-structured interviews of women, the authors of this book describe five epistemological positions through which women develop and evaluate their beliefs about the world. Crawford's overall goal is to demonstrate that using a different interpretive framework will yield very different impressions of a body of research. Crawford initially approaches the book through the lens of the feminist empiricist approach. Adherents of this position have prominently critiqued much sex difference research by arguing that many of the differences that arise are the result of faulty research. Good and unbiased research is likely to minimize the differences. Have the authors of *Women's Ways of Knowing* been able to conduct research that minimizes the problems typically associated with gender difference research? Crawford finds many methodological problems have confounded this research. This leads her to the conclusion that it may never be possible to overcome the problems of traditional empiricist research suggested by feminists. By demonstrating the difficulties involved in eliminating these problems, she concludes that the empiricist approach may not be a useful strategy for feminist psychologists. From this perspective, then, the book does not fare well. Taking another epistemological stance, Crawford describes the feminist standpoint position that promotes the idea that women, because of their special life circumstances, develop a unique perspective and have new and more accurate perspectives to bring to the research. Applying criteria from standpoint epistemology, Crawford finds that *Women's Ways of Knowing* yields insights that would be obscured from the empiricist point of view. Where empiricists seek to minimize difference, standpoint researchers seek out and value the differences. The book lives up to the promise offered by the standpoint epistemologists. However, these theorists must live with questions about the essentialized nature of their research.

Reflecting on the assumptions that guided her research with two colleagues a decade earlier, Nancy Datan describes the ways that life experiences and ideologies generated the hypotheses that guided their research. This research was an investigation into the ways that women in five different Israeli subcultures handled the onset of menopause. Her male colleagues, with some demographic data to support them, believed that menopause would be far more stressful to women who had borne few children than those women who had maximized their fertility by producing large families. Datan, on the other hand, felt that women who had developed options in life in addition to motherhood would be better prepared for the changes of menopause. Much to their surprise, they discovered that all the women were quite happy with the onset of menopause. Datan reflects on how the researchers' own life circumstances influenced what they were able to imagine about their interviewees. This led Datan to further reflection on how biases become confirmed in our thinking and stimulated her to re-examine the meanings of the Orthodox Jewish rituals surrounding menstruation. She concludes, similarly to Odeh, that one must sometimes walk in the other's path before jumping to easy conclusions guided by one's own life experiences. She highlights how her own aging process has given her new vantage points, and how one must recognize one's own position in the world, while trying to understand others.

Laura Brown poses the question of how one might view the world if the lesbian/gay perspective were central rather than peripheral. The usual orientation of psychology with its heterosexual vantage point, obscures many sensibilities that might be revealed if the lesbian/gay view were an integral organizer of experience. Lesbians and gay men experience a bicultural duality arising from aspects of their lives which reflect closeness with heterosexuality as well as their lesbian/gay orientation. This confluence of experience joined with a position on the margins provides new perspectives on the world, which stimulate a rethinking of behavioral parameters. When these ideas are developed with the aim of broadening paradigms in psychology it becomes evident that one must continually question "unquestionable" assumptions and search for the most revealing methods. Furthermore, centralizing the lesbian/gay experience makes possible new models of normalcy.

V. CONTESTED RELATIONS: FAMILY MEMBERS AND FRIENDS

The themes of this section emphasize how the multiplication of perspectives can reveal complex representations of social roles and relations. These contributions emphasize, from different vantage points, diverse ways of understanding two sets of relationships—ones centered on mother–daughter relations, a strong attractor of feminist theoretical interest, and male athletic friendships, a highly publicized and often examined form of male bonding.

Jane Flax reflects on the apparently unproblematic ways in which women and motherhood have been linked, especially through the theoretical perspectives that describe women as relational. She argues that by socially constructing women as primarily motivated by relationship, it becomes an easy step toward valorizing the relation between mother and child, thereby losing much of the potential for expressing both how rich and conflictual that relationship can be. Reflecting on both her psychoanalytic stance and her commitment as a feminist, Flax questions the assumptions that come with these positions. The various conflicting ideas she brings to her work, lead her to reflect on her experiences as a therapist and to look at how they may mirror that of mother and child. Describing her own relationship with a patient, she demonstrates how simple it is to assume the position of the good mother and to coerce her patient into a daughterly role, but the result of that is to drive underground the other aspects of the patient's behavior—aggression, sexuality, envy, and so forth that are absent from this glorified view of womanhood. She extends these ideas to the complexity of the relationship with the mother from the infant's earliest life. Both mother and child engage in multiple and complex interactions that rarely become an acknowledged part of our conceptions of this relationship.

Patricia Hill Collins examines the hegemony of the white Eurocentric construction of motherhood as it influences both white and black self concepts. Believing that it represents neither black history nor experience, she offers an Afrocentric perspective. Because recent research suggests that the African heritage has continued to exert an influence on African Americans she draws on this perspective for her model. She believes whites have denigrated black women through the stereotypes of "mammy" and "overpowerful matriarch." She offers an alternative model inspired by a long history of community-sharing in the nurturing of children and in the economic contributions of women to the family. Where these may run counter to idealized Eurocentric constructions of women's role as fulltime nurturer in a nuclear family, they have a long and honored tradition in West African cultures. Turning her attention to mother/daughter relationships, she finds a reflection of these ideals. While white American mothers may be grooming their daughters to assume a role of raising children within the confines of the nuclear family, a theme that seems to run through black mother/daughter relationships is the insistence on self-sufficiency through education and preparation for career as well as planning for marriage and a family.

In his focus on male athletes' friendships, Michael Messner also addresses a type of relationship that has repeatedly been described from a single point of view. Messner explores how men view their own friendships and asks the larger question of how these understandings fit in the overall relationship system to reproduce power and gender hierarchies. His choice of male athletes, both professional and recreational, is apt because this arena is a notorious bastion of male bonding and female exclusion and degradation. The production and reproduction of genders can be theorized in terms of various constructions of desire, sexuality, and intimacy. Messner shows that underneath the apparent bonding of these men lies the realities of often fierce competition. In the face of this competition, bonds are often cemented through engaging in

20

DAVIS AND GERGEN

sexist and homophobic discourse. By marginalizing gay males and treating woman as the "other," men construct a hierarchical gender order. Messner's study of male athletes' friendships moves from athletes' descriptions of their patterns of friendship to the way these relationships fit into a larger relational system and further, how, as currently constituted, they perpetuate power and sexist hierarchies within our culture.

VI. SEXUALITY AND PLEASURE: DE-FORMING DESIRE

Males and females are segregated in the service of maintaining sexual roles and relations. In naturalizing difference and desire, the constructed nature of sexuality can be suppressed. Both Leonore Tiefer and Michelle Fine demonstrate concern for a view of sexuality that is silent with respect to desire and pleasure. Celia Kitzinger and Sue Wilkinson consider the implications of an exclusive focus on heterosexuality.

Leonore Tiefer presents a history of the uses of the word "natural" as a form of explanation of human behavior. Nature has been able to function as a powerful form of explanation both historically and in the present because it is viewed as universal, prior to culture, and as a basic force at work in the world. Scholarly fields have frequently sought to enhance their credibility by defining themselves in terms of the natural. Sexology has fallen into this category. Tiefer points out the limitations that have arisen from the reliance on the concept of nature in describing a complex human interaction, such as sexual relations. In the field of sex therapy, when all energy becomes focused on external manifestations of sexual desire, such as an erection, there is a resultant disregard of multiple forms of sensuality and pleasure.

Michelle Fine presents an analysis of the multiple discourses surrounding sex education in the schools. Despite the reluctance of conservatives, sex education is widely accepted as an important subject in the schools, but, according to Fine, the content is strongly influenced by the ambivalence many feel about the public presentation of this subject matter. The result is a curriculum that presents sex, especially for girls, as an activity accompanied by multiple minefields that must be avoided. Fine argues that including "the discourse of desire" would allow girls to see themselves as agents who are in control of their own destiny. The current discourse of male needs and control encourages passive response on the part of girls.

Celia Kitzinger and Sue Wilkinson raise an important paradox for feminism. Despite the continuing feminist critique of heterosexuality as a representative of heteropatriarchy, large numbers of women continue to experience heterosexual activity as freely chosen and pleasurable. In light of this paradox, it becomes critical to continue to problematize heterosexuality and to analyze its position in the social construction of gender. They consider the question of whether one can find a way of theorizing that will incorporate heterosexuality without supporting the accompanying negative aspects of heteropatriarchy. They take up the point that by its very name heterosexuality emphasizes sexual opposition. This manner of constituting human relations reinforces oppressive aspects. To explain why most women do not embrace radical critiques and continue to engage in and justify heterosexuality, Kitzinger and Wilkinson examine theoretical positions that maintain a critique of patriarchy and simultaneously seek to justify heterosexual activity. They find theories that attempt to either maintain the myth of virginity or promote queer heterosexuality to be problematic. Rather than maintaining heterosexuality as the unmarked and natural choice for women, they urge that women at the very least understand how heterosexuality effects their oppression.

VII. GENDER AND IDENTITY: DIS-FIGURING THE BODY

Issues of embodiment, including the power of cultural icons to threaten women's self-images, have been of central concern to feminist scholars in the last two decades. Among a diverse set of issues, we have selected two pieces that deal with the ways in which the body is the site for cultural conflicts. Susan Bordo looks at how cultural obsessions are represented in the anorectic's struggles with her body. Although anorexia has often been looked at in terms of the problems of the individual, Bordo locates the problem with general cultural concerns. Thomas Gerschick and Adam Miller also address cultural issues in relation to the body. They take the examination of the effects of disabilities beyond the level of an individual problem to consider how they reflect social values. They argue that the experience of disabilities is socially constructed and intersects with cultural ideals of masculinity.

Looking at anorexia nervosa as a representation of "some of the central ills of our culture," Bordo describes the detachment of the body from the soul, as well as the current feeling of loss of control in our culture. She poses questions of why thinness has become such an obsession in our society and why it is associated almost exclusively with women. At a time when many people fear fat more than nuclear holocaust or even death, these questions beg to be asked. She discusses anorexia nervosa as being synchronous with three cultural axes: dualism, control, and gender/power. Like Tiefer, she believes that our bodies are not to be considered "natural" but socially constructed within our culture. Using historical and philosophical material as well as reports from young women struggling with anorexia, she demonstrates how these three axes incorporate many of the phenomenological experiences of anorexia.

Thomas Gerschick and Adam Miller argue that the traditional themes of masculinity: independence and physical power are linked to a strong and able body. Men who stand at the margins, unable to fill the traditional roles, are forced to rethink their views of masculinity and may be led to question the importance society attributes to these traits. In their analysis Gerschick and Miller deal with the impact disability has on the individual as well as how the

22

DAVIS AND GERGEN

disabled male constitutes a self image within the society. Although many seek to find ways to work within the system, there is a group of disabled men who reject or challenge the norms of society and seek to forge a new conception of disability and of masculinity.

VIII. POWER: MULTIPLY MESSAGED

An issue of ongoing interest to feminists has been power. Multiple perspectives on power complicate understandings of this difficult notion. For some feminists, access to power arises from one's location with respect to race, class, and gender. In order to understand behavior, it is necessary to consider the conjunction of social hierarchies and an individual's position with respect to them.

Lesley Miles looks at social constructions dealing with assaults to the integrity of the body. Concerned with discourse surrounding safe sex practices, specifically, ways to avoid AIDS, her analysis focuses on the conversations of black and white groups of South African women. Her results indicate that talk about sex is also talk about power, and in this society, men control the rules of the sexual interaction. Most women experience themselves in a no-win bind. If they request safe sex as a way of protecting themselves, the men feel aspersions are cast against them. Yet if they offer protection for the man, they imply a history of promiscuity that renders them undesirable. Analyses of women describing their sexual experiences reveal that there are several interlocking discourses surrounding any negotiation of safe sex. Lost in the attempt to prevent exposure to the deadly illness are implications of powerful sexual passions and the necessity to protect one's image of relative sexual purity.

Pierrette Hondagneu-Sotelo and Michael Messner explore what lies beneath public displays of masculine behavior. They believe that public appearances often belie the inequitable relationship existing between heterosexual partners. Thus, the "New Man," sensitive and publicly caring, has become not only acceptable, but laudable as a masculine persona. However, a closer look reveals that this man is often white, middle class, and professional and the nurturance he publicly displays may be only a superficial part of his behavior. In fact, his sensitivity may actually rely upon the labor of his wife or a poorly paid domestic servant. In contrast to the "New Man," Mexican immigrant men are often consigned to the role of "macho" men. The authors contend that despite apparent displays of power, which may be an attempt to redress lack of institutional power within the United States, there is, in fact, greater equality in their gender relations than there was in Mexico. Circumstances have forced the wife to work and often to assume a more autonomous role. Therefore the man has less power and distance from his wife than he had under the structure of their relationship in Mexico. The authors conclude that one cannot uncritically evaluate behavior apart from the cultural context.

Susan Oyama looks at the ways in which both biological theorists and feminists have made similar arguments with respect to women and war. While biologists may favor genetic interpretations, and feminists look toward the cultural, both position themselves with respect to the polarities in the nature/nurture conflict, and by implication involve themselves in essentialist arguments. The argument, from either position, states that women are essentially more peace-oriented than men and, if given the opportunity of power, would be more likely to avert aggression and war. Oyama finds these essentialist arguments flawed because they ignore complex levels of interrelationships. She argues that only through emphasizing multiple interactions and relationships will we be able to form an understanding of the ways in which a variety of features work in concert to influence behavior.

bell hooks examines the implications of the statement "the personal is political," the rallying cry of the feminist movement in the 1970s. Although an understanding of one's own position within society can be a powerful motivator to act for change, all too often women have failed to move beyond identifying their own experiences to acting politically. In order to create the kind of political power implied in this phrase, women not only have to be conscious of their own identity, but must understand the underlying power structure that creates that status.

IX. BREAKING OUT: DIAGNOSIS AND TREATMENT
AFTER MODERNITY

For psychologists the implications of a new social constructionist metatheory for therapeutic practices are far reaching. No longer seeking the truth of the case, but rather for new narratives, therapists are invited to look for novel constructions of reality. This series of chapters presents the authors' reframing of various clinical psychology issues—both conceptions of diagnosis and methods of treatment. The authors very consciously explore issues of power, gender equality, and hegemonic practices in the therapy setting.

Of central concern to many feminist constructionist critics are the diagnostic categories used in psychiatric practices and by health care managers. Jeanne Marecek illuminates how, over the course of psychiatric history, diagnoses and treatment have reflected cultural assumptions and have served to reinforce certain desired behaviors in women. Marecek's review of abnormal psychology textbooks reveals that twenty-five years of feminist scholarship have failed to alter the ways in which the field is conceptualized. She argues that abnormal psychology hides its contingent and prescriptive nature behind an image of a rigorous scientific discipline. Categories are presented as certain and true, not as the result of culturally constructed social norms which serve to control and constrain women's behavior. These diagnoses have worked hand in glove with current cultural views of women to "enforce norms of female domesticity, subordination, and subservience to men's sexual needs." Marecek believes that the critical theoretical and human issues arising from feminist scholarship are obscured within the field of psychology not only because of sexism, but also because of the image of psychology as a serious "scientific" discipline promoting objective knowledge, immune to the whims of social and cultural issues. She concludes by describing the dangerous implications for clinical practice when ideas become stuck in rigid reified categories.

Continuing the discussion of the dangers of an over-reliance on dominant discourses, Rachel Hare-Mustin describes how an uncritical assumption of major theoretical discourses leads family therapists to replicate the status quo. Contrary to therapy viewed as an uncovering that reaches to the core, the image she suggests is of a mirrored room that can only reflect the narratives people bring to it. If a discourse such as, "the equality between men and women," is unthinkingly accepted in the therapy room then the therapy will inevitably proceed from this point, thus obscuring other discourses of gender inequality. She envisions therapy as an introduction to new discourses allowing for the joint building of possibility rather than the reifying of what already exists.

Virginia Goldner, Peggy Penn, Marcia Sheinberg and Gillian Walker, discussing the relationship of violent couples, argue that an emphasis on battering alone is inadequate, and expand their therapeutic approach to investigate the dynamics that so strongly hold the couple together despite the abuse. While their interest is in the psychodynamics of the couple, they never indicate a parity of psychological problems within the couple or ignore the social implications of power imbalances. They choose in their therapy to acknowledge the harmfulness in the relationship as well as the factors that bind the couple together. Unless therapists and clients can construct a narrative to make sense of the ways in which the couple need each other, they cannot break the patterns of abuse. This multi-focused position allows for a richer psychological, social and political context in which to encourage therapeutic change.

X. POSTSCRIPT: A POSTMODERN MOMENT

We conclude with a piece by Mary Gergen in which she raises critical issues for a feminist social constructionist psychology. In so doing she replaces a linear rhetorical format with an interplay of her own ideas with the words of others. Her use of language is designed to stimulate the thoughts and imaginings of the reader rather than clarify specific points. She provokes vibrations that enable readers to oscillate into being constructions of their own formulations.

CONCLUSIONS

As editors of this book, we want to bring to diverse audiences a selection of readings that open up boundaries and encourage new ways of organizing views of the world. These pieces, which are among the best of some recent

25

work, are laden with powerful portents for the social sciences, psychology, in particular. We present their efforts to engender new conversations, new processes, new playing out of possibilities across a spectrum of interlocutors. Conversations begun here, we hope, will spiral out beyond the pages of our book, out from the silent rebuttals of lonely readers, beyond the classrooms where teachers instruct their students, into the coffee houses, carrels, and circles where those for whom gender issues are a concern, engage with one another. We are inviting our readers to join in the conversations now.

REFERENCES

Belenky, Mary, Clinchy, Blythe, Goldberger, Nancy, and Tarule, Jill (1986). *Women's ways of knowing: The development of self, voice, and mind*. New York: Basic Books.

Burr, Vivian (1995). *An introduction to social constructionism*. London: Routledge.

Butler, Judith (1990). *Gender trouble. Feminism and the subversion of identity*. London: Routledge.

Butler, Judith (1993). *Bodies that matter*. London: Routledge.

Curt, Beryl C. (1994). *Textuality and tectonics: Troubling social and psychological science*. Buckingham, England: Open University Press.

Daly, Mary (1978). *Gyn/ecology: The metaethics of radical feminism*. Boston: Beacon Press.

Eagly, Alice (1987). *Sex differences in social behavior: A social-role interpretation*. Hillsdale, NJ: Erlbaum.

Eagly, Alice (1995). The science and politics of comparing women and men. *American Psychologist, 50*, 145–158.

Elam, Diane (1994). *Feminism and deconstruction: Ms. en abyme*. London, New York: Routledge.

Farganis, Sondra (1994). *Situating feminism. From thought to action*. Thousand Oaks, CA: Sage.

Flax, Jane (1990). *Thinking fragments, psychoanalysis, feminism, & postmodernism in the contemporary west*. Berkeley: University of CA Press.

Fonow, Mary Margaret & Cook, Judith A. (Eds.) (1991). *Beyond methodology: feminist scholarship as lived research*. Bloomington: University of Indiana Press.

Fuss, Diana (1989). *Essentially speaking. Feminism, nature & difference*. London: Routledge.

Gergen, Kenneth J. (1985). The social constructionist movement in modern psychology. *American Psychologist, 40*, 266–275.

Gergen, Kenneth J. (1995). *Realities and relationships*. Cambridge: Harvard University Press.

Gergen, Mary M. (1988). Towards a feminist methodology. In M. Gergen (Ed.) *Feminist thought and the structure of knowledge (pp. 87–104)*. New York: New York University Press, 1988.

Gergen, Mary M. (1993). Feminist theory and the sex/gender variable in psychology. In Stam, H. J., Mos, L. P., Thorngate, W., & Kaplan, B. (Eds.). *Recent advances in theoretical psychology, Vol. 3*. New York: Springer-Verlag. 297–305.

Gergen, Mary M. (1994). Epistemology, gender, and history: Positioning the lenses of gender. *Psychological Inquiry, 5*, 86–92.

Gilligan, Carol (1982). *In a different voice: Psychological theory and women's development.* Cambridge, MA: Harvard University Press.

Grosz, Elizabeth A. (1994). *Volatile bodies: Toward a corporeal feminism.* Bloomington: Indiana University Press.

Haraway, Donna (1988). Situated knowledges: The science question in feminism and the privilege of partial perspective. *Feminist Studies, 14,* 575–599.

Harding, Sandra (1986). *The science question in feminism.* Ithaca: Cornell University Press; Milton Keynes, England: Open University Press.

Hare-Mustin, Rachel & Marecek, Jeanne (1990). *Making a difference: Psychology and the construction of gender.* New Haven, CT: Yale University Press.

Hartsock, Nancy C. M. (1983). *Money, sex and power.* New York: Longman.

Hekman, Susan (1990). *Gender and knowledge: Elements of a postmodern feminism.* Boston: Northeastern University Press.

Hyde, Janet, & Linn, Marcia C. (Eds.). (1986). *The psychology of gender: Advances through meta-analysis.* Baltimore: Johns Hopkins University Press.

Kitzinger, Celia (1987). *The social construction of lesbianism.* London: Sage.

Lather, Patti (1995). The validity of angels: Interpretive and textual strategies in researching the lives of women with HIV/AIDS. *Qualitative Inquiry, 1,* 41–68.

Maccoby, Eleanor, & Jacklin, Carol N. (1974). *The psychology of sex differences.* Stanford: Stanford University Press.

Marecek, Jeanne (1995). Gender, politics, and psychology's ways of knowing. *American Psychologist, 50,* 162–163.

Morawski, Jill G. (1994). *Practicing feminisms, reconstructing psychology: Notes on a liminal science.* Ann Arbor: Univ. of Michigan Press.

Oliver, Pam (1991). What do girls know anyway? Rationality, gender and social control. *Feminism & Psychology, 1,* 339–360.

Stacey, Judith. and Thorne, Barrie. (1985). The missing feminist revolution in sociology. *Social Problems, 32,* 310–316.

27

PART I
LINKING FEMINISM AND PSYCHOLOGY
Social Constructionist Re-visionings

REGARDING GENDER
Essentialism, Constructionism, and Feminist Psychology

Janis S. Bohan

DURING THE past decade and a half, a group of approaches to understanding women (represented by the work of Belenky, Clinchy, Goldberger, & Tarrule, 1986; Chodorow, 1978; Gilligan, 1982; Miller, 1976; and others) has gained wide popularity, both within and outside academia. Collectively, these models suggest that girls and women necessarily have different experiences than do boys and men and that these differential experiences generate distinctive modes of thinking, judging, relating, and so forth.

This notion of substantial differences between women's and men's modes of being has been a recurrent and pervasive theme in considerations of gen-

It was my intention that author's full first names be used in the reference section of this article. As I have argued elsewhere, the use of initials may support the presumption of male authorship, thereby contributing to the persistent invisibility of women and their work. Unfortunately, during the copyediting process (in accordance with the APA manual), initials were substituted for authors' first names by the editors of *Psychology of Women Quarterly*.

der, whether stressing or minimizing differences. Hare-Mustin and Marecek (1988, 1990) discussed how these two approaches, which they termed alpha bias and beta bias, respectively, have shaped psychology's understandings of gender despite the fact that the construction of gender as difference has failed either to resolve the paradoxes created by such renditions or to confront underlying issues of domination.

Historically, the vast majority of psychological considerations of gender have been maximalist or alpha biased and androcentric; sex differences have been regarded as fundamental to human nature, with male traits the valued norm. Only with the resurgence of feminism in the late 1960s was this dimorphism seriously questioned, and such challenges have since characterized much of feminist psychological theory and research (Crawford & Marecek, 1989; Deaux, 1984; Sherif, 1979; Unger, 1979).

Against this recent minimalist or beta biased background, the new approaches put forth by Gilligan, Miller, and others appear profoundly divergent. This "cultural feminism" presents traits deemed distinctively women's as indeed different from but equal or even preferable to those that characterize men in general. Thus, difference is affirmed, but the customary valuation of difference is turned on its head; women's ways of being are revered rather than demeaned.

This valuing of qualities traditionally associated with women is transformative. By elevating characteristics long identified as feminine, cultural feminists offer an alternative conception of women's place in the order of things and simultaneously promise to broaden the range of qualities regarded as worthy for all people. The effort to validate the intrinsic worth of "feminine" qualities arguably contributes importantly to the feminist goal of liberating women from oppression grounded in devaluation.

Yet, even as many rush to embrace this re-vision of gender, others urge caution. The debate between essentialist and constructionist views of gender is invoked in this critique, a debate whose concepts and terminology are often misunderstood and misrepresented. To clarify the meaning of essentialism and constructionism as they will be used here, I offer the following brief discussions of these two perspectives on gender.

ESSENTIALISM

Designating an approach as essentialist is not the same as saying that it argues for the biological determination of gender. The distinction between essentialist and constructionist views of gender lies not in the origin of gender qualities but in their location.

Essentialist views construe gender as resident within the individual, a quality or trait describing one's personality, cognitive process, moral judgement, etc. Thus, it is an essentialist stance to argue that "relationality" or a "morality of justice" is a quality possessed by the individual. Essentialist models, thus, portray gender in terms of fundamental attributes that are conceived as internal, persistent, and generally separate from the on-going experience of interaction with the daily sociopolitical contexts of one's life.[1]

CONSTRUCTIONISM

Just as essentialism is often misunderstood as biological determinism, the social construction of gender is often confused with the socialization of gender. The position urging that gender is socially constructed is not simply an assertion of the environmental origin of gender traits. Rather, the constructionist argument is that gender is not a trait of individuals at all, but simply a construct that identifies particular transactions that are understood to be appropriate to one sex.

Gender so defined is not resident in the person but exists in those interactions that are socially construed as gendered. From this view, relationality or morality is a quality of interactions not of individuals, and it is not essentially connected with sex. What it means to term a transaction feminine or masculine is socially agreed upon and is reproduced by the very process of participating in that transaction.

THE CONTRAST BETWEEN ESSENTIALISM AND CONSTRUCTIONISM

By way of analogy, consider the difference between describing an individual as friendly and describing a conversation as friendly. In the former case, "friendly" is construed as a trait of the person, an "essential" component to her or his personality. In the latter, "friendly" describes the nature of the interaction occurring between or among people. Friendly here has a particular meaning that is agreed upon by the participants, that is compatible with its meaning to their social reference groups, and that is reaffirmed by the process of engaging in this interaction. Although the essentialist view of gender sees it as analogous to the friendly person, the constructionist sees gender as analogous to the friendly conversation.

If "friendly" were gendered, an essentialist position might argue that women are more friendly than men. Whether this quality came from biological imperatives, from socialization, or from a combination of both, it is now a trait of women. A constructionist position would argue that the gendering of friendly transactions is the product of social agreements about the appropriateness of certain behavior. The differential exposure of men and women to those contexts that elicit friendly behavior results in a linkage between sex and friendliness, and friendliness becomes gendered.

THE CRITIQUE OF ESSENTIALISM

The models proffered by Belenky et al. (1986), Chodorow (1978), Gilligan (1982), and Miller (1976) represent essentialist construals of gender as defined

BOHAN

here. These understandings, although laudable for their affirmation of women's experience, also raise important theoretical, empirical, and political difficulties for feminist psychology. Although their enthusiastic welcome has served in some degree to bring women's experience to the fore, they demand the same critical political analysis that feminist psychology has accorded other less woman-centered theories. Among the concerns we must address are the following.

When We Say That Women Think, Make Moral Judgements, or Relate Differently Than Men, Which Women Do We Mean?

Both methodologically and theoretically, essentialist models are grounded in problematic universalizing assumptions. Research designs from which these models are derived have not systematically identified or sought out participants representing the diversity of women's experience (Auerbach, Blum, Smith, & Williams, 1985; Fine, 1985; Lerman, 1986; Lott, 1986). Theoretically, also, the exclusionary nature of these concepts is troublesome. Theories stressing mothering discount family groupings and child-rearing practices that vary from the nuclear family norm, and in so doing invalidate not only those women who are not mothers but also the experience of children raised in other living arrangements (Lerman, 1986; Lott, 1990).

The failure to acknowledge diversity among us may contribute to a misogynist agenda; Butler (1990) urged us to be cognizant of the "coercive and regulatory consequences" of a portrayal of women as a homogeneous class, a "seamless category" (p. 4). The point is not that each identifiable group of women does or does not approach the topics of concern in a similar manner. The point is that we do not know and dare not presume.

The experiences attributed to women, portrayed as contributing to their "nature," are not timeless and universal but are socially, historically, and politically located; essentialist models fail to acknowledge this situatedness (Nicholson, 1990). To presume that all women judge, think, or relate in a characteristic and universal manner denies the contextuality that, as psychologists, we know frames behavior.

Are the Qualities Attributed to Women in These Views Issues of Gender per se or Are They a Product of Oppression?

Hare-Mustin and Marecek (1988), Stack (1986), Westkott (1986), and others have argued that oppressed groups develop the ability to exist in two worlds—that of their immediate reference group and that of the dominant group—to abide by the demands of those in power.[2] This ability requires sensitivity to the expectations and responses of others; this vigilance is manifested as a mortality of caring, as a sense of self grounded in relationships, and as subjective and connected knowing.

If women's relationality is a product of oppression, as Miller (1976) suggested, then when we cherish our relationality, are we legitimizing the op-pression that created it (cf. Hare-Mustin & Marecek, 1990; Westkott, 1988)? This question has frightening political implications. If the oppressed can be led to value their own oppression, then liberation becomes impossible.

Imagine a scenario where women have begun to recognize their marginal-ization and to assert their personal and collective right to self-worth. Imagine that women are making notable if limited strides both in improved quality of life and personal autonomy and in raising the consciousness of their society to their oppression and the need for redress. Imagine, further, that the linger-ing product of that oppression is women's distinctive "way of being," a more relational, caring approach to others.

If you were a member of the long-dominant male power structure in this society, a group that wished to retain its hegemonic position, how might you proceed in the face of such challenges? First, no conscious conspiracy need direct such an undertaking; socially constructed understandings of what gen-der is and should be, what women are and should be, will suffice to guide both your traditionally empowered group and the response of the public at large. It will seem clear that your agenda is self-evidently right. I suggest that you could achieve your aim by appealing to women's caring nature, urging them to cherish the activities and roles they traditionally held and to abjure their striving for equality and visibility, which will now be portrayed as mis-guided.

Here are some suggested strategies for retaining power. You should call public attention to instances where the proposal for a return to traditional roles comes not from you but from among women's own numbers. At the same time, you should be vocal in your personal admiration for these quali-ties. Women will welcome your praise for qualities now seen as inherently theirs and inherently valuable, and it will offer no threat to your power to grant such acclaim, for these are traits of the disenfranchised.

You should employ and encourage public and political discourse that sup-ports your agenda. Phrases such as "the death of feminism," "saving the fami-ly," "the mommy track," "the biological clock," "the infertility epidemic," and "the new feminity" should be effective. You should encourage media cover-age that blazons across the front page commentary highlighting sex differ-ences and supporting "traditional" values. Serious scholarly and political criti-cism must be relegated to academic journals where it will go largely unno-ticed.

If effective, this strategy should result in a populace convinced of the merit of separate spheres and confortable with their own place in such a system. Critics will be largely unheard; those who are heard will appear resistant to the truth of common experience and hostile to the natural order.

The political realities underlying this chilling scenario have been the sub-ject of a number of serious scholarly analyses in recent years (e.g., Beckwith,

35

1984; Crawford, 1989; Faludi, 1991; Kahn & Yoder, 1989; Lott, 1988, 1990; Mednick, 1989; Poovey, 1988; Squire, 1989). If such a strategy succeeds in convincing women of the merit of a return to the separate spheres of the past, the aims and recent gains of feminism will be the likely casualties.

However, it might be argued, the work we consider here does not relegate women to devalued roles; indeed, here feminine qualities are cherished rather than demeaned. Certainly we must avoid participating in the devaluation of those traits that have traditionally been associated with women and that hold promise for improvement in the human condition: nurturance, sensitivity to others, connected knowing. Indeed, it is not only cultural feminists who have argued that "men's" modes of being are less rather than more noble. Sampson (1977, 1989, 1990), for example, has summarized considerable scholarship regarding the problematic nature of the western, masculine conception of the self-contained individual as the epitome of mental health and social evolution.

However, although we may cherish these qualities associated with women, wish them for ourselves, and also encourage them in men, both political experience and systematic research demonstrate that these traits are not those most respected by the culture. Collaboration with essentialist interpretations of gender might, if inadvertently, contribute to a recreation of earlier understandings of gender, with women deemed not different and equal but, once again, deficient.

Essentialist Models Have Troubling Implications for Collective Feminist Action

Further problems are created by the essentialist location of responsibility for a woman's experience and behavior within herself, the construal of gender as an aspect of the individual's personality structure. This position borders on victim blaming: Women's experience, including their marginalization and oppression, becomes a result of qualities within themselves, rather than a reflection of the social systems that shape their lives (cf. Fine, 1985; Kahn & Yoder, 1989; Lott, 1985, 1990; Sampson, 1977, 1990; Sarason, 1981; Scheman, 1983; Squire, 1989).

Operating from this understanding of gender, action undertaken to improve women's lot strives to change them, not the system. Thus, for instance, we encourage women to take assertiveness training rather than attending to the contextual forces that shape and interpret assertive interactions (cf. Gervasio & Crawford, 1989). We develop self-defense classes for women rather than working to change the beliefs that render women vulnerable and that condone violence against them. We attribute women's gender-prescribed behavior in relationships not to patriachal structures but to women's own codependence (cf. Brown, 1990).

It is doubtless easier to work for individual change, attributing failures to

individual inadequacies, than to confront vast and intransigent social institutions (cf. Albee, 1986; Caplan & Nelson, 1973; Squire, 1989). However, such
person-blame attributions ignore the omnipresent impact of power and its
differential distribution in society, belying the painful reality of the abuse of
power against women. To paraphrase Caplan and Nelson (1973), "a world dis-
astrously out of tune with [women's] needs is explained as a state of mind" (p.
202).

If we succumb to the temptation of compelling person-blame explanations, feminism is at risk of becoming a mental health rather than a social
change movement (cf. Mednick, 1989; Kahn & Jean, 1983). This is not to argue that women's mental health ought not to be a priority for feminist psychology; it is only to urge that it is not enough if feminist ideals are finally to
be achieved.

Although many feminists are in fact striving to change systems as well as
individuals, Fine and Gordon (1989) reminded us that "we exist at moments,
at the margins and among ourselves" (p. 146). Our individual efforts to reconstruct systems are critical but they are not adequate. However benevolent our
own purpose, the attribution of women's oppression to qualities within
themselves supports victim-blaming interpretations by others, charging
women with responsibility for the very dynamics that oppress them.

*To Label Particular Ways of Being as "Women's" Implies That Women Do Not Have
Access to Other Modes*

When we conflate gender with ways of knowing, relationality, or moral
judgement, we imply that these are women's ways of being and others are
men's ways (Crawford, 1989; Hare-Mustin & Marecek, 1988). It is but a short
step from affirming women's ways of being to disclaiming for women all other modes.

The argument may be that women possess these ways of being in addition
to modes traditionally attributed to men. Does this mean that men do not
possess the same range of potential as women? Some feminist theorists (e.g.,
Hartsock, 1983; Rose, 1986; Smith, 1974, 1987) have argued that women's
unique experience, particularly their marginality, does indeed grant them a
clearer perspective on reality than that available to men. Such feminist standpoint epistemologies (Harding, 1986) are beyond the scope of this article, but
they evoke concerns similar to those raised by essentialist positions discussed
here (Fuss, 1989; Gergen, 1988; Harding, 1991; Nicholson, 1990).

In a world where male is norm, qualities not explicitly identified as
"women's" are by default regarded as male traits. Men, too, are limited by this
dualistic view, and such bifurcated depictions of gender have been the subject
of numerous critiques (e.g., Hare-Mustin & Marecek, 1988, 1990; Morawski,
1985, 1990). However, the issue here is the selective attribution to women of

those modes of being that have been deemed inferior. Our declaration of these qualities as equally worthy does not alter the reality of their devaluation within society.

There is No Clear Evidence for Sex Differences in the Ways of Being Described by These Approaches

Despite the intuitive appeal apparent in the widespread acceptance of essentialist views of gender, a substantial literature testifies to their empirical inadequacies. Critics assessing the validity of these notions argue that their underpinnings reveal methodological problems, theoretical inconsistencies, and failures to replicate (e.g., Broughton, 1983; Crawford, 1989; Crawford & Marecek, 1989; Friedman, Robinson, & Friedman, 1987; Kahn & Yoder, 1989; Kerber et al., 1986; Lott, 1985; Mednick, 1989; Tavris, 1992).

This work raises an important question. If behavior is not differentiated by sex as portrayed by essentialist models, why have these depictions of gender enjoyed such widespread support, and why, as we have discussed them among ourselves, have they seemed to resonate so with women's personal experience?

THE PARADOX: WOMEN ARE DIFFERENT; IT IS NOT BECAUSE WOMEN ARE DIFFERENT

How can we reconcile the intuitive comfort of these ideas with the scholarly and political misgivings they raise? How can we respond to Greeno and Maccoby's (1986) warning: "women have been trapped for generations by people's willingness to accept their own intuitions about the truth of gender stereotypes" (p. 315)? A promising candidate for resolving this dilemma lies in the constructionist conception of gender.

The Social Construction of Gender

The foundational assertion of social constructionism is that we have no way of knowing with certainty the nature of reality. From this perspective, so-called knowledge does not reflect the discovery of a free-standing reality, existing apart from the knower and revealed by careful application of procedures. Rather, what we purport to know, what we see as truth, is a construction, a best understanding, based upon and inextricably intertwined with the contexts within which it is created. Among the most forceful of factors that shape our constructions of knowledge are the modes of discourse by which we exchange our perceptions and descriptions of reality. Thus, knowledge is a product of social interchange; what we call knowledge is simply what we agree to call truth (Berger & Luckmann, 1967; Bohan, 1990; Gergen, 1985; Unger, 1983).

In the process of thus agreeing to the reality of a phenomenon, we construct precisely that reality. Gender, for instance, is not an actual, free-standing

BOHAN

phenomenon that exists inside individuals, to be discovered and measured by social scientists. Rather, "gender" is an agreement that resides in social interchange; it is precisely what we agree it to be (Hare-Mustin & Marecek, 1988, 1990; Lorber & Farrell, 1991; Unger, 1989a).

Gender, from this understanding, is the meaning we have agreed to impute to a particular class of transactions between individuals and environmental contexts. One does not have gender; one does gender (West & Zimmerman, 1987). The factors defining a particular transaction as feminine or masculine are not the sex of the actors but the situational parameters within which the performance occurs. Thus, none of us is feminine or is masculine or fails to be either of those. In particular contexts, people do feminine; in others, they do masculine.

Unger and Crawford (1992) and Lott (1990) offered excellent summaries of the burgeoning literature that supports this interpretation. For example, Nancy Henley's (e.g., 1977) research on nonverbal communication demonstrated that women who hold positions of power behave toward their subordinates in a manner that would usually be described as "masculine." Similarly, Major (1987) found that women and men who enjoy comparable status in an occupational setting evidence similar values and behaviors, in contrast to the common assumption of sex differences in workplace values. In both cases, behavior is determined not by the sex of the actors but by the context of the work relationships, particularly power and status.

In other research, Zanna and Pack (1975) demonstrated that women behave in a more gender-traditional manner when interacting with a man whose attitudes toward gender are conservative than when relating to a man with more liberal views. Risman (1987) found that single fathers act more like mothers than like married fathers, behaving in a more "feminine" manner in response to the demands of their particular context. In both cases, gendered actions are shaped not by the sex but by the social location of the individual.

The disjunction between sex and gender evidenced in these examples illustrates that "gender" is not a trait inherent in individuals; rather, qualities usually seen as sex related are in fact contextually determined. Gender is revealed as simply the term given to a set of behavior-environment interactions that we have come to agree characterize members of one sex.

The question arises, how do we come to view certain interactions as feminine or masculine? The answer lies in the differential contexts of our experience (Lott, 1991). Women are far more likely to encounter situations that elicit feminine transactions (e.g., subordination) and men to encounter circumstances that elicit masculine (e.g., dominance), and this partitioning is a result of the self-sustaining nature of socially constructed knowledge.

The vast majority of situations in which we function entail gendered prescriptions and proscriptions. As we do gender "correctly," we legitimize the prescriptive quality of that circumstance for members of our sex, thus rein-

BOHAN

39

forcing and reproducing the gendering of those situations. Selective exposure of women and men to gendering contexts elicits behavior where sex is compatible with gender, thereby reinforcing the perception that gender is sex differentiated and sex defined. Thus, the continuing process of doing gender recreates the construction of gender.

Women are different, by virtue of their being women, but, paradoxically, that is not because they are women. The demands of social context constitute the primary determinant of our behaving in gendered ways (cf. Eagly, 1987; Lott, 1990). Experiences of women are different from those of men because, in large part, women encounter differentially gendered situations – and this process is circular and self-maintaining. Further, even when encountering what appear to be similar situations, women and men face discrepant prescriptions. Although a woman might free herself from the gendered demands of her social world and might occasionally or frequently do masculine, her experience remains different from that of a man. In such situations, she confronts the discrepancy between her actions and those expected of her, whereas he does not.

Because of the ubiquitous gendering of experience, we regularly encounter lessons in doing gender and consequences for failing to participate appropriately in gender transactions (West & Zimmerman, 1987). We become so familiar with this process that we come to experience it as a part of our makeup; we perceive ourselves as intrinsically gendered because gender so thoroughly suffuses our experience.

This identification with socially constructed understandings of gender guides our behavior, leading us, in general, to conform to gendered expectations and thus to do gender in a manner compatible with its construction in a particular social context. Further, our experience of gender as an aspect of internal identity and a "natural" quality of ourselves corroborates the social construction of gender as an intrapsychic trait intrinsically connected to sex.

In addition, the fundamental attribution error contributes to our overestimation of the role of personal factors and underestimation of situational forces that shape the gendered behavior of others as well. Thus, the social construction of gender, which entails both agreements about sex-specific qualities and a belief in gender's intrapsychic nature, guides both our own behavior and our assessment of others. We take this construction as reality, failing to see its sociohistorically situated nature.

Constructionism as Remedy to the Problems of Essentialism

The constructionist model ameliorates the several concerns regarding essentialist approaches to gender, although it also stimulates additional questions.

The Denial of Diversity

A constructionist position accommodates the necessity for recognizing diversity among women. Being a universal woman does not alone shape and gender one's experience. Distinctive circumstances of necessity generate different meanings of "gender" and elicit distinctive gender transactions, just as they order other aspects of individual women's realities. Sex is only one of the multiplicity of axes that frame women's lives; to focus solely on sex as defining of women's experience is to homogenize all women and to present a unidimensional picture of a multidimensional reality. Essentialism risks denying that multidimensionality; constructionism, with its focus on the centrality of context, embraces it.

However, the constructionist focus on diverse and distinctive contexts carries a risk as well: the threat of lapsing into an extreme of identity politics that particularizes the experience of each woman (Burman, 1990; Butler, 1990; Fuss, 1989; Nicholson, 1990). No two women share exactly the same nexus of identities; no two women exist in exactly the same set of framing contexts. If we take this to mean that no two women share the same reality, the resultant radical individualizing may shatter the sense of shared experience that must underlay collective political action on behalf of women (Bordo, 1990; Di Stefano, 1990). "The idea that anyone can speak for a Woman and for all women has become increasingly transparent," wrote Probyn (1990), "but how to speak without the comfort of a preliminary gesture toward the shared ground of women's common oppression is, however, unresolved" (p. 177).

Embracing Our Oppression

Because constructionism sees gender as residing in context rather than in the individual, the focus shifts from the person to the situation. Thus, the issue of power, the reality underlying women's oppression, is revealed in full light. We see that gender is exactly about power, and it becomes possible to recognize the role of power in the construction of gender, in its activation, and in its reproductive self-sustenance (cf. Hare-Mustin, 1991; Hare-Mustin & Marecek, 1988, 1990).

To illustrate the difference such a perspective makes, consider the case for relationality as a worthy human quality. Excising it from individual psyches and locating it firmly in context transforms our change strategies. Our task becomes the enhancement of contexts that elicit doing relationality, a far different undertaking from encouraging women to lay satisfied claim to relationality as a trait of their sex.

Political Risks

Constructionist understandings of gender leave us less vulnerable to the insidious and unacknowledged shaping forces of sociopolitical context that have haunted essentialist positions. From a stance sensitive to context, we are not easily persuaded that prescribed spheres are in any sense natural, enduring, or independent of their sociohistorical circumstances.

Neither are we at risk for blaming women for their own troubles; person-blame explanations fly in the face of the constructionist focus on social context. Further, constructionism is alert to the reciprocal consequences of knowledge production and is self-consciously value oriented in its theory and practice. A constructionist approach attends as much to its own impact on social beliefs and systems as to their impact on itself; it is vigilant in guarding against ideas that risk further victimizing victims of oppression.

However, some have argued that constructionism is itself an extremely risky position for feminist politics (e.g., Burman, 1990; Yeatman, 1990). If knowledge is always situational and there is no free-standing truth to be discovered by some disinterested means, then all views are equally "true." This reasoning leads to the charge that constructionism is irredeemably apolitical: if one truth is as good as another, where can one find a justification for political action? If misogynist bigotry is as valid a position as is feminist consciousness, how can we presume to take a political stance for feminism?

The constructionist reply invokes the argument for ethical responsibility. Although knowledge is situational, it is also explicitly value laden: The absence of an absolute truth does not provide—indeed, it does not tolerate—an escape from values issues. The privileging of feminist consciousness derives not from its more adequate access to an absolute and free-standing truth but from the humanity-enhancing values that are its foundation.[3]

Beyond this philosophical argument for the possibility of a politically informed constructionism, research demonstrates that constructionist views and political conviction are not, in fact, antithetical. Unger (1989b) reviewed results of her investigations into "personal epistemologies," which revealed that active feminists tend to hold a constructionist epistemological position. Further, she found that they are able to assume a stance that supports both individual change and social action. Unger argued that such a position is a realistic response to the recognition of both socially defined assumptions about gender (a constructionist interpretation) and the need for personal action (a feminist political commitment).

Another challenge to constructionism's political merit takes a more utilitarian tack. If essentialism is as "true" as constructionism, this approach queries, might essentialist models be strategically useful in uniting women toward political action? Others caution, however, that this maneuver risks salvaging an essentialism that could ultimately be employed toward antifeminist aims (Fuss, 1989; Squire, 1989).

The Designation "Women's Ways" Excludes Women From Other Ways of Being

The constructionist position reframes this issue by redefining gender. There are no "women's ways"; there are modes of being that we have agreed to understand as gendered. Thus, all modes of being are hypothetically available to people of either sex, given a context that elicits and supports them.

This resolution raises new questions and new challenges to feminist psychology. If women do indeed manifest alternative modes of being by virtue of selective exposure to contexts, what does this imply for social change? If, for example, transactions traditionally gendered as "feminine" are to be valued, what strategies can we develop for altering the persistent devaluation of such qualities, so that doing feminine becomes an aim rather than anathema? In valuing the contexts that encourage ways of being that have been traditionally construed as women's, will we embrace our subordination? And if we end oppression, do we lose relationality as a human quality?

The Absence of Evidence for Sex Differences

A constructionist analysis is easily comfortable with the absence of empirical support for sex differences in the qualities addressed here; indeed, a constructionist perspective would not anticipate sex differences but would look instead to context. Research intended to explore sex differences has in fact confirmed the centrality not of sex but of context (Unger & Crawford, 1992; Lott, 1990).

CONCLUSION

Elements of the essentialist-constructionist debate resist resolution at this juncture. Is essentialism bankrupt as an underpinning for feminist theory and politics – particularly feminism that celebrates diversity among women? Or are there elements here that can be parlayed into a women-affirming, politically informed psychology? Is constructionism the answer? Or are the questions that linger too damaging? In affirming diversity by attending to context, do we escape the danger of universalizing the experience of all women only to forge a politic of individual identity that denies any fundamental commonality among women and is therefore beyond the reach of collective feminist social activism? Will rendering gender a verb free us from the person-blame attributions that further damage victims and hamper social action, or does it risk plunging us into another abyss, this time one of rampant relativism, affirming any truth as equally valid, unchecked by feminist values?

43

Although the answers are not readily forthcoming, we must ask the questions nonetheless. We must look carefully at the political and social implications of our work – beyond the borders of our own laboratories, offices, and classrooms. We must be alert lest the gains thus far achieved by feminist efforts be dissolved by a reformulation of retreat as progress. We need to think carefully about how our own theories, research, and practice are shaped by social forces that are often unfriendly to women's realities, cultural diversity, and feminist aims. Stephanie Shields (1975) summed up her meticulous deconstruction of early American psychology's view of women with these words: "That science played handmaiden to social values cannot be denied" (p. 753). We must take care that we not let our own science play handmaiden to social values that we strive, as feminists, to alter.

BOHAN

NOTES

1. For instance, Gilligan wrote, "women's deference is rooted not only in their social circumstances but also in the substance of their moral concern" (1979, p. 440), clearly distinguishing "the substance of their moral concern" from the social circumstances of their lives.

2. This notion has roots outside psychology. It is reflected in Marxist analyses of women's roles (e.g., Engels, 1977) and has been evoked in depictions of the experience of people of color (e.g., Fanon, 1967; Freire, 1970; hooks, 1984).

3. Although the construal of feminist ideals as humanity enhancing is itself a value judgement, it is one I comfortably affirm as foundational to the personal and political aims of feminism.

REFERENCES

Albee, G. (1986). Toward a just society: Lessons from observations on the primary prevention of psychopathology. *American Psychologist, 41*, 891–898.

Auerbach, J., Blum, L., Smith, V., & Williams, C. (1985). On Gilligan's *In a different voice. Feminist Studies, 11*, 149–161.

Beckwith, B. (1984). How magazines cover sex difference research: Journalism abdicates its watchdog role. *Science for the People, 16*, 18–23.

Belenky, M. F., Clinchy, B. M., Goldberger, N. R., & Tarule, J. M. (1986). *Women's ways of knowing: The development of self, voice and mind.* New York: Basic Books.

Berger, P. L., & Luckmann, T. (1967). *The social construction of reality.* New York: Doubleday.

Bohan, J. S. (1990). Contextual history: A framework for re–placing women in the history of psychology. *Psychology of Women Quarterly, 14*, 213–228.

Bordo, S. (1990). Feminism, postmodernism, and gender skepticism. In L. Nicholson (Ed.), *Feminism/postmodernism* (pp. 133–156). New York: Routledge.

Broughton, J. M. (1983). Women's rationality and men's virtues: A critique of gender dualism in Gilligan's theory of moral development. *Social Research, 50*, 597–642.

Brown, L. (1990). What's addiction got to do with it: A feminist critique of codependence. *Psychology of Women: Newsletter of Division 35, American Psychological Association, 17*(1), 1, 3–4.

Burman, E. (1990). Differing with deconstruction: A feminist critique. In I. Parker & J. Shotter (Eds.), *Deconstructing social psychology* (pp. 208–220). London: Routledge.

Butler, J. (1990). *Gender trouble.* New York: Routledge.

Caplan, N., & Nelson, S. D. (1973). On being useful: The nature and consequences of psychological research on social problems. *American Psychologist, 28*, 199–211.

Chodorow, N. (1978). *The reproduction of mothering.* Berkeley: University of California Press.

Crawford, M. (1989). Agreeing to differ: Feminist epistemologies and women's ways of knowing. In M. Crawford & M. Gentry (Eds.), *Gender and thought: Psychological perspectives* (pp. 128–145). New York: Springer–Verlag.

Crawford, M., & Marecek, J. (1989). Psychology reconstructs the female, 1968–1988. *Psychology of Women Quarterly, 13*, 147–165.

Deaux, K. (1984). From individual differences to social categories: Analysis of a decade's research on gender. *American Psychologist, 39*, 105–116.

Di Stefano, C. (1990). Dilemmas of difference. In L. J. Nicholson (Ed.), *Feminism/postmodernism* (pp. 63–82). New York: Routledge.

Eagly, A. H. (1987). *Sex differences in social behavior: A social-role interpretation*. Hillsdale, NJ: Erlbaum.

Engels, F. (1977). The origin of the oppression of women. In R. Agonito (Ed.), *History of ideas on woman: A source book* (pp. 273–288). New York: Putnam.

Faludi, S. (1991). *Backlash: The undeclared war against American women*. New York: Crown.

Fanon, F. (1967). *Black skin, white mask* (C. L. Markmann, Trans.). New York: Grove.

Fine, M. (1985). Reflections on a feminist psychology of women. *Psychology of Women Quarterly, 9*, 167–183.

Fine, M., & Gordon, S. (1989). Feminist transformations of/despite psychology. In M. Crawford & M. Gentry (Eds.), *Gender and thought: Psychological perspectives* (pp. 146–174). New York: Springer–Verlag.

Freire, P. (1970). *Pedagogy of the oppressed* (M. B. Ramos, Trans.). New York: Seabury.

Friedman, W. J., Robinson, A. B., & Friedman, B. L. (1987). Sex differences in moral judgements? A test of Gilligan's theory. *Psychology of Women Quarterly, 11*, 37–46.

Fuss, D. (1989). *Essentially speaking: Feminism, nature and difference*. New York: Routledge.

Gergen, K. J. (1985). The social constructionist movement in modern psychology. *American Psychologist, 40*, 266–275.

Gergen, K. J. (1988). Feminist critique of science and the challenge of social epistemology. In M. M. Gergen (Ed.), *Feminist thought and the structure of knowledge* (pp. 27–48). New York: New York University Press.

Gervasio, A. H., & Crawford, M. (1989). Social evaluations of assertiveness: A critique and speech act reformulation. *Psychology of Women Quarterly, 13*, 1–25.

Gilligan, C. (1979). Woman's place in man's life cycle. *Harvard Educational Review, 49*, 431–446.

Gilligan, C. (1982). *In a different voice: Psychological theory and women's development*. Cambridge, MA: Harvard University Press.

Greeno, C. G., & Maccoby, E. E. (1986). How different is the "different voice"? *Signs: Journal of Women in Culture and Society, 11*, 310–316.

Harding, S. (1986). *The science question in feminism*. Ithaca, NY: Cornell University Press.

Harding, S. (1991). *Whose science? Whose knowledge?* Ithaca, NY: Cornell University Press.

Hare–Mustin, R. T. (1991). Sex, lies, and headaches: The problem is power. *Journal of Feminist Family Therapy, 3*, 39–61.

Hare–Mustin, R. T., & Marecek, J. (1988). The meaning of difference: Gender theory, postmodernism, and psychology. *American Psychologist, 43*, 455–464.

Hare–Mustin, R. T., & Marecek, J. (1990). *Making a difference: Psychology and the construction of gender*. New Haven, CT: Yale University Press.

Hartsock, N. C. (1983). The feminist standpoint: Developing the ground for a specifically feminist historical materialism. In S. Harding & M. B. Hintikka (Eds.), *Discovering reality: Feminist perspectives on epistemology, metaphysics, methodology, and philosophy of science* (pp. 283–310). Dordrecht, The Netherlands: D. Reidel.

45

BOHAN

Henley, N. (1977). *Body politics: Power, sex, and nonverbal communication.* Englewood Cliffs, NJ: Prentice–Hall.

hooks, b. (1984). *Feminist theory: From margin to center.* Boston: South End Press.

Kahn, A. S., & Jean, P. J. (1983). Integration and elimination or separation and redefinition: The future of the psychology of women as a discipline. *Signs: Journal of Women in Culture and Society, 8*, 659–671.

Kahn, A. S., & Yoder, J. D. (1989). The psychology of women and conservatism: Rediscovering social change. *Psychology of Women Quarterly, 13*, 417–432.

Kerber, L. K., Greeno, C. G., Maccoby, E. E., Luria, Z., Stack, C. B., & Gilligan, C. (1986). On *In a different voice:* An interdisciplinary forum. *Signs: Journal of Women in Culture and Society, 11*, 304–333.

Lerman, H. (1986). From Freud to feminist personality theory: Getting here from there. *Psychology of Women Quarterly, 10*, 1–18.

Lorber, J., & Farrell, S. A. (1991). *The social construction of gender.* Newbury Park, CA: Sage.

Lott, B. (1985). The devaluation of women's competence. *Journal of Social Issues, 41*, 43–60.

Lott, B. (1986). *Women's lives: Themes and variations in gender learning.* Monterey, CA: Brooks/Cole.

Lott, B. (1988). Separate spheres revisited. *Contemporary Social Psychology, 13*, 55–62.

Lott, B. (1990). Dual natures or learned behavior: The challenge to feminist psychology. In R. T. Hare-Mustin & J. Marecek (Eds.), *Making a difference: Psychology and the construction of gender* (pp. 65–101). New Haven, CT: Yale University Press.

Lott, B. (1991, August). *Social learning of gender: A feminist review.* Division 35 Presidential Address presented at the meeting of the American Psychological Association, San Francisco, CA.

Major, B. (1987). Gender, justice, and the psychology of entitlement. In P. Shaver & C. Hendrick (Eds.), *Review of personality and social psychology: Vol. 7. Sex and gender* (pp. 124–148). Beverly Hills, CA: Sage.

Mednick, M. T. (1989). On the politics of psychological constructs: Stop the bandwagon, I want to get off. *American Psychologist, 44*, 1118–1123.

Miller, J. B. (1976). *Toward a new psychology of women.* Boston: Beacon Press.

Morawski, J. G. (1985). The measurement of masculinity and femininity: Engendering categorical realities. *Journal of Personality, 53*, 196–223.

Morawski, J. G. (1990). Toward the unimagined: Feminism and epistemology in psychology. In R. T. Hare-Mustin & J. Marecek (Eds.), *Making a difference: Psychology and the construction of gender* (pp. 150–183). New Haven, CT: Yale University Press.

Nicholson, L. J. (Ed.). (1990). *Feminism/postmodernism.* New York: Routledge.

Poovey, M. (1988). Feminism and deconstruction. *Feminist Studies, 14*, 51–65.

Probyn, E. (1990). Travels in the postmodern: Making sense of the local. In L. J. Nicholson (Ed.), *Feminism/postmodernism* (pp. 176–189). New York: Routledge.

Risman, B. J. (1987). Intimate relationships from a microstructural perspective: Men who mother. *Gender and Society, 1*, 6–32.

Rose, H. (1986). Beyond masculinist realities: A feminist epistemology for the sciences. In R. Bleier (Ed.), *Feminist approaches to science* (pp. 57–76). New York: Pergamon.

Sampson, E. E. (1977). Psychology and the American ideal. *Journal of Personality and Social Psychology, 35*, 767–782.

BOHAN

Sampson, E. E. (1989). The challenge of social change for psychology: Globalization and psychology's theory of the person. *American Psychologist, 44*, 914–921.

Sampson, E. E. (1990). Social psychology and social control. In 1. Parker & J. Shotter (Eds.), *Deconstructing social psychology* (pp. 117–126). London: Routledge.

Sarason, S. B. (1981). An asocial psychology and a misdirected clinical psychology. *American psychologist, 36*, 827–836.

Scheman, N. (1983). Individualism and the objects of psychology. In S. Harding & M. B. Hintikka (Eds.), *Discovering reality: Feminist perspectives on epistemology, metaphysics, methodology, and philosophy of science* (pp. 225–274). Dordrecht, The Netherlands: D. Reidel.

Sherif, C. W. (1979). What every intelligent person should know about psychology and women. In E. C. Snyder (Ed.), *The study of women: Enlarging perspectives on social reality* (pp. 143–183). New York: Harper & Row.

Shields, S. A. (1975). Functionalism, Darwinism and the psychology of women: A study in social myth. *American Psychologist, 30*, 739–754.

Smith, D. (1974). Women's perspectives as a radical critique of sociology. *Sociological Inquiry, 44*, 7–13.

Smith, D. (1987). *The everyday world as problematic: A feminist sociology.* Boston: Northeastern.

Squire, C. (1989). *Significant differences: Feminism in psychology.* London: Routledge.

Stack, C. B. (1986). The culture of gender: Women and men of color. *Signs: Journal of Women in Culture and Society, 11*, 321–324.

Tavris, C. (1992). *The mismeasure of woman.* New York: Simon & Schuster.

Unger, R. K. (1979). Toward a redefinition of sex and gender. *American Psychologist, 34*, 1085–1094.

Unger, R. K. (1983). Through the looking glass: No wonderland yet! (The reciprocal relationship between methodology and models of reality). *Psychology of Women Quarterly, 8*, 9–32.

Unger, R. K. (1989a). *Representations: Social constructions of gender.* Amityville, NY: Baywood.

Unger, R. K. (1989b). Sex, gender, and epistemology. In M. Crawford & M. Gentry (Eds.), *Gender and thought: Psychological perspectives* (pp. 17–35). New York: Springer–Verlag.

Unger, R. K., & Crawford, M. (1992). *Women and gender: A feminist psychology.* New York: McGraw–Hill.

West, C., & Zimmerman, D. H. (1987). Doing gender. *Gender and Society, 1*, 125–151.

Westkott, M. (1986). *The feminist legacy of Karen Horney.* New Haven, CT: Yale University Press.

Westkott, M. (1988). *Female relationality and the idealized self.* Unpublished manuscript. University of Colorado, Boulder.

Yeatman, A. (1990). A feminist theory of social differentiation. In L. J. Nicholson (Ed.), *Feminism/postmodernism* (pp. 281–299). New York: Routledge.

Zanna, M., & Pack, S. (1975). On the self–fulfilling nature of apparent sex differences in behavior. *Journal of Experimental Social Psychology 11*, 583–591.

47

FEMINIST POSTSTRUCTURALISM AND DISCOURSE ANALYSIS

Nicola Gavey

IN THIS chapter I will discuss *feminist poststructuralism* (Weedon, 1987), which, I believe, is of great potential value to feminist psychologists. The theoretical underpinnings of feminist poststructuralism are transdisciplinary in origin and are radically different from much of psychology. It is, however, closely aligned with some poststructuralist enterprises within psychology and recent moves toward a postmodern psychology (e.g., Antaki, 1988; Gergen, 1985, 1988; Hare-Mustin & Marecek, 1988; Henriques, Hollway, Urwin, Venn, & Walkerdine, 1984; Sampson, 1985; Shotter & Gergen, 1989; Walker-

I would like to thank Sylvia Blood and Kathryn McPhillips for discussions that were helpful in the preparation of this article: Jeanne Marecek and two reviewers for helpful comments and editing: and Patti Lather for an inspiring seminar (unfortunately only days before the final draft of this article had to be finished). The research reported in this article was partially funded by a grant from the University of Auckland Research Fund.

dine, 1986).[1] While I am specifically addressing this discussion to psychologists, poststructuralist approaches are not disciplinary-bound. Therefore any apparent "containment" of this discussion within "psychology" is artificial.

Discourse analysis is an approach compatible with feminist poststructuralist theory. This "method" will be discussed, along with an example of discourse analysis from my research on the sexual coercion of women within heterosexual relationships.

FEMINIST POSTSTRUCTURALISM

Poststructuralism refers to a loose collection of theoretical positions influenced by, for example, post-Saussurean linguistics, Marxism (particularly Althusser's theory of ideology), psychoanalysis (especially Lacan's reworkings), feminism, the "new French feminists" (Kristeva, Cixous, Irigaray) and the work of Derrida, Barthes, and Foucault. Weedon (1987) claimed that poststructuralism offers a useful conceptual foundation for feminist practice. She described feminist poststructuralism as "a mode of knowledge production which uses poststructuralist theories of language, subjectivity, social processes and institutions to understand existing power relations and to identify areas and strategies for change" (pp. 40–41).

In the sections that follow, I will discuss feminist poststructuralism in relation to feminist psychologies and briefly outline what I regard as some of its key concepts. Work such as this, which attempts to identify and describe some of the "key features" of poststructuralism (in this case as they relate to psychology at least), is on somewhat shaky ground. It is in danger of fixing and oversimplifying the ideas, thus presenting them in a potentially stagnant and deradicalized form in which they may be adopted as new orthodoxy. Some people working along poststructuralist lines would be reluctant to label their approaches as "poststructuralist." An important part of poststructuralism is its resistance to definition or even identification, presumably because such practices represent an attempt to pin down an essence that does not exist.

Relationship to Feminist Psychologies

Feminist initiatives within psychology have tended to fall within the dominant positivist, empiricist research tradition of mainstream psychology (e.g., Lykes & Stewart, 1986; Wallston & Grady, 1985). Yet feminist criticisms of positivist social science research question some of the underlying assumptions of these approaches. For example, the possibility and virtues of "value-free" research and objectivity, the validity of laboratory research, the relationship between the researcher and the researched (and the power imbalance between the two), the mystification of scientific "expertise," and so on are all questioned by these critiques (e.g., Bograd, 1988; Hoff 1988; Kitzinger, 1987; Wallston, 1985; Wallston & Grady, 1985; Wilkinson, 1986; Yllo, 1988).

Mainstream psychology can be understood to fall within the *liberal human-*

ist tradition, which is so pervasive in contemporary Western society that it is a rarely recognized and rarely questioned "fundamental faith" (Kitzinger, 1987, p. 192). This lack of recognition is not surprising given that liberal humanism is, more often than not, the theoretical basis of "common sense" (Belsey, 1980; Weedon, 1987). It assumes that individuals share a unique essence of human nature (Weedon, 1987). It also involves an emphasis on rationality and "the dignity of the individual and his or her inalienable rights to justice, liberty, privacy, freedom of thought, and the pursuit of happiness irrespective of colour, class, creed, or gender" (Kitzinger, 1987, p. 191). Through the "indi-vidualistic focus of contemporary liberal psychology," Kitzinger (1987) ar-gued, "the personalization of the political is achieved" (p. 37). Thus, for in-stance, although liberal humanist values are not unworthy, the absence of metatheoretical concerns about power render them insufficient.

Even initiatives within feminist psychology that are related only tenuously to mainstream psychology (e.g., Belenky, Clinchy, Goldberger, & Tarule, 1986) share its humanist assumptions. For example, within these and other feminist analyses, there is considerable emphasis on, and privileging of, women's *experience*, which is often at least implicitly regarded as universal and transhistorical—an entity that is pure and essential. Women's language is re-garded as transparently reflecting women's unique experience. As such, to speak "from experience" has almost unquestionable authority in much femi-nist discourse. The importance of language as a constitutive process remains largely unrecognized.

A poststructuralist approach to experience is radically different. It assumes that "experience has no inherent essential meaning" (Weedon 1987, p. 34), and "in so far as it is meaningful experience is constituted in language" (Wee-don, 1987, p. 85; see also Belsey, 1980; Wetherell, 1986). This does not mean that experience does not exist or that it is not important, but rather that the ways in which we understand and express it are never independent of lan-guage.

Feminist emphasis on women's experience is important as a political strat-egy that has given voice to women's oppression by, and resistance to, patriar-chal prescriptions. Many feminists are highly committed to privileging women's experience in a positively redefined form. According to Derrida (quoted in Culler, 1982), this attempt to reverse the hierarchical relationship between men and women is an important phase in the deconstruction of this hierarchy. However, feminist theories that maintain this stance ultimately of-fer a less radical challenge to patriarchal discourse and power because they move "parallel to hegemonic discourse" (Weedon, 1987, p. 110) and adhere to the existent terms of the debate. As Lather (1988) noted, we "need to wrestle with the postmodern questioning of the lust for authoritative accounts if we are not to remain as much a part of the problem as of the solution ourselves" (p. 577). Feminist theorizing that posits essential, fixed qualities for women

51

GAVEY

and men (even if women's qualities are positively valued) can end up support-ing the status quo. Subversion requires a challenge to, rather than uncritical preservation of, the practices and forms of subjectivity (that is, ways of being, identities, desires, ways of behaving, and so on) required by existing social in-stitutions (Weedon, 1987).

Feminist poststructuralism is not necessarily inconsistent with other forms of feminism. For example in its insistence on social and historical specificity it shares common concerns with some socialist feminist theories. Also, the fem-inist recognition of the need for consciousness raising, or "subjective transfor-mation" (Henriques et al., 1984, p. 7), as necessary for significant social change, is a point with which feminist poststructuralism concurs. In fact, some feminist writers explicitly locate feminism within postmodernism gen-erally (e.g., Flax, 1987). Others (e.g., Bowles, 1984) believe that poststruc-turalists are merely reiterating what feminists have been saying all along. This certainly highlights the perception that there is important shared ground be-tween feminism and poststructuralism in general, clarifying the futility of di-chotomizing the two movements.

Approaches to Knowledge

Poststructuralist theory rejects the possibility of absolute truth and objectivity. As feminists have observed, dominant conceptions of reality and truth in pa-triarchal Western society have tended to be male constructions which reflect and perpetuate male power interests. Feminists' explorations of our own real-ities, as women, have tended to produce different truths, thus casting suspi-cion on the idea of one reality and one truth. Similarly, from a poststructural-ist perspective, knowledge is considered to be socially constructed, through "a specific kind of production with definite relations to the social and material world" (Venn, 1984, p. 150). Knowledge is transient and inherently unstable—there are few, if any, universal truths. Furthermore, knowledge is understood to be not neutral—it is closely associated with power. Those who have the power to regulate what counts as truth are able to maintain their access to material advantages and power.

Within poststructuralism a plurality of meanings is welcomed. Traditional science is considered to be just one discourse among many, no more or less valid as a means to truth and knowledge than other discursive forms such as literature. Although traditional scientific method may be utilized because of its rhetorical power or its utility in addressing technological problems, it is not thought to have any superior access to knowledge and truth. It is not privileged, as it is within mainstream psychology, as the best or only approach.

The structure of reality assumed for most scientific investigation is different from what is assumed within poststructuralism. For example, Culler (1982) noted, "Structuralists are convinced that systematic knowledge is possible; poststructuralists claim to know only the impossibility of this knowledge" (p.

22). If one's world view does not presume a pre-existent, fixed, universal structure of reality (human nature or development, for example) available to be discovered, then one may question what is the purpose of research and scholarship. Some feminists imply that it is the political ends of women's liberation (Acker, Barry, & Esseveld, 1983; Jaggar, 1983). Similarly, for constructionism (which is part of the developing postmodern movement within psychology), moral criteria are being reasserted as relevant to scientific practice (Gergen, 1985). For feminist post-structuralism, goals of scholarship would include developing understandings or theories that are historically, socially, and culturally specific, and that are explicitly related to changing oppressive gender relations. Rather than "discovering" reality, "revealing" truth, or "uncovering" the facts, feminist poststructuralism would, instead, be concerned with disrupting and displacing dominant (oppressive) knowledges.

Language

These approaches to knowledge are connected to the poststructuralist assertion that all meaning and knowledge is discursively constituted through language and other signifying practices (Belsey, 1980; Weedon, 1987; see also Black & Coward, 1981). Any interpretation or understanding of an object or event is made available through a particular discourse concerning or relating to that object or event.

Feminist poststructuralism is underpinned with the understanding that language (and discourse) constitutes subjectivity. Meaning is actively constituted through language and therefore is neither fixed nor essential. Meanings arise out of difference and distinctions, not out of direct and immediate essences and substances (Sampson, 1985, 1989). Furthermore, "common language is not innocent and neutral," but "riddled with the presuppositions of Western metaphysics" (Coward & Ellis, 1977, p. 123). This view of language is in marked contrast to the liberal humanist view of language as transparent and expressive, merely reflecting and describing (pre-existing) subjectivity and human experience of the world.

Discourse

Weedon's feminist poststructuralism is particularly influenced by the Foucauldian idea that language is always located in discourse. Discourse refers to an interrelated "system of statements which cohere around common meanings and values. . . . [that] are a product of social factors, of powers and practices, rather than an individual's set of ideas" (Hollway, 1983, p. 231). It is a broad concept referring to a way of constituting meaning which is specific to particular groups, cultures, and historical periods and is always changing. For Weedon (1987), discourse is a structuring principle of society that constitutes and is reproduced in social institutions, modes of thought, and individual subjectivity. So, for example, the discursive production of the desire to be a "good mother"

GAVEY

53

(which has particular material and political implications for women), would involve such things as "the child-care books, the hospital visits, the routine check-ups, the normalizing techniques which define satisfactory maternal health or development, and so on" (Henriques et al., 1984, p. 219). It is through discourse that material power is exercised and that power relations are established and perpetuated. And, at the same time, every discourse is "the result of a practice of production which is at once material, discursive and complex, always inscribed in relation to other practices of production of discourse" (Henriques et al., 1984, p. 106). Feminist poststructuralism maintains an emphasis on the material bases of power (for example, social, economic, and cultural arrangements) and the need for change at this level of discourse. This emphasis and insistence distinguishes it from some poststructuralist approaches that are highly abstract and apparently "apolitical" (Weedon, 1987).

Discourses are multiple, and they offer competing, potentially contradictory ways of giving meaning to the world. They offer "subject positions" for individuals to take up (Hollway, 1984; Weedon, 1987). These positions, or "possibilities" for constituting subjectivity (identities, behaviors, understandings of the world) vary in terms of the power they offer individuals. Discourses vary in their authority. The dominant discourses appear "natural," denying their own partiality and gaining their authority by appealing to common sense. These discourses, which support and perpetuate existing power relations, tend to constitute the subjectivity of most people most of the time (in a given place and time). So, for example, systems of meaning such as feminism are currently limited in their power because they are marginalized and unavailable as yet as subject positions to many women.

Individuals are not passive, however. Rather they are active and have "choice" when positioning themselves in relation to various discourses. For example, women can identify with and conform to traditional discursive constructions of femininity or they can resist, reject, and challenge them (to a greater or lesser extent). This is not a simple matter of rational choice however. Weedon suggested that consciousness, as fragmented and contradictory, is the product of a discursive battle for the subjectivity of the individual. For example, some women have chosen feminism as a system of meaning that is preferable for understanding their lives in this society at this time. Yet despite this choice some aspects of a feminist woman's subjectivity may still be gendered in traditionally feminine ways, and she may retain desires and behaviors incompatible with the goals of feminism (e.g., see Coward, 1984).

Subjectivity

Subjectivity is constituted or constructed through language and discourse. Subjectivity refers to "the conscious and unconscious thoughts and emotions of the individual, her sense of herself and her ways of understanding her relation to the world" (Weedon, 1987, p. 32).

Western psychology usually assumes that the individual has an essential, coherent, and unique nature and subjectivity. Poststructuralism does not. It seeks
to "decentre the subject"—to shift emphasis away from the individual as the
origin and guarantor of meaning, and as a "fully aware and self-present" agent
(Sampson, 1989, p. 14). In direct contrast to the humanist assumptions of a
unified, rational *self*, poststructuralism proposes *a subject* that is fragmentary,
inconsistent, and contradictory. Poststructuralism thus denies authenticity to
individual experience. It also denies the existence of an essential female nature—an important concept within some feminist discourses. It offers instead
a "contextualization of experience and an analysis of its constitution and ideological power" (Weedon, 1987, p. 125). It is, therefore, able to contend with
contradictions in experience, such as, the presence of desires and behavior inconsistent with women's liberation in women who see themselves as feminists. As Weedon suggested, an advantage of poststructuralism is its recognition of a "conscious awareness of the contradictory nature of subjectivity can
introduce the possibility of political choice between modes of femininity in
different situations and between the discourses in which they have their
meaning" (p. 87). It is possible, therefore, not to deny desires which may be
incompatible with liberation, "but rather to understand desires as produced
and therefore, potentially at least, as changeable" (Henriques et al., 1984, p.
219).

Experience as Text

Poststructuralist theory has probably been most developed within the field of
literary criticism (e.g., Belsey, 1980; Culler, 1982). A poststructuralist approach
to a fictive text regards it as an embodiment of various discourses available in
the social, cultural, and historical context of the author. The traditional notion
of authorship is challenged (Barthes, 1987; Foucault, 1979), as the author is
seen more as a reproducer of discourse than a creator of new thought. Literary texts provide important examples of various discourses in circulation at a
given time and in a given culture, but they are not regarded as providing great
original insights into "basic" human nature or social processes. Emphasis is
placed on the practice of reading, recognizing that there are numerous different *readings* of a text possible. There is no essential "true" meaning that resides
within the text; rather, different meanings are constructed on every reading.

Parallels can be drawn between the processes of analyzing and understanding literature and the processes of analyzing and understanding individuals'
behavior or their accounts of their experience (Potter, Stringer, & Wetherell,
1984). As language constitutes subjectivity, both fiction and individuals' self-
reports are examples of this constitution. At least two points are important
here with regard to psychology. First, the notion of experience (or behavior,
self-reports, etc.) as text implies that we should approach the reports and accounts of those we research as discursive productions and not as reflections

GAVEY

(accurate, distorted, or otherwise) of their "true" experience. Second, the poststructuralist emphasis on reading and the multiple meanings of texts reminds us that our understanding (reading) of our research data is really the constitution of such data, insofar as they are meaningful, and it is controlled by our own location in various discourses—for example, scientific, humanist, therapeutic, feminist, and so on.

DISCOURSE ANALYSIS

As one develops new theoretical understandings, one's ways of working shift. A way of working that is consistent with a feminist poststructuralist perspective is discourse analysis. This article presents discourse analysis as one tool for critical analysis, but by no means prescribes it as "the" new method.

Discourse analysis refers to a set of methods that have been used by workers with different theories of language in a variety of ways (e.g., van Dijk 1985). The particular form of discourse analysis that I present involves identifying the social discourses available to women and men in a given culture and society at a given time. These discourses provide subject positions, constituting our subjectivities, and reproducing or challenging existing gender relations (e.g., Hollway, 1984; Walkerdine, 1986). Close attention is paid to the social context of language and to its function in or relation to structures of power. One of the aims is to provide detailed, historically specific analyses which will enable us "to explain the working of power on behalf of specific interests and to analyze the opportunities for resistance to it" (Weedon, 1987, p. 41).

Potter and Wetherell (1987) note that one feature common to all forms of discourse analysis is that:

> Participants' discourse or social texts are approached *in their own right* and not as a secondary route to things "beyond" the text like attitudes, events or cognitive processes. Discourse is treated as a potent, action-oriented medium, not a transparent information channel. (p. 160, emphasis in original)

Discourse analysis involves the careful reading of texts (e.g., transcripts of conversations or interviews, or existent documents or records, or even more general social practices), with a view to discerning discursive patterns of meaning, contradictions, and inconsistencies. It is an approach that identifies and names language processes people use to constitute their own and others' understanding of personal and social phenomena. These processes are related to the reproduction of or challenge to the distribution of power between social groups and within institutions. Discourse analysis proceeds on the assumption that these processes are not static, fixed, and orderly but rather fragmented, inconsistent, and contradictory.

If this discussion of discourse analysis seems vague, it is perhaps because

56

GAVEY

there are no recipes or formulae. It is a form of analysis that is attentive both to detail in language and to the wider social picture. From the perspective of social psychologists, Potter and Wetherell (1987) emphasized:

> there is no *method* to discourse analysis in the way we traditionally think of an experimental method or content analysis method. What we have is broad theoretical framework concerning the nature of discourse and its role in social life, along with a set of suggestions about how discourse can best be studied and how others can be convinced findings are genuine. (p. 175, emphasis in original)

Just as there is no method in the usual sense for psychology, similarly the criteria for evaluating poststructuralist forms of discourse analysis bear little resemblance to traditional evaluative practices in mainstream psychology. (For a discussion on evaluating discourse analyses, see Potter & Wetherell, 1987.)

A DISCOURSE ANALYSIS APPROACH TO WOMEN'S EXPERIENCES OF SEXUAL COERCION WITHIN HETEROSEXUAL RELATIONSHIPS

In this section, I present an example of a discourse analysis from my ongoing research on women's experiences of sexual coercion within heterosexual relationships. One view of sexual victimization holds that it exists on a continuum of normative heterosexual practices which are socially constructed as involving an active, initiating male and a passive, responsive female (e.g., Gavey, 1988; Jackson, 1978; MacKinnon, 1983). From this perspective it makes limited sense to arbitrarily separate "rape" from "not rape," and "sexual coercion" from "noncoercive heterosexual sex." The majority of identified cases of rape and sexual abuse occur within what have been called "legitimate heterosexual relationships" (Gavey, 1988) or "potentially appropriate relationships" (Estrich, 1987) (e.g., Russell, 1982, 1984). Thus it is important to look at the full range of sexual coercion that occurs within such relationships. This range includes little discussed phenomena such as *social coercion* (e.g., engaging in sex only to avoid, for example, appearing "frigid" or old-fashioned) and *interpersonal coercion* (e.g., engaging in sex because it is the only way to stop a man's continual pleading) (Finkelhor & Yllo, 1983). These more normative forms of coercion include situations where the woman appears to *consent* to take part in an interaction despite not wanting to. Some of these forms of coercion, particularly social coercion, are rarely discussed in the literature on sexual victimization. I suggest this is because within the dominant discourses on heterosexuality, such behavior appears natural.

My research seeks to locate women's accounts of their experiences of heterosexual coercion in relation to specific discourses concerning sexuality and sexual violence in particular, and interpersonal relationships and gender relations more generally.

Presented on page 58 is a collection of extracts from the transcript of an

57

EXCERPTS FROM THE TRANSCRIPT OF AN INTERVIEW
WITH SUE DAVIS

1. Sue Davis: I just had no idea that he felt sexually attracted to me at all. I thought we were just good
2. friends, because we got on really well. And there was a New Year's party where he made it quite clear that,
3. you know, his manhood was going to be dashed if he didn't go to bed with me. And I got myself into the
4. situation where I knew that he was very vulnerable, and it didn't really mean a lot to me, and it seemed to
5. mean such a hell of a lot to him that I said yes. And it was not the greatest sexual experience I've ever had
6. anyway. I don't think it probably did much for him, because he realized that there wasn't much to it, and
7. so I don't think I did him any favors anyway, really. I would have been better to have found the right
8. words to say no.
9. (Gap of two pages)
10. Sue Davis: Um (pause) he just came and said he wanted to talk to me I think. "Come outside, come
11. outside." Something along that line, fairly insistently, because I was busy talking to someone else
12. and didn't really want to go and I remember I sort of went because he was so insistent. Um
13. (pause) and I didn't think I was naive in those days, but I certainly wasn't expecting him to be
14. (pause) you know he made it (pause) he said "Oh, come to Bruce's room" and I think then I figured
15. out what he wanted, but I figured if I went with him I would be able to sort of sit down and talk to
16. him and sort of say my line which I'd said quite a few times in the past by then, you know, "You're
17. a very attractive person, but (pause) um" And he was just so frantic that um (pause)
18. (Gap of half a page)
19. Interviewer: And then once you were out there he was quite frantic and (pause)
20. Sue Davis: Well he was sort of desperate to have sex and (pause)
21. Interviewer: How was he communicating that?
22. Sue Davis: Um, words, things like "Please Sue, please," you know, and physically. I can't
23. remember exactly how, but, you know, sort of, um (pause) he certainly didn't force me. Um I
24. somehow through the words got the feeling-although he never said it-that he'd never had sex
25. before. Um and I remember feeling the doomed "Oh shit!" you know. Um, as I said before it didn't
26. mean that much to me and it seemed to mean so much to him, so basically I lay down on the bed
27. and let him have sex, but it was not a mutually enjoyable sex. Basically he masturbated inside me
28. as far as I am concerned, and you know it was an inappropriate time (pause) it was all wrong
29. because, you know, if I had gone to bed with someone like that in another situation where we'd
30. cared about each other and we were going to be continuing that relationship I could have taught
31. him, um, but he was going off the next day, anyway. So as a first sexual experience it was lousy
32. for him-well I mean he came, but so what, you know, that was all. Um, and, you know I felt flat.
33. I didn't want to go and have sex with him in the first place. I had no idea that he felt that way
34. towards me.
35. (Gap of half a page)
36. Interviewer: What, if any, were some of the initial consequences of this event? (Gap of half a line)
37. Sue Davis: Um (pause) Well, he must have gone away with a fairly disillusioned attitude towards sex as far
38. as his first encounter had gone. I um felt just depressed about the whole incident. I didn't like it. I hadn't
39. wanted it, and I'd simply done it because I didn't want (pause) I seemed to have sex a lot at the time
40. because I didn't want to hurt someone's feelings. As though I was strong and they were not. Um, and I
41. know my feeling in those days was that sexual activity by itself isn't important, it was how I felt about
42. someone that made it important or not important. I still feel that way a bit. You know, it's (pause)
43. although I've been stuck with one person for many years it's (pause) sex without the love is just (pause) it's
44. no different from wiping your bottom after you've gone to the toilet, or brushing your hair. It's a physical
45. activity. It's an enjoyable one, um, well it can be an enjoyable one.
46. (Gap of one third of a page)
47. Interviewer: What feelings and thoughts do you have about this experience when you look back on
48. it?
49. Sue Davis: It makes me squirm a bit. Um, it's not one that I look back with any enthusiasm on,
50. whereas there are a lot of things I do look back with enthusiasm on, and, yeah, it was the motives.
51. the things that caused the behaviour were all wrong, and I thing that's the thing that makes me
52. not like it.

interview with a woman about her experiences of heterosexual coercion. Sue Davis (a pseudonym) is a Pakeha[2] woman who was 35 years old at the time of the interview. The conversation concerns an incident that was recalled in response to the question, "Have you ever had any sexual experiences that, looking back on, you feel uncomfortable about or regret in some way?" The incident happened 14 years before the interview, when she was 21 years old. Because Sue Davis describes herself as having "consented" to have sexual intercourse ("he certainly didn't force me"), it would not be regarded as an instance of sexual victimization by, for example, researchers taking a literal and de-contextualized reading of her account.

Because the reading process is constructive and not neutral, it is important to identify one's positions as a reader in relation to this text (even though such identification is unlikely to capture the nuances and complexity of these positions). My positions are currently, at least, feminist and poststructuralist in terms of theoretical perspectives, and female, heterosexual, Pakeha and educated in terms of my social location.

The main focus of the analysis is on the content of the text-that is, what was actually said. But, because language is a material and social process, the social and historical contexts of the account are also important. I examine this text for the presence of discourses relevant to women's experiences of social and interpersonal heterosexual coercion and for subject positions offered to women by these various discourses.

I will briefly discuss two related discursive themes in this text. These are the "permissive sexuality" discourse and the "male sexual needs" discourse (cf. Hollway, 1984). These discourses provide the respective possible subject positions of a "sexually liberated" woman for whom sex is "no big deal," and a woman who is responsive to and takes responsibility for male "needs." Sue Davis appears to have taken up these two positions. These discourses and subject positions can be understood in terms of their historical location, in a period from the early 1970s to the present, a time in the wake of the so-called sexual revolution for women.

Examples in the text of the "permissive sexuality" discourse include "it didn't mean that much to me" (lines 25–26) and "I seemed to have sex a lot at the time" (line 39; others appear in lines 41, 43–45). Examples of the positioning of taking responsibility for male sexuality include "his manhood was going to be dashed if he didn't go to bed with me" (line 3), and "he was sort of desperate to have sex" (line 20; others are found in lines 4, 4–5, 7, 12, 14–15, 15–16, 17, 26, 30–31, 31–32, 37, 39–40, 40).

These two discourses in conjunction, can render a woman almost "unrepeable" (Russell, 1982, p. 58) from the point of view of dominant discourses on sexuality and rape (except in a "classic" rape in which a stranger uses extreme violence). As Cherry (1983) noted, "in some instances, rapes literally 'don't exist' because the victim sees the coercive sexual experiences as natural and legitimate in the context of a structured power relationship between a man and a woman" (p. 252). Commenting on the sexual revolution, Hite (1977) addressed aspects of both the "permissive sexuality" and "male sexual needs" discourses:

> This glorification of the male "sex drive" and male orgasm "needs" amounts to justifying men in whatever they have to do to get intercourse—even rape—and defines the "normal" male as one who is "hungry" for intercourse. On the other hand, the definition of female sexuality as passive and receptive (but, since the sexual revolution, also necessary for a healthy woman) amounts to telling women to submit to this aggressive male "sex drive". (p. 465)

Given the subject positions adopted by Sue Davis, nonconsent in the situation she encountered would have been almost inconceivable. Thus the whole notion of consent and the meaning of choice in such contexts are rendered problematic. What is important here is that these subject positions reproduce a form of heterosexual gender relations in which women lack power.

One value of a poststructuralist approach is its assertion that subjectivity is produced through discourses that are multiple, possibly contradictory, and unstable. Sue Davis, for example, does not escape from any ill effects of this unwanted sexual experience. It left her feeling "flat" (line 32) and "depressed" (line 38) (see also, lines 7–8, and 49). This suggests that her experience was not constituted solely by her positionings in the permissive sexuality discourse and the male sexual needs discourse. The inconsistency and contradictions in her language (for example, at one stage she refers to feeling "the doomed 'Oh shit!'" [line 25], and the very next sentence, says "it didn't mean that much to me" [lines 25–26]) can be understood as the effect of a discursive battle between a positioning in the "permissive sexuality" discourse and another position within this or some other discourse and not articulated explicitly. This discourse might involve women's rights to "mutually enjoyable sex" (line 27) (which could be part of the "permissive sexuality" discourse) or some form of feminist discourse about the exploitation of women within heterosexual relationships. It is tempting to interpret this contradiction as indicating that her positioning in the permissive sexuality and male sexual needs discourses amounts to a false consciousness, and her negative feelings represent her true, authentic, real response. But such an interpretation is problematic because of its oversimplification and essentialism as well as its elitism and arrogance (Condor, 1986; Kitzinger, 1986; Marshall, 1986). Poststructuralists would suggest that some conflict of this kind is almost inevitable and is a potential source of change.

ADVANTAGES AND DISADVANTAGES OF FEMINIST POSTSTRUCTURALISM

There are some potential problems with a feminist poststructuralist approach for feminist psychologists. First, its anti-humanism and decentering of the in-

60

GAVEY

dividual is so inimical to many feminists and psychologists alike that they may reject it outright. Wilkinson (1986) found among the accounts of feminist research that she reviewed "a broad consensus regarding both the necessity of giving priority to female experience and of developing theory which is firmly situated in this experience" (p. 13). Feminist poststructuralism, of course, holds that female experience is never independent of social and linguistic processes and, in fact, is constituted by them. Hence it problematizes this approach to feminist research.

A second disadvantage is that poststructuralist theory is conceptually complicated, and often discussed in unfamiliar and therefore difficult language. This renders it to some extent inaccessible to people without certain sorts of backgrounds and the time to devote to indepth study of unfamiliar material. Belsey (1980) commented that this difficulty does not arise from "a perverse desire to be obscure" (p. 4), but rather: "to challenge familiar assumptions and familiar values in a discourse which, in order to be easily readable, is compelled to reproduce these assumptions and values, is an impossibility. New concepts, new theories, necessitate new, unfamiliar and therefore initially difficult discourses" (pp. 4–5). Thus, there may be no simple solution to this problem. This is of concern to feminists, especially those who give priority to combating elitism and sharing information outside formal education channels.

A third potential objection to poststructuralism is its relativism. As Flax (1987) noted:

61

> It is also appealing, for those who have been excluded, to believe that reason will triumph—that those who proclaim such ideas as objectivity will respond to rational arguments. If there is no objective basis for distinguishing between true and false beliefs, then it seems that power alone will determine the outcome of competing truth claims. This is a frightening prospect to those who lack (or are oppressed by) the power of others. (p. 625)

In a useful discussion of relativism in relation to postmodernism and feminism, Lather (in press) contends that relativism is only a problem if a foundational approach to knowledge is accepted: "All this hand-wringing about relativism can be framed primarily as a *liberal* response to the crisis of absolutism" (emphasis in original). My response to feminists' fears about relativism is to emphasize that it does not mean that we have to abandon our knowledges and values. Rather we must be aware that there is no sure way of guaranteeing or fixing them or of convincing others of their truth. Theory and research should be assessed in terms of their utility in achieving politically defined goals rather than their "truth value" (Kitzinger, 1986, p. 153).

What feminist poststructuralism offers us is a theoretical basis for analyzing the subjectivities of women and men in relation to language, other cultural practices, and the material conditions of our lives. It embraces complexity and contradiction and, I would suggest, surpasses theories that offer single-cause deterministic explanations of patriarchy and gender relations. It not only gives credence to women's active resistance to patriarchal power (as well as our oppression by it), but it also offers promising ways of theorising about change—all of which are important to feminism.

Feminist poststructuralism and other postmodern initiatives open up new ways of working for feminist psychologists. These include analysis of the socially constructed nature of human behavior, deconstruction of the assumptions within language and the processes of producing subjectivities, and discourse analysis of existing discursive fields and related subject positions. I hope this article will generate interest in poststructuralism among feminist psychologists. As that occurs, we will be able to develop our own more detailed and critical feminist poststructuralist understandings.

NOTES

1. Although the distinction between poststructuralism and postmodernism is not clear, and the terms are sometimes used interchangeably. I tend to assume that postmodernism refers to times and practices, and poststructuralism to theories which parallel and are part of these practices.

2. *Pakeha* refers to New Zealanders of European descent.

REFERENCES

Acker, J., Barry, K., & Esseveld, J. (1983). Objectivity and truth: Problems in doing feminist research. *Women's Studies International Forum, 6*, 423–435.

Antaki, C. (Ed.). (1988). *Analysing everyday explanation. A casebook of methods.* London: Sage.

Barthes, R. (1987). The death of the author (S. Heath, Trans.). In P. Barry, *Issues in contemporary critical theory* (pp. 53–55). Houndmills, Hampshire: MacMillan Education. (Original work published in 1968.)

Belenky, M. F., Clinchy, B. M., Goldberger, N. R., & Tarule, J. M. (1986). *Women's ways of knowing: The development of self, voice, and mind.* New York: Basic.

Belsey, C. (1980). *Critical practice.* London: Methuen.

Black, M., & Coward, R. (1981). Linguistic, social and sexual relations: A review of Dale Spender's *Man–Made Language. Screen Education, 39*, 69–85.

Bograd, M. (1988). Feminist perspectives on wife abuse: An introduction. In K. Yllo & M. Bograd (Eds.), *Feminist perspectives on wife abuse* (pp. 11–26). Newbury Park, CA: Sage.

Bowles, G. (1984). The uses of hermeneutics for feminist scholarship. *Women's Studies International Forum, 7*, 185–188.

Cherry, F. (1983). Gender roles and sexual violence. In E. R. Allgeier & N. B. McCormick (Eds.), *Changing boundaries: Gender roles and sexual behavior* (pp. 245–260). Palo Alto: Mayfield.

Condor, S. (1986). Sex role beliefs and "traditional" women: Feminist and intergroup perspectives. In S. Wilkinson (Ed.), *Feminist social psychology: Developing theory and practice* (pp. 97–118). Philadelphia: Open University Press.

Coward, R. (1984). *Female desire: Women's sexuality today*. London: Paladin.

Coward, R., & Ellis, J. (1977). *Language and materialism: Developments in semiology and the theory of the subject*. London: Routledge & Kegan Paul.

Culler, J. (1982). *On deconstruction: Theory and criticism after structuralism*. Ithaca, NY: Cornell University Press.

Estrich, S. (1987). *Real rape*. Cambridge, MA: Harvard University Press.

Finkelhor, D., & Yllo, K. (1983). Rape in marriage: A sociological view. In D. Finkelhor, R. J. Gelles, G. T. Hotaling, & M. A. Straus (Eds.), *The dark side of families: Current family violence research* (pp. 119–130). Beverly Hills: Sage.

Flax, J. (1987). Postmodernism and gender relations in feminist theory. *Signs: Journal of Women in Culture and Society, 12*, 621–643.

Foucault, M. (1979). What is an author? (K. Hanet, Trans.). *Screen, 20*, 13–33. (Original work published in 1969.)

Gavey, N. (1988, September). *Rape and sexual coercion within heterosexual relationships*. Paper presented at the XXIV International Congress of Psychology, Sydney, Australia.

Gergen, K. J. (1985). The social constructionist movement in modern psychology. *American Psychologist, 40*, 266–275.

Gergen, K. J. (1985, August). Toward a post–modern psychology. Invited address at the XXIV International Congress of Psychology, Sydney, Australia. (From *Wednesday Abstracts* XXIV International Congress of Psychology, August 28–September 2, 1988.)

Hare–Mustin, R. T., & Marecek, J. (1988). The meaning of difference: Gender theory, post–modernism, and psychology: *American Psychologist, 43*, 455–464.

Henriques, J., Hollway, W., Urwin, C., Venn, C., & Walkerdine, V. (1984). *Changing the subject: Psychology, social regulation, and subjectivity*. London: Methuen.

Hite, S. (1977). *The Hite report: A nationwide study of female sexuality*. Sydney: Summit Books.

Hollway, W. (1983). Heterosexual sex: Power and desire for the other. In S. Cartledge & J. Ryan (Eds.), *Sex and Love: New thoughts on old contradictions* (pp. 124–140). London: Women's Press.

Hollway, W. (1984). Gender difference and the production of subjectivity. In Henriques, J., Hollway, W., Urwin, C., Venn, C., & Walkerdine, V. (Eds.), *Changing the subject: Psychology, social regulation, and subjectivity* (pp. 227–263). London: Methuen.

Hoff, L. A. (1988). Collaborative feminist research and the myth of objectivity. In K. Yllo & M. Bograd (Eds.), *Feminist perspectives on wife abuse* (pp. 269–281). Newbury Park, CA: Sage.

Jackson, S. (1978). The social context of rape: Sexual scripts and motivation. *Women's Studies International Quarterly, 1*, 27–38.

Jaggar, A. M. (1983). *Feminist politics and human nature*. Totowa, NJ: Rowman & Allenheld.

Kitzinger, C. (1986). Introducing and developing Q as a feminist methodology: A study of accounts of lesbianism. In S. Wilkinson (Ed.), *Feminist social psychology: Developing theory and practice* (pp. 151–172). Philadelphia: Open University Press.

Kitzinger, C. (1987). *The social construction of lesbianism*. London: Sage.

Lather, P. (1988). Feminist perspectives on empowering research methodologies. *Women's Studies International Forum, 11*, 569–581.

63

GAVEY

Lather, P. (in press). Postmodernism and the politics of Enlightenment. *Educational Foundations*.

Lykes, M. B., & Stewart, A. J. (1986). Evaluating the feminist challenge to research in personality and social psychology: 1963–1983. *Psychology of Women Quarterly, 10*, 393–412.

MacKinnon, C. (1983). Feminism, Marxism, method, and the state: Toward feminist jurisprudence. *Signs: Journal of Women in Culture and Society, 8*, 635–658.

Marshall, J. (1986). Exploring the experiences of women managers: Toward rigour in qualitative methods. In S. Wilkinson (Ed.), *Feminist social psychology: Developing theory and practice* (pp. 193–209). Philadelphia: Open University Press.

Potter, J., Stringer, P., & Wetherell, M. (1984). *Social texts and context: Literature and social psychology*. London: Routledge & Kegan Paul.

Potter, J., & Wetherell, M. (1987). *Discourse and social psychology: Beyond attitudes and behaviour*. London: Sage.

Russell, D. E. H. (1982). *Rape in marriage*. New York: Macmillan.

Russell, D. E. H. (1984). *Sexual exploitation: Rape, child sexual abuse, and workplace harassment*. Beverly Hills: Sage.

Sampson, E. E. (1985). The decentralization of identity: Toward a revised concept of personal and social order. *American Psychologist, 40*, 1203–1211.

Sampson, E. E. (1989). The deconstruction of the self. In J. Shotter & K. J. Gergen (Eds.), *Texts of identity* (pp. 1–19). London: Sage.

Shotter, J., & Gergen, K. J. (Eds.). (1989). *Texts of identity*. London: Sage.

van Dijk, T. A. (1985). *Handbook of discourse analysis* (Vols. 1–4). London: Academic.

Venn, C. (1984). The subject of psychology. In Henriques, J., Hollway, W., Urwin, C., Venn, C., & Walkerdine, V. (Eds.), *Changing the subject: Psychology, social regulation, and subjectivity* (pp. 119–152). London: Methuen.

Walkerdine, V. (1986). Poststructuralist theory and everyday social practices: The family and the school. In S. Wilkinson (Ed.), *Feminist social psychology: Developing theory and practice* (pp. 57–76). Philadelphia: Open University Press.

Wallston, B. S. (1985). Feminist research methodology from a psychological perspective: Science as the marriage of agentic and communal. In M. Safir, M. T. Mednick, D. Israeli, & J. Bernard (Eds.), *Women's worlds: From the new scholarship* (pp. 226–223). New York: Praeger.

Wallston B. S., & Grady, K. E. (1985). Integrating the feminist critique and the crisis in social psychology: Another look at research methods. In V. E. O'Leary, R. K. Unger, & B. S. Wallston (Eds.), *Women, gender, and social psychology*. Hillsdale, NJ: Erlbaum.

Weedon, C. (1987). *Feminist practice and poststructuralist theory*. Oxford: Blackwell.

Wetherell, M. (1986). Linguistic repertoires and literary criticism: New directions for a social psychology of gender. In S. Wilkinson (Ed.), *Feminist social psychology: Developing theory and practice* (pp. 77–95). Philadelphia: Open University Press.

Wilkinson, S. (1986). Sighting possibilities: Diversity and commonality in feminist research. In S. Wilkinson (Ed.), *Feminist social psychology: Developing theory and practice* (pp. 7–24). Philadelphia: Open University Press.

Yllo, K. (1988). Political and methodological debates in wife abuse research. In K. Yllo & M. Bograd (Eds.), *Feminist perspectives on wife abuse* (pp. 28–50). Newbury Park, CA: Sage.

FEMINISM AND PSYCHOLOGY

Mary Brown Parlee

chapter 3

1996

THIS ESSAY originated as an oral presentation to an interdisciplinary group of feminist colleagues at the City University of New York in 1987. I revised and expanded it with similar readers in mind for publication. (It appeared in 1992.) By 1996 much had changed however, including the multiple meanings of feminism, psychology, the psychology of women, feminist psychology, women's studies, and feminist theory in the United States—and the social, political and economic conditions of women's lives around the world.

My own thinking and political consciousness have changed too, in ways that thwarted my initial efforts to revise and update this essay (rather than simply agree to its being reprinted) for a collection the editors anticipate will be read primarily by psychologists. Parts of it—both specific research studies and general theoretical/political sensibility—now seem out-of-date superceded by work I think is relevant and better.[1] But the lesson of the lecture traditionally given to first year medical students is all too apt here. "Half of what you will learn in the next four years will be essential for the practice of medicine, the other half will be out of date within a decade—problem is we don't know which is which." What is "out-of-date," what has been "super-seded" in my essay? The answer requires a nuanced intellectual, scientific, aes-thetic judgment and there is no simple answer: it depends on the knowledge and perspective and interests of . . .whom? The readers? The writer?

As a feminist I want to know who I am speaking with [writing for] in or-der to seek out and establish some common ground of assumptions, rele-vances, saliences in which a conversation might take root.[2] Thus I was reluc-tant to simply revise my essay into a narrative or linear argument from my own perspective about "feminism" and "psychology." I would have to disre-gard the facts that the intended readerships of the old and new version are different, and that my relationship to the material has changed as I have moved entirely out of psychology (institutionally and intellectually) and into women's studies and science studies and activism outside the academy.

Given the multiple and changing worlds I inhabit (and who does not?), I know that discursive objects such as "feminism," "social construction," "femi-nist theory," "psychology," "gender," and the like do not have fixed stable meanings. They are differently constructed in different conversations, in dif-ferent communities of practice: what is problematic in one community is tak-en for granted in another, what is central in one is unknown or irrelevant in another. In short, I am much more self-conscious about my participation in what Katie King (1994) calls "conversations" than I was even five years ago. And I take seriously her observation that "Feminists are not always clear about which conversations they are participating in at any time, who and what they are recruiting, making new alliances, new political versions [p. xi]." As I become clearer about this, however, a certain kind of linear narrative/ar-gument seems less possible—and certainly less rewarding—as a postmodern feminist project.

As King says, "It is not at all obvious that specific debates may simultane-ously inhabit several conversations at once, that objects such as "theory" may travel between and among many conversations, or that multiple objects con-structed in different conversations may appear "the same" as displayed under a single sign. "Theory" is sometimes many such political objects mis/dis/played by the single word [p. xi]." And the same is true of "feminism," "psychology," "psychology of women," "feminist psychology," "women's studies," and other taxonomic categories . . . . all of which appear in my 1992 text in ways that now seem wrong to me.

So, with the editors' encouragement, I decided to heighten the multiple, contradictory, shifting, and decentered meanings co-constructed by author, text, and readers rather than try to order, suppress, and deny them. I have left the 1992 version pretty much the way it appeared, with some additional ref-

66

PARLEE

erences to more recent work. It can be read on its own as an essay by a psychologist talking to feminists in interdisciplinary women's studies, including feminists in psychology who believe it is high time to go beyond critiques of psychology to the production of new psychological knowledge from a feminist perspective.[3]

But throughout that text I have inserted another: my reflections on the earlier text. These are shaped by the conversations in which I am now more deeply engaged—in interdisciplinary women's studies and science studies and in unnamed spaces where grass-roots feminist activists and academics struggle together to make theoretical conversations infused with the narratives of lived experiences. My hope is this strategy will illuminate one of the central concerns of the essay from its inception: the relations between feminists who are psychologists, feminists in other academic disciplines, and feminist activists—and the ways these are reflected in the production of psychological knowledge.

1992

Feminist psychological research has developed through stages similar to feminist scholarship in other disciplines (Fowkles and McClure, 1984; DuBois et al., 1985). First there was recognition and documentation of the neglect of women and women's experiences—or, more accurately, documentation of the fact that the experiences and actions of some men had been misleadingly presented as universal. Then came recognition that the concepts and theories developed to provide an understanding of men's experience are often inadequate for understanding women. This revelation led to the effort to identify and study neglected problems of particular interest to women or problems defined in the popular/political discourse as "women's issues." (See Parlee, 1975; 1979; 1985 for references.)

1996

This kind of triumphalist (or at least, if one takes it at face value, very optimistic) talk about stages in feminist scholarship was part of the Zeitgeist of feminist academic administrators in the early-mid 1980s. In retrospect I think it probably was part of a rhetorical strategy to gain support for women's studies programs and for proposals to "mainstream"Women's Studies into the traditional liberal arts curriculum. (Andersen, 1988, describes and reflects on such projects.) I heartily believed in the worth of such projects and still do.[4] However, the rhetoric always seemed to me to be curiously detached from reality on the ground, in the trenches of committees that establish curricular requirements, hire new faculty, approve doctoral dissertation topics, and pursue sexual harassment complaints. Clearly it would have been just as easy (and I think true) for me to describe three kinds of feminist contributions to psychology as to invoke the Whiggish notion of "stages" of "development." So I wonder why that talk of stages [or "kinds" of feminism, or of feminist critiques of science] was/is so pervasive, so easy to fall into.

Even more embarrassing from my current perspective, however, is the way I talked about "feminist psychological research"—unqualified—as if an unmarked category, work by feminists in academic psychology in North America, could stand in for much more diverse realities.

1992

During the dozen or so years covered by these three phases of feminists' interactions with traditional psychology)from the late '60s to the early '80s), feminist psychologists built an organizational base within the field.

1996

"Traditional psychology" is one of those nonspecific terms (like "mainstream psychology") that I now think are specious. It is vague and seems to invite contestation by those it purportedly references, or those who simply want to know more concretely what the conversation is about. And contests over what someone means by "mainstream psychology" seem unlikely to advance feminist projects. What vague phrases like "traditional psychology" do achieve, however, is implicitly create an oppositional and more highly valued category ("feminist psychology," "the psychology of women"). By implication, and sometimes explicitly, they also create a unified subject of this non-traditional, non-mainstream way of knowing—the "feminist psychologist."

68

But use of rhetorical strategies to create a purportedly unified subject, "feminist psychologist," seems more than a bit tendentious today, given the current range of feminists' views on the relations between feminism and psychology. This range of views has become more visible since the journal *Feminism & Psychology* was founded (1991), providing a marked contrast with most of the work published in the American Psychological Association's Division of the Psychology of Women journal *Psychology of Women Quarterly* and in *Sex Roles: A Journal of Research*.[5]

1992

Feminist women and some supportive men increasingly gained access to positions of power in professional organizations, positions affecting a wide range of activities important in determining what the knowledge base in psychology is or can be. (These include editorships of major journals, memberships on powerful boards and committees, key staff positions, major elective offices.) From some points of view, the impact of such activities by feminists has dramatically changed the way psychology functions as an organized discipline.

> Research articles submitted for review to journals published by the American Psychological Association (APA) are now reviewed "blind" (with the author's name and institutional affiliation removed)

PARLEE

These journals have officially adopted a policy of non-sexist language use (American Psychological Association, 1984), and it is reasonably well monitored and enforced

Guidelines for avoiding sexism in research have been published (McHugh, Koeske, and Frieze, 1986)

Substantial program time at national and regional conventions is in effect earmarked for feminist research about women, and as a consequence the media coverage of conventions very often focuses on research on women

Women are substantially represented (mostly by feminists) on major boards and committees of the American Psychological Association (APA) and other professional organizations

Within the APA Division of the Psychology of Women, furthermore, serious steps, reflected in allocation of scarce resources, have been taken to ensure the participation of "underrepresented groups" (women of color, lesbians, women of various ethnic backgrounds) in the decision-making functions of the division and of the organization as a whole. The networks and bibliographic resources necessary to make research by and about black women and Hispanic women accessible to a wide audience of psychologists are now available, as are texts and material for integrating research in the psychology of women into traditional subfields of psychology (Bronstein and Quina, 1988; Paludi, 1988). Feminist women are also active and effective in most of the other APA divisions: in clinical psychology and psychoanalysis as well as in social, developmental, industrial/organizational, educational psychology and so forth, and they work together with considerable political clout on issues arising within the organization as a whole.

1996

I still think psychology is better—fairer in procedures and richer in outcomes—because of the hard work some feminist psychologists put into making these and other institutional changes. I have become increasingly convinced, however, that the quotation William James offered when asked to comment on the success of psychophysics in dominating the newly emerging discipline of psychology, applies equally to the psychological knowledge produced by feminists once they/we became successfully institutionalized within the APA. "And everybody praised the duke/who this great fight did win/ "But what good cam of it at last?"/Quoth little Peterkin./ "Why that I cannot tell," said he; /But 'twas a famous victory."[6]

This is a view that many feminists who identify with the APA's Division of the Psychology of Women would probably disagree with very strongly. I would point to the contents of the *Psychology of Women Quarterly* as evidence for my view. So would they. My impression is that this gap has become increasingly wide during the past four or five years.[7]

69

PARLEE

1992

It is clear there have been substantial changes in psychology as a result of feminism, and it is likely research will continue in the future to include women, feminist issues, and gender as topics incorporated into the general knowledge base in psychology (Fine, 1985; Deaux, 1984), if not into the awareness and thinking of individual psychologists. Despite these real and important changes, however, I think, as Stacey and Thorne (1985) have argued for sociology, there is a missing feminist revolution in psychology.

1996

Stacey and Thorne's article is widely known, cited (and formerly discussed and now absorbed) among faculty and students in women's studies. I do not know if it is a shared reference point for feminists in psychology. Such uncertainty and doubts about how feminists in psychology are situated vis à vis the literature of interdisciplinary women's studies, is a main theme of this essay and one I think has become increasingly pertinent rather than less so during the past few years. I know the gap remains large when I hear feminists in psychology use words like "empirical," "data," "subject," "theory," with quite different meanings than they have for feminists in other disciplines, with no evident awareness (a prerequisite for analysis) of the differences.

1992

Women as subject matter and as professionals have been incorporated into—in the sense of grafted onto—psychology, but psychology has not been transformed in the sense usually meant by feminist scholars in the early days of enthusiastic self-consciousness about the enterprise (Dubois, 1983; Boxer, 1982; in psychology see Wallston, 1981; Unger, 1983; Wittig, 1985). In this sense, a transformation in psychology—a qualitative reshaping of the discipline—would result from putting experiences and activities of women at the center of the inquiry and shaping concepts, theories, and methods to articulate and provide an understanding of psychological phenomena from this perspective rather than from the perspective traditionally adopted in psychology—that of socially privileged men (Minnich, 1990).

In addition to the reasons Stacey and Thorne discussed (all of which seem also to apply), I think there is an equally important and usually unnoted reason why feminism has not had an impact on psychology at a more fundamental conceptual/methodological level. It has ultimately to do with the way scientific psychology presently function as part of the larger society (Sherif, 1979).[8]

In brief, I think it can be demonstrated that when psychological topics are formulated for research in traditional paradigms they are "deformed" in characteristic ways (Parlee, 1979; 1981). Psychological phenomena, events, and processes are stripped of their socio-cultural, political, and personal meanings as they are reformulated to fit the concepts and theories permitted by the narrow range of research methods that are compatible with a positivist view of science. Through its privileging of a narrow range of method (Lykes and Stewart, 1986) and the assumptions underlying them (Henley, 1986) psychology describes human activities in an ostensibly scientific language of a very particular kind, a language that enters public discourses regarding "social issues" (including gender relations) and more subtly and pervasively discourses concerning human beings in their relation to the social order.

The language of scientific psychology (re)presents the individual not as an agent who acts for reasons in a social and moral order but as a being subjected in natural-law-like ways to various causal influences conceptualized as variables or factors (Harré, 1984). For example, people may "have perceptions of danger" but do not fear anyone, they may "have self-schemas" but are not selves. This is not a concise technical language that can be unpacked into statements about what people do and why; it is jargon which systematically obscures the actor and reasons for acting through introduction of a scientistic terminology of cause and effect.[9]

To the extent the representations of persons in this mechanistic, agentless, non-moral language becomes part of public discourse (or part of the discourse of the educated elites), it deprives the general publics of the richer linguistic resources for self-interpretation and self-understanding inherent in the everyday language of persons, actions, reasons, motives, and values (Harré, 1983). These resources enable or even encourage people to experience and think of themselves as agents who can act politically and in other ways in a world of meaning toward ends they value. The mechanistic, pseudoscientific language of psychology thus plays its role in the reproduction of the existing social order by pervading public discourse and the interpretations of ourselves that are shaped by it, displacing a discourse more compatible with the self-interpretations necessary for people to act together for social change.[10].

If this is even a partly adequate analysis of the relationship of the methods, concepts, and language of mainstream psychology, particularly social psychology, to the larger culture, it is not surprising that the subfields of psychology most relevant to an understanding of social phenomena have proved extremely resistant to the kinds of fundamental conceptual changes envisaged by (among others) feminists. The forces shaping psychology from outside the discipline and perpetuating it in its present form are powerful compared with forces for change promoted from within by feminists.

1996

This is still a central point in my essay. However, I see it today as overstated in one respect ("mainstream psychology" gives a clue). I think by "psychology" here I mean U.S. "social psychology" of the sort covered by psychology text-

PARLEE

71

books of that name, and those areas of developmental and cognitive psychology that have been influenced by such work.

1992

Mainstream psychology [that is to say, experimental social psychology in the U.S.] in practice defines itself not by subject matter but by a particular conception of method and the assumptions and language associated with it. Therefore, feminists who are intellectually and personally oriented both to problems in the real world and to scientific psychological understanding[11] typically either have to give up their problem and action focus as they and it become incorporated into mainstream psychology or they have to create for themselves an interdisciplinary group of people with similar theoretical and practical interests.[12]

Feminist psychologists are fortunate in not having to create *de novo* an interdisciplinary context for their work. It is already partly there in feminist scholarship as a body of literature and a community of scholars, both of which are as accessible as psychological literature and organizations of psychologists. An analysis of citation patterns in the literature, however, would probably confirm the impression of many who participate in interdisciplinary activities that feminist psychology and psychologist are relatively isolated from feminist scholarship in other disciplines. [for confirmation see Parlee, 1991]. The more puzzling question then would seem to be not why feminist psychologists have had relatively little impact on mainstream psychology but why feminist psychology and feminist work in other disciplines and in the interdisciplinary matrix of feminist theory appear to have so little relationship to one another.[13]

To begin to answer the latter question, it is worth noting that some of the work in psychology best known to feminists outside psychology (most notably that of Carol Gilligan) has not been the focus of empirical research within psychology by feminists, primarily because the methods of traditional scientific psychology cannot be used to study it. However, some of the major topics in what is now the subfield called the psychology of women are conceptualized and researched in such a way that they appear to have had relatively little influence on or relationship to the work of feminist scholars in other disciplines. I want to show in what follows that Gilligan's work (and feminist psychological research on gender, language, and nonverbal communication) is compatible in its underlying assumptions with feminist research in other disciplines in a way more "mainstream" work on the psychology of women/gender probably is not.

1996

"Mainstream psychology of women" is of course much too vague! More seriously, I did not note explicitly that Gilligan was perhaps the best known *psy-*

chologist among women's studies scholars, but that a much larger "psychology" literature was and is very much part of interdisciplinary women's studies (where the term usually refers to psychoanalysis, psychoanalytic theory—Lacan, the French feminists, British object relations theorists). So far as I can tell from bibliographies of the work I read, academic (scientific) "psychology of women"—with some clear exceptions—is not part of conversations in interdisciplinary women's studies.

1992

Further, Gilligan's work (and, more generally, feminist thinking about psychological phenomena) can be expanded and clarified in the interdisciplinary context of feminist scholarship and theory more fruitfully than it can by being adapted to the mainstream social psychological methods and language now used by many psychologists interested in women and in gender. As such, and in light of the foregoing argument about the role of the paradigms of mainstream psychology in the reproduction of the social order, an analysis of key features of Gilligan's work and of feminist research on gender and language may suggest directions for future research that provides genuine understanding of the psychological component of human activities and promotes social change.

Carol Gilligan's research and writing have focused on three interrelated topics, all of which have both critical implications for traditional psychological theories and positive suggestions for future interdisciplinary feminist research. Some of her earlier and perhaps less well-known work was a fundamental critique from a feminist perspective of psychological theories of adult development (Gilligan, 1979; 1980). Such theories, she pointed out, conceptualize psychological growth and maturity (or positively valued "development") primarily in terms of increasing autonomy and independence.[14] For many women, Gilligan notes, the reality of interdependency in relationships and a concomitant experience of connectedness with others might be more salient and more highly valued. Theories of psychological development in adulthood and notions of maturity need to include both—as do real people.

Gilligan's insights about the possibly differential importance of separation and connectedness in the lives of women and men are elaborated in the two other topics of her work: moral reasoning and the related phenomenon of the experience of oneself in relation to others (Gilligan, 1977; 1982; Gilligan and Murphy, 1979; Murphy and Gilligan, 1980). As is by now common knowledge (though still not always reflected in the syllabi of psychology courses or the bibliographies of papers on moral development) the heart of Gilligan's critique is that the dominant theory and method in research on moral development, that of Lawrence Kohlberg, incorporates the same gender-biased assumptions that distort theories of adult development. The highest stage of moral reasoning, according to Kohlberg's theory, involves reasoning with general moral principles that treat each individual as an abstract entity, interchangeable with any and all others. This highest level, Kohlberg found, was less often reached by women. Where Kohlberg implicitly finds defect in women's moral reasoning, however, Gilligan finds difference—if researchers will only listen. Analyzing women's reasoning in an actual moral dilemma (as opposed to the gender- and class-biased hypothetical vignettes Kohlberg employed), Gilligan found that the women in her study often reasoned in terms of principles applying not to abstracted, isolated individuals but to particular persona whose individuality is specified in part by their relationships to others. For these women, moral principles involved not rights of abstract, interchangeable individuals but responsibilities for caring for particular, interdependent others. She proposed that the kind of moral reasoning Kohlberg identified and studied, a rights-based morality of justice, needs to be supplemented with a conception of a morality of care based on empathic appreciation of the concrete situation of particular others. In other work, Gilligan and her colleagues have explored empirically the idea that women's predominant mode of moral reasoning (a morality of care) is related to their sense of themselves in relation to others (Lyons, 1983; Pollack and Gilligan, 1982). For women, they have argued, the sense of self involves more connectedness with others than does men's (and separation is experienced as isolation and is frightening); men's sense of themselves, on the other hand, involves greater separation from others than does women's (and closeness is experienced as engulfment and is frightening). Working with a coding scheme related to Gilligan's, Nona Lyons claims her data show that such gender differences in the predominant mode of experiencing the self in relation to others are present from the teen-age years through late middle age.

74

1996

It would not be necessary now to describe Gilligan's work in such detail to any feminist audience/readership. It is, not as well-known however, to many psychologists who are not feminists. Long after Gilligan's work had become well known to feminists (in the mid 1980s) I was amazed to learn that a colleague's graduate seminar on moral development had not included her work: when asked about it he said there "had not been time" to "get to" Gilligan . . .

1992

Carol Gilligan clearly has provided an important corrective to a significant gender bias in theories of psychological development, theories of moral reasoning and of the self in traditional psychology. That it is not always acknowledged by traditional psychological researchers does not diminish the importance of her theoretical contribution.[15] The central ideas arising from Gilligan's critique, however, have been and can fruitfully be developed not in mainstream psychology in exactly her terms, but at psychology's edges, at its boundaries with other disciplines.

It should be emphasized that the present brief overview does not begin to do justice to the subtilty and complexity of the analyses of and commentaries on Gilligan's work that have come from scholars in disciplines other than psychology. Good examples of these—although they are of variable quality—can be found in the issue "Women and Morality" *Social Research* (Autumn, 1983), the collection of papers and commentaries on women and moral development in *New Ideas in Psychology* (1987, 5/2), "Science, Morality, and Feminist Theory" of the *Canadian Journal of Philosophy* (1987, supplementary volume 13), in Benhabib (1987), and in the volumes and articles cited in these works. As these critiques and commentaries evolve, they have contributed to the development of—or resonate with, in ways that can be mutually enriching—feminist work in the history and philosophy of science (Keller, 1985; Harding and O'Barr, 1987) and in philosophical moral and political theory (Kittay and Meyers, 1987; Held, 1992). When mainstream psychologists have addressed Gilligan's work, however, a primary focus has been on the question of whether or not there are gender differences in any of the phenomena described (Fishkin, Keniston, and MacKinnon, 1983; Brabeck, 1983; L. J. Walker, 1984). (Other psychologists working more at the edges of mainstream research traditions have formulated more interesting questions vis–à–vis the issues Gilligan raises—Haan, 1983; Haste, 1987; Bloom and Marecek, 1987.)

In addition to their intersection with moral philosophy and with feminist analyses of science—and moving in a different direction from most of the psychologists just mentioned—Gilligan's ideas might be usefully integrated with some of Dorothy Smith's work in sociology, particularly with ideas from Smith's (1979) classic analysis of what a sociology for women would look like. Smith's work implicitly suggests that independence and autonomy might be qualities especially valued by and salient for one particular group in this society—those whose work and family roles are structured in such as way as to render essential support work of others culturally and psychologically invisible. Such individuals—usually men who have wives, secretaries, and sometimes platoons of other invisible (often female) presences or technologies behind their supposedly individual achievements—might understandably build theories that articulate and validate the public (ideological) version of their own experiences. However, psychological theories of development stressing autonomy, independence, and separateness may describe the development of the consciousness of individuals in particularly privileged social locations rather than the psychological reality of these individuals' actual situations or selves as persons in a social order. In other words, autonomy might not be a feature of an individual's personality—as traditional psychological theories would have it—or even the actual possibility of relatively unconstrained actions by individuals in particularly privileged social locations. Rather, it might be a characteristic mode of awareness of one's dependence on others.

From this point of view, the psychological issues raised by Gilligan's work,

75

PARLEE

when integrated with Smith's, have to do with the discovery and analysis of differences between the ways some men and some women come to experience (become conscious of) the forms of their connectedness with others when some of their relationships of dependency are culturally rendered both psychologically and ideologically invisible. This is partly implicit in Gilligan's writing, but combining her work with Smith's shifts the emphasis in crucial ways by pointing to the role of social structure and ideology in the constitution of an individual's awareness of self and others. This formulation is related to and compatible with Chodorow's description of psychodynamic development within a structured social order (of which more below), a description which has had a major influence in interdisciplinary feminist theory.

The shift in emphasis that comes about when Gilligan's work is integrated with that of feminist sociologist Dorothy Smith is, of course, moving in a direction away from the traditional psychological question of whether men and boys "are" more "independent" (or "field independent") than girls and women. While even first-rate feminist psychologists such as Maccoby and Jacklin perforce took the question of "sex differences" seriously fifteen years ago (when that was how the relevant subfields of psychology formulated the issues—Maccoby and Jacklin, 1974), advances in feminist scholarship, in some areas of psychology, and in the thinking of many feminist psychologists have rendered the question moot for those interested in a psychological understanding of gender. Research on "sex differences"—now spoken of within the field as "gender differences" but not fundamentally reconceptualized—has the same scientific interest as does, for example, research on "age differences": that is, it is of no interest in serious work at the forefront on any particular psychological phenomenon. Thus most developmental psychologists tacitly recognize that "age" is not a "variable" and that focusing on age differences in, for example, problem solving does not illuminate the psychological processes involved and may not provide the most theoretically relevant articulation of comparison groups for investigating the phenomenon of interest.

It is probably instructive to note that while developmental psychologists would not speak of "age differences" in the abstract, some psychologists and most of the popular culture still speak of "sex differences" without qualification (as to differences in what? between which women and which men?). The question of "gender differences" in some particular phenomenon, I think, is one that retains its interest among some psychologists not because it reasonably derives from a set of scientific assumptions and data but because it is embedded in a culturally compelling, essentially political, discourse about "sex differences" and their origins in "nature" or [sic] "nurture." This is spoken of in some subfields of psychology as the question of "how biological and social factors interact," but the supposedly scientific formulation essentially replicates that of public discourse. (Both Keller, a scientist/historian, and deLauretis, a film critic, have given rich and cogent analyses of the empirical inadequacy and the negative political consequences for women of accepting this dichotomy as the basis of feminist inquiry—Keller, 1987; deLauretis, 1987. Rachel Hare-Mustin, a clinical psychologist, makes a related argument more likely to be accessible to psychologists —Hare-Mustin, 1987.) Given that the discourse shaping the research in psychology is non-scientific and comes primarily from outside the field, it is perhaps not surprising that as Gilligan's work has been incorporated into mainstream psychology, the constitutive transaction between selves and social structure that are foregrounded when Gilligan's work is integrated with Smith's have faded into the background. The post-Gilligan question in psychology all too often continues to be whether girls and women "are" more "interdependent" and more "relational" than boys and men, whether they "are" different in level or type of moral reasoning.

To further understand why Gilligan's work, particularly her work on the self, seems to be more compatible with and enriched by integration into disciplines other than psychology—and to understand also some of its limitations for feminist theory—it may be useful to consider it in light of interdisciplinary work by social psychologists and others in Great Britian and Europe which they call a "new psychology" (Harré, Clarke, and DeCarlo, 1985; Harrè and Gillet, 1994). Part of this "new psychology" (and it is that vis–à–vis mainstream U.S. psychology) involves a revision of the image of human nature that is embedded in and perpetuated by psychological theories.

In particular the new psychology rejects concepts and methods that implicitly conceptualize human beings as automata (beings that respond to causes rather than persons who act for reasons). The implicit conceptualization of persons as automata is currently introduced in mainstream U.S. psychology via the metaphor of person-as-computer or as an " information processing device."[16] (When behaviorism was the dominant perspective in psychology, persons were implicitly conceptualized as automata which "respond" to "stimuli" in the environment; now, after the "cognitive revolution," persons are implicitly conceptualized as automata which "process" " information" in the environment.)

The notion of a self, when formulated as a topic for empirical research, has proved difficult for U.S. psychologists to conceptualize in non-mechanistic terms (e.g., Markus and Sentis, 1981). Typically, the self is treated as an entity (a stimulus?) which is "perceived" (as in "self-perception") or something (a "self-schema") which is "had" in the sense of "owned" by some unspecified agent. A stimulus-response, cause and effect model or a model of a master computer program manipulating lower-level information processing modules prevails over a conceptualization of persons as active interpreters or makers of meaning.

Part of the appeal of Gilligan's work to many feminist psychologists, I believe, is that it uses everyday language for talking about selves and thereby im-

77

PARLEE

plies the possibility of a richer conception of the human person—as someone who seeks/makes meaning in a social and moral order, an agent who actively interprets and transforms the world according to the needs and purposes inherent in practical activities. This latter view of human nature is of course assumed by scholars in the humanities as well as by most laypeople. Differences between a view of persons as agents and the mechanistic conception currently dominating U.S. psychology, including much feminist psychology, is probably the most important single reason for the gap in communication between feminist psychologists and feminist scholars in other disciplines. Because the politically- and morally-grounded European social psychologists explicitly reject the image of people as automata and have begun to develop appropriate new methods of investigation, I think they represent a promising theoretical and empirical framework within which feminist psychology can develop (be transformed).

1996

If I were writing this today, I would try to be clearer that "richer conception of the human person" does not mean the unitary subject of modernism, but instead points to non-mechanistic discourses, resources which psychologists and other persons use strategically to accomplish and account for social action (Billig, 1987; Edwards and Potter, 1992; Henriques, Hollway, Irwin, Couze, and Walkerdine, 1984; Potter and Wetherell, 1987). I would also refer to this relatively new, richly social, and aware-of-power psychological approach consistently as its theorists/practitioners do, as discursive psychology, rather than as the "new" social psychology (of Harré and colleagues) which is a related but somewhat different tradition. Specific research projects conducted within/as discursive psychology can be found in Hollway, 1989; Billig, Condor, Edwards, Gane, Middleton, and Radley, 1988; Middleton and Edwards, 1990.

1992

Thinking about Gilligan's work on the self in the context of the new psychology, for example, might lead to a surprising reformulation. While they do not represent a single view, some psychologists involved in the new psychology (most notably Rom Harré) draw on the considerable cultural variation in conceptions of the self (Shweder and LeVine, 1984) to argue that for theoretical purposes the self is most fruitfully regarded not as an entity with attributes [or mental states and processes] but as a locally specific theory [discourse] which a social actor acquires [takes up, uses] in order to participate in a particular way in the discourses [discursive fields] in which she or he is engaged. In this view we do not so much "have" an inner, private self, which has particular properties and which "causes" our actions as we hold a theory of self [take up a subject position in a discourse] which allows us to make self-ascription (as in the avowal of an emotional state) and to otherwise participate in discourse in certain ways (Harré, 1984; Edwards and Potter, 1992; Hollway, 1989). This way of thinking of selves as socially constituted in language, of subjectivity as constructed in a semiotic discourse, represents an ontological shift from the view of the self as a schema or property of a material being, and it begins to connect in a way that conceptions of "self perceptions" and "self-schemas" do not with concerns about subjectivity and language as they have arisen in feminist literary and film criticism and in certain kinds of discourse analysis (see Alcoff, 1988).

In addition to its implicit conception of the person as agent, then, analysis of Gilligan's work can be seen as pointing to a second key assumption which may separate most feminist psychologists from feminist scholars in other disciplines: an assumption about the relationship of individual selves/subjectivity and the social order. Feminist scholars in disciplines other than psychology have drawn on Gilligan's work with unusual enthusiasm in part because it is almost universally read by feminists against a theoretical background previously laid out by Dorothy Dinnerstein (1976) and especially by Nancy Chodorow (1978).

Chodorow's work, central in feminist theory, persuasively argues for the necessity of a description of personality in sociologically grounded psychodynamic terms as central to an understanding of the ongoing reproduction of gender.[17] Chodorow's work explicitly and strongly emphasizes the dialectical, mutually constituting relationship between individual personality and social order. Like the "new" social psychologists, and very unlike traditional psychologists in the United States, her starting point is the social order, and she asks how individuals come into being as persons within it. For the reader with Chodorow in mind, then, Gilligan's description of gendered personalities offers a fuller characterization (with a focus on the individual) of a dialectical process necessarily manifested only in historically and culturally particular social arrangements of childrearing.

Brinton Lykes has suggested that Gilligan's work, even when read in the context of Chodorow, does not completely escape the assumptions of autonomous individualism she critiques in Kohlberg (Lykes, 1985). Although Gilligan's work is based on a conception of the person as an agent (and although this agent is not conceptualized with a masculine bias), Lykes argues that the underlying notion of self is still fundamentally that of a separate entity who interacts with (is connected with or related to) another separate entity. In this respect Gilligan has simply provided a " . . . 'female' variation of the dominant 'male' model of the egocentric contractual idea of the self." Social relations, and by extension the social order, are reduced in this conceptualization (which Popper, 1957, called "methodological psychologism") to interactions among individuals analytically conceived (and methodologically investigated) in asocial terms. The key feature of the social order—that it is structured, that individuals are differently located in it—is rendered invisible (or at least inconspicuous) by the persistence of the assumptions of autonomous individualism. (Margolis, 1987, offers a brief but spirited critique of this perspective.).

What is needed instead, Lykes said, is a psychological approach that takes as its starting point not the individual person but human activities—a unit of analysis that includes both the individual and her/his culturally defined environment as a dynamic, mutually constituting system. It is within human activities that the individuality of persons is articulated (comes into being) in relationships. Like Chodorow, Lykes thus connects the formation of selves with the particularities of social location, but her use of activity theory makes more explicit ways in which persons actively transform their worlds as they are formed by them. The conceptualization of the self as an individual, materially embodied entity is replaced in Lykes' work by the notion of "social individuality," which has meaning only as an articulation of a dialectical relationship of self and social. It is very difficult, as Lykes pointed out, to hold consistently the dialectical conception of social individuality in the face of habits of language use that describe the self in the terms of an ideology of autonomous individualism. The great virtue of Lykes' work, apart from its originality in contemporary terms and its connections with earlier, now-neglected traditions in psychology (Mead, H. S. Sullivan) is that it is grounded with a thriving theoretical perspective and body of empirical work known as activity theory [or sociohistorical psychology] (Wertsch, 1979, 1981; Vygotsky, 1978.1930). Unlike the work of Gilligan and Kohlberg, which rests on a conceptualization of the individual as separable from and prior to the social order, programmatic empirical exploration of social individuality can be readily undertaken within the tradition of activity theory. I think it represents a promising direction for future research by feminist psychologists who want to see their work integrated with feminist scholarship in other disciplines and who want to develop transformed psychological knowledge that is useful for social change.

1996

In some sense I still think this is right, but in practice (e.g., as in the new journal *Culture and Psychology*) sociohistorical psychology as a community of theorists and researchers has not been particularly sensitive to feminist concerns or aware of the relevant feminist literatures. Nevertheless, it is an interdisciplinary community from whom feminist psychologists can borrow useful theoretical and methodological tools for culturally-sensitive research in cultures very different from those in North America (e.g, see Scribner, 1990; Tobach et. al., in press).

1992

Apart from its particular contributions to psychology and to feminist scholarship in other disciplines what is most striking about Gilligan's work is the reaction to it both by academics and by popular audiences and professions outside the academy. A great many women say that the "different voice" Gilligan hears in women's moral reasoning (the focus on particulars of a person and situation, the "it depends on the circumstances" reluctance to reason with general principles about abstract entities) is one they know from their own experience but had never heard articulated and validated before.[18] The response is like the less wide-spread but similarly heartfelt reaction to Chodorow's and Dinnerstein's earlier descriptions of a related phenomenon (women's sense of a continuing connectedness with and awareness of others), and to Jean Baker Miller's more recent elaboration from a clinical perspective (Miller, 1984; see also Gilligan, Rogers, and Tolman, 1991; Belenky, Clinchy, Goldberger, and Tarule, 1986).

The fact that Gilligan's work speaks truth in some significant sense does not mean, of course, that we understand the social and cultural meaning of the popularity of her work. Her description of gender differences is not all that different from descriptions of women's special qualities that some feminists (and non-feminists) have offered in the past, although unlike feminists in the late 60s Gilligan does not simultaneously call for the social and cultural changes necessary to re-value, to really value, the qualities associated in this culture with some females.

So why is Gilligan's work so popular now? As Pauline Bart said in a slightly different but related context (Bart, 1977) we need to ask *cui bono?* Who benefits from this way of talking about gender? How can we explain the fact that the potentially harmful and destructive aspects of connectedness are so rarely named and explored? (Flax, 1978, is a pre-Gilligan exception.) How can we explain the fact that Gilligan's work has been taken up by men and by women in various educational settings with such extraordinary rapidity? (At the state level, for example, officials in New York have formed a committee to consider the implications of this work for curriculum revisions; it has already been incorporated into the ethics curriculum in at least one private school in New York City; feminist theologians use Gilligan's work as do at least some social work educators.) There has been an unprecedentedly rapid diffusion of Gilligan's ideas from academic psychology to what are sometimes called applied settings. Something is going on, having to do with the shaping of and control over the public discourse about gender. This is a phenomenon worthy of investigation in its own right by feminist scholars, apart from the use of the substantive content of Gilligan's work in their other research.

A significant feature of Gilligan's work may shed light on the ease and speed with which it has been "adopted". Although it uses the language of

81

agents rather than automata to describe human beings, it nevertheless implicitly retains a central assumption of mainstream psychology in (re)present-
ing the individual as conceptually separable from and prior to the social order.
Rather than providing a challenge or corrective to the culturally powerful
ideology of autonomous individualism, Gilligan's work is capable of being as-
similated into and interpreted as scientific support for the public, political discourse about gender (as "gender differences" and what is implicitly assumed
to be their biological-or-social causes).

Analysis of feminist research on language, gender, and nonverbal communication (Thorne and Henley, 1975; Thorne, Kramarae, and Henley, 1983;
Henley, 1977) further underscores the significance of assumptions about the
individual and the social order for the development of psychological knowledge that can be integrated with and enriched by feminist research and scholarship in other disciplines. As is the case in Chodorow's work, in the "new"
social psychology, and in Dorothy's Smith's kind of sociology, the starting
point in feminist work on language, gender and nonverbal communication is
the structured social order, and the focus is on transactions between persons
acting as agents within it. In this research, language use and nonverbal modes
of communication are conceptualized as a means through which individuals
express and recreate relations of dominance in the social order (Thorne and
Henley, 1975).

A paradigmatic example is Henley's (1977) research on touching: when
observations are made of occasions when one person touches another (in
contexts where it does not clearly have a sexual or affectionate meaning), the
pattern of touching between individuals is often nonreciprocal; the person in
a socially dominant position is the one who touches a social subordinate, but
not vice versa. Henley describes touching in such situations as a covert (and
deniable) assertion of power or dominance by the person who touches. If the
assertion is implicitly confirmed or acknowledged by the other's response
(when the subordinate permits the touch and does not reciprocate), then a
relationship of dominance is created in the face-to-face interaction relationship which re-creates (affirms, maintains, perpetuates) the power relationships
at the macro-social level (Thorne and Henley, 1975). In the theoretical
framework guiding this research, power is not something an individual "has"
or an attribute of a personality. It is shared meaning created in a mutually
confirming transaction between two persons, both of whom have to play
their part for that particular meaning to emerge. What such an analysis illuminates, of course, is the active role of both persons in creating power and dominance, in re-creating the macrosocial relations and structures of dominance
through microsocial processes of transactions.

From a feminist perspective, such an analysis is particularly important because it demonstrates significant circumstances in which women are not passive victims of their situation but can act as agents to alter the transaction and

PARLEE

to create new meanings. In Henley's analysis, the links between social structure, individual agents, social meaning and social change are made very clear—in a way Chodorow's work partly illuminates and Gilligan's much less so. In addition to nonverbal gestures, several other gender-related phenomena have been examined from the theoretical perspective outlined by Thorne and Henley (a perspective compatible with and increasingly integrated with ethnographic and other research on social identity and language use—e.g., Gumperz, 1982). For example (see Thorne and Henley, 1975; Thorne, Kramarae, and Henley, 1983), non-reciprocal use of the other person's first name (as opposed to title plus last name) has been shown to be related to relative status or power of two people in an interaction. Interruptions—disruption of smooth exchange of conversational turns—have also been extensively investigated as gender-related phenomena. Candace West and Don Zimmerman found that in many different kinds of settings, in conversations between friends or strangers, women are overwhelmingly more likely to be interrupted by men than men are by women. Similarly, Fishman has shown that the topic of conversations was overwhelmingly more likely to be determined by men than by women. In her recordings of talk between couples over long periods of time, Fishman found that conversational topics introduced by the men were almost always followed up by their female partners, whereas topics introduced by women often were dropped when no response (or only minimal response—"umhum") was forthcoming. As had previously been demonstrated for interruptions, Fishman found that the women did *not* passively accept their role in the conversation, but actively made efforts to engage their partner in conversation on topics they wanted to discuss. Devices like tag questions (do you think?) and introductory questions (guess what?) were repeatedly used by the women to keep their topic going—without conspicuous success. The men, on the other hand, simply did not have to engage in this kind of conversational "work" to discuss a topic they were interested in.

83

1996

Deborah Tannen's best-selling book *You Just Don't Understand* (1990) describes some of the same research on women's and men's communicative styles (see Henley, 1995, for an updated review and assessment). As Tavris (1992) and others have noted, however, Tannen's analysis strips out precisely what Thorne and Henley's emphasized. Tannen seems to assume "style" is a personal "variable" unrelated to power-asymmetries in the social relations of gender. So again, we need to ask: Why is Tannen's book a best-seller now?

1992

Although more recent research points to the need to qualify generalizations about "men" and "women" (which men? which women? under what circumstances?), it is also clear that "conversational politics" of this sort (Parlee,

PARLEE

1979) is a phenomenon that many women immediately recognize from their own experience. But I would suggest that unlike Gilligan's work which also evokes such recognition, this research [by Henley and others] does not incorporate the assumption that the individual and the social are conceptually separable—and that the social order does or should reflect the characteristics of individuals as described in the context-stripping research.

It is a very different thing to assume, as do researchers in the tradition Thorne and Henley represent, that persons act (in circumstances not of their own making) to create and recreate the social order. This both recognizes the reality that gender is a principle of social organization and shows how people can act to change it. A recent elaboration of this theoretical perspective is the landmark paper "Doing gender" by West and Zimmerman (West and Zimmerman, 1987; in many ways this formulation of gender was anticipated by psychologists Kessler and McKenna, 1978). In this paper the authors analyze gender as a feature of social organization that is continually reproduced through the activities of persons: gender is a practical accomplishment in situated human activities, not a property or mode of personality organization of an individual. In this view, gender (including the gendered social order) is continually made and remade in the flow of human activities; it is not a static property (either in the individual or in a social role) that casually influences these activities from the outside.

Like Lykes' research and the theoretical perspective she represents, the work by West and Zimmerman and by Thorne, Cramarae, and Henley presents a clear direction for feminist psychologists if they want to work with assumptions (about the person as agent and about the relation of persons and the social order) which enable their research both to be integrated with feminist work in other disciplines and with feminist theory and also contribute to a public discourse about gender that will support rather than suppress social change.

It is worth emphasizing that the theoretical perspective embodied in feminist work on language, gender and nonverbal communication [probably "discursive psychology" as characterized by Edwards and Potter (1992), toward which I now see I was groping in the 1992 essay] is simply incommensurable with the traditional psychological notion of gender as an attribute or mode of functioning or content of the "social cognition" of an individual conceptualized and measured socially (Potter and Wetherell, 1987). This is true both in terms of methods and in terms of the interpretation of data. For example, use of a "sex-role inventory" or other questionnaires as a method of investigation directed toward learning more about the individual will not capture—indeed will preclude and will deform in characteristic ways—the phenomena involved in "doing gender" because those phenomena are mutually constituted meaningful transactions between persons rather than intrapersona traits or mental responses to stimuli or ways of "processing information" within an individual.

Conceptions of personality in terms of traits, for instance, are highly problematic, and the problems have implications for both concepts and methods
of mainstream [!] psychological research on gender. Simply on semantic
grounds, it is clear that "aggression" (for example) refers to something happening between two or more people; the word cannot meaningfully be used
to describe an individual without reference to context. As an analytic concept
in scientific psychology, as opposed to an uncritical importation into psychology of popular talk, phenomena picked out by ordinary language as "aggression" occur between particular persons, under particular circumstances and
for reasons which need to be specified.[19]

In what can be seen as a linking of the notion of gender-associated "traits"
or beliefs about them (or in contemporary terms "gender schema") with the
conceptualization of gender as a practical accomplishment, Maltz and Borker
(1982) have suggested that some of the ways a person thinks about differences
in personality traits between men and women might be a (culturally/ideolog-
ically shaped) interpretation of what are in effect the situated, gender-creating
transactional phenomena West and Zimmerman describe. Women might be
thought to be more "concerned about other people" and more "tactful" than
men, for example, because—in settings where they want to accomplish certain goals and believe they can do so through particular linguistic strategies—
they ask their male conversational partner what he thinks, they talk about
topics he is interested in. Men might be interpreted as being more "decisive"
and "confident" than women because they speak—again, strategically and
purposefully—without interruptions. What Maltz and Border are pointing to
in their sociolinguistic analysis, then, is the possibility that trait descriptions of
personality represent culturally shaped, abstract generalizations inferred from
typical patterns of situated, meaningful, goal-directed interactions. These ab-
stractions are inferred from situated activities of persons but are characteristically (in this culture) conceptualized as personality traits and attributed to a
(de-contextualized) individual, thereby ideologically obscuring the meanings
of the transactions for the participants—and the way they recreate and reproduce a gendered social order. The challenge to feminists is to illuminate this
ideological function, not to work with concepts and methods that support
and perpetuate it.

I have tried to show in this essay that Gilligan's work and research on gender, language and nonverbal communication highlight the importance of two
issues about which assumptions are necessarily made in psychological research and theory. One is the conception of the person (as agent or as automaton) that is implicit in the concepts and methods of research. The other
is the conceptualization and methods for investigating the person in relation
to the social order. I believe that a clearer and more consistent commitment
to a conception of the person as agent and to a conception of social activity
as the starting point for psychological analysis will be helpful—indeed essen-

PARLEE

tial—if feminist psychological research is to be integrated with feminist scholarship in other disciplines and to lead to knowledge that is useful for understanding and social change.

To the extent that feminists use paradigms—methods and concepts and language—of traditional psychology that implicitly (re)present the person as an automaton and the social as arising from interactions among (fundamentally asocial) individuals, feminist psychological work has been and will be incorporated into mainstream psychology and has been and will be isolated from feminist scholarship in other disciplines. It seems to me this is not a politically or morally neutral possibility, since feminist psychology that adopts mainstream psychology's methods, concepts and language is likely to reproduce or at least leave unchallenged the ideological discourses that justify and recreate the social relations of gender.

Given the power and pervasiveness of the cultural and economic forces that shape and form the content and future directions of psychology from the outside, feminist psychologists' most productive and enriching alliances in the future undoubtedly lie with feminist scholars in other disciplines and with grass-roots feminist activists. Now that feminists have acquired at least some of the organizational base necessary to define new criteria for what constitutes excellence in psychological research, we can use it to redefine and transform feminist psychology by giving greater priority not to persuasion of and argument with mainstream psychologists but to an expanded and fruitful dialogue with other feminist scholars. Quite concretely, this might be begun in two ways. 1. Editors and reviewers could screen articles submitted for publication to ensure that they include references to, and enter into substantive dialogue with the ideas in scholarly work in at least one discipline outside psychology. 2. Editors set a strict limit (perhaps 50% to start) on the proportion of articles they publish in which questionnaires are the only method used for collection of data.

1996

Modest steps to be sure. But as chaos theory suggests, even the butterfly's wings can have unexpected and powerful consequences.

NOTES

1. Having worked in a developmental psychology program for several years I am aware of how the linear progression implied by developmental-like terms such as "updated" "superseded" conceals an implicit telos, a valued end point from which a coherent narrative is constructed of something called a "past." In science studies, too I frequently hear claims cast in terms of past and present that actually seem to be about different communities of practice. (e.g., "Nobody believes science is objective any more . . ." means [with a complex interplay of description and prescription] nobody in the speaker's community believes that or ought to, though most working scientists manifestly do.

2. This is not a problem for speakers or writers who do not have this concern, who simply assume they know who their listeners/readers are and speak accordingly. When they are right the monologue—linear narrative, argument—works for the intended, shared, purpose (Shankar-Perez, 1995). When they are wrong, however, listeners/readers know they are being talked "at" rather than "with" and they turn off, get angry (or use the situation as data for developing political analysis and strategy "from below").

3. For some recent and not so recent examples (among many) of feminists in psychology who have been doing this see: Crawford, Kippax, Onyx, Gault and Benton (1992), Fine (1992), Hare-Mustin and Marecek (1990), Hollway, (1989), Morawski (1994), Scarborough and Furumot (1987), Tiefer (1994), Ussher, (1989), Walkerdine, (1990), Wilkinson (1986).

4. As an administrator I sought and received funding from the Ford foundation to do one at CUNY.

5. The spectrum of views expressed by feminists in and about psychology seems likely to broaden even further with the editorial direction recently set for *The Psychology of Women Quarterly* (Russo, 1995).

6. When I elaborated this critique of work now usually referred to under the rubric of the "psychology of women" (Parlee, 1991) I was careful to note that some of my research has appeared in the journal of that name and is subject to the same critical analysis.

7. Two signs pointing in this direction are the newly clarified editorial policies for *The Psychology of Women Quarterly* (cited in note 5 above) and recent expressions of interest among some psychologists in Division 35 in "international/global psychology of women" which seem to retain—connceptually and methodologically—a decidedly North American perspective and sensibility.

8. During the past decade I have become increasingly aware of how serious an intellectual loss Carolyn Sherif's untimely death from cancer in 1982 was both to feminism and to psychology, as well as how it is a continuing personal loss for many who knew her. She would have much to contribute to some of the issues explored in this essay.

9. This became clear to me while I was working as an editor and writer at *Psychology Today* in 1978–79, when it was owned by the publishing company Ziff-Davis and edited by professional journalists. "Translations" of social psychology research results into plain English were often deemed obvious or trivial by the magazine's editors. (In 1983 *Psychology Today* was bought by the American Psychological Association and edited by journalists selected by psychologists; it did not prove a financial success.)

10. For examples of how the agentless, mechanistic language of U.S. experimental social psychology functions on a specific issue, see Henley, Miller and Beazley's (1995) and Lamb's (1991) analysis of how it obscures and evades the issue of who is responsible for violence against women.

11. Now I would not say "scientific psychological understanding" unless I were sure I could rely on a broad reading of "scientific"; it would probably have been clearer to say "systematic" understanding.

12. There is nothing unique to feminists about this. Environmental psychology is a field that faced such a choice several years ago, as did health psychology and feminist psychology.

87

PARLEE

13. One of the great dangers this isolation poses for intellectual life and for political change informed by research and theory is the danger of throwing out the baby with the bath. While many feminist scholars and activists rightly disregard psychological research based on methodological individualism and focused on persons (as "subjects") stripped from their social and physical contexts, there is the danger that they might mistake this for all that psychological analysis has to offer. Feminist psychologists, on the other hand, unnecessarily limit their methods and conceptual frameworks (and audiences) when they use methods from mainstream psychology that reformulate psychological phenomena into a mechanistic language that is inadequate to the complexity of the phenomena and incompatible with the interpretative understanding that is the goal of the humanities and some of the social sciences (Stacey and Thorne, 1985). That a focus on the difference between disciplines seeking causal explanations and those seeking interpretive understanding is the relevant one is underscored by Hyman's (1988) discussion of the impact of feminism on traditional disciplines. Hyman also thinks the distinction is important but, unlike Stacey and Thorne and myself, believes feminism has succeeded in changing the former but has not succeeded in its aim of "transform[ing] a political position into a scholarly pursuit" in the latter.

14. Levinson's discussion of a stage at midlife called "Becoming One's Own Man" is notable only for its truth in packaging; Erikson's conceptualization of an "identity crisis" in late adolescence puts similar emphasis on separation and independence as a prerequisite for development of satisfactory adult relationships.

15. One recent major research program in children's social development, for example, explicitly differentiates moral reasoning (used in Kohlberg's sense) from reasoning about what are called "personal concerns" (loyalty to family members over strangers, for example.) This resort to a stipulative definition of morality (in effect, defining it by stating it in a loud voice and simply ignoring the issues Gilligan raises) suggests that the bias in concepts and values which Gilligan has identified is very important indeed. As do the vitriolic—one might almost say shrill—attacks that have been made on her by some traditional psychologists and philosophers (Broughton, 1983; J. C. Walker, 1983).

16. Feminist psychology seems also to be becoming absorbed into this paradigm as feminist psychology/the psychology of gender/social psychology become increasingly amalgamated (see Lott, 1985 and Unger, 1985, for more positive views than I have of this development). Sandra Bem's work on gender schema theory, for example, is based on the "information processing" metaphor currently dominating social psychological research on "social cognition" (Bem, 1983; see also Bem 1993), as is feminist research on the self (Markus, Crane, Bernstein, and Siladi, 1982) and on the psychology of menstruation (Ruble and Brooks-Gunn, 1979). I have argued elsewhere that the "social cognition" paradigm (the interrelated set of methods, language, concepts, assumptions) is inadequate at least for understanding the psychological concomitants of the menstrual cycle (Parlee, 1988).

17. In *The Reproduction of Mothering,* Chodorow argues that the social arrangements whereby women mother both girls and boys—particularly the nuclear family—are integrally related to the sexual division of labor in the workplace. It is through particular forms of socially-organized childrearing that individuals are produced (as she puts it) with the psychological dispositions (the capacities, motivations, abilities) that are nec-

essary to reproduce existing work and family roles. She discusses these psychological dispositions and their development in terms of object relations theory, with separation/individuation being central to adult gender differences in, among other things, the phenomenal experience of relatedness to others. (Despite the generality of some of Chodorow's language, there has been considerable discussion of the limitations of her description to middle-class nuclear families in western industrialized societies, and her work is probably best read with this limitation in mind.

18. It is an empirical question whether the click of recognition is to be found primarily among white, educated, middle class North American women or whether the response is widespread among more diverse groups of women as Gilligan's unqualified descriptions of "women" implies.

19. This is part of what makes the description of premenstrual syndrome in terms of trait-like emotions (e.g., "anger," "irritability" conceptualized as attributes or properties of individuals) so insidious. It directs attention (talk) away from the social, moral realm, where a woman might have specific reasons for (justified) anger toward someone else, and locates it in the mechanistic realm of "causes" and effects. Researchers "measure" anger "in" women during the premenstrual phase; they do not talk with women about when, why, and at whom they are angry (Parlee, 1994). Again, cui bono?

REFERENCES [1992]

American Psychological Association (1984). Publication Manual (3rd ed). Washington, DC: American Psychological Association.

Alcoff, L. (1988). Cultural feminism vs post-structuralism: The identity crisis in feminist theory. SIGNS, 13, 405–436.

Bart, P. (1977). The mermaid and the minotaur: A fishy story that's part bull. Review of D. Dinnerstein, The mermaid and the minotaur. Contemporary Psychology, 834–835.

Bem, S. L. (1983). Gender schema theory and its implications for child development: Raising gender-aschematic children in a gender schematic society. SIGNS, 8, 598–616.

Bem, S. L. (1993). The lenses of gender: Transforming the debate on sexual inequality. New Haven, CT: Yale University Press.

Benhabib, S. (1987). The generalized and the concrete other: The Kolberg-Gilligan controversy and feminist theory. In S. Benhabib and D. Cornell (Eds.), Feminism as critique: On the politics of gender (pp. 77–95). Minneapolis: University Minnesota Press.

Bloom, A. H. and Marecek, J. (1987). The dual role of dialogue in moral development: A response to Philibert. New Ideas in Psychology, 5, 233–238.

Boxer, M. J. (1982). For and about women: The theory and practice of women's studies in the United States. SIGNS, 7, 661–695.

Brabeck, M. (1983). Moral development: Theory and research on differences between males and females. Developmental Review, 3, 274–291.

Bronstein, P. and Quina K. (Eds.), (1988). Teaching the psychology of people: Re-

PARLEE

sources for gender and sociocultural awareness. Washington, DC: American Psychological Association.

Broughton, J. M. (1983). Women's rationality and men's virtue: A critique of gender dualism in Gilligan's theory of moral development. *Social Research, 50,* 597–642.

Chodorow, N. (1978). *The reproduction of mothering.* Berkeley, CA: University California Press.

Deaux, K. (1984). From individual differences to social categories: Analysis of a decade's research on gender. *American Psychologist, 39,* 105–116.

de Lauretis, T. (1987). *Technologies of gender: Essays on theory, film, and fiction.* Bloomington, IN: Indiana University Press.

Dinnerstein, D. (1976). *The mermaid and the minotaur: Sexual arrangements and human malais.* New York: Harper and Row.

Du Bois E. C. (1983). Passionate scholarship: Notes on values, knowing, and method in feminist social science. In G. Bowles and R. D. Klein (Eds.), *Theories of women's studies.* Boston: Routledge and Kegan Paul.

Du Bois, E. C. Kelly, G. R., Kennedy, E. L., Korsmeyer, C. W. and Robinson, K. S. (Eds.), *Feminist Scholarship: Kindling the groves of academe.* Urbana: University of Illinois Press.

Erikson, E. (1968). *Identity: Youth and crisis.* New York: Norton.

Fine, M. (1985). Reflections of a feminist psychology of women: Paradoxes and prospects. *Psychology of Women Quarterly, 9,* 167–183.

Fine, M. (1992). *Disruptive voices: The possibilities of feminist research.* Ann Arbor: University of Michigan Press.

Fishkin, J., Keniston, K., and MacKinnon, C. (1983). Moral reasoning and political ideology. *Journal of Personality and Social Psychology, 27,* 109–119.

Flax, J. (1978). The conflict between nurturance and autonomy in mother-daughter relationships and within feminism. *Feminist Studies, 4,* 171–191.

Fowlkes, D. L. and McClure, C. S. (Eds.) (1984). *The genesis of feminist visions for transforming the liberal arts curriculum.* Birmingham AL: University Alabama Press.

Gilligan, C. (1977). In a different voice: Women's conception of self and morality. *Harvard Educational Review, 47,* 481–517.

Gilligan, C. (1979). Woman's place in a man's life cycle. *Harvard Educational Review, 49,* 431–446.

Gilligan, C. (1980). Restoring the missing text of women's development to life cycle theories. In D. C. McGuigan (Ed.), *Women's lives: New theory, research, policy.* Ann Arbor, MI: University of Michigan Center for Continuing Education of Women.

Gilligan, C. (1982). *In a different voice: Psychological theory and women's development.* Cambridge, MA: Harvard University Press.

Gilligan, C. and Murphy, J. M. (1979). Development from adolescence to adulthood: The philosopher and the dilemma of the fact. In D. Kuhn (Ed.), *Intellectual development beyond childhood.* San Francisco: Jossey-Bass.

Gumperz, J. J. (1982). *Language and social identity.* New York: Cambridge University Press.

Haan, N. (1983). An interactional morality of everyday life. In N. Haan, P. Rabinow, and W. Sullivan (Eds.), *Social science as moral inquiry.* New York: Columbia University Press.

Harding, S. and O'Barr, J. F. (1987). *Sex and scientific inquiry.* Chicago: University of Chicago Press.

Hare-Mustin, R. T. (1987). The gender dichotomy and developmental theory: A response to Sayers. *New ideas in Psychology, 5,* 261–265.

Hare-Mustin, R. T. and Marecek, J. (Eds.) (1990). *Making a difference: Psychology and the construction of gender.* New Haven, CT: Yale University Press.

Harré, R. (1983). An analysis of social activity. In J. Miller (Ed.), *States of mind.* New York: Pantheon.

Harré, R. (1984). *Personal being.* Cambridge, MA: Harvard University Press.

Harré, R. Clarke, D. and deCarlo, N. (1985). *Motives and mechanism: An introduction to the psychology of action.* New York: Methuen.

Haste, H. Why thinking about feeling isn't the same as feeling about thinking, and why post-androgyny is dialectical not regressive: A response to Philibert and Sayers. *New Ideas in Psychology, 5,* 215–222.

Henley, N. M. (1977). *Body politics: Power, sex, and nonverbal communication.* Englewood Cliffs, NJ: Prentice-Hall.

Henley, N. M. (1986). Feminist psychology and feminist theory. Carolyn Wood Sherif Memorial Lecture (Division 35), Annual Meeting of the American Psychological Association, Washington, DC.

Hyman, V. R. (1987–1988). Conflict and contradiction: Principles of feminist scholarship. *Academic Questions,* Winter, 5–14.

Joy, D. (Ed.) (1983). *Moral development foundations: Judeo-Christian alternatives to Piaget/Kohlberg.* Nashville: Abingdon.

Keller, E. F. (1985). *Reflections of gender and science.* New Haven: Yale University Press.

Keller, E. F. (1987). On the need to count past two in our thinking about gender and science. *New Ideas in Psychology, 5,* 275–288.

Kessler, S. J. and McKenna, W. (1978). *Gender: An ethnomethodological approach.* Chicago: University of Chicago Press.

Kittay, E. F. and Meyers, D. T. (Eds.) (1987). *Women and moral theory.* NJ: Rowman and Littlefield.

Lykes, M.B. and Stewart, A. J. (1986). Evaluating the feminist challenge to research in personality and social psychology: 1963–1983. *Psychology of Women Quarterly, 10,* 393–412.

Levinson, D. (1978). *The seasons of a man's life.* New York: Knopf.

Lott, B. (1985). The potential enrichment of social/personality psychology through feminist research and vice versa. *American Psychologist, 40,* 155–164.

Lykes, M. B. (1985). Gender and individualistic vs collectivist bases notions about the self. *Journal of Personality, 53,* 356–383.

Lyons, N. (1983). Two perspectives on self, relationships, and morality. *Harvard Educational Review, 53,* 125–145.

Maccoby, E. E. and Jacklin, C. N. (1974). *The psychology of sex differences.* Stanford, CA: Stanford University Press.

Maltz, D. N. and Borker, R. A. (1982). A cultural approach to male-female miscommunication. In J. J. Gumperz (Ed.), *Language and social identity.* New York: Cambridge University Press, 195–216.

PARLEE

Margolis, J. (1987). The middle ground in social psychology. *New Ideas in Psychology, 5,* 313–317.

Markus, H., Crane, M., Bernstein, S. and Siladi, M. (1982). Self-schemas and gender. *Journal of Personality and Social Psychology, 42,* 38–50.

Markus, H. and Sentis, K. (1981). The self in social information processing. In J. Suls (Ed.), *Psychological perspectives on the self.* Hillsdale, NJ: Lawrence Erlbaum Associates.

McHugh, M. C. Doeske, R. D. and Frieze, I. H. (1986). Issues to consider in conducting nonsexist psychological research: A guide to researchers. *American Psychologist, 41,* 879–890.

Miller, J. B. (1984). The development of women's sense of self. Wellesley, MA: Stone Center for Developmental Services and Studies at Wellesley College, Work-In-Progress Series.

Minnich, E. K. (1990). *Transforming knowledge.* Philadelphia: Temple University Press.

Morawski, J. (1994). *Reconstructing psychology: Notes on a liminal science.* Ann Arbor: University of Michigan Press.

Murphy, J. M. and Gilligan, C. (1980). Moral development in late adolescence: A critique and reconstruction of Kohlberg's theory. *Human Development, 23,* 77–104.

Paludi, M. A. (1988). *Exploring/Teaching the psychology of women: A manual of resources.* Albany, NY: SUNY Press.

Parlee, M. B. (1975). Psychology: Review essay. *SIGNS, 1,* 119–131.

Parlee, M. B. (1979). Conversational politics. *Psychology Today,* May, 48ff.

Parlee, M. B. (1979). Psychology and women: Review essay. *SIGNS, 5,* 121–133.

Parlee, M. B. (1981). Appropriate control groups in feminist research. *Psychology of Women Quarterly, 5,* 637–644.

Parlee, M. B. (1985). Psychology of women in the 80s: Promising problems. *International Journal of Women's Studies, 8,* 193–204.

Parlee, M. B. (1988). Menstrual cycle changes in moods and emotions: Causal and interpretive processes in the construction of emotions. In H. L. Wagner (Eds.), *Social psychophysiology and emotion: Theory and clinical applications.* Chichester: Wiley.

Pollack, S. and Gilligan, C. (1982). Images of violence in Thematic Apperception Test stories. *Journal of Personality and Social Psychology, 42,* 159–167.

Ruble, D. N. and Brooks-Gunn, J. (1979). Menstrual symptons: A social cognitive analysis of perception of symptoms. *Journal of Behavioral Medicine, 2,* 171–194.

Russo, N. F. (1995). Editorial. *PWQ: A scientific voice in feminist psychology. Psychology of Women Quarterly, 19,* 1–3.

Scarborough, E. and Furumoto, L. (1987). *Untold lives: The first generation of American women psychologists.* New York: Columbia University Press.

Sherif, C. W. (1979). Bias in psychology. In J. A. Sherman and E. T. Beck (Eds.), *The prism of sex: Essays on the sociology of knowledge.* Madison, WI: University of Wisconsin Press.

Shweder, R. A. and LeVine, R. A. (1984). *Culture theory: Essays on mind, self, and emotion.* New York: Cambridge University Press.

Smith, D. (1979). A sociology for women. In J. A. Sherman and E. T. Beck (Eds.), *The prism of sex: Essays on the sociology of knowledge.* Madison, WI. University of Wisconsin Press.

Stacey, J. and Thorne, B. (1985). The missing feminist revolution in sociology. *Social Problems, 32,* 310–316.

Strickland, L. H. (Ed.) (1984). *Directions in Soviet psychology.* New York: Springer-Verlag.

Thorne, B. and Henley, N. M. (Eds.) (1975). *Language and sex: Difference and dominance.* Rowley, MA: Newbury House Publishers.

Thorne, B. and Henley, N. M. (1975). Difference and dominance: An overview of language, gender, and society. In B. Thorne and N. M. Henley (Eds.), *Language and sex: Difference and dominance* (pp. 5–42). Rowley, MA: Newbury House Publishers.

Thorne, B. Kramarae, C., and Henley, N. M. (Eds.) (1983). *Language, gender and society.* New York: Harper and Row.

Unger, R. K. (1983). Through the looking glass: No wonderland yet! The reciprocal relation between methodology and models of reality. *Psychology of Women Quarterly, 8,* 9–32.

Unger, R. K. (1985). Epilogue: Toward a synthesis of women, gender, and social psychology. In V. E. O'Leary, R. K. Unger, and B. S. Wallston (Eds.), *Women, gender, and social psychology* (pp. 349–358). Hillsdale, NJ: Lawrence Erlbaum Associates.

Vygotsky, L. S. (1978). *Mind in society: The development of higher psychological processes.* Cambridge, MA: Harvard University Press. (Originally published 1930).

Walker, J. C. (1983). In a different voice: Cryptoseparatist analysis of female moral development. *Social Research, 50,* 665–695.

Walker, L. J. (1984). Sex differences in the development of moral reasoning: A critical review. *Child Development, 55,* 677–691.

Wallston, B. S. (1981). What are the questions in the psychology of women: A feminist approach to research. *Psychology of Women Quarterly, 5,* 597–617.

Walsh, M. R. (1987). *The psychology of women: Ongoing debates.* New Haven: Yale University Press.

Wertsch, J. V. (1979). From social interaction to higher psychological processes: A clarification and application of Vygotsky's theory. *Human Development, 51,* 1215–1221.

Wertsch, J. V. (trans. and Ed.) (1981). *The concept of activity in Soviet Psychology.* Armonk, NY: Sharoe.

West, C. and Zimmerman, D. (1987). Doing gender. *Gender and Society, 1,* 125–151.

Wilkinson, S. (Ed.) (1986). *Feminist social psychology: Developing theory and practice.* Milton Keynes: Open University Press.

Wittig, MA. (1985). Meta-theoretical dilemmas in the psychology of gender. *American Psychologist, 40,* 800–811.

93

PARLEE

REFERENCES [1996]

Andersen, M. L. (1988). Changing the curriculum in higher education. In E. Minnick, J. O'Barr, & R. Rosenfeld (Eds.), *Reconstructing the Academy: Women's Education and Women's Studies.* Chicago: University of Chicago Press, 36–68 (reprinted from *Signs, 12,* 2, Winter 1987).

Billig, M. (1987). *Thinking and arguing: A rhetorical approach to social psychology.* New York: Cambridge University Press.

Billig, M., Condor, S., Edwards, D., Gane, M., Middleton, D., & Radley, A. (1988). *Ideological dilemmas: A social psychology of everyday thinking.* Newbury Park, CA: Sage.

Crawford, J., Kippax, S., Onyx, J., Gault, U., & Benton, P. (1992). *Emotion and gender: Constructing meaning from memory.* Newbury Park, CA: Sage.

Edwards, D., & Potter, J. (1992). *Discursive psychology.* Newbury Park, CA: Sage.

Fine, M. (1992). *Disruptive voices: The possibilities of feminist research*. Ann Arbor, MI: University of Michigan Press.

Hare-Mustin, R. T., & Marecek, J. (Eds.). (1990). *Making a difference: Psychology and the construction of gender*. New Haven, CT: Yale University Press.

Harré, R., & Gillet, G. (1994). *The discursive mind*. Newbury Park, CA: Sage.

Henley, N. M. (1995). Body politics revisited: What do we know today? In P. J. Kalbfleisch & M. J. Cody (Eds.), *Gender, power, and communication in human relationships* (pp. 27–61). Hillsdale, NJ: Lawrence Erlbaum Associates.

Henley, N. M., Miller, M., & Beazley, J. (1995). Syntax, semantica, and sexual violence: Agency and the passive voice. *Journal of Language and Social Psychology, 14,* 60–84.

Henriques, J., Hollway, W., Urwin, C., Venn, C., & Walkerdine, V. (1984). *Changing the subject*. London: Methuen.

Hollway, W. (1989). *Subjectivity and method in psychology: Gender, meaning and science*. London: Sage.

Kessler, S. J., & McKenna, W. (1985). *Gender: An ethnomethodological approach*. Chicago: University of Chicago Press (originally published in 1978).

King, K. (1994). *Theory in its feminist travels: Conversations in U.S. women's movements*. Bloomington, IN: Indiana University Press.

Lamb, S. (1991). Acts without agents: An analysis of linguistic avoidance in journal articles on men who batter women. *American Journal of Orthopsychiatry, 61/2,* 250–257.

Middleton, D., & Edwards, D. (Eds.). (1990). *Collective remembering*. Newbury Park, CA: Sage.

Morawski, J. (1994). *Practicing feminism, reconstructing psychology: Notes on a liminal science*. Ann Arbor, MI: University of Michigan Press.

Parlee, M. B. (1991). Happy birth-day to *Feminism & Psychology*. *Feminism & Psychology, 1,* 39–48.

Parlee, M. B. (1994). The social construction of premenstrual syndrome: A case study of scientific discourse as cultural contestation. In M. G. Winkler & L. B. cole (Eds.), *The good body: Asceticism in contemporary culture* (pp. 91–107). New Haven, CT: Yale University Press.

Potter, J., & Wetherell, M. (1987). *Discourse and social psychology: Beyond attitudes and behavior*. Newbury Park, CA: Sage.

Russo, N. F. (1995). *PWQ:* A scientific voice in feminist psychology. *Psychology of Women Quarterly, 19,* 1–3.

Scarborough, E., & Furumoto, L. (1987). *Untold lives: The first generation of American women psychologists*. New York: Columbia University Press.

Scribner, S. (1990). A sociocultural approach to the study of mind. In G. Greenberg & E. Tobach (Eds.), *Theories of the evolution of knowing* (107–120). Hillsdale, NJ: Lawrence Erlbaum Associates.

Shankar-Perez, J. (1995). The coded garden: Gender, styles of narrative, and documentation for the Pilgrim Event Notification Application. Paper presented at The Women, Gender and Science Question conference, University of Minnesota, May 12–14.

Squire, C. (1989). *Significant differences—Feminism in psychology*. New York: Routledge.

Tannen, D. (1990). *You just don't understand*. New York: William Morrow.

Tavris, C. (1992). *Mismeasure of woman*. New York: Simon & Schuster.

Tiefer, L. (1995). *Sex is not a natural act & other essays*. Boulder, CO: Westview Press.

Tobach, E. Falmagne, R. J., Parlee, M. B., Martin, L. W., & Kapelman, A. S. (Eds.). (1995). *Mind and social practice: Selected writings by Sylvia Scribner*. New York: Cambridge University Press.

Ussher, J. (1989). *Psychology and the female body*. New York: Routledge.

Walkerdine, V. (1990). *Schoolgirl fictions*. London: Verso.

Wilkinson, S. (Ed.). (1986). *Feminist social psychology*. Milton Keynes: Open University Press.

PART II
CONNECTING WITH OTHERS
Research as Relational Practice

MAKING SENSE
Interviewing and Narrative Representation

Margery B. Franklin

PSYCHOLOGISTS, LIKE other social scientists, have long acknowledged the complex interweavings of methodology, epistemological assumptions, value groundings, and the nature of understanding generated through different forms of inquiry. However, until relatively recently, consideration of such interconnections has been dominated by mainstream voices or relegated to specialized discussions at the fringe. Even as aspects of feminist, social constructionist, and postmodernist thinking converge in a strong counterforce, the majority of academic research psychologists view new developments with skepticism, if not disdain; most journal limit themselves to articles couched in "scientific" terms, and graduate training continues to follow hallowed traditions of the field.

In this chapter, I describe and illustrate two aspects of a methodological approach still outside the mainstream: First, a qualitative interview process; second, the representation of interview material in narrative form. The third aspect of the approach, the comparative case study method, is mentioned briefly. I will refer to material and experience gathered in the first and second phases of a project focused on how women artists see the development of their work over the trajectory of their professional careers. The first phase of the project centered on one artist, a close friend (Franklin, 1989). As will become clear, this beginning significantly shaped subsequent work. In the second phase, I reinterviewed my friend and selected another six artists whose work I studied in some depth prior to beginning the interview process. Each of the seven is well established by professional criteria. With one exception, they are contemporaries. One is a photographer, two are sculptors, four are painters (Franklin, 1994).

THE INTERVIEW PROCESS

The study of women artists' work grew out of my interest in understanding a dramatic shift in my friend's work—a shift from large-scale abstract painting to small-scale figurative work in ceramic sculpture (Franklin, 1989). Following very informal conversation, I decided to phrase some questions and turn on a tape recorder. I had started to think of a "research project" focused on continuities, discontinuities, and transitions in artistic work. To establish anything verging on a formal interview when talking with my friend would have been extremely awkward and therefore counterproductive. I decided to violate every precept of academic psychology, and allow the "interviews" to become free-flowing conversations. Attempting to ground the approach I was using, I began to think more systematically about the interview process and soon discovered that many of my concerns and interests were shared by others. The relation of particular methodological strands to feminist thinking will be explored in the course of discussion.

Until quite recently, one model of the research interview displaced other possibilities.[1] This model, which I call the *information extraction* model, construes the interview as a situation in which the interviewer extracts from the interviewee an articulation of feelings, ideas, and/or knowledge. It is assumed that these feelings, ideas, and/or knowledge reside in the person and come forth in the interview with varying degrees of completeness and veracity—depending in part on the "openness" and "articulateness" of the interviewee, and in part on the skill of the interviewer in creating an appropriate environment. The interviewer always takes the active role of question-asker and the interviewee the passive role of respondent. The model involves a set of prescriptions that characterize the traditional approach to research interviewing in the social sciences. As we will see, each of these is disputed by adherents of other views. The prescriptions can be summarized as follows: (1) Use a standardized set of questions and ask them in a predetermined order; (2) don't respond substantively to what your interviewee says (this might "bias" subsequent responses); (3) be friendly enough to facilitate the information-extraction process but not more so; (4) do not express your own views, even if you think this would lead your "subject" to say more. The aim is to insure "scientific objectivity" and to obtain comparable material from different interviewees in a form that lends itself readily to coding and so to quantification. In traditional psychological circles, this form of interviewing is viewed as an alternative to the method of choice: the time-honored experiment in which variables are unambiguously designated and rigorously controlled.

Oakley (1981) suggests that the approach to interviewing designated here as the *information extraction* model reflects a masculine paradigm of how to do research. In addition to emphasizing the interview as a mechanical instrument of data collection and reducing the interviewer to a "question-asking and rapport-establishing" role, the model "appeals to such values as objectivity, detachment, hierarchy, and 'science' as an important cultural value . . ." (38). In a similar vein, Riger (cited in Reinharz, 1992, 24) argues that traditional research methods emphasize "objectivity, efficiency, separateness, and distance"—qualities that are identified with masculine values and modes of being. The significance of these identifications lies in their implications. As Keller (1985) suggests, we experience scientific endeavors in gendered terms: "hard," tough, and objectifying forms are identified as masculine, while "soft," tender minded, and subjectivized forms are identified as feminine—no matter who invented them.[2] As long as we live in a world where "masculine" modes of thinking and working are dominant, the softer, more tender minded approaches will be regarded with suspicion if not disdain. The task, then, is to show what is lost through the use of traditional methodologies, and what can be gained by other means.

101

Feminist scholars and others articulate a number of specific problems incurred by applying the traditional model. One set of problems concerns interview structure. I referred earlier to the fact that my artist friend would not have responded positively and productively, if at all, to a series of preformulated questions. The spontaneity of our exchange enabled her to articulate half-formed thoughts in a way that she, as well as I, found illuminating. Describing the emergence of her work in figurative ceramic sculpture, she created a metaphor not likely to occur as response to a pre-set question.

> It's like you're walking around with this enormous suitcase full of magic and you are never allowed to open it because the rules say that the things in that suitcase are not worthy of artistic consideration. Words, childhood memories, pretend, fantasy, archeology—all that. And so, until I could open that suitcase, I didn't really have anything to work with. It was like trying to paint with your hand tied behind your back. (From interview with MZ)

As Reinharz (1992) points out with reference to work by Gilligan (1982) and Belenky et al. (1986), asking some pre-formulated questions does not preclude having the interviewee take the lead. What is at issue is how such

FRANKLIN

questions are used and whether the interviewee is given sufficient opportunity to introduce and develop her own lines of thought. Reissman (1993) and Mishler (1986) emphasize the importance of posing questions in a way that opens up possibilities and encourages narrative accounts; closer focus can occur subsequently.

Another set of problems concerns the conduct of the interview. Prescriptions against responding to interviewees' questions not only interfere with establishing rapport but raise moral questions. Describing her study of the transition to motherhood, Oakley (1981) asks how she could avoid answering the women's urgent questions about aspects of pregnancy, deliver, and infant care.

> I was faced, typically, with a woman who was quite anxious about the fate of herself and her baby . . . who saw me as someone who could not only reassure but inform. I felt that I was asking a great deal from these women . . . And all this in the interests of "science" or for some book that might possibly materialize out of the research . . . (Oakley, 1981, 44).

Oakley resolved her dilemma by responding substantively to the women's questions, providing information or suggestions about how to obtain it. Other feminist researchers concur with Oakley's view that responsiveness, rather than distance, is not only appropriate but desirable in the interview context. Some go further by questioning prescriptions against expressing one's own views. Rather than introducing "influence" or "bias," the researcher's full participation (sometimes including self-disclosure) is seen as conducive to establishing the trust and reciprocity that facilitate open expression, and the possibility of an egalitarian relationship between interviewer and interviewee.[3] Perhaps it is obvious that not all feminist scholars would voice such views. The position designated as "feminist empiricism" by Harding (1991) does not take issue with the epistemological assumptions and methodological precepts of the *information extraction* interview mode. Furthermore, as Reinharz (1992) makes clear, feminist researchers may concur on underlying values and some aspects of desirable interview practice by take different positions on others—for example, the value and possible drawbacks of interviewing friends, the process of self-disclosure, the use of pre-set questions.

A second model of the interview, which I call the *shared understanding* view answers to many of the criticisms levelled against the *information extraction* model. Here, the interview is seen as a situation in which the interviewer attempts to gain understanding of how the interviewee experiences aspects of her own life and/or the world of objects and other persons. The interview is construed as an interpersonal situation and it is recognized that the interviewer's characteristics, sensitivity, and other qualities are likely to affect what is said. The "presence" and necessary participation of the interviewer is not viewed negatively, as in the preceding model. Further, it is asserted that the interview is a process during which meanings are not only brought forth but sometimes newly formed. For example, the interviewee may change her mind about something said or see relations not previously articulated. In contrast to the *information extraction* model, this model prescribes that: (1) the interview be semi-structured, following a guide rather than a predetermined set of questions; the interviewer is free to pursue lines of thinking introduced by the interviewee; (2) the interviewer comes to the interview as open-minded as possible, with few presuppositions; (3) the interviewer aims for clarification (by asking questions, providing tentative interpretations) but not at the risk of eradicating genuine ambiguity in the interviewee's view of what s/he is talking about; (4) the interviewer paraphrases or interprets while the interview is in process, encouraging the interviewee's responses and corrections; where possible, the interviewer may arrange a follow-up session to corroborate further interpretations. The aim is to obtain rich, nuanced descriptive material that reflects the interviewee's experience of her life world (or some part thereof) and lends itself to qualitative analysis in one or more modes—for example, identifying and categorizing central themes, or extracting core narratives. By calling this the *shared understanding* model, I draw attention to what seems a major theme: the idea that the interviewer should come to understand the interviewee's sense of her life experience from her perspective—the texture and feeling as well as the "facts"—through a process of exchange and even empathy. Such understanding does not preclude applying a theoretical framework that yields interpretations at another level from the interviewee's own.[4]

The most complete formulation of this model has been presented by Kvale (1983) who grounds the method in terms of phenomenological and hermeneutical modes of understanding. Although not necessarily drawing on Kvale's formulation, a number of feminist researchers advocate "phenomenological interviewing," which is geared toward in-depth understanding of the other's experience, and uses few prepared questions, allows changes of direction, and opportunity for corroboration of interpretations (Reinharz, 1992, 21). There seems some consonance between the underlying assumptions and aims of the *shared understanding* model and feminist standpoint epistemologies. As Harding says:

> The distinctive features of women's situation in a gender-stratified society are being used as resources in the new feminist research. It is these distinctive resources, which are not used by conventional researchers, that enable feminism to produce more accurate descriptions and theoretically richer explanations than does conventional research. (1991, 119)

These "distinctive resources" could include the kind of person-centered, deeply textured accounts of women's experience that a *shared understanding* interview process is designed to yield—particularly if the researcher takes into account issues of social positioning.[5]

Needless to say, proponents of the second model are highly critical of the

FRANKLIN

first model, identifying it with traditional positivistic approaches to research that they see as misguided and highly constricting. Proponents of the first model see adherents of the second (and third) models as unscientific, unsystematic, and "soft"—an accusation tied to gendered views of what constitutes scientific thinking, as already mentioned. The clinical research interview, as developed by Piaget, appears to draw on aspects of both models. The mode of questioning is flexible, carefully geared to the child interviewee's responses. On the other hand, the intention is to tap into underlying knowledge rather than to gain understanding of the other's lifeworld. In sum, in its classical version, the Piagetian interview uses aspects of practice identified with the second model while sharing some assumptions with the *infromation extraction* model.[6]

In the third model, which I call the *discourse model,* the interview is conceptualized as a situated speech event. Some assumptions are shared with the second model, but some are not—and emphases are redistributed. The idea of an ongoing interaction between two (or more) people, carried out in the medium of language, is paramount. It is assumed that both interviewer and interviewee have active roles in what transpires: The interviewer contributes, intentionally or unintentionally, to the spirit and perhaps the substance of the dialogue and so may shape it significantly. Assumptions that the interviewer can (or should) be "objective" and "distanced" (as required in the first model), or can bracket presuppositions (as in the second model), are called into question. Interviewers, like interviewees, necessarily see situations from a point of view infused with personal experience. It is deemed productive to draw on, rather than deny, the role of subjectivity (Hollway, 1989). The distribution of power, established in part prior to the interview (by relative social or professional position, etc.), and in part during it, will affect what is said and how. Most important (and more strongly than in the second model), meaning is formed, not merely expressed or reported, through the speaking that takes place in the interview process. While it may be premature to characterize this model in terms of prescriptions, the following are characteristic of its practice: (1) The interviewer enters into a conversational mode, and responds to interviewees' questions, perhaps even talking about her own experience; (2) while a topic or focus generally exists beforehand, exploration of new themes that arise in the exchange is encouraged; (3) cross-connections may develop: one interviewee may say something that can be used productively in subsequent interviews with others; (4) the interviewer attends to and, if desired, rearranges power relations between participants to the ends of establishing equality, or even a collaborative relationship. Obviously, this kind of move is intended to eradicate the inequality—the dominant/subordinate relation—that is seen as obtaining in the traditional interview and that tends to persist (although not condoned and perhaps modified) in the *shared understanding* view.

As can be seen, this model answers to additional concerns of feminist

scholars that were noted earlier—for example, issues surrounding power relations in the interview, and the degree and nature of the interviewer's participation. In the *information extraction* model, the interviewee is generally referred to as "subject" in line with the language (and assumptions) of the classic experiment. In the *shared understanding* view and the *discourse* models, the
interviewee is referred to as such or as "participant." The shift in language is
significant.

In both assumptions and mode of practice, the *discourse* model of the interview may be seen as consonant with the postmodern turn in psychology
(K. J. Gergen, 1992; Gergen & Gergen, 1991; Shotter, 1992) and with the position of feminist postmodernism identified by Harding.

Although I prefer to be a purist, I have found that my approach to interviewing draws on aspects of two models: the *shared understanding* model and
the *discourse* model. Striving to understand the interviewee's view of her development as an artist in phenomenological terms, I am aligned with the
shared understanding model. But I sometimes take a fairly active role in the interchange—more so than fits with this model. Second, I am interested in the
idea that the interviewee and I do not always agree. Does this mean that one
of us is off the mark? I prefer to see such divergence in terms of distinct
points of view, dual voices—a construction that is more consonant with the
discourse model. Third, I am interested in the issue of power relations—another emphasis of the *discourse* model. Because the artists I interviewed are as
professionally accomplished as I (in some cases, more so), the balance of power differs from that in most psychological research situations. This, together
with my egalitarian spirit and intent to develop a quasi-collaborative project,
influenced how I functioned in the interview—for example, when and how
much I probed. Fourth, I subscribe to the assumption of both models that
meaning is not merely expressed but often formed in the process of speaking.
However, the *discourse* model (and I have named it to reflect this feature)
places more emphasis on the meaning-constructive functions of language
than does the *shared understanding* view. Further, the *shared understanding* model seems to construe the interview as a guided monologue, while the *discourse*
model views it as a function of interactional context. At this point, my theoretical sympathies flow toward the *discourse* model but I see that my actual
practice draws from both models.[7]

ON NARRATIVE REPRESENTATION AND ANALYSIS

In recent years, a number of theorists have argued for the ubiquity and usefulness of narrative as a fundamental way of "making sense" (Bruner, 1986;
Polkinghorne, 1988; Reissman, 1993; Sarbin, 1986). Narrativizing makes
sense by ordering events (personal or otherwise) along a temporal dimension
and configuring these events in such a way that themes emerge (Polkinghorne, 1988; Ricoeur, 1981). In contrast, classification makes sense by group-

ing things into categories, displaying sameness and difference, and opening up possibilities for hierarchical as well as horizontal ordering (Bruner, 1986).

Interview material gathered in open-ended situations (the second and third models described above) lends itself to consideration in terms of narrative. Clearly, the decision to view material *qua* narrative, rather than in some other terms, is tied to views on how knowledge/understanding is made, what psychologists should be doing, and the sometimes hidden meanings of differing methodological approaches (including the question, touched on above, of consonance between specific models and particular feminist viewpoints). Further, as Mishler (1995) proposes, different approaches to narrative analysis vary in their assumptions, purposes, and procedures. In the comments to follow, I sketch some aspects of the approach that I take and show its application to material gathered in the interview study of women artists.

Speaking of narrative, I find it important to draw two kinds of distinctions: First, between the narrative presented in a particular situation and the underlying narrative that the person holds; second, between the speaker's (or interviewee's) narrative and the listener's (or interpreter's) narrative.

When I ask an artist to tell me about how she sees a particular phase of her work, or the transition from one phase to the next, she provides a *narrative representation* of that aspect of her life/work story—that is, a series of statements that describes and orders a number of actions and/or experiences.[8] *Narrative representations,* articulated and presented in some medium, must be distinguished from the semi-formulated, perhaps submerged narratives that lie beneath the surface. I call the latter *underlying narratives.* We may also assume that some experience exists in non-narrativized form—perhaps as images or "snapshots." A person telling aspects of a life story draws upon previously articulated *narrative representations* (stories told to self or others on previous occasions), semi-formulated *underlying narratives,* and non-narrativized experience. The form and content of the *narrative representation* are strongly shaped by situational factors, including how the teller perceives the listener, whether the listener participates actively, how this is taken by the speaker, and so forth. This is the sense in which all narrative representations must be seen as situated performances.[9]

To clarify the distinction between *narrative representations* that draw heavily on previously told stories and those that are more or less improvised on the spot, consider two extreme cases. Someone who has been interviewed several times previously about a particular aspect of that person's life (or otherwise "written" the story), is likely to draw upon a *pre-scripted narrative representation.* some modifications of form and content will occur as a function of situation and shifts in intention, but the major dimensions of the account are relatively unchanged. Portions of some of the artists' narratives gathered in my study seemed pre-scripted in this sense. I tend to view pre-scripted performances as one among other kinds of self-representation, not inherently less "genuine" although prepared for public consumption.[10]

On the other hand, when you ask someone about an aspect of her life that she has not previously thought about—for example, how she experienced changes in her body over time—she does not have a relevant *underlying narrative* to draw upon. In such situations, people draw on assorted memories and experiences, perhaps fragments of related narratives, to improvise a narrative representation. This representation may then be "stored" more or less intact, may settle in and become part of an already existing *underlying narrative,* or may fly out the window when the interview ends. I assume that even when narrative representations are "stored intact," thus available in scripted form for future use, changes will occur.

There are many sources of change. One is the process of telling itself, which involves oneself and/or others as audience. In a panel discussion that I organized, I listened to four of the artists I had interviewed address the question of continuities and changes in their work over time. For two, how they talked about continuity and change differed substantively from (although did not contradict) what they had said in the interviews. The particular form of changes suggested to me that the initial interviews provided an occasion for these artists to rethink some of their ideas about their own development— that is, to revise their *underlying narratives.* A more dramatic instance of revision was provided by my review of interviews with my friend over a period of ten years. The selection and ordering of events remained fairly stable across successive tellings, but the valuation of specific occurrences (for example, whether a particular work represented a "major turning point") as well as major organizing themes and other aspects of the life/work narrative changed considerably (Franklin, 1993).

There are many ways of analyzing *narrative representations;* only some of

107

THE INTERVIEWEE "Author"	THE INTERVIEWER "Interpreter"

Primary narrative representation
    prescripted
    improvisational
	Secondary narrative representation
	    theme/plot oriented
	    process oriented

Underlying narrative(s)	Constructed underlying narrative(s) and/or other schemas
Non-narrativized experience, memories & knowledge	

This diagram draws on, but does not follow, a diagram in Todorov (1990), 42.

FIGURE 1. Interviewee as "author and interviewer as "interpreter": Constructing narratives.

these qualify as narrative approaches. For example, content analysis that focuses on frequency of occurrence of particular items is not guided by considerations of narrative. Under the general rubric of narrative approaches, we find two broad strategies with different foci. The first focuses on the "stuff" of the narrative, the material that constitutes it, which includes aspects of structure (importantly, the arrangement manifested in "plot"), as well as what is generally called "content." I refer to this as *theme/plot* orientation.

Alternatively, one can look at a narrative (or portions of a narrative) in terms of structural components and **process**—for example, in terms of specific words and phrases used, how these are ordered and related to each other, options taken up or rejected, when pauses occur, whether there are interruptions, and so forth. Such approaches range from micro-analyses to macro-analyses.[11] This may be called a *process* approach.

To clarify the difference between the two general approaches, consider the following excerpt from the interview with painter LF. The interviewer is MF.[12]

1. MF: *When I wrote to you, I explained that I'm particularly interested in how artists see transitions in their work, times when their work is changing. Perhaps you could talk about how you see the phases in your work.*
2. LF: Well, for one thing, I'm more conscious of the phases, from one to the next, than I used to be.
3. MF: *Let's talk about that.*
4. LF: However, what I've noticed is a line of thinking, or a line of identity that runs through all the work.
5. The change is maybe less important than what's constant.
6. MF: *Yes, well, when I wrote to you, I explained that I'm interested in how artists see both continuities and changes in their work.*
7. LF: I started thinking about that a number of years ago.
8. Of course, I've painted abstract paintings without any break since art school.
9. And they changed a lot as I learned more and as I grow up.
10. As I change myself, my paintings change.
11. They change for all kinds of reasons,
12. but I found a piece that my mother had saved—my mother saved all my little paintings—it's a painting I did when I was about three or two and it had the same format that the paintings I did later have.
13. And I always felt that painting has to do with a kind of balance in the body.
14. That's an over-simplification
15. but the physicality of the painting is certainly connected with my body, and how I experience my body and the space I live in. That's the basic line, I think.

First consider this excerpt from a *themes/plot* point of view. The interviewee's *principal theme* comes through on lines 4 and 5: a **line of identity** runs through my work, constancy is more important than change. A *Subsidiary* (counter?) theme of **change** comes through on lines 8 and 9. The theme of

constancy is underlined with reference to childhood (line 12). At the same time, childhood activity and adult work are linked. A *related theme*—the indissoluble link between myself and my work, pivoting on the issue of change—comes through on line 10. *Elaboration/specification* of the principal theme occurs on line 15: the physicality of painting connected with the sense of my body in space (this theme is further developed later in the interview).

Looking at the excerpt from a macro *process* point of view, as contrasted with a *themes/plot* analysis, it's important to know that this exchange occurred about 30 minutes into the interview, after talking about the artist's background. At the start of this segment (line 1), I try to set the agenda, and I reinforce it after the interviewee's response (line 3). But she shifts the focus (lines 4 and 5). I accept this, but try to re-establish my credibility (line 6). On line 7, LF sort of acknowledges my fixing move, and goes on with her "story": a narrative organized around the theme of constancy that subsumes change. Much more detailed analysis of this sort can be done.

I see the two analytic strategies as complementary rather than exclusive. Until this point in my current work, I've used the first, but I would encourage an integrative approach that draws on both approaches (see, for example, Gee, 1991, and Mishler, 1995).

Let me now turn to the distinction between the interviewee's narrative and the interviewer's narrative. In our attempt to make sense within the world of social science, we renarrativize or otherwise analyze the "raw material" presented by the interviewee. Reading psychological studies that use interviews as "raw material," one often finds it difficult to tell where the interviewee's narrative leaves off and the investigator's narrative begins. Further, Mishler (1991) and Reissman (1993) make clear that even the apparently simple process of transcription involves a series of theory-laden decisions. Even those who are highly sophisticated on the issue of perspective sometimes blur boundaries as they attempt to develop an account that captures the other's experience. To underscore the importance of maintaining distinct perspectives, I refer to the interviewee's presented narrative as the *primary narrative representation* and to the investigator's narrative construction as the *secondary narrative representation*.[13]

Two examples will clarify the distinction between *primary* and *secondary* *narrative representations*. Photographer JL had been talking about her awareness of herself as a woman and how this entered into her work at various periods; she emphasized a recent shift and intensification in her awareness when she began to read feminist theory and to teach jointly with a feminist anthropologist.

1. JL: I've begun to feel that it's useful to me, and that difficult as it may be to get it, that it's somehow now in my work.
2. Even the notion of giving my work to —well, working with my sister,
3. the most successful part of the collaboration is when she writes on my im-

109

FRANKLIN

ages of her what she experienced in being photographed or in looking at the photographs.

4. And so giving back a voice.

5. MF: *And you feel that this particular kind of turn, one of the sources, or perhaps the primary source, has been feminist theory?*

6. JL:Yes.

10. MF: *Because I can see, knowing your previous work—I can see precursors.*

11. *When we spoke before, the way in which you talked about photography itself as a medium that is necessarily concerned with point of view, the relation of the camera and the photographer to what is being photographed, and this seems to me like an elaboration—*

12. JL:Yeah, I think so, I agree that those things are probably there (. . .)

13. So it might be that the best way to say it is:

14. these things were there, but once they found validation in a sense of community,

15. I was able to go further self-consciously, more purposefully.

16. It's good to be reminded that it was already there in many ways.

17. Sometimes perhaps whatever is your most current thinking kind of crowds out your earlier thinking.

In lines 1–4, the artist is elaborating on an earlier statement about how reading feminist theory affected her work. This is *primary narrative representation*. In line 5, I check my understanding. In lines 10 and 11, I provide a piece from the *secondary narrative representation* I'm in the process of constructing. In lines 12–17, the artist accepts my suggestion and incorporates it into her narrative representation, but at the same time re-asserts her sense that the new work represents a qualitative change, not as much a "continuation" as my phrasing might suggest.

As this example shows, offering pieces of one's *secondary narrative representation* during the interview may affect the interviewee's *primary narrative representation*. Here, the modification was minor, but one can easily imagine more extreme cases in which it might be appropriate to speak of co-construction of a narrative that falls somewhere between the "pure" forms of *primary* and *secondary*. Except when seeking clarity, I refrain from offering "reconstructions," in which case the *primary narrative* is unaffected by my interpretation. Also, there are instances where my reconstructions are ignored or explicitly rejected.

HS does very large oil paintings that could be classified as still lifes—vases, flowers, fabric, other objects. But she identifies herself as an abstract painter, concerned primarily with color, spatial relations, other formal concerns. She acknowledges that many of the objects she uses have "resonances," personal meanings that may also resonate for others, and that some of her titles direct viewers toward such resonances. In the second interview, I suggested to HS that she seemed to be moving away from purely formal concerns toward more intensified interest in resonances, associations, and metaphors—implying that there was movement or development in a particular direction. she made it very clear that she did not see her development this way:

> Themes are cyclical in my work. They've always been there and they keep spin-
> ning around and coming back. Sometimes they're formal concerns, say light and
> color; sometimes they're more about resonant objects, associations . . . I see it as
> a kind of wheel that's turning around.

Such formulations may exist prior to the interview or may take shape in the context of the conversation—in this case, to counter the interviewer's mis-construction. Now, do I revise the *secondary narrative representation* I'm constructing? That depends on how I see the artist's actual work over time *in relation to* what she has said. In this case, the interviewee's comments led me to question assumptions of "progress" in development that I tend to use even as I question standard models of development, and so entered into my thinking about other artists' work. But the point is that I try to avoid absorbing her view into mine, or *vice versa*. The voices are distinct, if interacting.

This plea for identifying distinct voices, and not assimilating others to our own, is closely linked to more encompassing questions concerning the kind of appropriation of the other that is recognized, at least among many feminists, as a hazard of social science research (Opie, 1992).

The main distinctions that I've made here are summarized in Figure 1. One could draw arrows to indicate relations and interactions. For example, *primary narrative representations* draw on *underlying narratives* and once articulated can sift down and become part of them. Also, we've seen that in an interview, *primary narrative representations* can be affected by secondary narrative representations, and so forth. The scheme as depicted in Figure 1 includes a component not yet mentioned: *constructed underlying narrative(s)*. While *secondary narrative representations* are certainly theory-guided, they remain closely tied to the specific phenomena of a particular case (that is, descriptive). Such narratives can become the "raw material" for another level of narrative construction, a level that draws on theoretical concepts transcending the particular case, and that is explicitly geared toward explanation. In constructing such underlying narratives the investigator can use established, codified theory (for example, psychoanalytic theory) or improvise theoretical formulations. I have used a notion of **converging streams** to interpret some instances of dramatic change in artists' work (Franklin, 1989, 1994). As one example, the beginning of DD's work with three dimensional structures, coming after struggles and explorations of almost two years, marks the beginning of the work she identifies with and is known for. DD had identified the streams, although not naming them as such, as she talked about what was going on in the period of struggles and explorations: Her memories of making shelters in childhood, viewing Egyptian structures at the Metropolitan Museum, a new valuing of autobiographical experience, keeping a journal and doing "free drawing."

However, the idea that a convergence of distinct streams (each with a history) issued in the new form of work is my formulation, part of my *constructed underlying narrative* of this case. (On the chart, the phrase "other schemas" is included with *constructed underlying narratives* to indicate alternatives to narrative construction at this level).

THE COMPARATIVE CASE STUDY

The cognitive case study approach as developed by Gruber (1980; see also Wallace, 1989) focuses on the creative person's work in the context of the life, and uses first person materials (such as journals, diaries, letters, and interviews) in conjunction with intensive study of the "work objects" to gain access to the work process and its vicissitudes. This represents one variant of the single case study approach. My use of interviews in conjunction with study of the work is connected to this tradition but departs from it in several ways. First, I have concentrated on how women artists *experience* the evolution of their work, and so place more emphasis on the first person account *per se*—not only what is said, but how it is said. Second, the interview—as contrasted with other first person statements—provides an opportunity for exchange of views between interviewee and interviewer. As we have seen, such exchanges can contribute significantly to the construction of both primary and secondary narratives. Third, like many of the researchers referred to in this chapter, I have used a comparative case study approach. In this approach, a number of people who have some things in common (such as gender, profession, age) are selected as participants. True to the idiographic tradition, each is viewed as an individual. But having several "cases" to contemplate provides a basis for articulating similarities and differences among individuals, sharpening perceptions through comparison, and possibly finding grounds for more encompassing statements.

* * *

In this chapter, I've identified and illustrated three components of a methodological approach that involves: (1) an approach to interviewing, (2) narrative analysis, and (3) a comparative case study method. In concluding, I want to make clear that I see these three components as fitting together: The open-ended, interactive interview provides material appropriate for analysis in terms of primary and secondary narrative representations (and underlying narratives). And vice versa: analysis in terms of narrative seems particularly appropriate to this kind of material, particularly if one is interested in development and patterns of change. Finally, the comparative case study method fits well with a perspectival point of view, with the idea of keeping voices distinct—even as it provides opportunity to explore how perspectives may converge.

NOTES

1. Bear in mind that this discussion does not concern models of the therapeutic interview, although there are some points of contact—particularly concerning issues of whether inner ideas and feelings are *expressed* or *formed* in the interchange.

2. Keller (1985, Ch. 4) is concerned to show the origins of these identifications in psychodynamic and cognitive developmental terms, arguing that the they are, on the one hand, more than metaphoric and, on the other hand, not "accidents" of culture.

3. Issues of power relations in the interview are probed by Mishler (1986) and Hollway (1989), among others. Hollway discusses the value of interviewing friends and friends of friends—"equals." To some extent, they become full participants in the research enterprise as she asks them to corroborate, or comment upon, her interpretations of transcript excerpts. Hollway also emphasizes the value of being able to establish genuine trust.

4. The tendency in social science to assimilate the interviewee's views to a pre-established theoretical framework or, more extremely, to appropriate the other's words, is discussed in the next section of the paper.

5. Riger (1992) remarks that arguments for feminist standpoint epistemologies "have stimulated rich and valuable portrayals of women's experience" but she voices reservations about feminist standpoint theory as a basis for science, suggesting that "this position seems to dissolve science into autobiography" (734). This kind of statement opens up an entire discourse on the meanings of "science" which cannot be explored here, but note Harding's counterarguments (Harding, 1991), including the argument that feminist standpoint epistemology generates a kind of "objectivity" not otherwise available. Morowski (1990) explores related issues.

6. Providing a hermeneutic interpretation of the Piagetian interview paradigm, Honey (1987) would take exception to my statement about underlying assumptions. Clearly, this is an arguable case.

7. For example, portions of most of my interviews are prompted monologues rather than taking dialogic form. To be sure, one can make fancy arguments for the idea that monologues are, at base, dialogues. However, coming down from the theoretical stratosphere, one recognizes that monologic speaking has a different dynamic than dialogic exchange.

8. I'm using the word "order" here as shorthand for the two interrelated aspects of narrativizing already mentioned, viz. temporal ordering, and configuring of parts into thematic wholes. Note that I'm not using a definition of narrative that calls on notions of canonical form—for example, that there has to be a problem followed by a resolution, or a "breach" in which expectations are jarred (see Chafe, 1990). In my view, such criteria should be used to distinguish "story" from other forms of narrative (or perhaps as criteria for well-formedness).

9. An alternative way of conceptualizing levels of narrative is presented by Reissman (1993).

10. I suggest that our tendency to denigrate pre-scripted versions reflects the view that what is "underneath" is more real than what shows (and perhaps almost a wish to elevate the interviewer/interpreter).

11. Such analyses often seem driven by discourse analyses developed within a lin-

guistic tradition, but have been used to infer emotional as well as cognitive meanings (see, for example, Labov & Fanshel, 1977). See Mishler (1995) for a recent discussion of different approaches to narrative analysis.

12. The artists are identified by name in the more detailed discussion of their work (Franklin, 1994). The use of line numbers here roughly designates meaning units.

13. This distinction corresponds, roughly, to Todorov's distinction between the author's narrative and the reader's narrative (Todorov, 1990). See Cohler (1991) and Kaplan (1991) on the distinction between a person's "life history" (existence/experience over time) and the "life story" ("the representation/interpretation of that experience by the person or someone else"); this distinction is similar to mine, but does not distinguish the person's unnarrativized and narrativized experience, or explicitly mark narrative representations of teller and interpreter (*primary* and *second narrative representations*, in my terminology).

REFERENCES

Belenky, M., Clinchy, B., Goldberger, N., and Tarule, J. (1986). *Women's ways of knowing.* New York: Basic Books.

Bruner, J. (1986). *Actual minds, possible worlds.* Cambridge, MA: Harvard University Press.

Bruner, J. (1990). *Acts of meaning.* Cambridge, MA: Harvard University Press.

Chafe, W. (1990). Some things that narratives tell us about the mind. In B. K. Fritton & A. D. Pellgrini (Eds.), *Narrative thought and narrative language.* Hillsdale, NJ: Lawrence Erlbaum Associates.

Cohler, B. J. (1991). The life story and the study of resilience and response to adversity. *Journal of Narrative and Life History, 1,* (2 & 3), 169–200.

Franklin, M. B. (1989). A convergence of streams: Dramatic change in the artistic work of Melissa Zink. In D. B. Wallace & H. E. Gruber (Eds.), *Creative people at work: Twelve cognitive case studies.* New York: Oxford University Press.

Franklin, M. B. (1993). An artist's evolution: Reconstructing the past. Contribution to symposium, Learning the subject (R. Albert, chair), Division 10, meetings of the American Psychological Association, Toronto, Canada.

Franklin, M. B. (1994). Narratives of change and continuity: Women artists reflect on their work. In M. B. Franklin & B. Kaplan (Eds.), *Development and the arts: Critical perspectives.* Hillsdale, NJ: Lawrence Erlbaum Associates.

Gee, J. (1991). A linguistic approach to narrative. *Journal of Narrative and Life History, 1,* (1), 15–39.

Gergen, K. J. (1992). Toward a postmodern psychology. In S. Kvale (Ed.), *Psychology and postmodernism.* Newbury Park, London, New Delhi: Sage Publications.

Gergen, K. J. & Gergen, M. M. (1991). Toward reflexive methodologies. In F. Steier (Ed.), *Research and reflexivity.* Newbury Park, London, New Delhi: Sage Publications.

Gilligan, C. (1982). *In a different voice.* Cambridge, MA: Harvard University Press.

Gruber, H. E. (1989). The evolving systems approach to creative work. In D. B. Wallace & H. E. Gruber (Eds.), *Creative people at work: Twelve cognitive case studies.* New York. Oxford University Press.

Harding, S. (1991). *Whose science, whose knowledge?* Ithaca, NY: Cornell University Press.

Hollway, W. (1989). *Subjectivity and method in psychology.* Newbury Park, London, New Delhi: Sage Publication.

Honey, M. A. (1987). The interview as text: Hermeneutics considered as a model for analyzing the clinically informed research interview. *Human Development, 30* (2), 69–82.

Kaplan, B. (1991). Animadversions on adversity, ruminations on resilience: A quasi-commentary on Bertram J. Cohler's article, "The life story and the study of resilience and response to adversity. *Journal of Narrative and Life History, 1,* (2 & 3), 201–211.

Keller, E. F. (1985). *Reflections on gender and science.* New Haven, CT: Yale University Press.

Kvale, S. (1983). The qualitative research interview: A phenomenological and hermeneutical mode of understanding. *Journal of Phenomenological Psychology, 14,* 171–196.

Labov, W. & Fanshel, D. (1977). *Therapeutic discourse.* New York: Academic Press.

Mishler, E. G. (1986). *Research interviewing: Context and narrative.* Cambridge, MA: Harvard University Press.

Mishler, E. G. (1991). Representing discourse: The rhetoric of transcription. *Journal of Narrative and Life History. 1* (4), 255–280.

Mishler, E. G. (1995). Models of narrative analysis: A typology. *Journal of Narrative and Life History, 5,* (2), 87–123.

Morawski, J. G. (1990). Toward the unimagined : Feminism and epistemology in psychology. In R. R. Hare-Mustin & J. Marecek (Eds.), *Making a difference: Psychology and the construction of gender.* New Haven, CT: Yale University Press.

Oakley, A. (1981). Interviewing women: A contradiction in terms. In H. Roberts (Ed.), *Doing feminist research.* London & New York: Routledge.

Opie, A. (1992). Qualitative research, appropriation of the "other" and empowerment. *Feminist Review, 40,* 52–69.

Polkinghorne, D. E. (1988). *Narrative knowing and the human sciences.* Albany, NY: State University of New York Press.

Polkinghorne, D. E. (1991). Narrative and self-concept. *Journal of Narrative and Life History, 1,* (2 & 3), 135–153.

Reinharz, S. (1992). *Feminist methods in social research.* New York & Oxford: Oxford University Press.

Reissman, C. K. (1993). *Narrative analysis.* Newbury Park, London, New Delhi: Sage Publications.

Ricoeur, P. (1981). The narrative function. In P. Ricoeur, *Hermeneutics and the human sciences.* (J. B. Thompson, Ed. & Trans.). Cambridge, UK: Cambridge University Press.

Riger, S. (1992). Epistomological debates, feminist voices: Science, social values, and the study of women. *American Psychologist, 47,* (6), 730–740.

Sarbin, T. R. (1986). Narrative as a root metaphor for psychology. In T. R. Sarbin (Ed.), *Narrative psychology.* New York: Praeger.

Shotter, J. (1992). 'Getting in touch': The meta-methodology of a postmodern science of modern life. In S. Kvale (Ed.), *Psychology and postmodernism*. Newbury Park, London, New Delhi: Sage Publications.

Todorov, T. (1990). *Genres in discourse*. New York: Cambridge University Press.

Wallace, D. B. (1989). Studying the individual: The case study method and other genres. In D. B. Wallace & H. E. Gruber, *Creative people at work*. New York: Oxford University Press.

WRITING ETHNOGRAPHY
Feminist Critical Practice

Carol B. Stack

MY FIRST anthropological study began in the early 1960s when I chronicled the northbound movement of African Americans from rural Mississippi, Arkansas, and Louisiana to Chicago—research that eventually led to the writing of *All Our Kin*.[1] Twenty years later, and back in the South, I watched daily the return of first-, second-, and third-generation urban dwellers following their own paths to rural southeastern homeplaces from midwestern and East Coast cities. I am currently completing a book about this dramatic return movement, *Call to Home: African Americans Reclaim the Rural South*.[2] Using both memories and field notes for studies done nearly twenty years apart, I try in this paper to reconstruct the nature of my own comfort and conflict as an ethnographer in these two studies. In the context of the politics and scholarship of the times, I explore the nuances of doing and writing ethnography as a white working-class woman. I do this by reconstructing two ethnographic projects, one from the 1960s and the second from the 1980s, from the perspective of the present and looking backward. Dramatizing both writer and subject in the historical context, I attempt to engage in writing culture as feminist critical practice.

The political energy of the 1960s was churning in "The Flats" (the fictive name of the African-American community that is the site of *All Our Kin*) as well as in nearby neighborhoods and communities. "Black Power" leadership ignited relationships across community boundaries and new alliances emerged out of coalition politics. I was invited to participate in meetings with a group of welfare mothers from "The Flats" who had begun a welfare rights organization. Those of us who were community workers and political activists believed that everything was in flux, and anticipated that traditional boundaries could be transformed. Those were the times of Martin Luther King, John Kennedy, civil rights, Black Power, welfare rights, and Vietnam. Personal and political experimentation crisscrossed race, gender, and class divisions. Working within and through a divisive generation gap (especially in white communities), young people under thirty believed that anything was possible. We allowed ourselves to take risks, especially around political action. We were inspired as political activism crossed race/class lines. And we perceived the possibility of social change as a collaboration among people who understood basic social truths about equity and human dignity. This undergirded our belief that acting on such truths would set us free; we produced moral imperatives for our times.

In 1968 I was twenty-eight, a white, working-class, politically active, single mother with a young son who was with me 'round the clock' in "The Flats." The following thoughts are a fragmented compendium of my experiences as a young anthropologist in the field. Looking back at my field notes and interviews, and reflecting on the lessons I learned, especially from my closest ally in the community, Ruby Banks, is a complex task in light of present-day challenges to ethnography. Ruby, who was also a single parent and the oldest daughter in a large extended family network, took on the challenge, and some of the fun, of teaching me to act appropriately as a woman, as a mother, and as a friend in "The Flats." In the manner that friends become "kin" if they seriously take on kin responsibilities, Ruby and her kinfolk included me as a part of their family. This, of course, did not happen immediately, but developed slowly as we came to depend upon one another to carry out the work of kinship, including the assumption of mutual responsibility for one another's children and other children in the kin group. This is more consequential than might be obvious, since many parents in "The Flats" were appalled at the widespread practice in mainstream culture of allowing strangers to "baby sit". Their critique also included a distrust of public and private day care centers run by outsiders. Ruby even carried notions of our "kinship" beyond "The Flats." For example, when she was sick in the hospital she claimed I was her "sister" so the nurses would let me visit. Despite looks of disbelief from nurses and other hospital staff who looked at me and saw a white woman, Ruby's sense of what constituted kin-like exchanges among friends rendered her claim to the hospital bureaucrats honest from her culturally constructed conception of fictive kinship. In the process, I learned to stretch my previously acquired notions of the boundaries of kinship.

Ruby attempted to teach me how to manage my life as a single woman in "The Flats." She warned me not to be alone with a man in the community. Included in her very careful instructions to me about interviewing men, was her certainty that if I let myself into an uncomfortable situation with a man and said "no," that I would be considered racist. Given my graduate training that included serious advice against developing sexual liaisons in the field (and startling examples of women anthropologists who had been murdered in the field for doing so), my emerging sense of feminist politics in 1968, my strong desire to maintain my primary relationships with women in "The Flats," and my goal of managing a research involvement that was not magnified by sexual/racial politics, I wholeheartedly agreed with Ruby's advice.

Despite an array of instructions on how to act appropriately in the community (which I often thought I would never grasp), and subtle tests of my knowledge and loyalty, there were long periods during my stay in the community when I was allowed to "forget" that I was white. In all seriousness, forgetting may have been a reflection of my own internal sense of comfort that developed over time. Ironically, I felt this transition about midway into the study, when people in the community began calling me "white Caroline." They did this in part so I wouldn't be confused with Ruby's niece, whom they began to call "black Caroline." My new nickname offered a wry twist on my identity: my "naming" was both a sign of acceptance and an unfeigned marker. People teased and commended me for acting right, observing that I must forget my own whiteness myself from time to time. But my lapses were quickly roused when I heard my nickname, which was used more in public than in the privacy of family life. My presence was public; my presence was named. I was "white Caroline."

As I look back there is no doubt that the meaning of my life was tied up with being in "The Flats." Within a small group of associates we created a situation of trust—a safety zone in which we pushed boundaries and experimented, nourishing one another's curiosities, not just the anthropologists'. From time to time a group of us would venture outside "The Flats" into the nearby white hangouts where people in "The Flats" felt they would not be safe without me. For example, we went to a couple of country and western bars a few miles from "The Flats." These adventures and inventions, however, were mere tokens compared to the world Ruby and her close friends opened up to me.

From Ruby and countless other single parents in "The Flats," I learned how rights and responsibilities for children were distributed within and across

119

STACK

kin groups. Their lives as single parents were far less isolated from kin and informal supports than the few white single parents I knew before I began my research in the late 1960s. During that time period I found myself alone as a single parent in the middle-class world of academics. During my stay in "The Flats," I was learning what I later came to realize were feminist strategies for surviving as a single parent within networks of friends and extended kin. My young child was with me, and we took turns with the children. I learned about child-keeping by practicing, which, of course, was a blessing to a single parent in the field. Over many months I learned women's strategies for negotiating kin, single motherhood, men, and the welfare system.

Near the completion of my fieldwork I reread *Tally's Corner,*[3] written by Elliot Liebow in 1967. Although I had read it earlier, I was startled by the fact that this now classic ethnography was almost entirely about individual men—men at the donut shop, on the corner, on the streets. In my own work I learned about women's connections to one another and their social/familial networks and through their eyes, about their connections to men. I asked different questions than Liebow and became fascinated with the role of women's networks in family survival. Liebow left unexamined where the women, children, and grandparents were. Where were the fathers, aunts, uncles, and cousins? I knew, and I wanted to write about the strength and resilience of women's ways of keeping families together.

When I stepped out of the field to write *All Our Kin*, in Langston Hughes' words in his short story, "Home," my "skin burned, I felt my color." I confronted my whiteness more utterly as a writer than as a researcher. I felt very alone and color-conscious as I began writing. I also felt, what looking back I might call a "white women's burden." Inside "The Flats," folks devised ways to blunt yet clarify color differences in our everyday experiences. When I began writing the ethnography I became color/politically conscious. I felt a strong sense of social responsibility to those I had studied, and I held a conviction that I could get the story right. I tried out every word I wrote on people I knew in "The Flats." I listened to their responses, argued, and tried again. I wanted the story to ring true to their experiences. When I finally wrote the book, I wrote in deep seriousness on the very first page of the introduction:

> This introduction anticipates curiosity about how a young white woman could . . . conduct a study of black family life, and provides a basis for evaluating the reliability and quality of the data obtained.[4]

This sample (and the tenor of the Introduction to *All Our Kin*) mirrors the rationalist assumptions of the times, implying a method for evaluating the reliability of the qualitative methods and the data presented in the book. The feminist critique of fieldwork and the writing of ethnography in the 1990s is far less sanguine with respect to what constitutes "good social science." The

120

STACK

flat accent on reliability and objectivity of data has been transformed through the filter of critical and feminist theory. Moreover, we are unconvinced that any attempt at clarifying our positionality does more than situate the perspective from which we believe we are "writing culture." The goal is to explore and experiment—to learn and write as much about our own understanding of how we locate our voice in our writing as possible. We acknowledge that how we position ourselves in our research and writing must be finely tuned with respect to the times, the region, the setting, and race/gender politics of the historical moment. From the vantage point of radical post-modern discourses "writing ethnography" is still on hold.[5] With a sharp turn toward the fragmentation of voices and stories, the process of writing ethnography has turned inward toward subjectivity. We could argue that ethnography itself has been taken as illusion, the fiction of the writer herself. Indeed, the more extravagant post-modern theorists undertake a pulverization of the modern subject itself.

The 1980s were fragmented by a backlash against the legacy of legal and moral commitments that stirred the 1960s and 1970s. Some of the legal and institutional mandates that took root have already been uprooted. Dialectic within and across political agendas had dominated an epoch of contradictions. We have witnessed a fragile and ephemeral attempt at the institutionalization of liberation values (affirmative action, for example), alongside the emergence of a "new right" morality. Nowhere in the country was this power struggle between, for example, forces such as Jesse Jackson and The New Right, fundamentalism and feminism, more graphic than in the South—or "New South."

What emerged in the 1980s was a "politics of rebuttal": new racisms and ethnic antagonisms co-existing with dramatic shifts in power, both individual and global, and connecting the two. Individuals and political groups fashioned new identities, new roles, and identities. Pro-choice new right feminists emerged, for example. Traditional coalitions were revisioned, and sometimes betrayed.

American dreams—downward mobility, joblessness, estranged Vietnam veterans, homelessness, loss of hope, new racisms, distrust, and a fear of new ideas—produced new sets of contradictions. These challenges took place in the context of deindustrialization in the North and South. At the same time institutions were hammering out some progressive agendas that were indeed legacies of the 1960s and 1970s. Nostalgia for the past was exposed by disillusioned youth dressing in 1960s garb, and population movements emerged among adults. For example, the "small town boom" of middle-aged migrants reinforced a longing for communities of memory.

In the 1980s I was a nearly middle-age professor, and my son was finishing high school. I was involved in ethnographic fieldwork among African Americans once again. This time I was studying people who were returning to rur-

STACK

al southern homeplace communities. My research site had moved from the Deep South migration of African-Americans to midwestern cities, to the return migration of people moving from the Northeast to the Southeast.

More often than not, my 80-year-old mother rather than my teenage son accompanied me as I probed the meaning of home to those returning to the rigid race/caste system of the rural South. We learned how effective women community workers were in achieving their dreams to improve the lot of rural women. They succeeded in creating day care for working women, bringing Title XX funds to rural communities, and creating coalitions across counties working toward rural economic development. In part because my mother was alone, and because she was genuinely welcomed by families in these rural communities, she often joined me in my study of families returning South. Together we also observed divisions between returnees and the oldtimers and their struggle over an appropriate political pace and plan for social change. We observed together how identity politics shaped tensions between generations. But even more unmistakable on the political horizon were differences across gender lines.

Call to Home focuses on the return South of African-American women and men bringing home "urban" knowledge, and on identity politics—how gender and ideology shape the commitments and political actions of women and men who return to rural southern homeplaces. The book is about the collision between the multiple notions and aspirations people bring home and the tight rope they walk in constructing workable identities in the South. Those who have returned have become artful in assuming personal and political identities appropriate to the situation at hand. I learned that on one level it was important for those who returned to be accepted back into the community as "homegirls" or "homeboys." However, many of the people who returned carry with them a political mission. They want to transform their homeplaces, and no matter how hard they try to be accepted within their communities, their more aggressive approach to social change labels them as "outsiders." In church, at local political meetings, or in the creation of coalitions across race lines, people enact multiple roles assuming the posture of "homegirl," "outsider," or "New Yorker" when appropriate. They also pay their respects to the rural elderly, and wrangle with differing identities depending on the situation, the moment, the nature of the coalition, the day, the audience, and their mood. Women and men talked about belonging and identity, about being and origins, about home, about place, about homeplace, and about locating their place and my place in the research setting.

Most of the people returning were in their forties, near my own age at that time, joining their grandparents and school-age children who had moved back home ahead of them. The parents of these return migrants were planning to return when they reached age sixty-five or had put in the necessary years working in the North so that they could bring retirement benefits home.

STACK

Recollecting my sensibilities from my fieldwork in the 1980s, I relive, as I now write, the complicated and painful deliberations of people attempting to explain how they negotiated their identities—who they were, and who they came to be back home. After three years of intense political work attempting to bring day care to eight rural counties in the Carolinas, one politically active young grandmother, Doris Moody, talked to me about how she labored to negotiate her place back home. "We belong and we don't," she told me. I learned how Doris tempered her political stance to meet the political situation. She was careful to avoid moving too fast, acting the part of "homegirl" when necessary. But she also shared her anxiety that if she and others accommodated to tradition too often they would give in sooner or later to the ways things had always been done.

In informal settings, in homes, and as we traveled long distances across rural counties to meetings and workshops, I listened and participated in discussions about rural day care, public funds, political elections, the Farmer's Home Administration, school systems, and farm loss. In contrast to my research in "The Flats," where I was intimately drawn into women's kin networks, I felt more like a colleague or long-term visitor than an adopted family member. The formalities and civility of southern tradition created a place, but not a "fictive" home for me. On the other hand, I was deeply connected to women-centered political organizations in rural counties attempting to write a feminist agenda around the needs of rural women. In contrast to the male-dominated black nationalist politics of the 1960s the leadership and organizing efforts of women was critical in these rural southern communities.

123

The women and men who returned home cross-cut many walks of life and economic circumstances. Some were college-educated, experienced professionals, others had acquired organizing skills and knowledge of public sector programs and funding. Yet others returned disheartened, houseless in the North, if not homeless. People often said that they returned changed—a different person from the person who left the South. Likewise my status and sensibilities had changed from my early research in "The Flats." Between 1975 and 1987 I was professor at Duke University, a director of a family policy center, and actively engaged in advocating reforms in state policy regarding families and children. I was nearly middle-aged and moderately middle-class. My son was in high school, my father had passed away, and my mother was elderly. Fortuitously, I returned to the field with a change in status somewhat similar to middle-class people who returned South. I was close to their age, and at the same life stage. As an outsider, I too was suspect, observed, and subject to unwritten rules, prescriptions, and restrictions.

In contrast to my fieldwork in the 1960s, this time I felt my color. The "insiders/outsiders" who returned were themselves working out their own places in rural home communities. I, too, was negotiating a space and became increasingly absorbed in how my own history affects the way I do ethnography. I was displaced far from home. How could I locate myself in the space/geography, and what would people ask of me? Had I experienced anything similar to their managing lives as both outsider and insider? My memories brought to mind my experience as the only working-class Jewish person in the community in which I grew up, and in all of the schools I attended from kindergarten through high school.

Sometimes working with women's political networks organizing around the needs of rural women, I was associated with the few white radicals who had moved into these rural communities in the 1970s and managed to maintain a power base as leaders in these alternative organizations. However, because people perceived that I was not seeking a power base, I was invited to meetings near the hub of coalition building and decision making. But this led to a difficult research delemma. Often I was pulled by contending factions who wanted me to understand/take their side in difficult, ongoing debates. My best teachers in negotiating this tension were women community workers who skillfully moved back and forth between offense and conciliation.

The battle ground over the construction of homeplace "identities" was located not only with respect to the white community, but all too painful, among and across generations of African Amercans in rural homeplaces as well. Among the many examples from my fieldwork, the following event illustrates multiple oscillations in the management of identities among politically active women within the course of a single evening.

Elders in these rural communities are treated with respect. A banquet arranged by local community organizers in honor of Miss Hammer, an elderly community leader, was held at a local hotel on a summer evening when my mother was visiting me in the field. At this event the tension between deference and respect for elders, some of whom risked their lives in early civil rights protests, and the politics of new leaders was brought into tension. The new leadership refused to perpetuate traditional brokerage systems between the local white and black power structures. They brought professionalized approaches and accountability to the management of local political organizations. They refused to immortalize the cachet of white pacemakers, those outsiders who retained power within local communities as organizers/leaders long after the civil rights movement.

At the banquet that evening, there was also a movement within the sponsoring organization to oust Mr. Jones, the remaining white "chair" of the organization. Mr. Jones was a long-term political associate of Miss Hammer's. They had started civil rights groups together. Although most of the anguish and debate took place in tense gatherings behind closed doors and in hotel rooms, the lines of argument and political coalitions divided across generations, and between newcomers and old-timers. My mother and I, guests of newcomers who initiated the debate, witnessed hurt feelings and deep emotions flowing over new leadership in the local organization.

STACK

Following the banquet my mother and Miss Hammer, age-mates and old acquaintances by that stage of my fieldwork (and the two oldest people present at the event), sat together to talk. People gathered around their memories. Everyone talked until all the dishes and favors and flowers were gone. My mother and Miss Hammer talked until the banquet room was turned into an empty hall with the exception of the chairs gathered around them in a circle. The many voices of resistance heard that evening in private spaces merged, for the moment into respectful "homegirl" voices in Miss Hammer's presence No final resolution that evening. A respect for the elderly.

Willingness to engage in discussion with an anthropologist is an indication of fortitude as well as state of mind. Dolores Dodson, for example, checked me out ahead of time. She learned from a friend that I had written a book and borrowed a tattered copy, which she read before agreeing to meet me. Late one afternoon I mastered her hand-drawn map, which I followed past several farms and two churches down endless dirt roads that led to her house. By the time I arrived, she had developed a critique of my work. We spent a couple of days comparing her experiences as a New Jersey social worker with my description of urban black families in midwestern cities. Amenable to building our relationship, Dolores was clear that she had something to teach me. One afternoon our conversation blossomed into a lively, overcroweded group discussion as friends and neighbors dropped in to visit. With everyone giving me personal notions of how I should go about this study, Dolores, lending support to my project, professed. "You see here a white woman capable of learning."

125

During our conversation she gave the go ahead to the women in the room, telling them about my current study and suggesting that they give me their notions of how I should go about it. Lending support to my project, my sponsor confessed to others that "It would be best, for the time being, if the white community was not aware of Carol's presence." In contrast to my experiences in "The Flats," Dolores and her neighbors asked me early on to be inconspicuous. The politics of race and power informed Dolores' belief that local whites viewed white outsiders who entered the black community as organizers stirring up trouble. However, these same women engaged the public sector at all levels—local, regional, and state—in their efforts to bring public funds to rural day care. As they got to know me they invited me to accompany them to public meetings and dropped their early misgivings about whether my presence could be known to the local white community.

A couple of months after I had arrived in New Jericho, one of the local communities in my study, Howard, a county attorney, arranged to meet with me over dinner for our second conversation. I waited until the last person left his office on Main Street. After a moment's pause he made clear that there was no public place where a white woman and a black man could eat together. "The word," he said, "would be all over town." It could destroy his reputa-

STACK

tion and his law practice. Hesitating, he suggested a take-out meal, which he volunteered to get, and sputtered softly, then out loud, that we weren't in New York City. "Can't even have a business meal together here." Home and the disposition of what constitutes "public spaces" deeply affected my research relationships with men in this study. In "The Flats" I was public, and could be seen in public with men (but not in private). In these rural southern townships in the 1980s, long after local whites were aware of my presence, men could/would not be in the public spaces of whites with me. My conversations with men, for the most part, took place in the privacy of homes sequestered several miles away from the town squares.

Doing fieldwork in the 1980s there was rarely a moment when the delicate balance of identity politics loosened its hold. However, when I returned to my post at the university and slowly began the process of writing ethnography, it was the height of the post-modern moment. For all theoretical purposes I suddenly felt ironically freed of my whiteness. I was subject as well as author, and as such won license to write about my own subjective, authentic experience. I could/should/would write a fragmented story of return migration in multiple voices, and reflect on the meaning of home through my own eyes. Mine was another voice. As a writer I could pay close attention to difference, ambiguity, shifting voices and roles. I too was seeing and being observed. Writing ethnography in these new times, I could shed the singularity of truth and improvise among shifting voices. I did this for a year or two while writing a draft of the book on return migration.

126

Reflecting back to the late 1960s and early 1970s, my sense of social responsibility as an ethnographer was enveloped in a search for truth. A discourse of moralism and power linked in part to the civil rights movement, to feminism, and to the anti-Vietnam movement, informed a generation of activist anthropologists. As feminists we made claims and created alliances as our sisters' keeper. We created a discourse that focused on the unity of women's lives; this unity became a struggle for agency that whitewashed women's lives. Given my own background growing up in a working-class family that struggled against poverty, I was personally alienated by race/class blinders in feminist theory and politics. However, interspersed among these prejudices, there were efforts among coalitions of women to counteract race/class bias in both theory and social policy. For example, working together with the local Welfare Rights Organization in "The Flats," we produced testimony against child support legislation (IV-D) that pitted low-income welfare mothers against divorced lower- and middle-income mothers. The National Organization of Women, on the other hand, testified in favor of this bill, ignoring the best interests of very poor women. My political commitments have been toward the construction of feminist research and policy agendas that take sensously relationships of race, class, and gender.

STACK

Agendas that tie research to social change can be at odds with current post-modern trends in the academy. In the latter part of the 1980s, the way was paved for ethnographers to go full circle, to shed ourselves of many notions, in particular, that we could tell another's truth. Gender itself became problematized, identities multiplied, class and race became complicated and fluid constructions. We were engaged in a discourse of relativism and inter-subjectivities in which we tried to deconstruct our own experiences and locate ourselves in our tale. In good spirit we tangled with multiple voices, and disentangled our own.

Critical theory and radical post-modern discourse have transformed ethnographic writing. Those of us still writing feminist ethnography face several dilemmas whose reconciliation is beyond the scope of this paper. We are still in dialogue over the departure from grand theory, the crisis of legitimation, claims of representation, and the predicament of voice and story for the writing of ethnography.

Whereas I was very careful to avoid claims that "The Flats" represented African-American culture in *All Our Kin*, I reluctantly look back on the functionalist mosaic of that early writing. I had been trained early on as an anthropologist to weave a coherent story, one in which the parts fit together and buttress the whole. I searched through my field notes for stories that fit together, to explain rights and responsibilities with respect to children. In those days, I am aware now, I paid less attention to the tensions and contradictions in people's experiences, and looked less for the disjunctures and contradictions in the stories. I painstakingly transcribed and presented their narratives word for word in a search for accuracy, with little puzzlement over the discontinuities or over the construction of the narrative itself.[6]

127

Critical theory and what we might call the humanity of understanding have taken us down a fascinating and important path away from a home-base, and we will never return. As anthropologists we are inside and outside the text, writing it and reading it, questioning its very construction, and searching for discontinuities and ambiguities with the narratives and the larger cultural texts. But in the end it is the ethnographer who lays her fingers on the keyboard to play the final note on the chorus of voices. Purged of an awesome and impossible claim that I write the "subject's" truth, I still believe it possible that the ethnographies I write reflect a progressive and feminist social agenda. As feminist ethnographers we take on a knotty paradox of social responsibility: we are accountable for the consequences of our writing, fully cognizant that the story we construct is our own.

STACK

NOTES

I am deeply grateful to the Editorial Board of Frontiers and to the critical stance of the reviewers for their suggested revisions for this article. I especially wish to thank

Louise Lamphere once again for her wisdom and tenacity. I also received intellectual support and helpful criticism from Jean Lave, Allison Wiley, Carol Smith, Nancy Scheper Hughes, Ann Ferguson, Amy Scharf, and Carol Chetkovich.

1. Carol B. Stack, *All Our Kin: Strategies for Survival in a Black Community* (New York: Harper and Row, 1972). "The Kindred of Viola Jackson" describes the migration north of 98 relatives moving from the rural South to midwestern cities.

2. Carol B. Stack, *Call to Home: African Americans Reclaim the Rural South* (New York: Basic Books, 1996).

3. Elliot Liebow, *Tally's Corner* (Boston: Little, Brown, 1967).

4. *All Our Kin*, xv.

5. For an important discussion of the construction of narrative, see Edward Bruner, "Ethnography as Narrative," in *The Anthropology of Experience*, ed. V. Turner and E. Bruner (Urbana, Ill.: University of Illinois Press, 1986) 145–150.

6. Gillis Deleuze and Felix Guattari, *Anti-Oedipus* (Minneapolis: University of Minnesota Press, 1983), and *A Thousand Plateaus* (Minneapolis: University of Minnesota Press, 1987).

STACK

DIALOGUE WITH GUATEMALAN INDIAN WOMEN
Critical Perspectives on Constructing Collaborative Research

M. Brinton Lykes

BETWEEN 1979 and 1983 50,000 to 100,000 Guatemalans were killed, thousands more were disappeared, over 400 rural villages were destroyed and between 100,000 and 200,000 Guatemalan children were orphaned [1, 2]. Although I have seen these figures many times since 1983 and listened to or read many personal testimonies of survivors of the military's violent counterinsurgency program in January of 1983 I knew very little either about the Guatemalan people's most recent struggle to redress gross economic, political and cultural repression or of the military's strategies for combatting their resistance. At the time I was completing the data collection stage of a study of

*The study reported in this paper was partially funded by grants from a Rhode Island College Faculty Scholars Award and from the Rhode Island College Research Fund. I would also like to thank members of my Feminist Methodology Research Group, Abigail J. Stewart and G. Ramsay Liem for their continuing support of this work. Finally, I would like to thank G. Ramsay Liem, Abigail J. Stewart and Rhode Unger for their comments on earlier drafts of this work.

alternative conceptualizations of the self [3, 4]. I was interviewing women in the United States who had been working in community- or work-based projects for social change in an effort to better understand the ways in which their notions of themselves as women were related to these activities. I was also working with a number of community-based women's projects for social change, and in the Latin American solidarity network. Through this work I traveled to Central America where I met several Guatemalans who spoke of their experiences, the need to flee their country, and their desire to develop stronger solidarity ties with women in the United States. At their initiative I agreed to join two friends to work on developing a national U.S. tour through which Guatemalan women could share their stories with mainstream women's groups. We networked with groups already working in the U.S. and designed a tour to both educate a new sector of the U.S. public about the situation of women and children in Guatemala and to raise funds to support refugees in Guatemala and in Mexico. Although my involvement in planning this tour grew out of political work in the feminist and Latin American struggles, because of my training and research interests I was also eager to learn more about how the Guatemalan women who came to the United States understood their experiences, about how they thought about and talked about their struggles and about how they understood themselves as Indian women. I was able initially to explore this last concern in a conversation with Juanita, one of the women on the tour.

130

INITIAL CONVERSATIONS: DECIDING TO COLLABORATE ON A RESEARCH PROJECT

In discussing her first experiences in the United States Juanita expressed concern over the orientation program that we had organized, and more particularly, over the response of one of the resource people we had invited to give her feedback on a "trial run" of her presentation. Upon completing her story Juanita was told by one of the listeners that it had been very moving but that it would not do for a U.S. audience because it was not clearly her "own" story. The critic suggested that Juanita's presentation had been a story of a family, of a community, not of an individual, and that in order to reach U.S. audiences Juanita had to be more personal, to describe her individual reality and how the events she recounted had affected her personally. Juanita told me how surprised and confused she had been by these comments, how she had been unsuccessful in her efforts to convince her critic that she had told her story, and that she remained confused about what women in the United States meant by telling one's story. For her, her story and the story of her people were synonymous (personal communication, 1983).

I returned frequently to this conversation and to my own growing concern about how the descriptions I was documenting in conversations with women in the United States might converge with or be distinguished from the reflec-

tions of women in or from a less individualistic, more comrnunity-based, society. Some of the Guatemalan Indian women with whom I had begun to
work, and others whose stories I was reading in testimonies, came from rural
communities steeped in rich traditions and ritual practices that affirmed community life but, simultaneously, rigid, yet complementary, gender roles that
maintained women's place within the home and community [5]. In addition,
these women had actively engaged in community-based projects to improve
their own and others' lives. From this perspective they shared certain experiences with the women I had been interviewing. Yet the social, political, economic and cultural contexts for this work differed dramatically. I was increasingly interested in how these women understood themselves as Indian
women as they were forced to journey from the Guatemalan Highlands to
life in exile in Mexico or the United States. I was also challenged to respond
to that "reality," to the violent repression that had necessitated their flight, that
was requiring new struggles of them as exiles.

BACKGROUND ON THE SITUATION IN GUATEMALA

Before the project could move forward I felt I needed to know more about
the history of the Guatemalan people with whom I had begun to work. I
read about the beauty and natural wealth of the country and about the ancient Mayan civilization [6]. This story describes four and a half centuries of
oppression and exploitation, from the destruction of life and community at
the time of the Conquest through the violent repression of the recent counterinsurgency. Yet this story is also one of continual resistance. Evidence of
major recent resistance efforts involving Indians and Ladinos include the development of a variety of organizations (e.g., unions, cooperatives, community development projects, student associations, Christian base communities and
guerrilla organizations). Most of these developed during the past twenty-five
years as part of an overall effort to break the minority's hold on power, particularly the ownership of over 80 percent of the land by less than 4 percent of
the farmers. These efforts are grounded in a struggle to establish a new power
base rooted in the economic, political, social and cultural concerns of the majority of the population.

131

LYKES

This most recent phase of the struggle for self-determination was met by
violent military action (especially between 1979 and 1983), action within the
context of a counterinsurgency strategy that led to the deaths of over 50,000
Guatemalans [1]. The worst of the systematic and brutal attacks against the
Guatemalan people were felt by the Indians of the Guatemalan Highlands
where over 400 rural villages have been destroyed [2]. Approximately one
million people are internal refugees within their country; another 150,000
have sought refuge in Mexico and between 100,000 and 200,000
Guatemalan children have been orphaned [1, 2, 7]. The extermination of entire villages and the massacre of children and the elderly suggest strongly that

the military project was intended not only to control revolutionary activity but to strike at and weaken or destroy key elements in Indian life, elements that give culture its coherence, elements that act as axes of community life and identity [8].

CONTINUING THE CONVERSATION

This violence, brutality and destruction was inflicted on particular individuals, each with his or her story, each a part of a community of friends and family that mourn her or his death or disappearance, each loss a statement about the military's strategies for controlling the population. The worst of these violent abuses of human rights and the army's penetration of all levels of civilian life have been documented, for example, in testimony before the Permanent People's Tribunal [9] from January 27 through 31, 1983 and in numerous publications by Americas Watch and other human rights groups. I confronted these facts in the stories of the women who toured the United States and in the testimonies I was reading.

I was able to travel to Guatemala and Mexico several times in 1985 and 1986 and experienced more directly the beauty of the land, the richness of the Mayan traditions, and simultaneously, in stark contrast, the population's fear, and despite massive repression, continuing resistance to efforts to silence the majority of the people. I was disturbed to realize how little I had known about the situation here, and found myself confronting not only the Guatemalan reality surrounding me but also the reality of the United States, of my professional development, of my community and of my personal relations. I also confronted a wall of silence about Guatemala from the mainstream press to the solidarity movement. As I began to penetrate that silence, to listen to personal testimonies and read human rights reports, I returned repeatedly to Falla's description of the counterinsurgency as a "partial genocide" [8].

This silence, constructed within the country, but sustained by the international community is an element in the strategy of counterinsurgency. The violent death or disappearance of a loved one is rarely publically recorded. When stories do appear in newspapers or on television events are frequently mystified, with the violent murder of women and children described as successful efforts to stop terrorism or to quiet communists who are described as disrupting community life. I remembered stories of the silence surrounding the Holocaust and asked myself repeatedly when and where I would speak.

Conversations with friends and colleagues when I returned from travels to the region furthered the process of breaking the silence about what I had seen, heard, and read. I next began a series of educational presentations and fundraising efforts on behalf of Guatemalan refugees, engaging my teaching and fundraising skills in efforts to speak to wider audiences. Through this I was able to follow through on the work begun in our "Woman to Woman" tour. But that was not enough. These felt like extra-curricular activities and I wanted to engage my skills as a psychologist in contributing to efforts to break the public silence surrounding this genocide. I wanted to contribute more directly to a process whereby the meaning of the events of the late 1970s and early 1980s from the point of view of those who had suffered most could be further developed and articulated.

I shared my concerns and hopes with a friend in Mexico. Although we agreed that human rights groups were publicizing the testimonies of victims of torture and abuse we felt that the meaning of these experiences to those who had suffered them and their broader social and political context was of necessity less well developed in the human rights reports. Much less well known, for example, were the detailed stories of the women and men who actively particpated in struggles for change in their communities, who resisted military repression, who may not have been physically abused, but who were forced to flee their country during the early 1980s. A number of Guatemalans living in exile had shared with my friend their sense of the importance of recording these stories, both as a record for the communities in exile and for those who have remained inside the country or have chosen to return as they continue the process of rebuilding their resistance movements. Specifically, the Center for Guatemala Studies, an interdisciplinary research center in Mexico City with whom my friend was affiliated, was interested in collecting the stories of Indian leaders and making these available to the communities in exile as resources in educational and community training programs. In addition to documenting earlier work in Guatemala they hoped to develop a record of the continuing work among Indian communities living in exile.

As we spoke my friend and I found that we also shared an interest in better understanding the conditions under which people come to understand themselves as actors contructing their future, as active participants in the social and political development of their people. We agreed that a project that documented the processes by which women, beginning with their immediate concerns, develop a political consciousness that is accompanied by action and gives social meaning to their activity, would contribute both to a better understanding of Guatemalan women's resistance efforts and, more generally, to our knowledge about the development of political self consciousness among women. The project was conceived thus as a concrete resource for existing Guatemalan communities, as a vehicle for exploring a more theoretical problem of interest to self theorists and to psychologists more generally, and as making a contribution to the collective task of breaking the silence surrounding Guatemala's recent history. We sought to document through oral history interviews some of the processes by which some representatives of the Guatemalan refugee communities in Mexico understand themselves and how their sense of who they are as Guatemalan Indian women is sustained and transformed in the experiences of being in exile.

133

LYKES

In this chapter I describe aspects of the ongoing collaboration between North American women and Guatemalan Indian women from my perspective as one of the North American women participants. What follows is a description and analysis of how the research itself developed. It includes a discussion of how we resolved some of the methodological challenges we confronted and provides a base from which to reflect on some of the ways we as women from different economic, cultural and racial groups are working together and independently to find our individual and collective voices to break the silence surrounding Guatemalan women's experiences, and thereby to contribute to an ongoing process of naming the meaning of these events.

DEVELOPING THE RESEARCH PROJECT

Although my colleague and I had identified several research questions and agreed that we would collaborate we did not have a strategy for proceeding. Our challenge as North American researchers was to clarify a strategy for addressing our interests in 1) theory-building about women's development of political self-consciousness and self-understanding; 2) speaking out about the realities of life for Indians in Guatemala and contributing to or supporting the Guatemalan struggle; and 3) documenting Guatemalan exiles' experiences for the Center's educational programming.

Research strategies I had learned in methods courses or through previous work fell far short of this challenge. My understanding of our field had been shaped in part by my resonance to McGuire's [10], Gergen's [11, 12] and Sampson's [13] criticisms of the experimentalist's claims to "objectivity" or scientific distance and this analysis was, broadly speaking, reflected in my earlier work. Yet despite general agreement among social psychologists that the "crisis literature" and its critical discussion of experimental social psychology (of its ahistoricity [14, 15] , its failure to take seriously the social context in which activity is embedded in describing social behavior [16-18] and its narrow data base [18]) had accurately captured the limitations of research in the field, mainstream journals continued to be dominated by studies using these methods [19]. The field's incorporation of this self-critical posture has not changed significantly its practice (see [20] for a similar argument concerning feminist criticisms). Although ideologically convinced that these critics were correct, it was the concrete problems I confronted in undertaking research with Guatemalan women that enabled me to depart more significantly from the quantitative methods of my training towards a more qualitative participatory model of research that would enable me both to better address the questions I was asking and to engage in research that is consistent with my social goals and commitments [19, 20-22].

Oral history interviews were selected as the appropriate method for this study because they are both sensitive to the single individual's experiences, enabling us to look at a woman's understanding of herself and her elaboration of the social meaning of her life, and to the Guatemalan community's long tradition of oral communication. Further, these stories are a rich record of the lives of a select number of Guatemalan women and can be examined not only for what is said but for how it is said [23, 24]. In addition, recording multiple stories facilitates better understanding of how individuals have responded to their experiences and enables the reconstruction of the collective experiences of a people as a basis for understanding what binds them together and creates an effective community. Finally, the open-ended interview that encourages the participant to tell her own story is sensitive to the developing collaborative relationship between ourselves and the participants, one that would both reflect and foster trust and sharing and complement our ongoing work and personal ties to Guatemalan Indian communities in Mexico.

Informed by a number of diverse strategies for developing our oral history method of collaborative research (see e.g., Langness and Frank's work on life stories [25], Frisch's historical approach [26] and Bertaux's [27] or Reinharz's [28] sociological perspectives) we began the more formal research project. Despite important theoretical differences in these distinctly disciplinary approaches to oral history (a discussion of which is beyond the scope of my chapter), we found that there were certain strategic issues that all researchers confront in collecting data that importantly shaped our work and provide an important lens through which to analyze and evaluate multicultural collaborative research. The remainder of this chapter will briefly discuss two of these issues, the identification of participants and the selection of a method, and discuss in some detail our process of "obtaining" informed consent. All three of these issues deal in some way with the question of control over the research process. Our experience suggests that assumptions of researcher control and participant powerlessness are implicit in these methods and that they contribute to and are shaped by the competing interests of researcher and participant that are part of and are played out in the research process.

WHO WOULD WE TALK WITH

The voices of this project are those of two North American women and a number of Guatemalan Indian women. Together the North American "researchers" have had ongoing involvement in and engagement with Guatemalans in the United States, Mexico and Guatemala for over ten years. The identification of Guatemalans who might have been interested in collaborating in this project was possible because of this previous work. This previous contact was particularly important given the political and social reality in Guatemala and the caution Guatemalans must exercise in speaking to anyone about their experiences. The need for such caution was expressed repeatedly by the women with whom we spoke. One woman turned off the tape recorder when she spoke of her husband's current work, fearing that he was such a well known leader that no precautions we would take could guarantee his anonymity. Because we were trusted friends we were allowed to record past activities. But the political realities for Guatemalans in exile and the public nature of our work are such that current activities were not recorded. These political realities framed and set limits on our collaboration as it developed.

"Subject selection" involved a process of articulating our interests to a number of different groups of Guatemalan women and continuing dialogue with those individuals or groups who expressed interest in the work and wanted to know more. The initial selection of which groups we would contact was shaped by our ongoing work with Guatemalans, the social, political and geographic realities within their communities, and a desire to focus the current study on the experiences of Quiché Indian women from the Guatemalan Highlands. This latter priority developed due to the particular impact that the violence of recent years has had on this group, the initial interest of a number of Quiché Indian women in the project and our knowledge that Guatemalan life differs significantly from group to group (e.g., there are 23 different linguistic groups, [5]) and from region to region. If our interviews were to give us a sense of the experiences of anyone beyond the individual woman with whom we spoke we felt that we needed to begin with women from only one of the twenty-three groups in one of the regions.

The decisions about which particular women would be interviewed emerged out of continuing conversations among ourselves as researchers, our contact people (who work with or are members of the communities described above) and individual women in these communities. Participation in the project reflects therefore both an individual's decision to tell her story and a decision about how her participation contributes to and is shaped by her own and her community's current experiences. Hence, although the decisions were made by individual researchers and participants, they also quite clearly reflect the individual's and her community's and/or organization's interests. Despite the fact that this research would be impossible without considerable overlap in interests among researchers and participants there are clear differences and potential, if not actual, competing interests among all participants.

For example, one group of women we approached expressed initial interest in the project and two members agreed to be interviewed. Serious health complications prevented both women from participating in their scheduled interviews. Although both interviews have been rescheduled subsequent conversations with others who work with this group suggest that the group's own more group-focused project (in contrast to our work of telling individual stories) may take precedence over participation in other activities, that is, for example, in our research. Although one could view both the initial reason for cancelling the appointments and the current hesitancy as individual excuses or changes in mind they are also reflective of broader group and community concerns. The health complications reflect symptoms that have developed in efforts to cope with the severe stressors of violence and exile and the lack of effective medical resources for the refugee community. The shift in focus towards putting more energy into their own group's project reflects, in part, an important tension between participating exclusively or primarily in activities with one's own organization and engaging with others in work that broadens the base of one's effort. It may also, in part, reflect renewed questions about our project, its goals, and its consequences for their work. Despite our contacts and ongoing work with Guatemalans we are outsiders and as such any collaboration must both bridge that difference and recognize the limits that it imposes.

Our response to the cancellation of these two interviews has been to reschedule conversations about the project before proceeding to conduct additional interviews. As a researcher this experience has been, on the one hand, frustrating and has "reduced my sample." As a collaborator, an activist, a seeker of knowledge and understanding of Guatemalan Indian women it has broadened my view of Indian women's experiences and provided an opportunity for elaborating and reflecting on my "agenda" in the project.

HOW WOULD WE PROCEED

Having identified some participants and agreed on an oral history method we needed to clarify the types of information we hoped to elicit, both in terms of developing an historical record and in terms of our more theoretical concerns. We developed a series of guiding questions that would provide a structure for our open-ended, in depth interviews and enable us to gather similar types of information from each participant. We conducted our first interview with these questions (see Appendix A). Not surprisingly, the interview strategy has been modified in collaboration with the Guatemalan participants to include a range of interactions and conversations that are broader in scope than the original questions.

Thus far, we have done intensive interviews with three Guatemalan Indian women and had lengthy conversations with several others. We have also spent a day with one of the women and her family and engaged in a focus group interview with four Guatemalan Indian women, including two who had been interviewed. All participants in the focus group had read the transcripts of the interview we had conducted, and together we discussed them. Whenever possible these conversations have been recorded. These different types of interactions have developed from the demands of the situation and from initiatives taken by some of the participants as they continue to identify ways in which this work intersects with and can be of service to their continuing activities. For example, the focus group interview was an opportunity to discuss divergent perspectives on the meaning of being an Indian woman and to reflect on some of the ways in which being in exile contributed to changing

LYKES

understandings of oneself. The views expressed in this discussion were later used as a basis from which to plan for conversations with other Indian women in an educational program women in the focus groups had designed to help other comañeras better understand their history and their current experiences.

As researchers our concern for the comparability of data from the different participants has dictated a continuing commitment to conduct an oral history interview with each of the "formal participants." However our additional conversations are key to the deepening of our understanding of Indian refugee women's reality and have made of this work a more truly collaborative project. The decision to incorporate multiple forms of interactions was a natural development of our process and has been one of the strengths of the method we are developing. Yet the amount of time I have been able to spend with these women (a total of five weeks in Mexico at two different time periods) has limited the number of interactions that we can have and suggests the role that material constraints (i.e., time) play in shaping research methods. The method described here derives from the different interests of the collaborators and our effort as researchers to develop a strategy that is responsive to these interests in the context of real material constraints of time and resources.

INFORMED CONSENT

Having seen the necessity for flexibility in the selection of participants and of a method, I was somewhat surprised by my own reaction to another convention of the research process that required similar flexibility, that is, the informed consent form. Before beginning this research I had carefully studied a number of informed consent forms from other oral history projects conducted in the United States. I had developed what I felt was a form that provided optimal protection of the identity of the participants and gave them a range of options concerning their continuing control over how the oral histories would be used. The Committee for the Protection of Human Subjects at my university provided useful comments and I felt satisfied with the final document. My sense was confirmed by a colleague with whom I shared my form who found it to be so thorough that she adopted it for her own field research and described it as an "empowering instrument." Nevertheless, in subsequent experience with the form I recognized assumptions that I had brought to the research project that belied my own articulated goals of collaboration.

Concretely, the form (see Appendix B) has been a major obstacle at the beginning of each interview. Intended to "protect the subjects of the research," the women with whom I spoke experienced it as a barrier or hurdle. My conversation with one of the women is illustrative. When I presented the form she suggested that she had already agreed to talk to me (otherwise she would not be there) and that by agreeing to tell her story she had indicated her consent. Her consent meant that whatever she would tell me was a part of our public record, to be used in support of the Guatemalan struggle as I understood that task. She found my choices concerning future use of the material as described on the form confusing and suggested that her signature was unnecessary, that we had already settled the question of the use of the material. When we had finally seemed to agree that she had *de facto* chosen Form A or unrestricted use and she checked this line she again refused to sign her name, indicating that she did not see why it was necessary.

My initial response to her hesitancy to sign was to interpret this as my failure to adequately communicate the purposes of the form or my faulty Spanish. I knew that the form *per se* was very much outside of her experiences and felt that I needed to "educate" her to its usefulness. I worried further that her reluctance to sign was an indication that she might have agreed to participate as a favor or without fully understanding the project and I became increasingly invested in trying to clarify the form and why it was an important document that protected her interests. The traditionally trained social psychologist in me reacted almost mechanically and upon reflection I realize that *I* was shifting the context of our relationship, one that had been collaboratively constructed to that point. My own somewhat automatic response as social scientist took on a life of its own and prevented me from responding to the experience itself.

By the third interview I began to discern that I was in fact misinterpreting the participants reality *and* our relationship. I had come to this project with a clear analysis of my power as Other, with my role as a university professor with a Ph.D. and as a white North American. Yet I was also a concerned researcher who was acutely aware of the ways in which researchers have taken advantage of subjects, misinterpreted their reality, and given them inadequate access to their own labor. I recognized the many ways in which the participant both makes her/himself vulnerable in sharing his/her story and has no real control over how the researcher reconstructs that story [29, 30]. I had therefore designed a form that I thought would address this imbalance of power, providing a base from which the participants could assert their agenda. I would, thereby, "empower" the participants.

My resocialization as a concerned researcher masked both my knowledge of the history of informed consent and its roots in the doctor-patient relationship and my knowledge base as an activist and political participant in the ongoing struggle of the Guatemalan people. On the one hand, I had failed to recognize that my form was constructed on the same foundation underlying all informed consent in social science research. The form both releases the sponsoring university or funding agency from any liability while enabling it to maintain a certain control over the researcher. Further, it gives control or license to the interviewer. As long as consent is given neither the sponsoring organization nor the researcher have responsibility for or to the participant.

LYKES

The former is not legally libel and the latter can now use the data in any way she or he, as scientist, determines. In sharp contrast to an ideology that recognizes the participant as subject with particular interests that I was communicating verbally and in our developing relationship, the form itself reflects an elaborate variation on more traditional documents. Although the elaboration places some limits on the license I as researcher can take with the participant's story, control remains in my hands. In addition, through introducing the form when I did I asserted my role as researcher, changing the terms of the previously established grounds for our interview. Reflecting on my experiences with the form revealed the complexity of both my role as researcher/activist and the constraints on developing collaboration between subjects in a context of real power imbalances. More importantly, I began to understand more clearly how previous analyses of the researcher-participant relationship, including my own, that described this power imbalance were still written from the perspective of the person in power, now the concerned researcher, and failed to understand the power of the participant. As the examples described above suggest the participants are not only aware of their power, they use it. Turning off the tape recorder, using the time of the interview to ask questions about the pre-Conquest history of Mayan Indians, and deciding what experiences to include in the telling of a story are three additional examples of the participants' role in constructing the collaboration, indices of her subjectivity. From this perspective the language of my form (for example, "this project is being undertaken by trained personnel for a serious scientific purpose and . . . careful attention to my [i.e., the participant's] general welfare will be provided throughout") is particularly paternalistic and gratuitous.

The basis for our (i.e., North American and Guatemalan) collaboration has been established long before we undertook this particular research project. The Guatemalan women evaluated our invitation to participate in the oral history project within the context of their community's ongoing struggle and a decision to develop ties with North American women was made in the context of ongoing systems that they have developed for decision making. In my decision to become involved in their lives and in their decision to include this project in their ongoing work we had, in a small and limited way, initiated a joint effort. Making these decisions, that is to interview and be interviewed, represented a concrete affirmation of mutual trust. The issue of consent had been settled. In some limited ways I had entered into their systems of social and political organizing, into their ongoing community dynamics with its many contradictions and conflicts. In other, also limited, ways their decision to be interviewed constituted their entry into my community. We have also, through the collaboration, begun a process of constructing a different reality, one that reflects the conversations that we are building together.

The informed consent form, which I introduced as a mechanism for "protecting the subjects" of the research project, was instead a barrier and forced me to confront the chasm between the needs and demands of research conducted within the boundaries of the university and the systems of trust and mistrust and of sharing and withholding that were already a part of this collaboration. In introducing a strategy that I thought I had constructed in a way to guarantee that the subjects or participants in the research maintained control over their words I was rather assuming that either I had control or needed to gain control over the process. I was, on the one hand, seeking to protect myself while, on the other hand, implicitly asserting that I needed to protect them from abuses of my control. The introduction of the form threatened to undermine our previously negotiated contractual arrangement of trust. Upon reflection I have come to see their resistance as a reaffirmation of that relationship, as an assertion of the control they know is theirs, and, finally, as a refusal to allow me to shift the grounds of my control. Their resistance to signing the informed consent form became an opportunity to more fully clarify both the meaning of the form and the developing meaning of our relationship. I have not jettisoned the form. Rather my current understanding of its meaning-in-context provides an alternative perspective from which to introduce a discussion of informed consent in our next oral history interview and increased clarification of the nature of the relationships developing in this project and how they shape the outcomes of our collaboration.

DISCUSSION

All research involves the selection of a method, identification of participants and development of an informed consent form. These are sometimes viewed as neutral, value free strategies for accomplishing the goal of testing a hypothesis or answering a research question. Concerned social scientists have identified some of the biases within research methods and sought to develop strategies that protect participants. As a first world North American woman and a concerned social scientist I was aware of the power and resources I brought to this collaboration when I began my work. (I was also aware of my weaknesses, for example, limited proficiency in Spanish and no proficiency in Quiché.) Minimally, I brought the power of my education, the power of being from the "first world," the power of access to methods of communication beyond the local community and the power of financial and professional resources to make these stories available. My recognition of my position enhanced my sensitivity to the power differential between researcher and participant and led to my efforts to develop strategies for empowering participants to redress this imbalance. By choosing to undertake a process of participatory, collaborative research I entered a process of negotiation with a number of Guatemalan women that revealed and challenged unexamined assumptions of power and control implicit in my research strategies. The negotiated relationship of trust, based in earlier conversation and shared solidarity in a broader political process, provided a context for re-examining some of my research strategies and clarifying the ways in which they functioned to maintain rather than re-duce the power imbalance between participant and investigator.

Rather than negate other considerations or analyses of the research process this analysis contributes to a developing understanding of collaborative re-search by documenting other dimensions underlying the power relations in the research process. In a process where there were a relatively high number of shared interests between researchers and participants the examples dis-cussed here provide evidence of competing interests between these parties and indicate how some of them are being confronted. The decision to engage in collaborative research does not *de facto* resolve competing interests. Nor does it minimize the importance of developing strategies for ensuring, for ex-ample, the anonymity of our informants, concerns that are even more critical in research with members of oppressed groups than in university based work with college sophomores. Rather it affirms a commitment on the part of both researcher and participant to engage the research process as subjects, as constructors of our own reality. The commitment to collaborative research and the ongoing negotiation, of the trusting relationship required by all col-laboration provides a context or framework for the work, and a baseline for understanding when one or another fails to treat the other as subject.

As suggested in this discussion I both underestimated the power of the par-ticipants at some points in our process and underestimated the power of the research strategies I was using (e.g., informed consent). Collaboration and trust do not negate power differentials; rather they create a bond between two active subjects who must then negotiate the power differential between them as they encounter it. This chapter describes several examples of these negotia-tions.

Recognition of the dynamics of power and control implicit in our research tools and of the differing forms of power and control the participants bring to the research situation suggest the importance that the research process itself plays in constructing the data that is being gathered. Although further elabo-ration of this point is beyond the scope of this chapter it is evident in the sto-ries that are being recorded and more obviously in the group conversations and reflections on the interviews that have been recorded that new meanings are constructed in and through this engaged collaboration. What is recorded are the stories of a person or of groups of persons that are constrained or fa-cilitated by the negotiated relationships between specific North American and Guatemalan compañeras.

The understanding of Guatemalan Indian women's experiences that emerges from this project is and will always be provisional. It draws its energy and forcefulness from the collaboration of a small number of Guatemalan In-dian women who are refugees in Mexico and an even smaller number of North American researchers who are committed to continuing involvement in solidarity with the people of Guatemala. The perspectives that emerge are particularly rich because they benefit from a self-consciously collaborative effort to understand the self-understanding of Guatemalan Indian women and their continuing participation in the struggles of their people. The text that emerges is a document built from the interactive process of reflection, of sharing, and of criticism. It documents one phase of a developing solidarity among women from different cultural, racial, class and national backgrounds who have engaged the common question of understanding Guatemalan women's experiences. It tells the stories of some Indian women and, by speaking to a community of psychologists and researchers, contributes to a broader collective process of breaking the silence surrounding Guatemala.

My personal decision to draw more fully on my professional expertise in my work with Guatemalans also reflects a turning point in my development as a psychologist. The work described here reflects collaborative research that is grounded in and derives from social and political commitment of solidarity with the people of Guatemala [31]. Although that commitment has been part of my work for a number of years it has been through participation in this research that I have been able to find more fully my voice as a North American feminist psychologist and the meaning of this experience is being mutually constructed in this collaboration.

APPENDIX A

GUIDELINE QUESTIONS FOR INTERVIEWS WITH GUATEMALAN INDIAN WOMEN

(English Version)

1. Experiences in family and community: Can you tell us about your experiences in childhood? in adolescence? in adulthood?
    (a) in your family, and
    (b) in your community.
2. What kinds of political involvements/experiences have you had? What have those experiences meant to you?
3. Did you participate in other groups or organizations in your community? What were those experiences like?
4. How has your participation changed you?
5. What people are most important in your life, what people have made the most differences in your life?
6. What has it meant to you to be an Indian?
7. What has it meant to you to be a woman?
8. Was religion or the church important in your life? Can you tell us about your experiences in the church or with religion?
9. Tell us about the situation before you came to Mexico.
10. Tell us about what you have done in the time you have been in Mexico.
11. What do you feel that you have accomplished in your life?
12. What do you want for your children?
13. Background information that did not come out in the conversation, including

LYKES

143

education (formal and informal; parents, self and children); size of family of origin and of current family; occupation (of self, spouse, parents).

14. Is there anything else you would like to tell us about; are there any questions you would like to ask of us; what has this experience been like for you?

APPENDIX A

(Spanish Version)

1. Experiencias en la familia y la communidad: Cuentos de tu niñez, juventud y ahora como adulta en relación a tu familia y tu comunidad.

2. ¿Qué tipo de participación o experiencia política hastenido tú? ¿Quó has ha significado en tu vida?

3. ¿Participabasen otros grupos u organizaciones en tu comunidad? ¿Cómo eran esas experiencias?

4. ¿Cómo te cambió tu participación?

5. ¿Quién(es) ha(n) sido las personas que más te han influenciado in to vida?

6. ¿Qué te ha significado ser indigena?

7. ¿Qué te ha significado ser mujer?

8. ¿Han tenido importancia en tu vida la religion o la iglesia?

9. Cuéntanos sobre tu situación immediatamente antes de venir a México.

10. Cuéntanos sobre lo que té has hecho desde la llegada a México (en tu familiar a qué te dedicas ...)

11. Hasta ahora, ¿qué has logrado en tu vida?

12. ¿Qué quieres para tus hijos?

13. Información generale: educación (formal y no formal) propia, de los padres e hijos; tamaño de su familiar de niñez y actual; a qué se dedica, en Guatemala, en Mexico-su esposo, los padres. ¿Habia viajado fuera de su comunidad antes de venir a Mexico?

14. Al fin: ¿Tienes otras cosas que quieres contar? ¿Otras experiencias? ¿Otras preguntas? ¿Qué te pareció esta experiencia de hablar de tu vida?

APPENDIX B INFORMED

CONSENT AGREEMENT

(English Version)

I agree to participate voluntarily in this study of Guatemalan women's experiences in family and community. My participation involves an oral history interview in which I will discuss my experiences in my family and community in Guatemala and in Mexico. I understand that the interview will take between 3 and 6 hours.

The material to be gathered will be recorded and will be transcribed. I will have the right to edit and correct the transcript of the interview during a period of 3 months after it is returned to me. The material will be kept strictly confidential until I have edited the transcript.

FORM A: After this time the tapes and transcripts will be available for use by students, scholars and others. The researcher may publish this material for the purposes of the project described here and may authorize publication of the transcripts or quotations from the transcripts in appropriate cases. (Unrestricted use.)

FORM B: After this time the tapes and transcripts will be available for use by students, scholars and others. The researcher will neither publish this material herself nor authorize publication of the transcripts or quotations from the transcripts during the interviewee's lifetime except with my written permission. (Restricted publication.)

FORM C: The tapes and transcripts will only be available for use by students, scholars and others for a period of years (specified by the interviewee) to those who obtain my written permission. The researcher will neither publish this material herself nor authorize publication of the transcripts or quotations from the transcripts during the interviewee's lifetime except with my written permission. (Restricted as to use and publication.)

I understand that this project is being undertaken by trained personnel for a serious scientific purpose and that careful attention to my general welfare will be provided throughout. Any questions I have about the project will be answered by the interviewer to the best of her ability. I understand that I am free not to answer any questions at any time.

I have read the above agreement. I understand what is being asked of me and am willing to participate in this project and to have the materials used in the ways described above.

_____
Interviewee's Signature

_____
Interviewer's Signature

_____
Date

APPENDIX B

(Spanish Version)

Voluntariamente doy mi acuerdó de participar en este estudio de las experiencias familiares y de sus comunidades vividas por mujeres guatemaltecas. Mi participación implica una entrevista de historica oral en la cual hablaré de mis experiencias en la familia y la comunidad, tanto en Guatemala como en Mexico. Entien do que la entrevista llevará de 3 a 6 horas.

Las entrevistas serán grabadas y transcritas. Reservo el derecho de revisar, editar y corregir la transcripcion de la entrevista durante un período de 3 meses después de que me la entreguen. Los contenidos no se publicarán hasta que yo los revise.

Marque una de las siguientes opciones:

Después de la revisión, los cassettes y sus transcripciones estarán disponibles para el uso de académicos, estudiantes y otros. La investigadora puede publicar los contenidos para los fines del proyecto aquí descritos y puede autorizar la

publicación de dichas transcripciones o citas de las mismas en casos apropria-
dos. (Uso ilimitado).

Después de la revisión, los cassettes y sus transcripciones estarán disponibles para el uso de académicas, estudiantes y otros. La investigadora ni
publicará las transcripciones o citas de las mismas, ni autorizará su publicación
durante la vida de la entrevistada sin pedir su permiso por escrito. (Publicación restringida).

Los cassettes y las transcripciones estarán disponibles únicamente para el
usos de académicos, estudiantes y otros a los que concedo mi permiso por escrito, durante un período de tiempo que yo defino. La investigadora ni publicará, ni autorizará su publicacion por otros, de los contenidos de las entrevistas durante la vida de la entrevistada, a menos que le dé mi permiso por escrito. (Uso y publicacion restringidos.)

Entiendo que este proyecto se está llevando a cabo por personas capacitadas
con fines científicos y que pondrán atención a la cuestión de mi seguridad.

Cualquier pregunta que yo peuda tener será respondida por la entrevistadora. Entiendo que no tengo que contestar todas las preguntas que me hagan
y que la decisión de no responder no implicará ninguna consecuencia negati-
va Para mí.

Yo he leido este acuerdo; entiendo los puntos y lo que se me estan pidien-
do. Estoy dispuesta a participar en este proyecto y a que los contenidos
pueden usarse de la manera marcada arriba.

146

_____

Firma entrevistada

_____

Firma entrevistadora

_____

Fecha

REFERENCES

1. C. Kruger and K. Enge, *Security and Development in the Guatemalan Highlands*,
   Washington Office on Latin America, Washington, D.C., 1985.
2. Amnesty International Publication, Guatemala: *The Human Rights Record*, London, United Kingdom, 1987.
3. M. B. Lykes, *Autonomous Individualism versus Social Individuality: Towards an Alternative Understanding of the Self,* University Microfilms International, #8416004, Ann
   Arbor, Michigan, 1984.
4. ——, Gender and Individualistic versus Collectivist Bases for Notions about the
   Self, *Journal of Personality,* 53, pp. 356–383, 1985.
5. R. Menchu, I, *Rigoberta Menchu: An Indian Woman in Guatemala*, with E. Burgos-
   Debray (ed. and intro.), translated by A. Wright, Verso Editions, London, 1984.
6. L. Frank and P. Wheaton, *Indian Guatemala; Path to Liberation: The Role of Christians
   in the Indian Process*, EPICA Task Force, Washington, D.C., 1984.

7. America's Watch and British Parliamentary Human Rights Group, *Human Rights in Guatemala: During President Cerenzo's First Year*, New York, 1987.

8. R. Falla, Vision de Pueblo Indigena del Genocidio que Sufre, (Sequndí Parte), Tribunal Permanente de los Pueblos. Excerpted in English in S. Jonas, E. McCaughan, and E. S. Martinez (eds. and trans.), *Guatemala: Tyranny on Trial*, Synthesis Publications, San Francisco, 1984.

9. S. Jonas, E. McCaughan, and E. S. Martinez (eds. and trans.), *Guatemala: Tyranny on Trial: Testimony of the Permanent People's Tribunal*, Synthesis Publications, San Francisco, 1984.

10. W. J. McGuire, The Yin and Yang of Progress in Social Psychology, *Journal of Personality and Social Psychology*, 26, pp. 446–456, 1973.

11. K. Gergen, Experimentation in Social Psychology: A Reappraisal, *European Journal of Social Psychology, 36*, pp. 1344–1360, 1978.

12. K. Gergen, The Positivist Image in Social Psychological Theory, in *Psychology in Social Context*, A. R. Buss (ed.), Irvington, New York, 1979.

13. E. E. Sampson, Scientific Paradigms and Social Values: Wanted - A Scientific Revolution, *Journal of Personality and Social Psychology, 36*, pp. 1332-1343, 1978.

14. L. Finison, *Social Action in Historical Perspective*, discussion-workshop at the meeting of the New England Social Psychological Association, Boston, April, 1980.

15. K. Gergen, Social Psychology as History, *Journal of Personality and Social Psychology, 26*, pp. 309-320, 1973.

16. A. R. Buss, The Emerging Field of the Sociology of Psychological Knowledge, *American Psychologist, 30*, pp. 988-1002, 1975.

17. E. G. Mishler, Meaning in Context: Is There Any Other Kind? *Harvard Educational Review, 49*, pp. 1-19, 1979.

18. E. G. Mishler, L. R. Amarasingham, S. T. Hauser, R. Liem, S. D. Osherson, and N. E. Waxler, *Social Contexts of Health, Illness, and Patient Care*, Cambridge University Press, Cambridge, 1981.

19. D. O. Sears, College Sophomores in the Laboratory: Influences of a Narrow Data Base on Social Psychology's View of Human Nature, *Journal of Personality and Social Psychology, 51* pp. 515-530, 1986.

20. M. B. Lykes and A. J. Stewart. Evaluating the Feminist Challenge to Research in Personality and Social Psychology: 1963-1983, *Psychology of Women Quarterly, 10*, pp. 393-411, 1986.

21. F. D. Miller and B. Zeitz, A Woman's Place is in the Footnotes, *Personality and Social Psychology Bulletin, 4*, pp. 511-514, 1978.

22. D. Spender, The Gatekeepers: A Feminist Critique of Academic Publishing, in *Doing Feminist Research*, H. Roberts (ed.), Routledge and Kegan Paul, Boston, 1981.

23. E. G. Mishler, The Analysis of Interview Narratives, *Narratology and Psychology*, Praeger Publishers, New York, 1985.

24. M. A. Paget, Experience and Knowledge, *Human Studies, 6*, pp. 67-90, 1983.

25. L. L. Langness and G. Frank, *Lives: An Anthropological Approach to Biography*, Chandler and Sharp, Novato, California, 1986.

26. Frish, Oral History and HARD TIMES: A Review Essay, *Oral History Review*, pp. 70-80, 1979.

27. D. Bertaux (ed.), *Biography and Society: The Life History Approach in the Social Sciences*, Sage, Beverly Hills, 1981.

28. S. Reinharz, *On Becoming a Social Scientist: From Survey Research and Participant Observation to Experiental Analysis*, Transaction Books, New Brunswick, New Jersey, 1984.

29. L. Stanley and S. Wise, *Breaking Out: Feminist Consciousness and Feminist Research*, Routledge and Kegan Paul, Boston, 1983.

30. A. Oakley, Interviewing Women: A Contradiction in Terms, in *Doing Feminist Research*, H. Roberts (ed.), Routledge and Kegan Paul, Boston, 1981.

31. B. DuBois, Passionate Scholarship: Notes on Values, Knowing and Method in Feminist Social Science, in *Theories of Women's Studies*, G. Bowles and R. D. Klein (eds.), Routledge and Kegan Paul, Boston, 1983.

LINGUISTIC REPERTOIRES AND LITERARY CRITICISM
New Directions for a Social Psychology of Gender

Margaret Wetherell

THE QUESTION this chapter addresses is how to analyse femininity and masculinity or construct a social psychology of women and men. Is femininity a set of traits - narcissism, dependence, communion and so on — developing naturally from biological differences, a set of psychological states fixed by the different experiences, limitations and potentialities of being a woman; or is it a set of stereotypes basic to roles and taken up by the people who adopt those roles?

All of these perspectives seem to obscure the main point about gender. I want to suggest that femininity and masculinity are ideological practices all the more effective because they appear as natural and inevitable results of biology or experience. The appearance of something coherent which could be explained as a property of the individual is precisely the effect of this ideological movement.

Habitual practice assigns children to one category or other. Name, identity and, later, type of occupation and access to resources become fixed by that sexual category. The symbolic and excessive importance of a sexual differentiation which seems vital only for the continuation and preservation of a certain kind of *status quo* is established and reinforced by family, media, and education. Actions and self-descriptions become, as a result, genderized, associated with just female or male, and then universalized so that the categories become homogeneous as well as separated, superordinate to other identities. As feminists appreciate, what in this way, becomes, taken for granted, and thus completely 'obvious', is also often the most difficult to penetrate and criticize.

Femininity and masculinity, examined closely, reduce to a set of codes or conventions and devices used to produce categorical difference. Gender, it will be argued, is not a matter of consistent unitary single identities, 'male' and 'female', but develops from contradictory and frequently fragmentary pieces of discourse, repertoires, and accounting systems available to individuals to make sense of their position, and which historically and contingently have come to be marked as feminine or masculine responses.

In turning this way to language and cultural practices of representation we will be following a track which may not be familiar to social psychologists but which will be to many others. The analysis developed here is an extension of earlier work (Potter *et al.*, 1984) and builds upon the concept of a linguistic repertoire (Potter and Mulkay, 1985). Help will be sought from literary critics and other cultural critics who have attempted to deconstruct the images of women and men offered in fiction, advertising, and more generally (Abel, 1982; Coward, 1984; Ellmann, 1979; Heath, 1982; Williamson, 1978), and from a recently elaborated model of the human subject as positioned ideologically (Adlam *et al.*, 1977; Coward and Ellis, 1977; Henriques *et al.*, 1984).

Initially, however, the argument will develop negatively through a critique of some standard socio-psychological approaches to gender, looking particularly at the definition and measurement of femininity and masculinity, themes of agency versus communion, or animus and anima, in the psychology of women and men. In order to argue for a reconceptualization of gender in social psychology, it is first necessary to see the problems with the existing framework.

COMMUNION AND AGENCY: THE EXIGENCIES OF GENDER MEASUREMENT

> It might seem quite a simple matter to obtain a measure of someone's femininity and masculinity, at least on the face of it. All that we require is some way of determining the degree to which people think that they conform to the characteristics typically associated with women and men, respectively. (Smith, 1985, p. 92)

The difficult part, indeed, is the definition of these characteristics and their status. Measurement then supposes that these traits will be enduring or displayed consistently across situations and are thus a meaningful attribute of the person.

In psychology, feminine and masculine have usually been understood in terms of a communion/agency, or alternatively expressivity/instrumentality, distinction. This distinction has been proposed in many guises from Jungian psychotherapy (de Castillejo, 1973; Johnson, 1976) to Bakan's (1966) dualities of human existence and Parson's and Bale's (1955) division of tasks in the household or group, and it is referred to in a number of chapters in the present volume. Bakan maintains, for instance, that:

> . . . a fundamental polarity underlies human existence at all levels from the cellular to the societal—the constructs of agency and communion . . . agency and communion are male and female principles, differentiating the aggregate of males from the aggregate of females . . . in psychological functioning, agency is seen in differentiation of self from the field, in intellectual functions involving separating and ordering, and in interpersonal styles involving objectivity, competition, exclusion, and distance; communion is seen in the merging of self with the field, in intellectual functions involving communication, interpersonal styles involving subjectivity, co-operation, acceptance and closeness. (quoted in Carlson, 1971, p. 271)

Thus, to put it more bluntly:

> Big boys are made of—independence, aggression, competitiveness, leadership, task orientation, outward orientation, assertiveness . . .

> Big girls are made of—dependence, passivity, fragility, low pain tolerance, non-aggression, non-competitiveness, inner orientation, interpersonal orientation, empathy, sensitivity, nuturance . . . (back cover publisher's blurb for Bardwick's *Psychology of Women*, 1971)

151

Jung claimed that two complementary but opposed principles, the anima (feminine) and the animus (masculine), of archetypal and mythical status, could be identified in the human psyche. Anticipating the modern emphasis on psychological androgyny, he argued that men not only contained animus aspects but also a smaller element of anima functions which would emerge from time to time, and similarly women were not only anima but also to some extent animus.

Precise specification of the nature of anima and animus is rare but a sense can be gained if we put together a pastiche of terms used by authors such as de Castillejo and Johnson. The animus-like agency is thus 'focussed consciousness and separation' of an 'impersonal collective character' involving 'reflection, deliberation, and self-knowledge', not to mention 'active achievement, cool reasonableness, mastery, penetration and the overcoming of the obstacles of nature'; the anima is more 'primaeval and oceanic, more closely

WETHERELL

tied to the original instinctive pattern' and manifested in 'diffuse awareness, natural contact with the living springs in the unconscious, values of life, unity, relationship and relatedness'. The anima is represented too by the following traits: 'waiting, passive, artistic, sense of the unbroken connection of all things, suffocating, inarticulate, raging vanity, conniving lust, pettiness'.

Unfortunately, women seem to benefit little from their animus side. Witness the following:

> . . . (femininity) expresses an attitude of spiritual waiting, and tending, and readiness for the meeting with its opposite which is a prerequisite for inner wholeness. Without this she becomes prey to the masculine within herself, a raging spirit of intellectual or physical activity to which no man can be related, and to which she can in no way relate herself. (de Castillejo, 1973, p. 57)

Although animus and anima are tied to the myths and tales told to make sense of the environment and human relations, by sleight of hand they also become more than that: as constitutive, biologically inevitable, patterns of consciousness. Developed in this form, de Castillejo and Johnson's anima and animus can quickly be rejected as semi-mystical ramblings, but, nonetheless, the more general agency and communion concepts to which they conform have become a powerful common sense in psychology, an implicit background knowledge which is never deconstructed but built upon as a foundation and correspondingly taken for granted.

Bem's (1974) Sex Role Inventory (the BSRI), for example, probably the most popular modern socio-psychological method for measuring gender identity, is clearly prey to this. Bem's aim in the inventory was to identify several gender options (feminine, masculine, or an androgynous combination of both) and operationalize these in questionnaire form. People completing the questionnaire could then determine their psychosexual identity. They were to read a list of traits presented then decide on the suitability of each trait as a self-description.

To select the items for inclusion in the inventory, Bem asked student judges to rate each of 400 personality characteristics in terms of its desirability for a woman or a man. Students were instructed not to think in terms of their own criteria for desirability but to intuit the kinds of criteria 'American society' would use. The complete inventory consists of 20 highly desirable feminine characteristics, 20 highly desirable masculine characteristics and 20 neutral or filler items. It is clear from examination of the BSRI that the agency/communion framework has been replicated by this procedure (feminine traits, for example, include warm and tender; masculine traits, aggressive and analytical).

In Bem's inventory, however, femininity and masculinity need not be tied to biological sex. Masculine females and feminine males are potential outcomes along with the androgynous (equally high in positive feminine and

152

WETHERELL

masculine traits) and the undifferentiated (equally low in positive feminine and masculine traits).

In this tradition of gender measurement, agency and communion have been linked to a much more modern set of assumptions about sex role stereotypes and the socialization process (Bem, 1974; 1975; 1976; Bem and Lenney, 1976; Bem et al., 1976). Bem states that 'the BSRI was founded on a conception of the sex-typed person as someone who has internalized *society's sex-typed standards* of desirable behaviour for men and women' (1974, p. 155, my emphasis). Despite being conventional and stereotypical this does not mean that these standards are not psychologically real for those who are sex typed. On the contrary, Bem maintains that people's behaviour can be predicted from their endorsement of stereotypes on the inventory; the other key word in the previous quotation, therefore, is 'internalized'.

Bem has gone on to institute a body of research which demonstrates this psychological reality, developing a programme of experiments which confirm that the psychologically feminine, for example, not only endorse the appropriate stereotypes on the inventory but behave in other situations in 'typically feminine' ways; and, moreover, that androgynous women and men are psychologically superior, in the sense of being better adjusted, more capable, human beings.

The conclusion arrived at by Bem *et al.* (1976) from one set of experimental results illustrates this trend:

> . . . only androgynous males were high in both instrumental and expressive domains; that is, only androgynous males were found to stand firm in their opinions as well as cuddle kittens, bounce babies, and offer a sympathetic ear to someone in distress. In contrast, the feminine male was low in independence, while the masculine male was low in nurturance. (p. 1022)

Empirical proof, apparently, that people live out the agency and communion scripts set out for them.

The social psychology of gender identity is thus characterized, first, by the need to find meaning in a feminine/masculine divide, and, second, by the desire to find the definitive content of those categories. These are usually understood in terms of some version of the agency/communion distinction and then fixed as a property of the individual across context and time.

As Smith (1985) points out, in many respects the BSRI and similar instruments are a considerable advance over earlier measures, representing the transition from a sex difference method to a more flexible stereotype or self-categorization approach. Sex differences are no longer assumed a *priori*, the inventory depends on willingness to categorize oneself in terms of a social consensus about what females and males should be like. It is not my aim in this chapter, however, to demonstrate the positive aspects of Bem's work in terms

153

WETHERELL

of the history of psychological research in this area, or indeed to criticize the methodological problems with the actual measurement procedure (cf. Smith, 1985; Eichler, 1980); rather, my intention is to examine the more global assumptions which underlie this tradition of work.

There seem to be three main grounds for suspecting that this kind of approach impedes the analysis of human relations and, in fact, may be more actively retrogressive. First, it seems probable that the force of femininity/masculinity discourse lies in the very assumption of a meaningful categorical difference rather than in the specific content identified through research as constitutive of that difference. Second, for this reason, Bem's inventory and others like it reinforce one set of 'imaginary identities', strengthening their ideological potential and legitimacy. Finally, there are problems with the model of the subject implicit not only in biologically inherent accounts but also in socialization notions of gender adoption.

Clifton *et al.* (1976) have demonstrated, with respect to the BSRI, that if people are asked to generate descriptions of various types of women (career woman, bunny, woman athlete, housewife, clubwoman) then only the image for 'housewife' matches the image of femininity or communion in the inventories. This not only illustrates the narrow realm from which Bem's gender stereotypes are drawn but points to a more fundamental problem.

Women athletes may rarely be seen by others as affectionate, gullible, tender, yielding, etc. or as 'feminine females' on Bem's scale, yet they are hardly immune from the ideological momentum of femininity discourse, as becomes apparent from even a cursory acquaintance with the traditions of sports broadcasting. For the woman athelete, it is the fact that she can be marked as 'feminine', whatever her attributes, and thus diminished, that is important. The possibility of categorization is more powerful than the content usually attributed to the categories.

Spender (1980) has called the general tendency for 'masculine' attributes and occupations to be valued and 'feminine' derogated and downgraded, the 'plus male, minus female' phenomenon. She documents cases where a certain type of linguistic construction (the tag question) becomes an indicator of control over a conversation when used by men, but where the same type of construction tends to be seen as a sign of weakness and hesitancy when used by women. We don't need to assume for one moment that there is only one correct interpretation of the meaning of the linguistic construction in question to see that in this case femininity and masculinity have become moveable categories. They have come to resemble the two possible readings that make up some well known visual illusions, either it is an old woman or it is a vase, either it is a dalmation dog or a pattern of leaves against a white background: the prior conceptualization or choice of reading determines the content and what can be seen. The content becomes shaped to the category.

The substance of femininity/masculinity categories may, in this way, be surprisingly flexible; women and men may be described in all kinds of ways, but what is vital for social reproduction is the possibility of difference and its value marking. It must be more useful, therefore, for the social scientist to examine how femininity/masculinity labels work to define situations and discourse, in combination with the power to have those labels accepted, i.e. creating content and organizing value; rather than identifying, as Bem does, the feminine or masculine as an inherent fixed property of certain states. Social psychologists could begin to investigate, for instance, how particular versions of sexual identity are adopted for characterizing one's own and others' actions in specific situations. Attention could be fruitfully directed to what is achieved by these different kinds of accounts.

A great deal seems to be missed that is crucial to the understanding of the social position of women and men, if we assume that the content of femininity or masculinity is unvarying and can be unproblematically 'discovered' once and for all, as one might discover what is inside a box. In this case the contents of the box could be constantly changing and can always be renegotiated; the important issue is how they are negotiated and often, to continue the analogy, the agreement that there are two boxes in the first place.

Paradoxically, in her most recent writings, Bem seems to have grasped parts of this point, although at the same time she continues to struggle to fix femininity and masculinity, but in a new guise as 'gender schema'. She writes:

> Even more importantly, however, the concept of androgyny is insufficiently radical from a feminist perspective because it continues to presuppose that there is a masculine and a feminine within us all, that is, that the concepts of masculinity and femininity have an independent and palpable reality rather than being themselves cognitive constructs derived from gender based schematic processing. A focus on the concept of androgyny thus fails to prompt serious examination of the extent to which gender organises both our perceptions and our social world. (Bem, 1981, p. 383)

155

Critics like Eichler (1980; cf. also Johnston, 1985) argued that androgyny was a meaningless ideal. As Eichler demonstrated, if our society was actually androgynous, the concept of androgyny itself could not exist, because sex (apart from in a strictly biological sense) would be considered an irrelevant variable and defunct as a term of reference for social organization (1980, p. 70). It is illogical to aim towards androgyny but to regard it at the same time as the combination of highly desirable feminine and masculine qualities. While conceding the point on androgyny, Bem, unfortunately, continues to maintain that gender identities can still be unilaterally defined, albeit as 'cognitive constructs'. Once again the implication is that gender conventions persist because they are internalized by individuals. But do they not persist because of their role in the reproduction of patriarchical social forms and because of their potential for flexible application?

WETHERELL

All this goes to show that this type of social psychology has effectively de-contextualized sex. Gender identities in the BSRI are viewed in the abstract, quite independently of the situations to which they might relate. In effect, a set of 'imaginary identities' is produced. The stereotypes or social consensus reflected by a small group of students become, in the inventory, reified into a normative standard, invariant across contexts, culture, and history, which constrains personality description.

Bem's attempt to discover gender as a literal state rather than to treat it as a metaphorical device could thus serve to bolster up the very ideological practice she hoped to defuse (through the concept of androgyny). This is the second problem with the BSRI. The gender identities produced results in ideological products (agency/communion) acquiring a tangible, measureable and constant reality through their representation as psychological, character variables. What, for instance, do the people who complete the BSRI learn? As Eichler and Johnston point out, they learn that their disposition is open to scientific test and, moreover, here is evidence that what people seem to believe about femininity is actually the case. 'Sex role stereotypes, as established, serve as a gauge for reality, rather than reality serving as a corrective for the stereotypes' (Eichler, 1980, p. 68). The otherwise highly tendentious and clearly reactionary fantasies of Jung, Bakan, etc. are in this way perpetuated. Their claim to be neutral descriptions of what is the case about women and men remains effectively unchallenged.

Following the general trend in social psychology as a whole, there has been little consideration of the power relationships or access to resources implicated in women as communion, men as agency schemes. In short, little feminism. The implications are clear, but seen as unproblematic or merely accepted as given.

Carlson, for instance, notes in her discussion of a more psychoanalytically oriented version of agency and communion:

> Central to Gutmann's formulation is the contrast between two kinds of 'maturational milieus' of men and women. Men inhabit an impersonal milieu—whether of business, battlefield, or prairie—a milieu governed by impersonal laws of nature, of economics, of the political order. Women inhabit the personal world of family, neighbourhood, community—a milieu governed by familiar forces of feelings, shared expectancies, predictabilities. (1971, p. 268)

Beware the woman who steps outside her ecological niche! It seems unfortunate, to say the least, that such admirable personal qualities should lead women into subjugated and oppressed positions.

Finally, we should examine the model of the human subject which underlies the social psychology of gender and accounts for some of its difficulties. It is unquestioned, as a central presupposition of psychometrics, that the human subject is unitary, coherent and consistent across situations, also in some way

WETHERELL

an 'individual' separated from, but influenced by, the rest of society (cf. the critique of socialization by Adlam *et al.*; 1977). Bem's inventory, for example, encourages the view that androgyny, femininity, and masculinity are traits which one either has or does not have. As an individual with a specific psychosexual identity you enter into relationships with other individuals with their own identities, producing and sustaining the social matrix.

This impression, however, is an illusion fostered by a method of measurement or style of investigation. Variability, contradiction and the construction of mental life through interaction, are carefully edited out of the record. A snapshot of a constrained either/or type of response at one moment in time is generalized to become a permanent psychological feature. Other methods of study, such as the collection of discourse for analysis, clearly demonstrate that variability and inconsistency are exactly the principal characteristics of any naturally occurring human justification, explanation or self-analysis (Potter, 1984; Potter and Litton, 1985). There seems no reason to believe that discourse about gender will prove an exception.

That is, if we look at how people talk about gender and sexuality and draw upon received notions to account for their own and others' behaviour, we might well find fragmentary rather than coherent references to 'femininity' and 'masculinity'. A multitude of contradictory and inconsistent self-characterizations depending on context might emerge, as opposed to one stable identity. A rapidly shifting discursive construction or creation of subject positions and group memberships might appear, acting as options to be taken up or rejected, by the interlocutor: far removed from an ordered intercourse between two fixed, 'already created', individuals.

How could social psychology cope with the possibility of people who are alternately 'androgynous', 'feminine' or 'masculine', and with a 'femininity' of ambiguous content outlined at one moment as expressive communion, but at another as instrumental and personal? Or a situation where, also, the repetition of these terms may signify more about the nature of divisions and power relations within a society, than the built-in character and temperament of the individual member?

Before making any suggestions, however, in answer to this question, it might be helpful to pause and consider a similar debate within feminist literary criticism. The terms of reference for this debate and method of resolution, although they may initially appear irrelevant, clarify the problem for the social psychologist, and further indicate the complexity of the dilemma.

WOMEN READING WOMEN

The development of feminist literary criticism has in many respects paralleled the investigation of femininity in social psychology (cf. Potter *et al.*; 1984, Chapter 1) but with the exception that a much more confident and sophisticated analysis of ideologically potent images has emerged. It is ironic that lit-

WETHERELL

157

erary criticism, through its dealings with fictional constructions, could advance the methods and theoretical analysis required to understand the regularities of gender operation in prosaic everyday life.

One of the first achievements of feminist critics was to bring to the foreground the social location of the author, displaying the consistent bias and distortion in male writers' descriptions of women. Critics like Ellmann (1979) and Millett (1969), in particular, have ensured that authors like Mailer, Miller and D. H. Lawrence can no longer be read with the same innocence. Their descriptions of women now appear contingent, questionable, risible and embarrassingly misogynist.

Ellmann claimed that four meta-principles govern the stereotypes of women found in literature and, by extension, have also influenced the critical assessment of female authors. First, sexual difference in texts is often achieved by a nature/art distinction. Rather like communion and agency, female functions are portrayed in literature as natural, unthinking, unself-conscious, while the male principle is assertive against nature, struggling rationally and self-consciously to improve and progress. Both can be seen as an ideal but the association with nature also demotes the female. Typically, says Ellmann, 'when the (male) observer reconsiders his own condition, and experiencing a revived gratification on its account, finds the same supposed thoughtlessness of others contemptibly naive' (1979, p. 62). Similarly in psychology, agency and communion are held up as equally ideal states, but it seems also that male agency just happens to fit men for high status and the exercise of power.

158

Second, there is the principle that female and male qualities are complementary; rather than covering the same spheres, they advantageously and, somehow, miraculously balance out. Third, there is the different base/superstructure notion of progress for women and men:

> Every feminine virtue implies a vice . . . women unfortunately are women, and
> their ideal is attained by rising above themselves . . . On the other hand, men are
> not men without effort and their ideal condition is attained by their becoming,
> and (with luck) remaining, simply men. (Ellmann, 1979, pp. 66–68)

Defective woman to supersexual ideal, versus subsexual male to proper sexual male, in 23 chapters.

Finally, Ellmann, unlike the social psychologist of gender, notes the fluidity of modern stereotypes, so that while the ascription of sex differences remains constant, the perceived content and evaluation varies widely. ('It is impossible for women to believe so much about themselves', 1979, p. 59). As argued in the last section, femininity and masculinity appear (it seems in fiction too) as highly unstable, contradictory states. The creation of difference and the organization of material which this allows, is the central achievement, even though the sense of the categorization may vary widely. A broader decon-

WETHERELL

struction of the mechanisms of gender labelling, following on from feminist critics' treatment of literature, must help the understanding of this process.

Feminist critics, besides their interest in the transmission of images of women, have principally sought to analyse the social position of the female author, and female experience, as a basis for writing. Novels written by women and subsequently displaced or forgotten have been rescued and re-evaluated. Attempts have been made to specify what has been seen as the unique and particular nature of women's writing style and the female literary tradition. Showalter (1982) has called this activity 'gynocritics' and sees it as combined with the 'androcentric criticism', illustrated by Ellmann and Millett's scholarly work, which deconstructs and reanalyses the presentation of women in the male literary tradition.

It is with the self-conscious development of androcentric and gynocentric criticism in feminist literary studies that the relevance to the social psychologist emerges. These activities immediately question the nature of sexual production and difference. Feminist literary critics cannot avoid deciding on the status, for instance, of the woman writer and reader, and the basis for the 'experience' or 'essential nature' she draws upon to produce or decode fiction. Different kinds of response have prevailed, but in some cases it seems clear that, as in social psychology, in deconstructing images of women, another image has often been privileged and left unexamined.

Gardiner (1981), for example, has claimed that the female psyche and social identity lead naturally to the choice of specific forms of literature (auto-biographical, fluid, escaping traditional narrative genres). We almost seem to be back again to 'oceanic' femininity, formless and tidal, but strangely at the same time personal and intimate. Other critics, (e.g. Burr-Evans, 1972) have asserted that women readers can learn unproblematically from women authors. Self-knowledge or 'the real experience of being a woman' follows from reading as though modern female authors were simply a more sophisticated version of the agony aunt.

Like Bem, these critics assume a common experience and essentially different psyche which separates women from men. It is on this basis that a female literary tradition has frequently been constructed. In the short term this has proved, as in psychology, to be no bad thing. In counterposing the dominance of male experience as the arbiter of taste with a feminine tradition, these critics reveal the contingency of male comment. What seemed a natural and obvious relation to the world, when contrasted with a different emphasis, can be seen as self-interested and exclusive. However, like the psychologist, the literary critic is still left with the problem of explicating the status of this feminine experience, confirmed or otherwise by texts, and with the suspicion that a woman-centred approach may ultimately fail to identify the reasons for the potency of textual images.

Culler puts this dilemma succinctly: 'Feminist readings,' he writes, 'are not

159

WETHERELL

produced by recording what happens in the mental life of the female reader as she encounters the words of *The Mayor of Casterbridge'* (1983, p. 49). That is, experience will not do as a ground for literary discovery, and, it is possible to add, if the reading is to be feminist or politically competent, just any woman's experience will not do either.

The difficulty with an appeal to experience, in particular a distinctively feminine experience, which female authors represent in their texts and which is recognized by the female reader as psychologically true, seems to be that the function of the text itself as a linguistic system or set of codes and patterns of signification becomes overlooked. Language is not a neutral reflection or representation of reality, it is *constitutive* of that typical experience, creating 'woman's nature', etc. As Furman (1980) puts it, in her argument for a genuinely textual feminism, the social and psychological significance of images cannot be sought in the personality behind the text which produces or reads it, but in the analysis of the language itself.

Literature becomes best viewed as a conglomeration of conventions for creating versions of reality. They are effective to the extent that the reader recognizes that reality as natural and unquestionable. The moment of recognizing 'a truth' about oneself in a novel (true because it appears to correspond with a current version of what one's experience was) should not, therefore, be the moment when analysis stops and knowledge is presumed to have been gained, but should become the starting point for another investigation of why that sense of recognition occurs in relation to the organization of the language itself, and the immediate questioning of the desirability of what has become 'obvious'.

It is in this sense that Coward (1980) has argued that properly feminist novels cannot be equated with just any woman-centred novel, or feminist criticism with the rescue of just any works based on women's experience. Not only, she argues, is there no common experience of womankind to refer to (otherwise how does one analyse the response of women of differing political orientations?) but many novels claiming to be based on archetypally female experience, (capable of 'changing women's lives' as their back covers maintain), have more in common with the narrative structures and expectations of that other class of 'woman-centred' novels, the popular romance.

A feminist criticism, according to its proponents, must thus be politically resonant, working effectively with a concept of ideology. Androcentric criticism must appreciate not only that women have been excluded and the images are unflattering, but also how entire structures of metaphor, unnoticed linguistic habits and genre demands have legitimated female marginality. Culler neatly draws this conclusion together by reproducing Showalter's argument. The feminist critic, Showalter notes, is concerned 'with the way in which the hypothesis of a female reader changes our apprehension of a given text, awakening us to the significance of sexual codes' (cited in Culler, 1983,

160

WETHERELL

p. 50). An integral activity, therefore, is investigating how the woman reader might have or could read 'as a man', endorsing and welcoming anti-female versions, and misogyny. Reading 'as a woman', becomes an acquired status, not a given one.

The position textual feminist literary criticism seems to have got to, then, is first, an emphasis on femininity/masculinity as shifting states, either in the encoding or decoding; and second, the view that these states are produced through language rather than being fundamentals which texts merely describe. This, incidentally, is what most distinguishes this approach from that taken by Bem and her contemporaries. Bem too sees femininity and masculinity as shifting, not necessarily linked to biological sex, but, as we saw, this displacement from physiology has not produced a social or political analysis of their function, only a retrenchment of individualism.

As a corollary to the two points above must go the recognition that human psychology and self-consciousness can no longer be seen as private, idiosyncratic realms, cut off from social relations. They are open to analysis through their material signs—the linguistic systems of which novels are simply one form. These systems subtly work to create and circulate a set of subject positions or identities which become the currency of human interaction and self-understanding.

As a logical extension of this frame of thought, recent feminist analyses have moved beyond the evaluation of 'great works' to the everyday: television programmes, advertisements and magazines (cf. Coward, 1984; Williamson, 1978; Winship, 1978). But how might the social psychology of gender become similarly feminist, and thus critical of, rather than subservient to, the social order? How might it become similarly sensitive to the organization and achievement of feminine and masculine subject positions in everyday speech, action and reaction?

THE SOCIO-PSYCHOLOGICAL STUDY OF 'FEMININITY' DISCOURSE

Although the argument cannot be developed extensively here, I want to suggest that through the concept of a 'lingustic repertoire' (cf. Potter and Mulkay, 1982; 1985; Potter and Litton, 1985) and the careful attention to discourse that this presumes, a progressive social psychology of gender might arise. This approach will necessarily assume that what is accessible for study, and thus its foundation, is the relatively autonomous ideological practices of a culture.

The function of an ideology is assumed here to be the elimination of the awareness of contradictions in material circumstances or perception of exploitation; mainly through the presentation of relationships (which seem important only for a particular kind of social arrangement) as natural or common sense. In this way sectional vested interests become general. In the case of gender, the analysis of ideology involves researching the construction of women as certain kinds of consumers, reproducers and agents/non-agents in

161

WETHERELL

the workforce (cf. Centre for Contemporary Cultural Studies, 1978): an outcome which requires the production of specifically 'female desires' (Coward,
1984) and 'appropriate' representations of ambition and place. This, then, is
the frame of reference for our study of gender.

What, however, is meant by a linguistic repertoire? Within a cultural system, as Coward (1984), Winship (1978) and others have demonstrated, it is
possible to identify meta-patterns or broad regularities in an ideology. For example, the pervading femininity/masculinity ideology has as a perennial feature the representation of male as norm and female as deviation, so that, to
take one case, 'progress' for women (and for society as a whole) is viewed unproblematically and as occurring when women are able to incorporate more
and more 'masculine' tasks and roles. There is much less impetus for men to
incorporate 'feminine' tasks. Spender's (1980) 'plus male, minus female' phenomenon would count as another type of organizing principle. Linguistic
repertoires are the substance which constitute these broad meta-themes. They
may engage femininity/masculinity directly through concerns with motherhood, child rearing, sexuality, breadwinning, etc., or through various different
subjects which may from time to time come to be specifically marked out
separately for women or for men (e.g. Coward's, 1984, analysis of food
pornography, ideal homes or 'our songs').

A repertoire consists of a set of recurrent and coherently related stylistic,
grammatical and lexical features, including seminal metaphors and tropes or
figures of speech. Just as one can point to the phonological, intonational and
accent patterns that make up the distinctive 'voice' attributed to a particular
social group, so one can also identify consistent linguistic patterns in terms of
content and mode of explanation. People, we have noted, are familiar with a
wide range of repertoires for a given topic and are quite capable of producing
discrepant and contradictory versions. Flexibility and variability of this kind
can be helpfully understood if the use of repertoires is related to functional
differences in the contexts in which they are produced and in interactional
goals. Repertoires can be characterized in terms of the guiding principle they
elucidate and the identification of stylistic regularities: what is consistently
omitted, for instance; the relation of subject to consequences; passive grammatical form, etc., define their boundaries.

A good illustration of the material discovered through this kind of discourse analysis can be found in a recent unpublished interview study conducted by Hilda Stiven (1985, in collaboration with myself and Jonathan Potter), which looked at female and male undergraduates' representations of children, careers, employment and achievement.

In general terms, first of all, Stiven found that whereas both women and
men students were what is usually described as 'career orientated', for women
this vision of their future could only be sustained for a limited time. Their
image of themselves in their 30s/40s, say, was comparatively blank and uncer-

162

WETHERELL

tain. There was some response, in other words, to the likely institutional barriers to come. However, unfortunately, the inadequate set of repertoires available to most respondents to make sense of their working lives would only admit individual solutions. For example, for some women happiness came from 'just being a housewife'; for others such domesticity was not a positive state of affairs but individual circumstances made it the only 'practical' outcome; alternatively, still other women might become, through their own efforts and talents, 'superwomen', combining career and family. They would provide a demonstration for men that it was possible to be woman and succeed as well. This demonstration was thought a necessary step before women as a whole could be taken seriously.

A great many of these women, that is, could only account for failure to achieve, or for the *status quo* for women, in terms of individual characteristics, or through instincts and a natural order which made domestic life inevitable and desirable. Their accounts, in fact, paralleled the traditional psychological analysis (Horner, 1972) which has it that women 'fear success' and this personality trait explains their low profile. In both cases explanations in terms of the structure and organization of society are obscured.

The particular repertoires which sustained this pattern fell into several categories. With regard to employment, for instance, a familiar repertoire was presented which has it that women are a problem for employers; or, adopting a phrase used by a number of respondents, they are 'a risk not worth taking'. The guiding principle here is that the employers' concerns are reasonable and the problem needs to be worked out by women within existing social structures. Through 'proving themselves equal' or 'being good at their job', women might persuade employers that they personally are a risk worth taking. The general impression gained from the interviews is that few of the women doubted their own ability to prove themselves as exceptions in this way; and perhaps as a result, if they fail to find an accommodating niche, they will be less likely to question the system within which they work, and more likely to attribute failure to contingent accidental factors.

163

This accounting system was generally combined with a repertoire concerning social change, which constructs change and progress as natural and inevitable processes. The history of women, therefore, could be represented as a story of gradual improvement up to the present day. This repertoire has several functions. First, it legitimates a positive view of society, as willing to solve problems and slowly combatting injustice; it rules out the necessity for 'drastic steps', particularly feminist movements which might 'go too far'; it renders personal intervention or action unnecessary; and it maintains the view that even though social change is potentially disruptive and negative, it can be contained, accommodated and diffused through slow progress.

The most notable internal contradictions revealed by Stiven's research concerned the tension between 'equal opportunities' and 'practical necessities' repertoires. Briefly, equal opportunities to work, freedom of choice and mutual decision making were claimed by most to be desirable ideals and a *sine qua non* of good relationships between husband and wife. Nonetheless, it was also understood that practical necessities and the 'nature of things' would result in the woman taking the primary responsibility for child rearing and that her career would be subordinate to her partner's. The equal opportunities repertoire satisfied one function, allowing for one kind of self-presentation expounding the ideal, while appeal to what usually must be the case, or to unfortunate realities, recognized and contributed to the actual *status quo*. It is not suggested that this contradiction is cynically proposed by, say, the male respondents. On the contrary it is a more general feature of the organization of discourse about female/male, both repertoires are sincerely held and one equally sincerely regretted. However, the contradiction is rarely noted by respondents. Although difficult to substantiate without a more extensive exposition, it was a case where inconsistency in response could very obviously be related to interactional goals and the context.

Stiven's findings could be understood as exemplars of what Tajfel (cf. 1981) has called *status quo*, social mobility, and social change belief structures. Williams and Giles (1978), for example, have argued that, as for other oppressed groups, distinct sub-groups of women can be identified according to their choice of strategy or perception of their social identity. Thus some women accept the *status quo* as legitimate; others seek to move as individuals into the more valued group, separating themselves as different from other women and adopting 'masculine' styles and norms. This may be typified by accepting training to become assertive, for example. Yet others attempt to change the very basis on which evaluation of superiority/inferiority is based through actively promoting social change. Parts of the repertoires described above (and others which emerged) could be understood in these terms.

However, one difficulty with this application, which immediately becomes apparent, arises from Williams and Giles' assumption that identity must be coherent and single so that their sub-groupings of women appear homogeneous and distinct. Stiven notes that many of her respondents showed mixtures and pieces of different repertoires, some of which appeared unambiguously *status quo* in orientation, others perhaps more reminiscent of a social mobility belief structure, and so on. Ultimately, they escaped easy categorization in terms of a global social identity.

This result highlights the very different model of the subject which would underlie a discourse approach to the study of gender. The unit of study is not the person but the linguistic repertoire or accounting system and its ideological implications. This emphasis allows us to make sense of diversity and contradictions in a manner prohibited by psychological analyses based on traits, biologies, or internalized sex role identities. We can respond to the variability and inconsistency evident in natural discourse which has in the past had to be

164

WETHERELL

repressed through a retreat to yes/no format questionnaires or strictly applied content analysis.

To the methodologist, this might seem a gain at the expense of the empirical certainty derived from neatly ordered response categories. However, it is normal practice with this type of discourse analysis (cf. Potter, 1985; Potter and Mulkay, 1982; Gilbert and Mulkay, 1984) to present the data or discourse on which any description of repertoires is based. This makes the process of interpretation manifest and allows for the reader to substantiate any disagreement. The method of construction is laid bare in a way not encountered in conventional presentation of results. It would, of course, also demonstrate the recurrent stylistic, grammatical and lexical features which distinguish repertoires and allow for their identification.

Finally, we should note that many of the repertoires identified through this kind of process will appear mundane and obvious. This is not surprising given that the aim is to examine the structure of everyday thought. But it is precisely at these points that society is reproduced and justified as people rationalize and make sense of their apparent place within it. By making the banal and commonsensical strange through analysis, it is possible to see in a new way something of how ideologies operate. This takes place at the level of individual understanding and explanation that social psychologists must consider their prime domain.

To summarize and conclude, the intention of this chapter has been to demonstrate why the socio-psychological study of gender is at an impasse. Social psychologists, it was suggested, have failed to capture the richness and subtlety of everyday conceptions of femininity and masculinity and, moreover, they have supported one kind of ideology in lieu of a critical examination. But, on a more positive note, it is clear that feminist literary critics have actively and productively confronted a similar dilemma about the definition and status of femininity. This debate clarifies the tools and emphases that a new social psychological approach might adopt and suggests that we can begin to learn from the upheavals and questionings in other disciplines. One thing is obvious: any new perspective such as the discourse analysis sketchily outlined in this section must be unavoidably political and thus in some way engaged with feminism.

165

WETHERELL

REFERENCES

Abel, E. (ed.) (1982). *Writing and Sexual Difference*. Brighton, Harvester Press.

Adlam, D., Henriques, J., Rose, N., Salfield, A., Venn, C. and Walkerdine, V. (1977). Psychology, ideology and the human subject. *Ideology and Consciousness 1,* 5-56.

Bakan, D. (1966). *The Duality of Human Existence*. Chicago, Rand McNally.

Bardwick, J. (1971). *Psychology of Women: A Study of Bio-Cultural Conflicts*. New York, Harper & Row.

Bem, S. (1974). The measurement of psychological androgyny. *Journal of Consulting and Clinical Psychology 42,* 155–162.

Bem, S. (1975). Sex-role adaptability: One consequence of psychological androgyny. *Journal of Personality and Social Psychology 31,* 634–643.

Bem, S. (1976). Probing the promise of androgyny. In: A. G. Kaplan and J. P. Bean (eds), *Beyond Sex-role Stereotypes.* Boston, Little, Brown and Co.

Bem, S. (1981). Gender schema theory: A cognitive account of sex-typing. *Psychological Review 66,* 354–364.

Bem, S. and Lenney, L. (1976). Sex-typing and the avoidance of cross-sex behaviour. *Journal of Personality and Social Psychology 33,* 48–54.

Bem, S., Martyna, W. and Watson, C. (1976). Sex-typing and androgyny: Further explorations of the expressive domain. *Journal of Personality and Social Psychology 34,* 1016–1023.

Burr-Evans, N. (1972). The value and peril for women of reading women writers. In: S. K. Cornillon (ed.), *Images of Women in Fiction: Feminist Perspectives.* Bowling Green, Ohio: Bowling Green University Press.

Carlson, R. (1971). Sex differences in ego functioning: Exploratory studies of agency and communion. *Journal of Consulting and Clinical Psychology 37,* 267–277.

Centre for Contemporary Cultural Studies. (1978). *Women Take Issue.* London, Hutchinson.

Clifton, A. K., McGrath, D. and Wick, B. (1976). Stereotypes of women: A single category? *Sex Roles 2,* 135–148.

Coward, R. (1980). Are women's novels feminist novels? *Feminist Review 5,* 53–65.

Coward, R. (1984). *Female Desire.* London, Paladin.

Coward, R. and Ellis, J. (1977). *Language and Materialism.* London, Routledge & Kegan Paul.

Culler, J. (1983). *On Deconstruction.* London, Routledge & Kegan Paul.

de Castillejo, I. (1973). *Knowing Woman: A Feminine Psychology.* London, Hodder and Stoughton.

Eichler, M. (1980). *The Double Standard.* New York, St. Martins Press.

Ellmann, M. (1979). *Thinking About Women.* London, Virago.

Furman, N. (1980). Textual feminism. In: S. McConnell-Ginet, R. Borker and N. Furman (eds), *Woman and Language in Literature and Society.* New York, Praeger.

Gardiner, J. K. (1982). On female identity and writing by women. In: E. Abel (ed.), *Writing and Sexual Difference.* Brighton, Harvester Press.

Gilbert, N. and Mulkay, M. (1984). *Opening Pandora's Box: A Sociological Analysis of Scientists' Discourse.* Cambridge, Cambridge University Press.

Heath, S. (1982). *The Sexual Fix.* London, MacMillan.

Henriques, J., Hollway, W., Urwin, C., Venn, C. and Walkerdine, V. (1984). *Changing The Subject.* London and New York, Methuen.

Horner, M. (1972). Toward an understanding of achievement-related conflicts in women. *Journal of Social Issues 28,* 157–176.

Johnson, R. A. (1976). *She: Understanding Feminine Psychology.* New York, Harper & Row.

Johnston, E. (1985). *The feminist challenge to psychology: sex-role stereotyping.* Unpublished Manuscript, University of St Andrews, Scotland, UK.

Millett, K. (1969). *Sexual Politics*. London; Rupert Hart-Davis.

Parsons, T. and Bales, R. (eds) (1955). *Family, Socialisation and Interaction Process*. Glencoe, Illinois, Free Press.

Potter, J. (1985). Testability, flexibility: Kuhnian values in scientists' discourse concerning theory choice. *Philosophy of the Social Sciences 14*, 303-330.

Potter, J. and Litton, I. (1985). Some problems underlying the theory of social representations. *British Journal of Social Psychology 24*, 81-90.

Potter, J. and Mulkay, M. (1982). Making theory useful: Utility accounting in social psychologists' discourse. *Fundamenta Scientiae 3*, 259-278.

Potter, J. and Mulkay, M. (1985). Scientists' interview talk. In: M. Brenner, J. Brown and D. Canter (eds), *The Research Interview: Uses and Approaches*. London, Academic Press.

Potter, J., Stringer, P. and Wetherell, M. (1984). *Social Texts and Context*. London, Routledge & Kegan Paul.

Showalter, E. (1982). Feminist criticism in the wilderness. In: E. Abel (ed.), *Writing and Sexual Difference*. Brighton, Harvester Press.

Smith, P. (1985). *Language, The Sexes and Society*. Oxford, Blackwell.

Spender, D. (1980). *Man-Made Language*. London, Routledge & Kegan Paul.

Stiven, H., Wetherell, M. and Potter, J. (1985). *Women in employment: an analysis of social representations*. Unpublished Manuscript, University of St. Andrews, Scotland, UK.

Tajfel, H. (1981). *Human Groups and Social Categories*. Cambridge, Cambridge University Press.

Williams, J. and Giles, H. (1978). The changing status of women in society: An intergroup perspective. In: H. Tajfel (ed.), *Differentiation Between Social Groups*. London, Academic Press.

Williamson, J. (1978). *Decoding Advertisements*. London, Boyars.

Winship, J. (1978). A woman's world: 'Woman'—an ideology of femininity. In: Centre for Contemporary Cultural Studies, *Women Take Issue*. London, Hutchinson.

PART III

CHALLENGING DIFFERENCES
Cultural Constraints and Narratives of Lives

FEMININITY AS PERFORMANCE

Valerie Walkerdine

chapter 8

INTRODUCTION

As girls at school, as women at work, we are used to performing. We are used, too, to dramaturgical metaphors which tell us that life is a performance in which we do nothing but act out a series of roles,[1] or indeed that these roles can be peeled away like layers of an onion to reveal a repressed core, a true self, which has been inhibited, clouded by the layers of social conditioning which obscure it.[2] Such views form much of the common sense of ideas about gender socialization in relation to education. Girls are conditioned into passivity, the story often goes; this is why they do badly at school: implicitly, femininity is seen as a series of roles, often imposed by agents of socialization, of whom the worst offenders are taken to be women: mothers and female teachers. But I want to tell a different story—one of female success, one which criticizes the idea that socialization works to render girls and women wimpish, feminine and passive.

Let me begin with an example, one which can be multiplied many times over. A woman teacher, one of my students, receives a well-deserved Distinction for her Master's degree. She received more or less straight As for all her work, but still she cannot believe that the Distinction belongs to her; it is as though the person with her name exists somewhere else, outside her body: this powerful person whom she cannot recognize as herself. Instead, she feels that she is hopeless, consistently panics about her performance and appears to have little confidence in herself. She can, however, express her views clearly and forcefully and the external examiner in her *viva* thanked her for the tutorial! I am sure this story has resonances for many women. Indeed, I am sure I related this story because I too have been constantly aware that the Valerie Walkerdine whom people speak well of feels as though it belongs to someone else, someone whom I do not recognize as me.

How is it that for many women, the powerful part of themselves has been so split off as to feel that it belongs to someone else? Here is no simple passive wimp femininity but a power which is desired, striven after, yet almost too dangerous to be acknowledged as belonging to the woman herself.

In this essay I shall explore this phenomenon, using work from both post-structuralism and psychoanalysis and data from my research on gender and schooling (Walkerdine *et al.*, 1989) to illustrate my arguments.

PERFORMANCE IN SCHOOL

There is a widespread myth that girls and women perform poorly in school. In the Girls and Mathematics Unit we investigated this issue in relation to mathematics in research, spanning several years and with children aged four to fifteen (Walkerdine *et al*, 1989). The first way in which I want to deal with the issue of performance is to challenge the idea that femininity equals poor performance and to concentrate rather on the ways in which femininity is read. What I am concerned to demonstrate is the discursive production of femininity as antithetical to masculine rationality to such an extent that femininity is *equated* with poor performance, even when the girl or woman in question is performing well. In other words, I am talking not about some essential qualities of femininity, but about the way in which femininity is read as a constellation of signs which mark it off as antithetical to 'proper' performance to an incredible degree. When we first became aware of this, Rosie Walden and I called it 'the just or only phenomenon' (Walden and Walkerdine, 1982). By this, we meant that whenever a positive remark was made about girls' performance in mathematics, particularly the strong sense that girls performed well in school up until the transfer at eleven, a remark would be brought in which suggested that the performance was to be accounted for by 'something which amounted to nothing'. In other words, no matter how well girls were said to perform, their performance was always downgraded or dismissed in one way or another. These pejorative remarks usually related to the idea that girls' performance was based on hard work and rule-following rather than brains or brilliance (in other words, what was supposed to underlie real mathematical performance).[3] This reading of girls' performance was consistent across schools and the age-range. In the younger age-groups it was common for teachers to talk about boys as having 'potential', a term often used to explain their poor performance. Throughout the sample of thirty-nine classrooms, not one teacher mentioned 'potential' within a girl. Quite the contrary, if a girl were performing poorly there was no way she could be considered good—indeed, if she were performing well it was almost impossible for her to escape pejorative evaluations, while boys, it seemed, no matter how poorly they performed, were thought to have hidden qualities:

> Very, very hard worker. Not a particularly bright girl . . . her hard work gets her to her standards.

This typical example of a comment about a girl can be compared with the following comment about a boy, of the kind that was never made about girls:

> . . can just about write his own name . . . not because he's not clever, because he's not capable, but because he can't sit still, he's got no concentration . . . very disruptive . . . but quite bright.

Indeed, it was as though boys did indeed in fantasy possess the 'phallus'[4] while girls represented a fictional 'lack' or absence. For whatever was said, again and again, the presence of certain attributes, like good performance, was read as an indication of a lack of something much more fundamental even when, as in the case of many boys, they did not perform well academically (see the quote above).

173

This led me to point out that in engaging with issues concerning the 'truth about women' it is necessary to avoid being caught in an empiricist trap in which we are led to attempt to prove the mathematical equivalence of girls (Walkerdine et al., 1989). For here we are not presented with something as straightforward as 'the evidence of our own eyes'. Here, girls are doing well yet they are said, in one way or another, 'not to have what it takes', while many boys, whose performance is poor, are said to possess something even when it is not visible in their performance. In order to examine and to understand such a situation I believe that we have to move away from a simple empiricism to a position in which we understand fact, fiction and fantasy as interrelated. It is to post-structuralism that I turn for an account which will allow us to examine how it comes about that gender difference is produced in fictional ways which have power in that they are part of the truth-effects of the regulation of children in classrooms. They form a basis of the 'truth about women', in this case the truth that women do not have rational powers of the

WALKERDINE

mind. Such a truth, I shall go on to argue, has to be desperately reasserted for fear that it is not true; only the paranoia of the powerful keeps it in circulation.

RATIONAL POWERS OF THE MIND

Counting girls' performance as evidence is not distinct from the issue of which it is taken to be evidence of. We have not only to debate about the data but also to engage with why this decision is made at all, what it means, and what its effects are in terms of practical consequences for girls' education. Classically (within philosophy, for example), the truth of such statements has been the subject of epistemological critiques. But the latter treat truth as though it were a timeless matter, separating the conditions of the production of truth from truth itself. The question that I want to pose is not 'Are the arguments true?' but 'How is this truth constituted, how is it possible, and what effects does it have?' Such questions, derived from the methodology of genealogy utilized by Foucault, can help us begin to take apart this truth about girls. Only if we understand its historical production and its effectivity can we begin to go beyond it. We shall argue that we can chart the historical antecedents of the position that females do not possess a capacity for reason or have 'mathematical minds', and so document how and why the arguments in support of that position have such a force now, and how we might challenge them.

Ideas about reason and reasoning cannot be understood historically outside of considerations about gender, and the development of science from the seventeenth century was intimately connected to the control of nature by man.[5] Discussions about female failure have focused on a minority of girls.[6] Of course, it is not surprising that later science 'discovered' the 'female intellect'.[7] Thus women, taken also to possess the capacity to reason, were allowed to enter the competition—if they had *enough* ability. But this means that the terms of the debate are never changed; women must still prove themselves equal to men. I have tried to show why we should not unquestioningly accept these terms but should question their very foundation. We are not duty-bound to accept existing truth conditions. We would argue that showing the truth about girls to be a production in which there are no *simple* matters of fact is a central and strategic part of our struggle.

Specific concepts within the development of education, which I have outlined elsewhere[8]—'the child' (gender unspecified) is taken to develop with a 'facilitating environment'. The two terms form a couple; a *child* developing in an *environment*. Further analysis suggests that the mother and the teacher both become part of the environment. They are defined by the very qualities that are opposite to those of 'the child', who is active, inquiring and whose activity leads to 'real understanding'. The teacher and the mother, by contrast, are not necessary to instruct but to watch, observe, monitor and facilitate devel-

174

WALKERDINE

opment. Teacher and mother are defined as 'passive' in relation to the child's 'active'. They are nurturant, facilitating, sensitive and supportive, and they know when to intervene but not to interfere.

This opposition is necessary to support the possibility of the illusion of autonomy and control upon which the child-centred pedagogy is founded.[9] In this sense, then, the 'capacity for nurturance' grounded in a naturalized femininity, the object of the scientific gaze, becomes the basis for woman's fitness for the facilitation of knowing and the reproduction of the knower, which is the support for, yet the opposite of, the production of knowledge. The production of knowledge is thereby separated from its reproduction and split along a sexual division which renders production and reproduction the natural capacities of the respective sexes.

The central concepts in the child-centred pedagogy and early mathematics education may themselves be regarded as signifiers—that is, aspects of discourse. That discourse claims to tell the truth about the universal properties of 'the child' which 'has concepts'. In this view, the attempts within psychology and mathematics, for example, may be seen as aspects of the attempt to construct a rationally ordered and controllable universe. We have argued that such an attempt is deeply bound up with the modern form of bourgeois government and the emergence of the modern state. It is also deeply involved with the attempt to describe and therefore regulate 'woman', 'the child', 'the working class', 'blacks' and 'the mad'.

The purpose of examining the conceptualizations which form the bedrock of modern practices is to draw out the key terms to the regime of truth which is constituted in and by the practices. My claim is that the discursive practices themselves—in producing the terms of the pedagogy, and therefore the parameters of practice—produce what it means to be a subject, to be subjected, within these practices. It can be stated that the terms in the discourse, such as *experience, discovery, stage*, etc., are signifiers which take their meaning from their position and function within the discourse itself: they enter as a relation. But this does not mean that there is a simple relation of representation between the material and the discursive. The discourse itself is a point of production and creation. When we say, then, that experience is created as a sign within the practice, or the *child* is produced as a subject, what we are talking about is the production of signs. If language does not represent reality, but rather the regulation of a practice itself produces a particular constellation and organization of the material and discursive practices, then it can be argued that something is produced. It is in this sense that Foucault's power/knowledge couple can be applied here.

By means of an apparatus of classification and a grading of responses 'the child' becomes a creation, and yet at the same time provides room for a reading of pathology. There are no behaviours which exist outside the practices for producing them, not at any rate in this particular sequence constellation

175

WALKERDINE

and with these particular effects. The discursive practice becomes a complex sign system in which signs are produced and read and have truth-effects: the truth of children is produced in classrooms. 'The child' is not coterminous with actual children, just as Cowie (1978) argued that the signifier 'woman' is not coterminous with actual women, but central to the argument is the specification of that relation that is between the signifier and signified. If children become subjects through their insertion into a complex network of practices, there are no children who stand outside their orbit. I use the concept of positioning[10] to examine further what happens when such readings are produced and how children become *normal* and *pathological*, fast and slow, rote-learning and real understanding, and so forth. In other words, the practices provide systems of signs which are at once systems of classification, regulation and normalization. These produce systematic differences which are then used as classifications of children in the class. It is the meaning of *difference* which is a central feature in the production of any sign system in terms of the relations with other signs within the discourse. Similarity, that is, those signs which are linked within the discourse also pile or heap together to provide evidence of a related classification. Thus *activity, doing, experience, readiness* and so forth operate in relations of similarity, while *rote-learning* and *real understanding* are signs of contrastive opposition, of difference. I will attempt to demonstrate that these signs are produced and that often one sign may be taken as an indicator of the presence of another (similarity). Thus, for example, *activity* heralds a signal system, a complex discursive practice, whose terms and limits may be specified. Within this, then, children become embodiments of 'the child', precisely because that is how the practice is set up: they are normal or pathological, and so forth. Their behaviour, therefore, is an aspect of a position, a multifaceted subjectivity, such that 'the child' describes only their insertion into this, as one of many practices. But the behaviours do not precede the practice precisely because their specificity is produced in these practices. This is why discourses of developmental psychology themselves can be understood not simply as providing a distortion of a real object, but may be read as evidence of *real understanding*, while passivity be read as coterminous with, or similar to, *rote-learning, rule-following.*

These produce the practices in which 'the child' becomes a sign to be read and a normal is differentiated from a pathological child. 'The child' develops through active manipulation of 'objects' in an 'environment'. Here all the practices become objects existing in a biologized environment. The Plowden Report is full of illustrations, all of which describe the school, the classroom, as an 'environment'. This sets up another aspect of the readings which are to be made. 'The child' is a unique individual, developing at 'his' own pace in an environment. The classroom therefore becomes the site of such development. However many children there are in a classroom, each is an individual—there is no sense of 'a class'. Indeed, it will be remembered that 'the class' forms a signifier in contrastive opposition to 'the child'. In this way, examining both the texts and practices themselves, it is possible to produce a reading of the pedagogy pre-existing object, 'the real child' which they fail to represent or describe adequately. If they are points of production, they have positive and not simply negative effects. In this sense they are our 'raw material'; the 'real' of a child is not something which can be known outside those practices in which its subjectivity is constituted. The signified forms a sign only out of fusion with the signifier. The signifier exists as a relation within a discourse. The material can be known as a relation only within a discursive practice. To say, therefore, that 'the child' is a signifier means that it must be united with a signified. Particular children therefore both become children—but also present behaviours to be read—which may be normal or pathological.

The question remains, of course, what precisely is it that produces these current truths? I have argued that current claims themselves rest upon a constant 'will to truth'[11] which, investing certainty in 'man', constantly seeks to find its Other and opposite in 'woman'. This truth is constantly reproven within classrooms in which the very apparatuses differentiate between success and its posited causes. This has profound material effects upon the life chances of girls.

It is suggested above that within current school mathematics practices, certain fantasies, fears and desires invest 'man' with omnipotent control of a calculable universe, which at the same time covers a desperate fear of and desire for the Other, 'woman'. 'Woman' becomes the repository of all the dangers displaced from the child, itself 'father' to the man. As I have argued, the necessity to prove the mathematical inferiority of girls is motivated not by a certainty but by a terror of loss. In all these respects, I have wanted to suggest a story in which these very fantasies, fears, desires become the forces that produce the actual effectivity of the construction of fact, of current discursive practices in which these fantasies are played out and in actual positions in such practices which, since they can be proved to exist, literally have power over the lives of girls and boys, as in Foucault's power/knowledge couple.

In this case, we could take the signifiers 'child', 'teacher' and 'girl', or the dichotomies 'active/passive', 'rote-learning/real understanding' as examples. We can ask how the contradictory positions created within these practices are lived, and how these effect the production of subjectivity—for example fears, desires, and fantasies.

The first and most important thing to state is that there are no unitary categories 'boys' and 'girls'. If actual boys and girls are created at the intersection of multiple positioning, they are inscribed as masculine and feminine. It follows, therefore, that girls can display 'real understanding' or boys 'nurturance'. What matters is the effects of these positions.

At first sight, it seems curious that such qualities could be displayed inside a pedagogy designed not only specifically to produce their opposite but also to

177

avoid their appearance at all costs. It is important that in this respect the pathologization of these qualities, linked to the fear of totalitarianism and authoritarianism, has related to certain developments in post-Freudian psychoanalysis, notably the work of Klein. However, much as their appearance is dreaded, it is also needed. Such ascriptions are frequently correlated with 'helpfulness', in which helpful children become an important part of the maintenance of calm, order and the smooth regulation of the classroom. Our research demonstrated that it is common for female teachers to fear such qualities as much as they want them.

In the classroom discourse itself, there appears to be an overt message concerning activity, exploration, openness, and so forth, derived from the child-centred pedagogy. However, our work in the primary classrooms suggests that the discourse of good behaviour, neatness and rule-following exists *covertly* alongside overt messages. It would have to be covert because it is the exact opposite of what is supposed to take place. Moreover, all those aspects—good behaviour, neatness and rule-following—are taken to be harmful to psychological and moral development. Thus they act as a fear- and guilt-inducing opposite. It is not surprising that teachers cannot afford to acknowledge the presence of such qualities in the classroom—if they do, they pathologize their appearance in girls, while failing to recognize that they are demanding the very qualities they simultaneously disparage. This possibility allows us to explore how girls come to desire in themselves qualities that appear the opposite from those of 'the child' that the pedagogy is set up to produce. Clearly, further investigations would have to engage with the classroom production of such contradictions, examining both the overt pedagogy and its covert shadow.

It is common in some psychoanalytic discourses, for example, to counterpose 'fantasy' to 'reality', yet it is this division that appears most questionable. After all, if it is true that some girls respond to the convert regulation of the classroom, we cannot say that such behaviour is pathological with respect to the real. It is precisely that certain aspects of the regulation of the practices are themselves suppressed. Simultaneously, the 'reality' of the child-centered pedagogy seems to be the object of an elaborate fantasy. It appears that here in the practices there circulates a vast and complex network of meanings, in which the play of desire, of teachers for children, of children for each other, envy, jealousy, rivalry, and so forth are continually created and re-created. It is not necessary to counterpose fantasy to reality, but to demonstrate how fantasies themselves are lived, played out and worked through in their inscriptions in the veridicality of discourses and practices.

I have begun to explore what this might mean elsewhere[12] but here we can take the analysis a little further, using the distinctions work and play, *rote-learning/rule-following* and *real understanding*. Work forms a relation in the 'old discourse'. In the new, children learn through doing, activity and play. Work forms an opposition of this. Work is bad because it relates to sitting in rows, regurgitating 'facts to be stored', not 'concepts to be acquired' through active exploration of the environment. Work, then, forms a metaphoric relation with rote-learning and rule-following. Each describes a practice, a mode of learning which is opposite and antithetical to the 'joy of discovery'. Play is fun. There are also other aspects of work, which could be further elaborated—it leads to resistance. Children regulated in this way do not become self-regulating. But work is also a category to be outlawed by a system of education set up in opposition to child labour. It constitutes a category which frees 'the child' to be something distinct, playful, not an adult, outside the field of productive labour, innocent, natural. Related therefore is a series of values, fantasies, fears, desires which are incorporated into the discursive practices. It follows that *work*, as constituted as an opposite of play, can be recognized as a difference, as everything which does not signify play. It can also be recognized as a danger-point, a point to be avoided. It is pathologized. It is learning by the wrong means; it is not 'natural' to 'the child'. If any child is observed 'doing work', this is likely to be understood as a problem. Hence the distinction between 'rote-learning' and 'real understanding' discussed earlier. First, what happens when a child produces high attainment as well as producing behaviour to be read as *work*? If play is the discourse of the school, through what discourse do children read their performance? If 'real understanding' is coterminous with the fantasy of possessing total power and control, how is it distinguished and what is the relation of this to 'getting the right answer', 'being certain', etc.? How does *possession of real understanding* provide fantasy, a chimera which has to be constantly and continually proved to exist out of a terror that lurking around every corner is its Other, rote-learning, work? Why is there such pressure, remorseless and unrelenting, to 'prove' that real understanding causes real attainment, and moreover that certain children have 'it' and that others just as surely do not, despite high attainment? What is invested?

One of the features of the apparatuses and technologies of the social, the modern production of truth through science, is that proof and practices for the production of evidence are central to the production of a truth; certainty of 'real understanding' is ceaselessly proved in practices even though the evidence is often ambiguous. Here we want not so much to dwell on the evidence itself as to question the motivation to provide proof, in particular of the opposition of *work* and play, rote and real.

Now, if the power of control over the universe invested in mathematical discourse is a fantasy, I am not setting out to demonstrate the *real* of the proof that girls *really* can do maths or boys actually do not have real understanding. Rather, we are interested in how those categories are produced as signs and how they 'catch up' the subjects, position them and, in positioning, create a truth. For is not girls' bid for 'understanding' the greatest threat of all to a uni-

versal power or a truth that is invested in a fantasy of control of 'women'?
Teachers will often go to great lengths to demonstrate that boys have real understanding. By the metaphoric chain created, activity is frequently read as a
sign of understanding. Understanding, then, is evidenced by the presence of
some attributes and the absence of others. It is activity—playing, utilization of
objects (Lego, for example) rule-breaking (rather than following)—and so
this can encompass naughtiness to the point of displays of hostility and conflict towards the teacher. All these and more are taken to be evidence. Conversely, good behaviour in girls, working hard, helpfulness, neat and careful
work, are all read as danger signs of a lack. The counter-evidence—hard work
in boys and understanding in girls—is also produced as evidence, but when it
is, other positions come into play (see Walkerdine, 1984). Evidence of real understanding, therefore, depends first upon a set of practices in which real understanding is the goal of an explicit framework of the 'activities' set up, as in
all the examples given here. Secondly, it is possible to read the correct accomplishment as the result of understanding, and failure produced through a lack
of requisite experience, readiness, concepts. Thirdly, the likelihood to favour
one explanation of success over another depends upon other characteristics
which define a real learner. However, boys frequently do not achieve terribly
well, yet evidence of failure is itself produced as evidence in support of understanding.

In these pedagogic practices, facilitating and nurturant Others (teachers,
mothers) are necessary to the facilitation of a 'natural' sequence of development in 'the child'. These contradictions are lived out by girls in pedagogic
practices. The very contradictions in the practice set girls up to achieve the
very thing which is simultaneously desired and feared—passivity. It is feared
in 'children', yet it is the very quality desired in nurturant care-givers, women
as mothers and teachers.

SPLITTING THE DIFFERENCE

If women being powerful within mathematical and pedagogic practices is so
threatening, it is hardly surprising that many women are fearful of recognizing power within themselves. No wonder the woman I mentioned in the Introduction has such difficulty in establishing that the person with a Distinction is actually herself. What she lives as a psychic problem is a profoundly social one, but a social one in which psychic processes are at the heart of the
matter. Women's success appears to present such a threat to masculine rationality, and to the bourgeois and patriarchal power which it underpins, that it
is very dangerous for women to admit their own power. How is that deep
contradiction lived for such women? Is femininity a performance, a defence
against the frightening possibility of stepping over the gender divide?

In this section of the paper I shall explore this issue, first with reference to
the work of Wendy Hollway (1982, 1989), who has discussed splitting in

couple relations, and the work of women psychoanalysts who have attempted to address this point, particularly Joan Riviere's (1985) work on womanliness as masquerade.

Wendy Hollway analyses adult heterosexual couple relations in terms of the way in which rationality and emotionality are split between partners, with the woman being taken to 'hold' the emotionality for the couple, a quality which the man also projects into her so that she can be the emotional one, meaning that as long as it is located in her, he does not have to come to terms with his own emotional vulnerability. Similarly, the man can hold rationality for the couple. Hollway analyses in great detail how this is achieved by the couple. The concept of splitting which she uses is derived from Kleinian psychoanalysis.[13] In Klein the split-off part of (in this case) 'man' is projected into and held by 'woman'; similarly rationality in woman cannot easily be accommodated and therefore has to be experienced as though it belonged to someone else. To put the argument in this way is completely different from the essentialist view of femininity in which certain characteristics simply do not belong to women, or a socialization account which treats the social as though it were added on to the psychic rather than seeing them as produced together.[14] Lacan[15] argued that 'woman' exists only as a symptom of male fantasy. What he meant was that the fantasies created under patriarchy (or the Law of the Father or Symbolic Order, as he calls it) create as their object not women as they really are but fantasies of what men both desire and fear in the Other. Women, then, become the repositories of such fantasies, and the effect for the psychic development of women themselves is extremely damaging and complex. Many psychoanalysts have attempted to engage with the problem presented by femininity under patriarchy. Freud tended to naturalize women's procreative function as a normal solution to the problem posed by the gendered splitting of rationality and emotionality. He did not investigate in great depth the elaborate fantasies which uphold the patriarchal and bourgeois order, and which I am suggesting are projected on to women. It is not surprising, then, that many women analysts who discovered the terrible confusions in their women patients around their power tended to essentialize them. The analysis I am suggesting here makes the essentializing tendency impossible. It is also true that there is no easy division between fantasy and an observable reality, since the social contains the elaborate fictions and fantasies of which I have written.

If masculinity and femininity may both be seen as defences against the qualities held by the Other, then there can be no natural division of the sexes, but a complex order through which difference is held in play. Joan Riviere (1985) presents an interesting analysis of femininity in relation to cases of women patients. In her paper "Womanliness as Masquerade' she gives the example of a woman academic who, after giving an academic paper, has to flirt with men, often picking a 'fatherly' type as object of her flirtation. Riviere suggests that such flirtation provides her with reassurance that she is, after all, a woman. It acts as a masquerade, an elaborate defence against her fear that her femininity is a mere charade. If the male gaze, in Lacan's terms, constructs the object of the gaze as a masquerade, what lies beneath the mask? Lacan would have us believe that there is nothing, or a confusion. However, we could equally well ask what it is that the fantasy of the phallus holds up. In the academic scenario it appears that the fantasy of femininity is kept in place by the discursive truths which define and regulate the evaluation of women's performance. The struggle both to perform academically and to perform as feminine must seem at times almost impossible. No wonder some of us split them apart in various ways, or have different conscious and unconscious methods for dealing with the unbearable contradiction.

To maintain this requires a tremendous amount of social and psychic labour. Luce Irigaray (1985) points clearly to these phallic fantasies and suggests that there is another libidinal organization for women that cannot be spoken in the present Symbolic Order. However, where Lacan presents women as a lack, Irigaray presents her as having Other desires screaming to be spoken. The feminine performance in this view is a defence not only against masculinity, but also against a powerful and active sexuality quite unlike that defined under patriarchy, although of course precisely that which is pathologized as bad or mad. Irigaray celebraces the plurality of woman as the plurality of sexual pleasure which does not have a goal of a single orgasm nor a single site of pleasure. Bronwyn Davies (1988) has explored women's sexual fantasies and also suggests that those fantasies are unlike the ones to which women are subjected. I am arguing, therefore, that to become the object of those fantasies—the ones which render women as the object of the male gaze—requires a tremendous amount of work to cover over not an essential femininity but a different set of desires and organization of pleasures (cf. Foucault) from those which can either clearly be articulated at the moment or are sanctioned in the practices in which femininity circulates as sign.

PEDAGOGIC STRATEGIES

If girls' and women's power is a site of struggle, constantly threatening the tenuous grasp of male academic superiority, then any engagement with these issues in practice cannot rest upon a rationalistic base of choice or equal opportunities. Not only must the fiction of the gendered splitting be taken apart, but the psychic struggle engaged in by girls and women to live out the impossibly contradictory positions accorded to us must be addressed, as must the paranoias of the powerful that understand women's success as a (conscious or unconscious) threat to their position of superiority, shaky as it is. This requires a strategy which engages with the educational politics of subjectivity, a politics which refuses to split the psychic from the social and attempts to understand the complexity of defence and resistance, and to find ways of dealing with them for teachers and students alike. Equal opportunities and models based on choice simply cannot engage with the complexity of the issues I have tried to spell out in this essay. Indeed, the danger is that when such strategies fail, as they do, educators will resort to existentialistic arguments, as they do, to explain, for example, the failure of girls to take 'non-traditional' subjects. Such essentialism is completely unwarranted, but working on fiction, fantasy and contradiction is to work in dangerous and threatening territory. It is that territory that we have to move into if we are to proceed in the struggle which recognizes that women, after all, can be very powerful indeed.

NOTES

1. See, for example, Hartnett et al. (1979).

2. Social conditioning is a term which is commonly used, and although it may once have referred to social learning theory, I think its roots in behaviourism are often forgotten.

3. This idea is discussed more fully in Walkerdine (1988) and Walkerdine et al. (1989).

4. This is a term used by Lacan (1977) to indicate not the real penis but the idea of male and patriarchal power invested in the possession of a penis. Possession of the phallus is both a metaphor and a fantasy.

5. In Walkerdine et al. we discuss at greater length the way in which physiological evidence is used to support the contention that educating girls would be physiologically dangerous by, in the end, affecting their capacity and desire to have children.

6. Of course, not all girls fail. (The discussions about failure concentrate on the failure of girls and women to enter higher-level careers requiring maths and to obtain higher-level passes in the subject, but the issue is generalized so that explanations for this are sought with respect to all girls; see Walkerdine et al.)

7. Higher education began to be open to women when the caring professions began to be based on the idea of the amplification of the capacities for maternal nurturance (see Walkerdine et al.)

8. Walkerdine (1984).

9. Walkerdine and Lucey (1989).

10. See Walkerdine et al. for a further discussion.

11. Cf. Foucault (1979).

12. Walkerdine et al.

13. See for example, Mitchell (1986).

14. Henriques et al. (1984).

15. Lacan.

REFERENCES

Cowie, E. (1978) 'Woman as Sign'. *m/f*, no. 1.

Davies, B. (1988) 'Romantic Love and Female Sexuality'. Unpublished paper.

Department of Education and Science (1967) *Children and their Primary Schools* (The Plowden Report). London, HMSO.

183

WALKERDINE

Foucault, M. (1979) *Discipline and Punish*. Harmondsworth, Penguin.

Hartnett, U., Boden, G. and Fuller, M. (1979) *Sex Role Stereotyping*. London, Tavistock.

Henriques, J., Hollway, W., Urwin, C., Venn, C. and Walkerdine, V. (1984) *Changing the Subject*. London, Methuen.

Hollway, W. (1982) 'Identity and Gender Difference in Adult Social Relations'.
Unpublished PhD thesis, University of London.

Hollway, W. (1989) *Subjectivity and Method in Psychology: Gender, Meaning and Science*. London, Sage.

Irigaray, L. (1985). *This Sex Which is not One*. Ithaca, NY, Cornell University Press.

Lacan, J. (1977) *Ecrits: A Selection*. London Tavistock.

Mitchell, J. ed. (1986) *The Selected Melanie Klein*. Harmondsworth, Penguin.

Riviere, J. (1985) 'Womanliness as Masquerade', in V. Burgin, J. Donald and C. Kaplan, eds, *Formations of Fantasy*. London, Methuen.

Walden, R. and Walkerdine, V. (1982) *Girls and Mathematics: The Early Years*. London, Heinemann.

Walkerdine, V. (1984) 'Developmental Psychology and the Child-centred Pedagogy', in Henriques *et al. Changing the Subject*. London, Methuen.

Walkerdine, V. (1988) *The Mastery of Reason*. London, Routledge.

Walkerdine, V. and The Girls and Mathematics Unit (1989) *Counting Girls Out*. London, Virago.

Walkerdine, V. and Lucey, H. (1989) *Democracy in the Kitchen*. London, Virago.

CHILDREN AND GENDER
Constructions of Difference

Barrie Thorne

WHEN I FIRST began observing in elementary schools as an ethnographer with gender on my mind, events like the following drew me and my notetaking like a magnet:

> On the playground, a cluster of children played "girls-chase-the-boys" or "boys-chase-the-girls" (they used both names). Boys and girls were by definition on different sides. In the back-and-forth of chasing and being chased, they used gender terms ("I'm gonna get that girl"; "Let's go after those boys") rather than individual names for members of the other side. In a combined fourth-and-fifth-grade classroom the teacher introduced a math game organized as girls against boys; she would write addition and subtraction problems on the board, and a member of each team would race to be the first to write the correct answer. As

This paper has benefited from helpful comments by Jane Collier, Cheris Kramarae, Deborah L. Rode, Judith Stacey, Candace West, and exspecially Avril Thorne.

the teacher wrote two scorekeeping columns headed "Beastly Boys" and "Gossipy Girls," several boys yelled out, "Noisy girls! Gruesome girls!" while some of the girls laughed. As the game proceeded, the girls sat in a row on top of their desks; sometimes they moved collectively, pushing their hips or whispering, "Pass it on." The boys stood along the wall, several reclining against desks. When members of either group came back victorious from the front of the room, they would do the "giving five" hand-slapping ritual with their team members.

On such occasions—when gender divisions were highlighted and "the girls" and "the boys" were defined as separate, opposing groups—I felt I was at the heart of children's gender relations. But these moments are not the whole of social life in elementary schools; at other times boys and girls interacted in relaxed rather than bounded and antagonistic ways. At example from the same fourth-and-fifth-grade classroom:

A student teacher had listed various activities on the board and asked students to choose one and sign up for it. Three boys and two girls had chosen to tape record a radio play. The teacher told them they could rehearse in the back of the room. They moved from their desks, settled in chairs at a round table (seated girl-boy-girl-boy-boy), and took turns leaning into the microphone and reading from the script. Now and then they stopped to talk and argue as a group.

I had to press myself to record the details of this situation; it seemed less juicy, less ripe for gendered analysis than the chasing sequence, the math game, or a same-gender group. This disparity in my perception of its relevance led me to ponder our frameworks for thinking about children and gender. These frameworks, which emphasize oppositional dichotomies, neatly fit situations in which boys and girls are organized as separate, bounded groups, and they obscure more relaxed, mixed-gender encounters. What kinds of frameworks can more fully account for the complexity of children's gender relations?

Is it "in the nature" of children that we should gear up different questions for them than we do for adults? Feminist scholarship has mostly centered upon the lives and experiences of adults; it has either ignored children, seen them as objects of adult (primarily women's) labor, or confined discussion of them to questions of "socialization" and "development."[1] In the last two decades our frameworks for thinking about adults and gender have moved beyond unexamined dualisms toward greater complexity. But when we focus on children, we tend to think in more simplistic ways—perhaps one reason for the lingering power of dualisms.[2]

THE DUALISTIC MODEL OF SEX DIFFERENCES

Most of the research on children and gender involves a search either for individual or for group sex differences. Both approaches conceptualize gender in terms of dualisms.

186

THORNE

Studies in the "individual sex differences" tradition typically set out to explore possible statistical correlations between individual sex/gender (usually understood as an unproblematic male/female dichtomy) and a specific piece of behavior or measure of personality. The pieces that have been studied range widely, including such personality traits as self-esteem, intellectual aptitudes like verbal or spatial ability, such motivational structure as need for affiliation, and specific behavior, for example, the amount of time spent in rough-and-tumble play. Extensive research has studied whether parents and teachers interact (for example, touch or talk) differently with girls and boys. Sex difference studies specify and gauge behavior (for example, with tests of spatial ability or measures of time spent in rough-and-tumble play or talking with a teacher), aggregate across many individuals, and then look for statistically significant correlations by sex.[3]

The results of sex difference research are always a matter of statistical frequency, for sex/gender differences are never absolutely, dichotomous. But where statistically significant differences are found, the language of frequency quickly slides into a portrayal of dualism ("boys engage in more rough-and-tumble play than girls"; "girls have greater verbal ability than boys"; "boys receive more teacher attention"). Many writers have cautioned against translating statistical complexity into a discourse of "the pinks and the blues," the tellingly dichotomous title of a popular television documentary on sex differences among children.[4] They have noted other related pitfalls in the sex difference approach, such as a bias toward reporting difference rather than similarity and a failure to distinguish statistical significance from the size of an effect.

But dichotomous portrayals may be unavoidable when one's basic strategy is to compare males and females. Individual sex categories[5]—female/male, woman/man, girl/boy—divide the population in half and are marked and sustained by daily social practices of gender display and attribution.[6] Sex difference research treats these categories as relatively unproblematic and continues binary framing with distinctions like similarity versus difference. Recent proposals to use phrases like "sex similarities and differences" or "sex-related differences," provide at best awkward and ambiguous tools for grasping the complexities of gender.

Although the situation is gradually beginning to change, sociologists and anthropologists have largely ceded the study of children to psychologists, who in turn have relegated the study of children to specialists in child development. The social science literature on children and gender reflects this division of labor. The focus has been more on individuals than on social relations, and the favored methods—laboratory experiments, observations organized around preset categories—strip human conduct from the contexts in which it is given meaning.

THORNE

187

GROUP DIFFERENCES

When psychologists, sociologists, and anthropologists of gender have studied the social relations of children, they have primarily relied on a model of group differences that is founded on the prevalence of gender separation in children's friendships and daily encounters. Every observational study of children's interactions in preschools, elementary schools, and junior high schools in the United States has found a high degree of gender separation in seating choices and in the groups children form.[7] In a study of sixth- and seventh-graders in a middle school whose enrollment was half Black and half white, Schofield found that while racial separation among the students was extensive, gender separation was even greater.[8]

After documenting widespread gender separation in children's social relations, most researchers have compared the separate worlds of boys and girls. The result is a by now familiar litany of generalized contrasts, usually framed as a series of dualisms: boys' groups are larger, and girls' groups are smaller ("buddies" versus "best friends"); boys play more often in public, and girls in more private places; boys engage in more rough-and-tumble play, physical fighting, and overt physical conflict than do girls; boys play more organized team sports, and girls engage in more turn-taking play; within same-gender groups, boys continually maintain and display hierarchies, while girls organize themselves into shifting alliances.[9]

There are problems with this separate worlds approach. Much of the literature, like that on individual sex differences, suffers from androcentrism: the "boys' world" is usually described first (as above) and more extensively; the less richly articulated "girls' world" seems explicitly (as in Lever's study)[10] or implicitly lacking.[11] Even where efforts are made to revalue the "girls' world" (as in Gilligan's reframing of Lever's work)[12] and to give both poles equal weighting, people still construe children's gender relations as polarities. The convention of separate worlds compresses enormous complexity into a series of contrasts: public/private, large/small, competitive/cooperative. It suggests a Victorian world of separate spheres writ small and contemporary.

Gender separation among children is not so total as the separate worlds rendering suggests, and the amount of separation varies by situation. For example, Luria and Herzog found that in a nursery school in Massachusetts two-thirds of playgroups were same-gender (one-third were mixed); 80 percent of playground groups of fifth- and sixth-graders in a public elementary school were same-gender (20 percent were mixed); in a private school, 63 percent of playground groups were same-gender (37 percent were mixed).[13] For many children in the United States, gender separation is more extensive on school playgrounds than in other daily settings. Girls and boys interact frequently in most elementary school classrooms, since adults organize much of the activity and usually rely on criteria other than gender. Children often report engaging in more cross-gender play in neighborhoods and in families

188

THORNE

than they do on school playgrounds; in these less populous situations they may have to cross gender and age categories to find playmates, and there are fewer witnesses to tease girls and boys who choose to be together.[14]

The occasions when girls and boys are together are as theoretically and socially significant as when they are apart, yet the literature on children's gender relations has largely ignored interaction between them. In much of the research on children's group life, "gender" has first been located in the separation of boys and girls and then in comparisons of same-gender groups.[15] Comparing groups of girls with groups of boys not only neglects the occasions when they are together but also ignores the complex choreography of separation and integration in children's daily interactions. Frequency counts provide snapshots of single moments, but they cannot teach us about the social processes by which gender is used—or overridden or ignored—as a basis for group formation.[16]

Finally, in relying on a series of contrasts to depict the whole, the separate worlds approach exaggerates the coherence of same-gender interaction and glosses extensive variation among boys and among girls. Characterizations of the "boys' world" suffer from a distortion akin to the "Big Man Bias" in anthropological ethnographies in which male elites are equated with men in general.[17] Larger, bonded groups of boys figure prominently in Joffe's ethnographic description of the "male subculture" of a preschool, Best's description of boys in an elementary school, Everhart's ethnography of a junior high and Cusick's of a high school, and Willis' study of working-class "lads" in a vocational secondary school in England.[18] Other less popular, disruptive, dominant, or socially visible boys—and girls (who remain invisible in the majority of school ethnographies)—appear at the edges of these portrayals, but their standpoints and experiences are voiced only indirectly. (Cusick reports that as a participant-observer he avoided "isolates"; "I was there to do a study not to be a friend to those who had no friends.")[19]

In the fourth-and-fifth-grade class in which I was a participant-observer,[20] a relatively stable group of four to six boys (often joined by a girl who successfully crossed gender boundaries) sat together in the classroom and the lunchroom and moved around the playground as a group, playing the team sports of every season. Because of the group's size, physicality, and social dominance, it *seemed* to be the core of the "boys' world" in that classroom—one more instance of the familiar generalization that boys are organized into "flocks" or "gangs." But other fourth-and-fifth-grade boys did not fit the model. Three of them were loners who avoided sports, preferred to stay indoors, and hung out at the edges of the playground. Three more were involved in an intense dyad-into-triad pattern similar to the social organization often generalized as typical of girls' friendships.[21] Two boys were recent immigrants from Mexico, spoke little English, were marginal in most classroom interaction, and on the playground often joined six to ten other Spanish-

189

THORNE

speaking, nonbilingual children in an ongoing game of dodgeball that was more mixed in gender and age than any other recurring playground group.

Depictions of girls' social relations have also masked considerable variation. While the fourth-and-fifth-grade girls I observed often used a language of "best friends" (dyads and triads did figure centrally in their social relationships), they also regularly organized into groups of five to seven doing "tricks" on the bars or playing jump rope. Hughes, who observed on an upper-middle-class school playground, and Goodwin, who observed Black children ages ten to thirteen in an urban neighborhood, also found that girls constructed larger groups and complex social networks.[22] Girls' social relations are usually depicted as more cooperative than those of boys, but ethnographers have documented patterns of dispute and competition in girls' interactions with one another, including ritual insults that are often said to be typical of boys.[23] Boys' social relations are usually claimed to be more hierarchical than girls', but type of activity affects mode of interaction. The group of neighborhood girls Goodwin studied constructed hierarchies when they played house (a form of pretend play that, tellingly for children's representations of families, involved continual marking of dominance).[24] But when the girls engaged in a task activity like making rings from the rims of glass bottles, their interactions were more collaborative and egalitarian.

FROM DUALISMS TO GENDER AS FLUID AND SITUATED

Instead of scrambling to describe girls (or girls' groups) in contrast to boys', we are beginning to develop more varied and complex ways of thinking about children and gender. This shift of interpretive conventions has been furthered by the work of anthropologists, folklorists, and sociologists, who are more prone than developmental psychologists to start with social relations and to emphasize social contexts and meanings.

Conceptualizing gender in terms of social relations breaks with the relatively static equation of gender with dichotomous difference. An emphasis on social relations is well developed in studies of social class and ethnicity. But what Connell calls "categoricalism" has hounded the study of gender: reliance on relatively unexamined, dichotomous sex (or gender) categories—male/female, woman/man, boy/girl—as tools of analysis.[25] I have already discussed this problem in sex difference research. It is also a problem in the use of gender as an untheorized binary variable,[26] and—coming from a quite different intellectual and political context—in feminist theories that take "women" and "men" as unproblematic categories.[27]

At the level of basic social categories, gender does operate more duallistically than class, race, or ethnicity. Our culture has only two sex categories, and every person is permanently assigned to one or the other with very few attempts to switch. In every situation each individual displays, and others attribute to her or him, characteristics associated with one or the other of the

190

THORNE

two categories.[28] The workings of social class and race and ethnic categories seem from the start to be far more complex and contingent than gender. Social class and ethnic categories are multiple, sometimes ambiguous, and may vary by situation. A person's social class or ethnicity may not be readily apparent, nor (as is the case with gender) do we always feel a need to know the class or ethnicity of those with whom we interact.

The distinctive features of sex categories lie behind what Wallman calls "the peculiar epistemology of sex"—the deep hold of dualisms on our ways of thinking about gender.[29] But dichotomous sex categories are only one part of the organizational and symbolic processes of gender. The two categories woman and man have multiple and changing meanings, as ethnographies of "femininities" and "masculinities" suggest.[30]

Shifting the level of analysis from the individual to social relations and from sex categories to the variable social organization and symbolic meanings of gender further unravels dichotomous constructions. When the topic is gender, there is no escaping the theme of difference. But the presence, significance, and meanings of differences are refocused when one asks about the social relations that construct differences—and diminish or undermine them.

How is gender made more or less salient in different situations? In specific social contexts, how do the organization and meanings of gender take shape in relation to other socially constructed divisions like age, race, and social class? How do children in varied positions (for example, popular, marginal, or more or less involved in teen culture) navigate and experience a given set of gender relations? By emphasizing variable social contexts and multiple standpoints and meanings, these questions open a more fluid and situated approach to gender.

SOCIAL CONTEXTS AND THE RELATIVE SALIENCE OF GENDER

Much of the research on children and gender has neglected the importance of social context. Children have been pulled from specificity and fixed by abstract stages of development. Studies of individual sex differences often generalize about girls versus boys without attending to variations in society and culture. A different perspective emerges when one shifts from individuals to group life, with close attention to social contexts.

Earlier I contrasted situations where gender is highly salient with those in which its importance is muted. When children play "boys-chase-the-girls," gender is basic to the organization and symbolism of the encounter. Group gender boundaries are charged with titillating ambiguity and danger,[31] and girls and boys become by definition separate teams or sides.

The idea of borderwork, used by Barth to analyze ethnic relations,[32] can also be used to conceptualize social relations maintained across yet based upon and strengthening gender boundaries. When girls and boys are organized as opposing sides in a math contest or in cross-gender chasing, members of both sides may express solidarity within their gender and playful and

191

THORNE

serious antagonism to the other. But borderwork is also asymmetric. Boys invade girls' games and scenes of play much more than girls invade boys'. Boys control far more playground space than girls. Girls are more often defined as polluting and boys as running the risk of contamination (for example, girls are more often defined as giving "cooties").[33] Difference is related to dominance in children's gender group arrangements, and the workings of power are complex. Girls do not always passively accept their devaluation, but sometimes challenge and derogate boys. They guard their play and respond angrily to invasions; they complain to adults.[34]

Moments of separation and of bounded interaction evoke perceptions of difference by participants and by the experts who observe them. In everyday life in schools, children and adults talk about the different "natures" of girls and boys primarily to justify exclusion or separation and in situations of gender conflict. Two examples from my field notes:

> A group of sixth-grade girls grabbed the football from the ongoing play of a group of boys [this was one of the few occasions when I saw a group of girls invade a group of boys on the playground]. The boys complained to the playground aide. She responded, "Why won't you let the girls play?" The boys replied, "They can't tackle; when we tackle 'em they cry."

> During lunchtime an aide who was frazzled by problems of discipline told the third-grade girls and boys they had to sit at separate tables. One girl turned to another and said, half in jest and half in earnest, "The boys are naughty and we're good."

Gender-marked moments seem to express core truths: that boys and girls are separate and fundamentally different as individuals and as groups. They help sustain a sense of dualism in the face of enormous variation and complex circumstances. But the complexities are also part of the story. In daily school life many situations are organized along lines other than gender, and girls and boys interact in relaxed and non-gender-marked ways. For example, children often play handball and dodgeball in mixed groups; girls and boys sometimes sit together and converse in relaxed ways in classrooms, the cafeteria, or the library. Collective projects, like the radio play described earlier, often draw girls and boys together and diminish the salience of gender.

Children's gender relations can be understood only if we map the full array of their interactions—occasions when boys and girls are together as well as those when they separate (Goffman coined the apt phrase "with-then-apart" to describe the periodic nature of gender segregation).[35] To grasp the fluctuating significance of gender in social life, we must examine encounters where gender seems largely irrelevant as well as those where it is symbolically and organizationally central.

Broadening the site of significance to include occasions where gender is

THORNE

both unmarked and marked is one of several analytic strategies that I believe can provide fuller understanding of children's gender relations. Our conceptual frameworks are whetted on the marked occasions. Extensive gender separation or organizing an event as boys against the girls sets off contrastive thinking and feeds an assumption of gender as dichotomous difference. By also seeing other contexts as relevant to gender, we can situate the equation of gender with dualism more accurately and understand something of the hold that conceptualization has on us in the thrall of our culture. By developing a sense of the whole and attending to the waning as well as the waxing of gender salience, we can specify not only the social relations that uphold but also those that undermine the construction of gender as binary opposition. We can also gain a more complex understanding of the dynamics of power.

MUTLIPLE DIFFERENCES

In specific social contexts, complex interactions among gender and such other social divisions as age, race, ethnicity, social class, and religion are another source of multiplicity. General terms like *intersecting differences* obscure the complex, sometimes contradictory dynamics of concrete situations. The range of possibilities is better evoked by Connell and colleagues, who observe that different social divisions and forms of inequality may "abrade, inflame, amplify, twist, dampen, and complicate each other."[36]

In the world of elementary schools, age is a more formally institutionalized social division than gender. Being in the first, fourth, or sixth grades determines daily activities and the company one keeps. Different grades may be allocated separate turfs in the lunchroom and the playground, and those who venture out of their age-defined territory may be chastised. In some situations children unite on the basis of age, which then becomes more salient than gender. One day a much disliked teacher who was on yard duty punished a fourth-grader for something he didn't do. He was very upset, and others from his classroom who were playing in the vicinity and witnessed or heard about the incident perceived a great injustice. Girls and boys talked about the situation in mixed clusters and joined as a group to argue with the adult.

Adults (including sociological observers) who work in schools are accorded privileges denied to children. They are not confined to specific lines, seats, and tables; they can move more freely through space; and they have institutionalized authority. Teachers and aides sometimes use their authority to construct and enhance gender divisions among children, as in the cases of the teacher who organized girls and boys into separate teams for classroom contests and the noontime aide who ordered boys and girls to sit at different tables. But adult practices also undermine gender separation between children in schools. In the United States there is a long tradition of mixed-gender public elementary schools, with girls and boys sharing a curriculum and with an ideology of treating everyone the same and of attending to individual needs. Some structural

193

THORNE

pressures run against separating girls and boys in daily school life, especially in classrooms.[37] Adult practices work in both directions, sometimes separating and sometimes integrating boys and girls. Overall, however, school-based observers have found that less gender separation takes place among children when adults control a situation than when children have more autonomy.[38]

When children have constructed sharp gender boundaries, few of them attempt to cross. But adults claim the privilege of freelancing. In the schools I studied, when boys and girls sat at separate tables in school cafeterias, teachers and aides of both genders sat at either table, and the presence of an adult sometimes created a wedge for more general mixed seating. When the fourth-and-fifth-graders drew names for a winter holiday gift exchange, they decided (in a discussion punctuated by ritual gender antagonism) that girls would give to girls and boys to boys. The teacher decided that she would draw with the boys and suggested that the aide and I (both women) draw with the girls. Our adult status altered the organization of gender.

A mix of age, gender, and ethnicity contributed to the marginalization of two Latino boys in the fourth-and-fifth-grade classroom. The boys were recent immigrants from Mexico and spoke very little English. They sat in a back corner of the classroom and sometimes worked at a side table with a Spanish-speaking aide. The other children treated them as if they were younger, with several girls who sat near them repeatedly monitoring the boys' activities and telling them what to do. When the children were divided by gender, other boys repeatedly maneuvered the Latino boys and another low-status boy into sitting next to girls. These spatial arrangements drew upon a gender meaning—an assumption that being by girls is contaminating—to construct ethnic subordination and marginality.

Gender display may symbolically represent and amplify social class divisions. The students in the two schools I studied were largely working class, but within that loose categorization children's different economic circumstances affected how they looked, especially the girls. It was easier to spot girls from impoverished families than boys because the girls' more varied clothing was less adaptable (as in the case of a mismatched top and bottom) than the T-shirts and jeans the boys wore. Girls' hairstyles were also more varied and complex, providing material for differentiated display of style and grooming, and grooming standards were more exacting for girls than for boys. A fifth-grade girl whose unkempt hair and mismatched old clothing marked her impoverished background was treated like a pariah, while the most popular girl had many well-matched outfits and a well-groomed appearance. The top and bottom rungs of girls' popularity (positions partly shaped by social class) were defined by heterosexual meanings when children teased about a particular boy "liking" or "goin' with" a specific girl. The teasers most frequently named either the most popular girl or the pariah as targets of a boy's liking—the most and least probable and polluting targets of desire.

Attention to the dynamics of social contexts helps situate gender in relationship to other lines of difference and inequality. The meanings of gender are not unitary but multiple, and sometimes contradictory.

MULTIPLE STANDPOINTS

Exploring varied standpoints on a given set of gender relations is another strategy for deconstructing a too coherent, dichotomous portrayal of girls' groups versus boys' groups and for developing a more complex understanding of gender relations. Children who are popular or marginal, those defined as troublemakers or good students, and those who are more or less likely to cross gender boundaries have different experiences of the same situations. Their varied experiences—intricately constructed by and helping to construct gender, social class, ethnicity, age, and individual characteristics—provide multiple vantage points on the complexity of children's social worlds.

An array of social types, including the bully, the troublemaker, the sissy, the tomboy, and the isolate populates both fictional and social science literature on children in schools. If we shift from types to processes, we can get a better hold on the experiences these terms convey. For example, the terms tomboy and sissy take complicated social processes—changing gender boundaries and a continuum of crossing—and reify them into individual essences or conditions (for example, "tomboyism"). Crossing involves definition, activity, and the extent to which a child has a regular place in the other gender's social networks. Boys who frequently seek access to predominantly female groups and activities ("sissies") are more often harassed and teased by both boys and girls. But girls who frequently play with boys ("tomboys") are much less often stigmatized, and they continue to maintain ties with girls, a probable reason that, especially in the later years of elementary school, crossing by girls is far more frequent than crossing by boys.[39]

When girls are accepted in boys' groups and activities without changing the terms of the interactions (one girl called it being a "buddy"), gender becomes low. Heterosexual idioms, which mark and dramatize gender difference, pose a threat to such acceptance; one can't be a "buddy" and "goin' with" at the same time. The fifth-grade girl who was "buddies" with a group of boys navigated the field of gender relations and meanings very differently than did girls who frequently initiated heterosexual chasing rituals. Unitary notions like the girls' world and girls versus boys are inadequate for this sort of analysis. Instead, one must grapple with multiple standpoints, complex and even contradictory meanings, and the varying salience of gender.

ETHNOGRAPHIES OF SCHOOLING

In developing a contextual and deconstructive approach to understanding gender and children's worlds, I have been influenced by the work of other ethnographers, whose methods bring sensitivity to social contexts and to the

195

THORNE

construction of meanings. Ethnographers of education who work within "social reproduction theory" (asking how schools reproduce inequalities, mostly of social class and gender) have emphasized students' varying subcultures, some more conforming and some created in opposition to the official structure of schools. In an ethnographic study of working class "lads" in a vocational school in England, Willis gave attention to gender as well as to social class (the primary focus of this tradition anchored in Marxist theories).[40] Resisting the middle-class authority of the school, the lads created an oppositional culture of aggression and joking tied to the working class "masculine" subculture of factory workers. The lads' subculture, different from that of more conforming boys, helped reproduce their class position.

Recent research within this tradition has finally moved girls from the periphery more toward the center of attention. In a study of fifth-graders in U.S. schools, Anyon analyzed strategies related to social class that girls used both to resist and to accommodate institutionalized attempts to enforce femininity.[41] For example, some girls used exaggerated feminine behavior to resist work assignments; those who were "discipline problems" rebelled both against the school and against expectations of them as girls.

Connell and his colleagues, who have studied girls and boys of different social classes in high schools in Australia, use the plural notions *masculinities* and *femininities* to articulate an array of subcultures and individual styles or types of identity.[42] (I find it problematic that they mix, rather than carefully distinguishing, individual and group levels of analysis.) They conceptualize gender and class as "structuring processes" and argue that each school has a "gender regime," constructing, ordering, and arbitrating between different kinds of masculinity and femininity. "The gender regime is in a state of play rather than a permanent condition."[43]

These studies are important in part because they break with the pervasive determinism of conventional "sex-role socialization" literature on gender and schools. Instead of simply "being socialized" (the imagery of children in much feminist literature), girls and boys are granted agency in constructing culture and resisting it as well as in adapting to dominant ideologies. By positing a complex and plural approach to gender, these ethnographies also challenge simplistic dualisms like "the male role versus the female role" or "girls' groups versus boys' groups."

But for all their value, these conceptualizations leave unresolved some of the issues I raised earlier. They analyze gender primarily by emphasizing separation between boys and girls and comparing the dynamics and subcultures of same-gender groups. While the groups and subcultures are multiple, a sense of deep division (separate worlds) between girls and boys persists. How far such divisions may vary by situation or subculture is not made clear. Dualistic assumptions poke through the multiplicity.

A second problem with Connell's work is that while the plural masculinities and femininities seem useful, the patterns these ethnographers describe sometimes seem more classificatory (an ever-finer grid for fixing gender) than anchored in a close analysis of social processes. By what criteria should a given pattern of interaction be seen as constructing a femininity or a masculinity, that is, as being relevant to the organization and meanings of gender? Some "social reproduction" ethnographers like Everhart largely ignore gender in their analyses of students' everyday interactions.[44] Others, for example, Anyon and Connell and his colleagues, refer the entire field of interaction to notions of gender.[45] This variation points to a more general question. Is gender always relevant? Do some parts of social life transcend it? If our challenge is to trace the threading of gender (and gender inequalities) through the complexity of social life, how can we determine when and how to invoke gendered interpretations?

These difficult questions suggest the need for finer conceptual tuning. In every situation we display and attribute core sex categories: gender does have ubiquitous relevance. But there is wide variation in the organization and symbolism of gender. Looking at social context shifts analysis from fixing abstract and binary differences to examining the social relations and contexts in which multiple differences are constructed, undermined, and given meaning.

This contextual approach to gender—questioning the assumption that girls and boys (and men and women) have different "essential natures" best understood in terms of opposition—clearly resonates with deconstructive, postmodernist tendencies in feminist thought.[46] I reached a deconstructive approach not by way of French theorists, however, but through the contextual and interpretive methods of ethnography.

Feminists have been more deconstructive and aware of multiplicities in thinking about adults than in thinking about children. We refer children's experiences to development and socialization, while granting adults a much broader scene of action. One way around that conceptual double standard is extending to children the frameworks (in this case, a fluid and contextual approach to gender) also used in analyzing the world of adults. In following that path, however, I have slid across a project that awaits close attention: grappling with differences of age, which, like gender, involve complex interactions of biology and culture. We should turn our critical attention to the dualism adult/child as well as to gender dualisms.

NOTES

1. See Barrie Thorne, "Re-Visioning Women and Social Change: Where Are the Children?" *Gender & Society* 1 (1987): 85–109. The invisibility of children in feminist and sociological thought can be documented by reviewing scholarly journals. Ambert analyzed issues of eight widely-read sociology journals published between 1972 and 1983. At the top of the journals in the proportion of space devoted to children, *Journal of Marriage and Family* had only 3.6 percent and *Sociology of Education* only 6.6 percent

197

of articles on children. The index for the first ten years of the feminist journal *SIGNS* has one entry under "child development," one under "child care," and four under "childbirth." See Anne–Marie Ambert, "Sociology of Sociology: The Place of Children in North American Sociology," in Peter Adler and Patricia A. Adler, eds., *Sociological Studies of Child Development* (Greenwich, Conn.: JAI, 1986) 1:11–31.

2. See M. Z. Rosaldo, "The Use and Abuse of Anthropology: Reflections on Feminism and Cross–Cultural Understanding," SIGNS 5(1980): 389–417.

3. For reviews of some of the research on sex differences see Eleanor Maccoby and Carol Jacklin, The Psychology of Sex Differences (Stanford: Stanford University Press, 1974), and Jere E. Brophy and Thomas L. Good, *Teacher-Student Relations* (New York: Holt, Rinehart, 1974).

4. For example, see Carol Jacklin, "Methodological Issues in the Study of Sex-Related Differences," *Developmental Review* 1 (1981): 266–73; Maccoby and Jacklin, *Psychology of Sex Differences*; and Maureen C. McHugh, Randi Daimon Keoske, and Irene Hanson Frieze, "Issues to Consider in Conducting Nonsexist Psychological Research," *American Psychologist* 41 (1986): 879–90.

5. Here is the inevitable footnote on terminology, one more example of the definitional fiddling so prevalent in the social science literature on sex and gender. This perpetual fiddling reflects our ongoing efforts to locate subject matter, to construct appropriate levels of analysis, and to grapple with difficult problems such as how to weigh and simultaneously grasp the biological and the cultural. I am currently persuaded that: (1) we should conceptually distinguish biological sex, cultural gender, and sexuality (desire), but (2) we should not assume that they are easily separable. One of our central tasks is to clarify their complex, often ambiguous relationships—kept alive in the term "sex/gender system" (a term first put forward in Gayle Rubin, "The Traffic in Women: Notes on the 'Political Economy' of Sex," in Rayna R. Reiter, ed., *Toward an Anthropology of Women* [New York: Monthly Review Press, 1975], 157–210). We should muse about why, after all our careful distinctions, we so easily slip into interchangeable use of *sex, gender,* and *sexual.*

The phrase *sex category* refers to the core, dichotomous categories of individual sex and gender (female/male; girl/boy; woman/man)—dualisms riddled with the complexities of biology/culture and age/gender. While these categories appear to be rock-bottom and founded in biology—hence "sex" category—they are deeply constructed by cultural beliefs and by social practices of gender display and attribution. *Gender* still seems serviceable as an all–purpose term linked with other words for finer conceptual tuning, e.g., "gender identity," "gender ideology," the social organization of gender." In my discussion of "sex difference" research I use "sex" rather than "gender" because that has been the (perhaps telling) verbal practice of that tradition.

6. See Suzanne J. Kessler and Wendy McKenna, *Gender: An Ethnomethodological Approach* (New York: John Wiley, 1978); Erving Goffman. "The Arrangement between the Sexes," *Theory and Society* 4 (1977): 301–36; Spencer E. Cahill, "Language Practices and Self–Definition: The Case of Gender Identity Acquisition," *Sociological Quarterly* 287 (1987): 295–311; and Candace West and Don H. Zimmerman, "Doing Gender," *Gender & Society* 1 (1987): 125–51.

7. See reviews in Marlaine E. Lockheed, "Sex Equity in Classroom Organization and Climate," in Susan B. Klein, ed., *Handbook for Achieving Sex Equity through Education* (Bal-

THORNE

timore: Johns Hopkins University Press, 1985), 189–217; and Eleanor Maccoby. "Social Groupings in Childhood: Their Relationship to Prosocial and Antisocial Behavior in Boys and Girls," in Dan Olweus, Jack Block, and Marian Radke–Yarrow, eds., *Development of Antisocial and Prosocial Behavior* (San Diego: Academic, 1985), 263–84.

8. Janet Schofield, *Black and White in School* (New York: Praeger, 1982).

9. See reviews in Daniel N. Maltz and Ruth A. Borker, "A Cultural Approach to Male–Female Miscommunication," in John J. Gumperz, ed., *Language and Social Identity* (New York: Cambridge University Press, 1983), 195–216; Barrie Thorne, "Girls and Boys Together... But Mostly Apart: Gender Arrangements in Elementary Schools," in Willard W. Hartup and Zick Rubin, eds., *Relationships and Development* (Hillsdale, N.J.: Lawrence Erlbaum, 1986), 167–84; and Maccoby, "Social Groupings."

10. Janet Lever, "Sex Differences in the Games Children Play," *Social Problems* 23 (1976): 478–87.

11. The invisibility and marginalization of girls in the extensive British literature on "youth subcultures" was first noted in Angela McRobbie and Jenny Garber, "Girls and Subcultures," in S. Hall and T. Jefferson, eds., *Resistance through Rituals* (London: Hutchinson, 1976).

12. Lever, "Sex Differences"; Carol Gilligan, *In a Different Voice* (Cambridge: Harvard University Press, 1982): 9–11.

13. Zella Luria and Eleanor Herzog, "Gender Segregation across and within Settings" (unpublished paper presented at 1985 annual meeting of the Society for Research in Child Development, Toronto).

14. Most observational research on the gender relations of preadolescent children in the United States has been done in schools. Goodwin's research on children in an urban neighborhood is a notable exception. See Marjorie Harness Goodwin, *Conversational Practices in a Peer Group of Urban Black Children* (Bloomington: Indiana University Press, in press).

15. Two decades ago there was a reverse pattern in research on adult interaction, at least in the literature on sociolinguistics and small groups. "Gender" was assumed to "happen" when men and women were together, not when they were separated. It took feminist effort to bring same–gender relations, especially among women (a virtually invisible topic in traditional research on communication), into that subject matter (see Barrie Thorne, Cheris Kramarae, and Nancy Henley, eds., *Language, Gender and Society* [Rowley, Mass.: Newbury House, 1983]). These inverse ways of locating gender—defined by the genders separating for children and by their being together for adults—may reflect age–based assumptions. In our culture, adult gender is defined by heterosexuality, but children are (ambivalently) defined as sexual. We load the interaction of adult men and women with heterosexual meaning, but we resist defining children's mixed–gender interaction in those terms. Traditional constructions of children and gender exemplify the ideal of latency.

16. See Barrie Thorne, "An Analysis of Gender and Social Groupings," in Laurel Richardson and Verta Taylor, eds., *Feminist Frontiers* (Reading, Mass.: Addison–Wesley, 1983), 61–63; and idem, "Girls and Boys Together," 170–71.

17. Sherry B. Ortner, "The Founding of the First Sherpa Nunnery, and the Problem of 'Women' as an Analytic Category," in Vivian Patraka and Louise Tilly, eds., *Feminist Re-Visions* (Ann Arbor: University of Michigan Women's Studies Program, 1984).

199

THORNE

18. Carole Joffe, "As the Twig Is Bent," in Judith Stacey, Susan Bereaud, and Joan Daniels, eds., *And Jill Came Tumbling After* (New York: Dell, 1974), 79–90; Raphaela Best, *We've All Got Scars* (Bloomington: Indiana University Press, 1983); Robert B. Everhart, *Reading, Writing and Resistance* (Boston: Routledge & Kegan Paul, 1983): Philip A. Cusick, Inside High School (New York: Holt, Rinehart and Winston, 1973).

19. Cusick, *Inside High School*, 168.

20. I was a participant–observer in two different elementary schools—for eight months in a largely working class school in California (there were about 500 students, 5 percent Black, 20 percent Hispanic, and 75 percent white), and for three months in a school of similar size, class, and racial/ethnic composition in Michigan. Most of the examples in this paper come from the California school, where I focused primarily on fourth– and fifth–graders. For further reports from this work, see my "Gender and Social Groupings"; "Girls and Boys Together"; and "Crossing the Gender Divide: What 'Tomboys' Can Teach Us about Processes of Gender Separation among Children" (unpublished paper presented at 1985 meeting of the Society for Research on Child Development, Toronto). See also Barrie Thorne and Zella Luria, "Sexuality and Gender in Children's Daily World," *Social Problems* 33 (1986): 176–90.

21. See Thorne and Luria, "Sexuality and Gender," 182–84.

22. Linda A. Hughes, "Beyond the Rules of the Game: Girls' Gaming at a Friends' School (unpublished Ph.D. diss., University of Pennsylvania Graduate School of Education, 1983); Goodwin, *Conversational Practices*.

23. Marjorie Harness Goodwin and Charles Goodwin, "Children's Arguing," in Susan Philips, Susan Steele, and Christina Tanz, eds., *Language, Gender, and Sex in Comparative Perspective* (Cambridge: University Press, 1988).

24. Goodwin, *Conversational Practices*.

25. R. W. Connell, "Theorising Gender," Sociology 12 (1985): 260–72. Also see R. W. Connell, *Gender and Power* (Stanford: Stanford University Press, 1987).

26. See Judith Stacey and Barrie Thorne, "The Missing Feminist Revolution in Sociology," *Social Problems* 32 (1985): 301–16.

27. This problem is analyzed in Connell, "Theorising Gender" and Gender and Power; Hester Eisenstein, *Contemporary Feminist Thought* (Boston: G.K. Hall, 1984); Jane Flax, "Postmodernism and Gender Relations in Feminist Theory," *SIGNS* 12 (1987): 621–43; Bell Hooks, Feminist Theory: From Margin to Center (Boston: South End, 1984); and Sylvia J. Yanagisako and Jane F. Collier, eds., *Gender and Kinship: Essays toward a Unified Analysis* (Stanford: Stanford University Press, 1987).

28. West and Zimmerman, "Doing Gender."

29. Sandra Wallman, "Epistemologies of Sex," in Lionel Tiger and Heather T. Fowler, eds., *Female Hierarchies* Chicago: Aldine, 1978). Also see Nancy Chodorow, "Feminism and Difference: Gender, Relation, and Difference in Psychoanalytic Perspective," "*Socialist Review* 46 (1979): 51–70; Rosaldo, "Use and Abuse of Anthropology"; and Yanagisako and Collier, "Feminism, Gender, and Kinship."

30. See Paul Willis, Learning to Labor (New York: Columbia University Press, 1977); and R. W. Connell, D. J. Ashenden, S. Kessler, and G. W. Dowsett, *Making the Difference: Schools, Families, and Social Division* (Boston: Allen & Unwin).

31. On the charged nature of socially constructed boundaries, see Mary Douglas, *Purity and Danger* (New York: Praeger, 1966).

32. Frederik Barth, *Ethnic Groups and Boundaries* (Boston: Little, Brown, 1969).

33. See Thorne, "Girls and Boys Together," 174–75.

34. In an ethnographic study of a multiracial school in England, Fuller found that that girls of varied social classes and ethnicities had somewhat different ways of responding to boys' efforts to control and devalue them. See Mary Fuller, "Black Girls in a London Comprehensive," in Rosemary Deem, eds., *Schooling for Women's Work* (London: Routledge & Kegan Paul, 1980), 52–65.

35. Goffman, "The Arrangement between the Sexes," 316. The phrase "sex (or gender) segregation among children" has been in widespread use, but as William Hartup suggested in comments at the 1985 meeting of the Society for Research in Child Development, the term segregation implies separation far more total and sanctioned than in most social relations among children in the United States.

36. R. W. Connell et al., *Making the Difference*, 182.

37. See David Tyack and Elisabeth Hansot, "Gender in American Public Schools: Thinking Institutionally," *SIGNS* 13 (1988): 741–60. British schools have institutionalized extensive gender separation, described in Sara Delamont. "The Conservative School? Sex Roles at Home, at Work and at School," in Stephen Walker and Len Barton, eds., *Gender, Class and Education* (Sussex: Falmer, 1983): 93–105.

38. See Luria and Herzog, "Gender Segregation," and Thorne, "Girls and Boys Together."

39. For a fuller analysis, see Thorne, "Crossing the Gender Divide."

40. Willis, *Learning to Labor*.

41. Joan Anyon, "Intersections of Gender and Class: Accommodation and Resistance by Working–Class and Affluent Females to Contradictory Sex–Role Ideologies," in Walker and Len Barton, eds., Gender, *Class and Education*, 1–19.

42. Connell et al., *Making the Difference*; S. Kessler, D. J. Ashenden, R. W. Connell, and G. W. Dowsett, "Gender Relations in Secondary Schooling," *Sociology of Education* 58 (1985): 34–48.

43. Kessler et al., "Gender Relations," 42.

44. Everhart, *Reading, Writing and Resistance*.

45. Anyon, "Intersections of Gender and Class"; Connell et al., *Making the Difference*.

46. On feminist postmodernism, see Flax, "Postmodernism and Gender Relations"; Sandra Harding, *The Science Question in Feminism* (Ithaca: Cornell University Press, 1986); and Toril Moi, *Sexual/Textual Politics* (London: Methuen, 1985).

201

LIFE STORIES
Pieces of a Dream

Mary Gergen

Mermaids' Songs
"I have heard the mermaids singing, each to each".

—T.S. Eliot

THE SONGS of mermaids are not like other songs. Mermaids' voices sing beyond the human range—notes not heard, forms not tolerated, and each to each, not one to many, one above all. If we imagine the mermaids, we might almost hear them singing. Their voices blending, so that each, in its own special timbre, lends to the harmony of the whole. So it might be as one writes—a voice in a choir at the threshold of sensibility. My voice shall be only one of many to be heard.

When you hear one voice it is the voice of authority, the father's voice. One voice belongs to an androcentric order. Will our singing mute the single voice before we drown?

"We need to learn how to see our theorizing projects as . . . 'riffing' between and over the beats of patriarchal theories" (Sandra Harding, 1986, 649).

This is an interwoven etude about life stories; it seeks to disrupt the usual narrative line, the rules of patriarchal form. I wish to escape the culturally contoured modes of discourse. Yet I, too, am mired in convention. If I write in all the acceptable ways, I shall only recapitulate the patriarchal forms. Yet, if I violate expectations too grievously, my words will become nonsense. Still, the mermaids sing.

> "Finding voices authentic to women's experience is appallingly difficult. Not only are the languages and concepts we have . . . male oriented, but historically women's experiences have been interpreted for us by men and male norms" (Kathryn Rabuzzi, 1988, 12).

We play at the shores of understanding. If you assent to the bending of traditional forms, then perhaps our collective act may jostle the sand castles of the ordered kingdom. We need one another, even if we do not always agree.

> "If we do our work well, 'reality' will appear even more unstable, complex, and disorderly than it does now" (Jane Flax, 1987, 643).

THE PARADOX OF THE PRIVATE: OUR PUBLIC SECRETS

When we tell one another our deepest secrets we use a public language. The nuances of consciousness, emotions both subtle and profound, inner yearnings, the whispering of conscience—all of these are created in the matrix of this language. The words form and deform around us as we speak and listen. We swim in a sea of words. Only that which is public can be private. We dwell in a paradox.

> "Individual consciousness is a socio-ideological fact. If you cannot talk about an experience, at least to yourself, you did not have it" (Caryl Emerson, 1983, 10).

Our cultures provide models not only for the contents of what we say but also for the forms. We use these forms unwittingly; they create the means by which we interpret our lives. We know ourselves via the mediating forms of our cultures, through telling, and through listening.

> "What created humanity is narration" (Pierre Janet, 1928, 42).

"Know thyself," a seemingly timeless motto, loses clarity when we hold that our forms of self-understanding are the creation of the unknown multitudes who have gone before us. We have become, we are becoming because "they" have set out the linguistic forestructures of intelligibility. What then does a personal identity amount to?

> "Every text is an articulation of the relations between texts, a product of inter-

GERGEN

textuality, a weaving together of what has already been produced elsewhere in discontinuous form; every subject, every author, every self is the articulation of an intersubjectivity structured within and around the discourses available to it at any moment in time" (Michael Sprinker, 1980, 325).

If self-understanding is derived from our cultures, and the stories we can tell about ourselves are prototypically performed, what implications does this have for our life affairs? The reverberations of this question will ring in our ears.

"Every version of an 'other' . . . is also the construction of a 'self'" (James Clifford, 1986, 23).

And, I add, every version of a self must be a construction of the other.

Our first mark of identity is by gender. We are called "boy" or "girl" in our first moment of life. Our personal identities are always genderized, then so must life stories be. I am concerned with the gendered nature of our life stories. What are manstories and womanstories? How do they differ? And what difference do these differences make?

"The literary construction of gender is always artificial . . . one can never unveil the essence of masculinity or femininity. Instead, all one exposes are other representations" (Linda Kauffman, 1986, 314).

205

This overture suggests the major themes. Countertones may resist articulation. You may not find what you want. The voices mingle and collide. Only in the confluence will the totality be fixed . . . temporarily.

DEFINING POWERS: DOUBTS ABOUT THE STRUCTURE

What do I mean by the narratives or stories of our lives? When we began our work on the traditional narrative, Kenneth Gergen and I described it as being composed of a valued end point; events relevant to this end point; the temporal ordering of these events toward the endpoint; the causal linkages between events (see also Gergen and Gergen, 1983; 1984; 1988).

Now I become uneasy. I wonder why this definition must be as it is. Doesn't a definition defend an order of discourse, an order of life? Whose lives are advantaged by this form and whose disadvantaged? Should we ask?

What are the forms of our life stories? We recognize them—a comedy, a tragedy, a romance, a satire. We know them as they are told. Their plots are implicated in their structures. A climax is a matter of form as well as content. Though separating form and content may be desirable from an analytic point of view, it is also arbitrary. (What are the forms of a womanstory and a manstory? How do they differ?)

GERGEN

"The dramatic structure of conversion . . . where the self is presented as the stage for a battle of opposing forces and where a climactic victory for one force—spirit defeating flesh—completes the drama of the self, simply does not accord with the deepest realities of women's experience and so is inappropriate as a model for women's life-writing" (Mary G. Mason, 1980, 210).

Should we question the ways in which patriarchal authority has controlled the narrative forms? We would be in good company. Many feminist literary critics have expanded this perspective (see also Shari Benstock, 1986; Rachel Duplessis, 1985; Sidonie Smith, 1987). Such writers as Virginia Woolf (1957, 1958) have also struggled with how male domination in literary forms has made some works great and others trivial, some worthy and some not. What has been judged by the figures of authority as correct has been granted publication, critical acclaim, and respect; the rest has often been ignored or abused.

". . . both in life and in art, the values of a woman are not the values of a man. Thus, when a woman comes to write a novel, she will find that she is perpetually wishing to alter the established values—to make serious what appears insignificant to a man and trivial what is to him important" (Virginia Woolf, 1958, 81).

Although androcentric control over literary forms is a serious matter, how much graver is the accusation that the forms of our personal narratives are also under such control? The relation between one and the other is strong, but the more pervasive nature and consequence of male-dominated life stories is certainly more threatening to me.

"Narrative in the most general terms is a version of, or a special expression of, ideology; representations by which we construct and accept values and institutions" (Rachel DuPlessis, 1985, x).

I would add, construct and accept ourselves!

Thus, I become increasingly skeptical of our classical definitions of the narrative. Judgments of what constitutes a proper telling are suspect on the grounds that what seem to be simple canons of good judgment, aesthetic taste, or even familiar custom may also be unquestioned expressions of patriarchal power. Under the seemingly innocent guise of telling a true story, one's life story validates the status quo.

GENDERIZING: TENDERIZING THE MONOMYTH

Myths have carried the form and content of narratives throughout the centuries. They tell us how great events occur as well as how stories are made. Joseph Campbell (1956) has analyzed these ancient myths. He proposes that there is one fundamental myth—the "monomyth." This myth begins as the

GERGEN

hero, having been dedicated to a quest, ventures forth from the everyday world. He goes into the region of the supernatural, where he encounters strange, dangerous, and powerful forces, which he must vanquish. Then the victorious hero returns and is rewarded for his great deeds. The monomyth is the hero's myth and the major manstory. (Where is the woman in this story? She is only to be found as a snare, an obstacle, a magic power, or a prize.)

> "The whole ideology of representational significance is an ideology of power" (Stephen Tyler, 1986, 131).

This monomyth is not just a historical curiosity. It is the basic model for the stories of achievement in everyday lives. Life stories are often about quests; they, like the monomyth, are stories of achievement. The story hangs on the end point— will the goal be achieved or not? In such stories all is subsumed by the goal. The heroic character must not allow anything to interfere with the quest.

Do you assume that a heroine is the same as a hero, except for gender? Some might say that narratives of heroes are equally available to women. I doubt this is so. Cultural expectations about how the two genders should express their heroism are clearly divergent.

Consider the central characters and the major plots of life stories codified in literature, history, or personal narrative; we could easily conclude that women do not belong, at least in the starring role. The adventures of the hero of the monomyth would make rather strange sense if he were a woman. If He is the subject of the story, She must be the object. In the System opposites cannot occupy the same position. The woman represents the totality of what is to be known. The hero is the knower. She is life; he is the master of life. He is the main character; she is a supporting actress. He is the actor; she is acted upon.

> "Although theroretically the hero was meant generically to stand for individuals of both sexes, actually, like so-called 'generic man,' the hero is a thoroughly androcentric construction" (Kathryn Rabuzzi, 1988, 10).

In general, the cultural repertoire of heroic stories requires different qualities for each gender. The contrast of the ideal narrative line pits the autonomous ego-enhancing hero single-handedly and single-heartedly progressing toward a goal versus the long-suffering, selfless, socially embedded heroine, being moved in many directions, lacking the tenacious loyalty demanded of a quest.

> "Culture is male, our literary myths are for heroes, not heroines" (Joanne Russ, 1972, 18).

GERGEN

207

The differences in our stories are not generally recognized in our culture. In a democratic society, with equal opportunity for all, we do not consider the absence of narrative lines as relevant to unequal representation of people in public positions of power. We do not turn to our biographies to help explain, for example, why so few women are the heads of organizations, climb mountains, or teach math classes, or why so few men are primary caretakers of children. Even when women are leaders in their professions, or exceptional in some arena of life, they find it difficult to tell their personal narratives in the forms that would be suitable to their male colleagues. They are in a cultural hiatus, with a paucity of stories to tell. (How does one become when no story can be found?)

"The emphasis by women on the personal, especially on other people, rather than on their work life, their professional success, or their connectedness to current political or intellectual history clearly contradicts the established criterion about the content of autobiography" (Estelle Jelinek, 1980, 10).

FEMINIST THEORIES AND GENDER DIFFERENCES

Various feminist theorists have emphasized the underlying family dynamics that may sustain our gendered stories. As Nancy Chodorow (1978), Dorothy Dinnerstein (1976), Jane Flax (1983), Carol Gilligan (1982), Evelyn Fox Keller (1983), and others have suggested, boys and girls are raised to regard their life trajectories differently. All children have as their first love object their mothering figure. However, boys are reared to separate from their mothers, and they learn to replace their attachment to mother with pride in masculine achievements and to derogate women and their relationships with them. Girls are not cut away from their mothers and forced to reidentify themselves. They remain embedded in their relations and do not learn the solitary hero role. But they must bear the burden of shame that the androcentered culture assigns to their gender.

This, then, is my theme: each gender acquires for personal use a repertoire of potential life stories relevant to their own gender. Understanding one's past, interpreting one's actions, evaluating future possibilities—each is filtered through these stories. Events "make sense" as they are placed in the correct story form. If certain story forms are absent, events cannot take on the same meaning.

"We assume that life produces the autobiography, as an act produces its consequence, but can we not suggest, with equal justice, that the autobiography project may itself produce and determine life" (Paul de Man, 1979, 920).

AUTOBIOGRAPHIES AS THE GENDERED STORIES OF LIVES

I have been studying the popular autobiographies of men and women. Of interest to me is not what is there, in the story lines, but what is missing. What is it that each gender cannot talk about—and thus cannot integrate into life stories and life plans? What can a manstory tell that a womanstory cannot, and vice versa?

> "What appears as 'real' in history, the social sciences, the arts, even in common sense, is always analyzable as a restrictive and expressive set of social codes and conventions" (James Clifford, 1986, 10).

In critical works concerning autobiography, women's narratives have been almost totally neglected (cf. Sayre, 1980; Olney, 1980; Smith, 1974). Women's writings have usually been exempted because they did not fit the proper formal mold. Their work has been more fragmentary, multidimensional, understated, and temporally disjunctive. "Insignificant" has been the predominant critical judgment toward women's autobiographies (and their lives) (Estelle Jelinek, 1980).

> "When a woman writes or speaks herself into existence, she is forced to speak in something like a foreign tongue" (Carolyn Burke, 1978, 844).

INTERPRETING THE STORIES

I look into autobiographies to discover the forms we use to tell a manstory, a womanstory. What story can I tell?

> "Autobiography reveals the impossibility of its own dream: what begins on the presumption of self-knowledge ends in the creation of a fiction that covers over the premises of its construction" (Shari Benstock, 1988, 11).

My materials are taken from many biographies. This chapter concentrates on but a few. In this way a sense of life may perhaps be felt. The quotations I have drawn from these texts are hardly proof of my conclusions; they are better viewed as illustrations to vivify my interpretations. Other interpretations can and should be made.

SEEKING THE QUEST

Traditional narratives demand an end point, a goal. Certain rhetorical moves are required by custom—concentrating on the goal, moving toward the point, putting events in a sequence, building the case (no tangents, please). Classical autobiographies delineate the life of cultural heroes—those who have achieved greatness through their accomplishments. We expect those who write their biographies must be such heroes.

> "Men tend to idealize their lives or to cast them into heroic molds to project their universal import" (Estelle Jelinek, 1980. 14).

209

GERGEN

How single-minded are these heroes in pursuit of their goals? How committed are the women who write their biographies? Does their story also fit the classic mold?

Listen to some of their voices.

Lee Iacocca's best-selling autobiography focused on his automotive career. His family life, in contrast, received scant attention. Iacocca's wife, Mary, was a diabetic. Her condition worsened over the years; after two heart attacks, one in 1978 and the other in 1980, she died in 1983 at the age of fifty-seven. According to Iacocca, each heart attack came after a crisis period in his career at Ford or Chrysler.

Iacocca wrote: "Above all, a person with diabetes has to avoid stress. Unfortunately, with the path I had chosen to follow, this was virtually impossible" (Lee Iacocca, 301).

Iacocca's description of his wife's death was not intended to expose his cruelty. It is a conventional narrative report—appropriate to his gender. The book (and his life) are dedicated to his career. Iacocca seems to have found it unimaginable that he could have ended his career in order to reduce his wife's ill health. As a manstory, the passage is not condemning; however, if we reverse the sexes, as a wife's description of the death of her husband or child, the story would appear callous, to say the least. Unlike Iacocca, a woman who would do such a thing would not be considered an outstanding folk hero.

Yeager is the autobiography of the quintessential American hero, the man with the "right stuff." His story is intensively focused on his career as a pilot in the air force. He was the father of four children born in quick succession, and his wife became gravely ill during her last pregnancy. Nothing, however, stopped him from flying. Constantly moving around the globe, always seeking the most dangerous missions, he openly states: "Whenever Glennis needed me over the years. I was usually off in the wild blue yonder" (Chuck Yeager and Leo James, 103).

America's favorite hero would be considered an abusive parent were his story regendered.

Richard Feynman, autobiographer and Nobel prize-winning physicist, was married to a woman who had been stricken with tuberculosis for seven years. During World War II, he moved to Los Alamos to work on the Manhattan Project developing the atomic bomb, and she was several hours away in a hospital in Albuquerque. The day she was dying he borrowed a car to go to her bedside.

He reports: "When I got back (yet another tire went flat on the way), they asked me what happened. 'She's dead. And how's the program going?' They caught on right away that I didn't want to moon over it" (Richard Feynman, 113).

Manstories tend to follow the traditional narrative pattern: becoming their own heroes, facing crises, following their quests, and ultimately achieving victory. Their careers provide them their central lines of narrative structuring, and personal commitments, external to their careers, are relegated to insignificant subplots.

What does one find among women authors?

"There is virtually only one occupation for a female protagonist—love, of course—which our culture uses to absorb all possible Bildung, success/failure, learning, education, and transition to adulthood" (Rachel DuPlessis, 1985, 182).

Beverly Sills, who became a star at the New York City Opera, all but gave up her singing career for two years to live in Cleveland because this was where her husband worked. She describes her thoughts: "Peter had spent all of his professional life working for the *Plain Dealer,* and he had every intention of eventually becoming the newspaper's editor-in-chief. I was just going to have to get used to Cleveland. My only alternative was to ask Peter to scuttle the goal he'd been working toward for almost twenty-five years. If I did that, I didn't deserve to be his wife. Not coincidentally, I began reevaluating whether or not I truly wanted a career as an opera singer. I decided I didn't . . . . I was twenty-eight years old, and I wanted to have a baby" (Beverly Sills and Lawrence Linderman, 120).

The only businesswoman in my sample, Sydney Biddle Barrows, also known by the title of her autobiography, *Mayflower Madam,* shows second thoughts about maintaining a then extremely successful business when it clashed with private goals:

"By early 1984 . . . . I realized that I couldn't spend the rest of my life in the escort business. I was now in my early thirties and starting to think more practically about my future—which would, I hoped, include marriage. As much as I loved my job, I had to acknowledge that the kind of man I was likely to fall in love with would never marry the owner of an escort service . . . . If I didn't want to remain single forever, I would sooner or later have to return to a more conventional line of work" (Sydney Biddle Barrows, 205).

Martina Navratilova discusses her feelings about going skiing after many years of foregoing this dangerous sport: "I made a decision in my teens to not risk my tennis career on the slopes, but in recent years I've wanted to feel the wind on my face again. . . . I wasn't willing to wait God-knows-how-many-years to stop playing and start living" (Martina Navratilova, 320).

Nien Cheng's *Life and Death in Shanghai* details her survival during years of imprisonment in China. Although her own survival might be seen as the major goal of her story, this focus is deeply compromised by her concerns with her daughter's welfare. "I hoped my removal to the detention house would free her from any further pressure to denounce me. If that were indeed the case .... I would be prepared to put up with anything" (Nien Cheng, 132).

Discovering that her daughter is dead greatly disturbs her own will to go on. "Now there was nothing left. It would have been less painful if I had died in prison and never known that Meiping was dead. My struggle to keep alive . . . . suddenly seemed meaningless" (ibid., 360).

For the women, the career line was important, but it was not an ultimate end point. Whereas men seemed to sacrifice their lives to careers, women seemed to tell the story in reverse. This is not to say that women avoided achieving goals. They, too, yearn for the joy of success. But men and women do not describe their feelings in the same way. Let us listen.

> Lee Iacocca: "My years as general manager of the Ford Division were the happiest period of my life. For my colleagues and me, this was fire-in-the-belly time. We were high from smoking our own brand—a combination of hard work and big dreams" (Lee Iacocca, 65).

> Chuck Yeager: "I don't recommend going to war as a way of testing character, but by the time our ended we felt damned good about ourselves and what we had accomplished. Whatever the future held, we knew our skills as pilots, our ability to handle stress and danger, and our reliability in tight spots. It was the difference between thinking you're pretty good, and proving it" (Chuck Yeager and Leo James, 88)

> Edward Koch: "I am the Mayor of a city that has more Jews than live in Jerusalem, more Italians than live in Rome . . . and more Puerto Ricans than live in San Juan.... It is a tremendous responsibility, but there is no other job in the world that compares with it . . . Every day has the possibility of accomplishing some major success" (Edward Koch, 359)

> When John Paul Getty drilled his first great oil well, he was overjoyed: "The sense of elation and triumph was–and–is always there. It stems from knowing that one has beaten nature's incalculable odds by finding and capturing a most elusive (and often a dangerous and malevolent) prey" (John Paul Getty, 28).

Male voices often have a tone of hostility, aggression, or domination. Their celebration of achievement seems to be the result of what is fundamentally an antagonistic encounter.

The ways that women's voices speak of achievements take a rather different slant.

> Martina Navratilova: "For the first time I was a Wimbledon champion, fulfilling the dream of my father many years before.... I could feel Chris patting me on the back, smiling and congratulating me.... Four days later, the Women's Tennis Association computer ranked me number 1 in the world, breaking Chris's four-year domination. I felt I was on top of the world" (Martina Navratilova, 190).

> Beverly Sills: "I think 'se pieta' was the single most extraordinary piece of singing I ever did. I know I had never heard myself sing that way before . . . the curtain began coming down very slowly . . . and then a roar went through that house

212

GERGEN

the likes of which I'd never heard. I was a little stunned by it: the audience wouldn't stop applauding" (Beverly Sills and Lawrence Linderman, 172).

Sydney Biddle Barrows: "I was motivated by the challenge of doing something better than everyone else . . . I was determined to create a business that would appeal to . . . men, who constituted the high end of the market . . . I was sure we could turn our agency into one hell of an operation—successful, elegant, honest, and fun" (Sydney Biddle Barrows, 48-49).

In the womanstories, the love of the audience response, the affection of the opponent, and the satisfaction of customers are the significant factors in their descriptions. The womanstory emphasizes continuity with others' goals, not opposition to them. In fact, one's opponent can be seen as a necessary part of one's success:

"You're totally out for yourself, to win a match, yet you're dependent on your opponent to some degree for the type of match it is and how well you play. You need the opponent; without her you do not exist" (Martina Navaratilova, 162).

EMOTIONAL INTERDEPENDENCY

What do these stories say about emotion interdependency—being with others and needing reciprocal affections? Here the manstory may be rather thin. Sticking to the narrative line may cut short their emotional lives, at least in print. But this is too black and white a message. Men have their buddies, their sidekicks, their intimate rivals, and compatriots. Perhaps the difference is that together they look outward, rather than at one another.

Let us look at how manstories allowed for the expression of relatedness and emotionality.

Ed Koch, reporting a conversation: "I've been Mayor for close to three years . . . I get involved in a lot of controversies and I make a lot of people mad at me, and so maybe at the end of these four years they'll say, 'he's too controversial and we don't want him!' And maybe they'll throw me out. That's okay with me. I'll get a better job, and you won't get a better Mayor" (Edward Koch, 227).

Chuck Yeager: "Often at the end of a hard day, the choice was going home to a wife who really didn't understand what you were talking about . . . or gathering around the bar with guys who had also spent the day in a cockpit. Talking flying was the next best thing to flying itself. And after we had a few drinks in us, we'd get happy or belligerent and raise some hell. Flying and hell-raising—one fueled the other" (Chuck Yeager and Leo James, 173).

John Paul Getty: "For some reason, I have always been much freer in recording my emotions and feelings in my diaries.... Taken as a whole, they might serve to provide insight into a father's true feeling about his sons. 1939

GERGEN

Los Angeles, California:
May 20: Saw George, a remarkable boy rapidly becoming a man. He is 5'9" tall and weighs 145 pounds.

Genève, Switzerland:
July 9: Drove to Ronny's school . . . Ronny is well, happy, and likes his school. His teachers give him a good report. He is intelligent and has good character, they say. Took Ronny and Fini to the Bergues Hotel for lunch and then to Chamonix. . .

Los Angeles:
December 10: Went to Ann's house (Ann Rork, my fourth wife who divorced me in 1935) and saw Pabby and Gordon, bless them. They are both fine boys" (John Paul Getty, 11).

Manstories seem to celebrate the song of the self. Emotional ties are mentioned as "facts" where necessary, but the author does not try to re-create in the reader emphatic emotional responses. The willingness to play the role of the "bastard" is seen in manstories, for example in Koch's remarks above, but women do not take this stance in their stories.

And about our heroines? What do their stories tell about their emotional interdependencies? How important are relationships to their life courses? Is there a womanstory, too?

Let us listen.

Beverly Sills: "One of the things I always loved best about being an opera singer was the chance to make new friends every time I went into a new production" (Beverly Sills and Lawrence Linderman, 229).

She wrote about how she and Carol Burnett had cried after finishing a television show together. "We knew we'd have nobody to play with the next day. After that we telephoned each other three times a day" (ibid., 280).

Martina Navratilova: "I've never been able to treat my opponent as the enemy, particularly Pam Shriver, my doubles partner and one of my best friends" (Martina Navratilova, 167).

Sydney Biddle Barrows emphasized in her book her ladylike upbringing, sensitive manners, and appreciation of the finer things of life. Her style of living was obviously challenged when she was arrested and thrown in jail.

On leaving a group of street-walking prostitutes with whom she had been jailed she wrote: "As I left the cell, everybody started shouting and cheering me on. 'Go get em, girlfren!' I left with mixed emotions. These girls had been so nice to me, and so open and interesting, that my brief experience in jail was far more positive than I could have imagined" (Sydney Biddle Barrows, 284)

The necessity of relating to others in a womanstory is especially crucial in Nien Cheng's narrative about solitary confinement. To avoid the bitter loneliness she adopted a small spider as a friend. She describes her concern for this spider: "My small friend seemed rather weak. It stumbled and stopped every few steps. Could a spider get sick, or was it merely cold? . . . It made a tiny web . . . forming something rather like a cocoon . . . when I had to use the toilet, I carefully sat well to one side so that I did not disturb it" (Nien Cheng, 155).

Though many other examples might be given, these illustrate the major differences I have found between the relatively more profound emotional interdependency and intimacy requirement of women, in the telling of their stories, and those of men. The important aspects of women's autobiographies depend heavily on their affiliative relationships with others. They seem to focus on these ties without drawing strong demarcations between their public world and "private" life. Their stories highlight the interdependent nature of their involvements and the centrality of emotional well-being to all facets of life much more vividly than men's stories do.

VOICES AS VERSES: FORMS AND FOAM

As stories are told, forms are re-created. The content belongs to the forms, and the forms control the content. Let us look at forms more closely.

> "Individuals have characteristic ways of navigating their lives. What is characteristic—the signature we need across episodes—exists at the level of narrative structure. We can analyze the structure of a life plot as symbolic in its own right" (Richard Ochberg, 1988, 1972).

215

Popular autobiographies of men are very similar in form. Their narrative lines tend to be linear (that is, strongly related to an explicit goal state, the career or quest) and progressive (the action moves toward this goal). Manstories also tend to be characterized by one or more major climaxes, usually related to career trajectories. The emphasis of a manstory on the single narrative line is evident from the beginning of the book. Edward Koch's autobiography, *Mayor,* for example, is totally devoted to his political carreer, especially as it "mirrors" the life of New York City from the mayor's office. Chapter I, entitled "A Child of the City," begins not with a biological childhood but with his political youth: "In March of 1975, when I was a U.S. Congressman from New York." Koch begins at a crisis point for the book's long-suffering heroine—not a flesh and blood woman, but New York City.

Chuck Yeager's book about his life as a pilot begins with a crash landing. Getty initiates his book with a sentence indicating that he was born in 1892 "and an active businessman since 1914" (John Paul Getty, vii). Physicist Feynman starts, "When I was about eleven or twelve I set up a lab in my house" (Richard Feynman, 3). Iacocca states, "You're about to read the history of a man who's had more than his share of success." (Lee Iacocca, xiv).

"The autobiographer confronts personally her culture's stories of male and female desire, insinuating the lines of her story through the lines of the patriarchal story that has been autobiography" (Sidonie Smith, 1987, 19).

Womanstories also contain a progressive theme related to achievement goals, but often the text emphasizes another facet of personal identity and deviates from one clear narrative line associated with career. Beverly Sills's first chapter recalls the last night she sang at the New York State Theater—a gala charity performance.

The event was not presented as a career triumph but as an emotionally significant "swan song." Sydney Biddle Barrows commences with a description of the annual meeting of the Society of Mayflower Descendants, of which she is a member, thus complexifying the question of how she became the owner of an escort service. Nien Cheng recalls her old home in Shanghai, her daughter asleep in her room. The importance of her daughter's activities plays a strong counterpoint to her own issues of existence. "Apple Trees" is the title of Martina Navratilova's first chapter; she begins: "I was three years old when my mother and father divorced" (Martina Navratilova, 1).

For female authors, the story forms available to them are much fuller (and more multiple in perspective) than for the men. Career successes and failures are mingled with other issues of great personal importance. Thus the story line becomes less clearly demarcated. The narrative threads are more complexly woven by the women. The story is about a person who is embedded in a variety of relationships, which all have some priority in the telling of the life. Ambiguity about any outcome complexifies the task of giving value to any particular event.

CAN STORIES AND LIVES BE CHANGED?

Throughout this composition I have illustrated how personal identities are construed through the gendered stories of lives. Autobiographies exemplify the repertoire of life-story forms by which "significant" members of a culture define themselves. Less important people, those who merely tell their stories to themselves and their private audiences, also use these forms. We all know ourselves, define our pasts, and project our futures as they fit into the acculturated story forms. But the forms for each gender are restrictive, and in many critical areas, such as achievement strivings and intimate relationships, men and women are inhibited from formulating selves that would allow for a different range of expressions and actions. Neither a man nor a woman can easily swap roles without the loss of social approval.

GERGEN

"The structure of autobiography, a story that is at once by and about the same individual, echoes and reinforces a structures already implicit in our language, a structure that is also (not accidentally) very like what we usually take to be the structure of self-consciousness itself: the capacity to know and simultaneously be that which one knows" (Elizabeth W. Bruss, 1980, 301)

I began this work with a special sensitivity to the losses that women have endured because they have been absent from the public sphere. I saw that because the story lines that lead a woman from childhood to maturity did not show the path by which strong achievement strivings could be satisfied without great personal sacrifice women could not become all they had the potential to be.

As I read the autobiographies of our "great" men, I confronted anew what many social critics, especially feminists, have frequently claimed: the goals, values, and method that sustain men's lives are antagonistic to other social values, those associated with women's narratives and lives. Particularly in re-visioning these stories, I saw the basic values of each clustering around themes of power versus themes of love.

Increasingly, as I read, what most needed change seemed to be not women's narratives, for them to become more like men's, but the reverse. Men, perhaps even more than women, needed new story lines, lines that were more muliplex, relational, and "messy." Both seemed imprisoned by their stories; both bound to separate pieces of the world, which if somehow put together would create new possibilities—ones in which each could share the other's dreams.

But how can we escape our story lines, our prisons made of words?

217

"Plots are dramatic embodiments of what a culture believes to be true... of all the possible actions people can do in fiction, very few can be done by women" (Joanne Russ, 1972, 4).

LANGUAGE: SOURCE AND SORCERESS

Language seems almost magical. Only through its powers to name can we identify our experiences and our persons. There are no social structures that bear upon us beyond this linguistic order. All that exists is within it. If we want to change our lives, we need to change our patterns of discourse. The "language games" constitute what there is to change.

Can we lift ourselves by our shoestrings?

"Individuals construct themselves as subjects through language, but individual subjects—rather than being the source of their own self-generated and self-expressive meaning-adopt positions available within the language at a given moment" (Felicity Nussbaum, 1988, 149)

Our narrative forms, our metaphors, our ways of communicating do not emerge from nothingness. They are embedded in the foundations of society.

Stories and their structural instantiations reverberate against and with one another. Are we prisoners of our father tongue? Yes . . ., mostly . . ., may be . . ., sometimes . . ., no. Perhaps we can at least wiggle a bit.

"In altering the images and narrative structures through which we compose the stories of our lives, we may hope to alter the very experiences of those lives as well" (Annette Kolodny, 1980, 258)

Many voices singing different tunes can sound noisy. Do you feel drowned out? We must sing like mermaids—and hope that a melody or two will be carried on the wind.

"Subversively, she rearranges the dominant discouse and the dominant ideology of gender, seizing the language and its power to turn cultural fictions into her very own story" (Sidonie Smith, 1987, 175).

How do we rearrange the melodies of talk? I will suggest some ways. Let us listen carefully as our words divide us and emphasize power differences among us. Let us resist these discordant tunes. (This will be less appealing at first to those whose words have been on everyone's lips.) Let us note, for example, that we call ourselves for some man long since dead. In a sense we belong to him. Let our names hang lightly in the air, or blow them away, if we wish.

"For a symbolic order that equates the ideas of the author with a phallic pen transmitted from father to son places the female writer in contradiction to the dominant definition of woman and casts her as the usurper of male prerogatives" (Domna Stanton, 1984, 13).

Let us listen to the metaphors we carry with us. Let us choose them carefully. Do we mimic our brothers who scoff at "soft" sciences and who love "hard" data? Do we feel the grasp of "sexual politics" at our throats?

"To change a story signals a dissent from social norms as well as narrative forms" (Rachel DuPlessis, 1985, 20).

Let us play with story lines. Let us not always conform to androcentric styles. Let us demure. Maybe stories don't need lines. Perhaps they need to step out of the queue and refuse to march in orderly progression. Let us not stick to the point. Let us improvise! (see also Gergen, 1990).

"The construction is nothing more than an improvisation" (George Rosenwald, 1988, 256).

Let us claim the tentative and fuzzy nature of all our linguistic formulations. Let us shake the tree of knowledge, unashamed. Let us eat the apple to the core and spit out "truth." Let us grant ourselves the pleasures of making and changing languages, as they transform us. Let us sing songs that will free us from the past and hum sweet dirges for androcentric systems as they drown.

AUTOBIOGRAPHICAL REFERENCES

Barrows, Sydney Biddle, with William Novak. 1986. *Mayflower Madam*. New York: Arbor House.

Cheng, Nien. 1986. *Life and Death in Shanghai*. New York: Penguin.

Feynman, Richard P. 1986. *"Surely You're Joking, Mr. Feynman!"* New York: Bantam Books.

Getty, J. Paul. [1976] 1986. *As I See It: An Autobiography of J. Paul Getty*. New York: Bantam Berkley.

Iacocca, Lee, with William Novak. 1984. *Iacocca: An Autobiography*. New York: Bantam Books.

Koch, Edward I., with William Rauch. 1986. *Mayor*. New York: Warner Books.

Navratilova, Martina, with George Vecsey. 1985. *Martina*. New York: Fawcett Crest.

Sills, Beverly, and Lawrence Linderman. 1987. *Beverly*. New York: Bantam Books.

Yeager, General Chuck, and Leo James. 1985. *Yeager: An Autobiography*. New York: Bantam Books.

GENERAL REFERENCES

Benstock, Shari. 1988. "Authorizing the Autobiography." In *The Private Self: Theory and Practice in Women's Autobiographical Writings*. Edited by S. Benstock. London: Routledge.

Bruss, Elizabeth W. 1980. "Eye for I: Making and Unmaking Autobiography in Film." In *Autobiography: Essays, Theoretical Critical*. Edited by J. Olney. Princeton, N.J.: Princeton University Press.

Burke, Carolyn G. 1978. "Report from Paris: Women's Writing and the Women's Movement." *Signs, Journal of Women in Culture and Society* 3:844.

Campbell, Joseph. 1956. *The Hero with One Thousand Faces*. New York: Bollingen.

Chodorow, Nancy. 1978. *The Reproduction of Mothering: Psychoanalysis and the Sociology of Gender*. Berkeley: University of California Press.

Clifford, James. 1986. "Introduction: Partial Truths." In *Writing Culture*. Edited by J. Clifford and G. Marcus. Berkeley: University of California Press.

de Man, Paul. 1979. "Autobiography as De-Facement." *Modern Language Notes* 94:920.

Dinnerstein, Dorothy. 1976. *The Mermaid and the Minotaur: Sexual Arrangements and the Human Malaise*. New York: Harper and Row.

DuPlessis, Rachel Blau. 1985. *Writing Beyond the Ending*. Bloomington: Indiana University Press.

Eliot, T.S. 1963. "The Love Song of J. Alfred Prufrock." In *Collected Poems, 1909-1962*. London: Faber and Faber.

Emerson, Caryl. 1983. "The Outer Word and Inner Speech: Bakhtin, Vygotsky, and the Internalization of Language." *Critical Inquiry* 10:245-264.

Flax, Jane. 1987. "Postmodernism and Gender Relations in Feminist Theory." *Signs, Journal of Women in Culture and Society* 12:621-643.

————. 1983. "Political Philosophy and the Patriarchal Unconsious: A Psychoanalytic Perspective on Epistemology and Metaphysics." In *Discovering Reality: Feminist Perspectives on Epistemology, Metaphysics, Methodology, and Philosophy of Science*. Edited by S. Harding and M.B. Hintikka. Dordrecht, Holland: D. Reidel.

Gergen, Kenneth J., and Mary M. Gergen. 1988. "Narrative and the Self as Relationship." In *Advances in Experimental Social Psychology*, vol. 21. Edited by L. Berkowitz. San Diego: Academic Press.

————. 1983. "Narrative of the Self." In *Studies in Social Identity*. Edited by K. Schiebe and T. Sarbin. New York: Praeger.

Gergen, Mary M. 1990. "A Feminist Psychologist's Postmod Critique of Postmodernism." *Humanistic Psychologist* 18:95-104.

Gergen, Mary M., and Kenneth J. Gergen. 1984. "Narrative Structures and Their Social Construction." In *Historical Social Psychology*. Edited by K. Gergen and M. Gergen. Hillsdale, N.J.: Erlbaum.

Gilligan, Carol. 1982. *In a Different Voice*. Cambridge, Mass.: Harvard University Press.

Harding, Sandra. 1986. "The Instability of the Analytical Categories of Feminist Theory." *Signs, Journal of Women in Culture and Society* 11:645-664.

Janet, Pierre. 1928. *L'Evolution de la memoire et la notion du temps*. Paris: L. Alcan.

Jelinek, Estelle C. 1980. *Women's Autobiography: Essays in Criticism*. Bloomington: Indiana University Press.

Kauffman, Linda S. 1986. *Discourses of Desire: Gender, Genre, and Epistolary Fictions*. Ithaca, N.Y.: Cornell University Press.

Keller, Evelyn Fox. 1983. "Gender and Science." In *Discovering Reality: Feminist Perspectives on Epistemology, Metaphysics, Methodology, and Philosophy of Science*. Edited by S. Harding and M.B. Hintikka. Dordrecht, Holland: D. Reidel.

Kolodny, Annette. 1980. "The Lady's Not for Spurning: Kate Millett and the Critics." In *Women's Autobiography: Essays in Criticism*. Edited by E. Jelinek. Bloomington: Indiana University Press.

Mason, Mary G. 1980. "Autobiographies of Women Writers." In *Autobiography, Essays Theoretical and Critical*. Edited by J. Olney. Princeton, N.J.: Princeton University Press.

Nussbaum, Felicity. 1988. "Eighteenth-Century Women's Autobiographical Common-places." In *The Private Self*. Edited by S. Benstock. London: Routledge.

Ochberg, Richard L. 1988. "Life Stories and the Psychosocial Construction of Careers." *Journal of Personality* 56:171-202.

Olney, James. 1980. *Autobiography: Essays Theoretical and Critical*. Princeton, N.J.: Princeton University Press.

Rabuzzi, Kathryn Allen. 1988. *Motherself: A Mythic Analysis of Motherhood*. Bloomington: Indiana University Press.

Rosenwald, George C. 1988. "A Theory of Multiple-Case Research." *Journal of Personality* 56:239-264.

Russ, Joanna. 1972. "What Can a Heroine Do? Or Why Women Can't Write." In *Images of Women in Fiction*. Edited by S. Koppelman Cornillon. Bowling Green, Ohio: University Popular Press.

Sayre, Robert F. 1980. "Autobiography and the Making of America." In *Autobiography, Essays Theoretical and Critical*. Edited by J. Olney. Princeton, N.J.: Princeton University Press.

Smith, Sidonie A. 1974. *Where I'm Bound: Patterns of Slavery and Freedom in Black American Autobiography*. Westport, Conn.: Greenwood Press.

————. 1987. *A Poetics of Women's Autobiography. Marginally and the Functions of Self-Representation*. Bloomington: Indiana University Press.

Sprinker, Michael. 1980. "Fictions of the Self: The End of *Autobiography*." In *Autobiography: Essays Theoretical and Critical*. Edited by J. Olney. Princeton, N.J.: Princeton University Press.

Stanton, Domna. 1984. *The Female Autograph*. Chicago: University Press.

Tyler, Stephen. 1986. "Post-Modern Ethnography: From Document of the Occult to Occult Documents." In *Writing Culture*. Edited by J. Clifford and G. Marcus. Berkeley: University of California Press.

Woolf, Virginia. [1929] 1957. *A Room of One's Own*. New York: Harcourt, Brace, Jovanovich.

————. 1958. *Granite and Rainbow*. New York: Harcourt, Brace, Jovanovich.

MASCULINITY AS HOMOPHOBIA
Fear, Shame, and Silence in the Construction of Gender Identity

Michael S. Kimmel

"Funny thing," [Curley's wife] said. "If I catch any one man, and he's alone, I get along fine with him. But just let two of the guys get together an' you won't talk. Jus' nothin' but mad." She dropped her fingers and put her hands on her hips. "You're all scared of each other, that's what. Ever'one of you's scared the rest is goin' to get something on you."

—John Steinbeck, *Of Mice and Men* (1937)

chapter 11

WE THINK of manhood as eternal, a timeless essence that resides deep in the heart of every man. We think of manhood as a thing, a quality that one either has or doesn't have. We think of manhood as innate, residing in the particular biological composition of the human male, the result of androgens or the possession of a penis. We think of manhood as a transcendent tangible property that each man must manifest in the world, the reward presented with great ceremony to a young novice by his elder for having successfully completed an arduous initiation ritual. In the words of poet Robert Bly (1990), "the

AUTHOR'S NOTE: This chapter represents a preliminary working out of a theoretical chapter in my forthcoming book, *Manhood: The American Quest* (in press). I am grateful to Tim Beneke, Harry Brod, Micheal Kaufman, Iona Mara-Drita, and Lillian Rubin for comments on earlier versions of the chapter.

structure at the bottom of the male psyche is still as firm as it was twenty thousand years ago" (p. 230).

In this chapter, I view masculinity as a constantly changing collection of meanings that we construct through our relationships with ourselves, with each other, and with our world. Manhood is neither static nor timeless; it is historical. Manhood is not the manifestation of an inner essence; it is socially constructed. Manhood does not bubble up to consciousness from our biological makeup; it is created in culture. Manhood means different things at different times to different people. We come to know what it means to be a man in our culture by setting our definitions in opposition to a set of "others"— racial minorities, sexual minorities, and, above all, women.

Our definitions of manhood are constantly changing, being played out on the political and social terrain on which the relationships between women and men are played out. In fact, the search for a transcendent, timeless definition of manhood is itself a sociological phenomenon—we tend to search for the timeless and eternal during moments of crisis, those points of transition when old definitions no longer work and new definitions are yet to be firmly established.

This idea that manhood is socially constructed and historically shifting should not be understood as a loss, that something is being taken away from men. In fact, it gives us something extraordinarily valuable—agency, the capacity to act. It gives us a sense of historical possibilities to replace the despondent resignation that invariably attends timeless, ahistorical essentialisms. Our behaviors are not simply "just human nature," because "boys will be boys." From the materials we find around us in our culture—other people, ideas, objects—we actively create our worlds, our identities. Men, both individually and collectively, can change.

In this chapter, I explore this social and historical construction of both hegemonic masculinity and alternate masculinities, with an eye toward offering a new theoretical model of American manhood.[1] To accomplish this I first uncover some of the hidden gender meanings in classical statements of social and political philosophy, so that I can anchor the emergence of contemporary manhood in specific historical and social contexts. I then spell out the ways in which this version of masculinity emerged in the United States, by tracing both psychoanalytic developmental sequences and a historical trajectory in the development of marketplace relationships.

CLASSICAL SOCIAL THEORY AS A HIDDEN MEDITATION OF MANHOOD

Begin this inquiry by looking at four passages from that set of texts commonly called classical social and political theory. You will, no doubt, recognize them, but I invite you to recall the way they were discussed in your undergraduate or graduate courses in theory:

224

KIMMEL

The bourgeoisie cannot exist without constantly revolutionizing the instruments of production, and thereby the relations of production, and with them the whole relations of society. Conservation of the old modes of production in unaltered form, was, on the contrary, the first condition of existence for all earlier industrial classes. Constant revolutionizing of production, uninterrupted disturbance of all social conditions, everlasting uncertainty and agitation distinguish the bourgeois epoch from all earlier ones. All fixed, fast-frozen relations, with their train of ancient and venerable prejudices and opinions are swept away, all new-formed ones become antiquated before they can ossify. All that is solid melts into air, all that is holy is profaned, and man is at last compelled to face with sober senses, his real conditions of life, and his relation with his kind. (Marx & Engels, 1848/1964).

An American will build a house in which to pass his old age and sell it before the roof is on; he will plant a garden and rent it just as the trees are coming into bearing; he will clear a field and leave others to reap the harvest; he will take up a profession and leave it, settle in one place and soon go off elsewhere with his changing desires . . . At first sight there is something astonishing in this spectacle of so many lucky men restless in the midst of abundance. But it is a spectacle as old as the world; all that is new is to see a whole people performing in it. (Tocqueville, 1835/1967)

Where the fulfillment of the calling cannot directly be related to the highest spiritual and cultural values, or when, on the other hand, it need not be felt simply as economic compulsion, the individual generally abandons the attempt to justify it at all. In the field of its highest development, in the United States, the pursuit of wealth, stripped of its religious and ethical meaning, tends to become associated with purely mundane passions, which often actually give it the character of sport. (Weber, 1905/1966)

225

We are warned by a proverb against serving two masters at the same time. The poor ego has things even worse: it serves three severe masters and does what it can to bring their claims and demands into harmony with one another. These claims are always divergent and often seem incompatible. No wonder that the ego so often fails in its task. Its three tyrannical masters are the external world, the super ego and the id. . . . It feels hemmed in on three sides, threatened by three kinds of danger, to which, if it is hard pressed, it reacts by generating anxiety. . . Thus the ego, driven by the id, confined by the super ego, repulsed by reality, struggles to master its economic task of bringing about harmony among the forces and influences working in and upon it; and we can understand how it is that so often we cannot suppress a cry: "Life is not easy!" (Freud, "The Dissection of the Psychical Personality," 1933/1966)

If your social science training was anything like mine, these were offered as descriptions of the bourgeoisie under capitalism, of individuals in democratic societies, of the fate of the Protestant work ethic under the ever rationalizing

KIMMEL

spirit of capitalism, or of the arduous task of the autonomous ego in psychological development. Did anyone ever mention that in all four cases the theorists were describing men? Not just "man" as in generic mankind, but a particular type of masculinity, a definition of manhood that derives its identity from participation in the marketplace, from interaction with other men in that marketplace—in short, a model of masculinity for whom identity is based on homosocial competition? Three years before Tocqueville found Americans "restless in the midst of abundance," Senator Henry Clay had called the United States "a nation of self-made men."

What does it mean to be "self-made"? What are the consequences of self-making for the individual man, for other men, for women? It is this notion of manhood—rooted in the sphere of production, the public arena, a masculinity grounded not in landownership or in artisanal republican virtue but in successful participation in marketplace competition—this has been the defining notion of American manhood. Masculinity must be proved, and no sooner is it proved that it is again questioned and must be proved again— constant, relentless, unachievable, and ultimately the quest for proof becomes so meaningless than it takes on the characteristics, as Weber said, of a sport. He who has the most toys when he dies wins.

Where does this version of masculinity come from? How does it work? What are the consequences of this version of masculinity for women, for other men, and for individual men themselves? These are the questions I address in this chapter.

226

MASCULINITY AS HISTORY AND THE HISTORY OF MASCULINITY

The idea of masculinity expressed in the previous extracts is the product of historical shifts in the grounds on which men rooted their sense of themselves as men. To argue that cultural definitions of gender identity are historically specific goes only so far; we have to specify exactly what those models were. In my historical inquiry into the development of these models of manhood[2] I chart the fate of two models for manhood at the turn of the 19th century and the emergence of a third in the first few decades of that century.

In the late 18th and early 19th centuries, two models of manhood prevailed. The *Genteel Patriarch* derived his identity from landownership. Supervising his estate, he was refined, elegant, and given to casual sensuousness. He was a doting and devoted father, who spent much of his time supervising the estate and with his family. Think of George Washington or Thomas Jefferson as examples. By contrast, the *Heroic Artisan* embodied the physical strength and republican virtue that Jefferson observed in the yeoman farmer, independent urban craftsman, or shopkeeper. Also a devoted father, the Heroic Artisan taught his son his craft, bringing him through ritual apprenticeship to status as master craftsman. Economically autonomous, the Heroic Artisan also cher-

KIMMEL

ished his democratic community, delighting in the participatory democracy of the town meeting. Think of Paul Revere at his pewter shop, shirtsleeves rolled up, a leather apron—a man who took pride in his work.

Heroic Artisans and Genteel Patriarchs lived in casual accord, in part because their gender ideals were complementary (both supported participatory democracy and individual autonomy, although patriarchs tended to support more powerful state machineries and also supported slavery) and because they rarely saw one another: Artisans were decidedly urban and the Genteel Patriarchs ruled their rural estates. By the 1830s, though, this casual symbiosis was shattered by the emergence of a new vision of masculinity, *Marketplace Manhood*.

Marketplace Man derived his identity entirely from his success in the capitalist marketplace, as he accumulated wealth, power, status. He was the urban entrepreneur, the businessman. Restless, agitated, and anxious, Marketplace Man was an absentee landlord at home and an absent father with his children, devoting himself to his work in an increasingly homosocial environment—a male-only world in which he pits himself against other men. His efforts at self-making transform the political and economic spheres, casting aside the Genteel Patriarch as an anachronistic feminized dandy—sweet, but ineffective and outmoded, and transforming the Heroic Artisan into a dispossessed proletarian, a wage slave.

As Tocqueville would have seen it, the coexistence of the Genteel Patriarch and the Heroic Artisan embodied the fusion of liberty and equality. Genteel Patriarchy was the manhood of the traditional aristocracy, the class that embodied the virtue of liberty. The Heroic Artisan embodied democratic community, the solidarity of the urban shopkeeper or craftsman. Liberty and democracy, the patriarch and the artisan, could, and did, coexist. But Marketplace Man is capitalist man, and he makes both freedom and equality problematic, eliminating the freedom of the aristocracy and proletarianizing the equality of the artisan. In one sense, American history has been an effort to restore, retrieve, or reconstitute the virtues of Genteel Patriarchy and Heroic Artisanate as they were being transformed in the capitalist marketplace.

Marketplace Manhood was a manhood that required proof, and that required the acquisition of tangible goods as evidence of success. It reconstituted itself by the exclusion of "others"—women, nonwhite men, nonnative-born men, homosexual men—and by terrified flight into a pristine mythic homosocial Eden where men could, at last, be real men among other men. The story of the ways in which Marketplace Man becomes American Everyman is a tragic tale, of striving to live up to impossible ideals of success leading to chronic terrors of emasculation, emotional emptiness, and a gendered rage that leave a wide swath of destruction in its wake.

227

KIMMEL

MASCULINITIES AS POWER RELATIONS

Marketplace Masculinity describes the normative definition of American masculinity. It describes his characteristics—aggression, competition anxiety—and the arena in which those characteristics are deployed—the public sphere, the marketplace. If the marketplace is the arena in which manhood is tested and proved, it is a gendered arena, in which tensions between women and men and tensions among different groups of men are weighted with meaning. These tensions suggest that cultural definitions of gender are played out in a contested terrain and are themselves power relations.

All masculinities are not created equal; or rather, we are all created equal, but any hypothetical equality evaporates quickly because our definitions of masculinity are not equally valued in our society. One definition of manhood continues to remain the standard against which other forms of manhood are measured and evaluated. Within the dominant culture, the masculinity that defines white, middle class, early middle-aged, heterosexual men is the masculinity that sets the standards for other men, against which other men are measured and, more often than not, found wanting. Sociologist Erving Goffman (1963) wrote that in America, there is only "one complete, unblushing male":

> a young, married, white, urban, northern heterosexual, Protestant father of college education, fully employed, of good complexion, weight and height, and a recent record in sports. Every American male tends to look out upon the world from this perspective. . . . Any male who fails to qualify in any one of these ways is likely to view himself . . . as unworthy, incomplete, and inferior. (p. 128)

This is the definition that we will call "hegemonic" masculinity, the image of masculinity of those men who hold power, which has become the standard in psychological evaluations, sociological research, and self-help and advice literature for teaching young men to become "real men" (Connell, 1987). The hegemonic definition of manhood is a man in power, a man *with* power, and a man of *power*. We equate manhood with being strong, successful, capable, reliable, in control. The very definitions of manhood we have developed in our culture maintain the power that some men have over other men and that men have over women.

Our culture's definition of masculinity is thus several stories at once. It is about the individual man's quest to accumulate those cultural symbols that denote manhood, signs that he has in fact achieved it. It is about those standards being used against women to prevent their inclusion in public life and their consignment to a devalued private sphere. It is about the differential access that different types of men have to those cultural resources that confer manhood and about how each of these groups then develop their own modifications to preserve and claim their manhood. It is about the power of these

KIMMEL

definitions themselves to serve to maintain the real-life power that men have over women and that some men have over other men.

This definition of manhood has been summarized cleverly by psychologist Robert Brannon (1976) into four succinct phrases:

1. "No Sissy Stuff!" One may never do anything that even remotely suggests femininity. Masculinity is the relentless repudiation of the feminine.
2. "Be a Big Wheel." Masculinity is measured by power, success, wealth, and status. As the current saying goes. "He who has the most toys when he dies wins."
3. "Be a Sturdy Oak." Masculinity depends on remaining calm and reliable in a crisis, holding emotions in check. In fact, proving you're a man depends on never showing your emotions at all. Boys don't cry.
4. "Give 'em Hell." Exude an aura of manly daring and aggression. Go for it. Take risks.

These rules contain the elements of the definition against which virtually all American men are measured. Failure to embody these rules, to affirm the power of the rules and one's achievement of them is a source of men's confusion and pain. Such a model is, of course, unrealizable for any man. But we keep trying, valiantly and vainly, to measure up. American masculinity is a relentless test.[3] The chief test is contained in the first rule. Whatever the variations by race, class, age, ethnicity, or sexual orientation, being a man means "not being like women." This notion of antifeminity lies at the heart of contemporary and historical conceptions of manhood, so that masculinity is defined more by what one is not rather than who one is.

MASCULINITY AS THE FLIGHT FROM THE FEMININE

Historically and developmentally, masculinity has been defined as the flight from women, the repudiation of femininity. Since Freud, we have come to understand that developmentally the central task that every little boy must confront is to develop a secure identity for himself as a man. As Freud had it, the oedipal project is a process of the boy's renouncing his identification with and deep emotional attachment to his mother and then replacing her with the father as the object of identification. Notice that he reidentifies but never reattaches. This entire process, Freud argued, is set in motion by the boy's sexual desire for his mother. But the father stands in the son's path and will not yield his sexual property to his puny son. The boy's first emotional experience, then, the one that inevitably follows his experience of desire, is fear—fear of the bigger, stronger, more sexually powerful father. It is this fear, experienced symbolically as the fear of castration, Freud argues, that forces the young boy to renounce his identification with mother and seek to identify with the being who is the

KIMMEL

actual source of his fear, his father. In so doing, the boy is now symbolically capable of sexual union with a motherlike substitute, that is, a woman. The boy becomes gendered (masculine) and heterosexual at the same time.

Masculinity, in this model, is irrevocably tied to sexuality. The boy's sexuality will now come to resemble the sexuality of his father (or at least the way he imagines his father)—menacing, predatory, possessive, and possibly punitive. The boy has come to identify with his oppressor; now he can become the oppressor himself. But a terror remains, the terror that the young man will be unmasked as a fraud, as a man who has not completely and irrevocably separated from mother. It will be other men who will do the unmasking. Failure will de-sex the man, make him appear as not fully a man. He will be seen as a wimp, a Mama's boy, a sissy.

After pulling away from his mother, the boy comes to see her not as a source of nurturance and love, but as an insatiably infantalizing creature, capable of humiliating him in front of his peers. She makes him dress up in uncomfortable and itchy clothing, her kisses smear his cheeks with lipstick, staining his boyish innocence with the mark of feminine dependency. No wonder so many boys cringe from their mothers' embraces with groans of "Aw, Mom! Quit it!" Mothers represent the humiliation of infancy, helplessness, dependency. "Men act as though they were being guided by (or rebelling against) rules and prohibitions enunciated by a moral mother," writes psychohistorian Geoffrey Gorer (1964). As a result, "all the niceties of masculine behavior—modesty, politeness, neatness, cleanliness—come to be regarded as concessions to feminine demands, and not good in themselves as part of the behavior of a proper man" (pp. 56, 57).

The flight from femininity is angry and frightened, because mother can so easily emasculate the young boy by her power to render him dependent, or at least to remind him of dependency. It is relentless; manhood becomes a lifelong quest to demonstrate its achievement, as if to prove the unprovable to others, because we feel so unsure of it ourselves. Women don't often feel compelled to "prove their womanhood"—the phrase itself sounds ridiculous. Women have different kinds of gender identity crises; their anger and frustration, and their own symptoms of depression, come more from being excluded than from questioning whether they are feminine enough.[4]

The drive to repudiate the mother as the indication of the acquisition of masculine gender identity has three consequences for the young boy. First, he pushes away his real mother, and with her the traits of nurturance, compassion, and tenderness she may have embodied. Second, he suppresses those traits in himself, because they will reveal his incomplete separation from mother. His life becomes a lifelong project to demonstrate that he possesses none of his mother's traits. Masculine identity is born in the renunciation of the feminine, not in the direct affirmation of the masculine, which leaves masculine gender identity tenuous and fragile.

Third, as if to demonstrate the accomplishment of these first two tasks, the boy also learns to devalue all women in his society, as the living embodiments of those traits in himself he has learned to despise. Whether or not he was aware of it, Freud also described the origins of sexism—the systematic devaluation of women—in the desperate efforts of the boy to separate from mother. We may *want* "a girl just like the girl that married dear old Dad," as the popular song had it, but we certainly don't want to be *like* her.

This chronic uncertainty about gender identity helps us understand several obsessive behaviors. Take, for example, the continuing problem of the schoolyard bully. Parents remind us that the bully is the least secure about his manhood, and so he is constantly trying to prove it. But he "proves" it by choosing opponents he is absolutely certain he can defeat; thus the standard taunt to a bully is to "pick on someone your own size." He can't, though, and after defeating a smaller and weaker opponent, which he was sure would prove his manhood, he is left with the empty gnawing feeling that he has not proved it after all, and he must find another opponent, again one smaller and weaker, that he can again defeat to prove it to himself.[5]

One of the more graphic illustrations of this lifelong quest to prove one's manhood occurred at the Academy Awards presentation in 1992. As aging, tough guy actor Jack Palance accepted the award for Best Supporting Actor for his role in the cowboy comedy *City Slickers*, he commented that people, especially film producers, think that because he is 71 years old, he's all washed up, that he's no longer competent. "Can we take a risk on this guy?" he quoted them as saying, before he dropped to the floor to do a set of one-armed push-ups. It was pathetic to see such an accomplished actor still having to prove that he is virile enough to work and, as he also commented at the podium, to have sex.

When does it end? Never. To admit weakness, to admit frailty or fragility, is to be seen as a wimp, a sissy, not a real man. But seen by whom?

MASCULINITY AS A HOMOSOCIAL ENACTMENT

Other men: We are under the constant careful scrutiny of other men. Other men watch us, rank us, grant our acceptance into the realm of manhood. Manhood is demonstrated for other men's approval. It is other men who evaluate the performance. Literary critic David Leverenz (1991) argues that "ideologies of manhood have functioned primarily in relation to the gaze of male peers and male authority" (p. 769). Think of how men boast to one another of their accomplishments—from their latest sexual conquest to the size of the fish they caught—and how we constantly parade the markers of manhood—wealth, power, status, sexy women—in front of other men, desperate for their approval.

That men prove their manhood in the eyes of other men is both a consequence of sexism and one of its chief props. "Women have, in men's minds,

231

such a low place on the social ladder of this country that it's useless to define yourself in terms of a woman," noted playwright David Mamet.

"What men need is men's approval." Women become a kind of currency that men use to improve their ranking on the masculine social scale. (Even those moments of heroic conquest of women carry, I believe, a current of homosocial evaluation.) Masculinity is a *homosocial* enactment. We test ourselves, perform heroic feats, take enormous risks, all because we want other men to grant us our manhood.

Masculinity as a homosocial enactment is fraught with danger, with the risk of failure, and with intense relentless competition. "Every man you meet has a rating or an estimate of himself which he never loses or forgets," wrote Kenneth Wayne (1912) in his popular turn-of-the-century advice book. "A man has his own rating, and instantly he lays it alongside of the other man" (p. 18). Almost a century later, another man remarked to psychologist Sam Osherson (1992) that "[b]y the time you're an adult, it's easy to think you're always in competition with men, for the attention of women, in sports, at work" (p. 291).

MASCULINITY AS HOMOPHOBIA

If masculinity is a homosocial enactment, its overriding emotion is fear. In the Freudian model, the fear of the father's power terrifies the young boy to renounce his desire for his mother and identify with his father. This model links gender identity with sexual orientation: The little boy's identification with father (becoming masculine) allows him to now engage in sexual relations with women (he becomes heterosexual). This is the origin of how we can "read" one's sexual orientation through the successful performance of gender identity. Second, the fear that the little boy feels does not send him scurrying into the arms of his mother to protect him from his father. Rather, he believes he will overcome his fear by identifying with its source. We become masculine by identifying with our oppressor.

But there is a piece of the puzzle missing, a piece that Freud, himself, implied but did not follow up.[6] If the pre-oedipal boy identifies with mother, he *sees the world through mother's eyes*. Thus, when he confronts father during his great oedipal crisis, he experiences a split vision: He sees his father as his mother sees his father, with a combination of awe, wonder, terror, and *desire*. He simultaneously sees the father as he, the boy, would like to see him—as the object not of desire but of emulation. Repudiating mother and identifying with father only partially answers his dilemma. What is he to do with that homoerotic desire, the desire he felt because he saw father the way that his mother saw father?

He must suppress it. Homoerotic desire is cast as feminine desire, desire for other men. Homophobia is the effort to suppress the desire, to purify all relationships with other men, with women, with children of its taint, and to ensure that no one could possibly ever mistake one for a homosexual. Homophobic flight from intimacy with other men is the repudiation of the homosexual within—never completely successful and hence constantly reenacted in every homosocial relationship. "The lives of most American men are bounded, and their interests daily curtailed by the constant necessity to prove to their fellows, and to themselves, that they are not sissies, not homosexuals," writes psychoanalytic historian Geoffrey Gorer (1964). "Any interest or pursuit which is identified as a feminine interest or pursuit becomes deeply suspect for men" (p. 129).

Even if we do not subscribe to Freudian psychoanalytic ideas, we can still observe how, in less sexualized terms, the father is the first man who evaluates the boy's masculine performance, the first pair of male eyes before whom he tries to prove himself. Those eyes will follow him for the rest of his life. Other men's eyes will join them—the eyes of role models such as teachers, coaches, bosses, or media heroes; the eyes of his peers, his friends, his workmates; and the eyes of millions of other men, living and dead, from whose constant scrutiny of his performance he will never be free. "The tradition of all the dead generations weighs like a nightmare on the brain of the living," was how Karl Marx put it over a century ago (1848/1964, p. 11). "The birthright of every American male is a chronic sense of personal inadequacy," is how two psychologists describe it today (Woolfolk & Richardson, 1978, p. 57).

That nightmare from which we never seem to awaken is that those other men will see that sense of inadequacy, they will see that in our own eyes we are not who we are pretending to be. What we call masculinity is often a hedge against being revealed as a fraud, an exaggerated set of activities that keep others from seeing through us, and a frenzied effort to keep at bay those fears within ourselves. Our real fear "is not fear of women but of being ashamed or humiliated in front of other men, or being dominated by stronger men" (Leverenz, 1986, p. 451).

This, then, is the great secret of American manhood: *We are afraid of other men*. Homophobia is a central organizing principle of our cultural definition of manhood. Homophobia is more than the irrational fear of gay men, more than the fear that we might be perceived as gay. "The word 'faggot' has nothing to do with homosexual experience or even with fears of homosexuals," writes David Leverenz (1986). "It comes out of the depths of manhood: a label of ultimate contempt for anyone who seems sissy, untough, uncool" (p. 455). Homophobia is the fear that other men will unmask us, emasculate us, reveal to us and the world that we do not measure up, that we are not real men. We are afraid to let other men see that fear. Fear makes us ashamed, because the recognition of fear in ourselves is proof to ourselves that we are not as manly as we pretend, that we are, like the young man in a poem by Yeats, "one that ruffles in a manly pose for all his timid heart." Our fear is the fear of humiliation. We are ashamed to be afraid.

Shame leads to silence—the silences that keep other people believing that we actually approve of the things that are done to women, to minorities, to gays and lesbians in our culture. The frightened silence as we scurry past a woman being hassled by men on the street. That furtive silence when men make sexist or racist jokes in a bar. That clammy-handed silence when guys in the office make gay-bashing jokes. Our fears are the sources of our silences, and men's silence is what keeps the system running. This might help to explain why women often complain that their male friends or partners are often so understanding when they are alone and yet laugh at sexist jokes or even make those jokes themselves when they are out with a group.

The fear of being seen as a sissy dominates the cultural definitions of manhood. It starts so early. "Boys among boys are ashamed to be unmanly," wrote one educator in 1871 (cited in Rotundo, 1993, p. 264). I have a standing bet with a friend that I can walk onto any playground in America where 6-year-old boys are happily playing and by asking one question, I can provoke a fight. That question is simple: "Who's a sissy around here?" Once posed, the challenge is made. One of two things is likely to happen. One boy will accuse another of being a sissy, to which that boy will respond that he is not a sissy, that the first boy is. They may have to fight it out to see who's lying. Or a whole group of boys will surround one boy and all shout "He is! He is!" That boy will either burst into tears and run home crying, disgraced, or he will have to take on several boys at once, to prove that he's not a sissy. (And what will his father or older brothers tell him if he chooses to run home crying?) It will be some time before he regains any sense of self-respect.

Violence is often the single most evident marker of manhood. Rather it is the willingness to fight, the desire to fight. The origin of our expression that one has a chip on one's shoulder lies in the practice of an adolescent boy in the country or small town at the turn of the century, who would literally walk around with a chip of wood balanced on his shoulder—a signal of his readiness to fight with anyone who would take the initiative of knocking the chip off (see Gorer, 1964, p. 38; Mead, 1965).

As adolescents, we learn that our peers are a kind of gender police, constantly threatening to unmask us as feminine, as sissies. One of the favorite tricks when I was an adolescent was to ask a boy to look at his fingernails. If he held his palm toward his face and curled his fingers back to see them, he passed the test. He'd looked at his nails "like a man." But if he held the back of his hand away from his face, and looked at his fingernails with arm outstretched, he was immediately ridiculed as a sissy.

As young men we are constantly riding those gender boundaries, checking the fences we have constructed on the perimeter, making sure that nothing even remotely feminine might show through. The possibilities of being unmasked are everywhere. Even the most seemingly insignificant thing can pose a threat or activate that haunting terror. On the day the students in my course

"Sociology of Men and Masculinities" were scheduled to discuss homophobia and male-male friendships, one student provided a touching illustration. Noting that it was a beautiful day, the first day of spring after a brutal northeast winter, he decided to wear shorts to class. "I had this really nice pair of new Madras shorts," he commented. "But then I thought to myself, these shorts have lavender and pink in them. Today's class topic is homophobia. Maybe today is not the best day to wear these shorts."

Our efforts to maintain a manly front cover everything we do. What we wear. How we talk. How we walk. What we eat. Every mannerism, every movement contains a coded gender language. Think, for example, of how you would answer the question: How do you "know" if a man is homosexual? When I ask this question in classes or workshops, respondents invariably provide a pretty standard list of stereotypically effeminate behaviors. He walks a certain way, talks a certain way, acts a certain way. He's very emotional; he shows his feelings. One woman commented that she "knows" a man is gay if he really cares about her; another said she knows he's gay if he shows no interest in her, if he leaves her alone.

Now alter the question and imagine what heterosexual men do to make sure no one could possibly get the "wrong idea" about them. Responses typically refer to the original stereotypes, this time as a set of negative rules about behavior. Never dress that way. Never talk or walk that way. Never show your feelings or get emotional. Always be prepared to demonstrate sexual interest in women that you meet, so it is impossible for any woman to get the wrong idea about you. In this sense, homophobia, the fear of being perceived as gay, as not a real man, keeps men exaggerating all the traditional rules of masculinity, including sexual predation with women. Homophobia and sexism go hand in hand.

The stakes of perceived sissydom are enormous—sometimes matters of life and death. We take enormous risks to prove our manhood, exposing ourselves disproportionately to health risks, workplace hazards, and stress-related illnesses. Men commit suicide three times as often as women. Psychiatrist Willard Gaylin (1992) explains that it is "invariably because of perceived social humiliation," most often tied to failure in business:

> Men become depressed because of loss of status and power in the world of men. It is not the loss of money, or the material advantages that money could buy, which produces the despair that leads to self-destruction. It is the "shame," the "humiliation," the sense of personal "failure." . . . A man despairs when he has ceased being a man among men. (p. 32)

In one survey, women and men were asked what they were most afraid of. Women responded that they were most afraid of being raped and murdered. Men responded that they were most afraid of being laughed at (Noble, 1992, pp. 105-106).

235

KIMMEL

HOMOPHOBIA AS A CAUSE OF SEXISM, HETEROSEXISM, AND
RACISM

Homohobia is intimately interwoven with both sexism and racism. The fear—sometimes conscious, sometimes not—that others might perceive us as homosexual propels men to enact all manner of exaggerated masculine behaviors and attitudes to make sure that no one could possibly get the wrong idea about us. One of the centerpieces of that exaggerated masculinity is putting women down, both by excluding them from the public sphere and by the quotidian put-downs in speech and behaviors that organize the daily life of the American man. Women and gay men become the "other" against which heterosexual men project their identities, against whom they stack the decks so as to compete in a situation in which they will always win, so that by suppressing them, men can stake a claim for their own manhood. Women threaten emasculation by representing the home, workplace, and familial responsibility, the negation of fun. Gay men have historically played the role of the consummate sissy in the American popular mind because homosexuality is seen as an inversion of normal gender development. There have been other "others." Through American history, various groups have represented the sissy, the non-men against whom American men played out their definitions of manhood, often with vicious results. In fact, these changing groups provide an interesting lesson in American historical development.

At the turn of the 19th century, it was Europeans and children who provided the contrast for American men. The "true American was vigorous, manly, and direct, not effete and corrupt like the supposed Europeans," writes Rupert Wilkinson (1986). "He was plain rather than ornamented, rugged rather than luxury seeking, a liberty loving common man or natural gentleman rather than an aristocratic oppressor or servile minion" (p. 96). The "real man" of the early 19th century was neither noble nor serf. By the middle of the century, black slaves had replaced the effete nobleman. Slaves were seen as dependent, helpless men, incapable of defending their women and children, and therefore less than manly. Native Americans were cast as foolish and naive children, so they could be infantilized as the "Red Children of the Great White Father" and therefore excluded from full manhood.

By the end of the century, new European immigrants were also added to the list of the unreal men, especially the Irish and Italians, who were seen as too passionate and emotionally volatile to remain controlled sturdy oaks, and Jews, who were seen as too bookishly effete and too physically puny to truly measure up. In the mid-20th century, it was also Asians—first the Japanese during the Second World War, and more recently, the Vietnamese during the Vietnam War—who have served as unmanly templates against which American men have hurled their gendered rage. Asian men were seen as small, soft, and effeminate—hardly men at all.

Such a list of "hyphenated" Americans—Italian-, Jewish-, Irish-, African-,

236

KIMMEL

Native-, Asian-, gay—composes the majority of American men. So manhood is only possible for a distinct minority, and the definition has been constructed to prevent the others from achieving it. Interestingly, this emasculation of one's enemies has a flip side—and one that is equally gendered. These very groups that have historically been cast as less than manly were also, often simultaneously, cast as hypermasculine, as sexually aggressive, violent rapacious beasts, against whom "civilized" men must take a decisive stand and thereby rescue civilization. Thus black men were depicted as rampaging sexual beasts, women as carnivorously carnal, gay men as sexually insatiable, southern European men as sexually predatory and voracious, and Asian men as vicious and cruel torturers who were immorally disinterested in life itself, willing to sacrifice their entire people for their whims. But whether one saw these groups as effeminate sissies or as brutal uncivilized savages, the terms with which they were perceived were gendered. These groups become the "others," the screens against which traditional conceptions of manhood were developed.

Being seen as unmanly is a fear that propels American men to deny manhood to others, as a way of proving the unprovable—that one is fully manly. Masculinity becomes a defense against the perceived threat of humiliation in the eyes of other men, enacted through a "sequence of postures"—things we might say, or do, or even think, that, if we thought carefully about them, would make us ashamed of ourselves (Savran, 1992, p. 16). After all, how many of us have made homophobic or sexist remarks, or told racist jokes, or made lewd comments to women on the street? How many of us have translated those ideas and those words into actions, by physically attacking gay men, or forcing or cajoling a woman to have sex even though she didn't really want to because it was important to score?

POWER AND POWERLESSNESS IN THE LIVES OF MEN

I have argued that homophobia, men's fear of other men, is the animating condition of the dominant definition of masculinity in America, that the reigning definition of masculinity is a defensive effort to prevent being emasculated. In our efforts to suppress or overcome those fears, the dominant culture exacts a tremendous price from those deemed less than fully manly: women, gay men, nonnative-born men, men of color. This perspective may help clarify a paradox in men's lives, a paradox in which men have virtually all the power and yet do not feel powerful (see Kaufman, 1993).

Manhood is equated with power—over women, over other men. Everywhere we look, we see the institutional expression of that power—in state and national legislatures, on the boards of directors of every major U.S. corporation or law firm, and in every school and hospital administration. Women have long understood this, and feminist women have spent the past three decades challenging both the public and the private expressions of men's power and acknowledging their fear of men. Feminism as a set of theories

237

KIMMEL

both explains women's fear of men and empowers women to confront it both publicly and privately. Feminist women have theorized that masculinity is about the drive for domination, the drive for power, for conquest.

This feminist definition of masculinity as the drive for power is theorized from women's point of view. It is how women experience masculinity. But it assumes a symmetry between the public and the private that does not conform to men's experiences. Feminists observe that women, as a group, do not hold power in our society. They also observe that individually, they, as women, do not feel powerful. They feel afraid, vulnerable. Their observation of the social reality and their individual experiences are therefore symmetrical. Feminism also observes that men, as a group, are in power. Thus, with the same symmetry, feminism has tended to assume that individually men must feel powerful.

This is why the feminist critique of masculinity often falls on deaf ears with men. When confronted with the analysis that men have all the power, many men react incredulously. "What do you mean, men have all the power?" they ask. "What are you talking about? My wife bosses me around. My kids boss me around. My boss bosses me around. I have no power at all! I'm completely powerless!"

Men's feelings are not the feelings of the powerful, but of those who see themselves as powerless. These are the feelings that come inevitably from the discontinuity between the social and the psychological, between the aggregate analysis that reveals how men are in power as a group and the psychological fact that they do not feel powerful as individuals. They are the feelings of men who were raised to believe themselves entitled to feel that power, but do not feel it. No wonder many men are frustrated and angry.

This may explain the recent popularity of those workshops and retreats designed to help men to claim their "inner" power, their "deep manhood," or their "warrior within." Authors such as Bly (1990), Moore and Gillette (1991, 1992, 1993a, 1993b), Farrell (1986, 1993), and Keen (1991) honor and respect men's feelings of powerlessness and acknowledge those feelings to be both true and real. "They gave white men the semblance of power," notes John Lee, one of the leaders of these retreats (quoted in *Newsweek*, p. 41). "We'll let you run the country, but in the meantime, stop feeling, stop talking, and continue swallowing your pain and your hurt." (We are not told who "they" are.)

Often the purveyors of the mythopoetic men's movement, that broad umbrella that encompasses all the groups helping men to retrieve this mythic deep manhood, use the image of the chauffeur to describe modern man's position. The chauffeur appears to have the power—he's wearing the uniform, he's in the driver's seat, and he knows where he's going. So, to the observer, the chauffeur looks as though he is in command. But to the chauffeur himself, they note, he is merely taking orders. He is not at all in charge.[7]

Despite the reality that everyone knows chauffeurs do not have the power,

238

KIMMEL

this image remains appealing to the men who hear it at these weekend work-shops. But there is a missing piece to the image, a piece concealed by the framing of the image in terms of the individual man's experience. That miss-ing piece is that the person who is giving the orders is also a man. Now we have a relationship *between* men—between men giving orders and other men taking those orders. The man who identifies with the chauffeur is entitled to be the man giving the orders, but he is not. ("They," it tuns out, are other men.)

The dimension of power is now reinserted into men's experience not only as the product of individual experience but also as the product of relations with other men. In this sense, men's experience of powerlessness is *real*—the men actually feel it and certainly act on it—but it is not *true*, that is, it does not accurately describe their condition. In contrast to women's lives, men's lives are structured around relationships of power and men's differential access to power, as well as the differential access to that power of men as a group. Our imperfect analysis of our own situation leads us to believe that we men need more power, rather than leading us to support feminists' efforts to re-arrange power relationships along more equitable lines.

Philosopher Hannah Arendt (1970) fully understood this contradictory ex-perience of social and individual power:

> Power corresponds to the human ability not just to act but to act in concert. Power is never the property of an individual; it belongs to a group and remains in existence only so long as the group keeps together. When we say of somebody that he is "in power" we actually refer to his being empowered by a certain number of people to act in their name. The moment the group, from which the power originated to begin with . . . disappears, "his power" also vanishes. (p. 44)

239

Why, then, do American men feel so powerless? Part of the answer is because we've constructed the rules of manhood so that only the tiniest fraction of men come to believe that they are the biggest of wheels, the sturdiest of oaks, the most virulent repudiators of femininity, the most daring and aggressive. We've managed to disempower the overwhelming majority of American men by other means—such as discriminating on the basis of race, class, ethnicity, age, or sexual preference.

Masculinist retreats to retrieve deep, wounded, masculinity are but one of the ways in which American men currently struggle with their fears and their shame. Unfortunately, at the very moment that they work to break down the isolation that governs men's lives, as they enable men to express those fears and that shame, they ignore the social power that men continue to exert over women and the privileges from which they (as the middle-aged, middle-class white men who largely make up these retreats) continue to benefit—regard-less of their experiences as wounded victims of oppressive male socializa-tion.[8].

KIMMEL

Others still rehearse the politics of exclusion, as if by clearing away the playing field of secure gender identity of any that we deem less than manly—women, gay men, nonnative-born men, men of color—middle-class, straight, white men can reground their sense of themselves without those haunting fears and that deep shame that they are unmanly and will be exposed by other men. This is the manhood of racism, of sexism, of homophobia. It is the manhood that is so chronically insecure that it trembles at the idea of lifting the ban on gays in the military, that is so threatened by women in the workplace that women become the targets of sexual harassment, that is so deeply frightened of equality that it must ensure that the playing field of male competition remains stacked against all newcomers to the game.

Exclusion and escape have been the dominant methods American men have used to keep their fears of humiliation at bay. The fear of emasculation by other men, of being humiliated, of being seen as a sissy, is the leitmotif in my reading of the history of American manhood. Masculinity has become a relentless test by which we prove to other men, to women, and ultimately to ourselves, that we have successfully mastered the part. The restlessness that men feel today is nothing new in American history; we have been anxious and restless for almost two centuries. Neither exclusion nor escape has ever brought us the relief we've sought, and there is no reason to think that either will solve our problems now. Peace of mind, relief from gender struggle, will come only from a politics of inclusion, not exclusion, from standing up for equality and justice, and not by running away.

240

NOTES

1. Of course, the phrase "American manhood" contains several simultaneous fictions. There is no single manhood that defines all American men; "America" is meant to refer to the United States proper, and there are significant ways in which this "American manhood" is the outcome of forces that transcend both gender and nation, that is, the global economic development of industrial capitalism. I use it, therefore, to describe the specific hegemonic version of masculinity in the United States, that normative constellation of attitudes, traits, and behaviors that became the standard against which all other masculinities are measured and against which individual men measure the success of their gender accomplishments.

2. Much of this work is elaborated in *Manhood: The American Quest* (in press).

3. Although I am here discussing only American masculinity, I am aware that others have located this chronic instability and efforts to prove manhood in the particular cultural and economic arrangements of Western society. Calvin, after all, inveighed against the disgrace "for men to become effeminate," and countless other theorists have described the mechanics of manly proof. (See, for example, Seidler, 1994.)

4. I do not mean to argue that women do not have anxieties about whether they are feminine enough. Ask any woman how she feels about being called aggressive; it sends a chill into her heart because her femininity is suspect. (I believe that the reason for the enormous recent popularity of sexy lingerie among women is that it enables

KIMMEL

women to remember they are still feminine underneath their corporate business suit—a suit that apes masculine styles.) But I think the stakes are not as great for women and that women have greater latitude in defining their identities around these questions than men do. Such are the ironies of sexism: The powerful have a narrower range of options than the powerless, because the powerless can also imitate the powerful and get away with it. It may even enhance status, if done with charm and grace—that is, is not threatening. For the powerful, any hint of behaving like the powerless is a fall from grace.

5. Such observations also led journalist Heywood Broun to argue that most of the attacks against feminism came from men who were shorter than 5 ft. 7 in. "The man who, whatever his physical size, feels secure in his own masculinity and in his own relation to life is rarely resentful of the opposite sex" (cited in Symes, 1930, p. 139).

6. Some of Freud's followers, such as Anna Freud and Alfred Adler, did follow up on these suggestions. (See especially, Adler, 1980.) I am grateful to Terry Kupers for his help in thinking through Adler's ideas.

7. The image is from Warren Farrell, who spoke at a workshop I attended at the First International Men's Conference, Austin, Texas, October 1991.

8. For a critique of these mythopoetic retreats, see Kimmel and Kaufman, Chapter 14.

REFERENCES

Adler, A. (1980). *Cooperation between the sexes: Writings on women, love and marriage, sexuality and its disorders* (H. Ansbacher & R. Ansbacher, Eds. & Trans.). New York: Jason Aronson.

Arendt, H. (1970). *On revolution.* New York: Viking.

Bly, R. (1990). *Iron John: A book about men.* Reading, MA: Addison-Wesley.

Brannon, R. (1976). The male sex role—and what it's done for us lately. In R. Brannon & D. David (Eds.), *The forty-nine percent majority* (pp. 1–40). Reading, MA: Addison-Wesley.

Connell, R. W. (1987). *Gender and power.* Stanford, CA: Stanford University Press.

Farrell, W. (1986). *Why men are the way they are.* New York: McGraw-Hill.

Farrell, W. (1993). *The myth of male power: Why men are the disposable sex.* New York: Simon & Schuster.

Freud, S. (1933/1966). *New introductory lectures on psychoanalysis* (L. Strachey, Ed.). New York: Norton.

Gaylin, W. (1992). *The male ego.* New York: Viking.

Goffman, E. (1963). *Stigma.* Englewood Cliffs, NJ: Prentice Hall.

Gorer, G. (1964). *The American people: A study in national character.* New York: Norton.

Kaufman, M. (1993). *Cracking the armour: Power and pain in the lives of men.* Toronto: Viking Canada.

Keen, S. (1991). *Fire in the belly.* New York: Bantam.

Kimmel, M. S. (in press). *Manhood: The American quest.* New York: Harper Collins.

Leverenz, D. (1986). Manhood, humiliation and public life: Some stories. *Southwest Review, 71,* Fall.

Leverenz, D. (1991). The last real man in America: From Natty Bumppo to Batman. *American Literary Review, 3.*

KIMMEL

Marx, K., & F. Engels. (1848/1964). The communist manifesto. In R. Tucker (Ed.), *The Marx-Engels reader*. New York: Norton.

Mead, M. (1965). *And keep your powder dry*. New York: William Morrow.

Moore, R., & Gillette, D. (1991). *King, warrior, magician lover*. New York: Harper Collins.

Moore, R., & Gillette, D. (1992). *The king within: Accessing the king in the male psyche*. New York: William Morrow.

Moore, R., & Gillette, D. (1993a). *The warrior within: Accessing the warrior in the male psyche*. New York: William Morrow.

Moore, R., & Gillette, D. (1993b). *The magician within: Accessing the magician in the male psyche*. New York: William Morrow.

Noble, V. (1992). A helping hand from the guys. In K. L. Hagan (Ed.), *Women respond to the men's movement*. San Francisco: HarperCollins.

Osherson, S. (1992). *Wrestling with love: How men struggle with intimacy, with women, children, parents, and each other*. New York: Fawcett.

Rotundo, E. A. (1993). *American manhood: Transformations in masculinity from the revolution to the modern era*. New York: Basic Books.

Savran, D. (1992). *Communists, cowboys and queers: The politics of masculinity in the work of Arthur Miller and Tennessee Williams*. Minneapolis: University of Minnesota Press.

Seidler, V. J. (1994). *Unreasonable men: Masculinity and social theory*. New York: Routledge.

Symes. L. (1930). The new masculinism. *Harper's Monthly*, 161. January.

Tocqueville, A. de. (1835/1967). *Democracy in America*. New York: Anchor.

Wayne, K. (1912). *Building the young man*. Chicago: A.C. McClurg.

Weber, M. (1905/1966). *The Protestant ethic and the spirit of capitalism*. New York: Charles Scribner's.

What men need is men's approval. (1993, January 3). *The New York Times*, p. C–11.

Wilkinson, R. (1986). *American tough: The tough-guy tradition and American character*. New York: Harper & Row.

Woolfolk, R. L., & Richardson, F. (1978). *Sanity, stress and survival*. New York: Signet.

KIMMEL

PART IV

OPEN TO INTERPRETATION
Multiple Lenses

POST-COLONIAL FEMINISM AND THE VEIL
Thinking the Difference

Lama Abu Odeh

SINCE THE Iranian Revolution of 1979, the issue of the veil has been the topic of heated debate in Arab countries, particularly those that witnessed strong fundamentalist movements. The fact that Iranian Islamicists who took power in Iran sanctioned the veil and penalized those women who chose not to wear it was either a seductive or, alternatively, a terrifying reminder to women in other Muslim countries of what it might be like for women under Islamicist rule. In countries like Jordan, Algeria and Egypt, where fundamentalist movements have mobilized many followers including large numbers of women whose adoption of the veil signified their initiation into the movement, the question of the legal sanction of the veil has aroused intense reactions from supporters and opponents alike. In this paper I try to explore the question of the veil from the complicated perspective of an Arab feminist, who both rejects the veil as a personal choice but also recognizes its empowering and seductive effect on Arab women. My discussion will be limited to the veil as it plays itself out in an Arab context, since this is what I am most familiar with. The analysis might, or might not, be true in other non-Arab Muslim countries. Also, my 'analysis' will be more of a personal journey of exploration and reflection, than a traditional academic analysis or a strictly scientific one.

For the purposes of this paper I shall use the term 'veil' to mean the current dress adopted by Muslim women in the Arab world, as followers of the contemporary fundamentalist movements. In its most common expression, the veil entails covering the woman's hair with a scarf that is ordinarily white, leaving the face to be exposed. All of the body is usually covered with a loose dress in dark colours, with buttons from top to bottom. Women typically wear Western clothes beneath this dress, which they take-off, along with the scarf, when they are in the sole company of women. These women do not usually cover their hands with gloves, nor do they wear make-up.

FROM NON-VEIL TO VEIL

In order to make sense of the veil as a social phenomenon one needs to inspect other types of women's dress that are distinguishable from the veil. This I will do, by noting the transitional step that these women have made in their dress, historically, from non-veil to veil.

I would like first, however, to locate the women who adopt the veil in terms of class. This will be rather difficult due to the complexity of class structure in postcolonial societies. In general, these women tend to belong to the urban lower and middle classes. Professionally, they work as civil servants, schoolteachers, secretaries in private enterprise, bank employees, nurses and university students. They are usually young, in their twenties and early thirties.

In the seventies, these women walked the streets of Arab cities wearing Western attire: skirts and dresses below the knee, high heels, sleeves that covered the upper arm in the summer; their hair was usually exposed, and they wore make-up. They differed from their mothers who pretty much dressed in the same way, in that they were more fashion conscious, more liberal in the colouring of their clothing and more generous in their make-up. Their mothers usually covered their hair with a scarf when they were in public, but only in a liberal rather than a rigid way (a good proportion of their hair showed underneath the scarf in contrast to the scarf of the fundamentalist dress which showed nothing).

If one were to freeze that 'moment' in the seventies, in an attempt to understand these women's relationship to their bodies, one would find it multi-layered and highly complex. In a way their bodies seemed to be a battlefield where the cultural struggles of postcolonial societies were waged. On the one hand, the Western attire which covered their bodies carried with it the 'capitalist' construction of the female body: one that is sexualized, objectified,

246

ODEH

It is not unusual to find the length of a girl's dress the object of family debate:

Father/brother: This dress is too short. No respectable girl would wear it. Ask your daughter (*addressing the mother*) to take it off.

Mother: Come on, let her be. Girls these days wear things like that.

Brother: Let her take it off. My friends follow girls on the streets who wear dresses that short. I won't have my sister going around dressed like that!

Girl: But it's so pretty. All my friends wear dresses that short.

Father/Brother: Maybe they do, but I won't have my daughter/sister walk in the streets with a dress like that.

The girl takes it off.

thingified etc. . . . But because capitalism never really won the day in post-colonial societies, where it managed to cohabit successfully with pre-capitalist social formations (traditionalism), these women's bodies were also simultaneously constructed 'traditionally': 'chattelized', 'propertized', terrorized as trustees of family (sexual) honour. The cohabitation in the female body of this double construction (the capitalist and the traditional) was experienced by these women as highly conflictual. The former seemed to push them to be seductive, sexy and sexual, the latter to be prudish, conservative and asexual. Whereas the former was supported by the attraction of the market (consumption of Western commodities), the latter was supported by the threat of violence (the woman is severely sanctioned, frequently by death, if she risks the family sexual honour).

247

Not infrequently, Arabic newspapers carry a story structured along the following lines: 'S.M. stabbed his sister K. in a coffee shop across from the university campus. The police are investigating the crime.' A possible scenario for the crime: the woman, a university student belonging to the middle or lower classes, is having coffee with a colleague. Somebody 'tips' her brother that she is involved in sexual relations with this man. Provoked by his sister's friendly public behaviour with another man, and shamed by other people's thinking that this public behaviour has in fact led to illicit sexual contact between them, the brother kills his sister in defence of family sexual honour. The time between the 'tip' and the actual murder is usually very brief. More concerned with the public perception than with the actual fact of the sister's conduct, the brother rushes to protect the family honour, promptly and unequivocally. After trial, the brother is imprisoned for one year only. His extenuating circumstance is committing a 'crime of honour', sanctioned in most Arab penal codes.

The above two stories are pointers on a continuum. The way the girl dress-

ODEH

es and how she behaves have heavy sexual significations. She is continuously subject to the test of 'honour' and reputation, that she never really passes once and for all. Her sense of disempowerment stems from the terror exercised over her body, death being its not infrequent extreme.

The ambivalence that these women felt about their bodies in the seventies was resolved by adopting the Islamic fundamentalist dress in the eighties. The length of her dress was no more the object of family debate, nor would she be caught having coffee with a colleague in public, thereby risking her own death. Rather than being engaged in keeping the impossible balance of the 'attractive prude' or the 'seductive asexual', these women chose to 'complete' the covering of their bodies, and 'consummate' their separation from men. I deliberately use the words 'complete' and 'consummate' because the veil was only the concealment of an already ambivalently covered body, rather than the radical transition from 'revealment' to 'concealment'. Likewise, the segregation of the veil was only the completion of an already ambivalent separation between the sexes.

THE VEIL AS EMPOWERMENT

I had earlier identified the women who adopt the veil as mostly working women or students, and young. An important part of their daily life is walking the streets and using public transport to go to work or to school and university. Public exposure of this kind has never been comfortable for women in Arab cities. Unfailingly subject to attention on the streets and on buses by virtue of being women, they are stared at, whistled at, rubbed against, pinched. . . Comments by men such as, 'what nice breasts you have', or 'how beautiful f. . . . you must be', or something more subtle in tone such as, 'what a blessed day this is that I have seen you', are not infrequent. Ordinarily, women avoid any kind of direct verbal exchange with men when they are so approached. They either give the man a look of disapproval, or simply look ahead dismayed, and continue on their way. Whatever their reaction, they are always conscious of being looked at. Exceptionally, a woman might engage in a verbal exchange with the man, such as when he is insistent in his approaches (he continues to rub his thigh against hers on the bus despite her attempts at keeping a distance away from him). She might retort angrily, 'Keep away from me you pig; don't you have sisters of your own?'. A dramatic public scene usually ensues, whereby the man jumps to his self-defence by denying the allegation, and the men on the bus condemning such kind of behaviour as, 'unworthy of a man who has sisters, and a sign of the corruption of youth these days'. The passengers might also chide the woman for not dressing more properly, implying that if she did, such kind of harassment might not have occurred. The bus driver might even gallantly ask the man to leave the bus.

A woman's willingness to raise objections to such male intrusions is notably different when she is veiled. Her sense of the 'untouchability' of her

ODEH

body is usually very strong in contrast to the woman who is not veiled. Whereas the latter would swallow the intrusions as inevitable and part of her daily life, trying to bypass them in all the subtle ways she can muster (by looking at the man angrily and moving away from him), the veiled woman on the other hand is more likely to confront the man with self-righteousness, 'have you no fear of Allah treating his believers in such a shameless fashion?' Public reaction is usually more sympathetic to her, the men on the bus making comments such as, 'Muslim women should not be treated like that. Young men should pray more and read the Quran.' It is also true to say that veiled women's exposure to male intrusions in the first place is considerably less than the others.

The importance of these daily experiences and their 'existential' effect on women, both veiled and non-veiled, is best understood when put in the context of Arab women's relationship to their bodies as I have tried to explore it above. Public sexual harassment seems to reinforce the non-veiled woman's ambivalence about her body making her powerless in the face of unwelcome intrusions. The problem doesn't seem to exist for veiled women, since adopting the veil was meant among other things to shield them from such sexual approaches so that when they are actually made, they are looked upon as being simply outrageous, both by the veiled women and the public.

THE VEIL AS DISEMPOWERMENT

As I wrote down the title of this section, I thought to myself that there are surely a hundred million ways in which the veil is disempowering to women. But as I searched in my mind for such examples, I discovered that those instances of disempowerment that I was thinking of reflected my own normative assumptions of how the world should be. In other words, they reflected my position as a feminist. Paradoxically enough, and feminist as I am, instances of the disempowerment of the veil did not present themselves to me as self-evident. Whereas it was obvious to me that the veil remedied the situation of sexual harassment on the street, by discouraging men from invading veiled women's space and by empowering them to raise objections when such invasions took place, it wasn't equally obvious to me that the veil actually weakened women and disabled them from confronting an uncomfortable daily experience. Even when I activated my own normative assumptions about how the world should be, instances of disempowerment did not become any more self-evident. For instance, my normative assumptions, as an Arab feminist, are based on the premise that Arab women should be able to express themselves sexually, so that they can love, play, tease, flirt and excite. In a social context, such as the one in the Arab world, where women can incur violent sanctions if they express themselves sexually, such acts carry important normative weight to me as a feminist. In them, I see acts of subversion and liberation.

ODEH

> In a conversation with a veiled fundamentalist woman in her late twenties, who is single, I ask, 'But don't you have sexual needs?'
> **She:** Sure I do.
> **I:** What do you do with them?
> **She:** Sure I have sexual needs, but nothing that is absolutely overwhelming and impossible to deal with. I occupy myself all the time. I read books. I love to read books on Islam. To be 'pure' as a single woman is my absolute priority. I do not let these things preoccupy my thinking. It is simply not an issue for me.

But loving, teasing, flirting and seducing was not the way these women normatively saw their sexuality. If in all these acts I saw pleasure and joy, they saw only evil. For them, a society in which the sexes interacted thus was undoubtedly corrupt. They therefore experienced the veil as normatively necessary: precisely because women should not go around seducing men (except the ones they are married to), then they should be veiled (from other men). The disempowerment of the veil that I reflected on seemed to express merely my panicked feminist self, one that saw the veil as threatening to its normative world and sexuality.

Unless I engaged in intellectual elitism by accusing these women of false consciousness and not knowing their own good, there was no way that I could point to instances of the disempowerment of the veil. What it all sounds like so far is a hopeless clash of normative visions.

In my late twenties and single myself, that was nothing my confused postcolonial feminist self could identify with.

As I wrote the above paragraph about my own normative vision of sexuality, I was fearfully conscious of my father's reaction.

> **Father:** What is this you're writing? Women going around seducing and teasing??!!
> **I:** . . .
> **Father:** Wipe it off. Do you want to shame me?? That's all I need!! My own daughter declaring to the world that she wants women to go around seducing and teasing! How can I show my face to the world??
> **I:** . . .
> **Father:** So this is what you want?? This is what your feminism is all about?? Women going around whoring??
> I, desperately searching for words that might fit into his conceptual scheme and finding none, remain silent.

PREACHING TO THE UNCONVERTED

What about those who are unconverted, neither feminist nor veiled? Those whose bodies and sexuality have not been constructed by the veil discourse, nor by the feminist one? What about those whose 'moment' in the seventies has lingered, whose ambivalence about their bodies has not been 'resolved' by the adoption of the veil? What does a feminist such as myself have to offer them and how do I fare in comparison with those who preach the veil? How could what I have to offer them be empowering?

I find that my position, and that of other feminists, is not devoid of ambivalence. We obviously fare worse when it comes to empowering women on the streets. If what we have as remedy is a long agenda of changing the laws, claiming our rights to walk the streets without harassment, and raising consciousness about the 'equality' of men and women, then what we have is terribly unattractive. It is long term (when the veil as remedy is immediate), sounds hopelessly utopian and demanding of women to engage in what sounds like difficult and impossible personal/political struggle. But what is even more serious than all this, in contrast to the look of social respectability that the veil bestows on those who wear it (sort of like the respectability of a woman dressed like a nun), we seem to offer women a discourse that will make them socially conspicuous, questionable and suspect. For the ambivalent woman of the seventies, already dogged in her pursuit for good reputation, what we offer her looks not only unattractive, but almost socially suicidal.

The situation is aggravated further by the fact that most such feminists are upper- or middle-class women, with material resources that enable them to avoid, to a great extent, uncomfortable experiences on the streets (most of them drive their own cars). They also invite instinctive hostility in lower-class women by virtue of their class position.

Even more, feminist discourse sounds quite foreign. It uses concepts such as 'equality' and 'freedom', which are on the one hand indeterminate and could be easily appropriated ('equality between men and women means that men should be women's superiors because they are more qualified'), but they are also concepts that need yet to become discourse in the postcolonial context ('why should women be free when men are not free either?'). Liberalism, which postcolonial feminism seems to be based on, has yet to win the day in these societies.

Regrettably for the feminist, the importlike quality of her discourse weakens her case even further. Seen as a Western product, feminism doesn't have an obvious list of victories the postcolonial feminist can lean on. Rape, pornography and family disintegration in the West are flaunted in the face of such a feminist as she proceeds to preach her politics. Rather than seeing feminism as a political response to these social phenomena, feminism is seen as its cause. It is because Western women have become 'emancipated' that they are on the streets to be raped, morally corrupt to be playmates, and selfish about their own lives to cause the disintegration of the family. In a crude, superficial, partial, empirical way, that might be true. But before the postcolonial feminist steps in to explain the complexity of the situation in the West, she finds herself silenced by the immediate, simple, straightforward almost magical rhetoric of the veil. But even if she is allowed to speak, she suddenly finds herself in the uncomfortable position of 'defending the West', an anomaly in itself in the postcolonial Muslim societies of the day.

SOLIDARITY WITH THE VEILED

So far I have constructed the veiled position and the feminist one as being sharply contrasted. I had indicated earlier that they seemed to me to represent a hopeless clash of normative visions. But let me step down a little bit and reshuffle the positions I have constructed. Who wants to talk about normative visions anyway? They often seem to lead nowhere.

Perhaps the feminist path and the veiled one criss-cross. Perhaps they do so to an extent that they are no longer singularly identifiable as such. To show how they might possibly do that we need to break them down and attack their coherence.

The coherence of the veiled position breaks down like this: the contemporary veil seeks to address sexual harassment on the street. It seeks to protect women on their way to work and to school. Its female subjects are socially conspicuous *a priori*: they are not women who are staying locked indoors. It has come to remedy the uncomfortable daily lives of single, young women, who are leaving the house seeking work and education. But the veil as rhetoric assumes that women should ideally be inconspicuous. They should be locked indoors out of men's way so as not to seduce them. They should not go out to work, their rightful place is in the house as wives and mothers, not as wage workers.

The veiled position thus seems to be self-deconstructing. If it seriously pursues its normative vision by inviting women to stay at home, then it loses its attractiveness and therefore its effectiveness as a tool. For it was women's conspicuousness that prompted them to adopt the veil in the first place.

Even more paradoxically, fundamentalist ideology, as the inspiration for the rhetoric of the veil, assumes that women should work only out of necessity, preferably work in professions that are considered feminine such as teaching and nursing, and once at the workplace they should minimize their contact with men to the greatest extent possible. Whether during their working hours, or during break-time, individual women and individual men should not be left alone. Men are presumed to be the leaders in any context, whether at work or at home. Women, who have adopted the veil for its empowering effect on the street as they go to work, can find themselves seriously disempowered if the veil carries its 'logic' to the workplace. Spatial and functional segregation between the sexes, as the fundamentalist ideology of the veil envisages for the workplace, could seriously affect the career prospects of veiled women. Since they live and work in a world where men are already the decision-makers, and the higher situated in the hierarchy of the workplace, minimizing contact between women and men could only possibly result in isolating women further from the positions of power and decision-making.

The ambivalence of their position as veiled women seeking work could be effectively utilized by feminists. Seeing this as a golden opportunity for joining hands with veiled women, feminists can offer their politics as remedy for the disempowerment veiled women can experience at the workplace. Liberal feminist demands such as equality in the distribution of responsibilities between men and women based on the qualifications of the individual, equality of promotion opportunities between the sexes, daycare facilities for women to nurture their children, can be offered to these women as empowering political rhetoric for them as wage workers. Such demands will undoubtedly resonate deeply in veiled women's experience at the workplace. Feminism could thus become the empowering politics of veiled women at work.

The ironic side about all this for feminists, is that all of a sudden they could find themselves joining hands with veiled women as 'comrades' in political action. The coherence of the feminist position could thus be open to question. Far from finding the beneficiaries of its rhetoric female subjects engaged in a struggle for free and equal interaction with men in a free play of sexuality, postcolonial feminism will have to adjust itself to the fact that its empowered subjects are veiled women. In other words, feminist women and veiled women are now sisters.

VEILED AND DIVIDED: THE BATTLE OVER THE BODY

I have so far talked about the veiled body as if it were monolithic. And even though I believe that the rhetoric of the veil seeks to construct a monolithic female sexuality for its followers, I do not however think that, on closer inspection, the community of the veiled reveals any such single construction. Veiled sexuality, it seems to me, reveals a multiplicity that is beyond the feminist's wildest expectations.

True, there are those who can be described as 'ideology incarnate'. Their relationship with their body replicates ideology so well that a shift in this construction looks almost hopeless. They are the leaders, the preachers, the passionate believers, the puritans. They are the ones whose public veiled self takes over, even when they are in the private quarters of women. Their bodies seem to adopt the daily rituals of the veil, where they come to look, for the more colour-loving aesthetic eye, rather bland, insipid and otherworldly. It is the body of the virtuous.

But there are also those in the community of the veiled who are tentative and wavering. Once secure in the company of women, they reveal bodies that are more colourful, lively and sexual. One is surprised at the shift their bodies make when they take the veil off. The bland face becomes colourful with creative make-up. The loose dress of the veil, once taken off, reveals underneath fashionable clothing, making a more individual and personal statement than the collective public one of the veil. Their sexuality appears to be more forthcoming, assertive and joyful. Once together, their interaction with each other is not devoid of seductiveness and flirtation. Their private bodies are almost unrelated to their public ones.

And there are also those whose private more colourful bodies, shyly but daringly, push to become more public. They wear make-up with the veil. They are more creative, fashion-conscious in public, constantly attempting to subvert the blandness of the veil. They invent a million ways to tie the scarf on their heads, which itself becomes more varied in colours than the more standard white. The loose dress of the veil suddenly becomes slightly tighter, more colourful, more daring in emulating Western fashions, even if it doesn't explicitly reveal more parts of the female body. One also notices them on the streets conversing with men, strolling with them, subverting the segregation that the veil imposes on the sexes.

And there are those who wear the veil, but retain a fiercely ambivalent relationship with it, so that wearing it is a conscious decision that is made almost every day. It is not uncommon to find them wearing it some days and taking it off others. 'Wearing the veil, I find sometimes encourages me to binge on food since my whole body is covered in public, and I tend to lose touch with it. I feel I need to take it off sometimes. I need the public voyeur's gaze to control myself.'

And, there are those who use their bodies and dress as a statement of opposition. They differentiate themselves in their environment by wearing the veil, and using it as a statement on female subordination in nonfundamentalist (pseudo-secular, pseudo-religious) Arab households in which they find themselves. Wearing the veil allows them to have a singular and individual voice: 'You are all not wearing the veil, but I AM. I am powerful enough to do it, and this is how I carve myself a space that you cannot reach. I disapprove of what you are, who you are, and what you think!'

Of course, a veiled woman is not necessarily either this or that. She could shift from one position to the other. At times colourful, other times bland, seductive and prudish, public and private. A veiled woman's subjectivity appears to be much more complicated than the simple word of the veil can possibly convey.

For the feminist, such multiplicity of veiled sexuality could be very exciting and promising of rich interaction and dialogue with veiled women. Her

ODEH

position accordingly could become more nuanced and multiple. Instead of dismissing them as the enemy, the threat, the falsely conscious, she could see them as the varied, divided, seemingly united, female community trying to survive in an environment that is hostile to them as much as it is to her. It is a multiplicity that invites conversation between the 'same', rather than the apartness of the 'other'.

THE FEMINIST RESITUATES HERSELF

In the section below, I shall refer to the 'rhetoric of the veil'. What I mean by it is the fundamentalist construction of the veil, as it is circulated ideologically. A woman who decides to wear the veil is usually subjected to a certain ideological indoctrination (by a fundamentalist preacher), about how every Muslim woman needs to cover her body so as not to seduce men, and how in doing this she obeys the word of Allah.

Otherwise, she would face his wrath on the day of judgement. I have already tentatively referred to it in the section entitled 'Solidarity with the veiled'. It is in relation to, and at the same time by means of, this 'official' rhetoric that the different women I have just described construct their position of ambivalence or subversion.

In my construction so far, I have largely ignored the question of power. What I mean by power in this context is the power attached to a particular discourse as the only possible representation of 'reality', to the exclusion of others. This is a particularly important issue for the postcolonial feminist who is interested in understanding and possibly impacting the female community of the veiled. The excitement over the multiplicity and richness of such a community for the postcolonial feminist might be immediately dampened by the ideological power of the veil over that community. This will still be the case, despite the variety and richness of veiled women's lives that could be read as subverting the rhetoric of the veil.

It is interesting to note that since the veiled women of the contemporary fundamentalist movements have adopted the veil as a political act (they were not born into it), the rhetoric of the veil has a strong hold over them, since it provided the rationale for their act. In articulating their lives and their relationship with their bodies, they can only engage in such rhetoric. This seems to have the effect, at the end of the day, of reifying the 'reality' of their daily lives, by disabling them from seeing the subversions and variations that exist or could exist to disrupt the ideology of the veil.

This seriously complicates the position of the feminist. In order to have a hearing with these women, she needs to 'hook up' with their conceptual system (rhetoric). But she also needs to do it in a way that subverts it and allows conceptual openings in it, through which veiled women can start to see their lives differently. This is a slippery road since she will always risk being over-

255

ODEH

The feminist: I like the way you wear your scarf. It's creative and most unusual.

Veiled woman: Thank you. I get bored with the way I look if I wear it the same every day.

The feminist: I thought the whole point was to wear it the same every day so that you don't attract attention to your body.

Veiled woman: It's just that I think that people need to look beautiful to others. That doesn't mean they have to seduce them. Allah is beautiful and He likes beauty.

The feminist: I agree with you. I think women can look beautiful without having to appear as if they are out to seduce men. I believe that women can look both proper and beautiful. In my opinion, you can do that either wearing the veil or even Western clothes. I, personally, feel more comfortable wearing the latter. The veil appears to me rather exaggerated.

Veiled woman: Except that Allah commanded us to wear the veil. But I've always believed that the important thing is how we feel inside. The important thing is that we feel pure inside, no matter what we wear, whether it is Western clothes or the veil.

whelmed by the 'logic' of the rhetoric, and thereby end up being rendered ineffective and immobilized by it. She will also find herself in the uncomfortable position of having to say things that she 'doesn't really mean' in order to have a hearing in the first place. Conscious of having to keep the balance of being both inside and outside the system, the feminist risks being pushed one side or the other.

"THEY HAVE EYES AND SEE NOT"
Gender Politics in the Diaspora Museum

Dafna N. Izraeli

THIS ARTICLE is a commentary on the construction and display of gender in an Israeli museum of social history—the Museum of the Jewish Diaspora, known in Hebrew as *Beit Hatefusot*. A source of considerable national pride, Beit Hatefusot ranks high on the list of "must see" for both tourists and Israelis. The military training of every soldier includes a study tour of the museum, which also organizes activities for Israeli students and provides programs in 14 languages for students from abroad and new immigrants. In other words, Beit Hatefusot is an important institution for the transmission of Jewish culture in Israeli society.

An official publication explains that Beit Hatefusot was not planned to be a shrine to the past. Instead, it presents the story of 2,500 years of Jewish dis-

I acknowledge my gratitude to the late Elia Dinur and to Judith Lorber for their contributions to improving this manuscript, to Rhoda Unger for encouraging me to pursue it, and to Susan Sered for her helpful comments.

persion as a living, stimulating experience. The aim of Beit Hatefusot is to explain what Jewish life is and has always been about and by doing so to enrich those who visit it. In this article, I decode the practices by which the museum constructs gender.

The apparent function of most museums of social history is to collect, preserve, and display authentic objects of social and historical importance and to make objectively valuable knowledge and culture equally accessible to all members of society. However, museums, as Bourdieu (1973) pointed out, also have a hidden function, to preserve social differentiation. The construction of gender in museums helps to produce the social and cultural differences between women and men that justify their unequal treatment (Lorber, in press).

The production and reproduction of culture are part of what Dorothy Smith (1987) called "the relations of ruling." Most people do not participate in the making of culture. The forms of thought and images we use do not arise directly or spontaneously out of people's everyday lives and relationships. Rather, they are the product of the work of specialists occupying the influential positions in the ideological apparatus (the educational system, communications, etc.). Our culture does not arise spontaneously; it is "manufactured" (Smith, 1987). Museums are locales in which the manufacturing process is implemented. The culture display is a reconstruction of events, the product of a process of interpretation, selection, and constitution of the facts as viewed through the prism of those responsible for its making. Deciphering the gender discourse embedded in the displays at the Beit Hatefusot museum reveals the way in which this museum contributes to the preservation of gender difference and inequality in Israeli society.

A museum is a display of a reality but is not reality itself. The display as constructed reflects the specific reality of the experts as well as their strategic decisions concerning how to convey that reality through the exhibits. Judaism's androcentric character constrains the decisions, but it does not determine what is displayed and what is omitted, what is highlighted and what is hidden, and whether women's lives—their role in the practice of Jewish life, their experiences and rituals—are given due importance or rendered invisible. Those decisions are left to the museum planners. They ultimately determine the display. "[C]ultural productions . . . are implicit or explicit narratives about gender" (Lorber, in press), and through the narratives they construct, the specialists reproduce and reinforce the androcentric theme in the story of the Jewish people.

THE BEIT HATEFUSOT MUSEUM DISPLAYS

The museum exhibits are organized thematically rather than chronologically. The name of each theme is predicated by the term *Gate*. In Hebrew, the term *Gate* takes on multiple meanings, including portal, chapter, or theme. The six

258

IZRAELI

major themes, according to the official release, "formed the main factors of Jewish survival": Gate of the Family, Gate of Community, Gate of Faith, Gate of Creativity, Gate Among the Nations, and Gate of Return (to Zion).

This article provides a guided tour of Beit Hatefusot viewed through a gender lens and points out how the museum constructs gender difference by assigning women and men to different roles, statuses, different forms of inter- action, and different locations in the display. As Gayle Rubin (1975) observed of the cultural emphasis on difference between women and men, "Far from being an expression of natural differences, exclusive gender identity is the suppression of natural similarities" (pp. 179–180). Also, gender difference is used in the display of Jewish life to construct male dominance and to margin- alize women. Far from being a reflection of historical reality, women's mar- ginalization, especially in the family, is the erasure of women's contribution to Jewish survival. This trivialization of women goes unnoticed by the visitor, who raises no eyebrow or question and to whom the display seems perfectly natural and factually acceptable. Few visitors leave saying "Hey, where are the women? Surely women did more than that?"

SCENES FROM FAMILY LIFE

The Family Gate is the first exhibit, as well it should be. The family— women's proverbial domain—has been and remains the mainstay of Jewish life. The term for housewife in Hebrew, *akeret habayit,* literally means *the essence of the home.* Elsewhere, say at the Gate of Creativity, the Gate of Faith, or the Gate of Redemption, women's invisibility could be too easily dis- missed as a historical fact.

At the approach to the Family Gate, on the wall facing the entrance, the caption reads PORTRAITS FROM THE PAST. Six large portraits display three men and three women. Under each portrait is an identifying caption. The men displayed are *Moses, Susskind of Trimberg,* and *Rabbi Jacob Sasportas.* The women are *Personifaction of Autumn, A Jewess from Poland,* and *A Jewess from Morocco.* The men are all real persons with names and/or titles. The women are members of categories.

A glass case below the portraits contains nine additional portraits from the past: six men, three women: *Rabbi Eliyahu Delmedigo, the Arraby Moor—the Chief Rabbi of Portugal, The Physician Ephraim Bueno, The Painter Maurycy Got- tlieb, Rabbi Samuel Jocob Haim Falk—The Ba'al Shem* (name of a famous Rab- bi) *of London, An East European Jew* (male), *Rebecca Gratz, Mrs. Asher Wertheimer,* and *A Jewish Bride.* All but one of the men have names. They also have achievements, as their titles bear out. Three are rabbis, one is a physician, and one a painter. Of the three women, only one woman has her own name and her right to fame is not mentioned. (She was a 19th century philanthropist who established and supported Jewish communal services in Philadelphia.) A

IZRAELI

second woman's claim to a name and a place in the display presumably rests on her having made a good marriage. The third woman is in a typically female generic category.

The first scene is constituted from white plaster figures. At center stage in the Circumcision scene, three men covered with prayer shawls participate in the ceremony—one of them holding the infant. Over to the side, at a distance from where the action is taking place, there-but-not-there, a number of women mind small children. As a group of tourists approaches, their guide explains in English, "The family exhibit is organized around two dominant themes—the life cycle of the Jew and the cycle of the holidays of Israel. The life cycle of the Jew begins with the circumcision of the newborn." But the life of the Jewish female child does not begin with a circumcision. I wonder whether the little girl's arrival was ever marked by any ritual at all. Maybe a small blessing? The museum is silent on the subject. Implicitly, the answer is no. The other visitors appear indifferent to the issue.

In the next scene, a young woman is seated by herself embroidering. The caption reads THE BABY'S SISTER EMBROIDERS A TORAH COVER FROM HIS SWADDLING CLOTH. The woman is identified in relation to her brother. She is only his sister. Her activity is also in relation to her brother. She is preparing the band he will use when he is called to the Torah at his bar-mitzva ceremony. The baby boy is just born and already there is a woman devotedly in his service.

The next scene— three displays in figures and pictures—portrays Torah study. Learning is of unparalleled value in Jewish life. Jews have always considered themselves as The People of the Book, and studying Torah is considered superior to observing almost all other religious obligations. The caption introducing the display reads THE JEWISH FAMILY PUT THE CHILD'S EDUCATION ABOVE EVERYTHING. A more accurate description of the exhibit would read "The Jewish Family put the little boy's education above everything." All three displays, historical and current, exclusively show little boys studying and their men teachers. One picture taken in recent decades is in a modern setting. The unarticulated message is that little girls did not learn Torah, do not learn, and need not learn. Why is there no picture of little girls studying Torah in Beit Yaakov, an educational network established for ultra-orthodox girls at the turn of the century? Will the museum anywhere tell the story of Sara Shnerer's successful struggle with the ultra-orthodox rabbis of Europe at the turn of the century to create the Beit Yaakov movement and thus make formal Jewish education available to girls? Education is so highly valued, and she made this treasure available to orthodox girls—surely her contribution would be recorded. Hard as I looked for her in the various exhibits I could find no trace of her anywhere. Perhaps her only claim— bringing literacy to women—was not path breaking or important enough to be included in the collective memory portrayed in Beit Hatefusot.

The bar-mitzva ceremony is next in the life cycle of the Jew, according to this museum. On show are two men flanking that Bar Mitzva Boy reading from the Torah against a background curtain (hiding the women folk?). The caption reads THE THIRTEEN YEAR OLD SON IS TOLD—NOW YOU ARE RESPONSIBLE FOR YOUR DEEDS. Thousands of young pupils will come through this exhibit. How will they ever learn from Beit Hatefusot that girls become responsible as well for their deeds at some point in life?

I ask a passing woman guide, "How come there are not more scenes with women in them?" "Because women are not circumcised and didn't have a bar mitzva," she replied as she brushed by me with a tone of disdain at my ignorance. It did not occur to her that things could be otherwise. I wanted to suggest that it might be more appropriate to open the family exhibit with a scene of a mother blessing the Sabbath candles, surrounded by her children whom she blessed in turn.[1] After all, our sages tell us that the Sabbath guarded over the Jewish people and the women guarded over the Jewish home. Surely, opening the family gate with an exhibit of a woman ushering in the Sabbath would reflect Jewish survival. But the guide was gone, and there was no one around with whom to share my thoughts.

The marriage is next. A wedding requires the bride, her mother, and her mother-in-law. Like the groom and father, they too are there for real; being who are, not quite props. Mazel Tov. The ceremony is underway. The sculptor froze in plaster the moment in the groom's life when all the significant women—his mother, wife, and mother-in-law—circle round him seven times. The women are united in a ritual of worship of a man. It is not the androcentricism of the museum curator that caused the bride, her mother, and her mother-in-law to circle the groom—that is also done at Ashkenazi weddings. It is the androcentricism of the museum curator that immortalized that moment in the ceremony rather than another or that omitted women's prewedding henna rituals and mikva (ritual bath) parties.

A slide projector reflects the final stage of life: a succession of paintings by an unknown artist, 14 slides depicting the process from deathbed to mourning. Women appear in only three. Their roles are visiting the sick, crying at the door of the bedroom while the men pray at the deathbed, and sewing the shrouds. Jewish history provides many additional options. In Roman times, women were hired as professional weepers. They could also have been there accompanying the dead, mourning, or comforting the mourners, but they are not.

SCENES FROM JEWISH HOLIDAYS

The display of the holidays in more recent times might be expected to tell a different story. However, there is monotonous repetition of women's blatant invisibility in the holiday cycle of the Jewish year. There are scenes from 10 different holidays. Three of these holidays, Passover, Hanukkah (Festival of

261

Lights), and Shaovut (Festival of Weeks), are displayed as family scenes that include women. In the displays representing the remaining seven holidays, only men appear: Purim—a little boy carrying *shalach manot,* the gifts that Jews traditionally send one another on Purim; Tabernacles—father and son praying together; Lag Ba'Omer—a Chassidic man standing over a bonfire, a Kabbalistic practice associated with the holiday and a favorite activity of the younger generation in contemporary Israel; Day of Holocaust and Valor (memorial day for those who died in the Holocaust)—an old man mourning by a graveside; and the Day of Independence—young boys in procession, brandishing national flags.

Do little girls not deliver gifts on Purim? Do women not traditionally make the blessing over the *etrog* and *lulav* in the *succah* during Tabernacles? Were women not murdered like men in the Holocaust? Do young girls not rejoice at the rebirth of the State? Is the mother, who throughout Jewish history ushered in the Sabbath—queen with her candle blessing and observed by her young children next-to-be blessed—not important enough to be immortalized, either as part of The Life Cycle of the Jew or The Holiday Cycle of the Jewish People?

The Day of Atonement is treated in a separate enclave. The major exhibit, a reproduction of a painting by Maurycy Gottlieb, is a painting of eight men and a boy in a synagogue, caught in a moment of prayer and devotion. Behind them and fully exposed, is the women's balcony. It is empty. Are women absent from the synagogue on the Days of Atonement? None are to be seen in the Gottlieb reproduction on display at Beit Hatefusot. The original painting at the Tel Aviv Museum, a copy of which hangs as a poster in the museum gift shop, tells a different story; that of a gallery filled with handsomely dressed women standing behind but above the men. The women in the painting here were erased, wiped out of the picture and so wiped out of history. Women's erasure from Jewish life is symbolically culminated in their absence from the Day of Atonement. Not one of the museum staff I asked could tell me why the women had been removed from the picture. Some assumed it was done "to prevent distraction from the main theme. . . . "

THE GENDER POLITICS OF MUSEUMS

Pedagogic action, of which museums are a specific case, have, according to Bourdieu (1973), a twofold arbitrariness about them (cf. Robbins, 1991). The content is arbitrary in the sense that it has no absolute reference and is only a reflection of the interests of the group controlling the context. The context within which culture is transmitted is arbitrarily determined by the power relations between groups in a society. Like other cultural institutions, museums contribute to the reproduction of the relations of ruling by serving as bearers of the dominant ideologies of the culture and as a medium for their transfer from generation to generation.

All significant positions of power in Israeli society are held almost exclusively by men. Men's interests and concerns and experiences are those that inform the culture. The culture that is transmitted thus reflects that of men's experiences, interests, and ways of knowing the world. As in other major religions, women have been historically excluded from the making of ideology of Jewish knowledge and of Jewish culture. Although throughout history women's contributions were important for the operation and preservation of society, their contributions were trivialized or marginalized and then erased by men's history. Dorothy Smith (1987, pp. 17–18) explained the significance of this exclusion.

> Being excluded, as women have been, from the making of ideology, of knowledge, and of culture means that our experience, our interests, our ways of knowing the world have not been represented in the organization of our ruling nor in the systematically developed knowledge that has entered into it.

Women's representation in museums, where knowledge, culture, and ideology are produced and disseminated, reproduces the historical practice of women's exclusion. It contributes to women's experiences, in the words of Sheila Rowbotham (1974), remaining "hidden from history."

The displays in the Museum of the Diaspora support and reproduce a hegemonic ideology[2] of Jewish life that is both androcentric and paternalistic. Its central features are hierarchically organized activities appropriated in individual and group activity, the outcome of which is to marginalize other kinds of activities. For example, the decision to represent family life through a life cycle of men's religious rituals (circumcision and bar mitzva), to show the groom as the central figure in the wedding ceremony, and to marginalize women in the depiction of the main mourning rituals are decisions that exclude women where Judaism says they are central, for example, the family. Hegemonic Judaism privileges activities typically performed by men and usually permitted only to men. Women's traditionally sung activities such as preparing the food for the family holiday meals and sending portions to the poor and needy, consecrating the home for the Sabbath and the holidays, calling on the sick, negotiating with non-Jewish shopkeepers every day in stores and market places, magically transforming the humble family room by day into a store and by night back to a bedroom, are nowhere highlighted on front stage in the history of the diaspora. This important museum symbolically annihilates women and reinforces the hegemonic Jewish view that institutionalizes men's centrality and their dominance over women.

Women's exclusion from the museum's history of the diaspora is not noticed by most visitors because what is rendered invisible is rarely missed. The fact that those who are controlled, less privileged, or excluded do not feel grieved by their condition is evidence of what Lukes (1974, p. 24) called the *third dimension* or hidden face of power.

263

IZRAELI

Is it not the supreme and most insidious exercise of power to prevent people, to whatever degree, from having grievances by shaping their perceptions, cognition and preferences in such a way that they accept their role in the existing order of things, either because they can see or imagine no alternative to it, or because they see it as natural and unchangeable, or because they value it as divinely ordained and beneficial?

The purpose of this study was to decode the practices by which gender was constructed and accomplished and to decipher the gender discourse embedded in the displays at the museum. Gender is, in Kessler and McKenna's (1978) term, accomplished through social practice. Museums accomplish gender through a complex chain of practical decisions, including whom to display and whom not to display, in what activity or inactivity, where and where not, in relation to whom and in relation to whom not. Once accomplished, the gender display becomes part of the collective memory of those who view it. The Diaspora Museum's version of Jewish history is transmitted to the next generation, who will visit the museum and view the culture on display as objective and external to themselves but also as a part of themselves and from which they learn about who they are.

Thus, Beit Hatefusot can be seen as a metaphor for the nonconscious ideology that marginalizes women in Israeli culture and results in their exclusion from such activities that are honored or glorified or bring money or power. Like so many other monuments in Israeli society, Beit Hatefusot reinforces a stereotypical world in which women remain nameless and voiceless and have no contribution to show for themselves. Stereotypes are manipulated politically to legitimize the preservation of male dominance. The trivialization and marginalization of women go unnoticed by the visitor, who raises no eyebrow or question, to whom the display seems perfectly natural and factually acceptable.

NOTES

1. At the entrance to the Family Gate, a pair of silver Sabbath candle sticks are encased and beneath them the caption: "The Jewish home on the Sabbath eve." The Jewish woman who makes the Jewish home is nowhere in sight. Among the hundreds, perhaps thousands of exhibits, I found only one small picture that portrays a woman lighting candles on the eve of the Day of Atonement as her two small children and another woman stand by.

2. Hegemony here means social ascendancy. The concept of hegemonic Judaism is adapted from Connell's (1987) use of hegemonic masculinity.

REFERENCES

Bourdieu, P. (1973). Cultural reproduction and social reproduction. In R. Brown (Ed.), *Knowledge, education and cultural change* (pp. 71–112). London: Tavistock.

Connell, R. W. (1987). *Gender & power.* Stanford, CA: Stanford University Press.

Kessler, S. J., & McKenna, W. (1978). *Gender: An ethnomethodological approach*. New York: Wiley.

Lorber, J. (1993). *Paradoxes of gender*. New Haven, CT: Yale University Press.

Lukes, S. (1974). *Power: A radical view*. London: Macmillan.

Robbins, D. (1991). *The work of Pierre Bourdieu*. Boulder, CO: Westview Press.

Rowbotham, S. (1974). *Hidden from history* (2nd ed.). London: Pluto Press.

Rubin, G. (1975). The traffic in women: Notes on the 'political economy' sex. In R. R. Reiter (Ed.), *Toward an anthropology of women* (pp. 157–210). New York: Monthly Review Press.

Smith, D. E. (1987). *The everyday world as problematic: A feminist sociology*. Boston: Northeastern University Press.

IZRAELI

AGREEING TO DIFFER
Feminist Epistemologies and Women's Ways of Knowing

Mary Crawford

"THE BRAIN: His and Hers;" "The Truth About Sex Differences;" "Just How the Sexes Differ;" "She and He: Different Brains?" and "The Gender Factor in Math: A New Study Says Males May Be Naturally Abler Than Females"—all are titles of recent features in mass–circulation magazines. When the popular press reports psychological research on sex differences, the message is that psychologists have discovered universal, fundamental differences that explain the behavior and social positions of women and men. Most of these "discoveries" are announced with no mention of the existence of contradictory evidence or diverse viewpoints within the field (Beckwith, 1984). But the extent and meaning of sex differences in personality, cognitive abilities, and behavior have been divisive issues among psychologists.

Feminist psychologists have a long tradition of skepticism about sex differences. Many of the first generation of women in the field devoted their research careers to demolishing their male colleagues' empirically indefensible beliefs about cognitive sex differences (Rosenberg, 1982). Their contemporary counterparts have, for the most part, maintained that research on sex differences should not be a major project for psychology and have characterized the literature as inconsistent, atheoretical, and inconclusive (Deaux, 1984; Sherif, 1979; Unger, 1979).

Recently, however, new claims have been made about modes of moral reasoning (Gilligan, 1982) and thinking (Belenky, Clinchy, Goldberger, & Tarule, 1986) more characteristic of women than men. These research projects, which are informed by feminist values, have been acclaimed as groundbreaking, revolutionary, and celebratory of women's strengths.

How can the new claims of difference best be evaluated? If masculinist values have undermined the validity of past sex difference research, do feminist values lead to more valid research or merely substitute a different set of biases? Given the long–standing minimization of difference in feminist psychology, can these new differences be accommodated? Can feminist psychologists agree on the question of difference, or must we agree to disagree?

Although the minimization and maximization of difference exist side by side in current feminist theorizing on the psychology of women (Hare–Mustin & Marecek, 1988), they have rarely been compared directly. Partly this is because most maximizing analyses are based on psychodynamically derived clinical evidence and most minimizing ones originate in quantitatively oriented experimental psychology. Outside psychology, the more impressionistic and qualitative models are often very influential. Witness, for example, the rapid acceptance and continuing influence in women's studies of Chodorow's (1978) *The Reproduction of Mothering*. Within psychology, however, proponents of each approach tend to dismiss the other. Debates among psychologists about the empirical validity of the work of Chodorow (1978) and Miller (1976), for example, often center on whether the verbal statements of clients as interpreted by their therapists constitute acceptable evidence about normal developmental processes (Rossi, 1981).

The question of how to evaluate claims of difference is complicated by the changes in research methods and values brought about by feminist scholarship. As in other disciplines, placing women at the center of inquiry has led to questioning fundamental assumptions underlying the theories and practices that define the discipline (McIntosh, 1983). In psychology, questioning has included the concept of objectivity, the assumption that methods are value–free (Crawford & Marecek, 1988; Sherif, 1979), and the utility of various epistemological stances.

In this chapter I examine research on "women's ways of knowing" (Belenky et al., 1986) from two epistemological stances (Harding, 1986). The first is a *feminist empiricist* view, which argues that sex bias in scientific research can be corrected by stricter adherence to rules of good research design and norms of correct interpretation. The second is a *feminist* standpoint view, which maintains that women's experiences as members of a subjugated group provide them with unique perspectives for understanding social relations. The two stances lead to very different judgments of the validity of *Women's Ways of Knowing* and its usefulness for women. Finally, I consider the popularization of the idea that there are uniquely feminine modes of thought, showing that difference takes on a third set of meanings when it leaves the academy and enters popular media.

WAYS OF KNOWING WOMEN'S WAYS OF KNOWING

In their book, Mary Belenky and her colleagues Blythe Clinchy, Nancy Goldberger, and Jill Tarule used structured interviews of 135 women to assess women's "ways of knowing:" that is, "perspectives from which women view reality and draw conclusions about truth, knowledge, and authority" (p. 3). Their interviewees were a diverse group of 90 selected students in six heterogeneous academic institutions (25 of whom had been interviewed earlier for a different research project) and 45 mothers who were clients in helping agencies (15 of whom were interviewed again a year after the initial contact).

The conceptual scheme used for classifying the women's responses built on the work of Perry (1970). Perry used a sequence of four yearly interviews with Harvard undergraduates of the 1950s and 1960s to describe how students' epistemological stances and understanding of themselves as knowers changed during the undergraduate years. (Perry believed that the Radcliffe women he tested followed the same developmental pattern as the Harvard men, and he did not report their results separately.)

Belenky et al. discerned five major epistemological positions in their interviewees: *silence*, in which women experience themselves as "mindless and voiceless and subject to the whims of external authority;" *received knowledge*, in which women perceive themselves as capable of taking in knowledge from external authorities but incapable of original thought; *subjective knowledge*, in which truth is perceived as personal and intuitive; *procedural knowledge*, in which women focus on applying objective procedures for learning and communicating; and *constructed knowledge*, in which all knowledge is seen as contextual and women value both objective and subjective ways of knowing, seeing themselves as creators as well as receivers of knowledge. Within the procedural category, the authors distinguish between *connected* and *separate* modes; the terms are taken from Gilligan (1982) and Lyons (1983) and are used to describe knowledge established through care and intimacy versus impersonal procedures.

Rather than quantitative or statistical analyses of their interview material, Belenky et al. relied on a qualitative content analysis. The number of women who held each perspective is not specified. The "silence" and "constructed knowledge" positions were rare, with not more than two or three women (about 2% of the sample) classified in each. "Almost half" of the women were

269

CRAWFORD

subjectivists; younger women were the majority of received knowers, and college students the majority of procedural knowers.

How do the methods and modes of interpretation of *Women's Ways of Knowing* fare when judged by the criteria feminist empiricist researchers have applied to masculinist claims of difference? How do they fare when judged as examples of feminist standpoint research? I now turn to a critical examination of *Women's Ways of Knowing* from these two contrasting epistemological perspectives.

BEYOND "SENTIMENTAL ROT AND DRIVEL:" FEMINIST EMPIRICISM AND SEX DIFFERENCE RESEARCH

An important contribution of feminist psychology from its inception has been to expose the exaggeration of sex difference in scientific research. The first generation of scientifically trained women devoted much research effort to challenging accepted wisdom about the extent and nature of differences. Helen Thompson Wooley, for example, conducted the first experimental laboratory study of sex differences in mental traits, using a variety of innovative measures. In interpreting her results she stressed the overall similarity of the sexes and the environmental determinants of observed differences, remarking acerbically in a 1910 *Psychological Bulletin* article that "there is perhaps no field aspiring to be scientific where flagrant personal bias, logic martyred in the cause of supporting a prejudice, unfounded assertions, and even sentimental rot and drivel, have run riot to such an extent as here" (p. 340). Among the women inspired by her work was Leta Stetter Hollingworth, who challenged the Darwinian view that women are innately less variable (and therefore less likely to be highly creative or intelligent) (Shields, 1982). The work of these women was influential in undermining biological determinism in psychology, opening the way for critical empirical research to replace unexamined assumptions about women's "natural" limitations (Rosenberg, 1982).

But an increase in the amount and sophistication of empirical research did not guarantee a less biased approach to the question of difference. Critics have again found it necessary to point out that the vast but atheoretical literature on sex differences resists coherent interpretation (Deaux, 1984; Maccoby & Jacklin, 1974; Unger, 1979) and have again charged that "psychology is replete with inconsequential, accidental, and incidental findings of 'sex differences'" that often are distorted, exaggerated, and miscited (Grady, 1981, pp. 632–633). Like their intellectual foremothers, they have concentrated on exposing both faulty methods and masculinist values and on showing how the two interact. Even recent advances in techniques for meta–analysis (Eagly, 1987; Hyde & Linn, 1986), which provide improved ways of aggregating and interpreting data from large numbers of studies, cannot wholly compensate for the biases in the original studies or ensure "objective" interpretation (Unger & Crawford, 1989).

270

In reaction to the exaggeration and politicization of sex differences in research, the project of feminist empiricism has been to show that with better (less biased and more sophisticated) research methods, sex differences diminish in frequency, reliability, and predictive power. It has claimed that the documentation of more such differences is far less interesting and important than other lines of research. At best, it claims, the reporting of sex differences is merely descriptive, not explanatory (Deaux, 1984; Unger, 1979). At worst, it is a fundamentally misguided attempt to justify the existence of unequal social categories. This work has had a great deal of conceptual and practical impact. It has not only demonstrated once again the exaggeration of sex difference in the scientific literature, it has delineated the methods and mechanisms of exaggeration.

The feminist empiricist critique of sex–biased methods has been nicely summarized by Jacklin (1981), who enumerated ten "ubiquitous" methodological flaws in difference research:

> The methodological issues in the study of sex–related differences include: 1) conceptualization of the term "difference," 2) failure to distinguish the significance of an effect from the size of an effect, 3) bias toward positive findings in the publishing . . . and reprinting of results, 4) confusion of within–sex differences with between–sex differences, 5) assuming that all sex–related differences are expressions of genetic or innate differences, 6) confusion of sex–of–stimuli effects with sex–of–subject effects, 7) interaction of sex–of–experimenter effects with sex–of–subject effects, 8) disregard of systematic differences in self–report of males and females, 9) reliance upon a narrow data base in terms of subject characteristics from which most sex–related differences are generalized, 10) the number of variables confounded with sex which make comparisons of sex difficult.

271

Though feminist psychologists have focused on claims of difference articulated by men (or people whose values were judged masculinist), the tools of this perspective can also be applied to women's (and feminists') claims. Has *Women's Ways of Knowing* succeeded in avoiding the "ubiquitous methodological problems" described by Jacklin (1981)? On the contrary, several of the logical and conceptual flaws Jacklin described are apparent in *Women's Ways of Knowing* and, from this perspective, are very probably the source of the spurious "difference" it discovers.

To begin with, it is impossible to demonstrate a sex difference (or a sex similarity) if only one sex is studied (the fourth error in Jacklin's list). Characterizing this error as "glaring, but common," Jacklin gives examples of studies that measured behaviors of only one sex and erroneously drew conclusions about differences between the sexes—for example, measuring the relationship between hormonal levels and mood only in women and concluding that only women show such relationship. Yet the claims of sex difference in *Women's*

CRAWFORD

Ways of Knowing are based on exactly this approach, studying people of one sex and speculating about how people of the other sex might or might not differ if they had also been studied. Whether men hold the epistemological positions characterized as "women's" ways of knowing remains an empirical question.

Perhaps Belenky et al. intended only to add information about women to already existing information about men, or to compare theoretical constructs about ways of thinking, regardless of gender, rather than to claim that their women's ways of knowing were in any way different from men's. But their analysis is based specifically on the premise that women's experience is different from men's and produces the differences between their sample and Perry's. Detailed comparisons with the men in Perry's (1970) study (and other research on male intellectual development) are made throughout the book, and although other factors, such as social class, are considered as possibly accounting for difference, sex itself is seen as central. Thus the study uses research on one sex to make claims about sex difference and then views the created difference as explainable by sex (cf. Unger, 1979).

This limitation is most clear when Belenky et al. (1986) explain the origins of differences in ways of knowing. Focusing on a male–oriented (competitive and individualistic) educational system, they conclude that women are uniquely and in their totality different from men in being harmed by competition and requiring a supportive environment. But differences in class size, teacher sex, and other factors may be as important in influencing classroom interaction as whether the student is female or male (Crawford & MacLeod, 1988). And, as Jacquelynne Eccles (Chapter 2) and others (e.g., Johnson & Johnson, 1987) have documented, highly competitive classrooms benefit a small minority even among white males.

Deciding what constitutes an appropriately comparable sample of women and men is another methodological problem. Jacklin (1981) maintains that the number of variables that are confounded with sex (error 10) is "the most pervasive problem in sex-related research." Even when a researcher makes a determined attempt to measure comparable males and females in the same study, it is often unclear what characteristics should be matched and which are irrelevant. Male and female college students who are matched on level of formal education will have very different backgrounds in mathematics, science, and the humanities, starting in high school (see Chapter 2) and will be concentrated in different courses of study in college. These differences may be irrelevant to some research questions but crucial to others. The comparisons made by Belenky et al. (1986) of their sample of women with Perry's (1970) sample of men are even more problematic than typical college–student comparisons because the two groups differed in many nontrivial ways. Perry's men were all Harvard undergraduates, a much more homogeneous group than Belenky et al.'s women in social class, age, ethnicity, and educational level. They were also part of a different age cohort. If one imagines a diverse 1970s sample of men including welfare clients, students at junior colleges and elite liberal arts colleges, older returning students, minority people, and victims of child abuse—that is, a male sample comparable to Belenky et al.'s females—the possible impact of factors other than gender can be conceptualized. Would any researcher expect such a sample to share the exact epistemological stances of 1950s Harvard undergraduates?

This is not to argue that researchers should study only Harvard undergraduates, or that women's and men's experiences in our culture are identical, even when they are "matched" by researchers. But the understanding of differences attributable to sex and gender is not served by indirect comparisons that confound sex and gender with many other variables.

A similar argument applies to claims about differences among women. Although the Belenky et al. sample of women differed in age, ethnicity, and class, these were not varied systematically, and therefore their contribution to the differences obtained *among women* cannot be assessed. The fact that all the "silenced" women were poor, most of the "subjectivists" young, and all the "procedural knowers" college students is uninterpretable. Whether these differences are class-related, age-related, dependent on level of formal schooling, or due to situational or methodological factors (e.g., students and nonstudents were given different forms of the interview schedule) is impossible to determine.

Other methodological confounds are evident in *Women's Ways of Knowing*. In comparing their women interviewees with Perry's men, the researchers recognize but discount the importance of the fact that the two groups were asked different questions in the context of different interview schedules. This bears some similarity to Jacklin's error (#6) of comparing males and females who are given "feminine" and "masculine" versions of a test, respectively. In addition, Perry's men were interviewed over four years, allowing a developmental picture to emerge for each individual. Although *Women's Ways of Knowing* is subtitled *The development of self, voice, and mind*, its authors acknowledge that it is not a developmental study. Most of the women were interviewed only once, making comparisons with Perry's men problematic on this dimension as well.

Finally, Jacklin (1981) notes that there is a sex-related difference in responding to self-report measures. Females are more willing or able to disclose personal feelings. She notes that "self-report may be the only possible way to study many aspects of adult feelings and behavior, but concern for the bias that this type of data collection produces must be taken into account. We should either attempt to estimate the defensiveness of subjects or attempt to validate the self-report measures more carefully than has been done" (pp. 270–271). Because Belenky and her colleagues developed an original questionnaire for their study, none of the traditional measures of validity and reliability are available.

273

CRAWFORD

The work of Gilligan (1982) has also been criticized from the feminist empiricist standpoint; some of those criticisms are relevant here because Gilligan's research provided a conceptual background for *Women's Ways of Knowing*. The two studies share the problem of having deduced sex differences from indirect comparisons. Gilligan's claim that women have a unique orientation of care and connectedness in moral decisionmaking is based largely on her study of real-life moral reasoning of women facing the crisis of an unwanted pregnancy. Studying a small sample of women, she compared their responses to those of men solving hypothetical moral dilemmas in earlier research by Kohlberg. The women in Gilligan's study should have been compared with men facing real-life dilemmas; for example, the men responsible for the unwanted pregnancies could have been questioned and their responses compared to those of the women (Colby & Damon, 1983). Unless similar women and men are compared in similar situations, claims of difference cannot be logically sustained. When direct comparisons are made, and occupational/educational background controlled, gender differences in ethical orientation and moral reasoning disappear (Walker, 1984). Thus the better controlled a study is the less likely it is to find "sex" differences (Jacklin, 1981).

By empiricist criteria then, *Women's Ways of Knowing* has methodological flaws and inadequacies that compromise its scientific validity. But uncovering methodological inadequacy in research done by feminist psychologists also uncovers epistemological contradictions and paradoxes in the feminist empiricist perspective. The implicit claim of this perspective is that, since androcentric values make for sexism in methods and the result is "bad science," feminists can remove bias and create "good science" by substituting a different set of researchers and a different set of values. Thus *Women's Ways of Knowing* and *In a Different Voice* can be seen as attempts to add a female (or feminist) perspective to scientific knowledge. But the empiricist argument that scientific methods, when properly applied, are value-neutral and capable of discovering objective facts about reality conflicts with the claim that women (or feminists) *as a group* produce better science than men (or nonfeminists). "Thus, feminist attempts to reform what is perceived as bad science bring to our attention deep logical incoherences and what, paradoxically, we can call empirical inadequacies in empiricist epistemologies" (Harding, 1986, p. 26).

"HAND, BRAIN, AND HEART:" FEMINIST STANDPOINT EPISTEMOLOGIES AND SEX DIFFERENCE RESEARCH

Feminist standpoint theorists maintain that scientists working from within women's unique position in social life can provide understandings of the natural and social world that are not possible from within men's social position. Although different theorists emphasize different aspects of women's experience as crucial in providing the basis for a distinctive epistemological stance, their theories all originate in the idea that "men's dominating position in social life results in partial and perverse understanding, whereas women's subjugated position provides the possibility of more complete and less perverse understanding" (Harding, 1986, p. 26). Hilary Rose (1983), for example, stresses the division of labor. Women's traditional work, she argues, is characterized by a unity of mental, emotional, and physical activity. When women bring their characteristic "caring labor" practices to scientific inquiry, they challenge the masculinist (and capitalist) division of scientific labor into classes of people who "do" (technicians, research assistants, custodians) and those who "think" (the scientists who generate and direct research projects). Rose also argues that a feminist epistemology must be grounded in the goals and practices of the women's movement. The goal of a science fully informed by feminism would be to increase women's knowledge and control of their own minds and bodies. Thus, according to Rose, a distinctive feminist standpoint emerges in the work of feminist researchers in areas of inquiry where work can be organized as "craft labor."

More generally, Fee (1986) defines feminist science in terms of three characteristics. First, it places women at the center of inquiry. Feminist psychologists have long criticized the discipline for overreliance on males as objects of study and for asking only masculinist questions (e.g., Sherif, 1979). Second, it reduces or eliminates the boundary between the knower and the object of study. In psychology, this would mean relinquishing the belief that only the "subject" is emotionally involved in the outcome of the research and is incapable of understanding her or his own experience without the aid of the "objective" experimenter. Third, it employs knowledge in order to liberate women, not to dominate or control them. Like Rose, Fee maintains that women (or feminists) make better scientists than men (or nonfeminists).

The feminist values orientation underlying the research by Belenky and her colleagues is clearly articulated in their book. They justify the study of women by maintaining that women's experience differs systematically from men's experience because women's position in society determines the social relations and activities in which women engage. Therefore the epistemological perspectives articulated by men do not represent the human experience but the male experience. To obtain complete and undistorted knowledge, women must be the focus of inquiry:

> In our study we chose to listen only to women. The male experience has been so powerfully articulated that we believed we would hear the patterns in women's voices more clearly if we held at bay the powerful templates men have etched in the literature and in our minds. (p. 9)

The study of women who vary in ethnicity, age, and social class also reflects feminist values of seeking to understand not only sexism but other forms of oppression:

275

CRAWFORD

> Including women from different ethnic backgrounds and a broad range of social classes enabled us to begin to examine and see beyond our own prejudices. It also allowed us to examine the injustices of the society by comparing women who were challenged and stimulated by the most elaborate of educations with women who were essentially uneducated. (pp. 13–14)

The researchers reflected practices of the women's movement in undertaking the task collectively, reaching conclusions by consensus and sharing authorship equally:

> During our work together, the four of us developed among ourselves an intimacy and collaboration which we have come to prize. We believe that the collaborative, egalitarian spirit so often shared by women should be more carefully nurtured in the work lives of all men and women. . . .

> In collaborating on writing this book we searched for a single voice—a way of submerging our individual perspectives for the sake of the collective "we." Not that we denied our individual convictions or squelched our objections to one another's points of view—we argued, tried to persuade, even cried at times when we reached an impasse of understanding—but we learned to listen to each other, to build on each others' insights, and eventually to arrive at a way of communicating as a collective what we believe. (p. ix)

The project also exemplifies Rose's conceptualization of feminist science as "craft labor" involving hand, brain, and heart (Rose, 1983). Belenky and her colleagues conducted the lengthy interviews themselves and devised a laborious method of content analysis. They describe this method as providing a qualitative, involved understanding of the phenomenological world of the interviewees rather than a distanced, pseudo-objective one.

From a feminist standpoint perspective then, *Women's Ways of Knowing* has strengths that are obscured by an empiricist perspective. In contrast to the minimization of difference that has characterized most feminist empiricism, feminist standpoint theorists seek out differences. Unlike masculinist claims about "women's natures," their claims of difference are based on values of respect for women's experience. *Women's Ways of Knowing,* as well as other claims of significant differences between women and men in personality structure (Chodorow, 1978; Miller, 1976), moral reasoning, and ethical orientation (Gilligan, 1982), is cast in a positive light when viewed as an example of a new, feminist approach to science.

Still, it is puzzling why the authors of *Women's Ways of Knowing* repeatedly compare the responses of their interviewees to Perry's. From a feminist standpoint perspective, their research project is not concerned with sex difference at all, but rather with illuminating women's experience. Comparisons with men should be superfluous. Moreover, it would only be expected that, as women and as feminists, Belenky, Clinchy, Goldberger, and Tarule would have

looked for and found different "ways of knowing" than Perry and his interviewers, even if they had interviewed the same people. Differences between
the two groups of respondents may be due to the interviewers as much as the
interviewees. Can research define "women's experience" without defining it
against men's experience? Are there limits to the importance of the researcher's social identity in determining the form and content of the data?
These remain relatively unexplored questions for feminist standpoint theorists.

Feminist standpoint epistemologies also raise the question of what constitutes the basis for a standpoint. Can a universalized "women's" standpoint exist when women differ by age, class, race, sexual preference, and ethnicity? Or
must theorists allow for the existence of multiple standpoints, those "hyphenated feminisms" such as black-lesbian or older-working-class women's perspectives? Can a woman ever legitimately study or write about women
whose standpoints differ from hers? These issues are real ones in contemporary feminist discourse. For example, Mohanty (1988) criticized the concept
of global feminism as based in mistaken attempts to describe the lives of Third
World women of color from the perspective of white, middle-class American
sociologists.

Feminist empiricism seeks to remediate sex bias by improving empirical
research, while the feminist standpoint approach attempts to develop a
uniquely feminist way of doing science (Harding, 1986). I have illustrated the
incompatibility of the two epistemologies, and some of their limitations, by
applying criteria derived from each to a feminist research project.

However, there is more to consider than epistemological stance when assessing the usefulness of research for women. In our individualistic culture,
psychology has a popular appeal unique among academic disciplines. And because our culture is also androcentric, psychological research that demonstrates sex differences is likely to be interpreted as demonstrating new sources
of biological deficiency in women. In the interpretation and popularization
of research, the social processes by which difference becomes a rationale for
oppression can be observed.

WOMEN'S NATURES: THE POP-PSYCH CONSTRUCTION OF REALITY

In the case of gender research, only a few discoveries reach the public at all
(Beckwith, 1984). When they do, a predictable set of events takes place, one
that researchers themselves can do little to control. A sex difference typically
will be interpreted as a deficiency or problem of *women*. It will be *di-
chotomized* and *universalized*—seen as characteristic of all women and no men.
It will be *essentialized*, or seen as having origins in women's essential (biological) natures. These processes, visible in the history of difference research, can
be expected to recur with feminist difference research. In this final section I

discuss the popularization of research on women's thinking and show how the processes of dichotomizing, universalizing, and essentializing occur.

That women have a different way of knowing seems on its way to becoming an established pop-psychological "fact," or, at the least, a "conceptual bandwagon" (Mednick, 1987). It is instructive to compare the media acceptance and endorsement of *In a Different Voice* and *Women's Ways of Knowing* with that of the most recent Hite report, *Women and Love* (Hite, 1987). (It should be noted that there are important differences in these projects. Hite is not a trained social scientist, and she used a mail survey rather than in–depth interviewing. However, her work bears at least superficial similarity to the others in its use of qualitative analysis of self–reports from nonrepresentative samples of women). Gilligan's work was lionized (e.g., Van Gelder, 1984), and *Ms. Magazine* pronounced her Woman of the Year. *Women's Ways of Knowing* was described as "a rich supply of resources for feminist analysis, public policy—and for theoretical and political struggles—for years to come" (Harding, 1987) and praised for its systematic, empirical approach (Hoffman, 1986) by feminist reviewers. It has also been awarded a Distinguished Publication Award from the Association for Women in Psychology. Its reception in the popular press has been positive. To one reviewer, the authors were "Joans of Arc guided by the sounds of women's voices" (Neustatdtl, 1986). To date, no reviewer has raised methodological issues. *Women and Love*, which was critical of men's behavior, was widely attacked as unscientific, methodogically flawed, murky and muddled, statistically deficient, and completely unrepresentative of "most women" (Hochschild, 1987; Shapiro, 1987; Wallis, 1987). Hite has been denigrated as an emotionally disturbed "pop-culture demagogue" (Barol & Brailsford, 1987).

Should feminists be concerned about the popular reception of *Women's Ways of Knowing?* One reason for its popularity may be that women find its ideas empowering (Mahlstedt, 1988). But even though the ideas are appealing from a feminist standpoint perspective, they may be distorted as they are disseminated. The culture will most readily authorize scientific research when it can be most easily enlisted to maintain male dominance (Mednick, 1987). Female superiority will not be authorized because the power to define "superior" and "inferior" remains with the dominant group (Bleier, 1984; Unger, 1987). The dangers of extolling feminine virtues were apparent to many of the pioneers of modern feminist psychology (Rosenberg, 1982). Difference—even though originally conceptualized as female strength, superiority, or virtue—is almost always transformed into "deficiency" for women. Because Western culture has long evaluated "masculine" reason and abstraction as inherently superior to "feminine" intuition and connection, the claim of "women's ways of knowing" is likely to be interpreted as further confirmation that rational thought is "male" (Hare-Mustin & Marecek, 1988).

Arguing that "difference" has long been both a way of construing the

278

CRAWFORD

meaning of gender and a source of justification for the oppression of women, some feminist theorists propose that gender as difference and as deficiency may be inseparable (Hare-Mustin & Marecek, 1988; Unger, 1979). In each of the oppositional pairs that constitute the building blocks of western thought—mind/body, fact/value, reason/emotion, culture/nature, and of course, masculine/feminine—the pole associated with men is more highly valued (Fee, 1986). At the individual level, the polarization and evaluation of oppositional pairs can readily be demonstrated with psychological techniques (Osgood & Richards, 1973). At the social level, there is abundant evidence that processes of social judgment lead to the equating of "male" with "superior" and "female" with "inferior." As Unger (1979) stated: "In sex, as in race, there are no separate but equal social categories" (p. 1092).

Once a category of behavior or personality becomes "gendered," it is increasingly seen as exclusively the property of one sex or the other. Gilligan's (1982) book is frequently cited, despite her disclaimers, in dichotomous terms—for example, as having "exploded on the psychological world with its clear argument explaining how women make moral judgments differently from men" (Neustatdtl, 1986, p. 38). Evidence that the two orientations described by Gilligan are *not* gender-related (Brabeck, 1983; Ford & Lowery, 1986; Walker, 1984) receives no media coverage. Similarly, the study by Belenky et al. is described as demonstrating a sex difference: "Even if they were glossed over (in the past), there are gender differences in the quest for knowledge, to finding self" according to the *Los Angeles Times* (Kovacs, 1986). And the difference is seen as separating all women from all men: "Just as the voice of conscience says different things to women than it does to men" (a reference to Gilligan's work), "the authors found that a different voice speaks to women when they ask themselves what it is they know," reports the *New York Times Book Review* (Neustatdtl, 1986). In *Women's Ways of Knowing*, dichotomizing is encouraged when the authors overgeneralize from their sample to all women (and from Perry's sample to all men) and when they fail to systematically examine variables other than sex. For example, they claim that women as a group have been harmed by a competitive educational system:

> Our interviews have convinced us that every woman, regardless of age, social class, ethnicity, and academic achievement, needs to know that she is capable of intelligent thought, and she needs to know it right away. Perhaps men learn this lesson before going to college, or perhaps they can wait until they have proved themselves to hear it. (p. 193)

This generalization is unwarranted without systematically separating sex from class, ethnicity, and other variables related to similarity between women and men. Feminist critics have pointed out that Gilligan (1982) also discounts factors such as class and religion, attributing all observed differences in moral reasoning to sex (Auerbach, Blum, Smith, & Williams, 1985; Lott, 1986). Yet

CRAWFORD

ethnicity and class are important factors in moral reasoning. Research on black Americans, although not directly comparable to Gilligan's, suggests that women and men frame moral choices similarly (Stack, 1986). Several theorists have suggested that apparent sex differences in moral reasoning may reflect women's subordinate social position and lack of power (Tronto, 1987). This view implies that the "ethic of care" will be expressed by powerless people generally rather than being characteristic of women (Hare-Mustin & Marecek, 1988).

Dichotomization has different consequences for men and women as groups. Men continue to be viewed as individuals and in terms of many possible social groupings, while women are viewed as women (Hare-Mustin & Marecek, 1988). Universalizing women tends to downplay the importance of immediate situational determinants of their behavior (McCullough, 1987). But much of gendered behavior is created in ongoing social interaction where not only gender but other factors come into play (Deaux & Major, 1987; Unger, 1987; West & Zimmerman, 1987). Global conclusions about women and competition, for example, beg the question of how women, and only women, could develop profound doubts about their abilities in an educational system in which most teachers are women, or how and why some women seek out and thrive in some competitive situations.

Do people move from one "way of knowing" to another as they respond to the novelty or difficulty of a learning situation, their status as members of a majority or minority group in the setting, the immediate behavior of higher status persons in a particular context, their expectations for themselves, or other factors? Would a student trained in mathematics and logic express the same epistemological position in describing her approach to math as in relating her attempts to solve a conflict with her parents? Might a poet be temporarily "silenced" on his first encounter with computer programming? Whether people would maintain consistent epistemological positions across situations such as these cannot, of course, be addressed by the retrospective report methods of Belenky et al., and it is not an appropriate question to ask of their data. One strength of the analysis in *Women's Ways of Knowing* is that it shows a diversity of approaches to knowledge. But if women are seen as holding particular epistemological positions as women, universalized questions about women become easy to ask (cf. on designing an education for women, Belenky et al. propose to start with the question "What does a woman know?" p. 198). Other questions, such as those that specify "Which women?" and "In what situations?" become more difficult to ask.

Once a sex difference is seen as categorically distinguishing the genders, it becomes "only natural" to assume that it is biologically based (Jacklin, 1981). Popular press accounts of sex differences in mathematics performance stress "math genes" and a male "hormonal edge" (Beckwith, 1984; Eccles & Jacobs, 1986). Even differences that are originally conceptualized as stemming from socially constructed experience become essentialized (Bleier, 1984; Unger, 1979) and seen as immutable. Chodorow (1978), for example, is explicit in rejecting Freud's notions of the biological origins of gendered personalities, and yet her work has frequently been misinterpreted as an essentialist account (Marecek, 1983). In *Women's Ways of Knowing* the endorsement of environmental causes of difference is undermined by references to the "naturalness" of some differences. For example, "women seem to take naturally to a non-judgmental stance. . . when someone said something they disagreed with or disapproved of, their instinct was not to argue" (pp. 116–117, emphasis added); or "many women take naturally to connected knowing" (p. 121, emphasis added). The more judgmental and analytical style attributed to men is not justified as natural or instinctive. Thus the way is opened for essentialist accounts of women's—and only women's—thinking.

These issues take on immediate practical importance when public policy may be based on presumed differences. Belenky et al., for example, suggest that educational systems be changed to meet what they see as women's unique needs for connected, noncompetitive, and nonhierarchical educational settings. But Fausto-Sterling (1985) argues that educational reforms emphasizing the special needs of women (based on differences in men's and women's thinking) have historically occurred whenever women are a majority in educational settings. Such reforms have functioned to segregate women and maintain power imbalances.

The operation of a sex and gender system can be seen in the popularization of research on women. Research that reports new ways that women differ from men or have special "women's" problems receives a great deal of attention (Crawford & Marecek, 1988). Research that reports similarities between women and men receives little. When a much-publicized difference fails to replicate in further investigations, either the new information is not reported or the argument for profound and immuatable differences simply shifts to another ground (Shields, 1982; Unger, 1979).

Perhaps the paradox is inherent: in challenging a system of subordination by gender, feminist psychologists have attempted to remediate sex bias in research and to demonstrate a uniquely feminine experience. But construing gender as a property of individuals, rather than as a set of interactive processes that form a system of subordination, leads back to the questions about the nature and meaning of difference that have preoccupied feminist psychology for so long.

Acknowledgments. Friends and colleagues helped me write this chapter by reading my first attempts and discussing the ideas with me. I thank Roger Chaffin, Rachel Hare-Mustin, Carol Farley Kessler, Deborah Mahlstedt, Mary McCullough, Pat Manfredi, Pat O'Neill, Donna Summerfield, and Rhoda Unger.

REFERENCES

Auerbach, J., Blum, L., Smith, V., & Williams, C. (1985). On Gilligan's *In a different voice*. *Feminist Studies, 11*, 149–161.

Barol, B., & Brailsford, K. (1987). Men aren't her only problem. *Newsweek, Nov.* 23, p. 76.

Beckwith, B. (1984) How magazines cover sex differences research. *Science for the People, 16*, 18–23.

Belenky, M.F., Clinchy, B.M., Goldberger, N.R., & Tarule, J.M. (1986). *Women's ways of knowing: The development of self, voice, and mind.* New York: Basic Books.

Bleier, R. (1984). *Science and gender: A critique of biology and its theories on women.* New York: Pergamon.

Brabeck, M. (1983). Moral judgment: Theory and research on differences between males and females. *Developmental Review, 3*, 274–291.

Chodorow, N. (1978). *The reproduction of mothering.* Berkeley: University of California Press.

Colby, A., & Damon, W. (1983). Listening to a different voice: A review of Gilligan's *In a different voice. Merrill–Palmer Quarterly, 29*, 473–481.

Crawford, M., & MacLeod, M. (1990). Sex roles in the college classroom: An assessment of the "chilly climate" for women. *Sex Roles, 23*, 101–122.

Crawford, M., & Marecek, J. (1988). *Psychology reconstructs the female: 1971–1988.* Paper presented at the Nags Head Conference on Sex and Gender, Nags Head, NC.

Deaux, K. (1984). From individual differences to social categories: Analysis of a decade's research on gender. *American Psychologist, 39*, 105–116.

Deaux, K., & Major, B. (1987). Putting gender into context: An interactive model of gender-related behavior. *Psychological Review, 94*, 369–389.

Eagly, A.H. (1987). *Sex differences in social behavior: A social role interpretation.* Hillsdale, NJ: Erlbaum.

Eccles, J.S., & Jacobs, J.E. (1986). Social forces shape math attitudes and performance. *Signs: Journal of Women in Culture and Society, 11*, 367–389.

Fausto–Sterling, A. (1985). *Myths of gender: Biological theoies about women and men.* New York: Basic Books.

Fee, E. (1986). Critiques of modern science: The relationship of feminism to other redical epistemologies. In R. Bleier (Ed.), *Feminist approaches to science.* New York: Pergamon.

Ford, M.R., & Lowery, C.R. (1986). Gender differences in moral reasoning: A comparison of the use of justice and care orientations. *Journal of Personality and Social Psychology, 50*, 777–783.

Gilligan, C. (1982). *In a different voice.* Cambridge: Harvard University Press.

Grady, K.E. (1981). Sex bias in research design. *Psychology of Women Quarterly, 5*, 628–636.

Harding, S. (1986). *The science question in feminism.* Ithaca, NY: Cornell University Press.

Hare-Mustin, R., & Marecek, J. (1988). The meaning of difference: Gender theory, postmodernism, and psychology. *American Psychologist, 43*, 455–464.

Hite, S. (1987). *The Hite report: Women and love. A cultural revolution in progress.* New York: Knopf.

Hochschild, A.R. (1987). Why can't a man be more like a woman? *New York Times Book Review*, Nov. 15, pp. 3, 32.

Hoffman, N.J. (1986). Feminist scholarship and women's studies. *Harvard Educational Review, 56*, 511–519.

Hyde, J.S., & Linn, M.C. (Eds.) (1986). *The psychology of gender: Advances through meta-analysis.* Baltimore: Johns Hopkins University Press.

Jacklin, C.N. (1981). Methodological issues in the study of sex-related differences. *Developmental Review, 1*, 266–273.

Johnson, D.W., & Johnson, R.T. (1987). *Learning together and alone: Cooperative, competitive, and individualistic learning.* Englewood Cliffs, NJ: Prentice–Hall.

Kovacs, D. (1986). Review of *Women's ways of knowing. Los Angeles Times*, Sept. 7, p. 10.

Lott, B. (1986). *Women's lives: Themes and variations in gender learning.* Monterey, CA: Brooks/Cole.

Lyons, N. (1983). Two perspectives on self, relationships, and morality. *Harvard Educational Review, 53*, 125–145.

Maccoby, E., & Jacklin, C. (1974). *The psychology of sex differences.* Stanford, CA: Stanford University Press.

Mahlstedt, D. (1988). Personal communication, May 25.

Marecek, J. (1983). *Identity and individualism in feminist psychology.* Paper presented at the Penn Women's Studies Conference, Philadelphia.

McCullough, M. (1987). *Analysis of "Feminist theory: From margin to center."* Unpublished manuscript.

McIntosh, P. (1983). *Interactive phases of curricular revision: A feminist perspective.* Working paper no. 124. Wellesley, MA: Wellesley College Center for Research on Women.

Mednick, M. (1987). *On the politics of psychological constructs: Stop the bandwagon, I want to get off.* Paper presented at Third International Interdisciplinary Conference on Women, Dublin, Ireland.

Miller, J.B. (1976). *Toward a new psychology of women.* Boston: Beacon Press.

Mohanty, C. (1988). Global feminism and its territories: Boundaries of politics and method. Presented at Feminist Thought for the Year 2000 Conference, Hamilton College, April 9.

Neustratdtl, S. (1986). They hear different vocies. *New York Times Book Review*, Oct. 5, p. 38.

Osgood, C.E., & Richards, M.M. (1973). From yang and yin to and or but. *Language, 49*, 380–412.

Perry, W.G. (1970). *Forms of intellectual and ethical development in the college years.* New York: Holt, Rinehart, & Winston.

Rose, H. (1983). Hand, brain, and heart: A feminist epistemology for the natural sciences. *Signs: Journal of Women in Culture and Society, 9*, 73–90.

Rosenberg, R. (1982). *Beyond separate spheres: Intellectual origins of modern feminism.* New Haven, CT: Yale University Press.

Rossi, A.S. (1981). On the reproduction of mothering: A methodological debate. *Signs: Journal of Women in Culture and Society, 6*, 492–500.

Scarborough, E., & Furumoto, L. (1987) *Untold lives: The first generation of American women psychologists.* New York: Columbia University Press.

283

Shapiro, L. (1987). Eavesdropping on women. *Newsweek*, Oct. 19, p. 86.

Sherif, C.W. (1979). Bias in psychology. In J.A. Sherman & E.T. Beck (Eds.) *The prism of sex: Essays in the sociology of knowledge*. Madison: University of Wisconsin Press.

Shields, S.A. (1982). The variability hypothesis: The history of a biological model of sex difference in intelligence. *Signs: Journal of Women in Culture and Society, 7*, 769–797.

Stack, C.B. (1986). The culture of gender: Women and men of color. *Signs: Journal of Women in Culture and Society, 11*, 321–324.

Tronto, J.C. (1987). Beyond gender difference to a theory of care. *Signs: Journal of Women in Culture and Society, 12*, 644–663.

Unger, R.K. (1979). Toward a redefinition of sex and gender. *American Psychologist, 34*, 1085–1094.

Unger, R.K. (August, 1987). The social construction of gender: Contradictions and conundrums. *Paper presented at the meeting of the American Psychological Association, New York.*

Unger, R.K., & Crawford, M. (1989). Methods and values in decisions about gender differences: Review of Alice H. Eagly, *Sex differences in social behavior: A social role interpretation. Contemporary Psychology.*

Van Gelder, L. (1984). *Carol Gilligan: Leader for a different kind of future. Ms.*, Jan., pp. 37–40, 101.

Walker, L. (1984). Sex differences in the development of moral reasoning: A critical review. *Child Development, 55*, 667–691.

Wallis, C. (1987). Back off, buddy. *Time*, Oct. 12, pp. 68–73.

West, C., & Zimmerman, D.H. (1987). Doing gender. *Gender & Society, 1*, 125–151.

Wooley, H.T. (1910). Psychological literature: A review of the recent literature on the psychology of sex. *Psychological Bulletin, 7*, 335–342.

CORPSES, LEPERS, AND MENSTRUATING WOMEN
Tradition, Transition, and the Sociology of Knowledge

Nancy Datan

THIS PAPER reexamines research on modernity and middle age, exploring the evolution of the questions that initiated the study as the findings affected the investigators. To put it more simply, where a report of current research allows researchers to say what they did, what they found, and what they make of it, this retrospective report of research initiated many years ago forces me to remember the questions that haunt me, admit the mistakes I made, and consider what I have learned with the passage of time.

My point of departure in this essay is a study of middle-aged women in five Israel subcultures who represented a quasi-continuum ranging from modern European women, probably more like our mothers than ourselves, to traditional Moslem Arab village women, whose large families and constricted lives are alien to the experience of the American social scientist. The study had its origins in a psychiatrist's observation that middle-aged women of Near Eastern origin and traditional cultures did not seem to suffer clinical depression associated with menopause and middle age: this depression, while rare, seemed confined to the more modern women of European origin. The clinical observation was confirmed by a review of national health statistics for the population of Israel, which prompted the medical sociologist Aaron Antonovsky and the psychiatrist Benjamin Maoz to consider whether modernity itself made aging more difficult for women. Their curiosity found expression in a grant application entitled "Socio-Cultural Patterns and the Involutional Crisis," which was approved for funding and assigned to Bernice Neugarten as project officer; it was she who put the grant application into my hands in 1967 and suggested that I might want to become involved in the study. I joined the project as a young mother of two; the guiding hypothesis of the study, that the small families of modern women constituted a "denial" of femininity that took its toll on the mental health of the women as fertility ceased at menopause, raised my hackles. I counterproposed that it would be modern women, from whom childbearing had long ago ceased and for whom other roles existed, who would make the transitions of middle age with ease. But, just to be sure, I got pregnant.

At this writing I am approaching the ages of the women who were subjects in that study; born between 1915 and 1924, they were between the ages of 45 and 54 when they were interviewed by us. My "insurance policy" baby has left for college. Ours was a study of women in transition: women whose origins represented points on a continuum ranging from tradition to modernity endured the transitions of middle age against the historical and social context of changing traditions, coupled with the transitions of immigration for the four Jewish subcultures of the study, the transitions of war and changing national boundaries for women in all five subcultures. We began to publish the findings from preliminary phases of the study immediately, as we discovered that we had misunderstood the meanings of tradition, modernity, and even the cultural significance of menstruation, childbearing, and menopause (Antonovsky, 1972, 1973; Antonovsky, Maoz, Datan, & Wijsenbeek, 1971; Datan, 1971, 1972, 1973; Datan, Maoz, Antonovsky, & Wijsenbeek, 1970; Maoz, 1973, 1975; Maoz, Datan, Antonovsky, & Wijsenbeek, 1970a; Maoz, Wijsenbeek, Antonovsky, & Datan, 1970b). The fieldwork and data analysis were completed in 1970; the findings from this four-phase study, which began with semistructured psychiatric interviews used to design a survey questionnaire, which followed and was in turn followed by a medical examination and a follow-up psychiatric interview, generated additional publications directly related to the study (Datan, Antonovsky, & Maoz, 1981) as well as new directions stimulated by it (Antonovsky, 1979; Datan, 1977; Datan, Antonovsky, & Maoz, 1984, 1985; Maoz, Antonovsky, Apter, Wijsenbeek, & Datan, 1977a,b; Maoz, Antonovsky, Apter, Datan, Rochberg, & Salomon, 1978). But it seemed to take us a decade to get the point. The point was that we had gone into the field—two men and one young woman—conceived that menopause would mean something very different to women who had planned and restricted childbearing, as compared to women whose family life cycle paralleled the biological life course as they began childbearing at marriage and ceased only at menopause. Exactly what was this difference in meaning? Well, that depended upon whether you asked Maoz, who was the first to notice clinical depression as a phenomenon of modern middle-aged women, Antonovsky, whose review of the national health statistics confirmed Maoz's impression, or me, who was young, modern by all the criteria in our survey, and anxious that the difference should be to my advantage. The point was that we were all wrong: regardless of childbearing history, regardless of whether middle age meant adjustment to the postparental phase of the family life cycle, or at the other extreme, might mean that mother and daughter bore children side by side and the home filling with grandchildren was not yet empty of young children–regardless of all these differences in childbearing history and the family of middle age, the women in our study welcomed the loss of fertility that menopause brought. And we did not believe them.

SEXISM AND AGEISM IN THE CONSTRUCTION OF HYPOTHESES

It seems clear in retrospect that our contradictory visions of middle age reflected the different life experiences of the investigators at least as much as they represented conflicting developmental models. We approached this study, I now believe, in the spirit of anthropologists suffering from "exotic bias," fortunate in two ways: first, we were outspoken advocates of our biases; second, our biases were mutually contradictory. I like to call the initial guiding hypothesis of the study the "male chauvinist pig hypothesis," since it proposes that the women most likely to enjoy mental health in middle age are those who spent their young adulthood barefoot and pregnant. Yet my colleagues–male, to be sure–had not made up this hypothesis out of whole cloth. To begin with, it fit the facts, such as they were—hospitalization for involutional psychosis, the clinical depression of middle age—was seen among modern women of Western origin, not among traditional women of Near Eastern origin. Moreover, this hypothesis was grounded in the psychoanalytic literature: Helena Deutsch (1945) termed menopause "the closing of the gates," as "omen of aging and death" (p. 478). Finally, the somewhat quantitative spirit of this hypothesis, that the more children a woman had borne the greater her fulfillment of her feminine potential–which I termed sarcastically the "rabbit theory of femininity"–was advocated by men who, although they were fathers, had never been pregnant. We spent a fiercely confrontational first year together debating the meanings of menstration and pregnancy as we designed the survey phase of the study, a year I also spent much of being pregnant.

For if masculinity accounted for a measure of my colleagues' "exotic bias," my youth accounted for that portion of mine. My own hypothesis, that mod-

DATAN

287

ern women had roles other than mother, that childbearing ceased long before fertility ended, that knowledge and alternatives–the hallmarks of modernity–made the modern woman's middle age an easier transition for her than for her traditional counterparts, was also grounded in facts and in its own literature. Demography supplied the facts of the modern woman's childbearing history; developmental psychology, and in particular the developmental task model of Havighurst and the research of Neugarten–at the time the only study of normal women's attitudes toward menopause–supported my hypothesis. As Antonovsky and Maoz believed the loss of fertility was salient, so did I: but where we believed it would be the women who had not exploited this potential to its fullest who would feel the loss, I believed it would be women who had no other potential to express who would feel the loss. When all the women of our study told us that the loss of fertility was welcome, we checked the data for computer error. Then we checked other responses for evidence of deception. When they were finally persuaded that women in all cultures were willing to share with us their sorrows and their joys, to tell us about the culture-specific meanings of menstruation and menopause, to express regret–as the Europeans did–that they had not borne larger families, or on the other hand, to regret–as the Persians did–the large families they had borne–then and only then did we believe them when we read over the responses that told us that they did not regret the loss of the capacity to bear children now. And even then I did not *quite* believe them–not in my bones, although I dutifully presented the finding to the Gerontological Society in 1971, acknowledging that it contradicted the psychoanalytic and psychiatric literature of the day. All the middle-aged women in the audience nodded their heads. Finally. Today I have a term for the temporal shortsightedness that blinded me then (and, in other respects, blinds me today); the narcissism of the life cycle, the temporal equivalent of ethnocentrism, the state of mind that causes me to flinch just a little when a colleague's two-year-old dashes into my office, to remember when I felt as she does now the omnipotence of young motherhood, and to feel, a little smugly, that real motherhood is the moment when a child graduates from college, that the first tooth or first word or first step is only a small miracle compared to the enormous miracle of a child's first existential dilemma, a first love. Today, finally, I believe what 1,148 women told me in 1968. And, thanks to the vigor with which I defended my earlier beliefs, I am a little more willing to hear about Alex's teeth, a little more willing to believe that Alex's mother does not really believe me when I describe a stage of motherhood that involves ex-boyfriends, applications to graduate school, and no diapers at all.

ETHNOCENTRISM IN THE CONSTRUCTION OF HYPOTHESES

If gender divided us, "modernity" united us, and our unity hindered us from understanding the limitations of our own culture. Masculinity on my col-

288

DATAN

leagues' part and youth of mine combined to create an overvaluation of fertility and childbirth–the motherhood of young adulthood. Cross-cultural research, as it is meant to do, showed us our limits. But where we disagreed on
the effects of modernity, we shared a concept of modernity that showed our
common origins in Western culture. To us, modernity meant coping; tradition
meant fatalism, passive acceptance, a network of ritual and taboo that constricted belief and behavior. We expected this to make a difference not just
with respect to the meaning of the loss of fertility, but in a broader sense:
middle age, my colleagues argued, would be more stressful for a modern
women growing older in a culture that valued youth and devalued old age;
menopause presented a signal of aging that was best accepted with the fatalism of tradition. I argued the converse, of course: that any transition was best
negotiated on the basis of a wide variety of alternatives and the active coping
skills that enabled the individual to choose wisely. We were not prepared to
find psychological well-being highest at the two extremes of our study,
among the modern Central European women and the traditional Moslem
Arab village women. And when this proved to be the case, our initial explanation was that this was due to cultural continuity: the Central European
women had immigrated to a country where theirs were the dominant cultural values: the Moslem Arab women lived in their relative security of small
farming villages where cultural values changed, but only slowly. The immigrant Jewish women from our transitional cultures–Turkey, Persia, and North
Africa–had grown to young adulthood in traditional cultures, and in immi-
grating across national borders had also immigrated through time to settle in
a culture where the traditional rewards no longer awaited them, but they
were unable to make use of the prerogatives of modernity.

No doubt there is much truth and perhaps some wisdom in this explanation. For I would now suggest that in the long run we are all in transition,
reared in a culture that changes around us as we grow out of it. If today I interviewed American women whose ages are those of my Israeli respondents, I
would be talking to the daughters of women born when the American
woman did not have the vote; the daughters of my respondents would be
adolescents or young adults who might choose engineering because they had
seen that a woman could be an astronaut, or who might choose political science or law because they had seen that a woman can run for vice-president.
My middle-aged respondents dreamed of a better life not for themselves, but
for their daughters. My mother advised me in 1960 to marry a man who
would let me use my brains; in 1984, I advised my daughter against the rab-
binate and in favor of physics, where jobs were certain. We are all time-travel-
ers; it is only because there is no way of standing still that it is so difficult to
see that we are in motion. And, too, the advocates of change may be using the
wrong measure: the year, or even the decade, is not the only measure of human progress. It is the generation–what my mother learned from her mother,

289

DATAN

what I learned from mine, what my daughter learns from me—which may be the unit of measure for changing social values. This I learned, considering the women in five Israeli subcultures whose psychological well-being was highest at the traditional and modern extremes.

PATRIARCHY RECONSIDERED: SEXISM AS ETHNOCENTRISM

It took a little longer to realize that cultural continuities and discontinuities were not the entire story. Our measures of tradition were intimately bound up with woman as "other", and tradition most certainly as somebody else's. Menopause was a convenient anchor, as Judaism shared with Islam cultural taboos on menstruating women, who were defined as ritually impure. Orthodox Judaism is conspicuous in modern Western religion for its attention to ritual purity. The menstruating woman must refrain from all contact with her husband—she cannot, for example, hand him his hat, but must set it on a table for him to pick up—for the duration of menstruation and for seven days after its cessation (Mishnah: Taharot: Niddah). In other words, traditional Jewish women spend half their adult life in a state of ritual uncleaness, in a tradition that identifies as the three chief source of ritual impurity corpses, lepers, and menstruating women (Mishnah: Taharot: Kelim). In Israel, where Judaism found a range of expression from orthodoxy to militant antitheism and the vocal rejection of ritual, Antonovsky, Moaz, and I were all closer to the secular than to the devout. And the more I learned about Orthodoxy, the more distance I sought between myself and the alien, and alienating, rituals that would signal my birth as a daughter with a period of uncleaness twice that which followed the birth of a son. If they wished, Antonovsky and Maoz could begin the day with the blessing recited by Orthodox Jewish men, praising Almighty God who had not created them women. I did not see much point in the woman's prayer of thanks to God for having created her according to his will; the many exclusions that followed—a woman may not participate in the reading of scriptures, may not bear witness in court, and so on—did not inspire gratitude. The whole of modernization, as reflected in our study (where modernity was associated with a lower percentage of women who described themselves as devout), the history of Judiasm (the Reform movement of Central Europe in the 19th century removed the exclusions Orthodoxy insisted on), even the history of the young state of Israel (which was born with an Equal Rights declaration)—all of it seemed to be a welcome rejection of the repellent taint of uncleaness associated with women in Jewish law (Exodus 32: 1-35).

I first discovered otherwise by reading Jewish law—a necessary prelude to a study that employed, somewhat obliquely, the degree of modernity as a measure of emancipation from the menstrual taboos common to Judaism and Islam. I began, therefore, with the menstrual taboos (Mishnah: Taharot), which begin by considering the colors of menstrual blood: "like the blood of a

wound," "like the color of sediment," "the shade of the bright-colored saf-
fron," "a color like that of water which has had the earth of the Valley of Beit
Kerem stirred into it," and finally, "the color of two parts of water mixed with
one part of the wine of Sharon." The imagery of the Talmudic writers, like
the customs of the Moslem women of our study, do not suggest uncleanliness
but rather ritual impurity–indeed, a concern that the menstruating woman
was potentially very enticing, to be fought off only through elaborate proscriptions. Centuries have diluted the original sense of power in religious tradition; secular American society has Christianity as its majority religion, with
no formal menstrual taboos at all–only "feminine sanitary protection" and related products sold to ameliorate what one can only suppose to be a woman's
natural state of uncleanness, an uncleanness to be scrubbed off in order to
achieve a sanitized and sexually attractive body–the very converse of the laws
and customs that recognize, through imagery if not by proclamation, the
power of female sexuality.

Thus to a casual onlooker, the Jewish woman is unclean; a closer look reveals that ritual impurity is a somewhat ambiguous expression of power. The
status of women in Jewish law, I found, has many examples of such ambiguities: for instance, although a woman may not bear witness in a religious court
of law, her word is accepted in a charge of rape. The study of middle age and
modernization that I began as a secular social scientist slowly became, in part
at least, a study of sexuality in Jewish tradition. To this study I brought another set of assumptions derived from cultural anthropology and evolutionary biology. In the tradition of anthropology, I began by assuming coherence in culture: where apparent contradication is seen by the outsider, the burden of
proof is on the social scientist. My second assumption is an evolutionary principle: enduring patterns of culture have survival value. The latter assumption
seems particularly defensible in the case of a people as beleaguered as the
Jews, who have never been numerous and who have nevertheless resisted ex-
tinction over the centuries. These two assumptions, cultural coherence and
survival imperatives, converge in the religious traditions that govern the expression of sexuality, where biological and cultural survival converge.

291

PATRIARCHY RECONSIDERED AGAIN: THE AMBIGUITIES OF MALE
DOMINANCE

Mary Douglas (1966) has pointed out that in any culture where male dominance is complete, menstrual taboos and other expressions of the fear of sexual pollution are not found. Women are simply controlled by force–frequently, lethal force. Conversely, whenever male dominance is incomplete, with
countervailing currents recognizing female power and reflecting protection
for women, she argues that the tensions of sexuality will be channeled into
some form of belief in sexual pollution. Following Mary Douglas, I propose
that the contradiction in Jewish tradition between an external social structure

DATAN

of apparent male dominance and the internal reality that protects women, in some cases at the expense of men, finds expression in an elaborate system of belief in sexual pollution. This belief system externalizes the ambivalence and mutual antagonisms that sex differences–in ancient Judaism as in any other primitive culture the primary source of social roles–tend to engender. The importance of this externalization is seen in the cultural complex of laws that assign secondary status to women, yet safeguard women against the brutal realities of pregnancy and childbearing while affirming sexual expressions in the service of family stability. This belief system, as Mary Douglas has put it, serves to protect the integrity of the body politic by guarding the ritual purity of the body physical, managing the tension induced by the contradiction between the formal social organization and the underlying dynamic culture that it serves.

Douglas's recognition of the cultural significance of ambiguity and conflict helped me recognize the ambiguities in our women's responses. The European Jewish women in our study came from the traditions of Western civilization and Zionism that had given rise to the Reform movement in Judaism and to the founding of a state with a declaration of equality of rights for every citizen regardless of religion, nationality, or sex. The Moslem Arab women had grown to young adulthood in a culture that permitted polygyny and was even more restrictive than Orthodox Jewish tradition. Yet it was the women at these two extremes who reported the highest psychological well-being on our survey. Furthermore, one European survivor of Auschwitz showed that the machinery of modernity can immobilize the human spirit as effectively as ritual and tradition: "I don't want menstruation to stop," she told us, "it stopped in Auschwitz." Finally, a Moslem Arab villager told us about her fear that with the West Bank now open her husband might, as a neighbor had done, take a second wife in Jordanian territory; "So I just keep him at home. I don't let him go to Tel Aviv." Not quite the subordinate, fatalistic woman we expected to typify traditional culture. We relearned some basic notions of cultural anthropology, particularly the difference between overt and covert power; more important, we learned something about ritual and tradition. What I term *ritual and tradition* is somebody else's coping strategies, which I know to be ineffectual, whereas my own coping strategies, which have not yet proven useless, I term *science and technology*. The women at the traditional and modern extremes of our study not only enjoyed greater cultural stability, but a larger measure of control over their own lives.

SEXISM AS SOCIAL SCIENCE: A PROBLEM IN THE SOCIOLOGY OF KNOWLEDGE

Finally, the study itself had a context that included not only the investigators but the scientific climate in which the investigation was carried out. The project entitled "Socio-Cultural Patterns and the Involutional Crisis," proposed as a study of woman's response to menopause and middle age, was funded. As the study drew to a close and we examined the pattern of our findings, it became apparent that we had a companion study: the husbands of our respondents, who could tell us how they felt about changes in the family life cycle, sexuality, marriage, children—all in the context of cultures that had been shown to vary dramatically. That study was proposed and funding was denied. It was rumored that a male reviewer had argued vehemently that there was no such thing as a male involutional crisis. This statement was made at a time when the midlife crisis of career for the male professional was just beginning to receive attention; but this is a crisis of affluence, a crisis of striving. What if there was a measure of truth in my colleagues' assertion that menopause, an inevitable change, was best met with passive acceptance? The study that proposed this to be the case was funded; the study that proposed to follow up this question with men was denied. It now seems to me that this was yet another instance of "woman as object," and I regret not only the lost opportunity to study these women's husbands, but the loss of the chance no scientist ever gets, to probe a reviewer's mind and find out just what seizes the imagination and gains support, what disturbs and evokes resistance. Precisely because we were fortunate to have competing resistances. this study allowed us to test not only our hypotheses but ourselves. The fate of the grant proposal that went unfunded prompts us to question the larger context in which the issues that are our life's blood—modernization, and the roles of women and men—are investigated or ignored.

293

REFERENCES

Antonovsky, A. Breakdown: A needed fourth step in the conceptual armamentarium of modern medicine. *Social Science and Medicine*, 1972, 6, 537-544.

Antonovsky, A. The utility of the breakdown concept. *Social Science and Medicine*, 1973, 7, 605-612.

Antonovsky, A. *Health, stress, and coping.* San Francisco: Jossey-Bass, 1979.

Antonovsky, A., Maoz, B., Datan, N., & Wijsenbeck, H. Twenty-five years later: A limited study of the sequellae of the concentration camp experience. *Social Psychiatry*, 1971, 6(4), 186-193.

Datan, N. *Women's attitudes toward the climacterium in five Israeli subcultures.* Ph.D. dissertation, University of Chicago, 1971.

Datan, N. To be a woman in Israel. *School Review*, 1972, 80(2), 319-332.

Datan, N. Your daughters shall prophesy: Ancient and contemporary perspective on the women of Israel. In M. Curtis & M. Chertoff (Eds.). *Israel: Social structure and change.* New Brunswick, N.J.: Transaction Books, 1973.

Datan, N. Ecological antecedents and sex-role consequences in traditional and modern Israeli sub-cultures. In A. Schlegel (Ed.), *Emergent women.* New York: Columbia University Press, 1977.

Datan, N., Antonovsky, A., & Maoz, B. *A time to reap: The middle age of women in five Israeli sub-cultures.* Baltimore, Md.: The Johns Hopkins University Press, 1981.

DATAN

Datan, N., Antonovsky, A., & Maoz, B. Multidisciplinary cross-cultural research: Perspectives from developmental psychology, medical sociology, and psychiatry. In J. K. Brown (Ed.). *Middle-aged women: Cross-cultural perspectives*. Bergin, 1984.

Datan, N., Antonovsky, A., & Maoz, B. Love, war, and the life cycle of the family. In K. McCluskey & H. W. Reese (Eds), *Life-span developmental psychology: Historical and cultural crises*. New York: Academic Press, 1985.

Datan, N. Maoz, B., Antonovsky, A., & Wijsenbeck, H. Climacterium in three cultural contexts. *Tropical and Geographical Medicine*, 1970, 22, 77–86.

Deutsch, H. *The psychology of women. Vol. II. Motherhood*. New York: Grune and Stratton, 1945.

Douglas, M. *Purity and Danger: An analysis of concepts of pollution and taboo*. London: Routledge and Kegan Paul, 1966.

Exodus 32: 1-35.

Maoz, B. *The perception of menopause in five ethnic groups in Israel*. Ph.D. dissertation, University of Leiden, Netherlands. Kupat Holim publication, 300 pp., 1973.

Maoz, B. Perception of menopause among five ethnic groups in Israel. *The Family Physician*, 1975, 4(2), 1-8.

Maoz, B., Antonovsky, A., Apter, A., Datan, N., Rochberg, J., & Salomon, Y. The effect of outside work on the menopausal woman. *Maturitas*, 1978, 1, 43-53.

Maoz, B., Antonovsky, A., Apter, A., Wijsenbeck, H., & Datan, N. Ethnicity and adaptation to climacterium. *Archiv fur Gynikologie*, 1977, 223, 9-18. (a)

Maoz, B., Antonovsky, A., Apter, A., Wijsenbeck, H., & Datan, N. The perception of menopause in five ethnic groups in Israel. *Acta Obstetricka Gynecologicka Scandanavia*, 1977, 65, 69-76. (b)

Maoz, B., Datan, N., Antonovsky, A., & Wijsenbeck, H. Female attitudes to menopause, *Social Psychiatry*, 1970, 5(1), 35-40. (a)

Maoz, B., Wijsenbeck, R., Antonovsky, A., & Datan, N. The climacterium and nonpsychotic disturbances in women. In L. Miller (Ed.), *Mental health in rapidly changing society. Jerusalem*, 1970 (b)

Mishnah: Nashim (Ketubot, Kiddushin); Taharot (Kelim, Niddah).

NEW VOICES, NEW VISIONS
Toward a Lesbian/Gay Paradigm
for Psychology

Laura S. Brown

AN INITIAL version of this article was given as the Division 44 Presidential Address at the Convention of the American Psychological Association, August 1988. For her invaluable help in making that first version come to life, I would like to thank my partner, Miriam Vogel, who got me through the first stage of my illness with love and courage, put up with my obsessing about writing this article for many months, then read the first draft and pointed out that which was still missing from my discussions. I'm also indebted to all of the presenters at the 1988 Advanced Feminist Therapy Institute, whose papers gave form and substance to my ideas. This version of the article owes a debt of gratitude to Jeanne Marecek, who invited its presence, and to two anonymous reviewers who made extremely helpful comments that allowed me to tie my own thinking into the feminist theoretical mainstream.

The use of full names in this article reflects a stylistic tradition of the Feminist Therapy Institute, which is to make the gender of a source visible to my readers. It is essential, in knowing how I came to my way of thinking, to know the perspectives of those who have influenced me.

The use of first-person pronouns to refer to lesbians and gay men is also a reflection of the feminist model of referring to one's own membership in a group about which one is writing.

VOICES LOST AND FOUND

What does it mean for psychology if the experiences of being lesbian and/or gay male, in all the diversity of meanings that those experiences can hold, are taken as core and central to definitions of reality rather than as a special topic tangential to basic understandings of human behavior, particularly human interactions? After all, just as there is no American Psychological Association division of the psychology of men or of white people, there is no special topic area called heterosexual studies in psychology. "Psychology," the official entity, values those experiences that are white, male, heterosexual, young, middle class, abled-bodied, and North American; thus has the universe of "human behavior" been defined. "Special topics," including lesbian and gay issues, have traditionally been defined as of special interest only, not in the core curriculum in reality or emotionally.

My raising of this essentially feminist question has roots both in personal experience and in a developing line of feminist theory. The personal experience, which was the catalyst for my thinking, has been both primary and most powerful and illustrates the feminist adage that the personal is political as well as theoretical. In 1987, I developed a supposedly untreatable neurological disorder of the voice called spastic dysphonia that left me literally speechless. For 3 months I had no voice: I experienced in an embodied way the powerlessness of the often-used metaphor of being unable to be heard. But rather than accepting the verdict of Western medical science that my disorder, because neurological, was untreatable, I pursued non-Western medical care: acupuncture and Chinese herbal medicine, cranial osteopathic manipulation, spiritual healing. By deciding to change the point of view from which I understood my disorder, I regained a voice: a new and often fragile one, but a voice, nonetheless. It was a jarring reminder of the importance of not taking the view from the mainstream as the only one there is, and one that intuitively led me to develop the thought process represented in this work. If I could have a new voice by changing the point of view from which I understood my problem, could such a new voice not also be raised within psychology, a voice that would reflect another set of my experiences in the world, those of a white North American lesbian?

Concurrent with my personal experiences, a developing line of feminist theory has raised questions about the nature of the observer's perspective in science. Such theory suggests that the pretensions of mainstream science to

296

BROWN

objectivity, or to encompassing the universe of knowledge and meaning, are in fact evidence of white, androcentric ways of understanding (Harding, 1986; Rose, 1983). Rose and Harding have joined other authors in attempting to redefine the conditions of discourse within the sciences, including psychology and other social sciences, so as to make central and visible the previously excluded experiences of women. These theorists have argued not only for the simple inclusion of women in the discourse, but also that the terms of the discourse be changed, be reinvented, in order to move from an androcentric to a feminist science. Sandra Harding (1986), in particular, has argued that a feminist science would be one in which categories of discourse and understanding would of necessity become destabilized in order to move beyond the deeply internalized structures of Western thinking. Feminist science and social science would ask questions from the female experience.

But let us move beyond that. What happens if what has previously been a conceptual ghetto, even within feminist psychology, is redefined as the center of the universe of understanding? If the ways of knowing and of legitimizing knowledge are opened to understandings that are rooted in the phenomenology of being gay or lesbian in the world, what new voices and visions become available? Does the way in which psychologists explore lesbian and gay issues become transformed by asking such questions? How has psychology so far been shaped through the distorted lens of heterosexist psychological science and practice? Beyond that, what happens if a lesbian/gay paradigm is used as core to psychological science and practice in general? How do psychologists change their understandings of such phenomena as intimacy, parenting, attraction, relationships, or gender, if they make assumptions based in experiences of being lesbian or gay?

297

In order to begin the process of answering such questions, the assumptions that lie within the questions themselves must be explored. Such questions assume first that current paradigms reflect a heterosexual reality, and second, that it is possible to identify what is meant by lesbian/gay reality in such a way as to address issues from that perspective.

HETEROSEXISM IN PSYCHOLOGY

The first assumption is based on the notion that the worldview of North American psychology, besides being biased by sexism, racism, and other exclusionary modal perspectives, views human behavior through the lens of heterosexual experience and is thus inherently heterosexist. What do I mean by that assertion? Concretely, this takes a number of forms. Our knowledge base is heterosexist. That is, it assumes heterosexuality and heterosexual forms of relating as the norm. More precisely, white, middle class, North American, married, Christian, able-bodied heterosexuality is defined as the norm. All other forms of experience are viewed in contrast to the norm. This non-conscious heterosexism manifests in myriad subtle ways; there are "couples,"

BROWN

meaning heterosexual couples, and then there are "lesbian and gay couples." There are "families," meaning nuclear, two-heterosexual-parent families, and "lesbian and gay families." And so on, ad nauseum. Even in the field of psychology of women, which has probably contributed more than any other field of psychology toward the movement to deconstruct psychology and dethrone the god of logical positivism (Hare-Mustin & Marecek, 1988), there are "women," and then there are "lesbians," tucked away in our own chapters of the textbooks. Lesbian experiences are seen as unique, offering little to the understanding of the norm. What occurs instead is that we are compared to the norm, in the past to demonstrate our pathology and, more recently, to affirm our normalcy Or we are simply categorized as an interesting variant of human experience, equal but still separate and always marginal.

This tendency to perceive lesbian and gay issues within the broadest scope of that term as tangential "special topics" robs psychology of much of its ability to understand human behavior. There are certain aspects of lesbian and gay experience which, if made central to all psychological inquiry, would change and expand the ability to comprehend both the intrapsychic and the interpersonal. But to use such a universe as core to hypothesis generation requires answering my second question regarding the definition of lesbian and gay experience.

DEFINING A LESBIAN AND GAY REALITY

In some ways, this is more complex and problematic than establishing the presence of heterosexism in psychology. This complexity exists largely because there is not one unitary lesbian and gay reality. Instead, there are multiple realities. The experience of being a white lesbian or gay man will be different from that of a lesbian or gay man of color and different within each ethnic group. The lesbian or gay man who comes from an orthodox religious background will be different from those who grew up in more religiously liberal settings. Also, a person's age cohort has a profound impact on the experience of being a sexual minority person, as does age of coming out and past history of overt heterosexual identity such as marriage. Class plays a powerful role in defining the experience and expression of being lesbian or gay. Moreover, North American lesbians and gay men live different realities than do our peers in other countries and cultures. Furthermore, constructions and parameters of gender separate the experiences of lesbians from those of gay men.

Even the concept of sexual orientation is one that is not clearly defined. Although, for the purpose of lesbian and gay right, we may adhere to the notion that sexual orientation is a fixed and relatively immutable phenomenon, clinically and experientially we are aware that it is a fluid, continuous one, with the words "lesbian" and "gay" encompassing a range of internal experiences and social constructions of attraction, arousal, identity, and affection (Greenberg, 1988; Kitzinger, 1987). Although there is a seductive pull to see

BROWN

ourselves as a unitary, and thus a united group, lesbians and gay men are more diverse than my own first minority group, Jews—where we joke that, "if there are two Jews. there are three schuls" (i.e. three opinions). Anyone who has been active in the lesbian and gay community will bear testimony to our variability and the challenges that this can present to the well-meaning gay pride parade organizer. Yet we are a nation of sorts; 10% of the U.S. population is larger than the total population of my partner's native country of The Netherlands. And all nations contain a certain amount of diversity.

So with all that diversity, are there within this "country" of internal experience those elements of being lesbian or gay male that are common to all and can be said to form a "lesbian and gay reality" from which to reconceptualize our study of human behavior? I would like to suggest that those common elements do exist cross-situationally, and that they are in fact central to my movement toward a new vision.

Biculturalism

The first among these common elements is the experience of biculturalism. Lesbians and gay men are always simultaneously participants in both heterosexual experience and lesbian and gay experiences. Our families of origin are usually comprised of heterosexual persons who participate in the privileges and rituals of the dominant heterosexual majority. Many of us have behaved heterosexually during our lifetimes, although we often revise the meaning of these aspects of our histories when we embrace a lesbian or gay identity. We are often very much in the position to "pass" for heterosexual and may experience discomfort with those aspects of ourselves or our peers that conform to cultural stereotypes of the "obvious" lesbian or gay man, while simultaneously cultivating certain aspects of those behaviors in more secure settings (Nestle. 1987). With rare exceptions, all lesbians and gay men must be in both cultures most of the time.

Marie Root (1988), writing on biracial identity development, pointed out that the experiences of the biracial person include having both minority and dominant cultures as part of one's family of origin. She suggested that this can lead to a sense of confusion and of non-fit in any context. While a person who is purely one minority group or another may feel free in the process of minority identity development to reject dominant culture, Root pointed out that for the biracial individual such a rejection also implies a rejection of a part of oneself. Biracial individuals are also often in the position of being able to choose to "pass" as members of the dominant culture and may feel ambivalence or distaste for those family members, often siblings and one parent, who are more physically like the devalued minority group and who threaten their passing status. In order to develop a functional biracial identity, the biracial person must develop ways to live within this matrix of complexity, to balance and value the differences that lie within.

299

BROWN

Extrapolating from Root's model, it may be that living and developing bi-culturally, while not unique to lesbian and gay men, is an experience that may create different ways of knowing and understanding oneself and one's reality. A healthy resolution of such conflicts of identity is one that must eschew either/or perspectives on who one is and embrace what is "other" within oneself. Such a successful resolution of a bicultural identity may create a propensity to view things on continua rather than in a polarized fashion. Being able to operate within grey areas and on middle grounds and balancing the demands of two divergent groups that are now internalized self-representations are characteristic of the experience of being gay or lesbian. Walter Williams's (1987) work on sexual identity among Native American cultures provides some confirmation for this idea. He noted that in many Native nations, the persons who occupied the interim space between the genders and whose behavior might be identified as gay or lesbian within white American culture, were perceived as seers, shamans, capable of greater wisdom than their clearly heterosexually defined peers. Different external factors may operate to influence the felt and lived experiences of this bicultural existence, and some lesbians and gay men, for example, lesbians or gay men of color in North America, actually may have multicultural identities.

This experience, like that of the biracial person, is distinct from that of members of racial and ethnic minorities in that even at the most intimate level of family relationships, there will be cultural differences and pulls to participate in the dominant culture in ways that do not exist for members of racial and ethnic minorities whose families share their group membership. The experience of having both self and other within one's identity development creates a singular and potentially powerfully heuristic model for self-understanding. The constant "management of difference" (deMonteflores, 1986) can lead to a rich and distinctive perspective on reality if we are willing to embrace and value it, rather than stigmatize it as not conforming to the dominant norm. The bicultural perspective of lesbians and gay men facilitates an understanding of the rules by which the mainstream culture operates, while simultaneously being able to envision new forms by which the same tasks might be accomplished.

Marginality

A second experience that informs a lesbian and gay reality is that of marginality. Even in the most supportive and accepting of settings, we carry the experience of existential "otherness." For many lesbians and gay men, the first awareness of who we were was simply that vague sense of difference and distance from the rituals of the heterosexual culture, of not understanding what our friends saw in the opposite gender, of watching to see how heterosexual courtship rituals were played out so that we could imitate them and fit in (Adair & Adair, 1978).

Mary Daly long ago pointed out how this "otherness" can allow women to see what is not seen, to know what is forbidden to know, because they are not sanctified as knowers (Daly, 1973). Harding (1986) argued that a feminist epistemology depends upon the valuing of "alienated," "bifurcated," or "oppositional" consciousnesses in theory making. Lesbian and gay male experience reflects this alienated, marginal worldview, no matter how well an individual lesbian or gay man appears to be integrated into the dominant social context.

It is no coincidence that one of the ways that political and religious conservatives attempt to undermine the movement against violence against women and children is to "lesbian-bait" its leadership (Schechter, 1982). In essence, what they are saying is that only a woman who is, as Adrienne Rich (1979) puts it, "disloyal to civilization" will be able to continue to break the patriarchy's silence on its crimes. It's no wonder that any man who attempts to analyze and move beyond the defined male gender roles is called "faggot": who else is enough outside the definition of the role to see alternate possibilities for male existence (Grahn, 1984)? In the catcalls of those who would annihilate lesbians and gay males lie germs of the truth; our experience of the world as outsiders may allow us to see differently, hear differently, and thus potentially challenge the conventional wisdom. We may be freer to see, speak and act other truths, to have, as Judy Grahn says, "another mother tongue."

These other truths can be powerful affirmations of our experience: they can also be frightening challenges to the culture of the mainstream and even to lesbians and gay men who are struggling with our own conflicting desires to both fit in and be who we are. One striking example of the outcomes of empowering our alienated lesbian and gay knowing has been in how we have created our families.

As asked by Dykewomon (1988) in a society caught up in sanctification of "The Family," can there be such a thing as a functional family under patriarchy? While this is also an essential feminist question found early in this wave of the U.S. women's movement in the work of Firestone (1970), lesbians and gay men have put that question into practice by the creation of families that are not patriarchal. Likewise, there may be a specifically lesbian way to raise children (Cooper, 1987), different from the power-unequal norms of the heterosexist family in which age differences are assumed inherently to connote power imbalance. Also challenged is the assumption that biological parents of both genders are necessary for the creation of emotionally healthy children, and the assumption that the only appropriate number of parents is two (Pollack & Vaughn, 1987). These challenges have not been without a price to the lesbian and gay male parents who have lost access to their children of blood or spirit for daring to raise such questions. Yet, many continue to raise them, knowing by looking in from the outside that the current paradigm of "family" cannot be the only one.

301

BROWN

Normative Creativity

A final common theme is that of being normatively different and thus creative. In other words, by lacking clear rules about how to be lesbian and gay in the world, we have made up the rules as we go along. For example, in their recent book on lesbian couples, Merilee Clunis and Dorsey Green (1988), discuss how they decided what was normative for lesbian couples. They put it rather simply: if a lot of lesbians seemed to be doing it, this must be the norm. And these norms challenge the dominant notions about what occurs in intimate interpersonal relationships; they question notions about how agency and communion function within a couple, about the healthy expression of dependency needs between adult partners. simply being lesbian or gay has been something we have had to invent for ourselves (Grahn, 1984), since whatever roadmaps the dominant culture offered have been full of wrong turns and uncharted territories. This need to invent for ourselves has been equal parts terrifying and exhilirating (*vide* the common theme of works on lesbian-and-gay-affirmative therapy regarding the problems due to the lack of clear models for lesbians and gay men). However, those who claim this as a positive and possibly unique aspect of our experience as lesbians and gay men begin to embrace the possibilites for actively deconstructing and re-creating our visions of human behavior far beyond the field of lesbian and gay studies.

In summary, there are three intertwined themes that define, cross-situationally, the experience of being lesbian and gay: biculturalism, with its requirements of juggling, balance, and living in and with ambiguity; marginality, with its perspective that is both outside and within the mainstream; and normative creativity, the ability to create boundaries that will work where none exist from tools that may be only partially suited to the task. If psychologists adopt these as guiding principles for their work where can and does this lead?

TOWARD A LESBIAN AND GAY PARADIGM FOR PSYCHOLOGY

A first and, for those in academic settings, somewhat risky step is to reevaluate the methodologies by which the knowledge base is generated. Mary Ballou (1988) has identified five epistemological perspectives that might be available for studying human behavior and pointed out how they lead to very different types of "revealed truths" when applied to inquiry. If scholars attempt to work from a valuing of the mixed, the ambiguous, the marginal, then it becomes extremely difficult to fit themselves solely within the logical positivist framework dominant in psychology. After all, such a framework assumes that phenomena are either A or B, and that if enough rigor is used in the design and test of a hypothesis, one truth can be found. This has a seductive flavor to it; as Harding (1986) pointed out, the tendency to perceive the universe in logical positivist terms is supported by such a wide variety of institutional and cultural structures that it "cannot be shucked off by mental hygiene and willpower alone" (p. 662). But this tendency must be continuously questioned since an exclusionary paradigm would not fit well with an application of lesbian and gay reality to the study of human behavior.

An alternative approach that draws upon lesbian and gay experience must allow for the use of many methodologies and the possibility of many, even conflicting, answers. A lesbian/gay psychology would be one of many truths, one in which a dialectical tension would constantly operate in such a manner as to stimulate new and wider inquiry. Rather than endless replications of the old, researchers would begin asking the questions not yet raised in the first place and then question further the answers received. If they allow their scholarship to live in as many realities as they do themselves, they find the possibility of many shades of meaning.

This has certainly been the case with my work in the area of psychotherapy ethics. By working from my lived experience as a white lesbian therapist practicing in the context of diverse lesbian communities, I've come to see ethical action as a continuous variable. One is not either ethical or nonethical, but changing and varying degrees of ethical at various levels of affective, cognitive, and behavioral expression during different periods of one's work as a therapist (Brown, 1985, 1987, 1988). I've found that simply having rules about what to do narrowed my thinking and excluded that which had never been considered, thus making it invisible. I've also learned that lesbian and gay male therapists, faced with situations unpredicted and unenvisioned by the ethics codes, have had to be creative in the development of norms that would allow us to behave ethically and yet still live within the realities of our communities (Gonsiorek, 1987; Hayden, 1987; Moss, 1987). For instance, the ethical principle regarding dual relationships (APA, 1981) gives little guidance about what to do when a therapist's former lover becomes lovers with a current client: notwithstanding, if that's what one has to deal with, and more than a few lesbian and gay male therapists have, the ethical principles for it are created along the way. The paradigms for ethical therapy evolving from lesbian and gay experience stress, not rules and regulations, but the relationship of the therapist to her or his community, and the relational context in which therapy takes place. This different perspective has allowed lesbian and gay therapists to both ask and answer questions that cannot even be raised in the conceptual universe of mainstream psychology ethics.

A second implication of adopting a paradigm for psychology that would embrace the themes of lesbian and gay experience would be a continuous reevaluation of taken-for-granted concepts in all aspects of psychology. For example, psychologists usually hold heterosexual couples as a norm simply because of their majority status. But it might be possible that what is normative for lesbian couples is in fact healthy for any intimate pair. In a paper written since her book was published, Dorsey Green (1988) raised this possibility when she discussed the issues of merger, fusion, and contact boundaries in re-

303

BROWN

lationships, suggesting that perhaps the merger that a healthy lesbian couple experiences is more normative and functional for intimate pairs than the illusion of autonomy and distance within a relationship that exists, she believed, in heterosexual couples simply as an artifact of gender roles. In other words, by taking the position of outsider and suggesting that the emperor in fact has no clothes, we may move psychology toward a deeper and more complex understanding of interpersonal relationships. This movement would have particular significance for the study of behaviors related to sexuality, gender role and identity, intimacy and bonding, and the development of family dynamics. While feminist psychology has commented at length on the problems of the "partriarchal, father-absent family" (Luepnitz, 1988), how might inquires be expanded by looking first at the functioning of healthy lesbian and gay families?

An analogy can be made here to work that develops non–North American cultural versions of psychology and that generates norms and hypotheses about development from within those cultural contexts. Carla Bradshaw (1988), in a paper on the interface between Japanese psychology and feminist therapy theory, pointed out how even the basic process of personality development is quite different when viewed through the lens of Japanese experience. Bradshaw pointed out that the concepts of dependence and individuation carry strikingly different meaning in Japanese culture from that in North American society and noted how behavior that would be considered pathological or pathogenic here represents normative and functional ways of being.

Similar work is underway in the Philippines to create a "Sikolohiyang Pilipino," Philippine psychology from within a Philippine cultural context (Protacio-Marcelino, 1988). The explicit aim of this work is to strip away North American concepts and ways of seeing from psychological theory and practice. It uses Philippine language and experience to develop an entirely new and different way of seeing and knowing human behavior. For example, Protacio-Marcelino analyzed the notion of "personality" in Western psychology, contrasting it with the eight different terms in Tagalog, one of the primary indigenous languages of the Philippines, that can define "personality" in terms of the context in which the person is found and the relationship of one actor to another. From the point of view of Philippine culture, a person has not one personality, but many, each determined by the relational context in which she or he is acting.

Clearly the diversity that exists within the lesbian and gay population makes the explication of a lesbian and gay psychology a challenging task. Or perhaps not; within any culture, however defined, there must be levels of difference to be accounted for by a psychology of that culture. However, the analogies hold in many ways. Protacio-Marcelino and her collegues (1988) spoke of how psychology in the Philippines was intellectually colonized by Americans; so, too, is American psychology colonized and dominated by heterosexual experience. By defining norms and terms from within lesbian and gay realities, psychologists ask themselves how these new paradigms might broaden the understanding of heterosexual realities as well.

Finally, by working from within lesbian and gay realities, the study of lesbian and gay issues will and must change. This new approach in no way denigrates that which has been done before and will continue to be done by way of research and practice in the field. Everything that has come before has allowed for the conceptual leaps in this article. But scholars have been constrained by working within the dominant paradigm so that only certain kinds of knowledge are pursued or revealed. To quote Audre Lorde (1984): "The master's tools will never dismantle the master's house," and such a renovation is what many lesbians and gay men in psychology had in mind when, a decade or more ago, we began to challenge the notion of homosexuality as psychopathology.

In challenging that one dearly held tenet of one branch of the tree of the behavioral sciences, we were, in the end, also challenging the whole structure, all of the assumptions that went into creating that idea. It's not certain that we realized that or even would have admitted how radical in fact this apparently simple goal was. To take the word out of the *Diagnostic and Statistical Manual* was simply one aspect of challenging the entire system of thinking that had allowed it to be placed there at all. Thus, the ideas suggested in this article are simply a carrying forward of that action. At the very first APA program on lesbian and gay issues, Barbara Love, (1975) suggested that lesbians might be the model of healthy female development. Her paper appealed intuitively to many, but few have yet to follow concretely the direction in which this non-psychologist lesbian activist was pointing: that is, to rearrange the norms and then to go about the business of seeking greater self-knowledge.

Some initial steps have been taken, both in psychology and in related fields of endeavor; the volume *Lesbian Psychologies* (Boston, Lesbian Psychologies Collective, 1987) provides an example of what is needed in the behavioral sciences. Some of the most exciting work developing from lesbian and gay paradigms is occurring in philosophy (Hoagland, 1988) and theology (Heyward, 1989). Both Sarah Lucia Hoagland and Carter Heyward proposed epistemologies that flow from the embodied experience of living as lesbians (Hoagland, 1988) or either lesbians or gay men (Heyward, 1989) and provide models that could be used for psychological inquiry as well.

In a paper I gave at APA in 1986 in a symposium on the state of the art in lesbian and gay affirmative psychotherapy (Brown, 1986), I suggested that lesbian and gay therapists were at a point where we needed to ask more complex questions about our work. I believe now that in order to ask those questions in satisfying ways, we need to use a lesbian/gay paradigm to construct the process of inquiry. For instance, one question raised in that earlier paper is "Why are so many lesbians in therapy?" It is now known thanks to the Na-

305

BROWN

tional Lesbian Health Care Survey, just how high the numbers are: 78% of their respondents were current or former therapy clients (Bradford & Ryan, 1987).

To avoid quick and easy answers to this question or answers that reflect the perspectives of the dominant culture on either lesbians or psychotherapy, the questions inside the questions must be asked, that is, create a dynamic tension within psychology. What does therapy mean in a lesbian and gay context? What associations arise to the word, what does it suggest to the sexual minority speaker and hearer, the sentence, "I'm in therapy." Who are the therapists and how do they see their work? Is the therapist, particularly the lesbian or gay male therapist working within their own communities, meaning something different at non-conscious levels by her or his choice of work than does the heterosexual therapist? What is the interaction of being in therapy with other experiences in the world as lesbians or gay men? Are we defining being in therapy as evidence of pathology, which has traditionally been the case? Or have lesbians and gay men re-visioned the meaning of therapy as prima facie evidence of health and health-seeking behaviors, as one useful and appropriate strategy for sanely managing to live in the ambiguity, which, in the final analysis, is the situation for most late 20th century Americans, not only those of us on the official margin?

This last question is one that quite directly flows from the lesbian/gay paradigm proposed here; that is, it is an outside question, one that sees strength in what has been called weakness, one that questions that which is taken for granted about the meaning of therapy in society. It is a question about the ritual of therapy that emphasizes how the context gives that ritual place and meaning. These are questions that go beyond the statistics and encourage a search for the meaning given to the experience by culture, context, and living in a particular way. And those are the sorts of questions that psychologists need to ask in all of their work.

In proposing this new voice and vision, I am raising more questions here than I am able to provide answers to. I'm not entirely certain myself of all the concrete implications of the paradigm that I'm suggesting; in writing this article, I have discovered just how much this idea still exists within me preconsciously, felt but unformed. Audre Lorde (1978), in *The Uses of the Erotic*, said that "in order to perpetuate itself every oppression must corrupt or distort those various sources of power within the culture of the oppressed that can provide energy for change." One such source of power is the process of owning and valuing as central one's experience even when the words are lacking in the dominant reality to describe it. My own thinking is still struggling through the muck of that distortion. It is my hope that by taking you with me as I continue that journey, I have set you to thinking, too, and that between us we will give form to what is still only a vague imagining on my part. We can pursue the comfort of the mainstream, or we can search for new voices and visions as psychology moves past its centenary with lesbian and gay psychology finally in place.

REFERENCES

Adair, N., & Adair C. 1978. *Word is out: Stories of some of our lives*. New York: New Glide Delta.

American Psychological Association [APA]. (1981). Ethnical principles of psychologists. *American Psychologist, 36*, 633-638.

Balloon, M. (1988, May). *Building feminist theory through feminist principles*. Paper presented at the Seventh Advanced Feminist Therapy Institute Conference, Seattle, WA.

Boston Lesbian Psychologies Collective (Eds.). (1987). *Lesbian psychologies: Explorations and challenges*. Urbana: University of Illinois Press.

Bradshaw, C. (1988, May). *Japanese psychology: What can Eastern thought contribute to feminist theory and therapy?* Paper presented at the Seventh Advanced Advanced Feminist Therapy Institute Conference, Seattle, WA.

Bradford, J., & Ryan, C. (1987). *National lesbian health care survey: Mental health implications*. Richmond: Virginia Commonwealth University Survey Research Laboratory.

Brown, L. S. (1985). *Power, responsibility, boundaries: Ethical concerns for the lesbian feminist therapist. Lesbian Ethics, 1*, 30–45.

Brown, L. S. (1986, August). A time to be critical: Directions and developments in lesbian-affirmative therapy. In B. Sang (Chair), *Lesbian and gay affirmative psychotherapy, State of the art*. Symposium presented at the Convention of the American Psychological Association, Washington, DC.

Brown, L. S. (1987, August). Beyond thou shalt not: Developing conceptual frameworks for ethical decision–making. In L. Garnets (Chair), *Ethical and boundary issues for lesbian and gay psychotherapists*. Symposium presented at the Convention of the American Psychological Association, New York, NY.

Brown, L. S. (1988). From perplexity to complexity: Thinking about ethics in the lesbian therapy community. *Women and Therapy, 8*, 13–26.

Clunis, D. M., & Green, G. D. (1988). *Lesbian couples*. Seattle: Seal Press.

Cooper, B. (1987). The radical potential in lesbian mothering of daughters. In S. Pollack & J. Vaughn (Eds.). *Politics of the heart: A lesbian parenting anthology* (pp. 233–240). Ithaca, NY: Firebrand Books.

Daly, M. (1973). *Beyond God the father: Toward a philosophy of women's liberation*. Boston: Beacon Press.

deMonteflores, C. (1986). Notes on the management of difference. In T. S. Stein & C. J. Cohen (Eds.), *Contemporary perspectives on psychotherapy with lesbians and gay men* (pp. 73–104). New York: Plenum Medical.

Dykewomon, E. (1988). Notes for a magazine, *Sinister Wisdom: A Journal for the Lesbian Imagination in the Arts and Politics* [Special Issue on Surviving Psychiatric Assault], 36, pp. 2–6.

Firestone, S. (1970). *The dialectic of sex*. New York: William Morrow.

Gonsiorek, J. (1987, August). Ethical issues for gay male therapists. In L. Garnets (Chair), *Ethical and boundary issues for lesbian and gay psychotherapists*. Symposium pre-

307

BROWN

sented at the Convention of the American Psychological Association, New York, NY.

Grahn, J. (1984). *Another mother tongue: Gay words, gay worlds*. Boston: Beacon Press.

Green, G. D. (1988, May). *Is separation really so great?* Paper presented at the Seventh Advanced Feminist Therapy Institute Conference, Seattle, WA.

Greenberg, D. (1988). *The construction of homosexuality*. Chicago: University of Chicago Press.

Harding, S. (1986). The instability of the analytical categories of feminist theory. *Signs: Journal of Women in Culture and Society, 11*, 645–664.

Hare–Mustin, R. T., & Marecek, J. (1988). The meaning of difference: Gender theory, post–modernism, and psychology. *American Psychologist, 43*, 455–464.

Hayden, M. (1987, January). *Clinical issues in boundary setting and maintenance*. Paper presented at a conference, Boundary Dilemmas in the Client–Therapist Relationship, Los Angeles, CA.

Heyward, C. (1989). *Touching our strength: The erotic as power and the love of god*. New York: Harper & Row.

Hoagland, S. L. (1988). *Lesbian ethics: Toward new value*. Palo Alto: Institute of Lesbian Studies.

Kitzinger, C. (1987). *The social construction of lesbianism*. London: Sage.

Lorde, A. (1978). *Uses of the erotic: The erotic as power*. Trumansburg, NY: Crossing Press.

Lorde, A. (1984). *Sister outsider*. Trumansburg, NY: Crossing Press.

Love, B. (1975, August). *A case for lesbians as role models for healthy adult women*. Paper presented at the convention of the American Psychological Association, Chicago, IL.

Moss, L. E. (1987, January). *The problem of overlapping relationships with clients*. Paper presented at a conference, Boundary Dilemmas in the Client-Therapist Relationship, Los Angeles, CA.

Nestle, J. (1987). *A restricted country*. Ithaca, NY: Firebrand Books.

Pollack, S., & Vaughn, J. (Eds.). (1987). *Politics of the heart: A lesbian parenting anthology*. Ithaca, NY: Firebrand Books.

Protacio–Marcelino, E. (1988, May). *Toward understanding the psychology of the Filipino*. Paper presented at the Seventh Advanced Feminist Therapy Institute, Seattle, WA.

Rich, A. (1979). *On lies, secrets, and silences*. New York: Norton.

Root, M. P. P. (1988, May). *Resolving "other" status: The process of identity development in biracial individuals*. Paper presented at the Seventh Advanced Feminist Therapy Institute, Seattle, WA.

Rose, H. (1983). Hand, brain, and heart: A feminist epistemology for the natural sciences. *Signs: A Journal of Women in Culture and Society, 9*, 73–90.

Schechter, S. (1982). *Women and male violence: The visions and struggles of the battered women's movement*. Boston: South End Press.

Williams, W. (1987). *Spirit and the flesh: Sexual diversity in American Indian culture*. Boston: Beacon Press.

308

BROWN

PART V

CONTESTED RELATIONS
Family Members and Friends

FORGOTTEN FORMS OF CLOSE COMBAT
Mothers and Daughters Revisited

Jane Flax

Women no doubt reproduce between them the peculiar, forgotten forms of close combat in which they engaged with
their mothers. Complicity in the non-said, connivance in the
unsayable, the wink of an eye, the tone of voice, the gesture,
the color, the smell: we live in such things, escapes from our
identity cards and our names, loose in an ocean of detail, a
data-bank of the unnameable. . . . In this weird feminine see-
saw that swings "me" out of the unnameable community of
women into single combat with another woman, it is perturb-
ing to say "I" . . . A piece of music whose so-called oriental civility is suddenly interrupted by acts of violence, murders,
bloodbaths: isn't that what "women's discourse" would be?
—Julia Kristeva, "Sabat Mater", *The Female Body in
Western Culture: Contemporary Perspectives*

chapter 17

FEMINIST WRITERS have provided powerful and persuasive accounts of the
psychological, political, and philosophical importance of mother-child relations and of their reverberations throughout our lives. This work has stimulated productive analyses of some of the patriarchal fantasies that underlie and
engender the productions of Western culture.[1] The frequent displacement of
fantasies from maternal to paternal sites even within psychological theorizing
has become more evident.[2] Our understanding of female subjectivity and human development is richer and more complex.

Despite these gains, I find the maternal turn so prevalent within recent
feminist theorizing increasingly disturbing and suspicious. I am convinced
this turn is neither accidental nor innocent. Deconstruction of the functions
within feminist discourses of maternal fantasies is urgently needed.[3] The following questions would be among those posed in such a deconstruction:
Why has the story of "woman" become the story of mothers and daughters?

Why have the conflicts, sacrifices, and confinements of these relations receded or been obscured in a valorization of women's connectedness? Why have mothers become central agents in the constitution of subjectivity? What purposes are served by this framing of the story? What aspects of female subjectivity are repressed or denied in this retelling? Where are stories of paternal power and relations of domination among women? What else determines gender identity? What are the relationships between gender and female subjectivity?

In 1976, Dinnerstein suggested myriad possible paths to pursue.[4] She brilliantly analyzes some of the fantasies about work mothers do. They help to relieve humans of a sense of responsibility and fallibility, of the limits of our powers, and the lack of coincidence between intent and outcomes. Evidently even Dinnerstein underestimated the power, prevalence, and persistence of these fantasies. They continue to reverberate throughout feminist discourses.

I will trace the operation of some of these fantasies through an interaction between a patient and myself. Then I will pursue their circulation through feminist theorizing more generally. I intend this analysis to provoke further conversation about the recurrent valorization of maternity and female relatedness within contemporary feminist discourses.

PASSIONATE ATTACHMENTS

Recently one of my patients arrived at her session in an agitated state. M is a white, professional woman in her late twenties from a relatively wealthy and socially prominent family. She told me the following story. M had dinner the previous week with a man from out of town whom she met on a business trip. After dinner (their first date), as they were walking away from the restaurant, he told her he did not have a place to spend the night. He claimed it was too late to return home. She named several hotels in the immediate neighborhood, but he pressured her to let him stay at her house. M demurred, saying there was nowhere for him to sleep. He said he did not mind sleeping on the floor. They discussed this for about ten minutes, and finally she agreed to let him stay with her.

At her house they talked and watched TV for a while (both sitting on the bed). Early in the morning M said she was exhausted and wanted to go to sleep. She changed into a sweatshirt and pants and went under the bed covers. A short time later she awoke to find the man under the covers with her, his hand on her shoulder, sighing loudly. She took his hand away, but he returned it to her body, moving it down her thigh and continuing to sigh. Again she flung the hand off, but he returned it. Finally she yelled at him, "what are you doing," took a blanket and went to sleep on the floor. He left early the next morning and later called her. She did not return the call.

The patient was very upset. She felt the man took advantage of her. She was also angry at herself for "being nice" and trying to avoid conflict by let-

FLAX

ting him stay. She called her mother to discuss the incident. Before M finished telling her about the dinner, her mother (as the patient felt it) began to criticize her for not giving the man a chance. The mother claimed her daughter was too particular. There must be something wrong with her; she had dated so many men but had found no one she wanted to marry. When would the daughter settle down? The daughter then continued to tell the mother the rest of her story. The mother began to criticize her daughter again; this time for being incautious. How could she let a man she hardly knew into her house? What was she thinking? How could her judgment be so poor?

The daughter felt furious and rejected by the mother. She could do nothing right; she would be condemned whether she gave the man a chance or not. She felt intruded upon and ashamed. Why couldn't her mother have empathy for her feelings? Why couldn't she help M figure out the regulation of distance, propriety and potential connections with men? What was her mother's agenda, other than wanting the daughter to be married? Why wasn't the daughter's professional success and power enough to please her? What was faulty in her handling of this situation, in her expectations of and response to her mother, and in her relations with men?

The context of the patient's questions included my three-year relationship with her. A major theme in M's therapy has been the lack of attunement between her parents and herself. This lack contributed to M's low sense of self-esteem and her insecurity. M's insecurity was exacerbated by a continual struggle between her sister and herself for first place in the family. She is ambivalent about sexuality, intimacy, and aggression.

In asking her questions she hoped for several contradictory responses. These include empathy for her pain, anger and shame about the situation and her mother's replies. She would like me to be a "good mother." A good mother would provide reassurance and restoration of her sense of self-worth and her capacity to love and be loved. She would encourage M to be a sexual being on her own terms. M also expects me to offer critical but sympathetic analyses of her behavior. She wants me to help her sort out conflicts about the wishes evoked by her mother. I am to assist M in resolving her ambivalence about sexuality and relations with men.

M's questions confronted me with a dilemma. This story, I felt then, and even more on reflection, exemplifies many problematic elements in the constitution of female subjectivity. These include sexuality, power, and relations between and fantasies about mothers and daughters. I bring a feminist sensitivity toward issues of power, gender, and rape to my therapy relations. I wish to avoid the culturally sanctioned tendency toward simplistic mother blaming. However, I also have the psychoanalyst's suspicion of split-off and denied feelings. These include envy, desire, aggression, ambivalence, and ambition. Women develop investments in certain kinds of relationships and images of the self, maternity, and "good" girls. These investments and passions affect

313

FLAX

mothers and daughters (and therapists) and the relationships between them.

My sometimes conflicting theoretical commitments influence my relations with patients, especially in the choice of interventions and the content of interpretations. In my relationship with M I have expressed my conflicting loyalties. I try to increase M's empathy for her mother's history while also encouraging M to explore her own split-off passions.

However, competing theoretical commitments are certainly not the only determinant of my interventions. I have also been influenced by our culture's fantasies of the good mother. My immediate response to M's questions was to empathize with the pain caused by the lack of attunement in her mother's response. I related it to the ongoing history of their relationship. My response to her question about what she wants from men was to highlight her need for a high level of emotional attunement in present relationships to repair the past. However, by focusing on connection and attunement, I also avoided M's rage. This feeling would have been evoked had I immediately suggested she look at her own behavior and motives more critically.

As I reflect upon this session, I grow more suspicious of my own behavior and motives. I wonder about what is gained and lost by focusing on relational (mother-daughter; therapist-patient) issues first. Does this perpetuate or reinforce certain fantasies and wishes of M and myself concerning being or having a good mother? Did I, like the mother, shut off access to the daughter's knowledge or experience of her sexuality to preserve our dyadic relationship? Shouldn't I also foster autonomous expressions of her sexuality and aggression? Am I encouraging M to shore up her identity as a blameless and attached daughter? By so readily assuming the role of the good mother, am I sustaining unrealistic and harmful fantasies of the perfectly attuned partner? How much frustration is necessary for the development of self-reflection and a realistic sense of agency and the necessary limits of any relationship?

In retrospect, I also wonder if I was doing M a disservice by withholding my questions about her ambivalence about sexuality, ambition, aggression, and power. A feminist sensitivity to date rape and sexual politics is certainly warranted. The man had access to contacts extremely useful for M's business. Yet, aren't ambiguities necessarily conveyed in sharing a bed with someone? Don't women sometimes wish to exploit a certain seductiveness or sexual tension for their own purposes, despite or even because of the fact that it can be used against them by men? Although women still suffer under male domination, can't sexual politics be played out by both genders?

From a feminist perspective it is reasonable to invite M to understand (not blame) her mother and the forces operating on her. It is certainly sensible for any mother to be concerned about her daughter's sexual vulnerability. M's mother expressed wishes widely shared in her community when she communicated the hope of having her daughter married. She grew up with very traditional white heterosexual middle-class expectations of women's place and marriage. In this mother's experience, tradition paid off. She enjoyed her marriage to a successful man, motherhood, and a second career when the children were older.

Yet, are my motives or effects so benign? Did I replicate or foreclose exploration of other less admirable behaviors? For example, shouldn't we pay attention to mothers' roles in regulating their daughters' sexuality? What about their envy in our youth-oriented, heterosexist culture of the daughter's potential pleasures and attractiveness to men? Can't mothers feel ambivalent that many career options are more thinkable to their daughters than they were to them?

What about this daughter's ambivalence about her mother's attachments? Why does the daughter still turn to her mother to mediate her relations with men and resolve her quandaries about sexuality, guilt, aggression, and autonomy? M experiences much rage and envy because her father and not she occupies central place in her mother's affections. She envies her mother's powerful and absorbing connection to her husband and her obvious pleasure in it. Why does she continue to hope her mother will change into a more satisfying partner for her?

WHOSE BODY IS IT ANYWAY?

M's story epitomizes the complex enmeshment of mothers and daughters in issues of subjectivity, embodiment, and sexuality. Mothers represent the impossible borders, the confounding of the dualities of Western culture.[2] A pregnant woman is simultaneously nature and culture; subject and other. A nursing mother is food (nature) and care (environment); her substance is inner and outer. "I'm in the milk and the milk's in me," sings a child in one of the stories I read to my son. The nursing mother's breast also transgresses the border between sexuality and maternity, between woman as the (man's) object of desire and as the mother of (his) children.

One strand of psychoanalytic thought, spun out of the work of Melanie Klein, stresses the centrality of the mother's body in the infant's fantasy life and development.[6] Her body is literally our first home and often the first source of food as well. As infants, her smell, feel, voice, and touch pervade our senses. They provide a bounded sense of space within which security and continuity become possible.

Yet this being is also our tormentor. She is the source of denial and frustration as well as gratification. Maddeningly separate from us, she has resources we desire within her, to give or not as she chooses. The feeding breast comes and goes, sometimes out of synch with the rhythms of the child's hunger and need. Each of us lives inside our own skin. What is in mother is not necessarily accessible or available to the child. Thus for daughter or son, connection with mother is suffused with desire, aggression, and ambivalence. Prebirth merger can never be restored. With each expression of desire or need we risk frustration, rejection, or damage to the other.

315

FLAX

While the question, to whom does the mother's breast belong, is enigmatic, another is equally so. To whom does the nursling's mouth belong? It signals and experiences a need, yet its satisfaction resides in part in the body of an Other. Hence food and love and feeding and control intermingle. This compounding provides rich material for the manifold potentialities of "eating disorders" and the disciplining of the body and its pleasures.[7] One of these pleasures we call "sexuality." Contrary to Freud's beliefs, these pleasures cannot be external to power (or civilization).[8] Power shapes their very "nature" and their naming as such. What can appear as sexuality depends upon complex networks of disciplinary practices, of power circulating between (among others) mothers and children, men and women.

Part of the painful interplay between many mothers and daughters is the initial evoking of desire and then forbidding it. Mothers often participate in turning daughters into objects of desire for men, not for themselves and not for women or their children. As my patient's mother implied (and my patient, too, believes), something is wrong with a grown woman without a husband, a man with property in her person/sexuality.

On the other hand, just as my patient did, many daughters turn to mothers for permission to be sexual and for information about how to do it properly. Frequently they are taught that some (but not too much) sexual display and exchange is necessary to "catch" a man. Daughters, of course, sometimes reject their mother's teachings. What do mothers think when their daughters develop different sexual orientations? How do mothers respond when daughters develop their own erotic interests outside the circuit of reproduction? How do mothers feel when their daughters decide not to become mothers? Of course I do not think mothers or daughters respond in any singular manner to these circumstances. I simply indicate how obscure so much of this terrian remains.

THE VIRGIN MOTHER

What is still missing from my patient's—and my—story? Daughters as well as sons have difficulties with and investments in managing the threatening content and unpredictable boundaries of embodiment, maternity, aggression, and female sexuality. The daughter's conflicts, resentment and ambivalence about the mother's individuality, sexuality, and power are often split off or repressed. The dyad's hostile feelings toward one another are often disavowed. Feelings such as envy, rage, and desire for control and suppression of difference are denied. Alternatively these feelings are assigned predominance solely in the constitution and psychodynamics of masculine identities.

Female sexuality outside the circuits of reproduction or relatedness is threatening to many women and men. Many men and women have trouble with the idea that they might simply be an object of women's desire or that sometimes women might experience sex as an end in itself. Sex is not necessarily imposed on women or something we suffer or enter into for its extrinsic rewards (a baby, feeling close to you).

This is part of the emotion stirred by abortion; that sex and motherhood are not intrinsically connected. "What if your mother aborted you?" a bumper sticker proclaims. This sticker intimates our terror of the maternal power over life and death. It also suggests our fear of the (potential) power of women to refuse to be mothers or to be perpetually in relations with others.

Without such denial or displacement the simplistic claims that the gender-based continuity of identity between mother and daughter has a predominantly beneficial influence in the constitution of feminine subjectivity would be less plausible. This continuity is said to provide a motive or ground for women's allegedly greater propensity for relatedness and connection. Some feminists celebrate the "female" virtues of (a now sanitized) connection and care. Relatedness and connection are seen as relatively straightforward and positive virtues.

Women are now praised for their greater immunity to "bad" forms of individuality. Bad forms of individuality are ones in which the nonrelational aspects of the self are given priority over maintaining connections with an Other. One must repress many aspects of experience to represent mother-daughter relations, connection, or relatedness in this way. The powerful connections established through hate or envy are defined away as "not genuine" forms of relatedness. The dangers, aggression, and potential abuses of or within relationships are rarely acknowledged. Connection can be represented as a relatively unproblematic good and as a basis for an alternative and implicitly superior subjectivity only after such repression has occurred.[9]

The construction of femininity within the circuit of mother/daughter provides a number of secondary gains. These include shielding the privilege of heterosexuality and reinforcing cultural prohibitions on women's aggression and wishes for separation. Images of maternity are desexualized.[10] The split between sexuality and maternity prevalent in our culture is replicated and recreated. The costs and deformations of contemporary femininity, so powerfully named by early radical feminists such as Rubin, recede from view.[11] Like all disowned material, these aspects of female subjectivity surface elsewhere.

Desexualized accounts of maternal practices also reinforce beliefs about sexuality and the dangers of the body/passion and mortality that are some of the most dubious aspects of contemporary white Western culture.[12] How often do white, middle-class women acknowledge that we actively participate in the constitution and deployment of our sexuality? How often do white heterosexual women admit that we like sex (sometimes), even or purposely outside a "meaningful" relationship or the gaze of an (masculine or feminine) Other?

317

FLAX

Feminist discourses are marked by their own unconscious fantasies about such matters.[13] For example, a curious dynamic has emerged in feminist writing. Female sexualities are increasingly disowned, deconstructed, projected outward, or made an effect of the actions of others as the maternal dimension of femininity is valorized (and homogenized). Sexuality becomes a mark of the victimization of women or is diffused into symbiotic merger.[14] Agency is shifted to maternity—or nowhere.[15] Sexuality may be exploited, distorted, and misshaped by patriarchal power and heterosexuality, but maternity is portrayed as a relatively free space for the constitution and expression of female virtue.

The conflation of woman/mother carries with it a necessary horizon of heterosexuality. Despite efforts by Rich among others, heterosexuality is protected and reinforced.[16] In a heterosexist society, the lack of questioning of how the mother got pregnant permits the almost automatic assumption of the existence somewhere of a man/husband/father to rest undisturbed. In our current discourses, woman/mother often presumes or requires the simultaneous existence of two related dyads: child/mother; father/mother. Consider, for example, the curious term "single" mother. How can a mother be single, since by definition she is a being in some relation to an Other? Obviously she is "single" because she "lacks" a husband; she operates outside the normal rules of the Name of the Father. Maternity without paternity is a deviant form.

Desexualized maternity also implies a lack of desire directed at the child. In psychoanalytic accounts the child has desire for the mother, and much is made of the girl's enforced shift from maternal to paternal love object. Yet what of the mother's desire? How does it shift between child and (adult) lover? In our justified concern with child abuse, are we denying the erotic charge of maternity, the bodily intimacy and the pleasures of that kind of knowledge of an Other? Can the child not bear the idea that it exists as an object for the mother, as much as she exists for it? What images do daughters have of their mothers as sexual beings, of passionate attachments that exclude and may come before and outside them? How does the daughter experience the father as a rival for the mother (not just the mother as a rival for him)?

What if your mother refuses her gaze, turns her attention elsewhere? Does not serve as your mirror, your nurturance, your ground of continuity of being or of the semiotic, fertile source of aesthetic meaning ungoverned by the Father's Law? If she is no longer outside, but inside, power? If she wields power not as care, nurturance, preservative love, but as assertion, need, or desire of her own? Or if she is off playing, with other women or men? Or in her own head? Can daughters stand to be cut off, outside the dyadic circuit? If their mothers don't need them to be women, do they need their mothers? If women don't need babies, do they need men?

FLAX

MOTHER'S WORK IS NEVER DONE: THE POLITICS OF MATERNAL FANTASIES

Feminists have barely begun to explore the mutually determining or constituting effects of maternity, sexuality, female subjectivity, and one's racial and class identities.[17] White feminists have paid too little attention to the ways race and class circulate through and stamp our discourses and choices of tropes, foregrounding certain images of femininity and marginalizing others. The generative effects of relationships of power and domination are rarely explored except in discussions of masculinity.

The constituting effects of racism in white feminist discourses continue to be obscured. The predominance of abstract and nonstituated maternal images serves to perpetuate white women's political innocence. We (white women) become complicit in the intersections of racism/sexism by not challenging the treatment of black mothers and by replicating purified images of white ones (nurturing, caring, empowering, ethical, etc.).[18]

By denying our own pleasures and expressions of aggression, assertion, and control, we represent ourselves as innocent victims outside circuits of power. As mothers, we are somehow universalized and freed from complicity in relations of domination. Our participation in and marking by racism disappears. This desexualized and deracialized "goodness" then becomes the basis of our ethical contribution to the public world. Desexualized white women can be "purely" mothers.

This status was denied black women in captivity. It was then turned against them in the many accusations against the black "matriarch".[19] Isn't it odd that white women are valorized for the very relation (nearly exclusive responsibility for the emotional care of their children) that is now declared to be the cause of innumerable ills in the black community?

Racism serves both white men and women by locating active sexuality as alien to white women, especially higher-class ones. Class operates similarly as in the construction of the pure wife and the loose servant. Traditionally, white women are portrayed as pure/superior, because, unlike black women, our sexuality is modest and constrained.[20] Absence of aggressive, self-generated, non-object-related sexuality is a mark of her race/class. In contrast to the more wild and dangerous sexuality of black men and women, white women's sexuality can be more easily controlled and satisfied. White men can claim to be the protectors of its "purity" and this legitimates their control over other men (potential defilers).

Property in women is an intrinsic aspect of the modern meanings of masculinity. Women's sexuality is inscribed as the possession (or contested terrain) and effect of men. Men's identity is partially defined/expressed by their control over female sexuality. The more women one has access to, the better man/person one is.[21] This ideal of masculinity has a regulatory effect. It influences men throughout the hierarchies of masculinity and even enters into

319

FLAX

ideas about emancipation and self-respect. As the characters in the recent Spike Lee movie, *Jungle Fever*, discuss, "liberation" for a black man is often taken to include control of "his own" women and sexual access to white ones.[22]

This view of women's sexuality as an effect and perogative of masculine power has been too uncritically adopted by some feminists. Feminists such as MacKinnon treat it as an accurate description of female sexuality. Instead such claims should be deconstructed. They reflect a complex mix of women's and men's struggles, resistance, wishes, and power. Control over female sexuality is exercised and resisted in various ways and for many conscious and unconscious purposes. Access to such control and the possibilities of successful resistance to it vary by race, geographic location, age, sexual identities, and class as well as gender. Sexuality does not spring from a space outside circuits of power; however, it is not simply a sum of their effects.

GOD IS DEAD, LONG LIVE MOTHER?

> If it is true that an ethics for the modern age is no longer to be confused with morality, and if confronting the problem of ethics means not avoiding the embarrassing and inevitable issue of the law but instead bringing to the law flesh, language, and jouissance then the reformulation of the ethical tradition requires the participation of women. Women imbued with the desire to reproduce (and to maintain stability); women ready to help our verbal species, afflicted as we are by the knowledge we are mortal, to bear up under the menace of death; mothers.[23]

Maternal fantasies serve ontological as well as political purposes. Note the slippage here, between women and mothers, reproduction and immortality; the evasion of human finitude. If feminism succeeds in displacing the Name of the Father, or God the Father and his traditional paternal functions, in whose Name will it be done? Will we install a regnant Holy Mother, and thus protect/ preserve the possibility of innocence?

Contemporary Western cultures glorify, denigrate, and isolate maternity. If women might say what they want of the maternal, it could be that we do not want to confront its limits and ambiguities. Mothers and daughters are complicit in evading our full, mutual disillusionment. Motherhood is a heterogenous and conflictual set of experiences, wishes, fantasies—some of which have nothing to do with the child. Mothers may sometimes have an interest in preserving life, but they cannot save the species or redeem our messy worlds. Maternity is not an essence, nor does it exhaust categories of woman or the feminine.

Perhaps such thinking reveals the recurrence of certain infantile fantasies—only I can satisfy the mother, she needs me (the child) to reach her unique being. Yet, motherhood is not an exclusionary state, separate and clearly differentiated from all others, Being a mother calls upon and evokes a heterogeneous set of capacities and feelings within a multiple subjectivity. While it might conflict with or require the temporary suspension of other capacities (as do many other practices) it does not transport anyone into a unique form of being. We go on hating, thinking, etc., as mothers and otherwise.

Daughterhood also is not the royal road to an understanding of woman, subjectivity, or gender. These are all shaped by heterogenous forces whose relative power is often undecidable in individual instances. It too is a status overdetermined by many factors including race, class, geography. Daughterhood is not the mirror image of motherhood. We will not exhaust its meanings by analysis of maternity; nor is maternity its necessary end or destination. The daughter's desire does not orginate or terminate in her relations with her mother.

Stories about mother–daughter relations reveal the recurrent power of our desire for a benign force or agent out there in the world looking out for us, attending to our needs, and ensuring their satisfaction. These wishes form part of the common ground upon which women and men form a community through sustaining fantasies about (maternal) possibilities. Certain fantasies about mothers ward off profound anxieties and discontents from which contemporary Westerners often suffer. Such stories can only serve their functions by the simultaneous operation of denial, evasion, and pushing other material to the margins, rendering contradictory aspects of maternity almost unspeakable. The existence of our wishes and the return of the repressed, with its undesired yet acted-upon knowledge, situates maternity as an inevitable space of contention.

We long for knowable origins that connect to guaranteed ends (including the goodness of our purposes and agency) and for a loving home." [24] We wish for a meaningful, purposive, orderly, continuous, stable, nurturing, friendly and comprehensible universe, and for secure roots. We would like protection against the multiple contingencies that destabilize but enable us to live finite lives in humanly constituted worlds. We want to be caught and held securely in an idealized mother's gaze. We ask her to assure us that someone is really still there, to protect us and catch us when we fall. Finitude, evil, death; all can be transcended in the rebirth of the holy, innocent child/mother. We promise to be good daughters if mother won't abandon us. Whose voice can we really hear? An echo, a delusion, a fantasy of a childhood always already past and yet disabling us still.

NOTES

1. See, for example, Wendy Brown, *Manhood and Politics: A Feminist Reading in Political Theory* (Totowa: Rowman & Littlefield, 1988); Sandra Harding and Merrill Hintikka, eds., *Discovering Reality: Feminist Perspectives on Epistemology, Metaphysics, Methodology, and the Philosophy of Science* (Boston: D. Reidel, 1983); Hanna Fenichel Pitkin, *For-

321

FLAX

tune is a Woman: Gender & Politics in the Thought of Niccolo Machiavelli (Berkeley: University of California Press, 1984); and Gayatri Chakravorty Spivak, "Feminism and Deconstruction Again: Negotiating with Unacknowledged Masculinism," in *Between Feminism & Psychoanalysis,* edited by Teresa Brennan (New York: Routledge, 1989).

2. Jane Flax, *Thinking Fragments: Psychoanalysis, Feminism and Postmodernism in the Contemporary West* (Berkeley: University of California Press, 1990), 73-88; Coppelia Kahn, "The Hand that Rocks the Cradle: Recent Gender Theories and Their Implications," in The *Mother Tongue: Essays in Feminist Psychoanalytic Interpretation,* edited by Shirley Nelson Garner, Claire Kahane, and Madelon Sprengnether (Ithaca: Cornell University Press, 1985); and Madelon Sprengnether, *The Spectral Mother: Freud, Feminism and Psychoanalysis* (Ithaca: Cornell University Press, 1990).

3. See, however, Elizabeth Abel, "Race, Class and Psychoanalysis? Opening Questions," in *Conflicts in Feminism,* edited by Marianne Hirsch and Evelyn Fox Keller (New York: Routledge, 1990); Patricia Boling, "The Democratic Potential of Mothering," *Political Theory* 19, 4 (November 1991): 606-625; Nancy Chodorow with Susan Contratto, "The Fantasy of the Perfect Mother," in Nancy Chodorow, *Feminism and Psychoanalytic Theory* (New Haven: Yale University Press, 1989); Hilary Manette Klein, "Marxism, Psychoanalysis, and Mother Nature," *Feminist Studies* 15, 2 (Summer 1989): 255-278; Domna Stanton, "Difference on Trial: A Critique of the Maternal Metaphor in Cixous, Irigaray and Kristeva," in The *Thinking Muse: Feminism and Modern French Philosophy,* edited by Jeffner Allen and Iris M. Young (Bloomington: Indiana University Press, 1989); Susan Suleiman, "Writing and Motherhood," in Garner, Kahane and Sprengnether, *The Mother Tongue,* (Itacha: Cornell University Press, 1985).

4. Dorothy Dinnerstein, *The Mermaid and the Minotaur: Sexual Arrangements and Human Malaise* (New York: Harper & Row, 1976).

5. See Kristeva; and Iris Young, "Breasted Experience: The Look and the Feeling," in Iris Young, *Throwing Like a Girl and Other Essays in Feminist Philosophy and Social Theory* (Indianapolis: Indiana University Press, 1990).

6. See especially Jessica Benjamin, *The Bonds of Love: Psychoanalysis, Feminism and the Problem of Domination* (New York: Pantheon, 1988); Dinnerstein, *The Mermaid and the Minotaur: Sexual Arrangements and Human Malaise* (New York: Harper & Row, 1976); Melaine Klein, *Love, Guilt and Reparation and Other Works 1921-1945* (New York: Delta, 1975); and D. W. Winnicott, *Through Paediatrics to Psycho-Analysis* (New York: Basic Books, 1975).

7. Susan Bordo, "Anorexia Nervosa: Psychopathology as the Crystallization of Culture," in *Feminism & Foucault: Reflections on Resistance,* edited by Irene Diamond and Lee Quinby (Boston: Northeastern University Press, 1988); Hilda Bruch, *The Golden Cage: The Engima of Anorexia Nervosa* (New York: Vintage, 1978); Kim Chernin, *The Hungry Self: Women, Eating and Identity* (New York: Harper, 1985); Patricia Moran, "Unholy Meanings: Maternity, Creativity and Orality in Katherine Mansfield," *Feminist Studies, 17,* 1 (Spring 1991): 105-126; and Susi Orbach, *Hunger Strike: The Anorectic's Struggle as a Metaphor for Our Age* (New York: Avon, 1986).

8. See Sigmund Freud, *Civilization and Its Discontents* (New York: W. W. Norton, 1961); and for contrary arguments, Michel Foucault, *The History of Sexuality, Volume 1: An Introduction* (New York: Vintage, 1980); *Michel Foucault: Politics, Philosophy, Culture: Interviews and Other Writings 1977-1984,* edited by Lawrence D. Kritzman (New York:

Routledge, 1988); Judith Butler, *Gender Trouble: Feminism and the Subversion of Identity* (New York: Routledge, 1990); and Biddy Martin, "Feminism, Criticism, and Foucault," in Diamond and Quinby, (Boston: Northeastern University Press, 1988).

9. Despite her protests, I believe Carol Gilligan's *In a Different Voice: Psychological Theory and Women's Development* (Cambridge: Harvard University Press, 1982) reads like this; as do the essays in *Women and Moral Theory*, edited by Eva Feder Kittay and Diana T. Meyers (Totowa: Rowman & Littlefield, 1987); and Jean Baker Miller, *Toward a New Psychology of Women* (Boston: Beacon, 1976).

10. For example, in Sara Ruddick's influential "Maternal Thinking," reprinted in *Mothering: Essays in Feminist Thinking*, edited by Joyce Trebilcot (Totowa: Rowman & Littlefield, 1984), sexuality is not discussed as an aspect of maternal practices.

11. Gayle Rubin, "The Traffic in Women: Notes on the 'Political Economy' of Sex," in *Toward an Anthropology of Women*, edited by Rayna Reiter (New York: Monthly Review Press, 1975); see also Shane Phelan, "Feminism and Individualism," *Women and Politics* 10, 4 (Summer 1991): 1-18.

12. Rosi Braidotti, *Patterns of Dissonance* (New York: Routledge, 1991), and the essays in *Gender/Body/Knowledge: Feminist Reconstructions of Being and Knowing*, edited by Alison M. Jaggar and Susan R. Bordo (Rutgers, NJ: Rutgers University Press, 1989) develop these themes.

13. Such fantasies play a part in the "sexuality debates" among feminists. See Carla Freccero, "Notes of a Post-Sex Wars Theorizer," and Teresa de Lauretis, "Upping the Anti *(sic)* in Feminist Theory," in Hirsch and Keller, eds., *Conflicts in Feminism*, (New York: Routledge, 1990); and Mariana Valverde, "Beyond Gender Dangers and Private Pleasure: Theory and Ethics in the Sex Debates," *Feminist Studies* 15, 2 (Summer 1989): 237-254.

14. Victimization is stressed by Catherine MacKinnon in *Feminism Unmodified: Discourse on Life and Law* (Cambridge: Harvard University Press, 1987); merger in Luce Irigaray, *This Sex Which Is Not One* (Ithaca: Cornell University Press, 1985).

15. Sara Ruddick, "Maternal Thinking," and "Preservative Love and Military Destruction: Some Reflections on Mothering and Peace," in Trebilcot, ed., *Mothering* (Totowa: Rowman & Littlefield). For a partial reconsideration, see Sara Ruddick, "Remarks on the Sexual Politics of Reason," in Kittay and Meyer, eds. *Women and Moral Theory* (Totowa: Rowman & Allenheld, 1987).

16. Adrienne Rich, "Compulsory Heterosexuality and Lesbian Existence," *Signs* 5, 4 (Summer 1980): 515-544.

17. But see Abel, "Race, Class and Psychoanalysis?" in Hirsch and Keller, eds., *Conflicts in Feminism* (New York: Routledge, 1990); Audre Lordre, *Sister Outsider* (Trumansburg, NY: Crossing Press, 1984); *Third World Women and the Politics of Feminism*, edited by Chandra Talpade Mohanty, Ann Russo, and Lourdes Torres (Bloomington: Indiana University Press, 1991); Evelyn Brooks Higginbotham, "African-American Women's History and the Metalanguage of Race," Signs 17, 2(Winter 1992): 251-274; Barbara Smith, "Introduction," in *Home Girls: A Black Feminist Anthology,* edited by Barbara Smith (New York: Kitchen Table Press, 1983); and Patricia J. Williams, *The Alchemy of Race and Rights* (Cambridge: Harvard University Press, 1991).

18. For more extensive critiques, see Deborah K. King, "Multiple Jeopardy, Multiple Consciousness: The Context of a Black Feminist Ideology," in *Black Women in*

323

FLAX

America: Social Science Perspectives, edited by Micheline R. Malson, et al. (Chicago: University of Chicago Press, 1990); and Elizabeth V. Spelman, *Inessential Woman: Problems of Exclusion in Feminist Thought* (Boston: Beacon, 1988).

19. Patricia Hill Collins, *Black Feminist Thought* (New York: Routledge, 1991); Angela Y. Davis, *Women, Race & Class* (New York: Random House, 1981); Bonnie Thornton Dill, "The Dialectics of Black Womanhood," and Diane Lewis, "A Response to Inequality: Black Women, Racism and Sexism," in Malson, et al., eds., *Black Women in America* (Chicago: University of Chicago Press, 1990).

20. Hazel V. Carby, "On the Threshold of Women's Era': Lynching, Empire and Sexuality in Black Feminist Theory," in *"Race," Writing and Difference*, edited by Henry Louis Gates (Chicago: University of Chicago Press, 1985); and Jacquelyn Dowd Hall, "'The Mind That Burns in Each Body': Women, Rape and Racial Violence," Barbara Omolade, "Hearts of Darkness," and Rennie Simson, "The Afro-American Female: The Historical Context of the Construction of Sexual Identity," in Ann Snitow, Christine Stansell and Sharon Thompson, eds., *Powers of Desire: The Politics of Sexuality* (New York: Monthly Review Press, 1983).

21. Carole Pateman, *The Sexual Contract* (Stanford: Stanford University Press, 1988).

22. See also Eldridge Cleaver, *Soul on Ice* (New York: Dell, 1968); bell hooks, *Yearning: Race, Gender, and Cultural Politics* (Boston: South End Press, 1990); Alice Walker, *In Search of Our Mothers' Gardens: Womanist Prose* (New York: Harcourt Brace Jovanovich, 1983), especially pp. 271-338; and Michele Wallace, *Black Macho and the Myth of the Superwoman* (New York: Dial, 1978).

23. Julia Kristeva, "Sabat Matter," in the *The Female Body in Western Culture: Contemporary Perspectives*, edited by Susan Rubin Suleiman (Cambridge: Harvard University Press, 1985), 117-118.

24. Biddy Martin and Chandra Talpade Mohanty, "Feminist Politics: What's Home Got To Do With It?" in *Feminist Studies/Critical Studies*, edited by Teresa de Lauretis (Bloomington: Indiana University Press, 1986).

THE MEANING OF MOTHERHOOD IN BLACK CULTURE AND BLACK MOTHER/DAUGHTER RELATIONSHIPS

Patricia Hill Collins

"WHAT DID your mother teach you about men?" is a question I often ask students in my courses on African-American women. "Go to school first and get a good education—don't get too serious too young." "Make sure you look around and that you can take care of yourself before you settle down," and "Don't trust them, want more for yourself than just a man," are typical responses from Black women. My students share stories of how their mothers encouraged them to cultivate satisfying relationships with Black men while anticipating disappointments, to desire marriage while planning viable alternatives, to become mothers only when fully prepared to do so. But above all, they stress their mothers' insistence on being self-reliant and re-sourceful.

These daughters from varying social class backgrounds, ages, family structures and geographic regions had somehow received strikingly similar messages about Black womanhood. Even though their mothers employed diverse teaching strategies, these Black daughters had all been exposed to common themes about the meaning of womanhood in Black culture.[1]

This essay explores the relationship between the meaning of motherhood in African-American culture and Black mother/daughter relationships by addressing three primary questions. First, how have competing perspectives about motherhood intersected to produce a distinctly Afrocentric ideology of motherhood? Second, what are the enduring themes that characterize this Afrocentric ideology of motherhood? Finally, what effect might this Afrocentric ideology of motherhood have on Black mother/daughter relationships?

COMPETING PERSPECTIVES ON MOTHERHOOD

The Dominant Perspective: Eurocentric Views of White Motherhood.

The cult of true womanhood, with its emphasis on motherhood as woman's highest calling, has long held a special place in the gender symbolism of white Americans. From this perspective, women's activities should be confined to the care of children, the nurturing of a husband, and the maintenance of the household. By managing this separate domestic sphere, women gain social influence through their roles as mothers, transmitters of culture and parents for the next generation.[2]

While substantial numbers of white women have benefited from the protections of white patriacrchy provided by the dominant ideology, white women themselves have recently challenged its tenets. On one pole lies a cluster of women, the traditionalists, who aim to retain the centraility of motherhood in women's lives. For traditionalists, differentiating between the experience of motherhood, which for them has been quite satisfying, and motherhood as an institution central in reproducing gender inequality, has proved difficult. The other pole is occupied by women who advocate dismantling motherhood as an institution. They suggest that compulsory motherhood be outlawed and that the experience of motherhood can only be satisfying if women can choose not to be mothers. Arrayed between these dichotomous positions are women who argue for an expanded, but not necessarily different role for women—women can be mothers as long as they are not *just* mothers.[3]

Three themes implicit in white perspectives on motherhood are particularly problematic for Black women and others outside of this debate. First, the assumption that mothering occurs within the confines of a private, nuclear family household where the mother has almost total responsibility for childdrearing is less applicable to Black families. While the ideal of the cult of true womanhood has been held up to Black women for emulation, racial oppression has denied Black families sufficient resources to support private, nuclear family households. Second, the assumption of strict sex-role segregation defining male and female spheres of influence within the family has been less applicable to African-American families than to white middle class ones. Finally, the assumption that motherhood and economic dependency on men are linked and that to be a "good" mother, one must stay at home, making motherhood a full-time "occupation", is similarly uncharacteristic of African-American families.[4]

Even though selected groups of white women are challenging the cult of true womanhood and its accompanying definition of motherhood, the dominant ideology remains powerful. As long as these approaches remain prominent in scholarly and popular discourse, Eurocentric views of white motherhood will continue to affect Black women's lives.

Eurocentric Views of Black Motherhood.

Eurocentric perspectives on Black motherhood revolve around two interdependent images that together define Black women's roles in white and in African-American families. The first image is that of the Mammy, the faithful, devoted domestic servant. Like one of the family, Mammy conscientiously "mothers" her white children, caring for them and loving them as if they were her own. Mammy is the ideal Black mother for she recognizes her place. She is paid next to nothing and yet cheerfully accepts her inferior status. But when she enters her own home, this same Mammy is transformed into the second image, the too-strong matriarch who raises weak sons and "unnaturally superior" daughters.[5] When she protests, she is labelled aggressive and nonfeminine, yet if she remains silent, she is rendered invisible.

The task of debunking Mammy by analyzing Black women's roles as exploited domestic workers and challenging the matriarchy thesis by demonstrating that Black women do not wield disproportionate power in African-American families has long preoccupied African-American scholars.[6] But an equally telling critique concerns uncovering the functions of these images and their role in explaining Black Women's subordination in systems of race, class and gender oppression. As Mae King points out, white definitions of Black motherhood foster the dominant group's exploitation of Black women by blaming Black women for their characteristic reactions to their own subordination.[7] For example, while the stay-at-home mother has been held up to all women as the ideal, African-American women have been compelled to work outside the home, typically in a very narrow range of occupations. Even though Black women were forced to become domestic servants and be strong figures in Black households, labelling them Mammys and matriarchs denigrates Black women. Without a countervailing Afrocentric ideology of motherhood, white perspectives on both white and African-American motherhood place Black women in a no-win situation. Adhering to these standards brings the danger of the lowered self-esteem of internalized oppression,

COLLINS

327

one that, if passed on from mother to daughter, provides a powerful mechanism for controlling African-American communities.

African Perspectives on Motherhood

One concept that has been constant throughout the history of African societies is the centrality of motherhood in religions, philosophies and social institutions. As Barbara Christian points out, "There is no doubt that motherhood is for most African people symbolic of creativity and continuity."[8]

Cross-cultural research on motherhood in African societies appears to support Christian's claim.[9] West African sociologist Christine Oppong suggests that the Western notion of equating household with family be abandoned because it obscures women's family roles in African cultures.[10] While the archetypal white, middle-class nuclear family conceptualizes family life as being divided into two oppositional spheres—the "male" sphere of economic providing and the "female" sphere of affective nurturing—this type of rigid sex role segregation was not part of the West African tradition. Mothering was not a privatized nurturing "occupation" reserved for biological mothers, and the economic support of children was not the exclusive responsibility of men. Instead, for African women, emotional care for children and providing for their physical survival were interwoven as interdependent, complementary dimensions of motherhood.

In spite of variation among societies, a strong case has been made that West African women occupy influential roles in African family networks.[11] First, since they are not dependent on males for economic support and provide for certain key dimensions of their own and their children's economic support, women are structurally central to families.[12] Second, the image of the mother is one that is culturally elaborated and valued across diverse West African societies. Continuing the lineage is essential in West African philosophies, and motherhood is similarly valued.[13] Finally, while the biological mother/child bond is valued, child care was a collective responsibility, a situation fostering cooperative, age stratified, woman-centered "mothering" networks.

Recent research by Africanists suggests that much more of this African heritage was retained among African-Americans than had previously been thought. The retention of West African culture as a culture of resistance offered enslaved Africans and exploited African-Americans alternative ideologies to those advanced by dominant groups. Central to these reinterpretations of African-American institutions and culture is a reconceptualization of Black family life and the role of women in Black family networks.[14] West African perspectives may have been combined with the changing political and economic situations framing African-American communities to produce certain enduring themes characterizing an Afrocentric ideology of motherhood.

COLLINS

ENDURING THEMES OF AN AFROCENTRIC IDEOLOGY OF MOTHERHOOD

An Afrocentric ideology of motherhood must reconcile the competing world views of these three conflicting perspectives of motherhood. An ongoing tension exists between efforts to mold the institution of Black motherhood for the benefit of the dominant group and efforts by Black women to define and value their own experiences with motherhood. This tension leads to a continuum of responses. For those women who either aspire to the cult of true womanhood without having the resources to support such a lifestyle or who believe sterotypical analyses of themselves as dominating matriarchs, motherhood can be an oppressive institution. But the experience of motherhood can provide Black women with a base of self-actualization, status in the Black community, and a reason for social activism. These alleged contradictions can exist side by side in African-American communities, families, and even within individual women.

Embedded in these changing relationships are four enduring themes that I contend characterize an Afrocentric ideology of motherhood. Just as the issues facing enslaved African mothers were quite different from those currently facing poor Black women in inner cities for any given historical moment, the actual institutional forms that these themes take depend on the severity of oppression and Black women's resources for resistance.

Bloodmothers, Othermothers, and Women-Centered Networks

In African-American communities, the boundaries distinguishing biological mothers of children from other women who care for children are often fluid and changing. Biological mothers or bloodmothers are expected to care for their children: But African and African-American communities have also recognized that vesting one person with full responsibility for mothering a child may not be wise or possible. As a result "othermothers," women who assist blood- mothers by sharing mothering responsibilities, traditionally have been central to the institution of Black motherhood.[15]

The centrality of women in African-American extended families is well known.[16] Organized, resilient women-centered networks of bloodmothers and othermothers are key in understanding this cenrality. Grandmothers, sisters, aunts, or cousins acted as othermothers by taking on childcare responsibilities for each other's children. When needed, temporary child care arrangements turned into long-term care or informal adoption.[17]

In African-American communities, these women-centered networks of community-based childcare often extend beyond the boundaries of biologically related extended families to support "fictive kin."[18] Civil rights activist Ella Baker describes how informal adoption by othermothers functioned in the Southern, rural community of her childhood:

329

COLLINS

My aunt who had thirteen children of her own raised three more. She had become a midwife, and a child was born who was covered with sores. Nobody was particularly wanting the child, so she took the child and raised him . . . and another mother decided she didn't want to be bothered with two children. So my aunt took one and raised him . . . they were part of the family.[19]

Even when relationships were not between kin or fictive kin, African-American community norms were such that neighbors cared for each other's children. In the following passage, Sara Brooks, a Southern domestic worker, describes the importance of the community-based childcare that a neighbor offered her daughter. In doing so, she also shows how the African-American cultural value placed on cooperative childcare found institutional support in the adverse conditions under which so many Black women mothered:

She kept Vivian and she didn't charge me nothin either. You see, people used to look after each other, but now it's not that way. I reckon it's because we all was poor, and I guess they put theirself in the place of the person that they was helpin.[20]

Othermothers were key not only in supporting children but also in supporting bloodmothers who, for whatever reason, were ill-prepared or had little desire to care for their children. Given the pressures from the larger political economy, the emphasis placed on community-based childcare and the respect given to othermothers who assume the responsibilities of childcare have served a critical function in African-American communities. Children orphaned by sale or death of their parents under slavery, children conceived through rape, children of young mothers, children born into extreme poverty, or children, who for other reasons have been rejected by their bloodmothers, have all been supported by othermothers who, like Ella Baker's aunt, took in additional children, even when they had enough of their own.

Providing as Part of Mothering

The work done by African-American women in providing the economic resources essential to Black family well-being affects motherhood in a contradictory fashion. On the one hand, African-American women have long integrated their activities as economic providers into their mothering relationships. In contrast to the cult of true womanhood where work is defined as being in opposition to and incompatible with motherhood, work for Black women has been an important and valued dimension of Afrocentric definitions of Black motherhood. On the other hand, African-American women's experiences as mothers under oppression were such that the type and purpose of work Black women were forced to do greatly impacted on the type of mothering relationships bloodmothers and othermothers had with Black children.

While slavery both disrupted West African family patterns and exposed enslaved Africans to the gender ideologies and practices of slaveowners, it simultaneously made it impossible, had they wanted to do so, for enslaved Africans to implement slaveowner's ideologies. Thus, the separate spheres of providing as a male domain and affective nurturing as a female domain did not develop within African-American families.[21] Providing for Black childrens' physical survival and attending to their affective, emotional needs continued as interdependent dimensions of an Afrocentric ideology of motherhood. However, by changing the conditions under which Black women worked and the purpose of the work itself, slavery introduced the problem of how best to continue traditional Afrocentric values under oppressive conditions. Institutions of community-based childcare, informal adoption, greater reliance on othermothers, all emerge as adaptations to the exigencies of combining exploitative work with nurturing children.

In spite of the change in political status brought on by emancipation, the majority of African-American women remained exploited agricultural workers. However, their placement in Southern political economies allowed them to combine childcare with field labor. Sara Brooks describes how strong the links between providing and caring for others were for her:

> When I was about nine I was nursin my sister Sally—I'm about seven or eight years older than Sally. And when I would put her to sleep, instead of me goin somewhere and sit down and play, I'd get my little old hoe and get out there and work right in the field around the house.[22]

Black women's shift from Southern agriculture to domestic work in Southern and Northern towns and cities represented a change in the type of work done, but not in the meaning of work to women and their families. Whether they wanted to or not, the majority of African-American women had to work and could not afford the luxury of motherhood as a noneconomically productive, female "occupation."

Community Othermothers and Social Activism

Black women's experiences as othermothers have provided a foundation for Black women's social activism. Black women's feelings of responsibility for nurturing the children in their own extended family networks have stimulated a more generalized ethic of care where Black women feel accountable to all the Black community's children.

This notion of Black women as community othermothers for all Black children traditionally allowed Black women to treat biologically unrelated children as if they were members of their own families. For example, sociologist Karen Fields describes how her grandmother, Mamie Garvin Fields, draws on her power as a community othermother when dealing with unfamiliar children.

> She will say to a child on the street who looks up to no good, picking out a name at random, "Aren't you Miz Pinckney's boy?" in that same reproving tone.

COLLINS

If the reply is, "No *ma'am*, my mother is Miz Gadsden," whatever threat there was dissipates.[23]

The use of family language in referring to members of the Black community also illustrates this dimension of Black motherhood. For example, Mamie Garvin Fields describes how she became active in surveying the poor housing conditions of Black people in Charleston.

> I was one of the volunteers they got to make a survey of the places where we were paying extortious rents for indescribable property. I said "we," although it wasn't Bob and me. We had our own home, and so did many of the Federated Women. Yet we still felt like it really was "we" living in those terrible places, and it was up to us to do something about them.[24]

To take another example, while describing her increasingly successful efforts to teach a boy who had given other teachers problems, my daughter's kindergarten teacher stated, "You know how it can be—the majority of children in the learning disabled classes are *our children*. I know he didn't belong there, so I volunteered to take him." In these statements, both women invoke the language of family to describe the ties that bind them as Black women to their responsibilities to other members of the Black community as family.

Sociologist Cheryl Gilkes suggests that community othermother relationships are sometimes behind Black women's decisions to become community activists. Gilkes notes that many of the Black women community activists in her study became involved in community organizing in response to the needs of their own children and of those in their communities. The following comment is typical of how many of the Black women in Gilkes' study relate to Black children: "There were a lot of summer programs springing up for kids, but they were exclusive . . . and I found that most of *our kids* (emphasis mine) were excluded."[26] For many women, what began as the daily expression of their obligations as community other-mothers, as was the case for the kindergarten teacher, developed into full-fledged roles as community leaders.

Motherhood as a Symbol of Power

Motherhood, whether bloodmother, othermother, or community othermother, can be invoked by Black women as a symbol of power. A substantial portion of Black women's status in African-American communities stems not only from their roles as mothers in their own families but from their contributions as community othermothers to Black community development as well.

The specific contributions Black women make in nurturing Black community development form the basis of community-based power. Community othermothers work on behalf of the Black community by trying, in the words of late nineteenth century Black feminists, to "uplift the race," so that vulnerable members of the community would be able to attain the self-reliance and independence so desperately needed for Black community development under oppressive conditions. This is the type of power many African-Americans have in mind when they describe the "strong, Black women" they see around them in traditional African-American communities.

When older Black women invoke this community othermother status, its results can be quite striking. Karen Fields recounts an incident described to her by her grandmother illustrating how women can exert power as community othermothers:

> One night . . . as Grandmother sat crocheting alone at about two in the morning, a young man walked into the living room carrying the portable TV from upstairs. She said, "Who are you looking for *this* time of night?" As Grandmother (described) the incident to me over the phone, I could hear a tone of voice that I know well. It said, "Nice boys don't do that." So I imagine the burglar heard his own mother or grandmother at that moment. He joined in the familial game just created: "Well, he told me that I could borrow it." "*Who* told you?" "John." "Um um, no John lives here. You got the wrong house."[27]

After this dialogue, the teenager turned around, went back upstairs and returned the television.

In local Black communities, specific Black women are widely recognized as powerful figures, primarily because of their contributions to the community's well-being through their roles as community othermothers. Sociologist Charles Johnson describes the behavior of an elderly Black woman at a church service in rural Alabama of the 1930s. Even though she was not on the program, the woman stood up to speak. The master of ceremonies rang for her to sit down but she refused to do so claiming, "I am the mother of this church, and I will say what I please." The master of ceremonies later explained to the congregation—"Brothers, I know you all honor Sister Moore. Course our time is short but she has acted as a mother to me . . . Any time old folks get up I give way to them."[28]

IMPLICATIONS FOR BLACK MOTHER/DAUGHTER RELATIONSHIPS

In her discussion of the sex-role socialization of Black girls, Pamela Reid identifies two complementary approaches in understanding Black mother/daughter relationships.[29] The first, psychoanalytic theory, examines the role of parents in the establishment of personality and social behavior. This theory argues that the development of feminine behavior results from the girls' identification with adult female role models. This approach emphasizes how an Afrocentric ideology of motherhood is actualized through Black mothers' activities as role models.

The second approach, social learning theory, suggests that the rewards and punishments attached to girls' childhood experiences are central in shaping women's sex-role behavior. The kinds of behaviors that Black mothers reward and punish in their daughters are seen as key in the socialization process. This approach examines specific experiences that Black girls have while growing up that encourage them to absorb an Afrocentric ideology of motherhood.

African-American Mothers as Role Models

Feminist psychoanalytic theorists suggest that the sex-role socialization process is different for boys and girls. While boys learn maleness by rejecting femaleness via separating themselves from their mothers, girls establish feminine identities by embracing the femaleness of their mothers. Girls identify with their mothers, a sense of connection that is incorporated into the female personality. However, this mother-identification is problematic because, under patriarchy, men are more highly valued than women. Thus, while daughters identify with their mothers, they also reject them because, in partiarchal families, identification with adult women as mothers means identifying with persons deemed inferior.[30]

While Black girls learn by identifying with their mothers, the specification of the female role with which Black girls identify may be quite different than that modeled by middle class white mothers. The presence of working mothers, extended family othermothers, and powerful community othermothers offers a range of role models that challenge the tenets of the cult of true womanhood.

Moreover, since Black mothers have a distinctive relationship to white patriarchy, they may be less likely to socialize their daughters into their proscribed role as subordinates. Rather, a key part of Black girls' socialization involves incorporating the critical posture that allows Black women to cope with contradictions. For example, Black girls have long had to learn how to do domestic work while rejecting definitions of themselves as Mammies. At the same time they've had to take on strong roles in Black extended families without internalizing images of themselves as matriarchs.

In raising their daughers, Black mothers face a troubling dilemma. To ensure their daughters' physical survival, they must teach their daughters to fit into systems of oppression. For example, as a young girl in Mississippi, Black activist Ann Moody questioned why she was paid so little for the domestic work she began at age nine, why Black women domestics were sexually harrassed by their white male employers, and why whites had so much more than Blacks. But her mother refused to answer her questions and actually became angry whenever Ann Moody stepped out of her "place."[31] Black daughters are raised to expect to work, to strive for an education so that they can support themselves, and to anticipate carrying heavy responsibilities in their families and communities because these skills are essential for their own survival as well as for the survival of those for whom they will eventually be responsible.[32] And yet mothers know that if daughters fit too well into the limited opportunities offered Black women, they become willing participants

COLLINS

in their own subordination. Mothers may have ensured their daughters' physical survival at the high cost of their emotional destruction.

On the other hand, Black daughters who offer serious challenges to oppressive situations may not physically survive. When Ann Moody became involved in civil rights activities, her mother first begged her not to participate and then told her not to come home because she feared the whites in Moody's hometown would kill her. In spite of the dangers, many Black mothers routinely encourage their daughters to develop skills to confront oppressive conditions. Thus, learning that they will work, that education is a vehicle for advancement, can also be seen as ways of preparing Black girls to resist oppression through a variety of mothering roles. The issue is to build emotional strength, but not at the cost of physical survival.

This delicate balance between conformity and resistance is described by historian Elsa Barkley Brown as the "need to socialize me one way and at the same time to give me all the tools I needed to be something else."[33] Black daughters must learn how to survive in interlocking structures of race, class and gender oppression while rejecting and trancending those very same structures. To develop these skills in their daughters, mothers demonstrate varying combinations of behaviors devoted to ensuring their daughter's survival—such as providing them with basic necessities and ensuring their protection in dangerous environments—to helping their daughters go farther than mothers themselves were allowed to go.

The presence of othermothers in Black extended families and the modeling symbolized by community othermothers offer powerful support for the task of teaching girls to resist white perceptions of Black womanhood while appearing to conform to them. In contrast to the isolation of middle class white mother/daughter dyads, Black women-centered extended family networks foster an early identification with a much wider range of models of Black womanhood which can lead to a greater sense of empowerment in young Black girls.

Social Learning Theory and Black Mothering Behavior

Understanding this goal of balancing the needs of physical survival of their daughters with the vision of encouraging them to transcend the boundaries confronting them sheds some light on some of the apparent contradictions in Black mother/daughter relationships. Black mothers are often described as strong disciplinarians and overly protective parents; yet these same women manage to raise daughters who are self-reliant and assertive.[34] Professor Gloria Wade-Gayles offers an explanation for this apparent contradiction by suggesting that Black mothers:

> do not socialize their daughters to be "passive" or "irrational." Quite the contrary, they socialize their daughters to be independent, strong and self-confident. Black mothers are suffocatingly protective and domineering precisely because

335

COLLINS

they are determined to mold their daughters into whole and self-actualizing persons in a society that devalues Black women.[35]

Black mothers emphasize protection either by trying to shield their daughters as long as possible from the penalties attached to their race, class and gender status or by teaching them how to protect themselves in such situations. Black women's autobiographies and fiction can be read as texts revealing the multiple strategies employed by Black mothers in preparing their daughters for the demands of being Black women in oppressive conditions. For example, in discussing the mother/daughter relationship in Paule Marshall's *Brown Girl, Brownstones,* Rosalie Troester catalogues some of these strategies and the impact they may have on relationships themselves:

> Black mothers, particularly those with strong ties to their community, sometimes build high banks around their young daughters, isolating them from the dangers of the larger world until they are old and strong enough to function as autonomous women. Often these dikes are religious, but sometimes they are built with education, family, or the restrictions of a close-knit and homogeneous community . . . this isolation causes the currents between Black mothers and daughters run deep and the relationship to be fraught with an emotional intensity often missing from the lives of women with more freedom.[36]

Black women's efforts to provide for their children also may affect the emotional intensity of Black mother/daughter relationships. As Gloria Wade-Gayles points out, "Mothers in Black Women's fiction are strong and devoted . . . but . . . they are rarely affectionate."[37] For far too many Black mothers, the demands of providing for children are so demanding that affection often must wait until the basic needs of physical survival are satisfied.

Black daughters raised by mothers grappling with hostile environments have to confront their feelings about the difference between the idealized versions of maternal love extant in popular culture and the strict, assertive mothers so central to their lives.[38] For daughters, growing up means developing a better understanding on the daughter's part that offering physical care and protection is an act of maternal love. Ann Moody describes her growing awareness of the personal cost her mother paid as a single mother of three children employed as a domestic worker. Watching her mother sleep after the birth of another child, Moody remembers:

> For a long time I stood there looking at her. I didn't want to wake her up. I wanted to enjoy and preserve that calm, peaceful look on her face, I wanted to think she would always be that happy . . . Adline and Junior were too young to feel the things I felt and know the things I knew about Mama. They couldn't remember when she and Daddy separated. They had never heard her cry at night as I had or worked and helped as I had done when we were starving.[39]

Renita Weems' account of coming to grips with maternal desertion provides another example of a daughter's efforts to understand her mother's behavior. In the following passage, Weems struggles with the difference between the stereotypical image of the super strong Black mother and her own alcoholic mother's decision to leave her children:

> My mother loved us. I must believe that. She worked all day in a department store bakery to buy shoes and school tablets, came home to curse out neighbors who wrongly accused her children of any impropriety (which in an apartment complex usually meant stealing), and kept her house cleaner than most sober women.[40]

Weems concludes that her mother loved her because she provided for her to the best of her ability.

Othermothers often play central roles in defusing the emotional intensity of relationships between bloodmothers and their daughters and in helping daughters understand the Afrocentric ideology of motherhood. Weems describes the women teachers, neighbors, friends, and othermothers that she turned to for help in negotiating a difficult mother/daughter relationship. These women, she notes, "did not have the onus of providing for me, and so had the luxury of talking to me."[41]

June Jordan offers one of the most eloquent analyses of a daughter's realization of the high personal cost Black women have paid as bloodmothers and othermothers in working to provide an economic and emotional foundation for Black children. In the following passage, Jordan captures the feelings that my Black women students struggled to put into words:

> As a child I noticed the sadness of my mother as she sat alone in the kitchen at night . . . Her woman's work never won permanent victories of any kind. It never enlarged the universe of her imagination or her power to influence what happened beyond the front door of our house. Her woman's work never tickled her to laugh or shout or dance. But she did raise me to respect her way of offering love and to believe that hard work is often the irreducible factor for survival, not something to avoid. Her woman's work produced a reliable home base where I could pursue the privileges of books and music. Her woman's work invented the potential for a completely different kind of work for us, the next generation of Black women: huge, rewarding hard work demanded by the huge, new ambitions that her perfect confidence in us engendered.[42]

Jordan's words not only capture the essence of the Afrocentric ideology of motherhood so central to the well-being of countless numbers of Black women. They simultaneously point the way into the future, one where Black women face the challenge of continuing the mothering traditions painstakingly nurtured by prior generations of African-American women.

NOTES

1. The definition of culture used in this essay is taken from Leith Mullings, "Anthropological Perspectives on the Afro-American Family," *American Journal of Social*

Psychiatry 6(1986), pp. 11–16. According to Mullings, culture is composed of "the symbols and values that create the ideological frame of reference through which people attempt to deal with the circumstances in which they find themselves," p. 13.

2. For analyses of the relationship of the cult of true womanhood to Black women, see Leith Mullings, "Uneven Development: Class, Race and Gender in the United States Before 1900," in *Women's Work, Development and the Division of Labor by Gender*, eds. Eleanor Leacock and Helen Safa (South Hadley, MA: Bergin & Garvey, 1986), pp. 41–57; Bonnie Thornton Dill, "Our Mothers' Grief: Racial Ethnic Women and the Maintenance of Families." Research Paper 4, Center for Research on Women (Memphis, TN: Memphis State University, 1986); and Hazel Carby, *Reconstructing Womanhood: The Emergence of the African-American Woman Novelist* (New York: Oxford University, 1987), especially chapter two.

3. Contrast for example, the Nationalist analysis of Selma Fraiberg, *Every Child's Birthright. In Defense of Mothering* (New York: Basic, 1977) to that of Jeffner Allen, "Motherhood: The Annihilation of Women," in *Mothering, Essays in Feminist Theory*, ed. Joyce Trebileot (Totawa, NJ: Rowan & Allanheld, 1983). See also Adrienne Rich, *Of Woman Born: Motherhood as Experience and Institution* (New York: Norton, 1976). For an overview of how Nationalists and feminists have shaped the public policy debate on abortion, see Kristin Luker *Abortion and the Politics of Motherhood* (Berkeley, CA: University of California. 1994).

4. Mullings, 1986, note 2 above; Dill, 1986; and Carby 1987. Feminist scholarship is also challenging Western notions of the family. See Barrie Thorne and Marilyn Yalom, eds., *Rethinking the Family* (New York: Longman, 1982).

5. Since Black women are no longer heavily concentrated in private domestic service, the Mammy image may be fading. In contrast, the matriarch image, popularized in Daniel Patrick Moynihan's *The Negro Farmily. The Case for National Action* (Washington, DC: U.S, Government Printing Office, 1965), is reemerging in public debates about the feminization of poverty and the urban underclass. See Maxine Baca Zinn, "Minority Families in Crisis: The Public Discussion," Research Paper 6, Center for Research on Women (Memphis, TN: Memphis State University, 1987).

6. For an alternative analysis to the Mammy image, see Judith Rollins, *Between Women. Domestics and Their Employers* (Philadelphia: Temple University, 1985). Classic responses to the hypothesis include Robert Hill, *The Strengths of Black Families* (New York: Urban League, 1972); Andrew Billingsley, *Black Families in White America* (Englewood Cliffs, NJ: Prentice-Hall, 1968); and Joyce Ladner, *Tomorrow's Tomorrow* (Garden City, NY: Doubleday, 1971). For a recent analysis, see Linda Burnham, "Has Poverty Been Feminized in Black America?" *Black Scholar* 16 (1985), pp. 15–24.

7. Mae King, "Thee Politics of Sexual Stereotypes," *Black Scholar* 4 (1973), pp. 12–23.

8. Barbara Christian, "An Angle of Seeing. Motherhood in Buchi Emecheta's *Joys of Motherhood* and Alice Walker's *Meridian*," in *Black Feminist Criticism,* ed. Barbara Christian (New York: Pergamon, 1985), p. 214.

9. See Christine Oppong, ed., *Female and Male in West Africa* (London: Allen & Unwin, 1983); Niara Sudarkasa. "Female Employment and Family Organization in West Africa," in *The Black Woman Cross-Culturally*, ed. Filomina Chiamo Steady (Cambridge, MA: Schenkman, 1981), pp. 49–64; and Nancy Tanner. "Matrifocality in In-

donesia and Africa and Among Black Americans," in *Woman, Culture, and Society*, eds. Michelle Rosaldo and Louise Lamphere (Stanford, CA: Stanford University, 1974), pp. 129–156.

10. Christine Oppong, "Family Structure and Women's Reproductive and Productive Roles: Some Conceptual and Methodological Issues," in *Women's Roles and Population Trends in the Third World*, eds. Richard Anker, Myra Buvinic and Nadia Youssef (London: Croom Heim, 1982), pp. 133–150.

11. The key distinction here is that, unlike the matriarchy thesis, women play central roles in families and this centrality is seen as legitimate. In spite of this centrality, it is important not to idealize African women's family roles. For an analysis by a Black African feminist, see Awa Thiam, *Black Sisters Speak Out: Feminism and Oppression in Black Africa* (London: Pluto. 1978).

12. Sudarkasa, 1981.

13. John Mbiti, *African Religions and Philosophies* (New York: Anchor, 1969).

14. "Interpreting the African Heritage in Afro-American Family Organization," in *Black Families*, ed. Harriette Pipes McAdoo (Beverly Hills, CA: Sage, 1981), pp. 37–53; and Deborah Gray White, *Ar'nt I a Woman? Female Slaves in the Plantation South* (New York: W.W. Norton, 1984).

15. The terms used in this section appear in Rosalie Riegle Troester. "Turbulence and Tenderness: Mothers, Daughters and 'Othermothers' in Paule Marshall's *Brown Girl, Brownstones*," SAGE: A Scholarly Journal on Black Women 1 (Fall 1984) pp. 13–16.

16. See Tanner's discussion of matrifocality, 1974; see also Carrie Allen McCray, "The Black Woman and Family Roles," in *The Black Woman*, ed. LaFrances Rogers-Rose (Beverly Hills, CA: Sage, 1980), pp. 67–78; Elmer Martin and Joanne Mitchell Martin, *The Black Extended Family* (Chicago: University of Chicago, 1978); Joyce Aschenbrenner, *Lifelines, Black Families in Chicago* (Prospect Heights, IL: Waveland, 1975); and Carol B. Stack, *All Our Kin* (New York: Harper & Row 1974).

17. "Martin and Martin, 1978; Stack, 1974; and Virginia Young. "Family and Childhood in a Southern Negro Community," *American Anthropologist* 72 (1970), pp. 269–288.

18. Stack, 1974.

19. Ellen Cantarow, *Moving the Mountain: Women Working for Social Change* (Old Westbury, NY- Feminist Press, 1980), p. 59.

20. Thordis Simonsen, ed., *You May Plow Here, The Narrative of Sara Brooks* (New York: Touchstone, 1986), p. 181.

21. White 1985; Dill, 1986; Mullings, 1986, note 2 above.

22. Simonsen, 1986, p. 86.

23. Mamie Garvin Fields and Karen Fields, *Lemon Swamp and Other Places, A Carolina Memoir* (New York: Free Press, 1983), p. xvii.

24. Ibid, p. 195.

25. Cheryl Gilkes, "'Holding Back the Ocean with a Broom,' Black Women and Community Work," in Rogers-Rose, 1980, pp. 217–231; "Going Up for the Oppressed: The Career Mobility of Black Women Community Workers," *Journal of Social Issues* 39 (1983), pp. 115–139.

26. Gilkes, 1980, p. 219.

339

COLLINS

27. Fields and Fields, 1983, p. xvi.

28. Charles Johnson, *Shadow of the Plantation* (Chicago: University of Chicago, 1934, 1979), p. 173.

29. Pamela Reid, "Socialization of Black Female Children," in *Women: A Developmental Perspective*, eds. Phyllis Berman and Estelle Ramey (Washington, DC: National Institute of Health, 1983).

30. For works in the feminist psychoanalytic tradition, see Nancy Chodorow, "Family Structure and Feminine Personality," in Rosaldo and Lamphere, 1974; Nancy Chodorow, *The Reproduction of Mothering* (Berkeley, CA: University of California, 1978); and Jane Flax, "The Conflict Between Nurturance and Autonomy in Mother-Daughter Relationships and Within Feminism," *Feminist Studies* 4 (1978), pp. 171–189.

31. Ann Moody, *Coming of Age in Mississippi* (New York: Dell, 1968).

32. Ladner, 1971; Gloria Joseph, "Black Mothers and Daughters: Their Roles and Functions in American Society," in *Common Differences*, ed. Gloria Joseph and Jill Lewis (Garden City, NY: Anchor, 1981), pp. 75–126; Lena Wright Myers, *Black Women, Do They Cope Better?* (Englewood Cliffs, NJ: Prentice-Hall, 1980).

33. Elsa Barkley Brown, "Hearing Our Mothers' Lives," paper presented at Fifteenth Anniversary of African-American and African Studies at Emory College, Atlanta, 1986. This essay will appear in the upcoming Black Women's Studies issue of *SAGE: A Scholarly Journal on Black Women*, Vol. VI, No. 1.

34. Joseph, 1980; Myers, 1980.

35. Gloria Wade-Gayles, "The Truths of Our Mothers' Lives: Mother-Daughter Relationships in Black Women's Fiction," *SAGE: A Scholarly Journal on Black Women* 1 (Fall 1984), p. 12.

36. Troester, 1984, p. 13.

37. Wade-Gayles, 1984, p. 10.

38. Joseph, 1980.

39. Moody, 1968, p. 57.

40. Renita Weems, "'Hush. Mama's Gotta Go Bye Bye: A Personal Narrative," *SAGE: A Scholarly Journal on Black Women* 1 (Fall 1984), p. 26.

41. Ibid, p. 27.

42. June Jordan, *On Call, Political Essays* (Boston: South End Press, 1985), p. 145.

LIKE FAMILY
Power, Intimacy, and Sexuality in Male Athletes' Friendships[1]

Michael A. Messner

The locker room had become a kind of home to me... I often enter tense and uneasy, disturbed by some event of the day. Slowly my worries fade as I see their unimportance to my male peers. I relax, my concerns lost among relationships that are warm and real, but never intimate, lost among the constants of an athlete's life. Athletes may be crude and immature, but they are genuine when it comes to loyalty. The lines of communication are clear and simple. . . We are at ease in the setting of satin uniforms and shower nozzles.

—Bill Bradley (1977)

chapter 19

INTRODUCTION

THROUGHOUT MOST of this century, it was commonly believed that men who worked together, fought together, and played together within public institutions such as the workplace, the military, and sport tended to form deep and lasting friendships. Men, it was believed, enjoyed the Truly Great Friendships, while women's friendships with each other were characterized by shallow cattiness and gossip. Moreover, social commentators such as Lionel Tiger (1969) and George Gilder (1973) argued that civilization itself rests on the foundation of men's "natural" tendency to bond together in public life. This highly romanticized view of men's friendships was turned on its head in the mid-1970s by a new perspective, which was inspired by a revived feminist movement. Men's liberationists began to examine the quality of men's friendships with other men, and found them wanting. Men's friendships, it was argued, tend to be destructively competitive, homophobic, and emotionally impoverished (Balswick, 1976; Farrell, 1975; Fasteau, 1974; Morin & Garfinkel, 1978; Pleck & Sawyer, 1974).

By the mid-1980s, the social-scientific literature tended to echo this emphasis on the "emotional limits" and "impoverishment" of men's friendships, especially when compared categorically with women's friendships. In the forefront of this perspective were adherents of feminist psychoanalytic theory, who argued that early developmental differences, grounded in the social structure of mothering, created deeply rooted (unconscious) differences between women and men (Chodorow, 1978; Dinnerstein, 1976). As a result of these internalized gender identity differences, males develop more "positional" identities (with fears of intimacy), while females develop more "relational" identities (with fears of separation) (Gilligan, 1982; Rubin, 1983). One result of these differences, according to Rubin (1985), is that women tend to enjoy deep, intimate, meaningful, and lasting friendships, while men have a number of shallow, superficial, and unsatisfying "acquaintances." Rubin characterizes the dominant form of men's friendships with other men as "bonding without intimacy."

By the late 1980s, this negative characterization of men's friendship had itself been called into question. Following Cancian's (1987) observation that since the Industrial Revolution, social conceptions of love and intimacy have become "feminized," Swain (1989) argues that Rubin and others have been guilty of judging men's friendships against the standard of the type of intimate relationships that women tend to construct. Women tend to place a very high value on *talk*—and indeed, for a relationship to be "intimate," there must be a willingness and ability to verbally and mutually share one's inner life with another (Rubin, 1983, 1985). Since men friends tend to *do things* with each other, rather than spending their time talking about their inner lives, they are engaged in "bonding without intimacy." Swain asserts that if we instead examine men's friendships from the point of view of men, rather than through a "feminine model," we see that men's friends are in fact characterized by a "covert style of intimacy" (p. 71). Men already have an "active style of intimacy," and should not be forced to learn "feminine-typed skills to foster intimacy in their relationships" (p. 85). In short, women and men tend to experience and define intimate friendship in different ways, and neither should be judged by the standard of the other.

This chapter aims to shed light on this ongoing debate through an examination of men's friendships within a specific social institution—organized sports. At issue in this debate, I will argue, is the question: From whose standpoint should we examine men's friendships? If we judge men's friendships through an idealized feminine standard, men's friendships will appear impoverished. It is valuable and important to understand how men experience and define their own friendships. But in analyzing gender difference in friendship patterns, it is crucial to move beyond the "separate but equal" stance, where

MESSNER

women's friendships are evaluated through a feminine standpoint, and men's friendships through a masculine standpoint. As we ask what men's friendships mean to men, we also need to ask the femin*ist* (not femin*ine*) question: How do these male friendship patterns fit into an overall system of power? This means examining both the quality of men's friendships with each other and the ways that male friendships and peer groups construct men's attitudes and relationships toward women. This is the task of this chapter. Through a concrete examination of men's friendships within the institution of sport, I hope to shed light on the complexity of men's friendships—both in terms of individual men's experience of friendships, and in terms of the role of men's friendships in constructing the larger gender order. Through an analysis of in-depth interviews with 30 male former athletes of diverse age, race, and socioeconomic status,[2] I will describe and analyze male athletes' friendships with each other. Then I will examine the ways that men's friendships and peer groups serve to construct their relationships with —and attitudes about —women.

THE PARADOX OF MEN'S FRIENDSHIPS IN SPORT

Years after the end of an athletic career, it is not uncommon to hear men talk almost reverently of their friendships with former teammates. For instance, Gene,[3] a former professional football player, said:

> The guys I played with, I had the utmost respect for. Because once you've been through training camp together, and those hard times together, you learn to know and feel things about 'em that can't anyone else ever feel if they haven't been in those situations with 'em. The most important persons are your teammates, and to be loved and respected by them means more than anything—more than the money aspect, if a guy would tell the truth about it.

343

These kinds of statements were not reserved for former professional athletes. Jim, who played football, basketball, and baseball through high school, spoke of his relationships with teammates with similar reverence:

> I'd say that most of my meaningful relationships have started through sports and have been maintained through sports. There's nothing so strong, to form that bond, as sports. Just like in war, too—there are no closer friends than guys who are in the same foxhole together trying to stay alive. You know, hardship breeds friendships, breeds intense familiarity. . . You have to commonly endure something together—sweat together, bleed together, cry together. Sports provide that.

This (often highly romanticized) sense that close friendships between men are forged in "adversity," through "enduring hardship" together, was a common theme in former athletes' discussions of their friendships with teammates. But despite almost universal agreement that sports provided a context

MESSNER

in which this kind of mutual respect, closeness, even love among men did develop, there was usually a downside to men's descriptions of their relationships with teammates. For instance, Brent, a former high school basketball player said that in his early teens, his relationship with this best friend was a "sports rivalry." He described this friendship as:

> [A] sort of love-hate relationship. There were times when we. . . I remember fighting him. I remember getting into fights, but at the same time I remember going to his house and having good times. It was never a real deep relationship.

It is this sort of ambiguity that was most characteristic of men's descriptions of their relationships with teammates. "Forged in battle," these are often the closest relationships that these men ever have; yet athletic battles as often take place among teammates as they do with other teams. This ambiguity can be examined as a manifestation of the development of masculine identities within the competitive, hierarchical world of athletic careers.

THE TEAM STRUCTURE: ANTAGONISTIC COOPERATION

The public face that a team attempts to present to the rest of the world is that of a "family," whose shared goal of winning games and championships bonds its individual members together. But the structure of athletic careers is such that individuals on teams are constantly competing against each other—first for a place on the team, then for playing time, for public recognition and star status, and eventually, just to stay on the team. Rather than being purely cooperative enterprises, then, athletic teams are characterized by what Riesman (1953) calls "antagonistic cooperation." In sport, just as in the modern bureaucratic corporation, "a cult of teamwork conceals the struggle for survival" (Lasch, 1979, p. 209).

Coaches attempt to mitigate the potentially negative consequences of this individual struggle for survival by emphasizing the importance of "team play." In fact, several men said that having learned to "play a role" on a team, rather than needing to be the star, was a valuable lesson they learned through sports. For them, teamwork was an exciting and satisfying experience. As Jon, a former high school basketball player, put it: I like the feeling of getting on a team where you might not have the best individuals, but with teamwork and somehow a sense of togetherness, you can knock somebody off that's better than you.

This sort of satisfaction, though, appeared to be more common among young males like Jon who knew that they were not stars, who knew that their futures did not lie in athletic careers. As he put it:

> I would never have gotten my name in the newspaper—maybe if I had been a better scorer, but I never was. The way I would make my niche in basketball was obviously by being a good passer—I always got a thrill out of it.

344

MESSNER

For those who did see themselves as stars (or potential stars), who were committed to athletic careers, the competition with teammates was very real and often very intense. Athletes have developed their own ways of dealing with the structured reality that one teammate's success might mean one's own demotion. For instance, the fact that new players on a team often pose a threat to the veterans is dealt with through ritualized testing and hazing of rookies. A former pro football player, Billy, said that as a rookie on his college football team, he had to "earn the respect" of the older players before being accepted as a teammate. He did this by "getting knocked on my butt by them," and then in turn, "knocking them on their butts. After that, they respected me." Nathan, another former pro football player, agreed that "you get your respect, but you have to earn it. . . . They won't just give it to you right off." Part of the ritual involves showing the proper deference to the veteran players, not appearing so "cocky." One year, Nathan said:

> A rookie came in, and the veterans hadn't even come to camp yet, and this guy was talking about what he was going to do to [the team's veteran defensive stars], how he was gonna be the leading pass receiver. He lasted about 2 days. They hurt him, and I think he stayed in the training room about 2 weeks. Came out, lasted another day, and they sent him back. Finally he had to be cut from the team. People were popping him, right, just because he had a loud mouth.

Once a team is formed, a coach does his best to channel these sorts of internal antagonisms toward an external "enemy" (Sabo & Panepinto, 1990). As Gene explained:

345

> No matter what you hear about teams—they don't get along, they fight each other—you just try to let some outsider come in and come up fightin' one of 'em. It'd be like two brothers who fight like cats and dogs, but you let somebody else mess with one of them and he's gotta be ready to deal with both of them at one time. Same thing: A team *is* a family. It *has* to be.

Lurking just below the surface of this "family" rhetoric, though, lies intense, often cutthroat competition. Several men told me of difficult, even destructive relationships that developed between themselves and teammates as a result of competition for individual rewards and recognition. This was especially true in cases where two players were vying to be seen as the star of the team. Jim told of a high school basketball game in which his teammate/rival was "basket-hanging," and had gotten 26 easy points by halftime, which put him within 5 points of the school record.

> I must have fed Tim [the ball] eight times in the first half. At halftime, our center says to me, "Hey, this is bullshit. I'm getting all the rebounds, and I haven't gotten a shot. Why can't Tim get a few rebounds instead of all the [easy baskets] at the other end?" So I said, "Oh, I'll take care of that," 'cause I was the one throwing

him the ball all the time. So I'd get the outlet pass and I'd just bring it up. Tim ended up with 28 points. I'm sure he still begrudges that—I mean, he could have broken every record in the book, but anybody who could make a layup could have done that.

The intensity of this kind of competition between teammates can actually increase as one moves up the ladder of athletic careers, where the stakes are higher. Chris told me that through college, friendships with basketball teammates were important and meaningful to him, but when he got to the professional ranks, he found it was "all business," with little room for the development of close friendships:

> [When you get] to pro ball, all of a sudden you got assholes out there. It's the money. The competition is greater. You're dealing with politics. I was drafted second round. They had a lot of draft picks and it was real cutthroat. So you see a lot of good players come and go. It was tight. You're dealing with money. You're dealing with jobs. It's a business, and that really turned me off. I had dreamed it would be *everything*, and I got there and it was a job. You know, a fuckin' job where a man screams at your ass.

At times, these sorts of antagonisms are racially oriented. Thomas, for instance, described his shock in his first year of pro football in finding that black players were second-class citizens on his team:

> There was no togetherness on that team. Race had a lot to do with it. And money. They didn't want no brother making no money . . . You know, a white player would walk into the damn locker room and tell one of the brothers, "Turn off that damn nigger music' I don't want to hear that shit!" And the brother would go over and turn the music off! Boy, oh boy, when the guy turned off the music, that just about blew my mind! I said to myself, this cat ain't got no heart. . . And then they went after me, 'cause I'm the rookie, the number-one draft choice. They wanted me to sing. *I ain't singing: Fuck 'em. I'm a grown man. I ain't gonna sing.* Then they tried to get me on the football field and I ended up fuckin' around and hurtin' a couple of people 'cause I knew what they were gonna do. It didn't take me very long to get 'em quiet.

Few men described such overly antagonistic racial conflicts on the team, yet most did say that informal relationship networks on teams tended to be organized along racial lines. For instance, Larry, a black man who had played college football recalled that: "For the most part, the white guys hung out with each other, and the brothers hung out with the brothers." Nevertheless, several white and black men told me that through sports they had their first real contact with people from different racial groups, and for a few of them, good friendships began. Unfortunately, most of these friendships were not strong enough to persist outside the context of the team situation, where social, cultural, peer, and familial pressures made it difficult to nurture and maintain cross-racial friendships.[4]

How do we explain men's tendency to describe their friendships with team-mates both in highly romanticized terms of "family" and as destructively competitive? First, the structured system of "antagonistic cooperation" clearly puts teammates into ambiguous relationships with each other. Yet the structure of the athletic context does not fully or adequately explain the experi-ence of the participants. We also need to consider the gendered psychological and emotional tendencies that these males brought to their athletic experi-ences.[5]

As I outlined earlier, Rubin (1983; 1985) argues that men's early develop-mental experiences have left them with a deep fear of intimacy (which she defined as the ability and willingness to mutually share one's inner life with another person).[6] As a result, though men do want to spend time with other men, they tend to maintain emotional distance between themselves by orga-nizing their time together around an activity that is external to themselves. As Jim stated above, "Sports provide that." Here men can enjoy the company of other men—even become close—without having to become intimate in ways that may threaten their "firm ego boundaries," and thus their fragile masculine gender identities.

We can now begin to make sense of former professional basketball player Bill Bradley's (1977) seemingly paradoxical description of his relationships with his teammates as "warm and real, but never intimate." Bradley seems most comforted here by the simultaneous existence of a certain kind of *close-ness* with a clear sense of *boundaries and distance*. This seeming paradox is ex-plained when we consider it in light of the interaction between masculine gender identity and the gendered structure of sport as a social institution: The hierarchical and rule-bound structure of athletic careers, and especially the structure of "antagonistic cooperation" on the team, dovetails with men's am-bivalent need to develop closeness without intimacy with other men.[7] In short, competitive activities such as sports mediate men's relationships with each other in ways that allow them to develop a powerful bond together, while at the same time preventing the development of what Rubin calls "in-timacy."

Thus far, I have argued that the depth of athletes' friendships with each other is limited by the affinity between the structure of sport and the structure of developing masculine gender identities. But to simply leave it that men's friendships constitute "bonding without intimacy" belies the depth of affec-tion that so many of these men expressed for each other. In fact, my research

MESSNER

suggests that male athletes do tend to develop what Swain (1989, p. 72) calls "covert intimacy." a "private, often nonverbal, context-specific form of communication." Whereas women's style of intimacy emphasizes the importance of talk, in men's covert intimacy, "closeness is in the 'doing,'" and "actions speak louder than words and carry greater interpersonal value" (p. 77).

Though it appears to be true that "men and women have different styles of intimacy that reflect the often-separate realms in which they express it" (Swain, p. 78), there is a danger in adopting a stance of simply viewing men's and women's friendships as "separate but equal." For instance, Swain discusses a man who told him that "a couple of girls picked up [him and his friend] and we got laid and everything . . . after, [he and his friend] went out and had a few beers and compared notes." Swain (p. 77) concludes that "though this sort of quote might imply sexual exploitation . . . the commonality gained from a shared life experience did provide meaningful interaction among the men." Clearly, this talk among men is "meaningful interaction" *when examined from the point of view of the men.* But rather than simply viewing male friends' sexual talk about women in terms of its functions for male friendships, it is also crucial to examine the ways that this kind of talk among men might contribute to the construction of a certain kind of attitudes toward and relationships with women. In other words, I am suggesting that we move away from examining men's friendships with each other from a *feminine* standpoint (Rubin), or from a *masculine* standpoint (Swain), and instead ask feminist questions: How are male athletes' friendships with each other affected by—and in turn affect—their attitudes toward and relationships with women? And how do these attitudes and relationships contribute to the construction of the larger gender order?

SEXUALITY AND SEXUAL ATTITUDES

"Big Man on Campus." "Sexual Athlete." For many, these terms conjure up the dominant cultural image of the athlete on campus: He is extremely popular, self-assured, and (hetero) sexually active. Other boys and young men are envious of the ease with which he can "get women." My interviews at times revealed a grain of truth to this popular sterotype of the athlete. Chris, for instance, said that even as a second-string professional basketball player, it was:

(J)ust the good life [laughs]—I mean, you could wave at one way up in the 15th row, and after the game, she's standin' right there by the locker room . . . that's what makes it fun, you know.

Similarly, when asked how he related to others when in school, Thomas said:

I liked to be the big man on campus, and sports was a highlight because it gave me that opportunity. *Everybody* knew who I was. Big Tom. *Everybody* knew who I was.

348

MESSNER

On the surface, these two statements would seem to affirm the dominant sterotype of the athlete as a confident young man at ease with himself and with his sexuality among his peers. Interestingly though, when asked about their *specific* relationships with females, a very different picture emerged. "Big Tom," for instance, stated:

> Girls, in high school, were really not prime in my life [laughs]—. . . When I was in high school, I thought I was an ugly guy. You know, being under a lot of pressure, and being so much bigger than everybody, and everybody's always looking at you. In high school, you don't know what looks *mean*— it could be good, it could be bad. At one time I felt like I was a freak, so I was more or less into myself. I don't think I had one girlfriend.

This sense of awkwardness and insecurity with respect to girls and women seemed almost universal among the men I interviewed. David's shyness in high school was compounded by his low-class status, so for him, sports became an escape from dealing with girls:

> No doubt I was shy, and I think it had to do with the fact that if I did make a date with a girl, how was I gonna' go? What was I gonna spend? 'Cause I had none of it. So I just used sports as an escape.

Clarence, a high school football player, had similar problems with girls:

> In my senior year [of high school], I remember dating all these girls, [but] I wasn't sexually active. I hadn't had intercourse—I might have done a little petting, but never any genital stuff. I think I was popular, and was seen as an attractive boy, but I didn't have a sense of it. I just thought I was absolutely ugly as hell.

Several of the men I interviewed recalled hoping that being seen as an athlete would give them the confidence to overcome their insecurity with girls. Jon said that he had hoped that being on the high school basketball team would help him overcome his shyness "and make it easier to talk with girls. It didn't." But several of these men reported that they did eventually develop ways to "talk to girls," despite their shyness. For instance, Eldon, a black former college track and field competitor, said that in high school:

> I was lame, as they called it. So I didn't know how to do women so well. My stepmother threw a 16th birthday party for me and invited a lot of friends, and I remember that day, trying on a lot of the roles that I saw guys playing, and it kind of shocked me because the women took it seriously, you know. That was a big turning point for me. I didn't particularly like, especially, some of the black modes of relating to women, I thought were *stupid*—just *nonsense*—sweet nothings seemed silly to me. [But] anyway, I tried it, my version of it, and to my surprise some woman took it seriously. That meant it was possible [laughs]. . .

Calvin, a former college basketball player, described a similar transformation from tortured shyness with girls in high school to developing a "rap" with women in college:

> I was just scared, and bashful, and shy. I did not know what to say or what to do. It was very uncomfortable. This was a very bad time, 'cause you're always around a lot of girls at parties . . . very uncomfortable in groups and with individuals . . . Finally [I went] off to college and went to the extreme of trying to attract a lot of girls, [and was] semi-successful. You knew you had to have a date on Fridays, and knew you had to have one on Saturdays, and so you just walked through the student union, and you'd just have this rap you'd thought of, and you'd just put it on. It was peer pressure. . . I'm naturally a shy person . . . but somehow in college I was able to somehow fall into the right kinds of things to do and say.

We can see from these stories that developing a "rap" with women becomes an almost ritualized way that a young man helps himself overcome an otherwise paralyzing shyness, a sense of "lameness" when trying to relate to women. Developing a "rap" with women involves a certain dramaturgy, a conscious self-manipulation ("you'd just put it on"), and one result is that girls and women become the objects of men's verbal manipulation. And this specific form of verbal manipulation of women does not spring naturally or magically from men's shyness. Rather, it is socially learned through the male peer group. Notice that Eldon learned to "do women" by watching his male peers. And Calvin, though somewhat mystified as to how he was able "somehow" to overcome his shyness and "fall into the right things to say," also cites "peer pressure" as a motivating force. Clearly, an analysis of the development of men's sexual relationships with women must take into account the ways that male peer groups structure attitudes and feelings about sexuality and emotional commitment to women.

In his study of male college fraternities, Lyman (1987) argues that there is an erotic basis to the fraternal bond in male homosocial groups. In the past, the key to maintaining the male bond was the denial of the erotic. Organized sport, as it arose in the nineteenth and early twentieth centuries was based, in part, on a Victorian antisexual ethic. First, it was believed that homosocial institutions such as sport would "masculinize" young males in an otherwise "feminized" culture, thus preventing homosexuality.[8] And second, the popular (and "scientific") belief in the "spermatic economy" held that "the human male possessed a limited quantity of sperm that could be invested in various enterprises, ranging from business through sport to copulation and procreation. In this context, the careful regulation of the body was the only path to the conservation of energy" (Mrozek, 1983, p. 20). As Crosset (1990, p. 53) points out, in a social context which held that young men's precious energies would be drained off should they expend too much sperm, sport was elevated as the key "to regenerate the male body and thus make efficient use of male energy."

Some of the older men in my study went through adolescence and early adulthood when the remnants of the ideology of the "spermatic economy" were still alive. Eldon, for instance, said that as a young runner, from the late 1940s through the mid-1950s, he had been "a bit cautious about sex, because I still had some old-fashioned notions about sexual energy [being] competitive with athletic stuff." Most of these men, though, came of age during the sexual revolution of the 1960s and early 1970s, when the dominant credo became, "If it feels good, do it." As a result, the male peer group, within the athletic context, became a place where sexual activity and *talk* of sexual activity (real or imagined) were key components of the peer status-system.

But if the bond among men is erotic, and the culture is increasingly telling them "if it feels good, do it," what is to prevent the development of sexual relations among these young men who are playing, showering, dressing, and living together in such close quarters? The answer is that the erotic bond among male friends and teammates is neutralized through overt homophobia, and through the displacement of the erotic toward women as objects of sexually aggressive talk and practice in the male peer group. In boyhood, adolescent, and young adult male peer groups, "fag," "girl," and "woman" are insults that are used almost interchangeably. Through this practice, heterosexual masculinity is collectively constructed through the denigration of homosexuality and feminity as "not-male." For example, Bill, a former high school football and basketball player, described how his athletic male peer group helped to structure his own public presentation of his sexuality:

351

I was shy [with girls]—I hung out more with guys. I never dated. I never was real intimate with anyone. It was just kinda scary because I thought I'd get teased by my peers.

(For not being involved with women?)

For being involved! But you *gotta* be involved to the point where you get 'em into bed, you know, you *fuck 'em*, or something like that, yeah, that's real important [laughs]—but as far as being intimate, or close, I wasn't. And that wasn't real important. Just so I could prove my heterosexuality it was real important. But I always wanted to look good to females—'cause I didn't have the personality [laughs]—*to get 'em into bed!* So I wanted to be able to have the *body* and the, uh, the sort of friends around who, uh, who admired me in some sort of way, to have that pull.

This sort of use of women as objects of sexual conquest is important for gaining status in athletic male peer groups, but also tends to impoverish young males' relationships with females. As Neal, a former high school football player put it, he and his friends on the team used to:

[T]ell a lot of stories about girls. I guess it was a way to show our masculinity. . . [But] I never got emotionally involved with any of the girls I went out with. I never got close to any of them.

The link between young males' tendency to "tell [sexual] stories about girls" and their lack of intimacy with girls and young women is an important one. As Lyman points out, young males commonly use sexually aggressive stories and jokes as a means of "negotiating" the "latent tension and aggression they feel toward each other." And they also are using this joking relationship to "negotiate the tension they felt between sexual interest in the girls and fear of commitment to them . . . [they use] hostile joking to negotiate their fear of the 'loss of control' implied by intimacy" (Lyman, 1987, p. 156). Thus, while talk of sex with females bonds the males together, the specific forms of sexual talk (sexual objectification and conquest of women) help males deal with their terror of intimacy with women (which many of them described, above, as "shyness," "Lameness," and such). Again, in the words of Lyman (p. 151): "In dealing with women, the group separated intimacy from sex, defining the male bond as intimate but not sexual (homosocial), and relationships with women as sexual but not intimate (heterosexual)."

In fact, male peer groups tend to police their own members in terms of intimacy with females. Though male peer groups routinely confer high status on one who is sexually active (or says he is), they also commonly respond to a friend who starts to spend a lot of time with a girlfriend by taunting him that he is "pussywhipped." The result of this kind of lockerroom culture is that many young men end up suffering from a kind of "'sexual schizophrenia.' Their minds lead them toward eroticism while their hearts pull them toward emotional intimacy" (Sabo, 1989, p. 39). Some young men deal with this split by keeping their emotional attachments with females a secret, while continuing to participate in lockerroom discussions about sexuality with their male peers. Frank, a former high school basketball and tennis player, had one such relationship in high school:

We started sneaking around and going out late at night and no one else knew. I didn't tell any of my friends. . . We got along great, sexually and emotionally, though she said I didn't express my feelings enough. . . .

In a very real sense, these young males' relationships with girls and women— whether sexual or not—were *constructed through* (indeed, were often distorted by and subordinated to) their friendships with their male teammates.

At times, the male peer group's policing of its members' relationships with females took on a racial angle. Larry, for instance, said that when he was a college football player:

[T]he biggest conflict we had was black males dating white girls. . . The white males would call up the white females and call them whores, bitches, and prosti-

MESSNER

tutes—you know, insulting language, like "if you ball him, you'll ball anybody, so come over here and ball me, too."

In this case, then, the peer group was not only policing intimacy with women, but also attempting to impose controls on interracial sexuality.

The need to prove one's manhood through sexual conquests of women was experienced as a burden by many young heterosexual males, and was sometimes complicated by racial tensions, but it was especially oppressive for gay men. In this youth, Mike had thrown himself into sports, rather than into dancing, largely because he was terrified that people might find out that he was gay. Sports allowed him to construct a masculine public image. Yet within sports, this meant that he had constantly to construct a heterosexual image:

> I hated high school. I mean, I just didn't know who I was. I think I had quite a bit of negative self-esteem at that time, 'cause I really felt different . . . I mean, I didn't drink, I didn't like to screw around, and this was what all my friends did, so I felt compelled to go along with this stuff, and all the time hating it . . . I dated some women, some that I loved because they were just really fine people—uh, physically, there was not a great deal of passion. *For males*, there was a passion . . . [But] homophobia was rampant, especially in athletics. You see, I think a lot of atheletes go into athletics for the same reason I did. They need to prove their maleness. And I did, I really admit it. I wanted to be viewed as a male. Otherwise I would be a dancer today. I wanted the male, macho image of an athlete. . . I felt I've gotta hide this thing—'cause I know what they were thinking: If I were gay, they would see me as less than a man, *or not a man*. So I'm gonna *be a man*, 'cause *that's what I am*. So I was protected by a very hard shell—and I was *clearly* aware of what I was doing . . . just as a lot of gay men are aware that they're living a lie . . . it's a terrible thing to live with.

Though his secret knowledge of his own homosexuality made this process a much more *conscious* one for Mike ("I was *clearly* aware of what I was doing"), his public construction of manhood-as-heterosexual was not all that different from what his straight counterparts were doing. Whether gay or straight, the denial and denigration of gayness and femininity (in one's self and in others) were important keys to these young men's construction of masculine identities and status in their male peer group.[9] As Mike said:

> Go into any locker room and watch and listen, and you'll hear the same kind of garbage—I call it garbage now, and I thought it was garbage then, but I felt compelled to go along with it, because I wanted that image. . . . And I know others who did, too. I know a *lot* of athletes are gay. And I think a lot of athletes are attracted to athletics because they're fighting feelings of tenderness—not necessarily gay—but they're fighting feminine qualities. . . . I know a lot of football players who very quietly and very secretly like to paint, or play piano, and they do it quietly because this to them is threatening if it's known by others.

353

The pressure to be seen by one's peers as "a man"—indeed, the pressure to see one's *self* as "a man"—kept most young males in conformity (at least on the surface) with this homophobic and sexist locker-room "garbage." Conformity with sexist and homophobic locker-room culture was a way—for gay as well as for non-gay men—to publicly construct their gender identities. But gay athletes were far more likely to see this construction of identity *as a conscious strategy* than were heterosexual athletes (Pronger, 1990). As Brittan (1989, p. 41) explains, "In everyday life most heterosexuals do not have to do too much identity work because they tend to function in contexts in which heterosexuality is taken for granted."

For a few, though, conformity with what Mike called locker-room "garbage" led them to question—even reject—the jock culture and the specific form of masculinity and sexuality that predominated there. Brent, for instance, said that toward the end of high school:

> I really got turned off to the way the guys were relating to the girls. It was really ugly in certain ways, like just treating them like objects, totally judging them by their surface appearances, talking amongst themselves in really abusive language about girls, how they're gonna do this or that to them. . . I thought it was wrong. I thought that people shouldn't be treated that way. I started to realize that the way I related to women was *not* the way these guys were relating to them, and therefore I didn't want to relate with them on that level. So I started to distance myself from the same activities, and started to feel really alienated from my buddies.

354

This sort of realization about—and rejection of—the sexist treatment of women was a rare exception to the rule. And it is significant that this realization was made by a young athlete who several years earlier had come to realize that he was not a "career athlete." That he had already begun to disengage from his athletic career meant that he had less invested in the athletic male peer group. For young men who were fully committed to athletic careers, this sort of rejection of one of the key bonds of the male peer group would have amounted to career suicide. So whether they liked it or not, most went along with it. And when the "garbage" went beyond verbal sparring and bragging about sexual conquests to actual behavior, peer group values encouraged these young men to treat females as objects of conquest. Frank described a "night on the town" with his male friends. He was a virgin in high school and terrified at his own lack of sexual experience. But when they hit the town, he said, "We were like wolves hunting down prey. Dave told me, 'If a girl doesn't give it up in 60 seconds, drop her!'"

It is this sort of masculine peer group dynamic that is at the heart of the rape culture (Beneke, 1982; Herman, 1984). Kanin (1984) argues that college men who have experienced pressure from their current male friends to engage in sexual activity are more likely to commit acquaintance rape. Similarly, Koss and

MESSNER

Dinero (1988, p. 144) find in their national study that "involvement in peer groups that reinforce highly sexualized views of women" is an important predictor of "sexually aggressive behavior" by college males. And Warshaw (1988, p. 112) concludes from her research on date and acquaintance rape that "Athletic teams are breeding grounds for rape [because they] are often populated by men who are steeped in sexist, rape-supportive beliefs." Indeed, sportswriter Rich Hoffman states in a story in the *Philadelphia Daily News* that between 1983 and 1986, a U.S. college athlete was reported for sexual assault an average of once every 18 days (cited in Warshaw, 1988, p. 113).

Only a fraction of male athletes actually rape women. The (mostly verbal) sexual objectification of women that is an important basis of male athletes' friendships with each other actually hurts young males by making intimacy with women more difficult to develop. But ultimately, it is women who pay the price for young men's tendency to use sexual talk of women to mediate their relations with other men. Johnson (1988, p. 119) argues:

> That the peer group's pressure to be heterosexual occurs in a context in which women are sex-objectified may well have the consequence of making it difficult for males to become sexually aroused in a relationship in which they do not feel dominant over the female. If one learns about sexuality in the context of being rewarded by other males for "scoring," for "getting pussy" or just "getting *it*," then this does not augur well for egalitarian sex.

CONCLUSION

355

Feminist scholars argue that sport is an institution constructed largely through gender relations (Bryson, 1987; Hall, 1988; Messner, 1988; Theberge, 1981). The feminist critique of sport has revealed that within athletics, specific kinds of masculine identity, values, attitudes, and relationships are constructed (Kidd, 1987; Messner, 1987; Messner & Sabo, 1990; Sabo, 1985). Though an individual athlete may feel as though his athletic career is a lonely, individual quest for success, in fact, he is actively participating in a social process of masculine gender identity construction. And this identity construction is accomplished through relationships with others within institutional contexts (Connell, 1990).

When I asked former athletes to talk about the kinds of friendships that they had with teammates, most of them immediately dropped into the language of "family." This was not too surprising. Like family relations, friendships with teammates are often among the closest relationships that young men develop. But underneath the talk of respect, love, and closeness among teammates lies another reality: Athletic teams, like families, are also characterized by internal antagonisms rooted in hierarchy. And these socially structured competitive antagonisms among teammates are exacerbated by boys' and young men's tendency to fear certain kinds of closeness with others.

This is not to say that men do not develop intimate friendships among athletic teammates. The men I interviewed developed a kind of *covert intimacy*, an intimacy that is characterized by *doing together*, rather than by mutual talk about their inner lives. That the men whom I interviewed valued these friendships is beyond question. In fact, they often spoke reverently of the friendships they developed while involved in athletic careers. But I have suggested in this chapter that in evaluating men's friendships, it is desirable to move beyond either judging them (negatively) from a *feminine* standpoint, or observing that, from a *masculine* standpoint, men value the particular kinds of intimacy they have with male friends. Instead, I have argued that it is important to look at men's covert intimacy in the larger context of structured power relations between men and women, and between men and other men. When examined in this way, we can see that, though men often feel good about their athletic friendships, the fact that these kinds of friendships are often cemented by sexist and homophobic talk (and, at times, actions) suggests that men's covert intimacy within sports plays a part in the construction of a larger gender order in which men's power over women is reasserted (often through sexuality). Moreover, it is revealed that through these kinds of athletic friendships and peer-group dynamics, heterosexual men marginalize gay men, while policing and limiting any "feminine" tendencies in themselves. Homophobia discounts the possible existence of erotic desire among men, while aggressive sexuality expressed toward women displaces the erotic bond among men toward a devalued female object. As a result, the bond among males is cemented, while the ability to develop egalitarian relationships with either males or females is impoverished.

Overall, these sorts of relationships among men contribute to the construction of a gender order that is dominated by heterosexual males. But there are contradictions in this construction of masculinity that suggest potential avenues for change. First, individually, men's lives are emotionally impoverished by the limits of the kinds of relationships that they commonly develop in organized sports. It is possible that the recognition of these limits will lead some men to reject the promise of masculine power and status in favor of joining together with women in constructing a more humane world and more egalitarian relationships. Perhaps more important, concrete analyses of men's identities and relationships in sport reveal that, although their collective actions serve to construct men's overall power and privilege over women, men do not equally share the fruits of this privilege. What we observe in sport is the construction of a *dominant form* of masculinity—what Connell (1987) calls "hegemonic masculinity."

Outside of sport—and indeed, submerged within sport—there are clearly groups of marginalized and subordinated men who are oppressed by narrow constructions of hegemonic masculinity. The example of gay athletes, discussed above, is a case-in-point. And poor and ethnic minority male athletes,

MESSNER

though they often see sport as an arena in which to construct a respected masculine identity, are far more often than not locked into their subordinate class and racial status because of their single-minded focus on sports success (Messner, 1989). If gay men, poor men, and minority men can reject these narrow conceptions of masculinity (which ultimately oppress them), there is the possibility that they might see in feminism a key to the development of an egalitarian society. For it is only within the context of egalitarianism that truly intimate friendships can develop asnd flourish.

NOTES

1. This chapter is part of a larger study published as *Power at Play: Sports and the Problem of Masculinity* (Beacon Press, 1992). I thank Bob Blauner, Pierrette Hondag-neu-Sotelo, Michael Kimmel, Peter Nardi, and Don Sabo for comments and sugges-tions on earlier drafts of this work.

2. My research aimed at exploring and interpreting the meanings that males them-selves attribute to their participation in athletic careers. The tape-recorded interviews were semistructured, and took from 1½ to 6 hours to conduct. I asked each man to talk about four broad eras in his life: (a) his earliest experiences with sports in boy-hood; (b) his athletic career; (c) retirement or disengagement from the athletic career; and (d) life after the athletic career. In each era, I focused the interview on the mean-ings of "success and failure," and on the boy's/man's relationships with family, with other males with women, and with his own body. Most of the men I interviewed had been involved in the (U.S.) "major sports"—football, basketball, baseball, track. All had at some time in their lives based their identities largely on their roles as athletes and could therefore be said to have had "athletic careers." Twelve had played organized sports through high school, 11 had played through college, and 7 had been profession-al athletes. At the time of the interviews, most had been retired from playing organized sports for at least 5 years. Their ages ranged from 21 to 48, with the median at 33. Fourteen were black, 14 were white, and 2 were Latino.

3. All names of interviewees used in this article are pseudonyms.

4. C.R.L. James' eloquent description of a painful reunion that he had with a for-mer cricket teammate/friend seems to capture the essence of cross-racial friendships that develop in the athletic context: "We had nothing to say to each other, our social circles were too different, and he never came again. He went to Europe to study med-icine and years afterwards, when we were grown men, I met him once or twice. We greeted each other warmly, but I was always embarrassed and I think he was too. There was a guilty feeling that something had gone wrong with us. Something had. The school-tie can be transplanted, but except on annual sporting occasions the old school-tie cannot be. *It is a bond of school only on the surface. The link is between family and friends, between members of the class or caste*" (James, 1983, p. 41, emphasis added).

5. Duquin (1984), in her comparison of male and female college athletes, found that female athetes are more likely to bring "an ethic of care" to their athletic experi-ences, while males are more likely to employ "the orientation of self-interest." This suggests that men's gendering identities are more consistent with the hierarchical structure and the value on individual competition that characterize the current sports world. Men would be more likely to be comfortable with the kinds of relationships

357

MESSNER

that are developed in this world, while women would be more likely to attempt to find ways to develop more intimate relationships with teammates. This difference might also explain why female athletes are more likely to attribute the causes of their successes to factors "external" to themselves (coaches, teammates, family, luck), while males are more comfortable taking individual credit for their successes (see McHugh, Duquin, & Frieze, 1978).

6. Rubin's definition of "intimacy," while helpful in constructing her typology of gender differences in friendship patterns, is class biased. Her emphasis on *verbalization* of one's "inner life" is based on a very upper-middle-class, therapeutic definition of initimacy, which might ignore or devalue other, nonverbal forms of expression that might be more common in social groups who are not so immersed in the professional/therapeutic culture.

7. In the words of Ian Craib, the relationship between structure and personality is best viewed as an "elective affinity. The 'normal' structure and operation of institutions, as they have developed in modern capitalist society, makes use of, and perhaps routinely (though not necessarily) confirms the routine structure and processes of the male personality" (Craib, 1987, p. 737).

8. Here are some of the roots of the still-popular misconception that male homosexuality is connected to some essential "femininity," a confusion of *sexual identity* with *gender identity*. This confusion is clearly a cultural manifestation (see W. L. Williams, 1986).

9. C. L. Williams (1989) observes that homophobia and misogyny are a common part of basic training for male Marines.

REFERENCES

Balswick, J. (1976). The inexpressive male: A tragedy of American Society. In D. David & R. Brannon (Eds.), *The forty-nine percent majority* (pp. 55–67). Reading, MA: Addison-Wesley.

Beneke, T. (1982). *Men on rape.* New York: St. Martin's Press.

Bradley, B. (1977). *Life on the run.* New York: Bantam.

Brittan, A. (1988). *Masculinity and power.* Oxford & New York: Basil Blackwell.

Bryson, L. (1987). Sport and the maintenance of masculine hegemony. *Women's Studies International Forum, 10,* 349–360.

Cancian, F. M. (1987). *Love in America: Gender and self-development.* Cambridge: Cambridge University Press.

Chodorow, N. (1978). *The reproduction of mothering.* Berkeley: University of California Press.

Connell, R. W. (1987). *Gender and power,* Palo Alto, CA: Stanford University Press.

Connell, R. W. (1980). An iron man: The body and some contradictions of hegemonic masculinity. In M. A. Messner & D. F. Sabo (Eds.), *Sport, men and the gender order: Critical feminist perspectives* (pp. 83–96). Champaign, IL: Human Kinetics.

Craib, I. (1987). Masculinity and male dominance. *The Sociological review, 38,* 721–743.

Crosset, T. (1990). *Masculinity, sexuality, and the development of early modern sport.* In M. A. Messner & D. F. Sabo (Eds.), *Sport, men and the gender order: Critical-feminist perspectives* (pp. 45–54). Champaign, IL: Human Kinetics.

Dinnerstein, D. (1976). *The mermaid and the minotaur: Sexual arrangements and human malaise.* New York: Harper Colophon.

Duquin, M. (1984). Power and authority: Moral consensus and conformity in sport. *International Review for Sociology of Sport, 19*, 295–304.

Farrell, W. (1975). *The liberated man.* New York: Bantam.

Fasteau, M. F. (1974). *The male machine.* New York: McGraw–Hill.

Gilder, G. (1973). *Sexual suicide.* New York: Bantam.

Gilligan, C. (1982). *In a different voice: Psychological theory and women's development.* Cambridge, MA: Harvard University Press.

Hall, M. A. (1988). The discourse on gender and sport: From femininity to feminism. *Sociology and Sport Journal, 5*, 330–340.

Herman, D. (1984). The rape culture. In J. Freeman (Ed.). *Women: A feminist perspective* (3rd ed.) (pp. 20–38). Mountain View, CA: Mayfield.

James, C.R.L. (1983). *Beyond a boundary.* New York: Pantheon.

Johnson, M. M. (1988). *Strong mothers, weak wives: The search for gender equality.* Berkeley: University of California Press.

Kanin, E. J. (1984). Date rape: Differential sexual socialization and relative deprivation. *Victimology, 9*, 95–108.

Kidd, B. (1987). Sports and masculinity. In M. Kaufman (Ed.), *Beyond patriarch: Essays by men on pleasure, power, and change* (pp. 250–265). Toronto: Oxford University Press.

Koss, M. P., & Dinero, T. E. (1988). Predictors of sexual aggression among a national sample of male college studies. In R. A. Prentky & V. Quinsey (Eds.), *Human Sexual Aggression: Current Perspectives. Annals of the New York Academy of Sciences, 528*, 133–146.

Lasch, C. (1979). *The culture of narcissism.* New York: Warner.

Lyman, P. (1987). The fraternal bond as a joking relationships: A case study of sexist jokes in male group bonding. In M. S. Kimmel (Ed.), *Changing men: New directions in research on men and masculinity* (pp. 148–163). Newbury Park, CA: Sage.

McHugh, M. C., Duquin, M. E., & Frieze, I. H. (1978). Beliefs about success and failure: Attribution and the female athlete. In C. A. Oglesby (Ed.), *Women and sport: From myth to reality* (pp. 173–191). Philadelphia: Lea & Farber.

Messner, M. (1987). The meaning of success: The athletic experience and the development of male identity. In H. Brod (Ed.), *The making of masculinities: The new men's studies* (pp. 193–210). Boston: Allen & Unwin.

Messner, M. (1988). Sports asnd male domination: The female athlete as contested ideological terrain. *Sociology of Sport Journal, 5*, 197–211.

Messner, M. (1989). Masculinities and athletic careers. *Gender & Society, 3*, 71–88.

Messner, M. A., & Sabo, D. F. (Eds.). (1990). *Sport, men and the gender order: Critical feminist perspectives.* Champaign, IL: Human Kinetics.

Morin, S. F., & Garfinkel, E. M. (1978). Male homophobia. *Journal of Social Issues, 34*(1).

Morozek, D. J. (1983). *Sport and the American Mentality: 1880–1910.* Knoxville: University of Tennessee Press.

Pleck, J., & Sawyer, J. (Eds.). (1974). *Men and masculinity.* Englewood Cliffs, NJ: Prentice–Hall.

Pronger, B. (1990). Gay jocks: A phenomenology of gay men in athletics. In M. A. Messner & D. F. Sabo (Eds.), *Sport, men and the gender order: Critical feminist perspectives* (pp. 141–152). Champaign, IL: Human Kinetics.

Riesman, D. (1953). *The lonely crowd: A study of the changing American character.* New Haven: Yale University Press.

359

MESSNER

Rubin, L.d B. (1983). *Intimate strangers: Men and women together*. New York: Harper & Row.

Rubin, L. B. (1985). *Just friends: The role of relationship in our lives*. New York: Harper & Row.

Sabo, D. (1985). Sport, patriarchy and male identity: New questions about men and sport. *Arena Review, 9*, 1–30.

Sabo, D. (1989, Winter/Spring). The myth of the sexual athlete. *Changing Men: Issues in Gender, Sex, and Politics, 20*, 38–39.

Sabo, D. F., Penepinto, J. (1990). Football ritual and the social reproduction of masculinity. In M. A. Messner & D. F. Sabo (Eds.), *Sport, men and the gender order: Critical feminist perspectives* (pp. 115–126). Champaign, IL: Human Kinetics.

Swain, S. (1989). Covert intimacy: Closeness in men's friendships. In B. J. Risman & P. Schwartz (Eds.), *Gender in intimate relationships: A microstructural approach* (pp. 71–86). Belmont. CA: Wadsworth.

Theberge, N. (1981). A critique of critiques: Radical and feminist writings on sport. *Social Forces, 60*, 2.

Tiger, L. (1969). *Men in groups*. London: Nelson.

Warshaw, R. (1988). *I never called it rape*. New York: Harper & Row.

Williams, C. L. (1989). *Gender differences at work: Women and men in nontraditional occupations*. Berkeley: University of California Press.

Williams, W. L. (1986). *The spirit and the flesh: Sexual diversity in American Indian cultures*. Boston: Beacon.

PART VI
SEXUALITY AND PLEASURE
De-forming Desire

SEXUAL BIOLOGY AND THE SYMBOLISM OF THE NATURAL[1]

Leonore Tiefer

chapter 20

INTRODUCTION

THE LANGUAGE and standpoint of the "natural" have been used to legitimate claims in many different academic disciplines, but contemporary feminists have criticized discussions of "nature" as little more than "rationalizations
of inequality" (Lowe & Hubbard, 1983). Sexology, however, still heavily favors
the language of the "natural," and this emphasis will provide the focus of the
present paper. Sexologists love to debate the contributions of "nature versus
nurture" when it comes to matters in sexuality such as gender differences,
sexual orientation, sex drive, transsexualism, and changes due to aging, but
feminists need to take a closer look at what is really meant by sexologists' use
of "nature."

This analysis begins with examples and discussion of the uses of "nature"
and "naturalism" in sexology, and a review of what some historians and
philosophers of science have had to say about such language. Then we will

turn to some specifically feminist criticisms of naturalism language and imagery, and following that, briefly describe how postmodernist scholarship rejects naturalism language. Finally, we will return to some practical dilemmas with regard to the use of naturalism language in contemporary sexology, using research and treatment of "impotence" as the example.

USES OF "NATURE" AND "NATURALISM" IN SEXOLOGY

While many of us may think that sex is "natural," have we ever stopped to ask ourselves what we mean by that term or what is our evidence for such a claim? Let's begin by looking at five examples of how naturalism language has been used in sexology.

1. The whole of sexual experience for both the human male and female is constituted in two . . . separate systems . . . that coexist *naturally* . . . . The biophysically and psychosocially based systems of influence that *naturally* coexist in any woman [can] function in mutual support. . . . Based on the manner in which an individual woman internalizes the prevailing psychosocial influence, her sexual value system may or may not reinforce her *natural* capacity to function sexually. One need only remember that sexual function can be displaced from its *natural* context temporarily or even for a lifetime in order to realize the . . . import [of sexual value system]. (219). . . . It seems more accurate to consider female orgasmic response as an acceptance of *naturally* occurring stimuli that have been given erotic significance by an individual sexual value system than to depict it as a learned response (297) (Masters & Johnson, 1970, emphasis added)

2. Present-day legal determinations of sexual acts which are acceptable, or "*natural*," and those which are "contrary to *nature*," are not based on data obtained from biologists, nor from *nature* herself (Kinsey, Pomeroy, & Martin, 1948, 202, emphasis added).

3. It is an essential part of our conceptual apparatus that the sexes are a polarity and a dichotomy in *nature* (Greer, 1971, 15, emphasis added).

4. The *nature* of the society in which a people live clearly plays a significant part in shaping the patterns of human sexual behavior . . . . Human societies appear to have seized upon and emphasized a *natural*, physiologically determined inclination toward intercourse between males and females, and to have discouraged and inhibited many other equally *natural* kinds of behavior. We believe that under purely hypothetical conditions in which any form of social control was lacking, coitus between males and females would prove to be the most frequent type of sexual behavior (Ford & Beach, 1951, 19).

5. This *natural* instinct which with all conquering force and might demands fulfillment (Kraft-Ebing, *Psychopathia Sexualis,* 1886, 1, from Weeks, 1985, 69)

Raymond Williams (1976), a noted historian of culture, identifies three meanings for the term "nature," locating their origins in seventeenth century European political debates. He begins his discussion by saying that "nature" is "perhaps the most complex word in the language (219)." That is not a trivial observation, and we would do well to remember it. An examination of how

Williams' three meanings apply to naturalism language in sexology will help us understand the immense power of the term.

The first meaning Williams sees for nature is *essential quality,* as seen in the final sexology quotation, "the nature of the society in which a people live. . . ." The "nature" of the society means here "the essential quality" of the society. Nature here is metaphor for bottom, bedrock, and essence, which makes it a *powerful* signifier. By generalization, anything called "natural" also gains the powerful connotation of basic and bedrock.

The second meaning Williams identifies for nature is as *inherent force directing the world.* This meaning can be seen in the second sexology quotation above, which uses the phrase "contrary to nature." This particular phrase, which can to this day be found in many legal texts, means that some sexual act is judged to oppose a higher force directing the world, making nature here a successor or stand-in for God. This use is connoted in the popular phrase, "Don't fool with Mother Nature."

The third use Williams identifies is nature as *material world,* particularly as *fixed* material world. This seems to be the most common usage in the sexological quotations above. For example, the third quotation says the sexes are "a dichotomy in nature," which seems to mean that the sexes have a fixed relation in the material world. The first quotation calls female orgasm natural, that is, female orgasm is claimed to definitely exist in the material world. The second quotation is asserting, "Present-day legal determinations are not based on data obtained from Nature herself," suggests that such claims are not based in the material world, but are human-made. Independence from culture, some sort of objective existence, is connoted by this particular meaning.

Perhaps now it is clear why the terms "nature" and "natural" are so often used for their immense rhetorical power to justify and legitimize. By emphasizing that something is *in nature,* we give it a special solidity that invokes a validity for nature *by contrast with culture,* as if anything human-made might be "artificial" and temporary, but that things prior to and outside human culture are more trustworthy. The so-called "laws of nature," for example, are somehow above human politics, somehow "more real" than "merely" the product of some legislative process (Shiebinger, 1986). The adjective "natural" confers a "pre-cultural" authority; it connotes a layer before or under culture. One's "sexual" nature, then, connotes a sexuality solid and valid, prior to the vagaries of human-made culture.

There are two additional aspects of the rhetorical power conveyed to sexual matters by the use of "natural" language. The first is *universality.* If part of the meaning of "natural" is "human but prior to culture," then anything natural should be universal to the human condition. This assumption of universality gives tremendous rhetorical power to the language of "nature" as it is used with regards to sexuality.

Finally, "natural" usually implies *biological,* since what else human could be

TIEFER

universal, pre-social, and essential, but our anatomy and physiology? The solid materialism of biology is contrasted with culture in most uses of "nature" in sexology. If we think orgasm is natural, for example, it is because we think orgasm is a universal, biological reality; if intercourse is natural, it is because we think it is a human universal based in biology; if sexuality itself is "natural," then it is thought to be universal and somehow basically biological.

THE NEED FOR LEGITIMACY IN SEXOLOGY

I suggest that the term "natural" is used so frequently in sexologic discourse because academics studying sexuality need *justification and legitimation* for their work. "Nature" and "natural" are used rhetorically in order to *persuade* audiences that sexuality is important and studyable, not so as to describe or give information arising as a result of empirical research (Simons, 1989).

In the sexological quotations above, this rhetorical effect is most apparent in the reiterated uses of naturalism language by Masters and Johnson (1970), where the powerful legitimizing connotations of nature are invoked repeatedly to support certain claims about sexual capacity. No new information is provided by the repeated assertions of naturalism—they serve only to call up pre-social, universal, and biological connotations.

Sex researchers' need for legitimacy and respectability cannot be overestimated, especially in the United States, with its history of repressive sexual values (Freedman & D'Emilio, 1988). Many sexologists still resonate with this story told by George Corner (1961), one of the 20th century's pioneer sex endocrinologists:

> In 1922 the National Research Council was called upon by influential groups . . . to bring together existing knowledge and to promote research upon human sex behavior and reproduction . . . The Committee for Research in Problems of Sex [formed] with financial support from the Rockefeller Foundation, successfully undertook to encourage research on a wide range of problems of sex physiology and behavior. The younger readers of this book will hardly be able to appreciate the full significance of [this]. . . . It represented a major break from the so-called Victorian attitude which in the English-speaking countries had long impeded scientific and sociologic investigation of sexual matters and placed taboos on open consideration of human mating and childbearing as if these essential activities were intrinsically indecent. To investigate such matters, even in the laboratory with rats and rabbits, required of American scientist . . . a certain degree of moral stamina. A member of the Yerkes Committee once heard himself introduced by fellow scientist to a new acquaintance as one of the men who had 'made sex respectable.' (P. x)

TIEFER

SEX IS SEX

In addition to underscoring the concern over respectability, which continues to pervade U.S. sex research (cf. Abramson, 1990), I chose this quotation to highlight my final point about the uses of naturalism language. Notice the phrase Corner uses: *"To investigate such matters, even in the laboratory with rats and rabbits."* The language of naturalism, with its implications of biological universality, allows us to claim that the focus of our research is on the same "sexuality," even when we replace human subjects with rats and rabbits (Hall, 1974). We can study "sexual" behaviors and hormone-behavior interactions in all species, and easily think we are looking at the same, or at least related, phenomena. This particular implication can be seen every time a television "Nature" series on sexuality glides easily from courting or mating pictures of bugs to fish to antelope to teenagers. This universality and biologism within sexology is the fundamental slippery slope supported by the language and metaphor of "nature" that must be challenged by feminists.

ORIGINS OF THE USE OF NATURE AND NATURALISM

I alluded earlier to sources of the uses and meanings of nature and naturalism in seventeenth century European history. Once we see that the use of these terms originated in a *particular* time for *particular* purposes, it may help us see more clearly the rhetoric involved in their contemporary use. This abbreviated discussion does not begin to do justice to the depth or complexities of the historical topics, but I hope it represents the central ideas.

Philosophers and historians of science have suggested that the use of nature-language and imagery in seventeenth century Britain and Europe served both to reinforce democratic factions within contemporary political struggles and to promote the new "scientific" methods and theories (Bloch & Bloch, 1980). Anti-monarchial writers of the time called on "nature" and the "laws of nature" to provide an authority and legitimacy alternative to the traditional authority of kings and popes.

European political philosophers of the sixteenth and seventeenth centuries invoked a hypothetical "state of nature," subject to the "laws of nature," to support the right of people to resist the prevailing doctrine of the divine right of kings and to resist the all-pervasive influence of the Roman Catholic church. We can see how naturalism language could invoke a pre-social design for the world (Williams' second definition), which could offer greater legitimacy for revolutionary struggle than the mere historical legitimacies of states. Appeals to the reason and dignity of persons as given by a universal, pre-social "human nature" could support claims for universal human rights, aspirations, and equality (Schiebinger, 1986).

At the same time, nature, this time meaning material world (Williams' third meaning), was invoked throughout the writings of seventeenth century scientists such as Francis Bacon and Rene Descartes as nature waiting to be tamed and controlled through "man's" use of reason. Emancipated from ignorance and fear, making use of the new economic and technological opportunities of the time, "man" would "master nature," "rip the veil from nature,"

367

TIEFER

etc. The laws of nature were just waiting for discovery by the human mind—an image still popular today.

To summarize, the rhetorical use of "nature" and "natural" to refer to subjects and laws pre-social, universal, and biological thus arose for political purposes during a time of intense sociopolitical conflict and change. Wherever legitimacy is required, we should not be surprised to hear naturalism language used because of its immense rhetorical power.

FEMINIST CHALLENGE TO THE LANGUAGE OF NATURALISM

The language and implications of naturalism have been a special target of attack during the current women's movement (Lowe & Hubbard, 1983). From the very first, feminist assaults on the ideology of male supremacy attacked assumptions about male and female nature underlying sex-role stereotyping and women's social, economic, and political oppression. Feminists recognized that naturalism language was often used in the contemporary normative sense of good, healthy, and moral while also carrying the old connotations of natural as biologically based, fixed, and presocial. Feminists worried that the justifying power of the metaphor of naturalism would turn "what is" into "what should be," an outcome rarely of benefit to women.

The explosive rise of sociobiology in the mid-1970s provided timely confirmation. Biological, evolutionary, and animal research were recruited to justify the status quo. Donald Symons' (1979) sociobiology text, for example, argued that

368

> there is a female human nature and a male human nature and these natures are extraordinarily different, though the differences are to some extent masked . . . by moral injunctions (Geertz, 1980)

And what are these different sexual natures? Symons (1979) described permanent gender differences in desire, jealousy, sexual pleasure, the brain, orgasm, wishes for partner variety, i.e., in the whole familiar list of twentieth century Western white middle class gender differences in sexual script. Yet, as reviewers in *Science,* the *Quarterly review of Biology* and the *New York Review of Books* all pointed out, Symons' evidence consisted of a hit-or-miss search for universals in the animal and human research literatures. It was no surprise to feminists when his book included a critique of feminist political demands. Thus is it always, feminists would say, when nature is valorized.

The first wave of feminist theory and research was directed to painstakingly correcting ideas about women, showing how socialization and social structure exert more influence than any sort of "natural" inevitability or biological determinism. For example, in practically any psychological study, differences within groups of men and women ("intrasex differences") are greater than differences between men and women ("intersex differences"). Michael Lewis (1974), for example, observed that within-sex differences were at least as great

TIEFER

as between-sex differences in many measures made of children's behavior. Ironically, however, the title of his paper was "Early sex differences in socioemotional development," and the point about intrasex vs. intersex differences was lost. This has happened time and time again. It seems that reporting larger intragroup than intergroup differences just isn't very interesting.

Ruth Bleier (1986) finally concluded that claims about sex differences, especially those linked to biology, are, like Banquo's ghost, impossible to kill. If it isn't the size of brains, then it's mathematical ability; if it isn't impulses towards aggression, then it's interhemispheric transfer of information; if it isn't preferences in types of play activities, then it's pleasure in genital sexuality. A modern society built on sex differences requires continual authoritative reinforcement ("scientific findings"), and the media, as Lynda Birke (1986) and others have shown, compliantly provide this support. The media dichotomize and polarize men and women. Studies demonstrating sex differences will be regularly featured in the *New York Times,* for example, and those with biological measures will usually make the front page!

In the face of this wall of resistance, a new feminist strategy of scholarship emerged in the 1980s. Researchers no longer struggled to correct false ideas of female nature or to show the social distortion of natural female capacity by institutionalized oppression, but now worked to challenge the very notion of "the natural" altogether by using the idea of social construction. Donna Haraway (1986) illustrated this strategic shift in her influential essay, "Primatology is politics by other means," arguing

369

> The past, the animal, the female, nature: these are the contested zones in the discourse of primatology . . . [but] rarely will feminist contests for scientific meaning work by replacing one paradigm with another, by proposing . . . alternative accounts and theories. Rather, as a form of narrative practice or story-telling, feminist practice in primatology has worked more by altering a 'field' of stories or possible explanatory accounts, by raising the cost of defending some accounts, by destabilizing the plausibility of some strategies of explanation . . . feminist science is about changing possibilities. (Haraway, 1986, 115, 81)

Thus, while Haraway supports liberal feminist research efforts to challenge existing theories of gender difference by showing female primates capable of competition, mobility, aggression, and sexual assertion (e.g., the work of Jane Lancaster), Haraway also argues that showing that females are "just like and therefore just as good as males" is ultimately a doomed strategy that perpetuates the focus on gender as difference.

The type of work illustrated by narrative analysis, however, analyzing existing theories as "narratives" and proposing new narratives in substitution, will conflict with sex research's needs for legitimacy that we discussed earlier. You'll recall George Corner's comment in *Sex and Internal Secretions* that studying the sex physiology and behavior of rats and rabbits was the only way

TIEFER

early researchers had of getting into the otherwise risque and dangerous area of sex research. That is, biological narrative could confer legitimacy! Carolyn Sherif knew this a decade ago when she argued that reductionism wouldn't disappear until the prestige hierarchy within science changed:

> What psychology defined as basic was dictated by slavish devotion to the more prestigious disciplines. Thus, a physiological or biochemical part or element was defined as more basic than a belief that Eve was created from Adam's rib, not because the former can necessarily tell us more about a human individual, but because physiology and biochemistry were more prestigious than religious history or sociology (Sherif, 1979, 100)

Acquiring legitimacy through alliance with and identification with respectable and well-established fields has often governed twentieth century scientific choices. Feminists, eager to "destabilize the plausibility of these strategies of explanation," have been at pains to uncover the historical particularities contributing to scientific developments. Gail Hornstein (1989), for example, has shown how the move to quantify psychological phenomena allowed the new field of psychology, particularly in the United States, to differentiate itself from philosophy. New techniques would define phenomena in a new way, amateurs could be weeded out by sophisticated language, and psychology could qualify as science (as defined by the natural sciences). The history of sex research will tell the same tale about the inclusion and exclusion of methods and theories. A decade ago (Tiefer, 1983, 1986a) I discussed some of the reasons feminists criticize contemporary science, stressing how biological sex research is tied to anachronistic notions of male and female nature. But because of the prestige hierarchies of science, which themselves have come to seem "natural," it will be difficult to shift scientific paradigms.

POSTMODERN SCHOLARSHIP AND "DENATURALIZATION"

Postmodern scholarship cannot be apprehended simply, but needs to be mentioned in any critique of the use and symbolism of naturalism. Suffice it to say that scholars in many disciplines are identifying and calling "postmodern" a fundamental shift in worldview and the construction of reality. Political philosopher Jane Flax (1987) has put it this way:

> Postmodern discourses are all "deconstructive" in that they seek to distance us from and make us skeptical about beliefs concerning truth, knowledge, power, the self and language that are often taken for granted within and serve as legitimation for contemporary Western culture.
>
> Postmodern philosophers seek to throw into radical doubt [such factors as] the existence of a stable, coherent self. . . . [whether] Reason and its "science" . . . can provide an objective, reliable and universal foundation for knowledge . . . [that] Reason itself has transcendental and universal qualities . . . .[that] Language is merely the medium through which representation occurs (624–5)

"Discourses," of course, can take many forms: scientific or academic treatises, diaries, poems, statements made on the analyst's couch, lullabies, or filmscripts, among others. Postmodernism is all about relativism and multiple points of view. It's about contextualizing observations and concepts. It's about acknowledging change and the difficulty of definitive pronouncements. It's about permanent instability.

It denies the validity of universal generalization and substitutes the point of view that no perspective offers a privileged access to "the way things really are." Recently, Bill Simon (1989) titled a commentary on the status of sex research, "The Postmodernizaion of Sex," and identified the "emergent consensus about the absence of consensus(18)" as the central theme of postmodernism, "a sense of being forced to an unexpected and often discomforting pluralism" (19).

How does postmodernism relate to the idea of "the natural?" Obviously, creating skepticism concerning truth, knowledge, power, the self, and language is going to come down hard on nature and naturalism! Simon (1989) says that postmodernism *is about* denaturalization in general and sexual denaturalization in particular. "In effect . . . what is implied is the reading of the sexual 'against the grain,' i.e., reinterpreting the predominant biological explanatory concepts as metaphorical illusions." (Simon, 1989, p. 24) Sexuality, like everything else, is a social construction (Tiefer, 1987). Social, not natural. This perspective has so far had its strongest impact on the history of sexuality (Duggan, 1990) and the notion of sexual object choice or sexual identity (Boswell, 1990). By putting categories, concepts, metaphors, and methods up for grabs, postmodernism offers an extraordinary theoretical opportunity to create sexual understandings beyond those based on Enlightenment naturalism.

A CONTEMPORARY ILLUSTRATION

In case the reader thinks that this has all been an academic exercise, and that sexologists are not really caught in the flytrap of natural-talk and imagery, let me provide a real-life illustration. I work in a hospital/medical center urology department dealing with men who are referred with complaints of erectile dysfunction. I participate in their initial evaluation and diagnosis and supervise trainees who provide sex therapy for appropriate couples.

Daily, I experience the clash of my postmodern perceptions of diversity and social construction with the naturalized perceptions held by patients and physicians of penile erections and impotence. Patients come in the door, "I can't get an erection. I can't have sex. Fix it." Period. The end. There is a thing, "the erection." It's necessary for the thing, "sex." These are not matters of construction or negotiation. They exist. They are real.

I sit there, like a time-traveller dropped into a strange century or culture. My urologist colleagues are comfortable and unperturbed by the patients' straightforward discourse. They seem confident that they can measure this erection thing in the daytime and the nighttime, that they can diagnose it,

371

prognose it, take pictures of it, measure it with lots of expensive gadgets, treat it pharmacologically, create it surgically, fix it up, and it's always the same thing. Meanwhile, I am still back at the beginning wondering what is this thing, the erection, that's necessary for that thing, sex? If ever there was an example of nature, isn't it an erection? If there ever was anything suited for biological study, isn't it an erection? If there ever was anything pre-social and universal, isn't it an erection?

Well, no! To me, there is no such thing as erection as an entity. It's a means to a variety of socially constructed ends—pleasure, gender-affirmation, procreation, power. So, why do we ask patients only about their erection; why don't we talk to them about pleasure, power, and gender? The answer is that our hospital work is part of a social construction. Our conversations seem to be about the penis, but they're really about the construction of masculinity. The men don't want to have an erection to dry their socks on, they want it because they have learned that the *natural* expression of masculinity is to have one frequently and easily for the practice or capability of heterosexual intercourse. Knowing one can have an erection for intercourse, *whether one actually does it or not,* is being a man. The growing domain of impotence research and treatment is part of the contemporary construction of masculinity (Tiefer, 1986b, 1994).

But, here I am, a postmodernist, committed to diversity and relativism, thinking human physiology is to be regarded as merely providing a set of physical possibilities and saying nothing about use or meaning. Various states of the penis might or might not have anything to do with pleasure or procreation or display or domination or anxiety or hypochondriasis or ego-satisfaction. But as long as we just talk about the erection, we'll never get to acknowledge these other issues.

Frank Beach, the pre-eminent animal sex researcher, my major professor in graduate school, used to say about sex, in his blunt Midwestern style, "You can't be a carpenter without a hammer!" But postmodern deconstruction of the natural shows that you *can* be a carpenter without a hammer, or you can have different hammers for different occasions, or that your coworker can find something of hers to use as a hammer, or that you could decide together to forget the idea of hammer and build something a little different. But you can't do that, if you feel that carpenter and hammer are natural, that is, biological, universal, presocial, imperative, essential, and in the modern construction, normal. Don't tell me this is just semantics. An entire industry, and a large part of many real people's real lives, is banking on the proposition that you can't be a carpenter without a hammer.

CONCLUSION

The perspective that biological sex research is more basic because the findings appear closer to nature, that is, pre-social and more generalizable, can be traced to European Enlightenment era definitions of nature and the natural world and the particularities of Enlightenment era politics. Its persistence can be traced to the power of masculinist discourse. However, this construction is coming under challenge from many directions. As historian Ludmilla Jordanova (1989) writes,

> Over the last 20 years or so historians have become aware of the need to unpack the processes through which "naturalization" takes place, whereby ideas, theories, experiences, languages, and so on, take on the quality of being "natural," permitting the veiling of their customary, conventional and social characteristics. Understanding such naturalization is integral to the project of delineating and explaining the precise nature of scientific and medical power. (Jordanova, 1989,5)

Biological sex research is popular because it reinforces traditional ideas and because other types of research have been dismissed or ignored (Tiefer, 1995). But there are other ways to think about the sexual, and I can guarantee that once you start, it's very hard to go back.

NOTES

1. This paper is a revised version of a talk given to the International Academy of Sex Research, Sigtuna, Sweden, 1990, which is reprinted in original form in Leonore Tiefer (1995) *Sex is not a natural act and other essays,* Boulder: Westview.

REFERENCES

Abramson, P. R. (1990). Sexual science: Emerging discipline or oxymoron. *Journal of Sex Research, 27,* 147–165.

Birke, L. (1986). *Women, feminism and biology: The feminist challenge.* NY: Methuen.

Bleier, R. (1986). Sex differences research: Science or belief? In Bleier, R. (Ed.) *Feminist approaches to science.* NY: Pergamon.

Bloch, M. & Bloch, J. H. (1980). Women and the dialectics of nature in 18th century French thought. In MacCormack, C. P. & Strathern, M. (Eds.) *Nature, culture and gender.* Cambridge: Cambridge University Press.

Boswell, J. (1990). Concepts, experience and sexuality. *Differences, 2,* 67–87.

Corner, G. W. (1961). Foreward. In Young, W. C. (Ed.) *Sex and internal secretions, Vol I.* 3rd ed. Baltimore: Williams and Wilkins.

Duggan, L. (1990). Review essay: From instincts to politics: Writing the history of sexuality in the U.S. *Journal of Sex Research, 27,* 95–109.

Flax, J. (1987). Postmodernism and gender relations in feminist theory. *Signs, 12,* 621–644.

Ford, C. S. & Beach, F. A. (1951). *Patterns of sexual behavior.* NY: Harper and Row.

Freedman, E. B. & D'Emilio, J. (1988). *Intimate matters: A history of sexuality in America.* New York: Harper & Row.

Geertz, C. (1980, Jan 24). Review of *The evolution of human sexuality* in *New York Review of Books.*

Greer, G. (1971). *The female eunuch.* NY: McGraw-Hill.

373

Hall, D. L. (1974). Biology, sex hormones and sexism in the 1920s. *Philosophical Forum, 5,* 81–96.

Haraway, D. (1986). Primatology is politics by other means. In Bleier, R. (Ed.) *Feminist approaches to science.* NY: Pergamon.

Hornstein, G. (1989). Quantifying psychological phenomena: Debates, dilemmas and implications. In Morawski, J. G. (Ed.) *The Rise of Experimentation in American Psychology.* New Haven: Yale University Press.

Jordanova, L. (1989). *Sexual visions: Images of gender in science and medicine between the 18th and 20th centuries.* Madison: University of Wisconsin Press.

Kinsey, A. C., Pomeroy, W. B. & Martin, C. E. (1948). *Sexual behavior in the human male.* Philadelphia: W. B. Saunders.

Lewis, M. (1975). Early sex differences in the human: Studies of socioemotional development. *Archives of Sexual Behavior, 4,* 329–335.

Lowe, M. & Hubbard, R. (Eds.) (1983). *Woman's nature: Rationalizations of inequality.* New York: Pergamon Press.

Masters, W. H. & Johnson, V. E. (1970). *Human sexual inadequacy.* Boston: Little, Brown.

Schiebinger, L. (1986). Skeletons in the closet: The first illustrations of the female skeleton in the 18th C. anatomy. *Representations,* number 14, 42–82.

Sherif, C. (1979). Bias in psychology. In Sherman, J. A. & Beck, E. T. (Eds.) *The prism of sex: Essays in the sociology of knowledge.* Madison: University of Wisconsin Press.

Simon, W. (1989). Commentary on the status of sex research: The postmodernization of sex. *Journal of Psychology and Human Sexuality, 2,* 9–37.

Simons, H. (1989). Introduction. In Simons, H. (Ed.) *Rhetoric in the human sciences.* Newbury Park, CA: Sage.

Symons, D. (1979). *The evolution of human sexuality.* NY: Oxford University Press.

Tiefer, L. (1983). A political perspective on the use of gender as an independent variable. Paper delivered at International Academy of Sex Research, Harriman, NY.

Tiefer, L. (1986a). Methodology of research on female sexuality. Paper delivered at International Academy of Sex Research, Amsterdam.

Tiefer, L. (1986b). In pursuit of the perfect penis: The medicalization of male sexuality. *American Behavioral Scientist. 29,* 579–599.

Tiefer, L. (1987). Social constructionism and the study of human sexuality. In Shaver, P. & Hendrick, C. (Eds.). *Sex and gender.* Newbury Park: Sage Publications.

Tiefer, L. (1995). *Sex is not a natural act and other essays.* Boulder: Westview.

Weeks, J. (1985). *Sexuality and its discontents.* London: Routledge & Kegan Paul.

Williams, R. (1976). *Keywords: A vocabulary of culture and society.* NY: Oxford University Press. (rev. ed, 1983).

SEXUALITY, SCHOOLING, AND ADOLSCENT FEMALES
The Missing Discourse of Desire

Michelle Fine

SINCE LATE 1986, popular magazines and newspapers have printed steamy stories about education and sexuality. Whether the controversy surrounds sex education or school-based health clinics (SBHCs), public discourses of adolescent sexuality are represented forcefully by government officials, New Right spokespersons, educators, "the public," feminists, and health-care professionals. These stories offer the authority of "facts," insights into the political controversies, and access to unacknowledged fears about sexuality (Foucault, 1980). Although the facts usually involve the adolescent female body, little has been heard from young women themselves.

This article examines these diverse perspectives on adolescent sexuality and, in addition, presents the views of a group of adolescent females. The article is informed by a study of numerous current sex education curricula, a year of negotiating for inclusion of lesbian and gay sexuality in a citywide sex education curriculum, and interviews and observations gathered in New York

City sex education classrooms.[1] The analysis examines the desires, fears, and fantasies which give structure and shape to silences and voices concerning sex education and school-based health clinics in the 1980s.

Despite the attention devoted to teen sexuality, pregnancy, and parenting in this country, and despite the evidence of effective interventions and the widespread public support expressed for these interventions (Harris, 1985), the systematic implementation of sex education and SBHCs continues to be obstructed by the controversies surrounding them (Kantrowitz et al., 1987; Leo, 1986). Those who resist sex education or SBHCs often present their views as based on rationality and a concern for protecting the young. For such opponents, sex education raises questions of promoting promiscuity and immortality, and of undermining family values. Yet the language of the challenges suggests an affect substantially more profound and primitive. Gary Bauer, Undersecretary of Education in the U.S. Department of Education, for example, constructs an image of immortality littered by adolescent sexuality and drug abuse:

> There is ample impressionistic evidence to indicate that drug abuse and promiscuity are not independent behaviors. When inhibitions fall, they collapse across the board. When people of any age lose a sense of right and wrong, the loss is not selective. . . . [T]hey are all expressions of the same ethical vacuum among many teens. . . . (1986)

376

Even Surgeon General C. Everett Koop, a strong supporter of sex education, recently explained: "[W]e have to be as explicit as necessary. . . . You can't talk of the dangers of snake poisoning and not mention snakes" (quoted in Leo, 1986, p. 54). Such commonly used and often repeated metaphors associate adolescent sexuality with victimization and danger.

Yet public schools have rejected the task of sexual dialogue and critique, or what has been called "sexuality education." Within today's standard sex education curricula and many public school classrooms, we find: (1) the authorized suppression of a discourse of female sexual desire; (2) the promotion of a discourse of female sexual victimization; and (3) the explicit privileging of married heterosexuality over other practices of sexuality. One finds an unacknowledged social ambivalence about female sexuality which ideologically separates the female sexual agent, or subject, from her counterpart, the female sexual victim. The adolescent woman of the 1980s is constructed as the latter. Educated primarily as the potential victim of male sexuality, she represents no subject in her own right. Young women continue to be taught to fear and defend in isolation from exploring desire, and in this context there is little possibility of their developing a critique of gender or sexual arrangements.

FINE

PREVAILING DISCOURSES OF FEMALE SEXUALITY
INSIDE PUBLIC SCHOOLS

> If the body is seen as endangered by uncontrollable forces, then presumably this is a society or social group which fears change—change which it perceived simultaneously as powerful and beyond its control. (Smith-Rosenberg, 1978, p. 229)

Public schools have historically been the site for identifying, civilizing, and containing that which is considered uncontrollable. While evidence of sexuality is everywhere within public high schools—in the halls, classrooms, bathrooms, lunchrooms, and the library—official sexuality education occurs sparsely: in social studies, biology, sex education, or inside the nurse's office. To understand how sexuality is managed inside schools, I examined the major discourses of sexuality which characterize the national debates over sex education and SBHCs. These discourses are then tracked as they weave through the curricula, classrooms, and halls of public high schools.

The first discourse, *sexuality as violence*, is clearly the most conservative, and equates adolescent heterosexuality with violence. At the 1986 American Dreams Symposium on education, Phyllis Schlafy commented: "Those courses on sex, abuse, incest, AIDS, they are all designed to terrorize our children. We should fight their existence, and stop putting terror in the hearts and minds of our youngsters." One aspect of this position, shared by women as politically distinct as Schlafly and the radical feminist lawyer Catherine MacKinnon (1983), views heterosexuality as essentially violent and coercive. In its full conservative form, proponents call for the elimination of sex education and clinics and urge complete reliance on the family to dictate appropriate values, mores, and behaviors.

Sexuality as violence presumes that there is a causal relationship between official silence about sexuality and a decrease in sexual activity—therefore, by not teaching about sexuality, adolescent sexual behavior will not occur. The irony, of course, lies in the empirical evidence. Fisher, Byrne, and White (1983) have documented sex-negative attitudes and contraceptive use to be negatively correlated.

In their study, sex-negative attitudes do not discourage sexual activity, but they do discourage responsible use of contraception. Teens who believe sexual involvement is wrong deny responsibility for contraception. To accept responsibility would legitimate "bad" behavior. By contrast, Fisher et al. (1983) found that adolescents with sex-positive attitudes tend to be both more consistent and more positive about contraceptive use. By not teaching about sexuality, or by teaching sex-negative attitudes, schools apparently will not forestall sexual activity, but may well discourage responsible contraception.

The second discourse, *sexuality* as victimization, gathers a much greater following.

377

FINE

Female adolescent sexuality is represented as a moment of victimization in which the dangers of heterosexuality for adolescent women (and, more recently, of homosexuality for adolescent men) are prominent. While sex may not be depicted as inherently violent, young women (and today, men) learn of their vulnerability to potential male predators.

To avoid being victimized, females learn to defend themselves against disease, pregnancy, and "being used." The discourse of victimization supports sex education, including AIDS education, with parental consent. Suggested classroom activities emphasize "saying no," practicing abstinence, enumerating the social and emotional risks of sexual intimacy, and listing the possible diseases associated with sexual intimacy. The language, as well as the questions asked and not asked, represents females as the actual and potential victims of male desire. In exercises, role plays, and class discussions, girls practice resistance to trite lines, unwanted hands, opened buttons, and the surrender of other "bases" they are not prepared to yield. The discourses of violence and victimization both portray males as potential predators and females as victims. Three problematic assumptions underlie these two views:

–First, female subjectivity, including the desire to engage in sexual activity, is placed outside the prevailing conversation (Vance, 1984).

–Second, both arguments present female victimization as contingent upon unmarried heterosexual involvement-rather than inherent in existing gender, class, and racial arrangements (Rubin, 1984). While feminists have long fought for the legal and social acknowledgement of sexual violence against women, most have resisted the claim that female victimization hinges primarily upon sexual involvement with men. The full range of victimization of women-at work, at home, on the streets-has instead been uncovered. The language and emotion invested in these two discourses divert attention away from structures, arrangements, and relationships which oppress women in general, and low-income women and women of color in particular (Lorde, 1978).

–Third, the messages, while narrowly anti-sexual, nevertheless buttress traditional heterosexual arrangements. These views assume that as long as females avoid premarital sexual relations with men, victimization can be avoided. Ironically, however, protection from male victimization is available primarily through marriage-by coupling with a man. The paradoxical message teaches females to fear the very men who will ultimately protect them.

The third discourse, *sexuality as individual morality*, introduces explicit notions of sexual subjectivity for women. Although quite judgmental and moralistic, this discourse values women's sexual decisionmaking as long as the decisions made are for premarital abstinence. For example, Secretary of Education William Bennett urges schools to teach "mortality literacy" and to educate towards "modesty," "chastity," and "abstinence" until marriage. The lan-

378

FINE

guage of self-control and self-respect reminds students that sexual immortali-ty breeds not only personal problems but also community tax burdens.

The debate over morality in sex education curricula marks a clear contra-diction among educational conservatives over whether and how the state may intervene in the "privacy of families." Non-interventionists, including Schlafly and Onalee McGraw, argue that educators should not teach about sexuality at all. To do so is to take a particular moral position which subverts the family. Interventionists, including Koop, Bennett, and Bauer, argue that schools should teach about sexuality by focusing on "good values," but dis-agree about how. Koop proposes open discussion of sexuality and the use of condoms, while Bennett advocates "sexual restraint" ("Koop AIDS Stand As-sailed," 1987). Sexuality in this discourse is posed as a test of self-control; indi-vidual restraint triumphs over social temptation. Pleasure and desire for women as sexual subjects remain largely in the shadows, obscured from ado-lescent eyes.

The fourth discourse, a *discourse of desire*, remains a whisper inside the offi-cial work of U.S. public schools. If introduced at all, it is as an interruption of the ongoing conversation (Snitow, Stansell, & Thompson, 1983). The naming of desire, pleasure, or sexual entitlement, particularly for females, barely exists in the formal agenda of public schooling on sexuality. When spoken, it is tagged with reminders of "consequences"–emotional, physical, moral, repro-ductive, and/or financial (Freudenberg, 1987). A genuine discourse of desire would invite adolescents to explore what feels good and bad, desirable and undesirable, grounded in experiences, needs, and limits. Such a discourse would release females from a position of receptivity, enable an analysis of the dialectics of victimization and pleasure, and would pose female adolescents as subjects of sexuality, initiators as well as negotiators (Golden, 1984; Petchesky, 1984; Thompson, 1983).

379

In Sweden, where sex education has been offered in schools since the turn of the century, the State Commission on Sex Education recommends teach-ing students to "acquire a knowledge . . . [which] will equip them to experi-ence sexual life as a source of happiness and joy in fellowship with other [people]" (Brown, 1983, p. 88). The teachers' handbook goes on, "The many young people who wish to wait [before initiating sexual activity] and those who have had early sexual relations should experience, in class, [the feeling] that they are understood and accepted" (p. 93). Compared this to an exercise suggested in a major U.S. metroplitan sex education curriculum: "Discuss and evaluate: things which may cause teenagers to engage in sexual relations be-fore they are ready to assume the responsibility of marriage" (see Philadelphia School District, 1986; and New York City Board of Education, 1984).

A discourse of desire, though seldom explored in U.S. classrooms, does oc-cur in less structured school situations. The following excerpts, taken from group and individual student interviews, demonstrate female adolescents' subjective experiences of body and desire as they begin to articulate notions of sexuality.

In some cases young women pose a critique of marriage:

> I'm still in love with Simon, but I'm seeing Jose. He's OK but he said, "Will you be my girl?" I hate that. It feels like they own you. Like I say to a girlfriend, "What's wrong? You look terrible!" and she says, "I'm married!" (Millie, a 16-year-old student from the Dominican Republic)

In other cases they offer stories of their own victimization:

> It's not like last year. Then I came to school regular. Now my old boyfriend, he waits for me in front of my building every morning and he fights with me. Threatens me, gettin' all bad.... I want to move out of my house and live 'cause he ain't gonna stop no way. (Sylvia, age 17, about to drop out of twelfth grade)

Some even speak of desire:

> I'm sorry I couldn't call you last night about the interview, but my boyfriend came back from [the] Navy and I wanted to spend the nigth with him, we don't get to see each other much. (Shandra, age 17, after a no-show for an interview)

In a context in which desire is not silenced, but acknowledged and discussed, conversations with adolescent women can, as seen here, educate through a dialectic of victimization and pleasure. Despite formal silencing, it would be misleading to suggest that talk of desire never emerges within public schools. Notwithstanding a political climate organized around the suppression of this conversation, some teachers and community advocates continue to struggle for an empowering sex education curriculum both in and out of the high school classroom.

Family life curricula and/or plans for a school-based health clinic have been carefully generated in many communities. Yet they continue to face loud and sometimes violent resistance by religious and community groups, often from outside the district lines (Boffey, 1987; "Chicago School Clinic," 1986; Dowd, 1986; Perlez, 1986a, 1986b; Rohter, 1985). In other communities, when curricula or clinics have been approved with little overt confrontation, monies for training are withheld. For example, in New York City in 1987, $1.7 million was initially requested to implement training on the Family Life education curriculum. As sex educators confronted community and religious groups, the inclusion of some topics as well as the language of others were continually negotiated. Ultimately, the Chancellor requested only $600,000 for training, a sum substantially inadequate to the task.[2]

In this political context many public school educators nevertheless continue to take personal and professional risks to create materials and foster class-

380

FINE

room environments which speak fully to the sexual subjectivities of young women and men. Some operate within the privacy of their classrooms, subverting the official curriculum and engaging students in critical discussion. Others advocate publicly for enriched curricula and training. A few have even requested that community-based advocates not agitate for official curricular change, so "we [teachers] can continue to do what we do in the classroom, with nobody looking over our shoulders. You make a big public deal of this, and it will blow open."[3] Within public school classrooms, it seems that female desire may indeed be addressed when educators act subversively. But in the typical sex education classroom, silence, and therefore distortion, surrounds female desire.

The blanketing of female sexual subjectivity in public school classrooms, in public discourse, and in bed will sound familiar to those who have read Luce Irigaray (1980) and Helen Cíxous (1981). These French feminists have argued that expressions of female voice, body, and sexuality are essentially inaudible when the dominant language and ways of viewing are male. Inside the hegemony of what they call The Law of the Father, female desire and pleasure can gain expression only in the terrain already charted by men (see also Burke, 1980). In the public school arena, this constriction of what is called sexuality allows girls one primary decision—to say yes or no—to a question not necessarily their own. A discourse of desire in which young women have a voice would be informed and generated out of their own socially constructed sexual meanings. It is to these expressions that we now turn.

381

The Bodies of Female Adolescents: Voices and Structured Silences

If four discourses can be distinguished among the many positions articulated by various "authorities," the sexual meanings voiced by female adolescents defy such classification. A discourse of desire, though absent in the "official" curriculum, is by no means missing from the lived experiences or commentaries of young women. This section introduces their sexual thoughts, concerns, and meanings, as represented by a group of Black and Latina female adolescents—students and dropouts from a public high school in New York City serving predominantly low-income youths. In my year at this comprehensive high school I had frequent opportunity to speak with adolescents and listen to them talk about sex. The comments reported derive from conversations between the young women and their teachers, among themselves, and with me, as researcher. During conversations, the young women talked freely about fears and, in the same breath, asked about passions. Their struggle to untangle issues of gender, power, and sexuality underscores the fact that, for them, notions of sexual negotiation cannot be separated from sacrifice and nurturance.

The adolescent female rarely reflects simply on sexuality. Her sense of sexuality is informed by peers, culture, religion, violence, history, passion, authority, rebellion, body, past and future, and gender and racial relations of power (Espin, 1984; Omolade, 1983). The adolescent woman herself assumes a dual consciousness–at once taken with the excitement of actual/anticipated sexuality and consumed with anxiety and worry. While too few safe spaces exist for adolescent women's exploration of sexual subjectivities, there are all too many dangerous spots for their exploitation.

Whether in a classroom, on the street, at work, or at home, the adolescent female's sexuality is negotiated by, for, and despite the young woman herself. Patricia, a young Puerto Rican woman who worried about her younger sister, relates: "You see, I'm the love child and she's the one born because my mother was raped in Puerto Rico. Her father's in jail now, and she feels so bad about the whole thing so she acts bad." For Patricia, as for the many young women who have experienced and/or witnessed sexual violence, discussions of sexuality merge representations of passion with violence. Often the initiator of conversation among peers about virginity, orgasm, "getting off," and pleasure, Patricia mixed sexual talk freely with references to force and violence. She is a poignant narrator who illustrates, from the female adolescent's perspective, that sexual victimization and desire coexist (Benjamin, 1983).

Sharlene and Betty echo this braiding of danger and desire. Sharlene explained: "Boys always be trying to get into my panties," and Betty added: "I don't be needin' a man who won't give me no pleasure but take my money and expect me to take care of him." This powerful commentary on gender relations, voiced by Black adolescent females, was inseparable from their views of sexuality. To be a woman was to be strong, independent, and reliable–but not too independent for fear of scaring off a man.

Deidre continued this conversation, explicitly pitting male fragility against female strength: "Boys in my neighborhood ain't wrapped so tight. Got to be careful how you treat them. . . . "She reluctantly admitted that perhaps it is more important for Black males than females to attend college, "Girls and women, we're stronger, we take care of ourselves. But boys and men, if they don't get away from the neighborhood, they end up in jail, on drugs or dead . . . or wack [crazy]."

These young women spoke often of anger at males, while concurrently expressing a strong desire for male attention: "I dropped out 'cause I fell in love, and couldn't stop thinking of him." An equally compelling desire was to protect young males–particularly Black males–from a system which "makes them wack." Ever aware of the ways that institutional racism and the economy have affected Black males, these young women seek pleasure but also offer comfort. They often view self-protection as taking something away from young men. Lavanda offered a telling example: "If I ask him to use a condom, he won't feel like a man."

In order to understand the sexual subjectivities of young women more completely, educators need to reconstruct schooling as an empowering context in which we listen to and work with the meanings and experiences of gender and sexuality revealed by the adolescents themselves. When we refuse that responsibility, we prohibit an education which adolescents wholly need and deserve. My classroom observations suggest that such education is rare.

Ms. Rosen, a teacher of a sex education class, opened one session with a request: "You should talk to your mother or father about sex before you get involved." Nilda initiated what became an informal protest by a number of Latino students: "Not our parents! We tell them one little thing and they get crazy. My cousin got sent to Puerto Rico to live with her religious aunt, and my sister got beat 'cause my father thought she was with a boy." For these adolescents, a safe space for discussion, critique, and construction of sexualities was not something they found in their homes. Instead, they relied on school, the spot they chose for the safe exploration of sexualities.

The absence of safe spaces for exploring sexuality affects all adolescents. It was paradoxical to realize that perhaps the only students who had an in-school opportunity for critical sexual discussion in the comfort of peers were the few students who had organized the Gay and Lesbian Association (GALA) at the high school. While most lesbian, gay, or bisexual students were undoubtedly closeted, those few who were "out" claimed this public space for their display and for their sanctuary. Exchanging support when families and peers would offer little, GALA members worried that so few students were willing to come out, and that so many suffered the assaults of homophobia individually. The gay and lesbian rights movement had powerfully affected these youngsters, who were comfortable enough to support each other in a place not considered very safe–a public high school in which echoes of "faggot!" fill the halls.

In the absence of an education which explores and unearths danger and desire, sexuality education classes typically provide little opportunity for discussions beyond those constructed around superficial notions of male heterosexuality (see Kelly, 1986, for a counterexample). Male pleasure is taught, albeit as biology.

Teens learn about "wet dreams" (as the onset of puberty for males), "erection" (as the preface to intercourse), and "ejaculation" (as the act of inseminating). Female pleasures and questions are far less often the topic of discussion. Few voices of female sexual agency can be heard. The language of victimization and its underlying concerns–"Say No," put a brake on his sexuality, don't encourage–ultimately deny young women the right to control their own sexuality by providing no access to a legitimate position of sexual subjectivity. Often conflicted about self-representation, adolescent females spend enormous amounts of time trying to "save it," "lose it," convince others that they have lost or saved it, or trying to be "discreet" instead of focusing their energies in ways that are sexually autonomous, responsible, and pleasurable. In

FINE

classroom observations, girls who were heterosexually active rarely spoke, for fear of being ostracized (Fine, 1986). Those who were heterosexual virgins had the same worry. And most students who were gay, bisexual, or lesbian remained closeted, aware of the very real dangers of homophobia.

Occasionally, the difficult and pleasurable aspects of sexuality were discussed together, coming either as an interruption, or because an educational context was constructed. During a social studies class, for example, Catherine, the proud mother of two-year-old Tiffany, challenged an assumption underlying the class discussion—that teen motherhood devastates mother and child; "If I didn't get pregnant I would have continued on a downward path, going nowhere. They say teenage pregnancy is bad for you, but it was good for me. I know I can't mess around now, I got to worry about what's good for Tiffany and for me."

Another interruption came from Opal, a young Black student. Excerpts from her hygiene class follow.

Teacher: Let's talk about teenage pregnancy.

Opal: How come girls in the locker room say, "You a virgin?" and if you say "Yeah" they laugh and say "Ohh, you're a virgin. . . ." And some Black teenagers, I don't mean to be racial, when they get ready to tell their mothers they had sex, some break on them and some look funny. My friend told her mother and she broke all the dishes. She told her mother so she could get protection so she don't get pregnant.

Teacher: When my 13-year-old (relative) asked for birth control I was shocked and angry.

Portia: Mothers should help so she can get protection and not get pregnant or diseases. So you was wrong.

Teacher: Why not say "I'm thinking about having sex?"

Portia: You tell them after, not before, having sex but before pregnancy.

Teacher (now angry): Then it's a fait accompli and you expect my compassion? You have to take more responsibility.

Portia: I am! If you get pregnant after you told your mother and you got all the stuff and still get pregnant, you the fool. Take up hygiene and learn. Then it's my responsibility if I end up pregnant. . . .

Field Note, October 23, Hygiene Class

Two days later, the discussion continued.

Teacher: What topics should we talk about in sex education?

Portia: Organs, how they work.

Opal: What's an orgasm?

[laughter]

Teacher: Sexual response, sensation all over the body. What's analogous to the male penis on the female?

Theo: Clitoris.

Teacher: Right, go home and look in the mirror.

Portia: She is too much!

Teacher: Why look in the mirror?

Elaine: It's yours.

Teacher: Why is it important to know what your body looks like?

Opal: You should like your body.

Teacher: You should know what it looks like when it's healthy, so you can recognize problems like vaginal warts.

Field Note, October 25, Hygiene Class

The discourse of desire, initiated by Opal but evident only as an interruption, faded rapidly into the discourse of disease – warning about the dangers of sexuality.

It was in the spring of that year that Opal showed up pregnant. Her hygiene teacher, who was extremely concerned and involved with her students, was also quite angry with Opal: "Who is going to take care of that baby, you or your mother? You know what it costs to buy diapers and milk and afford child care?"

Opal, in conversation with me, related, "I got to leave [school] 'cause even if they don't say it, them teachers got hate in their eyes when they look at my belly." In the absence of a way to talk about passion, pleasure, danger, and responsibility, this teacher fetishized the latter two, holding the former two hostage. Because adolescent females combine these experiences in their daily lives, the separation is false, judgmental, and ultimately not very educational.

Over the year in this high school, and in other public schools since, I have observed a systematic refusal to name issues, particularly issues that caused adults discomfort. Educators often projected their discomfort onto students in the guise of "protecting" them (Fine, 1987). An example of such silencing can be seen in a (now altered) policy of the school district of Philadelphia. In 1985 a student informed me, "We're not allowed to talk about abortion in our school." Assuming this was an overstatement, I asked an administrator at the District about this practice. She explained, "That's not quite right. If a student asks a question about abortion, the teacher can define abortion, she just can't discuss it." How can definition occur without discussion, exchange, conversation, or critique unless a subtext of silencing prevails (Greene, 1986; Noddings, 1986)?

Explicit silencing of abortion has since been lifted in Philadelphia. The revised curriculum now reads:

Options for unintended pregnancy:

(a) adoption

(b) foster care

(c) single parenthood

(d) teen marriage

(e) abortion

385

FINE

A footnote is supposed to be added, however, to elaborate the negative consequences of abortion. In the social politics which surround public schools, such compromises are apparent across cities.

The New York City Family Life Education curriculum reads similarly (New York City Board of Education, 1984, p. 172):

List: The possible options for an unintended pregnancy. What considerations should be given in the decision on the alternatives?

–adoption

–foster care

–mother keeps baby

–elective abortion

Discuss:

–religious viewpoints on abortion

–present laws concerning abortion

–current developments in prenatal diagnosis and their implication for abortion issues

–why abortion should not be considered a contraceptive device

List: The people or community services that could provide assistance in the event of an unintended pregnancy

Invite: A speaker to discuss alternatives to abortion; for example, a social worker from the Department of Social Services to discuss foster care.

One must be suspicious when diverse views are sought only for abortion, and not for adoption, teen motherhood, or foster care. The call to silence is easily identified in current political and educational contexts (Fine, 1987; Foucault, 1980). The silence surrounding contraception and abortion options and diversity in sexual orientations denies adolescents information and sends the message that such conversations are taboo—at home, at church, and even at school.

In contrast to these "official curricula," which allow discussion and admission of desire only as an interruption, let us examine other situations in which young women were invited to analyze sexuality across categories of the body, the mind, the heart, and of course, gender politics.

Teen Choice, a voluntary counseling program held on-site by non-Board of Education social workers, offered an instance in which the complexities of pleasure and danger were invited, analyzed, and braided into discussions of sexuality. In a small group discussion, the counselor asked of the seven ninth graders, "What are the two functions of a penis?" One student responded, "To pee!" Another student offered the second function: "To eat!" which was followed by laughter and serious discussion. The conversation proceeded as the teacher asked, "Do all penises look alike?" The students explained, "No, they are all different colors!"

The freedom to express, beyond simple right and wrong answers, enabled these young women to offer what they knew with humor and delight. This discussion ended as one student insisted that if you "jump up and down a lot, the stuff will fall out of you and you won't get pregnant," to which the social worker answered with slight exasperation that millions of sperm would have to be released for such "expulsion" to work, and that of course, it wouldn't work. In this conversation one could hear what seemed like too much experience, too little information, and too few questions asked by the students. But the discussion, which was sex-segregated and guided by the experiences and questions of the students themselves (and the skills of the social worker), enabled easy movement between pleasure and danger, safety and desire, naïveté and knowledge, and victimization and entitlement.

What is evident, then, is that even in the absence of a discourse of desire, young women express their notions of sexuality and relate their experiences. Yet, "official" discourses of sexuality leave little room for such exploration. The authorized sexual discourses define what is safe, what is taboo, and what will be silenced. This discourse of sexuality mis-educates adolescent women. What results is a discourse of sexuality based on the male in search of desire and the female in search of protection. The open, coed sexuality discussions so many fought for in the 1970s have been appropriated as a forum for the primacy of male heterosexuality and the preservation of female victimization.

387

THE POLITICS OF FEMALE SEXUAL SUBJECTIVITIES

In 1912, an education committee explicitly argued that "scientific" sex education "should . . . keep sex consciousness and sex emotions at the minimum" (Leo, 1986). In the same era G. Stanley Hall proposed diversionary pursuits for adolescents, including hunting, music, and sports, "to reduce sex stress and tension . . . to short-circuit, transmute it and turn it on to develop the higher powers of the men [sic]" (Hall, 1914, pp. 29, 30). In 1915 Orison Marden, author of *The Crime of Silence*, chastised educators, reformers, and public health specialists for their unwillingness to speak publicly about sexuality and for relying inappropriately on parents and peers, who were deemed too ignorant to provide sex instruction (Imber, 1984; Strong, 1972). And in 1921 radical sex educator Maurice Bigelow wrote:

> Now, most scientifically-trained women seem to agree that there are no corresponding phenomena in the early pubertal life of the normal young woman who has good health (corresponding to male masturbation). A limited number of mature women, some of them physicians, report having experienced in the

FINE

pubertal years localized tumescence and other disturbances which made them definitely conscious of sexual instincts. However, it should be noted that most of these are known to have had a personal history including one or more such abnormalities such as dysmenorrhea, uterine displacement, pathological ovaries, leucorrhea, tuberculosis, masturbation, neurasthenia, nymphomania, or other disturbances which are sufficient to account for local sexual stimulation. In short such women are not normal. . . . (p. 179)

In the 1950s public school health classes separated girls from boys. Girls "learned about sex" by watching films of the accelerated development of breasts and hips, the flow of menstrual blood, and then the progression of venereal disease as a result of participation in out-of-wedlock heterosexual activity.

Thirty years and a much-debated sexual revolution later (Ehrenreich, Hess, & Jacobs, 1986), much has changed. Feminism, the Civil Rights Movement, the disability and gay rights movements, birth control, legal abortion with federal funding (won and then lost), and reproductive technologies are part of these changes (Weeks, 1985). Due both to the consequences of, and the backlashes against, these movements, students today do learn about sexuality–if typically through the representations of female sexuality as inadequacy or victimization, male homosexuality as a story of predator and prey, and male heterosexuality as desire.

Young women today know that female sexual subjectivity is at least not an inherent contradiction. Perhaps they even feel it is an entitlement. Yet when public schools resist acknowledging the fulness of female sexual subjectivities, they reproduce a profound social ambivalence which dichotomizes female heterosexuality (Espin, 1984; Golden, 1984; Omolade, 1983). This ambivalence surrounds a fragile cultural distinction between two forms of female sexuality: consensual sexuality, representing consent or choice in sexuality, and *coercive* sexuality, which represents force, victimization, and/or crime (Weeks, 1985).

During the 1980s, however, this distinction began to be challenged. It was acknowledged that gender-based power inequities shape, define, and construct experiences of sexuality. Notions of sexual consent and force, except in extreme circumstances, became complicated, no longer in simple opposition. The first problem concerned how to conceptualize power asymmetries and consensual sexuality. Could consensual female heterosexuality be said to exist within a context replete with structures, relationships, acts, and threats of female victimization (sexual, social, and economic) (MacKinnon, 1983)? How could we speak of "sexual preference" when sexual involvement outside of heterosexuality may seriously jeopardize one's social and/or economic wellbeing (Petchesky, 1984)? Diverse female sexual subjectivities emerge through, despite, and because of gender-based power asymmetries. To imagine a female sexual self, free of and uncontaminated by power, was rendered naive (Foucault, 1980; Irigaray, 1980; Rubin, 1984).

FINE

The second problem involved the internal incoherence of the categories. Once assumed fully independent, the two began to blur as the varied practices of sexuality went public. At the intersection of these presumably parallel forms–coercive and consensual sexualities–lay "sexual" acts of violence and "violent" acts of sex. "Sexual" acts of violence, including marital rape, acquaintance rape, and sexual harassment, were historically considered consensual. A woman involved in a marriage, on a date, or working outside her home "naturally" risked receiving sexual attention; her consent was inferred from her presence. But today, in many states, this woman can sue her husband for such sexual acts of violence; in all states, she can prosecute a boss. What was once part of "domestic life" or "work" may, today, be criminal. On the other hand, "violent" acts of sex, including consensual sadomasochism and the use of violence-portraying pornography, were once considered inherently coercive for women (Benjamin, 1983; Rubin, 1984; Weeks, 1985). Female involvement in such sexual practices historically had been dismissed as nonconsensual. Today such romanticizing of a naive and moral "feminine sexuality" has been challenged as essentialist, and the assumption that such a feminine sexuality is "natural" to women has been shown to be false (Rubin, 1984).

Over the past decade, understandings of female sexual choice, consent, and corecion have grown richer and more complex. While questions about female subjectivities have become more interesting, the answers (for some) remain deceptively simple. Inside public schools, for example, female adolescents continue to be educated as though they were the potential *victims* of sexual (male) desire. By contrast, the ideological opposition represents only adult married women as fully consensual partners. The distinction of coercion and consent has been organized simply and respectively around age and marital status–which effectively resolves any complexity and/or ambivalence.

The ambivalence surrounding female heterosexuality places the victim and subject in opposition and derogates all women who represent female sexual subjectivities outside of marriage–prostitutes, lesbians, single mothers, women involved with multiple partners, and particularly, Black single mothers (Weitz, 1984). "Protected" from this derogation, the typical adolescent woman, as represented in sex education curricula, is without any sexual subjectivity. The discourse of victimization not only obscures the derogation, it also transforms socially distributed anxieties about female sexuality into acceptable, and even protective, talk.

The fact that schools implicitly organize sex education around a concern for female victimization is suspect, however, for two reasons. First, if female victims of male violence were truly a social concern, wouldn't the victims of rape, incest, and sexual harassment encounter social compassion, and not suspicion and blame? And second, if sex education were designed primarily to prevent victimization but not to prevent exploration of desire, wouldn't there be more discussions of both the pleasures and relatively fewer risks of disease

389

or pregnancy associated with lesbian relationships and protected sexual intercourse, or of the risk-free pleasures of masturbation and fantasy? Public education's concern for the female victim is revealed as deceptively thin when real victims are discredited, and when nonvictimizing pleasures are silenced.

This unacknowledged social ambivalence about heterosexuality polarizes the debates over sex education and school-based health clinics. The anxiety effectively treats the female sexual victim as though she were a completely separate species from the female sexual subject. Yet the adolescent women quoted earlier in this text remind us that the female victim and subject coexist in every woman's body.

TOWARD A DISCOURSE OF SEXUAL DESIRE AND SOCIAL ENTITLEMENT: IN THE STUDENT BODIES OF PUBLIC SCHOOLS

I have argued that silencing a discourse of desire buttresses the icon of woman-as-victim. In so doing, public schooling may actually disable young women in their negotiations as sexual subjects. Trained through and into positions of passivity and victimization, young women are currently educated away from positions of sexual self-interest.

If we re-situate the adolescent woman in a rich and empowering educational context, she develops a sense of self which is sexual as well as intellectual, social, and economic. In this section I invite readers to imagine such a context. The dialectic of desire and victimization—across spheres of labor, social relations, and sexuality—would then frame schooling. While many of the curricula and interventions discussed in this paper are imperfect, data on the effectiveness of what is available are nevertheless compelling. Studies of sex education curricula, SBHCs, classroom discussions, and ethnographies of life inside public high schools demonstrate that a sense of sexual and social entitlement for young women can be fostered within public schools.

Sex Education as Intellectual Empowerment

Harris and Yankelovich polls confirm that over 80 percent of American adults believe that students should be educated about sexuality within their public schools. Seventy-five percent believe that homosexuality and abortion should be included in the curriculum, with 40 percent of those surveyed by Yankelovich et al. (N = 1015) agreeing that 12-year-olds should be taught about oral and anal sex (see Leo, 1986; Harris, 1985).

While the public continues to debate the precise content of sex education most parents approve and support sex education for their children. An Illinois program monitored parental requests to "opt out" and found that only 6 or 7 of 850 children were actually excused from sex education courses (Leo, 1986). In a California assessment, fewer than 2 percent of parents disallowed their children's participation.

And in a longitudinal 5-year program in Connecticut, 7 of 2,500 students requested exemption from these classes (Scales, 1981). Resistance to sex education, while loud at the level of public rhetoric and conservative organizing, is both less vocal and less active within schools and parents' groups (Hottois & Milner, 1975 1975; Scales, 1981).

Sex education courses are offered broadly, if not comprehensively, across the United States. In 1981, only 7 of 50 states actually had laws against such instruction, and only one state enforced a prohibition (Kirby & Scales, 1981). Surveying 179 urban school districts, Sonnenstein and Pittman (1984) found that 75 percent offered some sex education within senior and junior high schools, while 66 percent of the elementary schools offered sex education units. Most instruction was, however, limited to 10 hours or less, with content focused on anatomy. In his extensive review of sex education programs, Kirby (1985) concludes that less than 10 percent of all public school students are exposed to what might be considered comprehensive sex education courses.

The progress on AIDS education is more encouraging, and more complex (see Freudenberg, 1987), but cannot be adequately reviewed in this article. It is important to note, however, that a December 1986 report released by the U.S. Conference of Mayors documents that 54 percent of the 73 largest school districts and 25 state school agencies offer some form of AIDS education (Benedetto, 1987). Today, debates among federal officials–including Secretary of Education Bennett and Surgeon General Koop–and among educators question when and what to offer in AIDS education. The question is no longer whether such education should be promoted.

Not only has sex education been accepted as a function of public schooling, but it has survived empirical tests of effectiveness. Evaluation data demonstrate that sex education can increase contraceptive knowledge and use (Kirby, 1985; Public/Private Ventures, 1987). In terms of sexual activity (measured narrowly in terms of the onset or frequency of heterosexual intercourse), the evidence suggests that sex education does not instigate an earlier onset or increase of such sexual activity (Zelnick & Kim, 1982) and may, in fact, postpone the onset of heterosexual intercourse (Zabin, Hirsch, Smith, Streett, & Hardy, 1986). The data for pregnancy rates appear to demonstrate no effect for exposure to sex education alone (see Dawson, 1986; Marsiglio & Mott, 1986; Kirby, 1985).

Sex education as constituted in these studies is not sufficient to diminish teen pregnancy rates. In all likelihood it would be naive to expect that sex education (especially if only ten hours in duration) would carry such a "long arm" of effectiveness. While the widespread problem of teen pregnancy must be attributed broadly to economic and social inequities (Jones et al., 1985), sex education remains necessary and sufficient to educate, demystify, and improve contraceptive knowledge and use. In conjunction with material opportunities for enhanced life options, it is believed that sex education and access to contraceptives and abortion can help to reduce the rate of unintended

391

FINE

pregnancy among teens (Dryfoos, 1985a, 1985b; National Research Council, 1987).

School-Based Health Clinics: Sexual Empowerment

The public opinion and effectiveness data for school-based health clinics are even more compelling than those for sex education. Thirty SBHCs provide on-site health care services to senior, and sometimes junior, high school students in more than 18 U.S. communities, with an additional 25 communities developing similar programs (Kirby, 1985). These clinics offer, at a minimum, health counseling, referrals, and follow-up examinations. Over 70 percent conduct pelvic examinations (Kirby, 1985), approximately 52 percent prescribe contraceptives, and 28 percent dispense contraceptives (Leo, 1986). None performs abortions, and few refer for abortions.

All SBHCs require some form of general parental notification and/or consent, and some charge a nominal fee for generic health services. Relative to private physicians, school-based health clinics and other family planning agencies are substantially more willing to provide contraceptive services to unmarried minors without specific parental consent (consent in this case referring explicitly to contraception). Only one percent of national Planned Parenthood affiliates require consent or notification, compared to 10 percent of public health department programs and 19 percent of hospitals (Torres & Forrest, 1985).

The consequences of consent provisions for abortion are substantial. Data from two states, Massachusetts and Minnesota, demonstrate that parental consent laws result in increased teenage pregnancies or increased numbers of out-of-state abortions. The Reproductive Freedom Project of the American Civil Liberties Union, in a report which examines the consequences of such consent provisions, details the impact of these statutes on teens, on their familial relationships, and ultimately, on their unwanted children (Reproductive Freedom Project, 1986). In an analysis of 1985, this report documents over 7,000 pregnancies in teens aged 13-17, 3,500 of whom "went to state court to seek the right to confidential abortions, all at considerable personal cost." The report also notes that many of the pregnant teens did not petition the court, "although their entitlement and need for confidential abortions was as strong or more so than the teenagers who made it to court. . . . Only those minors who are old enough and wealthy enough or resourceful enough are actually able to use the court bypass option" (Reproductive Freedom Project, p. 4).

These consent provisions, with allowance for court bypass, not only increase the number of unwanted teenage pregnancies carried to term, but also extend the length of time required to secure an abortion, potentially endangering the life of the teenage woman, and increasing the costs of the abortion. The provisions may also jeopardize the physical and emotional well-being of some young women and their mothers, particularly when paternal

FINE

consent is required and the pregnant teenager resides with a single mother. Finally, the consent provisions create a class-based health care system. Adolescents able to afford travel to a nearby state, or able to pay a private physician for a confidential abortion, have access to an abortion. Those unable to afford the travel, or those who are unable to contact a private physician, are likely to become teenage mothers (Reproductive Freedom Project, 1986).

In Minneapolis, during the time from 1980 to 1984 when the law was implemented, the birth rate for 15- to 17-year-olds increased 38.4 percent, while the birth rate for 18- and 19-year-olds–not affected by the law–rose only .3 percent (Reproductive Freedom Project, 1986). The state of Massachusetts passed a parental consent law which took effect in 1981. An analysis of the impact of that law concludes that". . . the major impact of the Massachusetts parental consent law has been to send a monthly average of between 90 and 95 of the state's minors across state lines in search of an abortion. This number represents about one in every three minor abortion patients living in Massachusetts" (Cartoof & Klerman, 1986). These researchers, among others, write that parental consent laws could have more devastating effects in larger states, from which access to neighboring states would be more difficult.

The inequalities inherent in consent provisions and the dramatic consequences which result for young women are well recognized. For example, twenty-nine states and the District of Columbia now explicitly authorize minors to grant their own consent for receipt of contraceptive information and/or services, independent of parental knowledge or consent (see Melton & Russo, 1987, for full discussion; National Research Council, 1987; for a full analysis of the legal, emotional, and physical health problems attendant upon parental consent laws for abortion, see the Reproductive Freedom Project report). More recently, consent laws for abortion in Pennsylvania and California have been challenged as unconstitutional.

Public approval of SBHCs has been slow but consistent. In the 1986 Yankelovich survey, 84 percent of surveyed adults agree that these clinics should provide birth control information; 36 percent endorse dispensing of contraceptives to students (Leo, 1986). In 1985, Harris found that 67 percent of all respondents, including 76 percent of Blacks and 76 percent of Hispanics, agree that public schools should establish formal ties with family planning clinics for teens to learn about and obtain contraception (Harris, 1985). Mirroring the views of the general public, a national sample of school administrators polled by the Education Research Group indicated that more than 50 percent believe birth control should be offered in school-based clinics; 30 percent agree that parental permission should be sought, and 27 percent agree that contraceptives should be dispensed, even if parental consent is not forthcoming. The discouraging news is that 96 percent of these respondents indicate that their districts do not presently offer such services (Benedetto, 1987; Werner, 1987).

Research on the effectiveness of SBHCs is consistently persuasive. The three-year Johns Hopkins study of school-based health clinics (Zabin et al.; 1986) found that schools in which SBHCs made referrals and dispensed contraceptives noted an increase in the percentage of "virgin" females visiting the program as well as an increase in contraceptive use. They also found a significant reduction in pregnancy rates: There was a 13 percent increase at experimental schools after 10 months, versus a 50 percent increase at control schools; after 28 months, pregnancy rates decreased 30 percent at experimental schools versus a 53 percent increase at control schools. Furthermore, by the second year, a substantial percentage of males visited the clinic (48 percent of males in experimental schools indicated that they "have ever been to a birth control clinic or to a physician about birth control," compared to 12 percent of males in control schools). Contrary to common belief, the schools in which clinics dispensed contraceptives showed a substantial postponement of first experience of heterosexual intercourse among high school students and an increase in the proportion of young women visiting the clinic prior to "first coitus."

Paralleling the Hopkins findings, the St. Paul Maternity and Infant Care Project (1985) found that pregnancy rates dropped substantially in schools with clinics, from 79 births/1,000 (1973) to 26 births/1,000 (1984). Teens who delivered and kept their infants had an 80 percent graduation rate, relative to approximately 50 percent of young mothers nationally. Those who stayed in school reported a 1.3 percent repeat birth rate, compared to 17 percent nationally. Over three years, pregnancy rates dropped by 40 percent. Twenty-five percent of young women in the school received some form of family planning and 87 percent of clients were continuing to use contraception at a 3-year follow-up. There were fewer obstetric complications; fewer babies were born at low birth weights; and prenatal visits to physicians increased relative to students in the control schools.

Predictions that school-based health clinics would advance the onset of sexual intimacy, heighten the degree of "promiscuity" and incidence of pregnancy, and hold females primarily responsible for sexuality were countered by the evidence. The onset of sexual intimacy was postponed, while contraception was used more reliably. Pregnancy rates substantially diminished and, over time, a large group of males began to view contraception as a shared responsibility.

It is worth restating here that females who received family planning counseling and/or contraception actually postponed the onset of heterosexual intercourse. I would argue that the availability of such services may enable females to feel they are sexual agents, entitled and therefore responsible, rather than at the constant and terrifying mercy of a young man's pressure to "give in" or of a parent's demands to "save yourself." With a sense of sexual agency

FINE

and not necessarily urgency, teen girls may be less likely to use or be used by pregnancy (Petchesky, 1984).

Nontraditional Vocational Training: Social and Economic Entitlement

The literature reviewed suggests that sex education, access to contraception, and opportunities for enhanced life options, in combination (Dryfoos, 1985a, 1985b; Kirby, 1985; Select Committee on Children, Youth and Families, 1985), can significantly diminish the likelihood that a teenager will become pregnant, carry to term, and/or have a repeat pregnancy, and can increase the likelihood that she will stay in high school through graduation (National Research Council, 1987). Education toward entitlement–including a sense of sexual, economic, and social entitlement–may be sufficient to affect adolescent girls' views on sexuality, contraception, and abortion. By framing female subjectivity within the context of social entitlement, sex education would be organized around dialogue and critique, SBHCs would offer health services, options counseling, contraception, and abortion referrals, and the provision of real "life options" would include nontraditional vocational training programs and employment opportunities for adolescent females (Dryfoos, 1985a, 1985b).

In a nontraditional vocational training program in New York City designed for young women, many of whom are mothers, participants' attitudes toward contraception and abortion shifted once they acquired a set of vocational skills, a sense of social entitlement, and a sense of personal competence (Weinbaum, personal communication, 1986). The young women often began the program without strong academic skills or a sense of competence. At the start, they were more likely to express more negative sentiments about contraception and abortion than when they completed the program. One young woman, who initially held strong antiabortion attitudes, learned that she was pregnant midway through her carpentry apprenticeship. She decided to abort, reasoning that now that she has a future, she can't risk losing it for another baby (Weinbaum, paraphrase of personal communication, 1986). A developing sense of social entitlement may have transformed this young woman's view of reproduction, sexuality, and self.

The Manpower Development Research Corporation (MDRC), in its evaluation of Project Redirection (Polit, Kahn, & Stevens, 1985) offers similar conclusions about a comprehensive vocational training and community-based mentor project for teen mothers and mothers-to-be. Low-income teens were enrolled in Project Redirection, a network of services designed to instill self-sufficiency, in which community women served as mentors. The program included training for what is called "employability," Individual Participation Plans, and peer group sessions. Data on education, employment, and pregnancy outcomes were collected at 12 and 24 months after enroll-

395

FINE

ment. Two years after the program began, many newspapers headlined the program as a failure. The data actually indicated that at 12 months, the end of program involvement, Project Redirection women were significantly *less likely* to experience a repeat pregnancy than comparison women; *more likely* to be using contraception; *more likely* to be in school, to have completed school, or to be in the labor force; and twice as likely (20 percent versus 11 percent, respectively) to have earned a Graduate Equivalency Diploma. At 24 months, however, approximately one year out of the program, Project and comparison women were virtually indistinguishable. MDRC reported equivalent rates of repeat pregnancies, dropout, and unemployment.

The Project Redirection data demonstrate that sustained outcomes cannot be expected once programs have been withdrawn and participants confront the realities of a dismal economy and inadequate child care and social services. The data confirm, however, the effectiveness of comprehensive programs to reduce teen pregnancy rates and encourage study or work as long as the young women are actively engaged. Supply-side interventions–changing people but not structures or opportunities–which leave unchallenged an inhospitable and discriminating economy and a thoroughly impoverished child care/social welfare system are inherently doomed to long-term failure. When such programs fail, the social reading is that "these young women can't be helped." Blaming the victim obscures the fact that the current economy and social welfare arrangements need overhauling if the sustained educational, social, and psychological gains accrued by the Project Redirection participants are to be maintained.

In the absence of enhanced life options, low-income young women are likely to default to early and repeat motherhood as a source of perceived competence, significance, and pleasure. When life options are available, however, a sense of competence and "entitlement to better," may help to prevent second pregnancies, may help to encourage education, and, when available, the pursuit of meaningful work (Burt, Kimmich, Goldmuntz, & Sonnenstein, 1984).

Femininity May Be Hazardous to Her Health: The Absence of Entitlement

Growing evidence suggests that women who lack a sense of social or sexual entitlement, who hold traditional notions of what it means to be female–self-sacrificing and relatively passive–and who undervalue themselves, are disproportionately likely to find themselves with an unwanted pregnancy and to maintain it through to motherhood. While many young women who drop out, pregnant or not, are not at all traditional in these ways, but are quite feisty and are fueled with a sense of entitlement (Fine, 1986; Weinbaum, personal communication, 1987), it may also be the case that young women who do internalize such notions of "femininity" are disproportionately at risk for pregnancy and dropping out.

The Hispanic Policy Development Project reports that low-income female sophomores who, in 1980, expected to be married and/or to have a child by age 19 were disproportionately represented among nongraduates in 1984. Expectations of early marriage and childbearing correspond to dramatic increaes (200 to 400 percent) in nongraduation rates for low-income adolescent women across racial and ethnic groups (Hispanic Policy Development Project, 1987). These indicators of traditional notions of womanhood bode poorly for female academic achievement.

The Children's Defense Fund (1986) recently published additional data which demonstrate that young women with poor basic skills are three times more likely to become teen parents than women with average or above-average basic skills. Those with poor or fair basic skills are four times more likely to have more than one child while a teen; 29 percent of women in the bottom skills quintile became mothers by age 18 versus 5 percent of young women in the top quintile. While academic skill problems must be placed in the context of alienating and problematic schools, and not viewed as inherent in these young women, those who fall in the bottom quintile may nevertheless be the least likely to feel entitled or in control of their lives. They may feel more vulnerable to male pressure or more willing to have a child as a means of feeling competent.

My own observations, derived from a year-long ethnographic study of a comprehensive public high school in New York City, further confirm some of these conclusions. Six months into the ethnography, new pregnancies began showing. I noticed that many of the girls who got pregnant and carried to term were not those whose bodies, dress, and manner evoked sensuality and experience. Rather, a number of the pregnant women were those who were quite passive and relatively quiet in their classes. One young woman, who granted me an interview anytime, washed the blackboard for her teacher, rarely spoke in class, and never disobeyed her mother, was pregnant by the spring of the school year (Fine, 1986).

Simple stereotypes, of course, betray the complexity of circumstances under which young women become pregnant and maintain their pregnancies. While U.S. rates of teenage sexual activity and age of "sexual initiation" approximate those of comparable developed countries, the teenage pregnancy, abortion, and childbearing rates in the United States are substantially higher. In the United States, teenagers under age fifteen are at least five times more likely to give birth than similarly aged teens in other industrialized nations (Jones et al., 1985; National Research Council, 1987). The national factors which correlate with low teenage birthrates include adolescent access to sex education and contraception, and relative equality in the distribution of wealth. Economic and structural conditions which support a class-stratified society, and which limit adolescent access to sexual information and contraception, contribute to inflated teenage pregnancy rates and birthrates.

397

This broad national context acknowledged, it might still be argued that within our country, traditional notions of what it means to be a woman–to remain subordinate, dependent, self-sacrificing, compliant, and ready to marry and/or bear children early–do little to empower women or enhance a sense of entitlement. This is not to say that teenage dropouts or mothers tend to be of any one type. Yet it may well be that the traditions and practices of "femininity" as commonly understood may be hazardous to the economic, social, educational, and sexual development of young women.

In summary, the historic silencing within public schools of conversations about sexuality, contraception, and abortion, as well as the absence of a discourse of desire–in the form of comprehensive sex education, school-based health clinics, and viable life options via vocational training and placement–all combine to exacerbate the vulnerability of young women whom schools, and the critics of sex education and SBHCs, claim to protect.

CONCLUSION

Adolescents are entitled to a discussion of desire instead of the anti-sex rhetoric which controls the controversies around sex education, SBHCs, and AIDS education. The absence of a discourse of desire, combined with the lack of analysis of the language of victimization, may actually retard the development of sexual subjectivity and responsibility in students. Those most "at risk" of victimization through pregnancy, disease, violence, or harassment–all female students, low-income females in particular, and non-heterosexual males–are those most likely to be victimized by the absence of critical conversation in public schools. Public schools can no longer afford to maintain silence around a discourse of desire. This is not to say that the silencing of a discourse of desire is the primary root of sexual victimization, teen motherhood, and the concomitant poverty experienced by young and low-income females. Nor could it be responsibly argued that interventions initiated by public schools could ever be successful if separate from economic and social development. But it is important to understand that by providing education, counseling, contraception, and abortion referrals, as well as meaningful educational and vocational opportunities, public schools could play an essential role in the construction of the female subject–social and sexual.

And by not providing such an educational context, public schools contribute to the rendering of substantially different outcomes for male and female students, and for male and female dropouts (Fine, 1986). The absence of a thorough sex education curriculum, of school-based health clinics, of access to free and confidential contraceptive and abortion services, of exposure to information about the varieties of sexual pleasures and partners, and of involvement in sustained employment training programs may so jeopardize the educational and economic outcomes for female adolescents as to constitute

398

FINE

sex discrimination. How can we ethically continue to withhold educational treatments we know to be effective for adolescent women?

Public schools constitute a sphere in which young women could be offered access to a language and experience of empowerment. In such contexts, "well-educated" young women could breathe life into positions of social critique and experience entitlement rather than victimization, autonomy rather than terror.

NOTES

1. The research reported in this article represents one component of a year–long ethnographic investigation of students and dropouts at a comprehensive public high school in New York City. Funded by the W.T. Grant Foundation, the research was designed to investigate how public urban high schools produce dropout rates in excess of 50 percent. The methods employed over the year included: in–school observations four days/week during the fall, and one to two days/week during the spring; regular (daily) attendance in a hygiene course for twelfth graders; an archival analysis of more than 1200 students who compose the 1978–79 cohort of incoming ninth graders; interviews with approximately 55 recent and long–term dropouts; analysis of fictional and autobiographical writings by students; a survey distributed to a subsample of the cohort population; and visits to proprietary schools, programs for Graduate Equivalency Diplomas, naval recruitment sites, and a public high school for pregnant and parenting teens. The methods and preliminary results of the ethnography are detailed in Fine (1986).

2. This information is derived from personal communications with former and present employees of major urban schools districts who have chosen to remain anonymous.

3. Personal communication.

REFERENCES

Bauer, G. (1986). *The family: Preserving America's future.* Washington, DC: U.S. Department of Education.

Benedetto, R. (1987, January 23). AIDS studies become part of curricula. *USA Today,* p. D1.

Benjamin, J. (1983). Master and slave: The fantasy of erotic domination. In A. Snitow, C. Stansell, & S. Thompson (Eds.), *Powers of desire* (pp. 280–299). New York: Monthly Review Press.

Bennett, W. (1987, July 3). Why Johnny can't abstain. *National Review, 56,* pp. 36–38.

Bigelow, M. (1921). *Sex-Education.* New York: Macmillan.

Boffey, P. (1987, February 27). Reagan to back AIDS plan urging youths to avoid sex. *New York Times,* p. A14.

Brown, P. (1983). The Swedish approach to sex education and adolescent pregnancy: Some impressions. *Family Planning Perspectives, 15*(2), 92–95.

Burke, C. (1980). Introduction to Luce Irigaray's "When our lips speak together." *Signs, 6,* 66–68.

Burt, M., Kimmich, M., Goldmuntz, J., & Sonnenstein, F. (1984). *Helping pregnant ado-*

lescents: Outcomes and costs of service delivery. Final Report on the Evaluation of Adolescent Pregnancy Programs. Washington, DC: Urban Institute.

Cartoof, V., & Klerman, L. (1986). Parental consent for abortion: Impact of the Massachusetts law. *American Journal of Public Health, 76,* 397–400.

Chicago school clinic is sued over birth control materials. (1986, October 16). *New York Times,* p. A24.

Children's Defense Fund. (1986). *Preventing adolescent pregnancy: What schools can do.* Washington, DC: Children's Defense Fund.

Children's Defense Fund. (1987). *Adolescent pregnancy: An anatomy of a social problem in search of comprehensive solutions.* Washington, DC: Children's Defense Fund.

Cixous, H. (1981). Castration or decapitation? Signs, 7, 41–55.

Dawson, D. (1986). The effects of sex education on adolesent behavior. *Family Planning Perspectives, 18,* 162–170.

Dowd, M. (1986, April 16). Bid to update sex education confronts resistance in city. *New York Times,* p. A1.

Dryfoos, J. (1985a). A time for new thinking about teenage pregnancy. *American Journal of Public Health, 75,* 13–14.

Dryfoos, J. (1985b). School–based health clincis: A new approach to preventing adolescent pregnancy? *Family Planning Perspectives, 17*(2), 70–75.

Ehrenreich, B., Hess, E., & Jacobs, G. (1986). *Re-making love.* Garden City, NY: Anchor Press.

Espin, O. (1984). Cultural and historical influences on sexuality in Hispanic/Latina women: Implications for psychotherapy. In C. Vance (Ed.), *Pleasure and danger* (pp. 149–164). Boston: Routledge & Kegan Paul.

Fine, M. (1986). Why urban adolescents drop into and out of school. *Teachers College Record, 87,* 393–409.

Fine, M. (1987). Silencing in public school. *Language Arts, 564,* 157–174.

Fisher, W., Byrne, D., & White, L. (1983). Emotional barriers to contraception. In D. Byrne & W. Fisher (Eds.), *Adolescents, sex, and contraception* (pp. 207–239). Hillsdale, NJ: Lawrence Erbaum.

Foucault, M. (1980). *The history of sexuality* (Vol. 1.). New York: Vintage Books.

Freudenberh, N. (1987). *The politics of sex education.* HealthPAC Bulletin. New York: HealthPAC.

Golden, C. (1984, March). *Diversity and variability in lesbian identities.* Paper presented at Lesbian Psychologies Conference of the Association of Women in Psychology.

Greene, M. (1986). In search of a critical pedagogy. *Harvard Education Review, 56,* 427–441.

Hall, G. S. (1914). Education and the social hygiene movement. *Social Hygiene, 1* (1 December), 29–35.

Harris, L., and Associates. (1985). *Public attitudes about sex education, family planning and abortion in the United States.* New York: Louis Harris and Associates, Inc.

Hispanic Policy Development Project. (1987, Fall). *1980 high school sophmores from poverty backgrounds: Whites, Blacks, Hispanic look at school and adult reposnsibilties,* Vol. 1, No. 2. New York: Author.

Hottois, J., & Milner, N. (1975). *The sex education controversy.* Lexington, MA: Lexington Books.

Imber, M. (1984). Towards a theory of educational origins: The genesis of sex education. *Educational Theory, 34*, 275–286.

Irigaray, L. (1980). When our lips speak together. *Signs, 6*, 69.

Jones, E., Forrest, J., Goldman, N., Henshaw, S., Lincoln, R., Rosoff, J., Wesoff, C., & Wulf, D. (1985). Teenage pregnancy in developed countries. *Family Planning Perspectives, 17*(1), 55–63.

Kantrowitz, B., Hager, M., Wingert, S., Carrol, G., Raine, G., Witherspoon, D., Huck, J., & Doherty, S., (1987, February 16). Kids and contraceptives. *Newsweek,* pp. 54–65.

Kelly, G. (1986). *Learning about sex.* Woodbury, NY: Barron's Educational Series.

Kirby, D. (1985). *School-based health clinics: An emerging approach to improving adolescent health and addressing teenage pregnancy.* Washington, DC: Center for Population Options.

Kriby, D., & Scales, P. (1981, April). An analysis of state guidelines for sex education instruction in public schools. *Family Relations,* pp. 229–237.

Koop, C. E. (1986). *Surgeon General's report on acquired immune deficiency syndromed.* Washington, DC: Office of the Surgeon General.

Koop's AIDS stand assailed. (1987, March 15). *New York Times,* p. A25.

Leo, J. (1986, November 24). Sex and schools. *Time,* pp. 54–63.

Lorde, A. (1980, August). *Uses of the erotic: The erotic as power.* Paper presented at the Fourth Berkshire Conference on the History of Women, Mt. Holyoke College.

MacKinnon, C. (1983). Complicity: An introduction of Andrea Dworkin's "Abortion," Chapter 3, "Right–Wing Women." *Law and Inequality, 1*, 89–94.

Marsiglio, W., & Mott, F. (1986). The impact of sex education on sexual activity, contraceptive use and premarital pregnancy among American teenagers. *Family Planning Perspectives, 18*(4), 151–162.

Melton, S., & Russon, N. (1987). Adolescent abortion. *American Psychologist, 42*, 69–83.

National Research Council. (1987). *Risking the future: Adolesenct sexuality, pregnancy and childbearing* (Vol. 1). Washington, DC: National Academy Press.

New York City Board of Education. (1984). *Family living curriculum including sex education.* Grades K through 12. New York City Board of Education, Division of Curriculum and Instruction.

Noddings, N. (1986). Fidelity in teaching, teacher education, and research for teaching. *Harvard Educational Review, 56*, 496–510.

Omolade, B. (1983). Hearts of darkness. In A. Snitow, C. Stansell, & S. Thompson (Eds.), *Powers of desire* (pp. 350–367). NY: Monthly Review Press.

Perlez, J. (1986a, June 24). On teaching about sex. *New York Times,* p. C1.

Perlez, J. (1986b, September 24). School chief to ask mandatory sex education. *New York Times,* p. A36.

Petchesky, R. (1984). *Abortion and woman's choice.* New York: Longman.

Philadelphia School District. (1986). Sex education curriculum. Draft.

Polit, D., Kahn, J., & Stevens, D. (1985). *Final impacts from Project Redirection.* New York: Manpower Development Research Center.

Public/Private Ventures. (1987, April). *Summer training and education program.* Philadelphia: Author.

Reproductive Freedom Prefect. (1986). *Parental consent laws on abortion: Their catastroph-*

ic impact on teenagers. New York: American Civil Liberties Union.

Rohter, L. (1985, October 29). School workers shown AIDS film. *New York Times*, p. B3.

Rubin, G. (1984). Thinking sex: Notes for a radical theory of the politics of sex. In C. Vance (Ed.), *Pleasure and danger* (pp. 267–319). Boston Routledge & Kegan Paul.

St. Paul Maternity and Infant Care Project. (1985). *Health services project description.* St. Paul, MN: Author.

Scales, P. (1981). Sex education and the prevention of teenage pregnancy: An overview of policies and programs in the United States. In T. Ooms (Ed.), *Teenage pregnancy in a family context: Implications for policy* (pp. 213–253). Philadelphia: Temple University Press.

Schlafly, P. (1986). Presentation on women's issues. American Dreams Symposium, Indiana University of Pennsylvania.

Selected group to see original AIDS tape. (1987, January 29). *New York Times*, p. B4.

Smith–Rosenberg, C. (1978). Sex as symbol in Victorian purity: An ethnohistorical analysis of Jacksonian American. *American Journal of Sociology, 84*, 212–247.

Snitow, A., Stansell, C., & Thompson, S. (Eds.). (1983). *Powers of desire.* New York: Monthly Review Press.

Sonnenstein, F., & Pitman, K. (1984). The availability of sex education in large city school districts. *Family Planning Perspectives, 16*(1), 19–25.

Strong, B. (1972). Ideas of the early sex education movement in American, 1890–1920. *History of Education Quarterly, 12*, 129–161.

Thompson, S. (1983). Search for tomorrow: On feminism and the reconstruction of teen romance. In A. Snitow, C. Stansell & S. Thompson (Eds.), *Powers of desire* (pp. 367–384). New York: Monthly Review Press.

Torres, A., & Forest, J, (1985). Family planning clinic services in the United States, 1983. *Family Planning Perspective, 17*(1), 30–35.

Vance, C. (1984). *Pleasure and danger.* Boston: Routledge & Kegan Paul.

Weeks, J, (1985). *Sexuality and its discontents.* London: Routledge & Kegan Paul.

Weitz, R. (1984). What price independence? Social reactions to lesbians, spinsters, widows and nuns. In J. Freeman (Eds.), *Women: A feminist perspective* (3rd ed.). Palo Alto, CA: Mayfield.

Werner, L. (1987, November 14). U.S. report asserts administration halted liberal "anti–family agenda." *New York Times*, p. A12.

Zabin, L., Hirsch, M., Smith, E., Streett, R., & Hardy, J. (1986). Evaluation of a pregnancy prevention program for urban teenagers. *Family Planning Perspectives, 18*(3), 119–126.

Zelnick, M., & Kim, Y. (1982). Sex education and its association with teenager sexual activity, pregnancy and contraceptive use. *Family Planning Perspectives, 14*(3), 117–126.

VIRGINS AND QUEERS
Rehabilitating Heterosexuality?

Celia Kitzinger
Sue Wilkinson

chapter 22

SOME YEARS ago, one of us had a Portuguese neighbor who, about six months after the birth of her first child, burst into tears one day, and said, "I am not a real woman." Looking at her elegantly made-up face, her expensive dress and jewelry, and the child in her arms, it took some time to work out what she meant: since the birth of her child, she had not sexual intercourse with her husband. "I am not a real woman" appeared to be a literal translation of a Portuguese phrase. It was one of the clearest demonstrations of the extent to which, at least in modern Western cultures, being a "real woman" means engaging in heterosexual sexual activity. Heterosexuality *constitutes* women as "real" women and men as "real" men (Wittig 1992). Those of us who are not heterosexual lose authenticity as members of our own sex and become "the third sex"—*unsexed* or *degendered*.

Heterosexuality reinscribes male/female divisions by its very definition: "hetero" means other, different; "heterosexuality" means sexual involvement with one who is other, one who is different—man with woman, woman with man. The otherness of the "other" sex, the "differentness" of man from woman, is thereby immediately reinforced. There are, of course, many ways in which human beings differ from each other: "heterosexuality" *could* mean sex between two people of different racial or ethnic backgrounds (regardless of their sex), or between two people of different religious or political persuasions, or between two people from different socioeconomic groups. Instead, "heterosexuality" marks what is seen, in some sense, as the fundamental "difference"—the male/female division.

From the beginning of first-wave feminism, feminists have produced searing critiques of heterosexuality, pointing in particular to the abuses associated with heterosexual sex (child sexual abuse, rape in marriage, clitoridectomy, wife-beating, sexual slavery), and to the compulsory nature of heterosexuality in a society that systematically inculcates and rewards heterosexuality while punishing and rendering lesbianism invisible. Such critiques, advanced from a range of different feminist perspectives (including liberal and socialist feminisms) have often left open the possibility of a (potentially) nonabusive and noncompulsory heterosexuality, freely chosen by women in egalitarian and personally rewarding relationships with men. The radical feminist critique of heterosexuality, by contrast, critiques even purportedly noncompulsory and nonabusive heterosexuality as *reinscribing sex differences, and hence, inevitably, women's subordination and men's power.* This latter critique would seem to render heterosexuality political anathema for feminists.

Many feminists, however, have expressed the belief that heterosexuality can be rescued and rehabilitated. Indeed, some of the very same theorists who propose the radical critique nonetheless retain the possibility of some kind of heterosexuality exempt from this analysis. In this article, we discuss and evaluate two such attempts, both (in their contemporary manifestations) originating from lesbian feminists. The first, "virgin heterosexuality" (a heterosexuality which does not reinscribe, but rather resists "maleness" and "femaleness") is advanced by Marilyn Frye, first at a speech given at the National Women's Studies Association annual conference in June 1990, published in *off our backs* later than same year (prompting a flood of letters in response), and subsequently revised as a chapter in her book, *Willful Virgin* (1992). The second rehabilitatory attempt, "queer heterosexuality" (a heterosexuality which not only does not reinscribe, but which actively subverts, "maleness and "femalness") is an offshoot of postmodernist and queer theory, the former often identified with Judith Butler's enormously influential book, *Gender Trouble* (1990), the latter with activist groups such as Queer Nation and OutRage. In this article we discuss the attempts of "virgin" and "queer" theorist to rehabilitate heterosexuality. We analyze, from a radical feminist perspective, the problem associated with both rehabilitory attempts and consider their implications.

VIRGIN HETEROSEXUALITY: RESISTING "SEX"

In what seems an attempt to retain heterosexual women's allegiance to feminist politics, lesbian feminist Marilyn Frye offers the possibility of rehabilitating heterosexuality by reviving the historical meaning attached to the word
"virgins." This term originally meant not women without experience of heterosexual intercourse but rather "females who are willing to engage in chosen
connections with males, who are wild females, undomesticated females, thoroughly defiant of patriarchal female heterosexuality" (1992, 134). The question, then, is whether it is possible for a contemporary woman to become a
"virgin" in this sense: to retain freedom of choice to take or to reject male
lovers; to have many male lovers, but never be possessed or captured, to be
"one-in-herself," unexploited, not in a man's control. Is it possible for women
to enjoy sexual interactions which "are not sites where people with penises
make themselves men and people with vaginas are made women" (Frye 1992,
134)?

Frye's own answer to this question is somewhat ambiguous. Many women
heard her original speech, and the article based on it, as answering "no," and
as claiming lesbianism as an essential component of feminism. What she actually says is this:

> I think everything is against it, but *it's not my call*. I can hopefully imagine, but the
> counter-possible creation of such a reality is up to those who want to live it, if
> anyone does. (1992, 136; emphasis in original)

405

In putting the burden of creating "heterosexual virginity" onto those women
who wish to engage in sexual connection with men, while maintaining independence and autonomy, Frye poses an important challenge to heterosexual
feminists, and her analysis has far-reaching implications for radical feminist
theory. We raise three key concerns here: (1) the politics of penetration; (2)
the method of heterosexual virginity; and (3) the problem of power.

First, in suggesting that sexual intercourse is compatible with virginity,
Frye's analysis runs counter to a long-standing radical feminist political analysis of the politics of penile-vaginal penetration. It is *precisely* penile-vaginal
penetration, rather than any other acts of heterosexual sex, which has been
critiqued by those who point to the particular set of cultural and political
meanings attached to penile penetration of women (being "had," "possessed,"
"taken," "fucked"), meanings which are "oppressive, humiliating and destructive" (Duncker 1993, 148). The Leeds Revolutionary Feminist Group argued
that:

> No act of penetration takes place in isolation. Each takes place in a system of re-
> lationships that is male supremacy. As no individual woman can be "liberated"
> under male supremacy, so no act of penetration can escape its function and its
> symbolic power. (1981, 7)

KITZINGER/WILKINSON

This analysis of penile penetration is independent of whether or not a particular woman happens to enjoy penile-vaginal penetration—although these
two arguments have often been confused, as though the experience of "pleasure" in sexual intercourse somehow mitigates against its oppressive function.
Although for some women, penetration "can feel like one more
invasion...[and is] less pleasurable than other forms of sexual contact" (Gill
and Walker 1993, 70), many others can, and do, take pleasure from the experience of penile-vaginal penetration and want to distinguish between "compulsory" or "abusive" penetration and "consensual" penetration:

> Penetration is not always rape. Having experienced penetration which was, I
> know the enormous difference between the feeling of fear, anxiety and disem-
> bodiment which come with forced sex, and the feeling of intimacy, oneness and
> sensuality which comes with intercourse which is not. (Rowland 1993, 77)

> If there is safety, trust and love in the relationship, having the man's penis inside
> your vagina can signify as the ultimate in closeness. . . I want to open to him. He
> wants to be wanted by me, and therefore welcomed inside me. He wants to give
> me something: I want to be given. . . I get pleasure from feeling his penis inside
> my vagina because it means feeling him (with all that means about loving, ac-
> cepting and respecting this particular person) inside me. (Hollway 1993)

In a sociopolitical context in which many women have long been denied a
right to sexual desires and pleasures, attempts to experience pleasure are represented by some feminists and sex radicals as a struggle against oppression:
expansion of the "possibilities, opportunities and permissions for pleasure" is
part of a "necessary feminist strategy on sexual matters" (Vance 1992, xvi).
Within radical feminist analyses, however, women's pleasure is not a "pure"
erotic force welling up from within, but rather is seen as having been constructed under heteropatriarchy. Male power does not simply deny and repress women's sexuality; it also actively constructs it. It is neither the relative
scarcity nor the impoverished quality of female heterosexual organsm that
concerns many radical feminists; rather, as Jeffreys (1990) argues, it is a serious
problem that, despite the conditions of women's oppression, women can have
orgasms in heterosexual sex. According to this analysis, heterosexual pleasure
(and much lesbian and gay male sexual pleasure too) is based on the eroticizing of subordination (Dworkin 1987; Jeffreys 1990; Kitzinger 1994; MacKinnon 1987). Frye's analysis simply sidesteps this radical feminist critique.

Moreover, some women are virgins in the modern sense of the term:
women whose vaginas are untouched by any penis (Jo 1993). Accepting the
analysis of penile-vaginal penetration as inherently oppressive (and/or simply
disliking the sensations it produces), other women—and, indeed some men
(e.g., Stoltenberg 1990)—either refuse heterosexual sex altogether, or choose
heterosexual sex that does not include intercourse itself. This rebellion against

KITZINGER/WILKINSON

the "coital imperative" (Jackson 1984, cited in Gavey 1993, 100) is difficult for women to achieve in the context of heterosexual relationships. "For several years of my life I was raped," says Amanda Sebestyen. "I was penetrated against my will because I didn't dare insist on any other kind of sex. And I *still* have a fight any time I start a sexual relationship with a man" (1982, 235). If heterosexual sexual intercourse is not seen as a key site of oppression, then women's valiant attempts to resist it are reduced to mere acts of personal preference. Of course, some women happen to dislike sexual intercourse (and prefer not to do it), whereas others happen to like it, but liking or disliking it is not the point here: personal preferences do not address the key question of the function of intercourse in maintaining women's oppression. The refusal of coitus, whether or not accompanied by a more general refusal to engage in any form of sex with men, has long been a deliberate strategy of resistance for feminists (cf. Jeffreys 1985). The political imperatives guiding these choices are obscured by Frye's reversion to an archaic definition of virgin.

Second, it is not at all clear how "virginity" (in Frye's terms) can be accomplished, and what the methods are by which a woman can remain "free", "sexually and hence socially her own person" (Frye 1992, 133), when engaging in heterosexual sexual intercourse and otherwise connecting with men. If the refusal of penile-vaginal penetration is conceptualized as resistance to heteropatriarchal oppression, then women's "voluntary" engagement in coitus can be (and often is) characterized as compliance with, or capitulation to, the enemy—rather than as free choice (Leeds Revolutionary Feminist Group 1981). Despite her intentions, Rich's (1980) concept of "compulsory heterosexuality" has, paradoxically, been used to promote the notion of a "freely chosen", "consensual" heterosexuality (Brunet and Turcotte 1988, 455), and to some extent Frye's concept of virgins is dependent on such a notion: that women have, as Warner says, "freedom of choice: to take [male] lovers or reject them" (1990, 15). The methods for living heterosexual feminist virginity could begin to "make sense" (according to Frye) if they included the following: refusal to attire or decorate the body in way that signal female compliance with male-defined femininity; defense of women-only spaces; refusal of male protection and the institution of marriage (despite the economic pressures); and ardent passion for, and enduring friendships with, other virgins, including lesbians. Some women do attempt such "virginal" strategies: "woman-identified radical feminist" Robyn Rowland (1993), for example, takes responsibility for her choice to be heterosexual; is not married; lives apart from her male partner 75 percent of the time; and identifies her "crucially important" commitment to "putting women first." In parallel with these demands on women in heterosexual relationships, heterosexual feminist Naomi Wolf (1993) has produced an account of what is needed from "the men we love" for successful feminist heterosexual relationships. Among the defining criteria of such men, she includes the following: they "understand that we are engaged in a cross-cultural relationship . . . and that they know little of our world"; they "don't hold a baby as if it's still squirming, unidentifiable catch from the sea . . . don't tell women what to feel about sexism . . . are willing to read the books we love . . . undertake half the care and cost of contraception . . . make a leap of imagination to believe in the female experience . . . don't drive without gender glasses on . . . know that just because sex can be irrational doesn't mean we're insane."

Such models for living positive feminist heterosexual virginity are dependent on a great deal of unacknowledged social privilege. Many women are trapped in marriages with men for whom such demands are irrelevant and many others have marriage and/or other heterosexual partnerships denied them for reasons of racism, class oppression, or disability. Others are forcibly separated from their male partners (and children) by war, famine, political intrigue, scarcity of work, or economic necessity. The woman who, forced by her own poverty or the exigencies of her country's national debt, leaves her family to work as a domestic servant or as a migrant coffee picker may well be apart from her husband for 75 percent (or more) of the time, but where is her opportunity to "invent and embody modes of living positive virginity"?

Third, Frye's analysis fails to centrally address the radical feminist critique of heterosexuality that she herself advances: the function of heterosexuality in constructing us as "men" and as "women", and hence as oppressor and oppressed. Sexuality, as Catherine MacKinnon says, "is a social construct, gendered to the ground" (1987, 149). Heterosexuality is a key mechanism through which male dominance is achieved. Male dominance is "not an artificial overlay" upon heterosexuality that can somehow be stripped away to leave an uncorrupted, pure, sexual interaction; rather it is intrinsic to heterosex itself:

> It has often been asserted that [sissy] men have too much in common with women for either of them to feel much excitement. There is no gap for the spark to jump. You get two sweet, nice people together, and nobody's going to do anything except with the permission of the other, assuming that anyone has the "balls" to bring the subject up. . . . Opposites attract . . . women want real men, and that's all there is to it. (Hunter 1993, 159)

More than this, there is a strong link between heterosexuality and masculinity, such that "heterosexuality is largely conceptualized *unthinkingly* as a relationship between women and *masculine* males" (Hunter 1993, 163)—that is, between subordinated and dominator.

Many feminist theorists have analyzed the extent to which sex is eroticized power difference and have critiqued the phenomenon that Jeffreys (1990) labels "heterosexual desire"—by which she means not just desire between women and men, but the eroticizing of dominance and submission. The problem for feminists is not just man's eroticizing of power, but also women's eroticizing of *powerlessness*. Erotic excitment, according to this analysis, is modeled on a heterosexual pardigm constructed around power difference. When (as in lesbian or gay male sex) the sex (as in "gender") hierarchy is missing, other social stratifications (e.g., race, class) or specially constructed power differentials (as in sadomasochism) can sometimes be eroticized (Jeffreys 1993).

As we have noted, critiques of heterosexual sexual activity often proceed as though sexual pleasure—or lack of it—was the sole criteron on which a feminist assessment could be made; yet, for many women, the problem is their serious political concern about how sexual pleasure is produced, and the form that such pleasure takes. Segal (1983) points out that "it does not feel like personal liberation to be able to orgasm to intensely masochistic fantasies"; and Bartky's decision "not to pursue men whose sadism excited me" (1993, 42) was made at the cost of "the powerful erotic charge" found in such relationships. Jeffreys recommends that women seek to shut down those sexual responses which eroticize subordination: "The question we have to ask ourselves is whether we want our freedom or whether we want to retain heterosexual desire" [1990, 134]. Frye's acceptance of heterosexual desire and activity as unproblematic parts of the virgin's repertoire represents a failure to engage with this radical feminist critique.

In sum, then, although Frye's portrayal of virgin heterosexuality may seem attractive—particularly in its links with feminist traditions of defying patriarchal conventions and reclaiming or investing feminist alternatives—it is not convincing, either as a strategy for resisting the traditional inscription of "woman", or as a means of rehabilitating heterosexuality. Frye's analysis overlooks heterosexual sexual intercourse as a key site of women's oppression and resistance; is unclear as to the methods by which virgin heterosexuality is to be accomplished under heteropatriarchy; and, most important from the radical feminist perspective, does not address the central role of heterosex in reinscribing "sex" as power relations.

409

QUEER HETEROSEXUALITY: SUBVERTING "SEX"

In recent years the word "queer," long used as a term of insult and self-loathing, has been reclaimed by lesbians, gay men, bisexuals, transvesites, and transexuals as a proud declaration of nonconformist sexualities: "We're here, we're queer; get used to it!" In place of the medicopsyciatric "homosexual," or the euphemistic and self-justificatory "gay", the word "queer" is seen as confrontational and as underscoring the fact that we are "queer" ("deviant" and "abnormal") to a world in which normality is defined in rigid and suffocating terms:

> The insistence on queer—a term defined against "normal" and generated precisely in the context of terror—has the effect of pointing out a wide field of

normalization, rather than simple tolerance, as the site of violence. (Warner 1990)

The notion of "queer heterosexuality" has come to refer to those people who, while doing what is conventionally defined as "heterosexuality," nonetheless do so in ways which are transgressive of "normality." Just as Marilyn Frye and others have expanded the notion of "virgin" to include a particular way of doing heterosex, so the queer theorists have expanded the notion of "queer" to include, among other things, a particular way of doing heterosex.

Like "virgin" theorists, "queer" theorists start from the position that "straight sex" *reinscribes* its participants as "man" and "woman." Queer theory differs from virgin theory in that, whereas the concept of "virgin" heterosexuality denotes the doing of heterosex while *resisting* being "sexed," "queer" heterosexuality denoted the doing of [what used to be called] heterosex while *actively subverting* its constructive function. Rather than simply *resisting* the equation between sex (as activity) and sex (as gender), queer theory explicitly acknowledges this link, and by deliberately drawing attention to and playing with it, attempts to denaturalize and hence subvert the equation. "Fucking with gender" implies the possibility of doing sex in such a way that it not merely resists, but actively disrupts normative definitions of "sex" and "gender."

Influenced by, and in many ways an offshoot of postmodermism, it is nonetheless possible to critique queer theory without engaging in an attack on the whole of the postmodernist and poststructuralist movements, some aspects of which (especially the notion of disciplinary power) have been found useful by many feminists, ourselves included (see also Weedon 1987; Diamond and Quinby 1988). In this section of the article, our focus is on queer theory (rather than on postmodernism) and, more narrowly still, on that aspect of queer theory that relates to heterosexuality. In general, queer theory aims to deconstruct and confound normative categories of gender and sexuality, exposing their fundamental unnaturalness. There are no "true" gender identities or natural sexes: rather maleness and femaleness are "performances" or "simulations." Maleness and femaleness are

> *performative* in the sense that the essence or identity that they otherwise purport to express are *fabrications* manufactured and sustained through corporal signs and other discursive means . . . an illusion discursively maintained for the purposes of the regulation of sexuality within the obligatory frame of reproductive heterosexuality. (Butler 1990, 136)

"Simulation" means not a replica of something that actually exists, but an identical copy for which there has never been an original. Disneyland, for example, has been described as a simulation whose function in proclaiming its status as "unreal" precisely to make the rest of the United States look "real" (Baudrillard 1988). Gender, too, is conceived as an exact copy of some-thing that never really existed in the first place: there is no "real," underlying male-ness or femaleness on which we base our performances. The postmodern body "is the body of the mythological Trickster, the shape-shifter or indeter-minate sex and changeable gender . . . who continually alters her/his body, creates and recreates a personality . . . and floats across time from period to period, place to place" (Bordo 1993, 144, paraphrasing Smith-Rosenberg 1985). This is, in the language of postmodernism, indicative of an identity in flux, a protean fantasy, an intricate textual dance, a narrative heteroglossia, a choreography of multiplicity, and a celebration of a transcendent polyvocal self at a time when "the rigid demarcations of the clear and distinct Cartesian universe are crumbling, and the notion of the unified 'subject' is no longer tenable" (Bordo 1993, 144). In this theory of fluctuating and continually al-tering selves, sex is an area "of fashion and style rather than biology and iden-tity" (Chapkis 1986, 138). "Being" man or woman is conceptualized not as core identity, but rather as "a put-on, a sex toy" (Schwichtenberg 1993, 135) or as a "temporary positioning" (Gergen 1993, 64).

In conceptualizing what have previously been seen as "core" identities (man/woman; hetero/homosexual) as no more than fluctuating fashions or performances, queer theory, like postmodernism more generally, expresses the hope for future abolition of such divisive patriarchal binarisms, ushering in the age of the post-lesbian and—of course—the post-heterosexual. In this imagined world ("this world of my fantasy," Gergen 1993, 64), man does not exist, nor woman either; hence, the concepts of heterosexuality, homosexuali-ty and bisexuality are literally unthinkable. The sex of the person you have sex with is not only irrelevant in terms of social meaning and identity: it is also unspecifiable, because "sex-as-gender" is no longer a meaningful concept. Many feminists (Gergen 1993; Ruby 1993) and sex radicals (Sprinkle 1992) are attracted by the deconstructive power of queer theory, which vividly un-couples the inscription of gender through heterosexuality; however, this vi-sion of the future uncoupling of "heterosex" and "gender" is not, of course, specific to postmodernist and queer theory: it has a long (though rarely ac-knowledged) history within radical feminism (e.g., Radicalesbians 1970; Pier-cy 1979), as well as in the early writings of both the British and the North American gay liberation movements. What is distinctive about postmodern and queer (as opposed to radical feminist) theory is the strategy envisioned for getting "there" from "here."

The notion of "queer heterosexuality" is one component of the postmod-ern strategy for transition into the brave new world of the future. Such a world would have no use for the concept of "queer heterosexuality" because there would be no such thing as heterosexuality, no men and women to per-form it, nor any heteronormativity against which to be positioned as "queer."

411

In the interim, queer theorists give "queer heterosexuals" a walk-on role. "There are times," says queer theorist Cherry Smyth (1992), "when queers may choose to call themselves heterosexual, bisexual, lesbian or gay, or none of the above." According to Schwichtenberg, one could "come out" and participate in a range of identities "such as a lesbian heterosexual, a heterosexual lesbian, a male lesbian, a female gay man, or even a feminist sex-radical" (1993, 141). Another writer offers this list: "There are straight queers, biqueers, tranny queers, lez queers, fag queers, SM queers, fisting queers" (Anonymous leaflet 1991, cited in Smyth 1992, 17). Although queer heterosexuality is rarely explored in any detail (and still less are queer heterosexuals themselves queuing up to describe their experiences), the notion of the "queer heterosexual" has become established in queer theory. It has gained (a limited) currency not, apparently, because many people are convinced of either its possibility or its desirability, still less because it names significant contemporary identities, but because queer heterosexuality is a necessary component of "gender-fucking" (Butler 1990).

If all is artifice, simulation and performance, if "sex" is only a passing fashion, there is no point in opposing this by looking for some underlying reality or truth about "men" and "women," rather, the strategy becomes to actively participate in the artifice precisely in order to underscore the fragility of "sex" and "gender" as *artifice*. This strategy is described by queer theorists as "gender play" (Schwichtenberg 1993), "gender bending" (Braidotti 1991) or, most popularly in the queer movement, as "gender-fuck" or "fucking with gender." The gender-fuck is supposed to "deprive the naturalizing narratives of compulsory heterosexuality of their central protagonists: 'man' and 'woman'" (Butler 1990, 146) and to illustrate the social constructedness of "sex," in all its multiple meanings.

This key queer strategy, the gender-fuck, is about parody, pastiche, and exaggeration. It replaces resistance to dominant cultural meanings of sex with carnivalesque reversals and transgressions of traditional gender roles and sexualities, which revel in their own artificiality. Media figures like Boy George and Annie Lennox have been cited as gender benders (Braidotti 1991, 122-3), but the most famous example of contemporary gender-fucking is undoutedly Madonna, described as both a "postmodern feminist heroine" (Kaplan 1987 in Mandzuick 1993, 169; Schwichtenberg 1993, 132) and as a "queer icon" (Henderson 1993, 108). Her postmodern "queerness" lies in the way in which she is "dressing up and acting out to *expose* the constructedness of what in other settings passes as 'natural' male, female, or heterosexual" (Henderson 1993, 122).

This same celebration of denaturalization is evident in the work of lesbian photographers often called queer. The controversial collection of lesbian photography, *Stolen Glances*, by Fraser and Boffin (1991) (the latter explicitly identifies herself as queer in Smyth 1992), was compiled not in the "attempt to naturalize a 'lesbian aesthetic . . . but rather to celebrate that there is no natural sexuality at all," and out of an interest in "subversive strategies of representation" (p. 21): these photos include Boffin's images of lesbian Casanovas in a Victorian cemetery and Della Grace's portrayal of a lesbian couple, one in gestapo cap, chains and black leather, the other in a bridal veil. Sex radicals such as Grace are often admired by queer theorists for their transgressive gender-fucking strategies, and are increasingly drawing on queer theory as an explanatory framework. *Love Bites*, a collection of photographs by Della Grace, has been cited by Smyth (1992) as an example of gender-fucking: one photograph, "Lesbian Cock," shows two lesbians dressed in leather and biker caps, both sporting moustaches and one holding a lifelike dildo protruding from her crotch.

> Lesbian feminists think things like lesbians giving blow-jobs to dildos should be kept quiet. . . . [F]or women to indulge in gender-fucking somehow isn't acceptable. But lesbians do. Lesbians even have "gay male sex." (Grace, quoted in Smyth 1992, 44)

A varied selection of lesbians, bisexuals, gay men, transsexuals, transvesites and sex radicals have claimed (or been ascribed) the "queer" label and have been lauded for their gender-fucking prowess. In the name of queer, some lesbians reclaim butch-fem roles as "changeable costuming" (MacCowan 1992, 300), and some gay men reclaim camp as "the pervert's revenge on authenticity" (Dollimore 1991). Transvestism (and cross-dressing) "draws the binary logic of sexual identity into question" (Bristow 1992). Transsexuals have a part to play because "the surgical removal and implantation of body parts reveals that one's flesh can be cut, so to speak, like a suit" (Bristow 1992) and because symbolically speaking "we are all transsexuals" (Baudrillard 1988). Hermaphrodites, too, are "a pornotopian escape from . . . rigid binarism" (Williams 1992, 261) and Annie Sprinkle, "Post-Porn Post-Modernist" and "bi-girl" (Sprinkle 1992), sometimes bracketed with Madonna as a queer performance artist (Williams 1992, 234), delights in the gender-fucking ambiguity of her "first time with a F2M-transsexual-surgically-made hermaphrodite." With queer support for such a dazzling variety of "perversions," and given that the "biological sex" of sexual partners is dismissed in favor of gender as performance, it is hardly surprising that "many queer activists are wondering what's stopping gay men and lesbians from developing a sexual politics that also embraces bi- and heterosexuals" (Pickering 1992).

But here imagination falters. Despite the fact that queer politics includes many bisexuals (Kennedy 1992) and supports lesbians having sex with men as "transgressive" (Wilson 1992), lesbian and bisexual queer theorists have not offered any details on "queer heterosex." It is as though merely the doing of sex with men is (for a lesbian, or for one who also has sex with women) transgressive in and of itself, and need not be subjected to further analysis.

KITZINGER/WILKINSON

Even if this were true (which we don't accept), heterosexual sex for straight women cannot fulfill this allegedly transgressive function: does it then become a "queer-approved" activity only if it violates some other purported taboos—if it's sadomasochistic, or fetishistic, perhaps? Queer theorists have never satisfactorily answered the question, What makes straight heterosexuality "queer"?

From a radical feminist perspective, then, our first critism of queer heterosexuality is that (as with virgin heterosexuality) its proponents offer little or no indication of the methods for doing it. Queer heterosexuality is advanced as a conceptual and practical possibility, a supporting cameo role in the queer masquerade, but its characterization is largely content free. Extrapolating from queer theory more generally, it would obviously have to be a form of heterosexuality that "fucked with gender," that is, actively transgresses, parodies and subverts the "woman subordinate," "male dominant" sexual equation. It is not clear that, as a political strategy, this is any more sophisticated than is reclaiming as feminist the female dominatrix scenes of male pornography or celebrating women's fantasies of raping men.

A second problem with the notion of queer heterosexuality is that, by definition, it elides heterosexuality and homosexuality as sexually—and hence politically—equivalent, sometimes literally so:

> The sexual ambiguities, finally, are just that—ambiguous. We do not know for sure that Madonna does not kiss a woman, nor do we know for sure that she does. In a pop cultural universe that makes heterosex abundant and abundantly clear, allusions to homosex are nice but not enough. Postmodernism's playful indeterminacy becomes gay activism's short shrift. (Henderson 1993, 113)

The presentation of lesbianism and heterosexuality as interchangeable is not as radical as queer theorists would have us believe. It was Kinsey's (Kinsey, Pomeroy, and Martin 1948; Kinsey et al. 1953) famous invention of the "homosexual-heterosexual" continuum (borrowed in part from Freud's [1977] theories of innate bisexuality and polymorphous perversity) that set the stage for a widespread dissolution within psychology of any specific differences between lesbians and heterosexual women (cf. Kitzinger, 1987). The presentation of lesbianism and heterosexuality as equivalent betrays the underlying liberalism of queer theory. As the meanings of heterosexuality and homosexuality become blurred within a fantasy world of ambiguity, indeterminacy. and charade, the material realities of oppression and the feminist politics of resistance are forgotten:

> It is difficult . . . to acknowledge the divided self and engage the pleasure of masquerade while at the same time fighting a strikingly antagonistic legal and social system for your health, your safety, your job, your place to live, or the right to raise your children. (Henderson 1993, 123)

414

KITZINGER/WILKINSON

Third, in promoting a flexible polysexuality (mono-, bi-, tri-, multitranssexuality; categories to be transgressed and transcended), queer and postmodern theory provide renewed justification for heterosexual women's refusal to notice that they *are* heterosexual—or for their tendency to dismiss such an observation as unimportant, based on transitory and provisional attributions. Asked to identify themselves as heterosexual, many feminists react with defensive anger:

> Why address me so categorically as a heterosexual? Why was anyone so sure? Because I am married? Or because my husband seems "straight"? Is it about my hairdo or my shoes or the things I have said, or not said? . . . Perhaps it is a political question. Do I not belong to some inner circle? Is there a conspiracy afoot? How did the heteros get picked out? (Gergen 1993, 62)

Gergen draws explicitly on postmodernism to defend her refusal of the "heterosexual" label, paying "a special tribute to Judith Butler for her book, *Gender Trouble: Feminism and the Subversion of Identity*, from which I borrow heavily in this text" (1993, 64). Using such theories, then, the lesbian feminist insistence that heterosexual feminists make their choice intelligible (Frye 1992, 55-6) is, at best, sidestepped as unnecessary; at worst, dismissed as meaningless.

Finally, queer theory is centrally antagonistic to much of radical feminist theory. This is partly because queer theorists see all forms of feminism as totalizing "grand narratives," whose meanings and values must be subverted and thrown into question along with the other explanatory frameworks in politics, science and philosophy, mere fodder for deconstruction in the postmodern age. More than this, however, queer politics is often expressed in terms explicitly oppositional to feminism, especially radical feminism, characterized as "moralistic feminist separatism" (Smyth 1992, 36). "Queer" functions as apologia of justification for much behavior seen by radical feminism as damaging to women and lesbians: imitation of gay male sexuality, the defense of pornography, and sadomasochism. There is no attempt to problematize pleasure, much less to engage with radical feminist attempts to do so (Jeffreys 1990; Kitzinger and Kitzinger 1993; Kitzinger and Perkins 1993), other than to characterize these as repressive, restrictive and tolalitarian in effect or intent. We cannot, then, as radical feminists, turn to queer theory in any attempts to salvage heterosexuality from radical feminist critiques, because queer theory simply ignores or mocks such critiques.

In this section, then, we have outlined attempts to rehabilitate heterosexuality by subverting it as "queer." Although queer theory appeals to those attracted by its sense of possibility, its promise of fun, and its celebration of pleasure, we find it seriously lacking as a feminist political strategy. Its propositions are unclear; it falsely attributes sexual and political equivalence to hetero- and homosexuality; it permits heterosexual women to continue ignoring, and

415

failing to render problematic, their heterosexuality; and it is in direct conflict with key tenets of radical feminist politics.

REHABILITATING HETEROSEXUALITY?

As we have shown, neither virgin nor queer theory offers a coherent feminist agenda sufficient for the rehabilitation of heterosexuality. At this point we would like to raise the question as to *why* heterosexuality is so vigorously defended, even (or perhaps, especially)—it seems—by lesbians? Why are some feminists apparently so desperate to continue the doing of heterosexual sex that they are prepared to accept such bizarre concepts as virgin and queer heterosexuality in order to justify themselves? The lengths to which feminists (including lesbians) are prepared to go in defending sex with men is surely a clue to its political importance.

To some extent, and despite the bravado of the language in which both are couched, we see virgin and queer theory as defeatist. Recognizing the failure of lesbian feminism to communicate radical political analyses of heterosexuality and acknowledging the strong hold that heterosexuality apparently exerts on so many women (even those who could choose, even those who once did choose, lesbianism) (Bartky 1993), it is perhaps easier to revert to attempts to reform heterosexuality, exploring what feminist goals might be achievable *within* that institution, rather than attacking the institution per se. The abandonment of the radical critique of heterosexuality as inherently oppressive can be read as a tacit admission of defeat.

In an increasingly right-wing political climate, this defeat is perhaps not surprising. Many oppressed groups are moving toward coalition politics: radical feminist critiques of heterosexuality, often experienced as criticism and rejection of individual heterosexual feminists, can stand in the way of working together effectively, and lesbians have often felt compelled to mute our criticisms in the interests of immediate survival. The possibility offered by Frye's "virgin heterosexuality" (that one can, after all, be a heterosexual and a feminist) must, whatever demands it makes on the practice of that heterosexuality, be far more appealing to many heterosexual women than is the characterization of them as "collaborators with the enemy" (Leeds Revolutionary Feminist Group 1981). Queer theory, too, despite its purportedly more confrontational stance, is far more accommodating of heterosexuality than is radical feminism's theory of political lesbianism: Smyth (1992, 36) even raises as a possibility (and leaves unanswered) the question: "Is straight SM automatically queer, while a monogamous 'vanilla' lesbian couple living in suburbia isn't?" This explicit endorsement and validation of particular kinds of heterosexuality *at the expense of lesbianism* is a striking development of queer theory, and one that feeds into heterosexual feminists' oft-voiced retort that "lesbian relationships aren't perfect either" (Rowland 1993, 77; Jacklin 1993, 35). It is hardly surprising, then, that heterosexual feminists are seduced by queer theo-

416

ry's "wit," "ingenuity," "panache" (Beloff 1993), and "great possibilities for freedom" (Gergen 1993, 63-4) far more often than they are enthused by the rage and rigor of radical lesbian feminism.

Both virgin and queer theory bypass key radical feminist concerns. Earlier feminist analyses of sexual intercourse are crucially absent from Frye's "virgin" paper. Worse by far than mere omission, queer theory actively *reverses* earlier radical feminist critiques—for example, transsexualism, sadomasochism, and pornography, (Dworkin 1982; Raymond 1982; Linden et al. 1982) and celebrates its own "inclusiveness," actively welcoming not only straights and bisexuals, but also transsexuals, transvestites, sadomasochists and pornographers under the queer umbrella. Lesbian queers endorse as progressive "alliances between pro-sex anti-censorship lesbians and like-minded gay men . . . so opening up the possibility of new models for the expansion of lesbian erotic possibilities," whereas "equal, nuturing" sex is characterized as "prepubescent" (Smyth 1992, 37). The "transgressive" impulse of queer theory manifests itself at least as much against feminism as against heteropatriarchy. Such aspects of the queer movement render it less a symptom of the "defeat" of, and more an indication of the "backlash" against, feminism (Kitzinger and Wilkinson, 1994).

What seems to be missing, in these continuing attempts to rehabilitate heterosexuality, is any sense that it is still necessary to critique and analyze it as an oppressive mechanism of social control. Enthusiastic renditions of blow jobs on a dyke's strap-on dildo or descriptions of how to do a "politically correct" blow job with a man (avoid the "erotic phallic-power associations" of kneeling, and try the "69" position, Dennis 1992, 162-3) simply ignore crucial aspects of the radical feminist critique of heterosexuality. For many women, heterosexuality still has the status of a compulsory institution; for many, it is still in the context of heterosexuality that they are abused. Any serious attempt to rehabilitate heterosexuality must, at the very least, address these material realities, making heterosexuality worthy of feminist support must be more than the luxury of a few socially and economically privileged partners of "new men." More than this, given the radical critique of heterosexuality as a primary site for the reinscription of gender-based patterns of dominance and submission, the models of heterosexuality advanced by virgin and queer theorists are seriously incomplete or flawed. It is unclear how "virgins" can mysteriously evade the implications of the heterosexual act; and implausible that "queers," through "playing" with genderized symbols of power and powerlessness, can hope to "subvert" them.

It is perhaps worth noting that the notions of both "queer" and "virgin" heterosexuality derive primarily from, and are being developed by, people who do not so identify themselves: queers are rarely exclusively heterosexual, and virgin heterosexuality is, says Frye, "not my call." Such theorists have developed or appropriated particular angles on heterosexuality in the interest of

417

developed queer or radical lesbian theory more generally. When heterosexual feminists (even relatively privileged ones) are asked to contribute their theorectical understandings of heterosexuality (as in Wilkinson and Kitzinger, 1993), their analyses are much less optimistic as to the possibility of successfully combining heterosexuality and feminism. They speak—in voices far more hesitant than those of the lesbian and gay "virgin" and "queer" theorists—of painful contradiction, struggle and compromise. We are still a long way from having a politically and theoretically adequate solution to the problem of heterosexuality. Meanwhile, in the vast majority of heterosexual realtionships, which are neither "virgin" nor "queer," heterosexual sexual activity repeatedly reinscribes biological and social maleness and femaleness, continually constructing women as women and men in order to ensure male dominance and female subordination. In this way, nothing changes: heterosexuality continues to mean what it has always meant under heteropatriarchy, and to serve the same sociopolitical function.

REFERENCES

Bartky, S. 1993. Hypatia unbound: A confesion. In *Heterosexuality: A "Feminism & psychology" reader*, edited by S. Wilkinson and C. Kitzinger. London: Sage.

Baudrillard, J. 1988. *Selected writings*, edited by Mark Poster. Stanford: Stanford Univeristy Press.

Beloff, H. 1993. Review of Stolen glances: Lesbians take photographs, edited by T. Boffin and J. Fraser, *Feminism & Psychology* 3:272–4.

Bordo, S. 1993. "Material girl": The effacements of postmodern culture. In *The Madonna connection: Representational politics, subcultural identities, and cultural theory*, edited by C. Schwichtenberg. Boulder, CO: Westview.

Braidotti, R. 1991. *Patterns of dissonance: A study of women in contemporary philosophy*. Cambridge: Polity.

Bristow, J. 1992. Cross-dress, transgress. *Observer*, 3 May.

Brunet, A., and L. Turcotte. 1988. Separatism and radicalism. In *For lesbians only: A separatist anthology*, edited by S.L. Hoagland and J. Penelope. London: Onlywomen.

Butler, J. 1990. *Gender trouble: Feminism and the subversion of identity*. London: Routledge.

Dennis, W. 1992. *Hot and bothered: Men and women, sex and love in the 1990s*. London: Grafton/HarperCollins.

Diamond, I., and L. Quinby. eds. 1988. *Feminism and Foucault: Reflections on resistance*. Boston, MA: Northeastern University Press.

Dollimore, J. 1991. *Sexual dissidence: Augustine to Wilde, Freud to Foucault*. Oxford: Clarendon.

Duncker, P. 1993. *Heterosexuality: Fictional agendas. In Heterosexuality: A "Feminism & Psyhology" reader*, edited by S. Wilkinson and C. Kitzinger. London: Sage.

Dworkin, A. 1982. Pornography: Men possessing women. London: The Women's Press.

———.1987. *Intercourse*. London: Arrow/Century-Hutchinson.

Fraser, J. and T. Boffin. 1991. Tantalizing glimpses of stolen glances: Lesbians take photographs. *Feminist Review 38*:20–32.

Freud, S. 1977. *On sexuality*. Penguin Freud Library, vol. 7. London: Penguin.

Frye, M. 1990. Do you have to be a lesbian to be a feminist? *off our backs* (August/September): 21–3.

———.1992. *Willful virgin: Essays in feminism, 1976-1992*. Freedom, CA: The Crossing.

Gavey, N. 1993. Technologies and effects of heterosexual coercion. In *Heterosexuality: A "Feminism & Psychology" reader*, edited by S. Wilkinson and C. Kitzinger. London: Sage.

Gergen, M. 1993. Unbundling our binaries—genders, sexualities, desires. In *Heterosexuality: A "Feminism & Psychology" reader*, edited by S. Wilkinson and C. Kitzinger. London: Sage.

Gill, R. and R. Walker. 1993. Heterosexuality, feminism, contradiction: On being young, white, heterosexual feminists in the 1990s. In *Heterosexuality: A "Feminism & Psychology" reader*, edited by S. Wilkinson and C. Kitzinger. London: Sage.

Henderson, L. 1993. Justify our love: Madonna and the politics of queer sex In *The Madonna connection: Representational politics, subcultural identities, and cultural theory*, edited by C. S. Schwichtenberg. Boulder, CO: Westview.

Hollway, W. 1993. Theorizing heterosexuality: A response. *Feminism & Psychology* 3(3):412–7.

Hunter, A. 1993. Same door, different closet: A heterosexual sissy's coming-out party. In *Heterosexuality: A "Feminism & Psychology" reader*, edited by S. Wilkinson and C, Kitzinger. London: Sage.

Jacklin, C.N. 1993. How my heterosexuality affects my feminist politics. In *Heterosexuality: A "Feminism & Psychology" reader*, edited by S. Wilkinson and C. Kitzinger. London: Sage

Jeffreys, S. 1985. *The spinster and her enemies: Feminism and sexuality 1880-1930*. London: Pandora.

———.1990. *AntiClimax: A feminist perspective on the sexual revolution*. London: The Women's Press.

———.1993. *The lesbian heresy*. London: The Women's Press.

Jo, B. 1993. 'Virgin' means never having been heterosexual—Virgins do exist. *off our backs* (January): 22.

Kennedy, M. 1992. Two sides to sexuality, *Guardian*, 4 September.

Kinsey, A. C., W. B. Pomeroy, and C. E. Martin. 1948. *Sexual behavior in the human male*. Philadelphia: W. B. Saunders Co.

Kinsey, A. C., W.B. Pomeroy, and C.E. Martin, and P.H. Gebhard. 1953. *Sexual behavior in the human female*. Philadephia: W.B. Saunders.

Kitzinger, C. 1987. *The social construction of lesbianism*. London Sage.

———.1994. Problematizing pleasure. Radical feminist deconstructions of sexuality and power. In *Gender and power*, edited by H.L. Radtke and H. J. Stam. London: Sage.

Kitzinger, C., and R. Perkins. 1993. *Changing our minds: Lesbian feminism and psychology* New York: New York University Press; London: Onlywomen.

Kitzinger, J., and C. Kitzinger. 1993. 'Doing it': Lesbian representations of sex. In *Outwrite: Popularizing lesbian texts*, edited by G. Griffin. London: Pluto.

419

Leeds Revolutionary Feminist Group. 1981. Political lesbianism: The case against heterosexuality. In *Love your enemy? The debate between heterosexual feminism and political lesbianism*, edited by Onlywomen Press. London: Onlywomen.

Linden, R. R., D. R. Pagano, D. Russell, and S.L. Star, eds. 1982. *Against sadomasochism: A radical feminist analysis*. East Palo Alto, CA: Frog in the Well

MacKinnon, C. A. 1987. *Feminism unmodified: Discourses on life and law*. Cambridge, MA: Harvard University Press.

Mandzuik, R. 1993. Feminist politics and postmodern seductions: Madonna and the struggle for political articulation. In *The Madonna connection: Representational politics, subcultural identies, and cultural theory*, edited by C. Schwichtenberg. Boulder, CO: Westview.

Pickering, B. 1992. Queer street fighters. *Guardian*, 8 September

Piercy, M. 1979. *Woman on the edge of time*. London: The Women's Press.

Radicalesbians. 1970. The woman identified woman (leaflet) reprinted in *For lesbians only: A separatist anthology*, edited by S. L. Hoagland and J. Penelope. London: Onlywomen.

Raymond, J. 1982. *The transsexual empire*. London: The Women's Press.

Rich, A. 1980. Compulsory heterosexuality and lesbian existence. *Signs: Journal of Women in Culture and Society* 5:631–60.

Rowland, R. 1993. Radical feminist heterosexuality: The personal and the political. In *Heterosexuality: A "Feminism & Psychology" reader*, edited by S. Wilkinson and C. Kitzenger. London: Sage.

Ruby, J. 1993. A lesbian feminist fucks with gender. *off our backs* 32:4–5, 20–1.

Schwichtenberg, C. 1993. Madonna's postmodern feminism: Bringing the margin to the center. In *The Madonna connection: Representational politics, subcultural indentities, and cultural theory*, edited by C. Schichtenberg. Boulder, CO: Westview.

Segal, L. 1983. Sensual uncertainty, or why the clitoris is not enough. In *Sex and Love: New thoughts on old contradictions*, edited by S. Carledge and J. Ryan. London: The Women's Press.

Smyth C. 1992. *Lesbians talk queer nations*. London: Scarlet.

Sprinkle, A. 1992. My first time with a F2M-transsexual-surgically-made hermaphrodite. In *Discontents: New queer writers*, edited by D. Cooper. New York: Amethyst.

Stoltenberg, J. 1990. *Refusing to be a man*. London: Fontana.

Warner, M. 1990. Fear of a queer planet, *Social Text* 9:12–31.

Weedon. C. 1987. *Feminist practice and poststructuralist theory*: Oxford: Blackwell.

Wilkinson, S., and C. Kitzinger. eds. 1993. *Heterosexuality: A "Feminism & Psychology" reader* London: Sage.

Williams. L. 1992. Pornographies on/scene, or diff'rent strokes for diff'ent folks. In *Sex exposed: Sexuality and the pornography debate*, edited by L. Segal and M. McIntosh. London: Virago.

Wilson, E. 1992. Crossed wires in the gender debate. *Guardian* 2 (May).

Wittig. M. 1992. *The straight mind*. Boston: Beacon.

PART VII

GENDER & IDENTITY
Dis-Figuring the Body

ANOREXIA NERVOSA
Psychopathology as the Crystallization of Culture

Susan Bordo

Historians long ago began to write the history of the body. They have studied the body in the field of historical demography or pathology; they have considered it as the seat of needs and appetites, as the locus of physiological processes and metabolisms, as a target for the attacks of germs or viruses; they have shown to what extent historical processes were involved in what might seem to be the purely biological "events" such as the circulation of bacilli, or the extension of the lifespan. But the body is also directly involved in a political field; power relations have an immediate hold upon it; they invest it, mark it, train it, torture it, force it to carry out tasks, to perform ceremonies, to emit signs.

—Michel Foucault, Discipline and Punish

I believe in being the best I can be, I believe in watching every calorie ...

Crystal Light television commercial

chapter 23

INTRODUCTION

IN 1983, preparing to teach an interdisciplinary course in "Gender, Culture, and Experience," I felt the need for a topic that would enable me to bring feminist theory alive for a generation of students that seemed increasingly suspicious of feminism. My sister, Binnie Klein, who is a therapist, suggested that I have my class read Kim Chernin's *The Obsession: Reflections on the Tyranny of Slenderness*. I did, and I found my Reagan-era students suddenly sounding like the women in the conciousness-raising sessions that had first made me aware of the fact that my problems as a woman were not mine alone. While delighted to have happened on a topic that was so intensely meaningful to them, I was also disturbed by what I was reading in their journals and hearing in the privacy of my office. I had identified deeply with the general themes of Chernin's book. But my own disordered relations with food had never reached the point of anorexia or bulimia, and I was not prepared for the discovery that large numbers of my students were starving, binging, purging, and filled with self-hatred and desperation. I began to read everything I could find on eating disorders. I found that while the words and diaries of patients were enormously illuminating, most of the clinical theory was not very helpful. The absence of cultural perspective—particularly relating to the situation of women,—was striking.

As a philosopher, I was also intrigued by the classically dualistic language my students often used to describe their feelings, and I decided to incorporate a section on contemporary attitudes toward the body in my metaphysics course. There, I discovered that although it was predominantly my female students who experienced their lives as a perpetual battle with their bodies, quite a few of my male students expressed similar ideas when writing about running. I found myself fascinated by what seemed to me to be the cultural emergence of a set of attitudes about the body which, while not new as *ideas*, were finding a special kind of embodiment in contemporary culture, and I began to see all sorts of evidence for this cultural hypothesis. So began a project that has since occupied a good deal of my attention and that has, I believe, progressively been validated. In 1983, the body practices and attitudes that I viewed as supporting my tentative intuitions were a mere ripple on the cultural scene compared to the place I have watched them assume since then.

"Anorexia Nervosa: Psychopathology as the Crystallization of Culture," first published in 1985, was the result of my initial exploration of the various cultural axes to which my students' experiences guided me in my "Gender, Culture, and Experience" and metaphysics courses. "The Body and the Reproduction of Femininity: and "Reading the Slender Body," both first published in 1989, are in a sense an extension of that earlier piece, in that they explore the dynamics of further axes on which eating disorders are located: the historically female psychological disorders, changes in historical attitudes toward what constitutes "fat" and "thin," and the structural tensions of consumer society. These axes are not, however, meant to make up an exhaustive list. Ultimately, these essays do not so much explain eating disorders as *follow* them through a series of cultural interconnections and intersections.

Since the "Anorexia Nervosa" essay first appeared, in 1985, there has, of course, been an explosion of written material, media attention, and clinical study devoted to eating disorders. I have not attempted to incorporate new studies or statistics into these previously published pieces, although much of the new information strongly bears out my observations and interpretations. Nor have I tried to bring my original formulations into line with developments in my thinking. I have chosen instead to let the evolution of my ideas–and in some cases the evolution of the phenomena themselves–manifest themselves through the essay.

BORDO

EATING DISORDERS, CULTURE, AND THE BODY

Psychopathology, as Jules Henry has said, "is the final outcome of all that is wrong with a culture."[1] In no case is this more strikingly true than in that of anorexia nervosa and bulimia, barely known a century ago, yet reaching epidemic proportions today. Far from being the result of a superficial fashion phenomenon, these disorders, I will argue, reflect and call our attention to some of the central ills of our culture–from our historical heritage of disdain for the body, to our modern fear of loss of control over our future, to the disquieting meaning of contemporary beauty ideals in an era of greater female presence and power than ever before.

Changes in the incidence of anorexia[2] have been dramatic.[3] In 1945, when Ludwig Binswanger chronicled the now famous case of Ellen West, he was able to say that "from a psychiatric point of view we are dealing here with something new, with a new symptom."[4] In 1973, Hilde Bruch, one of the pioneers in understanding and treating eating disorders, could still say that anorexia was "rare indeed."[5] Today, in 1984, it is estimated that as many as one in every 200-250 women between the ages of thirteen and twenty-two suffer from anorexia, and that anywhere from 12 to 33 percent of college women control their weight through vomiting, diuretics, and laxatives.[6] The New York Center for the Study of Anorexia and Bulimia reports that in the first five months of 1984 it received 252 requests for treatment, as compared to the 30 requests received in all of 1980.[7] Even correcting for increased social awareness of eating disorders and a greater willingness of sufferers to report their illnesses, these statistics are startling and provocative. So, too, is the fact that 90 percent of all anorectics are women, and that of the 5,000 people each year who have part of their intestines removed as an aid in losing weight 80 percent are women.[8]

Anorexia nervosa is clearly, as Paul Garfinkel and David Garner have called it, a "multidimensional disorder," with familial, perceptual, cognitive, and, possibly, biological factors interacting in varying combinations in different individuals to produce a "final common pathway."[9] In the early 1980s, with growing evidence, not only of an overall increase in frequency of the disease, but of its higher incidence in certain populations, attention has begun to turn, too, to cultural factors as significant in the pathogenesis of eating disorders.[10] Until very recently, however, the most that could be expected in the way of cultural or social analysis, with very few exceptions, was the (unavoidable) recognition that anorexia is related to the increasing emphasis that fashion has placed on slenderness over the past fifteen years.[11] This, unfortunately, is only to replace one mystery with another, more profound than the first.

What we need to ask is *why* our culture is so obsessed with keeping our bodies slim, tight, and young that when 500 people were asked what they feared most in the world, 190 replied, "Getting fat."[12] In an age when our children regularly have nightmares of nuclear holocaust, that as adults we should give *this* answer—that we most fear "getting fat"—is far more bizarre than the anorectic's misperceptions of her body image, or the bulimic's compulsive vomiting. The nightmares of nuclear holocaust and our desperate fixation on our bodies as arenas of control–perhaps one of the few available arenas of control we have left in the twentieth century—are not unconnected, of course. The connection, if explored, could be significant, demystifying, instructive.

So, too, we need to explore the fact that it is women who are most oppressed by what Kim Chernin calls "the tyranny of slenderness," and that this particular oppression is a post-1960s, post-feminist phenomenon. In the fifties, by contrast, with middle-class women once again out of the factories and safely immured in the home, the dominant ideal of female beauty was exemplified by Marilyn Monroe—hardly your androgynous, athletic, adolescent body type. At the peak of her popularity, Monroe was often described as "femininity incarnate," "femaleness embodied"; last term, a student of mine described her as "a cow." Is this merely a change in what size hips, breasts, and waist are considered attractive, or has the very idea of incarnate femaleness come to have a different meaning, different associations, the capacity to stir up different fantasies and images, for the culture of the eighties? These are the sorts of questions that need to be addressed if we are to achieve a deep understanding of the current epidemic of eating disorders.

The central point of intellectual orientation for this essay is expressed in its subtitle. I take the psychopathologies that develop within a culture, far from being anomalies or aberrations, to be characteristic expressions of that culture; to be, indeed, the crystallization of much that is wrong with it. For that reason they are important to examine, as keys to cultural self-diagnosis and self-scrutiny. "Every age," says Christopher Lasch, "develops it own peculiar forms of pathology, which express in exaggerated form its underlying character structure."[13] The only aspect of this formulation with which I would disagree, with respect to anorexia, is the idea of the expression of an underlying, unitary cultural character structure. Anorexia appears less as the extreme expression of a character structure than as a remarkably overdetermined *symptom* of some of the multifaceted and heterogeneous distresses of our age. Just as anorexia function in a variety of ways in the psychic economy of the anorexic individual, so a variety of cultural currents or streams converge in anorexia, find their perfect, precise expression in it.

I will call those streams or currents "axes of continuity": axes because they meet or converge in the anorexic syndrome; continuity because when we locate anorexia on these axes, its family resemblances and connections with other phenomena emerge. Some of these axes represent anorexia's *synchronicity* with other contemporary cultural practices and forms–bodybuilding and jogging, for example. Other axes bring to light *historical* connections: for in-

426

BORDO

stance, between anorexia and earlier examples of extreme manipulation of the female body, such as tight corseting, or between anorexia and long-standing traditions and ideologies in Western culture, such as our Greco-Christian traditions of dualism. The three axes that I will discuss in this essay (although they by no means exhaust the possibilities for cultural understanding of anorexia) are the *dualist axis*, the *control axis*, and the *gender/power axis*.[14]

Throughout my discussion, it will be assumed that the body, far from being some fundamentally stable, acultural constant to which we must *contrast* all culturally relative and institutional forms, is constantly "in the grip," as Foucault puts it, of cultural practices. Not that this is a matter of cultural *repression* of the instinctual or natural body. Rather, there is no "natural" body. Cultural practices, far from exerting their power *against* spontaneous needs, "basic" pleasures or instincts, or "fundamental" structures of body experience, are already and always inscribed, as Foucault has emphasized, "on our bodies and their materiality, their forces, energies, sensations, and pleasures."[15] Our bodies, no less than anything else that is human, are constituted by culture.

Often, but not always, cultural practices have their effect on the body as experienced (the "lived body," as the phenomenologists put it) rather than the physical body. For example, Foucault points to the medicalization of sexuality in the nineteenth century, which recast sex from being a family matter into a private, dark, bodily secret that was appropriately investigated by such specialists as doctors, psychiatrists, and school educators. The constant probing and interrogation, Foucault argues, ferreted out, eroticized and solidified all sorts of sexual types and perversions, which people then experienced (although they had not done so originally) as defining their bodily possibilities and pleasures. The practice of the medical confessional, in other words, in its constant foraging for sexual secrets and hidden stories, actually *created* new sexual secrets—and eroticized the acts of interrogation and confession, too.[16] Here, social practice changed people's *experience* of their bodies and their posibilities. Similarly, as we shall see, the practice of dieting—of saying no to hunger—contributes to the anorectic's increasing sense of hunger as a dangerous eruption from some alien part of the self, and to a growing intoxication with controlling that eruption.

The *physical* body can, however, also be an instrument and medium of power. Foucault's classic example in *Discipline and Punish* is public torture during the Ancien Régime, through which, as Dreyfus and Rabinow put it, "the sovereign's power was literally and publicly inscribed on the criminal's body in a manner as controlled, scenic and well-attended as possible."[17] Similarly, the nineteenth-century corset caused its wearer actual physical incapacitation, but it also served as an emblem of the power of culture to impose its designs on the female body.

Indeed, female bodies have historically been significantly more vulnerable than male bodies to extremes in both forms of cultural manipulation of the

BORDO

body. Perhaps this has something to do with the fact that women, besides *having* bodies, are also *associated* with the body, which has always been considered woman's "sphere" in family life, in mythology, in scientific, philosophical, and religious ideology. When we later consider some aspects of the history of medicine and fashion, we will see that the social manipulation of the female body emerged as an absolutely central strategy in the maintenance of power relations between the sexes over the past hundred years. This historical understanding must deeply affect our understanding of anorexia and of our contemporary preoccupation with slenderness.

This is *not* to say that I take what I am doing here to be the unearthing of a long-standing male conspiracy against women or the fixing of blame on any particular participants in the play of social forces. In this I once again follow Foucault, who reminds us that although a perfectly clear logic, with perfectly decipherable aims and objectives, may characterize historical power relations, it is nonetheless "often the case that no one was there to have invented" these aims and strategies, either through choice of individuals or through the rational game plan of some presiding "headquarters.[18] We are not talking, then, of plots, designs, or overarching strategies. This does not mean that individuals do not *consciously* pursue goals that in fact advance their own position. But it does deny that in doing so they are consciously directing the overall movement of power relations or engineering their shape. They may not even know what that shape is. Nor does the fact that power relations involve domination by particular groups—say, of prisoners by guards, females by males, amateurs by experts—entail that the dominators are in anything like full control of the situation or that the dominated do not sometimes advance and extend the situation themselves.[19] Nowhere, as we shall see, is this collaboration in oppression more clear than in the case of anorexia.

THE DUALIST AXIS

I will begin with the most general and attenuated axis of continuity, the one that begins with Plato, winds its way to its most lurid expression in Augustine, and finally becomes metaphysically solidified and scientized by Descartes. I am referring, of course, to our dualistic heritage: the view that human existence is bifurcated into two realms or substances: the bodily or material, on the one hand; the mental or spiritual, on the other. Despite some fascinating historical variations which I will not go into here, the basic imagery of dualism has remained fairly constant. Let me briefly describe its central features; they will turn out, as we will see, to comprise the basic body imagery of the anorectic.

First, the body is experienced as *alien*, as the not-self, the not-me. It is "fastened and glued" to me, "nailed" and "riveted" to me, as Plato described it in the *Phaedo*.[20] For Descartes, the body is the brute material envelope for the inner and essential self, the thinking thing; it is ontologically distinct from that inner self, is as mechanical in its operations as a machine, is, indeed, comparable to animal existence.

Second, the body is experienced as *confinement and limitation*: a "prison," a "swamp," a "cage," a "fog"—all images that occur in Plato, Descartes, and Augustine—from which the soul, will, or mind struggles to escape. "The enemy ["the madness of lust"] held my will in his power and from it he made a chain and shackled me," says Augustine.[21] In the work of all three philosophers, images of the soul being "dragged" by the body are prominent. The body is "heavy, ponderous," as Plato describes it; it exerts a downward pull.[22]

Third, the body is the *enemy*, as Augustine explicitly describes it time and again, and as Plato and Descartes strongly suggest in their diatribes against the body as the source of obscurity and confusion in our thinking. "A source of countless distractions by reason of the mere requirement of food," says Plato; "liable also to diseases which overtake and impede us in the pursuit of truth; it fills us full of loves, and lusts, and fears, and fancies of all kinds, and endless foolery, and in very truth, as men say, takes away from us the power of thinking at all. Whence come wars, and fightings, and factions? Whence but from the body and the lusts of the body."[23]

And, finally, whether as an impediment to reason or as the home of the "slimy desires of the flesh" (as Augustine calls them), the body is the locus of *all that threatens our attempts at control*. It overtakes, it overwhelms, it erupts and disrupts. This situation, for the dualist, becomes an incitement to battle the unruly forces of the body, to show it who is boss. For, as Plato says, "Nature orders the soul to rule and govern and the body to obey and serve."[24]

All three—Plato, Augustine, and, most explicitly, Descartes—provide instructions, rules, or models of how to gain control over the body, with the ultimate aim—for this is what their regimen finally boils down to—of learning to live without it.[25] By that is meant: to achieve intellectual independence from the lure of the body's illusions, to become impervious to its distractions, and, most important, to kill off its desires and hungers. Once control has become the central issue for the soul, these are the only possible terms of victory, as Alan Watts makes clear:

> Willed control brings about a sense of duality in the organism, of consciousness in conflict with appetite. . . . But this mode of control is a peculiar example of the proverb that nothing fails like success. For the more consciousness is individualized by the success of the will, the more everything outside the individual seems to be a threat—including . . . the uncontrolled spontaneity of one's own body. . . . Every success in control therefore demands a further success, so that the process cannot stop short of omnipotence.[26]

Dualism here appears as the offspring, the by-product, of the identification of

429

BORDO

the self with control, an identification that Watts sees as lying at the center of Christianity's ethic of anti-sexuality. The attempt to subdue the spontaneities of the body in the interests of control only succeeds in constituting them as more alien and more powerful, and thus more needful of control. The only way to win this no-win game is to go beyond control, to kill off the body's spontaneities entirely—that is, to cease to *experience* our hungers and desires.

This is what many anorectics describe as their ultimate goal. "[I want] to reach the point," as one put it, "when I don't need to eat at all."[27] Kim Chernin recalls her surprise when, after fasting, her hunger returned: "I realized [then] that my secret goal in dieting must have been the intention to kill off my appetite completely."[28]

It is not usually noted, in the popular literature on the subject, that anorexic women are as obsessed with *hunger* as they are with being slim. Far from losing her appetite, the typical anorectic is haunted by it—in much the same way that Augustine describes being haunted by sexual desire—and is in constant dread of being overwhelmed by it. Many describe the dread of hunger," of not having control, of giving in to biological urge," to "the craving, never satisfied thing,"[29] as the "original fear" (as one puts it),[30] or, as Ellen West describes it, "the real obsession." "I don't think the dread of becoming fat is the real . . .neurosis," she writes, "but the constant desire for food. . . . [H]unger, or the dread of hunger, pursues me all morning. . . . Even when I am full, I am afraid of the coming hour in which hunger will start again." Dread of becoming fat, she interprets, rather than being originary, served as a "brake" to her horror of her own unregulatable, runaway desire for food.[31] Bruch reports that her patients are often terrified at the prospect of taking just one bite of food, lest they never be able to stop.[32] (Bulimic anorectics, who binge on enormous quantities of food–sometimes consuming up to 15,000 calories a day[33]—indeed *cannot* stop.)

These women experience hunger as an alien invader, marching to the tune of its own seemingly arbitrary whims, disconnected from any normal self-regulating mechanisms. Indeed, it could not possibly be so connected, for it is experienced as coming from an area *outside* the self. One patient of Bruch's says she ate breakfast because "my stomach wanted it," expressing here the same sense of alienation from her hunger (and her physical self) as Augustine's when he speaks of his "captor," "the law of sin that was in my member."[34]

Bruch notes that this "basic delusion," as she calls it, "of not owning the body and its sensations" is a typical symptom of all eating disorders. "These patients act," she says, "as if for them the regulation of food intake was outside [the self]."[35] This experience of bodily sensations as foreign is, strikingly, not limited to the experience of hunger. Patients with eating disorders have similar problems in identifying cold, heat, emotions, and anxiety as originating in the self.[36]

While the body is experienced as alien and outside, the soul or will is described as being trapped or confined in this alien "jail," as one woman describes it.[37] "I feel caught in my body," "I'm a prisoner in my body":[38] the theme is repeated again and again. A typical fantasy, evocative of Plato, imagines total liberation from the bodily prison: "I wish I could get out of my body entirely and fly!"[39] "Please dear God, help me. . . . I want to get out of my body, I want to get out!"[40] Ellen West, astute as always, sees a central meaning of her self-starvation in this "ideal of being too thin, of being *without a body*."[41]

Anorexia is not a philosophical attitude; it is a debilitating affliction. Yet, quite often a highly conscious and articulate scheme of images and associations–virtually a metaphysics–is presented by these women. The scheme is strikingly Augustinian, with evocations of Plato. This does not indicate, of course, that anorectics are followers of Plato or Augustine, but that the anorectic's metaphysics makes explicit various elements, historically grounded in Plato and Augustine, that run deep in our culture.[42] As Augustine often speaks of the "two wills" within him," one the servant of the flesh, the other of the spirit," who "between them tore my soul apart," so the anorectic describes a "spiritual struggle," a "contest between good and evil," often conceived explicitly as a battle between mind or will and appetite or body.[43] "I feel myself, quite passively," says West, "the stage on which two hostile forces are mangling each other."[44] Sometimes there is a more aggressive alliance with mind against body: "When I fail to exercise as often as I prefer, I become guilty that I have let my body 'win' another day from my mind. I can't wait 'til this semester is over. . . . My body is going to pay the price for the lack of work it is currently getting. I can't wait!"[45]

In this battle, thinness represents a triumph of the will over the body, and the thin body (that is to say, the nonbody) is associated with "absolute purity, hyperintellectuality and transcendence of the flesh. My soul seemed to grow as my body waned; I felt like one of those early Christian saints who starved themselves in the desert sun. I felt invulnerable, clean and hard as the bones etched into my silhouette."[46] Fat (that is to say, becoming all body) is associated with the taint of matter and flesh, "wantonness,"[47] mental stupor and mental decay.[48] One woman describes how after eating sugar she felt "polluted, disgusting, sticky through the arms, as if something bad had gotten inside."[49] Very often, sexuality is brought into this scheme of associations, and hunger and sexuality are psychically connected. Cherry Boone O'Neill describes a late-night binge, eating scraps of leftovers from the dog's dish:

> I started slowly, relishing the flavor and texture of each marvelous bite. Soon I was ripping the meager remains from the bones, stuffing the meat into my mouth as fast as I could detach it.
> [Her boyfriend surprises her, with a look of "total disgust" on his face.]
> I had been caught red-handed . . . in an animalistic orgy on the floor, in the

431

BORDO

dark, alone. Here was the horrid truth for Dan to see. I felt so evil, tainted, pagan. . . . In Dan's mind that day, I had been whoring after food.[50]

A hundred pages earlier, she had described her first romantic involvement in much the same terms: "I felt secretive, deceptive, and . . . tainted by the ongoing relationship" (which never went beyond kisses).[51] Sexuality, similarly, is "an abominable business" to Aimee Liu; for her, staying reed-thin is seen as a way of avoiding sexuality, by becoming" androgynous," as she puts it.[52] In the same way, Sarah, a patient of Levenkron's, connects her dread of gaining weight with "not wanting to be a 'temptation' to men."[53] In Liu's case, and in Sarah's, the desire to appear unattractive to men is connected to anxiety and guilt over earlier sexual abuse. Whether or not such episodes are common to many cases of anorexia,[54] "the avoidance of any sexual encounter, a shrinking from all bodily contact," is, according to Bruch, characteristic of anorectics.[55]

THE CONTROL AXIS

Having examined the axis of continuity from Plato to anorexia, we should feel cautioned against the impulse to regard anorexia as expressing entirely modern attitudes and fears. Disdain for the body, the conception of it as an alien force and impediment to the soul, is very old in our Greco-Christian traditions (although it has usually been expressed most forcefully by male philosophers and theologians rather than adolescent women!).

But although dualism is as old as Plato, in many ways contemporary culture appears *more* obsessed than previous eras with the control of the unruly body. Looking now at contemporary American life, a second axis of continuity emerges on which to locate anorexia. I call it the *control axis*.

The young anorectic, typically, experiences her life as well as her hungers as being out of control. She is a perfectionist and can never carry out the tasks she sets herself in a way that meets her own rigorous standards. She is torn by conflicting and contradictory expectations and demands, wanting to shine in all areas of student life, confused about where to place most of her energies, what to focus on, as she develops into an adult. Characteristically, her parents expect a great deal of her in the way of individual achievement (as well as physical appearance), yet have made most of the important decisions for her.[56] Usually, the anorexic syndrome emerges, not as a conscious decision to get as thin as possible, but as the result of her having begun a diet fairly casually, often at the suggestion of a parent, having succeeded splendidly in taking off five or ten pounds, and then having gotten hooked on the intoxicating feeling of accomplishment and control.

Recalling her anorexic days, Aimee Liu recreates her feelings:

The sense of accomplishment exhilarates me, spurs me to continue on and on. It provides a sense of purpose and shapes my life with distractions from insecurity. . . . I shall become an expert [at losing weight]. . . . The constant downward

432

BORDO

trend [of the scale] somehow comforts me, gives me visible proof that I can exert control.[57]

The diet, she realizes, "is the one sector of my life over which I and I alone wield total control."[58]

The frustrations of starvation, the rigors of the constant physical activity in which anorectics engage, the pain of the numerous physical complications of anorexia: these do not trouble the anorectic. Indeed, her ability to ignore them is further proof to her of her mastery of her body. "This was something I could control," says one of Bruch's patients. "I still don't know what I look like or what size I am, but I know my body can take anything."[59] "Energy, discipline, my own power will keep me going," says Liu. "Psychic fuel, I need nothing and no one else, and I will prove it. . . . Dropping to the floor, I roll. My tailbone crunches on the hard floor. . . . I feel no pain. I will be master of my own body, if nothing else, I vow."[60] And, finally, from one of Bruch's patients: *"You make of your own body your very own kingdom where you are the tyrant, the absolute dictator."*[61]

Surely we must recognize in this last honest and explicit statement a central modus operandi for the control of contemporary bourgeois anxiety. Consider compulsive jogging and marathon-running, often despite shin splints and other painful injuries, with intense agitation over missing a day or not meeting a goal for a particular run. Consider the increasing popularity of triathlon events such as the Iron Man, whose central purpose appears to be to allow people to find out how far they can push their bodies—through long-distance swimming, cycling, and running—before they collapse. Consider lawyer Mike Frankfurt, who runs ten miles every morning: *"To run with pain is the essence of life."*[62] Or consider the following excerpts from student journals:

The best times I like to run are under the most unbearable conditions. I love to run in the hottest, most humid and steepest terrain I can find. . . . For me running and the pain associated with it aren't enough to make me stop. I am always trying to overcome it and the biggest failure I can make is to stop running because of pain. Once I ran five of a ten-mile run with a severe leg cramp but wouldn't stop–it would have meant failure.[63]

When I run I am free. . . . The pleasure is closing off my body—as if the incessant pounding of my legs is so total that the pain ceases to exist. There is no grace, no beauty in the running—there is the jarring reality of sneaker and pavement. Bright pain that shivers and splinters sending its white hot arrows into my stomach, my lung, but it cannot pierce my mind. I am on automatic pilot—there is no remembrance of pain, there is freedom—I am losing myself, peeling out of this heavy flesh. . . . Power surges through me.[64]

None of this is to dispute that the contemporary concern with fitness has nonpathological, nondualist dimensions as well. Particularly for women, who have historically suffered from the ubiquity of rape and abuse, from the culturally instilled conviction of our own helplessness, and from lack of access to facilities and programs for rigorous physical training, the cultivation of strength, agility, and confidence clearly has a positive dimension. Nor are the objective benefits of daily exercise and concern for nutrition in question here. My focus, rather, is on a subjective stance, become increasingly prominent, which, although preoccupied with the body and deriving narcissistic enjoyment from its appearance, takes little pleasure in the *experience* of embodiment. Rather, the fundamental identification is with mind (or will), ideals of spiritual perfection, fantasies of absolute control.

Not everyone, of course, for whom physical training is a part of daily routine exhibits such a stance. Here, an examination of the language of female body-builders is illustrative. Body-building is particularly interesting because on the surface it appears to have the opposite structure to anorexia: the body-builder is, after all, building the body *up*, not whittling it down. Body-building develops strength. We imagine the body-builder as someone who is proud, confident, and perhaps most of all, conscious of and accepting of her physicality. This is, indeed, how some female body-builders experience themselves:

> I feel . . . tranquil and stronger [says Lydia Cheng]. Working out creates a high everywhere in my body. I feel the heat. I feel the muscles rise, I see them blow out, flushed with lots of blood. . . . My whole body is sweating and there's few things I love more than working up a good sweat. That's when I really feel like a woman.[65]

Yet a sense of joy in the body as active and alive is *not* the most prominent theme among the women interviewed by Trix Rosen. Many of them, rather, talk about their bodies in ways that resonate disquietingly with typical anorexic themes.

There is the same emphasis on will, purity, and perfection: "I've learned to be a stronger person with a more powerful will . . . pure concentration, energy and spirit." "I want to be as physically perfect as possible." "Body-building suits the perfectionist in me." "My goal is to have muscular perfection."[66] Compulsive exercisers—whom Dinitia Smith, in an article for New *York magazine* calls "The New Puritans"—speak in similar terms: Kathy Krauch, a New York art director who bikes twelve miles a day and swims two and a half, says she is engaged in "a quest for perfection." Mike Frankfurt, in describing his motivation for marathon running, speaks of "the purity about it." These people, Smith emphasizes, care little about their health: "They pursue self-denial as an end in itself, out of an almost mystical belief in the purity it confers."[67]

Many body-builders, like many anorectics, unnervingly conceptualize the body as alien, not-self:

I'm constantly amazed by my muscles. The first thing I do when I wake up in the morning is look down at my "abs" and flex my legs to see if the "cuts" are there. . . . My legs have always been my most stubborn part, and I want them to develop so badly. Every day I can see things happening to them. . . . I don't flaunt my muscles as much as I thought I would. I feel differently about them; they are my product and I protect them by wearing sweaters to keep them warm.[68]

Most strikingly, body-builders put the same emphasis on *control*: on feeling their life to be fundamentally out of control, and on the feeling of accomplishment derived from total mastery of the body. That sense of mastery, like the anorectic's, appears to derive from two sources. First, there is the reassurance that one can overcome all physical obstacles, push oneself to any extremes in pursuit of one's goals (which, as we have seen, is a characteristic motivation of compulsive runners, as well). Second, and most dramatic (it is spoken of time and again by female body-builders), is the thrill of being in total charge of the shape of one's body. "Create a masterpiece," says Fit magazine. "Sculpt your body contours into a work of art." As for the anorectic—who literally cannot see her body as other than her inner reality dictates and who is relentlessly driven by an ideal image of ascetic slenderness—so for the body-builder a purely mental conception comes to have dominance over her life: "You visualize what you want to look like . . . and then create the form." "The challenge presents itself: to rearrange things." "It's up to you to do the chiseling; you become the master sculptress." "What a fantasy, for your body to be changing! . . . I keep a picture in my mind as I work out of what I want to look like and what's happened to me already."[69] Dictation to nature of one's own chosen design for the body is the central goal for the body-builder, as it is for the anorectic.

The sense of security derived from the attainment of this goal appears, first of all, as the pleasure of control and independence.

"Nowadays," says Michael Sacks, associate professor of psychiatry at Cornell Medical College, "people no longer feel they can control events outside themselves—how well they do in their jobs or in their personal relationships, for example—but they can control the food they eat and how far they can run. Abstinence, tests of endurance, are ways of proving their self-sufficiency."[70] In a culture, moreover, in which our continued survival is often at the mercy of "specialists," machines, and sophisticated technology, the body acquires a special sort of vulnerability and dependency. We may live longer, but the circumstances surrounding illness and death may often be perceived as more alien, inscrutable, and arbitrary than ever before.

435

BORDO

Our contemporary body-fetishism expresses more than a fantasy of self-mastery in an increasingly unmanageable culture, however. It also reflects our alliance *with* culture against all reminders of the inevitable decay and death of the body. "Everybody wants to live forever" is the refrain from the theme song of *Pumping Iron*. The most youth-worshipping of popular television shows, "Fame," opens with a song that begins, "I want to live forever." And it is striking that although the anorectic may come very close to death (and 15 percent do indeed die), the dominant experience throughout the illness is of *invulnerability*.

The dream of immortality is, of course, nothing new. But what is unique to modernity is that the defeat of death has become a scientific fantasy rather than a philosophical or religious mythology. We no longer dream of eternal union with the gods; instead, we build devices that can keep us alive indefinitely, and we work on keeping our bodies as smooth and muscular and elastic at forty as they were at eighteen. We even entertain dreams of halting the aging process completely: "Old age," according to Durk Pearson and Sandy Shaw, authors of the popular *Life Extension*, "is an unpleasant and unattractive affliction."[71] The mega-vitamin regime they prescribe is able, they claim, to prevent and even to reverse the mechanisms of aging.

Finally, it may be that in cultures characterized by gross excesses in consumption, the "will to conquer and subdue the body" (as Chernin calls it) expresses an aesthetic or moral rebellion.[72] Anorectics initially came from affluent families, and the current craze for long-distance running and fasting is largely a phenomenon of young, upwardly mobile professionals (Dinitia Smith calls it "Deprivation Chic").[73] To those who are starving *against* their wills, of course, starvation cannot function as an expression of the power of the will. At the same time, we should caution against viewing anorexia as a trendy illness of the elite and privileged. Rather, its most outstanding feature is powerlessness.

THE GENDER/POWER AXIS

Ninety percent of all anorectics are women. We do not, of course, need to know that particular statistic to realize that the contemporary "tyranny of slenderness" is far from gender-neutral. Women are more obsessed with their bodies than men, less satisfied with them,[74] and permitted less latitude with them by themselves, by men, and by the culture. In a 1984 *Glamour* magazine poll of 33,000 women, 75 percent said they thought they were "too fat." Yet by Metropolitan Life Insurance Tables, themselves notoriously affected by cultural standards, only 25 percent of these women were heavier than their optimal weight, and a full 30 percent were below that weight.[75] The anorectic's distorted image of her body—her inability to see it as anything but too fat—although more extreme, is not radically discontinuous, then, from fairly common female misperceptions.

Consider, too, actors like Nick Nolte and William Hurt, who are permitted a certain amount of softening, of thickening about the waist, while still retaining romantic-lead status. Individual style, wit, the projection of intelligence, experience, and effectiveness still go a long way for men, even in our fitness-obsessed culture. But no female can achieve the status of romantic or sexual ideal without the appropriate *body*. That body, if we use television commercials as a gauge, has gotten steadily leaner since the mid 1970s.[76] What used to be acknowledged as an extreme required only of high fashion models is now the dominant image that beckons to high-school and college women. Over and over, extremely slender women students complain of hating their thighs or their stomachs (the anorectic's most dreaded danger spot); often, they express concern and anger over frequent teasing by their boyfriends. Janey, a former student, is 5′10″ and weights 132 pounds. Yet her boyfriend Bill, also a student of mine, calls her "Fatso" and "Big Butt" and insists she should be 110 pounds because (as he explains in his journal for my class) "that's what Brooke Shields weighs." He calls this "constructive criticism" and seems to experience extreme anxiety over the possibility of her gaining any weight: "I can tell it bothers her yet I still continue to badger her about it. I guess that I think that if I continue to remind her things will change faster."[77] This sort of relationship, in which the woman's weight has become a focal issue, is not at all atypical, as I have discovered from student journals and papers.

Hilda Bruch reports that many anorectics talk of having a "ghost" inside them or surrounding them, "a dictator who dominates me," as one woman describes it;" a little man who objects when I eat" is the description given by another.[78] The little ghost, the dictator, the "other self" (as he is often described) is always male, reports Bruch. The anorectic's *other* self—the self of the uncontrollable appetites, the impurities and taints, the flabby will and tendency to mental torpor—is the body, as we have seen. But it is also (and here the anorectic's associations are surely in the mainstream of Western culture) the *female* self. These two selves are perceived as at constant war. But it is clear that it is the male side—with its associated values of greater spirituality, higher intellectuality, strength of will—that is being expressed and developed in the anorexic syndrome.[79]

What is the meaning of these gender associations in the anorectic? I propose that there are two levels of meaning. One has to do with fear and disdain for traditional female roles and social limitations. The other has to do, more profoundly, with a deep fear of "the Female," with all its more nightmarish archetypal associations of voracious hungers and sexual insatiability.

Adolescent anorectics express a characteristic fear of growing up to be mature, sexually developed, and potentially reproductive women. "I have a deep fear," says one," of having a womanly body, round and fully developed. I want to be tight and muscular and thin."[80] Cherry Boone O'Neill speaks explicitly of her fear of womanhood.[81] If only she could stay thin, says yet another, "I

437

BORDO

would never have to deal with having a woman's body; like Peter Pan I could stay a child forever."[82] The choice of Peter Pan is telling here—what she means is, stay a *boy* forever. And indeed, as Bruch reports, many anorectics, when children, dreamt and fantasized about growing up to be boys.[83] Some are quite conscious of playing out this fantasy through their anorexia; Adrienne, one of Levenkron's patients, was extremely proud of the growth of facial and body hair that often accompanies anorexia, and especially proud of her" skinny, hairy arms."[84] Many patients report, too, that their father had wanted a boy, were disappointed to get "less than" that, or had emotionally rebuffed their daughter when she began to develop sexually.[85]

In a characteristic scenario, anorexia develops just at the outset of puberty. Normal body changes are experienced by the anorectic, not surprisingly, as the takeover of the body by disgusting, womanish fat. "I grab my breasts," says Aimee Liu," says Aimee Liu, "pinching them until they hurt. If only I could eliminate them, cut them off if need be, to become as flat-chested as a child again."[86] The anorectic is exultant when her periods stop (as they do in *all* cases of anorexia[87] and as they do in many female runners as well). Disgust with menstruation is typical: "I saw a picture at a feminist art gallery," says another woman. "There was a woman with long red yarn coming out of her, like she was menstruating. . . . I got that *feeling*—in that part of my body that I have trouble with . . . my stomach, my thighs, my pelvis. That revolted feeling."[88]

Some authors interpret these symptoms as a species of unconscious feminist protest, involving anger at the limitations of the traditional female role, rejection of values associated with it, and fierce rebellion against allowing their futures to develop in the same direction as their mothers' lives.[89] In her portrait of the typical anorexic family configuration, Bruch describes nearly all of the mothers as submissive to their husbands but very controlling of their children.[90] Practically all had had promising careers which they had given up to care for their husbands and families full-time, a task they take very seriously, although often expressing frustration and dissatisfaction.

Certainly, many anorectics appear to experience anxiety about falling into the life-style they associate with their mothers. It is a prominent theme in Aimee Liu's *Solitaire*. Another woman describes her feeling that "[I am] full of my mother . . . she is in me even if she isn't there" in nearly the same breath as she complains of her continuous fear of being" not human . . . of ceasing to exist."[91] And Ellen West, nearly a century earlier, had quite explicitly equated becoming fat with the inevitable (for an elite woman of her time) confinements of domestic life and the domestic stupor she associates with it:

> Dread is driving me mad . . . the consciousness that ultimately I will lose everything; all courage, all rebelliousness, all drive for doing; that it—my little world—will make me flabby, flabby and fainthearted and beggarly.[92]

Several of my students with eating disorders reported that their anorexia had developed after their families had dissuaded them from choosing or forbidden them to embark on a traditionally male career.

Here anorexia finds a true sister-phenomenon in the epidemic of female invalidism and "hysteria" that swept through the middle and upper-middle classes in the second half of the nineteenth century.[93] It was a time that, in many ways, was very like our own, especially in the conflicting demands women were confronting: the opening up of new possibilities versus the continuing grip of the old expectations. On the one hand, the old preindustrial order, with the father at the head of a self-contained family production unit, had given way to the dictatorship of the market, opening up new, nondomestic opportunities for working women. On the other hand, it turned many of the most valued "female" skills—textile and garment manufacture, food processing—out of the home and over to the factory system.[94] In the new machine economy, the lives of middle-class women were far emptier than they had been before.

It was an era, too, that had been witnessing the first major feminist wave. In 1840, the World Anti-Slavery Conference had been held, at which the first feminists spoke loudly and long on the connections between the abolition of slavery and women's rights. The year 1848 saw the Seneca Falls Convention. In 1869, John Stuart Mill published his landmark work "On the Subjection of Women." And in 1889 the Pankhursts formed the Women's Franchise League. But it was an era, too (and not unrelatedly, as I shall argue later), when the prevailing ideal of femininity was the delicate, affluent lady, unequipped for anything but the most sheltered domestic life, totally dependent on her prosperous husband, providing a peaceful and comfortable haven for him each day after his return from his labors in the public sphere.[95] In a now famous letter, Freud, criticizing John Stuart Mill, writes:

> It really is a still-born thought to send women into the struggle for existence exactly as men. If, for instance, I imagine my gentle sweet girl as a competitor it would only end in my telling her, as I did seventeen months ago, that I am fond of her and that I implore her to withdraw from the strife into the calm uncompetitive activity of my home.[96]

This is exactly what male doctors *did* do when women began falling ill, complaining of acute depression, severe headaches, weakness, nervousness, and self-doubt.[97] Among these women were such noted feminists and social activists as Charlotte Perkins Gilman, Jane Addams, Elizabeth Cady Stanton, Margaret Sanger, British activist Josephine Butler, and German suffragist Hedwig Dohm. "I was weary myself and sick of asking what I am and what I ought to be," recalls Gilman,[98] who later went on to write a fictional account of her mental breakdown in the chilling novella The Yellow Wallpaper. Her doctor, the famous female specialist S. Weir Mitchell, instructed her, as Gilman

439

BORDO

recalls, to "live as domestic a life as possible. Have your child with you all the time. . . . Lie down an hour every day after each meal. Have but two hours intellectual life a day. And never touch pen, brush or pencil as long as you live."[99]

Freud, who favorably reviewed Mitchell's 1887 book and who advised that psychotherapy for hysterical patients be combined with Mitchell's rest cure ("to avoid new psychical impressions"),[100] was as blind as Mitchell to the contribution that isolation, boredom, and intellectual frustration made to the etiology of hysteria. Nearly all of the subjects in *Studies in Hysteria* (as well as the later Dora) are acknowledged by Freud to be unusually intelligent, creative, energetic, independent, and, often, highly educated. (Berthe Pappenheim—"Anna O.'"—as we know, went on after recovery to become an active feminist and social reformer.) Freud even comments, criticizing Janet's notion that hysterics were "psychically insufficient," on the characteristic coexistence of hysteria with "gifts of the richest and most original kind."[101] Yet Freud never makes the connection (which Breuer had begun to develop)[102] between the monotonous domestic lives these women were expected to lead after they completed their schooling, and the emergence of compulsive daydreaming, hallucinations, dissociations, and hysterical conversions.

Charlotte Perkins Gilman does make that connection. In *The Yellow Wallpaper* she describes how a prescribed regime of isolation and enforced domesticity eventuates, in her fictional heroine, in the development of a full-blown hysterical symptom, madness, and collapse. The symptom, the hallucination that there is a woman trapped in the wallpaper of her bedroom, struggling to get out, is at once a perfectly articulated expression of protest and a completely debilitating idée fixe that allows the woman character no distance on her situation, no freedom of thought, no chance of making any progress in leading the kind of active, creative life her body and soul crave.

So too for the anorectic. It is indeed essential to recognize in this illness the dimension of protest against the limitations of the ideal of female domesticity (the "feminine mystique," as Betty Friedan called it) that reigned in America throughout the 1950s and early 1960s—the era when most of their mothers were starting homes and families. This was, we should recall, the era following World War II, an era during which women were fired en masse from the jobs they had held during the war and shamelessly propagandized back into the full-time job of wife and mother. It was an era, too, when the "fuller figure," as Jane Russell now calls it, came into fashion once more, a period of "mammary madness" (or "resurgent Victorianism," as Lois Banner calls it), which glamorized the voluptuous, large-breasted woman.[103] This remained the prevailing fashion tyranny until the late 1960s and early 1970s.

But we must recognize that the anorectic's protest, like that of the classical hysterical symptom, is written on the bodies of anorexic women, not embraced as a conscious politics—nor, indeed, does it reflect any social or political understanding at all. Moreover, the symptoms themselves function to preclude the emergence of such an understanding. The idée fixe—staying thin—becomes at its farthest extreme so powerful as to render any other ideas or life-projects meaningless. Liu describes it as "all encompassing."[104] West writes: "I felt all inner development was ceasing, that all becoming and growing were being choked, because a single idea was filling my entire soul."[105]

Paradoxically—and often tragically—these pathologies of female protest (and we must include agoraphobia here, as well as hysteria and anorexia) actually function as if in collusion with the cultural conditions that produced them.[106] The same is true for more moderate expressions of the contemporary female obsession with slenderness. Women may feel themselves deeply attracted by the aura of freedom and independence suggested by the boyish body ideal of today. Yet, each hour, each minute spent in anxious pursuit of that ideal (for it does not come naturally to most mature women) is in fact time and energy taken from inner development and social achievement. As a feminist protest, the obsession with slenderness is hopelessly counterproductive.

It is important to recognize, too, that the anorectic is terrified and repelled, not only by the traditional female domestic role—which she associates with mental lassitude and weakness—but by a certain archetypal image of the female: as hungering, voracious, all-needing, and all-wanting. It is this image that shapes and permeates her experience of her own hunger for food as insatiable and out of control, that makes her feel that if she takes just one bite, she will not be able to stop.

441

Let us explore this image. Let us break the tie with food and look at the metaphor: hungering . . . voracious . . . extravagantly and excessively needful...without restraint . . . always wanting . . . always wanting too much affection, reassurance, emotional and sexual contact, and attention. This is how many women frequently experience themselves, and, indeed, how many men experience women. "Please, God, keep me from telephoning him," prays the heroine in Dorothy Parker's classic" A Telephone Call,"[107] experiencing her need for reassurance and contact as being as out of control and degrading as the anorectic does her desire for food. The male counterpart to this is found in Paul Morel in Lawrence's *Sons and Lovers*: "Can you never like things without clutching them as if you wanted to pull the heart out of them?" he accuses Miriam as she fondles a flower. "Why don't you have a bit more restraint, or reserve, or something. . . . You're always begging things to love you, as if you were a beggar for love. Even the flowers, you have to fawn on them."[108] How much psychic authenticity do these images carry in 1980s America? One woman in my class provided a stunning insight into the connection between her perception of herself and the anxiety of the compulsive dieter. "You know," she said, "the anorectic is always convinced she is taking up too much space, eating too much, wanting food too much. I've never felt that

BORDO

way, but I've often felt that I was *too much*—too much emotion, too much need, too loud and demanding, too much *there*, if you know what I mean."[109]

The most extreme cultural expressions of the fear of woman as "too much"–which almost always revolve around her sexuality—are strikingly full of eating and hungering metaphors. "Of woman's unnatural, insatiable lust, what country, what village doth not complain?" queries Burton in *The Anatomy of Melancholy*.[110] "You are the true hiennas," says Walter Charleton, "that allure us with the fairness of your skins, and when folly hath brought us within your reach, you leap upon us and devour us."[111]

The mythology/ideology of the devouring, insatiable female (which, as we have seen, is the image of her female self the anorectic has internalized) tends historically to wax and wane. But not without rhyme or reason. In periods of gross environmental and social crisis, such as characterized the period of the witch-hunts in the fifteenth and sixteenth centuries, it appears to flourish.[112] "All witchcraft comes from carnal lust, which is in women *insatiable*," say Kramer and Sprenger, authors of the official witch-hunters handbook, *Malleus Malificarum*. For the sake of fulfilling the "*mouth* of the wom . . .[women] consort even with the devil."[113]

Anxiety over women's uncontrollable hungers appears to peak, as well, during periods when women are becoming independent and are asserting themselves politically and socially. The second half of the nineteenth century, concurrent with the first feminist wave discussed earlier, saw a virtual flood of artistic and literary images of the dark, dangerous, and evil female: "sharp-teethed, devouring" Sphinxes, Salomes, and Delilahs, "biting, tearing, murderous women." "No century," claims Peter Gay, "depicted woman as vampire, as castrator, as killer, so consistently, so programmatically, and so nakedly as the nineteenth."[114] No century, either, was so obsessed with sexuality—particularly female sexuality—and its medical control. Treatment for excessive "sexual excitement" and masturbation in women included placing leeches on the womb,[115] clitoridectomy, and removal of the ovaries (also recommended for "troublesomeness, eating like a ploughman, erotic tendencies, persecution mania, and simple 'cussedness'")[116] The importance of female masturbation in the etiology of the "actual neurosis" was a topic in which the young Freud and his friend and colleague Wilhelm Fliess were especially interested. Fliess believed that the secret to controlling such "sexual abuse" lay in the treatment of nasal "genital spots"; in an operation that was sanctioned by Freud, he attempted to "correct" the "bad sexual habits" of Freud's patient Emma Eckstein by removal of the turbinate bone of her nose.[117]

It was in the second half of the nineteenth century, too, despite a flurry of efforts by feminists and health reformers,[118] that the stylized "S-curve," which required a tighter corset than ever before, came into fashion.[119] "While the suffragettes were forcefully propelling all women toward legal and political emancipation," says Amaury deRiencourt, "fashion and custom imprisoned

442

BORDO

her physically as she had never been before."[120] Described by Thorstein Veblen as a "mutilation, undergone for the purpose of lowering the subject's vitality and rendering her permanently and obviously unfit for work," the corset indeed did just that.[121] In it a woman could barely sit or stoop, was unable to move her feet more than six inches at a time, and had difficulty in keeping herself from regular fainting fits. (In 1904, a researcher reported that "monkeys laced up in these corsets moped, became excessively irritable and within weeks sickened and died"!)[122] The connection was often drawn in popular magazines between enduring the tight corset and the exercise of self-restraint and control. The corset is "an ever present monitor," says one 1878 advertisement, "of a well-disciplined mind and well-regulated feelings."[123] Today, of course, we diet to achieve such control.

It is important to emphasize that, despite the practice of bizarre and grotesque methods of gross physical manipulation and external control (clitoridectomy, Chinese foot-binding, the removal of bones of the rib cage in order to fit into the tight corsets), such control plays a relatively minor role in the maintenance of gender/power relations. For every historical image of the dangerous, aggressive woman there is a corresponding fantasy—an ideal femininity, from which all threatening elements have been purged—that women have mutilated themselves *internally* to attain. In the Victorian era, at the same time that operations were being performed to control female sexuality, William Acton, Richard von Krafft-Ebing, and others were proclaiming the official scientific doctrine that women are naturally passive and "not very much troubled with sexual feelings of any kind."[124] Corresponding to this male medical fantasy was the popular artistic and moral theme of woman as ministering angel; sweet, gentle, domestic, without intensity or personal ambition of any sort.[125] Peter Gay suggests, correctly, that these ideals must be understood as a reaction-formation to the era's "pervasive sense of manhood in danger," and he argues that few women actually fit the "insipid goody" (as Kate Millett calls it) image.[126] What Gay forgets, however, is that most women *tried* to fit—working classes as well as middle were affected by the "tenacious and all-pervasive" ideal of the perfect lady.[127]

On the gender/power axis the female body appears, then, as the unknowing medium of the historical ebbs and flows of the fear of woman as "too much." That, as we have seen, is how the anorectic experiences her female, bodily self: as voracious, wanton, needful of forceful control by her male will. Living in the tide of cultural backlash against the second major feminist wave, she is not alone in constructing these images. Christopher Lasch, in *The Culture of Narcissism*, speaks of what he describes as "the apparently aggressive overtures of sexually liberated women" which "convey to many males the same message—that women are *voracious, insatiable,*" and call up "early fantasies of a possessive, suffocating, *devouring* and castrating mother."[128]

Our contemporary beauty ideals, by contrast, seemed purged, as Kim

Chernin puts it, "of the power to conjure up memories of the past, of all that could remind us of a woman's mysterious power."[129] The ideal, rather, is an "image of a woman in which she is not yet a woman": Darryl Hannah as the lanky, newborn mermaid in *Splash*; Lori Singer (appearing virtually anorexic) as the reckless, hyperkinetic heroine of *Footloose*; the Charley Girl; "Cheryl Tiegs in shorts, Margaux Hemingway with her hair wet; Brooke Shields naked on an island;"[130] the dozens of teenage women who appear in Coke commercials, in jeans commercials, in chewing gum commercials.

The images suggest amused detachment, casual playfulness, flirtatiousness without demand, and lightness of touch. A refusal to take sex, death, or politics too deadly seriously. A delightfully unconscious relationship to her body. The twentieth century has seen this sort of feminine ideal before, of course. When, in the 1920s, young women began to flatten their breasts, suck in their stomachs, bob their hair, and show off long colt-like legs, they believed they were pursuing a new freedom and daring that demanded a carefree, boyish style. If the traditional female hourglass suggested anything, it was confinement and immobility. Yet the flapper's freedom, as Mary McCarthy's and Dorothy Parker's short stories brilliantly reveal, was largely an illusion—as any obsessively cultivated sexual style must inevitably be. Although today's images may suggest androgynous independence, we need only consider who is on the receiving end of the imagery in order to confront the pitiful paradox involved.

Watching the commercials are thousands of anxiety-ridden women and adolescents (some of whom may well be the very ones appearing in the commercials) with anything but an unconscious relation to their bodies. They are involved in an absolutely contradictory state of affairs, a totally no-win game: caring desperately, passionately, obsessively about attaining an ideal of coolness, effortless confidence, and casual freedom. Watching the commercials is a little girl, perhaps ten years old, whom I saw in Central Park, gazing raptly at her father, bursting with pride: "Daddy, guess what? I lost two pounds!" And watching the commercials is the anorectic, who associates her relentless pursuit of thinness with power and control, but who in fact relentless pursuit of thinness with power and control, but who in fact destroys her health and imprisons her imagination. She is surely the most startling and stark illustration of how cavalier power relations are with respect to the motivations and goals of individuals, yet how deeply they are etched on our bodies, and how well our bodies serve them.

NOTES

This essay was originally published in the Philosophical Forum 17, no.2 (Winter 1985). I wish to thank all those in the audiences at Le Moyne, D'Youville, and Bennington who commented on my presentations, and Lynne Arnault, Nancy Fraser, and Mario Moussa for their systematic and penetrating criticisms and suggestions for the

444

BORDO

Forum version. In addition, I owe a large initial debt to my students, particularly Christy Ferguson, Vivian Conger, and Nancy Monaghan, for their observations and insights.

1. Jules Henry, *Culture Against Man* (New York: Alfred A. Knopf, 1963).

2. When I wrote this piece in 1983, the term anorexia was commonly used by clinicians to designate a general class of eating disorders within which intake-restricting (or abstinent) anorexia and bulimia-anorexia (characterized by alternating bouts of gorging and starving and/or gorging and vomiting) are distinct subtypes (see Hilde Bruch, *The Golden Cage: The Enigma of Anorexia Nervosa* [New York: Vintage, 1970], P. 10; Steven Levenkron, *Treating and Overcoming Anorexia Nervosa* [New York: Warner Books, 1982], p. 6; R. L. Plamer, *Anorexia Nervosa* [Middlesex: Penguin, 1980], pp. 14, 23-24; Paul Garfinkel and David Garner, Anorexia Nervosa: A Multidimensional Perspective [New York: Brunner/Mazel, 1982], p. 4). Since then, as the clinical tendency has been increasingly to emphasize the differences rather than the commonalities between the eating disorders, bulimia has come to occupy its own separate classificatory niche. In the present piece I concentrate largely on those images, concerns, and attitudes shared by anorexia and bulimia. Where a difference seems significant for the themes of this essay, I will indicate the relevant difference in a footnote rather than overcomplicate the main argument of the text. This procedure is not to be taken as belittling the importance of such differences, some of which I discuss in "Reading the Slender Body."

3. Although throughout history scattered references can be found to patients who sound as though they may have been suffering from self-starvation, the first medical description of anorexia as a discrete syndrome was made by W. W. Gull in an 1868 address at Oxford (at the time he called the syndrome, in keeping with the medical taxonomy of the time, hysteric apepsia). Six years later, Gull began to use the term *anorexia nervosa*; at the same time, E. D. Lesegue independently decribed the disorder (Garfinkel and Garner, *Anorexia Nervosa*, pp. 58–59). Evidence points to a minor "outbreak" of anorexia nervosa around this time (see John Jacobs Brumberg, *Fasting Girls* [Cambridge: Harvard University Press, 1988]0, a historical occurrence that went unnoticed by twentieth-century clinicians until renewed interest in the disorder was prompted by its reemergence and striking increase over the past twenty years (see note 11 of "Whose Body Is This?" for sources that document this increase). At the time I wrote the present piece, I was not aware of the extent of anorexia nervosa in the second half of the nineteenth century.

4. Ludwig Binswanger, "The Case of Ellen West," in Rollo May, ed., *Existence* (New York: Simon and Schuster, 1958), P. 288. He was wrong, of course. The symptom was not new, and we now know that Ellen West was not the only young woman of her era to suffer from anorexia. But the fact that Binswanger was unaware of other cases is certainly suggestive of its infrequency, especially relative to our own time.

5. Hilde Bruch, *Eating Disorders* (New York: Basic Books, 1973), p. 4.

6. Levenkron, *Treating and Overcoming Anorexia Nervosa*, p. 1; Susan Squire, "Is the Binge-Purge Cycle Catching?" Ms. (Oct. 1983).

7. Dinitia Smith, "The New Puritans," *New York Magazine* (June 11, 1984): 28.

8. Kim Chernin, *The Obsession: Reflections on the Tyranny of Slenderness* (New York: Harper and Row, 1981), pp. 63, 62.

9. Garfinkel and Garner, *Anorexia Nervosa*, p. xi. Anorectics characterically suffer

445

BORDO

from a number of physiological disturbances, including amenorrhea (cessation of menstruation) and abnormal hypothalamic function (see Garfinkel and Garner, *Anorexia Nervosa*, pp. 58–89, for an extensive discussion of these and other physiological disorders associated with anorexia; also Eugene Garfield, "Anorexia Nervosa: The Enigma of Self-Starvation," *Current Contents* [Aug. 6, 1984]: 8–9). Researchers are divided, with arguments on both sides, as to whether hypothalamic dysfunction may be a primary cause of the disease or whether these characteristic neuroendocrine disorders are the result of weight loss, caloric deprivation, and emotional stress. The same debate rages over abnormal vasopressin levels discovered in anorectics, touted in tabloids all over the United States as the "explanation" for anorexia and key to its cure. Apart from such debates over a biochemical predisposition to anorexia, research continues to explore the possible role of biochemistry in the self-perpetuating nature of the disease, and the relation of the physiological effects of starvation to particular experiential symptoms such as the anorectic's preoccupation with food (see Bruch, *The Golden Cage*, pp. 7–12; Garfinkel and Garner, *Anorexia Nervosa*, pp. 10–14).

10. Initially, anorexia was found to predominate among upper-class white families. There is, however, widespread evidence that this is now rapidly changing (as we might expect; no one in America is immune from the power of popular imagery). The disorder, it has been found, is becoming more equally distributed, touching populations (e.g., blacks and East Indians) previously unaffected, and all socioeconomic levels (Garfinkel and Garner, *Anorexia Nervosa* pp. 102–3). There remains, however, an overwhelming disproportion of women to men (Garfinkel and Garner, *Anorexia Nervosa*, pp. 112–13).

11. Chernin's *The Obsession*, whose remarkable insights inspired my interest in anorexia, remains the outstanding exception to the lack of cultural understanding of eating disorders.

12. Chernin, *The Obsession*, pp. 36–37. My use of the expression "our culture" may seem overly homogenizing here, disrespectful of differences among ethnic groups, socioeconomic groups, subcultures within American society, and so forth. It must be stressed here that I am discussing ideology and images whose power is precisely the power to homogenize culture. Even in pre-mass-media cultures we see this phenomenon: the nineteenth-century ideal of the "perfect lady" tyrannized even those classes who could not afford to realize it. With television, of course, a massive deployment of images becomes possible, and there is no escape from the mass shaping of our fantasy livers. Although they may start among the wealthy elite ("A woman can never be too rich or too thin"), media-promoted ideas of femininity and masculinity quickly and perniciously spread their influence over everyone who owns a TV or can afford a junk magazine or is aware of billboards. Changes in the incidence of anorexia among lower-income groups (see note 10, above) bear out this point.

13. Christopher Lasch, *The Culture of Narcissism* (New York: Warner Books, 1979), p. 88.

14. I choose these three primarily because they are where my exploration of the imagery, language, and metaphor produced by anorexic women led me. Delivering earlier versions of this essay at colleges and conferences, I discovered that one of the commonest responses of members of the audiences was the proffering of further axes; the paper presented itself less as a statement about the ultimate meaning or causes of a phenomenon than as an invitation to continue my "unpacking" of anorexia as a crystallizing formation. Yet the particular axes chosen have more than a purely autobio-

graphical rationale. The dualist axes serve to identify and articulate the basic body imagery of anorexia. The control axis is an exploration of the question "Why now?" The gender/power axis continues this exploration but focusses on the question "Why women?" The sequence of axes takes us from the most general, most historically diffuse structure of continuity—the dualist experience of self–to ever narrower, more specified arenas of comparison and connection. At first the connections are made without regard to historical context, drawing on diverse historical sources to exploit their familiar coherence in an effort to sculpt the shape of the anorexic experience. In this section, too, I want to suggest that the Greco-Christian tradition provides a particularly fertile soil for the development of anorexia. Then I turn to the much more specific context of American fads and fantasies in the 1980s, considering the contemporary scene largely in terms of popular culture (and therefore through the "fiction" of homogeneity), without regard for gender difference. In this section the connections drawn point to a historical experience of self common to both men and women. Finally, my focus shifts to consider, not what connects anorexia to other general cultural phenomena, but what presents itself as a rupture from them, and what forces us to confront how ultimately opaque the current epidemic of eating disorders remains unless it is linked to the particular situation of women.

The reader will notice that the axes are linked thematically as well as through their convergence in anorexia: the obsession with control is linked with dualism, and the gender/power dynamics discussed implicitly deal with the issue of control (of the feminine) as well.

15. Michel Foucault, *The History of Sexuality*. Vol. 1: *An Introduction* (New York: Vintage, 19800, p. 115.

16. Foucault, *History of Sexuality*, pp. 47–48.

17. Hubert L. Dreyfus and Paul Rabinow, *Michel Foucault: Beyond Structuralism and Hermeneutics* (Chicago: University of Chicago Press, 1983), p. 112.

18. *Foucault, History of Sexuality*, p. 95.

19. Michel Foucault, *Discipline and Punish* (New York: Vintage, 1979), p. 26.

20. Plato, Phaedo, in *The Dialogues of Plato*, ed. and trans. Benjamin Jowett, 4th ed., rev. (Oxford: Clarendon Press, 1953), 83d.

21. St. Augustine, *The Confessions*, trans. R. S. Pine-Coffin (Middlesex: Penguin, 1961), p. 164.

22. *Phaedo* 81d.

23. *Phaedo* 66c. For Descartes on the body as a hindrance to knowledge, see *Conversations with Burman* (Oxford: Clarendon Press, 1976), p. 8, and *Passions of the Soul in Philosophical Works of Descartes*, 2 vols., trans. Elizabeth S. Haldane and G. R. T. Ross (Cambridge: Cambridge University Press, 1969), vol. 1, p. 353.

24. *Phaedo* 80a.

25. Indeed, the Cartesian "Rules for the Direction of the Mind," as carried out in the *Meditations* especially, are actually rules for the transcendence of the body—its passions, its senses, the residue of "infantile prejudices" of judgment lingering from that earlier time when we were "immersed" in body and bodily sensations.

26. Alan Watts, *Nature, Man, and Woman* (New York: Vintage, 1970), p. 145.

27. Bruch, *Eating Disorders*, p. 84.

28. Chernin, *The Obsession*, p. 8.

29. Entry in student journal, 1984.

447

BORDO

30. Bruch, *The Golden Cage*, p. 4.

31. Binswanger, "The Case of Ellen West," p. 253.

32. Bruch, Eating Disorders, p. 253.

33. Levenkron, Treating and Overcoming Anorexia Nervosa, p. 6.

34. Bruch, *Eating Disorders*, p. 270; Augustine, Confessions, p. 164.

35. Bruch, *Eating Disorders*, p. 50.

36. Bruch, *Eating Disorders*, p. 254.

37. Entry in student journal, 1984.

38. Bruch, *Eating Disorders*, p. 279.

39. Aimee Liu, *Solitaire* (New York: Harper and Row, 1979), p. 141.

40. Jennifer Woods, "I Was Starving Myself to Death," Mademoiselle (May 1981): 200.

41. Binswanger, "The Case of Ellen West," p. 251 (emphasis added).

42. Why they should emerge with such clarity in the twentieth century and through the voice of the anorectic is a question answered, in part, by the following two axes.

43. Augustine, *Confessions*, p. 165; Liu, *Solitaire,* p. 109.

44. Binswanger, "The Case of Ellen West," p. 343.

45. Entry in student journal, 1983.

46. Woods, "I Was Starving Myself to Death," p. 242.

47. Liu, *Solitaire*, p. 109.

48. "I equated gaining weight with happiness, contentment, then slothfulness, then atrophy, then death." (From case notes of Binnie Klein, M.S.W., to whom I am grateful for having provided parts of a transcript of her work with an anorexic patient.) See also Binswanger, "The Case of Ellen West," p. 343.

49. Klein, case notes.

50. Cherry Boone O'Neill, *Starving for Attention* (New York: Dell, 1982), p. 131.

51. O'Neill, *Starving for Attention*, p. 49.

52. Liu, *Solitaire*, p. 101.

53. Levenkron, *Treating and Overcoming Anorexia Nervosa*, p. 122.

54. Since the writing of this piece, evidence has accrued suggesting that sexual abuse may be an element in the histories of many eating-disordered women (see note 2 in "Whose Body Is This?").

55. Bruch, *The Golden Cage*, p. 73. The same is not true of bulimic anorectics, who tend to be sexually active (Garfinkel and Garner, *Anorexia Nervosa*, p. 41). Bulimic anorectics, as seems symbolized by the binge-purge cycle itself, stand in a somewhat more ambivalent relationship to their hungers than do abstinent anorectics. See "Reading the Slender Body," in this volume, for a discussion of the cultural dynamics of the binge-purge cycle.

56. Bruch, *The Golden Cage*, p. 33.

57. Liu, *Solitaire*, p. 36.

58. Liu, *Solitaire*, p. 46. In one study of female anorectics, 88 percent of the subjects questioned reported that they lost weight because they "liked the feeling of will power and self-control" (G. R. Leon, "Anorexia Nervosa: The Question of Treatment Emphasis," in M. Rosenbaum, C. M. Franks, and Y. Jaffe, eds., *Perspectives on Behavior Therapy in the Eighties* [New York: Springer, 1983], pp. 363–77).

59. Bruch, *Eating Disorders*, p. 95.

60. Liu, *Solitaire*, p. 123.

61. Bruch, *The Golden Cage*, p. 65 (emphasis added).

62. Smith, "The New Puritans," p. 24 (emphasis added).

63. Entry in student journal, 1984.

64. Entry in student journal, 1984.

65. Trix Rosen, *Strong and Sexy* (New York: Putnam, 1983), p. 108.

66. Rosen, *Strong and Sexy*, pp. 62, 14, 47, 48.

67. Smith, "The New Puritans," pp. 27, 26.

68. Rosen, *Strong and Sexy*, pp. 61-62.

69. Rosen, *Strong and Sexy,* pp. 72, 61. This fantasy is not limited to female bodybuilders. John Travolta describes his experience training for *Staying Alive*: "[It] taught me incredible things about the body . . . how it can be reshaped so you can make yourself over entirely, creating an entirely new you. I now look at bodies almost like pieces of clay that can be molded." ("Travolta: 'You Really Can Make Yourself Over,'" *Syracuse Herald-American*, Jan. 13, 1985.)

70. Smith, "The New Puritans," p. 29.

71. Durk Pearson and Sandy Shaw, *Life Extension* (New York: Warner, 1982), p. 15.

72. Chernin, *The Obsession*, p. 47.

73. Smith, "The New Puritans," p. 24.

74. Sidney Journard and Paul Secord, "Body Cathexis and the Ideal Female Figure," *Journal of Abnormal and Social Psychology 50*: 243-46; Orland Wooley, Susan Wooley, and Sue Dyrenforth, "Obesity and Women–A Neglected Feminist Topic," *Women's Studies Institute Quarterly* 2 (1979): 81-92. Student journals and informal conversations with women students have certainly borne this out.

75. "Feeling Fat in a Thin Society," *Glamour* (Feb. 1984): 198.

76. The same trend is obvious when the measurements of Miss America winners are compared over the past fifty years (see Garfinkel and Garner, *Anorexia Nervosa*, p. 107). Some evidence has indicated that this tide is turning and that a more solid, muscular, athletic style is emerging as the latest fashion tyranny.

77. Entry in student journal, 1984.

78. Bruch, *The Golden Cage*, p. 58.

79. This is one striking difference between the abstinent anorectic and the bulimic anorectic: in the binge-and-vomit cycle, the hungering female self refuses to be annihilated, is in constant protest. And, in general, the rejection of femininity discussed here is not typical of bulimics, who tend to strive for a more "female"-looking body as well.

80. Entry in student journal, 1983.

81. O'Neill, *Starving for Attention*, p. 53.

82. Entry in student journal, 1983.

83. Bruch, *The Golden Cage*, p. 72; *Bruch, Eating Disorders*, p. 277. Others have fantasies of androgyny: "I want to go to a party and for everyone to look at me and for no one to know whether I was the most beautiful slender woman or handsome young man" (as reported by therapist April Benson, panel discussion, "New Perspectives on Female Development," third annual conference of the Center for the Study of Anorexia and Bulimia, New York, 1984).

449

BORDO

84. Levenkron, *Treating and Overcoming Anorexia Nervosa*, p. 28.

85. See, for example, Levenkron's case studies in *Treating and Overcoming Anorexia Nervosa*, esp. pp. 45, 103; O'Neill, *Starving for Attention*, p. 107; Susie Orbach, *Fat Is a Feminist Issue* (New York: Berkley, 1978), pp. 174-75.

86. Liu, *Solitaire*, p. 79.

87. Bruch, *The Golden Cage*, p. 65.

88. Klein, case study.

89. Chernin, *The Obsession*, pp. 102-3; Robert Seidenberg and Karen DeCrow, *Women Who Marry Houses: Panic and Protest in Agoraphobia* (New York: McGraw-Hill, 1983), pp. 88–97; Bruch, *The Golden Cage*, p. 58; Orbach, *Fat Is a Feminist Issue*, pp. 169-70. See also my discussions of the protest thesis in "Whose Body Is This?" and "The Body and the Reproduction of Femininity."

90. Bruch, *The Golden Cage*, pp. 27–28.

91. Bruch, *The Golden Cage*, p. 12.

92. Binswanger, "The Case of Ellen West," p. 243.

93. At the time I wrote this essay, I was unaware of the fact that eating disorders were frequently an element of the symptomatology of nineteenth-century "hysteria"—a fact that strongly supports my interpretation here.

94. See, among many other works on this subject, Barbara Ehrenreich and Dierdre English, *For Her Own Good* (Garden City: Doubleday, 1979), pp. 1–29.

95. See Martha Vicinus, "Introduction: The Perfect Victorian Woman," in Martha Vicinus, ed., *Suffer and Be Still: Women in the Victorian age* (Bloomington: Indiana University Press, 1972), pp. x-xi.

96. Ernest Jones, *Sigmund Freud: Life and Work* (London: Hogarth Press, 1956), vol. 1, p. 193.

97. On the nineteenth-century epidemic of female invalidism and hysteria, see Ehrenreich and English, *For Her Own Good*; Carroll Smith-Rosenberg, "The Hysterical Woman: Sex Roles and Conflict in Nineteenth-Century America," Social Research 39, no. 4 (Winter 1972): 652–78; Ann Douglas Wood, "The 'Fashionable Diseases': Women's Complaints and Their Treatment in Nineteenth Century America," *Journal of Interdisciplinary History* 4 (Summer 1973).

98. Ehrenreich and English, *For Her Own Good*, p. 2.

99. Ehrenreich and English, *For Her Own Good*, p. 102.

100. Sigmund Freud and Josef Breuer, *Studies on Hysteria* (New York: Avon, 1966), p. 311.

101. Freud and Breuer, *Studies on Hysteria*, p. 141; see also p. 202.

102. See especially pp. 76 ("Anna O."), 277, 284.

103. Marjorie Rosen, *Popcorn Venus* (New York: Avon, 1973); Lois Banner, *American Beauty* (Chicago: University of Chicago Press, 1983), pp. 283–85. Christian Dior's enormously popular full skirts and cinch-waists, as Banner points out, are strikingly reminiscent of Victorian modes of dress.

104. Liu, *Solitaire*, p. 141.

105. Binswanger, "The Case of Ellen West," p. 257.

106. This is one of the central themes I develop in "The Body and the Reproduction of Femininity."

107. Dorothy Parker, *Here Lies: The Collected Stories of Dorothy Parker* (New York: Literary Guild of America, 1939), p. 48.

108. D. H. Lawrence, *Sons and Lovers* (New York: Viking, 1958), p. 257.

109. This experience of oneself as "too much" may be more or less emphatic, depending on such variables as race, religion, socioeconomic class, and sexual orientation. Luise Eichenbaum and Susie Orbach (*Understanding Women: A Feminist Psychoanalytic Approach* [New York: Basic Books, 1983]) emphasize, however, how frequently their clinic patients, nonanorexic as well as anorexic, "talk about their needs with contempt, humiliation, and shame. They feel exposed and childish, greedy and insatiable" (p. 49). Eichenbaum and Orbach trace such feelings, moreover, to infantile experiences that are characteristic of all female development, given a division of labor within which women are the emotional nurturers and physical caretakers of family life. Briefly (and this sketch cannot begin to do justice to their rich and complex analysis): mothers unwittingly communicate to their daughters that feminine needs are excessive and bad and that they must be contained. The mother does this out of a sense that her daughter will have to learn the lesson in order to become properly socialized into the traditional female role of caring for others—of feeding others, rather than feeding the self—and also because of an unconscious identification with her daughter, who reminds the mother of the "hungry, needy little girl" in herself, denied and repressed through the mother's *own* "education" in being female: "Mother comes to be frightened by her daughter's free expression of her needs, and unconsciously acts toward her infant daughter in the same way she acts internally toward the little-girl part of herself. In some ways the little daughter becomes an external representation of that part of herself which she has come to dislike and deny. The complex emotions that result from her own deprivation through childhood and adult life are both directed inward in the struggle to negate the little-girl part of herself and projected outward onto her daughter" (p. 44). Despite a real desire to be totally responsive to her daughter's emotional needs, the mother's own anxiety limits her capacity to respond. The contradictory messages she sends out convey to the little girl "the idea that to get love and approval she must show a particular side of herself. She must hide her emotional cravings, her disappointments and her angers, her fighting spirit. . . . She comes to feel that there must be something wrong with who she really is, which in turn must mean that there is something wrong with what she needs and what she wants. . . . This soon translates into feeling unworthy and hesitant about pursuing her impulses" (pp. 48-49). Once she has grown up, of course, these feelings are reinforced by cultural ideology, further social training in femininity, and the likelihood that the men in her life will regard her as "too much" as well, having been schooled by their own training in masculine detachment and autonomy.

(With boys, who do not stir up such intense identification in the mother and who, moreover, she knows will grow up into a world that will meet their emotional needs [that is, the son will eventually grow up to be looked after by his future wife, who will be well trained in the feminine arts of care], mothers feel much less ambivalent about the satisfaction of needs and behave much more consistently in their nurturing. Boys therefore grow up, according to Eichenbaum and Orbach, with an experience of their needs as legitimate, appropriate, worthy of fulfillment.)

The male experience of the woman as "too much" has been developmentally explored, as well, in Dorothy Dinnerstein's ground-breaking *The Mermaid and the Minotaur: Sexual Arrangements and Human Malaise* (New York: Harper and Row, 1976). Dinnerstein argues that it is the woman's capacity to call up memories of helpless infancy,

451

BORDO

primitive wishes of "unqualified access" to the mother's body, and "the terrifying erotic independence of every baby's mother" (p. 62) that is responsible for the male fear of what he experiences as "the uncontrollable erotic rhythms" of the woman. Female impulses, a reminder of the autonomy of the mother, always appear on some level as a threatening limitation to his own. This gives rise to a "deep fantasy resentment" of female impulsivity (p. 59) and, on the cultural level, "archetypal nightmare visions of the insatiable female" (p. 62).

110. Quoted in Brian Easlea, *Witch-Hunting, Magic, and the New Philosophy* (Atlantic Highlands, N.J.: Humanities Press, 1980), p. 242 (emphasis added).

111. Quoted in Easlea, *Witch-Hunting*, p. 242 (emphasis added).

112. See Peggy Reeve Sanday, *Female Power and Male Dominance* (Cambridge: Cambridge University Press, 1981), pp. 172–84.

113. Quoted in Easlea, *Witch-Hunting*, p. 8.

114. Peter Gay, *The Bourgeois Experience: Victoria to Freud. Vol. 1: Education of the Senses* (New York: Oxford University Press, 1984), pp. 197–201, 207.

115. Chernin, *The Obsession*, p. 38.

116. Ehrenreich and English, *For Her Own Good*, p. 124.

117. See Jeffrey Masson's controversial *The Assault on Truth: Freud's Suppression of the Seduction Theory* (Toronto: Farrar Straus Giroux, 1984) for a fascinating discussion of how this operation (which, because Fliess failed to remove half a meter of gauze from the patient's nasal cavity, nearly killed her) may have figured in the development of Freud's ideas on hysteria. Whether or not one agrees fully with Masson's interpretation of the events, his account casts light on important dimensions of the nineteenth-century treatment of female disorders and raises questions about the origins and fundamental assumptions of psychoanalytic theory that go beyond any debate about Freud's motivations. The quotations cited in this essay can be found on p. 76; Masson discusses the Eckstein case on pp. 55–106.

118. Banner, *American Beauty*, pp. 86–105. It is significant that these efforts failed in large part because of their association with the women's rights movement. Trousers like those proposed by Amelia Bloomer were considered a particular badge of depravity and aggressiveness, the *New York Herald* predicting that women who wore bloomers would end up in "lunatic asylums or perchance in the state prison" (p. 96).

119. Banner, *American Beauty*, pp. 149–50.

120. Amaury deRiencourt, *Sex and Power in History* (New York: David McKay, 1974), p. 319. The metaphorical dimension here is as striking as the functional, and it is a characteristic feature of female fashion: the dominant styles always decree, to one degree or another, that women *should not take up too much space*, that the territory we occupy should be limited. This is as true of cinch-belts as it is of foot-binding.

121. Quoted in deRiencourt, *Sex and Power in History*, p. 319.

122. Kathryn Weibel, *Mirror, Mirror: Images of Women Reflected in Popular Culture* (New York: Anchor, 1977), p. 194.

123. Christy Ferguson, "Images of the Body: Victorian England," philosophy research project, Le Moyne College, 1983.

124. Quoted in E. M. Sigsworth and T. J. Wyke, "A Study of Victorian Prostitution and Venereal Disease," in Vicinus, ed., *Suffer and Be Still*, p. 82.

125. See Kate Millett, "The Debate over Women: Ruskin vs. Mill," and Helene E.

Roberts, "Marriage, Redundancy, or Sin: The Painter's View of Women in the First Twenty-Five Years of Victoria's Reign," both in Vicinus, ed., *Suffer and Be Still.*

126. Gay, The Bourgeois Experience, p. 197; Millett, "Debate over Women," in Vicinus, ed., *Suffer and Be Still*, p. 123.

127. Vicinus, "Introduction," p. x.

128. Lasch, *The Culture of Narcissism*, p. 343 (emphasis added).

129. Chernin, *The Obsession*, p. 148.

130. Charles Gaines and George Butler, "Iron Sisters," *Psychology Today* (Nov. 1983): 67.

453

GENDER IDENTITIES AT THE CROSSROADS OF MASCULINITY AND PHYSICAL DISABILITY

Thomas J. Gerschick
Adam Stephen Miller

Whatever the physically impaired may think of himself, he is attributed a negative identity by society, and much of his social life is a struggle against this imposed image. It is for this reason that we can say that stigmatization is less a by-product of disability than its substance. The greatest impediment to a person's taking full part in his society are not his physical flaws, but rather the tissue of myths, fears, and misunderstandings that society attaches to them. (Murphy, 1990)

chapter 24

TWO SETS of social dynamics converge in the lives of men with physical disabilities: the demands embodied in what sociologist R. W. Connell calls hegemonic masculinity and the stigmatization of people with disabilities. On the one side, hegemonic masculinity privileges men who are strong, courageous, aggressive, independent, self-reliant, and career-oriented. On the other, society perceives and expects people with disabilities to be weak, pitiful, passive, and dependent. This article seeks to sharpen our understanding of the cre-

We would like to thank our informants for sharing their time, experiences, and insight. Additionally, we would like to thank the following people for their comments on earlier drafts of this work: Sandra Cole, Harlan Hahn, Michael Kimmel, Michael Messner, Don Sabo, and Marg Weigers. We, of course, remain responsible for its content. We are indebted to Kimberley Brow and Erika Gottfried for background research and interview transcriptions. This research supported by a grant for the Undergraduate Research Opportunity Program at the University Michigan.

ation, maintenance, and recreation of gender identities by men who by birth, accident, or illness find themselves at the crossroads of these social forces.

Hegemonic masculinity is comprised of the socially dominant conceptions, cultural ideals, and ideological constructions of what is appropriate masculinity. It operates in three realms: personal; cultural and institutional and in the organization and use of the body (Connell 1990a, 1991, 1987). Gender, then, operates not only on an individual level but also as a collective practice and process (West & Zimmerman, 1987).

"To say that a particular form of masculinity is hegemonic," maintains Connell (1990b), "means that it is culturally exalted and that its exaltation stabilizes a structure of dominance and oppression in the gender order as a whole" (p. 94). Thus within it, there is a hierarchy within sexes: men over other men, as well as between the sexes: men over women.

Among the characteristics attributed to masculinity that are preferentially privileged and rewarded in U.S. dominant culture are strength, courage, endurance, stoicism, tenacity, and independence, especially economic independence. Despite the fact that these characteristics and ideals are primarily based in fantasy rather than reality, they are the standard against which men are judged.

For some men, access to dominant masculinity is blocked due to race and ethnicity, social class, sexual orientation, or similar factors. For others, such as men with physical disabilities, physical limitations and social stigma prevent access. Those who do not, and/or cannot, reflect the hegemonic standard of masculinity are subordinated and marginalized.

Men with physical disabilities are marginalized and stigmatized because they undermine the typical role of the body in U.S. culture. The body is a central foundation of how we define ourselves and how we are defined by others. As many of us know from painful personal experience, it is a way of determining value, which in turn translates into status and prestige. Additionally, men's bodies allow them to demonstrate the socially valuable characteristics of toughness, competitiveness, and ability (Messner, 1992). Thus, one's body and relationship to it provide a way to apprehend the world and one's place in it. The bodies of men with disabilities serve as a continual reminder that they are at odds with the expectations of the dominant culture.

Anthropologist Robert Murphy (1990), drawing on his own experience as a man who developed a disability later in life, observed:

> Paralytic disability constitutes emasculation of a more direct and total nature. For the male, the weakening and atrophy of the body threaten all the cultural values of masculinity: strength, activeness, speed, virility, stamina, and fortitude. (p. 94)

It is broadly accepted that identity is constructed in relation to others. For men with physical disabilities, then, gender identity and practice are created

GERSCHICK/MILLER

and maintained at the crossroads of marginalization and stigmatization. These men have limited access to cultural resources to help them negotiate the gender order. As a consequence, they are constrained and face limited options. Given the marginalized status of people with disabilities and the demands of prevailing masculinity, it is no wonder that they experience what Murphy (1990) calls, "embattled identities" (p. 104).

GOALS OF THE RESEARCH

Seeking to advance the growing body of literature on marginalized and alternative masculinities and identity, we ask the following set of questions: How do men with physical disabilities respond to the demands of hegemonic masculinity and their marginilization? How do they reconcile the associated expectations with their reality? How do they define masculinity for themselves and what are the sources of these definitions? To what degree do their responses contest and/or perpetuate the current gender order? That is, what are the political implications of different gender identities and practices?

The experiences of men with physical disabilities are important because they illuminate both the insidious power and limitations of contemporary masculinity. These men have insider knowledge of what the subordinated know about the gender order (Janeway, 1980). Additionally, the gender practices of some men exemplify alternative visions of masculinity that are obscured but available to men in our culture. Finally, they allow us to elucidate a process of paramount importance: how men with physical disabilities find happiness, fulfillment, and a sense of self-worth in a culture that has, in essence, denied them the right to their own identity, including their own masculinity.

457

THE THREE "R" FRAMEWORK

While no two construct their sense of masculinity in exactly the same way, there appear to be three dominant patterns men with physical disabilities use to cope with their situations.[1] These patterns can be conceived of in relation to the standards inherent in dominant masculinity. We call them the three Rs: *reformulation*, which entails men's redefinition of hegemonic characteristics on their own terms: *reliance*, reflected by sensitive or hypersensitive adoptions of particular predominant attributes; and *rejection*, characterized by the renunciation of these standards and either the creation of their own principles and practices or the denial of masculinity's importance in their lives. However, one should note that no man *entirely* follows any one of these patterns in defining his sense of self. Rather, for heuristic reasons, it is best to speak of the major and minor ways each man uses these three patterns.

For example, a man with physical disabilities may rely on dominant standards in his view of sexuality and occupation, but also reformulate the prevailing ideal of independence. Therefore, we discuss the primary way in

GERSCHICK/MILLER

which a man with disabilities relates to hegemonic masculinity's standards, while recognizing that his coping mechanism is a more complex combination of strategies. In doing so, we avoid "labeling" men and assigning them to arbitrary categories.

REFORMULATION

Men who reformulate predominant standards in defining their masculinity tend not to overtly contest these standards, but—either consciously or unconsciously—they recognize in their own condition an inability to meet these ideals as they are culturally conceived. They respond to an ideal by reformulating it, shaping it along the lines of their own abilities, perceptions, and strengths, and they define their manhood along these new lines.

An example of this comes Damon, a 72-year-old quadriplegic who survived a spinal-cord injury in an automobile accident 10 years ago. Damon says that he has always desired, and had, control of his life. While Damon now requires round-the-clock personal care assistants (PCAs), he asserts that he is still a very independent person:

> I direct all of my activities around my home where people have to help me to maintain my apartment, my transportation which I own and direction in where I go. I direct people how to get there and I tell them what my needs will be when I am going and coming and when to get where I am going.

Damon says that his sense control is more than mere illusion; it is a reality others know of as well. This reputation is important to him:

> People know from Jump Street that I have my own thing and I direct my own thing. And if they can't comply with desire, they won't be around. . . . I don't see any reason why people with me can't take instructions and get my life on just as I was having it before, only thing I'm not doing it myself. I direct somebody else to do it. So, therefore, I don't miss out on very much.

Hegemonic masculinity's definition of independence privileges self-reliance and autonomy. Damon requires substantial assistance: indeed, some might term him "dependent." However, Damon's reformulation of the independence ideal, accomplished in part through a cognitive shift, allows him to think otherwise.

Harold, a 46-year-old polio survivor, described a belief and practice akin to Damon's. Also a quadriplegic, Harold similarly requires PCAs to help him handle daily necessities. Harold termed his reliance on and control of PCAs "acting through others":

> When I say independence can be achieved by acting through other people, I actually mean getting through life, liberty, and the pursuit of happiness while utilizing high quality and dependable attendant care services.

As with Damon, Harold achieves his perceived sense of independence by controlling others. Harold stressed that he does not count on family or friends to do favors for him, but *employs* his PCAs in a "business relationship" he controls. Alternatives to family and friends are used whenever possible because most people with disabilities do not want to burden or be dependent on their families any more than necessary (Murphy, 1990).

Social class plays an important role here. Damon and Harold have the economic means to afford round-the-clock assistance. While none of our informants experienced economic hardship, many people with disabilities depend on the welfare system for their care, and the amount and quality of assistance they receive would make it much more difficult to conceive of themselves as independent.

A third man who reformulates predominant demands is Brent, a 45-year-old administrator. He told us that his paraplegic status, one that he has lived with since he was 5-years-old, has often cast him as an "outsider" to society, and that this status was particularly painful in his late adolescence, a time when the "sexual revolution" was sweeping America's youth:

> A very important measure of somebody's personhood—manhood—was their sexual ability. . . . What bothers me more than anything else is the stereotypes, and even more so, in terms of sexual desirability. Because I had a disability, I was less desirable than able-bodied people. And that I found very frustrating.

His experiences led him to recast the hegemonic notion that a man's relations with a partner should be predominantly physical into an idea of the importance of emotional relations and trust. This appears to be key to Brent's definition of his manhood:

459

> For me that is my measure of who I am as an individual and who I am as a man—my ability to be able to be honest with my wife. Be able to be close with her, to be able to ask for help, provide help. To have a commitment, to follow through and to do all those things that I think are important.

As Connell (1990a) notes, this requires a capacity to not only be expressive, but also to have feelings worth expressing. This clearly demonstrates a different form of masculine practice.

The final case of reformulation comes from Robert, a 30-year-old survivor of a motorcycle accident. Able-bodied for much of his life, Robert had the accident when he was 24, leaving him paraplegic. Through 5 years of intensive physical therapy, he has regained 95% of his original function, though certain effects linger to this day.

Before his accident, Robert had internalized many of the standards of dominant masculinity exemplified by frequenting bars, leading an active sex life, and riding a motorcycle. But, if our research, and the body of autobiographical works from men with physical disabilities, has shown anything, it is that coming to terms with a disability eventually changes a man. It appears to have transformed Robert. He remarked that, despite being generally "recovered," he has maintained his disability-influenced value system:

> I judge people on more of a personal and character level than I do on any physical, or I guess I did, but you know important things are guys that have integrity, guys that are honest about what they are doing that have some direction in their life and know what, you know, peace of mind and what they stand for.

One of the areas Robert said took longest to recover was his sexuality—specifically, his confidence in his sexual ability. While Robert said sexual relations are still important to him today, like Brent he has reformulated his previous, largely hegemonic notion of male sexuality into a more emotionally and physically egalitarian model:

> I've found a whole different side to having sex with a partner and looking at satisfying the partner rather than satisfying myself, and that has taken the focus off of satisfying myself and being the big manly stud and concentrating more on my partner and that has become just as satisfying.

However, reformulation does not yield complete severance from prevailing masculinity's standards as they are culturally conceived. For instance, despite his reformulative inclinations, Robert's self-described "macho" attitude continued in some realms during his recovery. He, and all others we interviewed, represent the complexity of gender patterns; no man's masculinity falls neatly into any one of the three areas.

For instance, though told by most doctors that his physical condition was probably permanent, Robert's resolve was unyielding. "I put my blinders on to all negative insight into it and just totally focused on getting better," he said. "And I think that was, you know, a major factor on why I'm where I'm at today." This typifies the second pattern we identified—reliance on hegemonic masculinity's standards. It is ironic, then, that Robert's tenacity, his never-ending work ethic, and his focused drive to succeed, are largely responsible for his almost-complete recovery. While Robert has reformulated much of his earlier sense of masculinity, he still relies on this drive.

Perhaps the area in which men who reformulate most closely parallel dominant masculinity is the emphasis they place on their occupation. Our sample is atypical in that most of our informants were professionally employed on a full-time basis and could therefore draw on class-based resources, whereas unemployment among people with disabilities is very high. Just as societal members privilege men who are accomplished in their occupation, Harold finds both "purpose," and success, in his career: "No one is going to

460

GERSCHICK/MILLER

go through life without some kind of purpose. Everyone decides. I wanted to be a writer. So I became a writer and an observer, a trained observer."

Brent said that he draws much of his sense of self, his sense of self-esteem, and his sense of manhood from his occupational accomplishments. Initially, Brent denied the importance of the prevailing ideal that a man's occupational worth is derived from his "breadwinner" status:

> It is not so important to be the breadwinner as it is to be competent in the world. You know, to have a career, to have my name on the door. That is what is most important. It is that recognition that is very important to me.

However, he later admitted that being the breadwinner still was important to him, though he denied a link between his desires and the "stereotypical" conception of breadwinner status. He maintained that "it's still important to me, because I've always been able to make money." Independence, both economic and physical, were important to all of our informants.

Rejection of hegemonic ideals also occurs among men who primarily rely on a reformulative framework. Harold's view of relationships with a partner dismisses the sexually powerful ideal: "The fact of the matter is that I'm not all that upset by the fact that I'm disabled and I'm a male. I mean, I know what I can do." We will have more to say about the rejection of dominant conceptions of sexuality below.

In brief summary, men whose primary coping pattern involves reformulation of dominant standards recognize their inability to meet these ideals as they are culturally conceived. Confident in their own abilities and values, and drawing from previous experience, they confront standards of masculinity on their own terms. In doing so, they distance themselves from masculine ideals.

461

RELIANCE

However, not all men with physical disabilities rely on the approach of men who reformulate. Many men are concerned with others' views of their masculinity and with meeting the demands of hegemonic masculinity. The second pattern, reliance, involves the internalization of many more of the ideals of predominant masculinity, including physical strength, athleticism, independence, and sexual prowess. Just as some men depend on reformulation for much of their masculine definition, others, despite their inability to meet many of these ideals, rely on them heavily. As such, these men do not seem to be as comfortable with their sense of manhood; indeed, their inability to meet society's standards bothers them very much.

These men find themselves in a double blind that leaves them conflicted. They embrace dominant conceptions of masculinity as a way to gain acceptance from themselves and from others. Yet, they are continuously reminded in their interactions with others that they are incomplete. As a result, the

GERSCHICK/MILLER

identity behind the facade suffers; there are, then, major costs associated with this strategy.

The tension between societal expectations and the reality of men with physical disabilities is most clearly demonstrated by Jerry, a 16-year-old who has juvenile rheumatoid arthritis. While Jerry is physically able to walk for limited distances, this requires great effort on his part; consequently, he usually uses a wheelchair. He is concerned with the appearance of his awkward walking. "I feel like I look a little, I don't know, more strange when I walk," he said.

The significance of appearance and external perception of manliness is symptomatic of the difficulty men with physical disabilities have in developing an identity and masculinity free of others' perceptions and expectations. Jerry said:

> I think it [others' conceptions of what defines a man] is very important because if they don't think of you as one, it is hard to think of yourself as one or it doesn't really matter if you think of yourself as one if no one else does.

Jerry said that, particularly among his peers, he is not seen as attractive as the able-bodied teenagers; thus he has difficulty in male-female relations, beyond landing an occasional date. "[The girls believe] I might be a 'really nice person,' but not like a guy per se," he said. "I think to some extent that you're sort of genderless to them." This clearly represents the emasculation and depersonalization inherent in social definitions of disability.

However, Jerry said that he faces a more persistent threat to his autonomy—his independence and his sense of control—from others being "uncomfortable" around him, and persisting in offering him assistance he often does not need. He said this makes him "angry," though he usually doesn't refuse the help out of politeness. Thus, with members of his social group, he participates in a "bargain": they will socialize with him as long as he remains in a dependent position where they can "help" him.

This forced situational passivity leads Jerry to emphasize his autonomy in others. For instance, Jerry avoids asking for help in nearly all situations. This is directly tied to reinforcing his embattled manhood by displaying outward strength and independence:

> If I ever have to ask someone for help, it really makes me like feel like less of a man. I don't like asking for help at all. You know, like even if I could use some, I'll usually not ask just because I can't, I just hate asking . . . [a man is] fairly self-sufficient in that you can sort of handle just about any situation in that you can help other people and that you don't need a lot of help.

Jerry has internalized the prevailing masculine ideal that a man should be independent; he relies on that ideal for his definition of manhood. His inability to meet this ideal—partly through his physical condition, and partly from how others treat him—threatens his identity, and his sense of manhood, which must be reinforced even at the expense of self-alienation.

One should not label Jerry a "relier" simply from these struggles. Being only 16 years of age—and the youngest participant in our study—Jerry is still developing his sense of masculinity, and, as with many teenagers, both able bodied and disabled, he is trying to fit into his peer group. Furthermore, Jerry continues to mature and develop his self-image and sense of masculinity. A follow-up interview in 5 years might show a degree of resolution to his struggles.

Such a resolution can be seen in Michael, a 33-year-old manager we interviewed, who also internalizes many of the standards of hegemonic masculinity. A paraplegic from an auto accident in 1977, Michael struggled for many years after his accident to come to terms with his condition.

His struggles had several sources, all tied into his view of masculinity's importance. The first is that before his accident he accepted much of the dominant conception of masculinity. A high-school student, farm hand, football and track star at the time, Michael said that independence, relations with the women he dated, and physical strength were central to his conception of self.

After his accident, Michael's doctors told him there was a 50-50 chance that he would regain the ability to walk, and he clung to the hope. "I guess I didn't understand it, and had hope that I would walk again," he said. However, he said he was "depressed" about his situation, "but not so much about my disability I guess. Because that wasn't real yet."

But coming home 3 months after his accident did not alleviate the depression. Instead, it heightened his anxiety and added a new component—vulnerability. In a span of 3 months, Michael, in essence, had his sense of masculinity, and his security in himself, completely stripped away. He was in an unfamiliar situation, and far from feeling strong, independent, and powerful, he felt vulnerable and afraid: "No one," he remarked, "can be prepared for a permanent disability."

His reliance on dominant masculinity, then, started with his predisability past, and continued during his recovery as a coping mechanism to deal with his fears. The hegemonic standard Michael now strives most to achieve is that of independence. It was central to him before, and is central to his sense of masculinity at present. Indeed, it is so important that it frustrates him greatly when he needs assistance. Much like Jerry, he refuses to ask for it:

> I feel that I should be able to do everything for myself and I don't like . . . I don't mind asking for things that I absolutely can't do, like hanging pictures or moving furniture or having my oil changed in my car but there are things that I'm capable of doing in my chair like jumping up one step. That I feel like I should be able to do and I find it frustrating when I can't do that sometimes . . . I don't like asking for [help I don't think I need]. It kind of makes me mad.

463

When asked if needing assistance was "unmanly," Michael replied, "There's probably some of that in there." For both Michael and Jerry, the independence ideal leads to risk-taking behavior in order to prove to themselves that they are more than their social definition.

Yet, much like Robert, Michael has reformulated his view of sexuality. He says that his physical sexuality "makes him feel the most masculine," apparently another reliant response with a stereotypical emphasis on sexual performance. However, it is more complicated. Michael said that he no longer concentrates on pleasing himself, as he did when able bodied, but that he now has a more partner-oriented view of sexuality. "I think that my compensation for my feeling of vulnerability is I've overcompensated by trying to please my partner and leave little room to allow my partner to please me . . . some of my greater pleasure is exhausting my partner while having sex." Ironically, while he focuses more on his partner's pleasure now than ever before, he does so at his own expense.

Thus, sex serves multiple purposes for Michael—it gives him, and his partner, pleasure; it reassures his fears and his feelings of vulnerability; and it reconfirms his masculinity. This is neither strictly reliance nor reformulation, but both.

While independence and sexuality are both extremely important to Scott, a 34-year-old rehabilitation engineer, he emphasizes a third area for his sense of manhood—athletics. Scott served in the Peace Corps during his 20s, working in Central America. He described his lifestyle as "rigorous" and "into the whole sports thing," using a mountain bike as his primary means of transportation and recreation. He was also an avid hockey player in his youth, and spent his summers in softball leagues.

Scott acquired a polio-like virus when he was 25-years-old that left him permanently paraplegic, a situation that he did not initially accept. In an aggressive attempt to regain his physical ability, and similar to Robert, Scott obsessively attacked his rehabilitation:

> [I was] thinking, that's always what I've done with all the sports. If I wasn't good enough I worked a little harder and I got better. So, I kept thinking my walking isn't very good now. If I push it, it will get better.

But Scott's athletic drive led not to miraculous recovery, but overexertion. When ordered by his doctors to scale back his efforts, he realized he could not recover strictly through tenacity. He is now ambivalent about his limitations. He clearly does not feel like a failure: "I think that if I wouldn't have made the effort, I always would have wondered could I have made a difference." Following the athlete's code of conduct, "always give 110%," Scott attacked his recovery. But when his efforts were not enough—when he did not "emerge victorious"—he accepted it, as an athlete would. Yet, his limitations also frustrate him at times and in different areas.

For example, though his physical capacity is not what it was, Scott maintains a need for athletic competition. He plays wheelchair basketball, and is the only wheelchair participant in a city softball league. However, he has not returned to hockey, the sport he loved as a youngster; in fact, he refuses to even try the sled-based equivalent.

Here is Scott's frustration. His spirit of athleticism is still alive, but he laments the fact that he cannot compete exactly as before:

> [I miss] the things that I had. I played hockey, that was my primary sport for so many years. Pretty much I did all the sports. But, like I never played basketball, I never liked basketball before. Which is why I think I can play now. See, it would be like the equivalent to wheelchair hockey. Some friends of mine have talked to me about it, [but] I'm not really interested in that. Because it wouldn't be real hockey. And it would make me feel worse, rather that better.

In this respect, Scott has not completely come to terms with his limitations. He still wants to be a "real" athlete, competing in the same sports, in the same ways, with the same rules, with others who share his desire for competition. Wheelchair hockey, which he derogatorily referred to as "gimp hockey," represents the antithesis of this for him.

Scott's other responses add to this emphasis. What he most dislikes about having a disability is "That I can't do the things that I want to be able to do," meaning he cannot ride his bike or motorcycle, he cannot play "real" hockey, and that he can no longer live a freewheeling, spontaneous lifestyle. Rather, he has to plan ahead of time where he is going and how he will get there. The frustration caused by having to plan nearly every move was apparent in almost all of our interviews.

However, on the subject of independence, Scott said, "I think I'm mostly independent," but complained that there were some situations where he could not meet his expectations and had to depend on his wife. He said that usually this was not a "major issue," but "there's still times when, yeah, I feel bad about it, or you know it's the days where she doesn't feel like it, but she kind of has to, that's what bothers me the most I guess." Thus, he reflects the general desire among men with disabilities not to be a burden of any kind upon family members.

Much of the time, Scott accepts being "mostly independent." His reliance on the ideals of athleticism and independence plays a significant part in his conception of masculinity and self. However, Scott has also learned, though to a limited degree, to let go of this previous ideals and to accept a different, reformulated, notion of independence and competition. Yet, he cannot entirely do so. His emphasis on athletics and independence is still strong, and there are many times when athletics, and acceptance, conflict.

However, one should stop short of a blanket assessment of men who rely on hegemonic masculinity standards. "Always" is a dangerous word, and "men who rely on hegemonic standards are always troubled" is a dangerous statement. An apparently exceptional case among men who rely on hegenomic standards comes from Aaron, a 41-year-old paraplegic. Rather than experiencing inner turmoil and conflict, Aaron is one of the most upbeat individuals we interviewed. Aaron said that before his 1976 accident, he was "on top of the world," with a successful business, a commitment to athletics that included basketball shoot-arounds with NBA prospects, and a wedding engagement. Indeed, from the time of his youth, Aaron has relied on such hegemonic standards as sexuality, independence, athleticism, and occupational accomplishment.

For example, when asked what masculinity meant to him before his accident, Aaron said that it originally meant sexual conquest. As a teen, he viewed frequent sexual activity as a "rite of passage" into manhood. However, by his 20s, he "started to settle down and think about a long-term, committed relationship."

Aaron said he had also enjoyed occupational success, and that this success was central to his definition of self, including being masculine. Working a variety of jobs ranging from assembly-line worker to white-collar professional, Aaron said "I had been very fortunate to have good jobs which were an important part of who I was and how I defined myself."

Aaron said that much of his independence ideal came from his father. When his parents divorced, Aaron's father explained to him that, though he was only five, he would have to be "the man of the house." Aaron took this lesson to heart, and strived to fulfill this role both in terms of independence and providing for the family. "My image of manhood was that of a provider," he said, "one who was able to make a contribution to the financial stability of the family in addition to dealing with the problems and concerns that would come up."

His accident, a gunshot wound injuring his spinal cord, left him in a completely dependent condition. Predictably, Aaron could not immediately cope with this. "My whole self-image itself was real integrally tied up with the things I used to do," he said. "I found my desire for simple pleasures to be the greatest part of the pain I had to bear."

His pain increased when he left the hospital. His financé had left him, and within 2 years he lost "everything that was important to me"—his house, his business, his savings, most of his friends, even, for a while, his hope.

However, much as with Robert, Aaron's resiliency eventually turned his life around. Just as he "hit bottom," he began telling himself, that "if you hold on long enough, if you don't quit, you'll get through it." He gave himself 5 years to recover, sold his wheelchair, and either crawled or used leg braces with crutches for mobility. Additionally, he attacked his therapy with the vengeance he had always devoted to athletics. "I'd never been confronted with a situation in my entire life before that I was not able to overcome by the efforts of my own merit," he said. "I took the same attitude toward this."

Further, he reasserted his sexuality. Though he then wore a colostomy bag, he resumed frequent sexual intercourse, taking the attitude that "this is who I was and a woman was either going to have to accept me as I was, or she's got to leave me the ... alone."

However, he realized after those 5 years that his hard work would not be rewarded nor would he be miraculously healed. Figuring that "there's a whole lot of life that I need to live and this wasn't the most efficient way to live it," he bought a new sport wheelchair, found a job, and became involved in wheelchair athletics. In this sense, a complex combination of all three patterns emerged in Aaron, as reliance was mixed with reformulation and rejection.

Furthermore, his soul searching led him to develop a sense of purpose in his life, and a reason for going on:

> [During my recovery] I felt that I was left here to enrich the lives of as many people as I could before I left this earth, and it gave me a new purpose, a new vision, a new mission, new dreams.

The 5 years of agony and conflict gave way to success and fulfillment. His wheelchair basketball team won the national championship. He landed a job as a reporter, and, to fulfill his "purpose," did a series of "abilities reports" about independent living, educating the public about disability rights long before the Disability Rights Movement had gained national attention. Today, he is president and CEO of a nonprofit disability rights organization.

Tenacity, the quest for independence, athletics, and sexuality carried Aaron through his recovery. Many of these ideals, which have their source in his father's teachings, remain with him today, as he continues to be active in athletics (everything from basketball to softball to scuba diving), to assert his sexuality, and to aim for complete autonomy. To Aaron, independence, both physical and financial, is more than just a personal ideal. It is one that should be shared by all people with disabilities. As such, he aspires to be a role model for others:

> The work that I am involved in is to help people gain control over their lives and I think it's vitally important that I walk my talk. If ... we hold ourselves out to be an organization that helps people gain control over their lives, I think it's vitally important for me as the CEO of that organization to live my life in a way that embodies everything that we say we're about.

Clearly, Aaron is not the same man he was before his disability. He says his maturity and his experience with disability have "made [him] stronger," and that manhood no longer simply means independence and sexual conquest. Manhood also means:

> being responsible for one's actions, being considerate of another's feelings, being sensitive to individuals who are more vulnerable than yourself, to what their needs would be, standing up on behalf of and fighting for those who cannot

speak out for themselves, fight for themselves. It means being willing to take a position and be committed to a position even when it's inconvenient or costly to take point of view and you do it only because of the principle involved.

This dovetails significantly with his occupation, which is of great importance to him. But, as alluded to above, Aaron's reliance on occupation cannot be seen as mere reliance on the hegenomic conception of occupational achievement. It is more a reformulation of that ideal from self-achievement to facilitating the empowerment of others.

Nevertheless, Aaron's struggle to gain his current status, like the struggle of others who rely on hegemonic masculinity's standards, was immense. Constructing hegemonic masculinity from a subordinated position is almost always a Sisyphean task. One's ability to do so is undermined continuously by physical, social, and cultural weakness. "Understandably, in an effort to cope with this stress [balancing the demands for strength and the societal perception of weakness]," writes political scientist Harlan Hahn (1989), "many disabled men have tended to identify personally and politically with the supposed strength of prevalent concepts of masculinity rather than with their disability" (p.3). To relinquish masculinity under these circumstances is to court gender annihilation, which is untendable to some men. Consequently, relying on hegemonic masculinity becomes more understandable (Connell, 1990a, p. 471).

REJECTION

Despite the difficulties it presents, hegemony, including that related to gender, is never complete (Janeway, 1980; Scott, 1985). For some men, resistance takes the form of creating alternative masculine identities and subcultures that provide them with a supportive environment. These men are reflected in the final pattern: rejection. Men who follow this pattern do not so much share a common ideology or set of practices, rather they believe that the dominant conception of masculinity is wrong, either in its individual emphases or, as a practice. Some of these men develop new standards of masculinity in the place of the ones they have rejected. Others, seemingly, choose to deny masculinity's importance, though this does not mean they are effeminate or prefer androgyny. Instead, they emphasize their status as "persons", under the motto of "people first." This is especially true of those who are active in the Disability Rights Movement.

Alex, a 23-year-old first-year law student, survived an accident that left him an incomplete quadriplegic when he was 14. Before that time, he felt he was an outsider at his private school because he eschewed the superficial, athletically oriented and materialistic atmosphere. Further, he said the timing of the accident, when many of his peers were defining their social roles, added to this outsider perspective in that it made him unable to participate in the highly social role-forming process. "I didn't learn about the traditional roles of sexuality and whatever the rules are for such behavior in our society until later," he said. "Because of my physical characteristics, I had to learn a different set of rules."

Alex describes himself as a "nonconformist." This simple moniker is central to his conception of selfhood and masculinity. Alex, unlike men who primarily reformulate these tenets, rejects the attitudinal and behavioral prescriptions of hegemonic masculinity. He maintains that his standards are his own—not society's—and he scoffs at commonly held views of masculinity.

For example, Alex blamed the media for the idea that men must be strong and attractive, stating "the traditional conception is that everyone has to be Arnold Schwartzenegger . . . [which] probably lead[s] to some violence, unhappiness and things like that if they [men] don't meet the standards."

As to the importance of virility and sexual prowess, Alex said, "There is a part of me that, you know, has been conditioned and culturated and knows those [dominant] values," but he sarcastically laughed at the notion of a man's sexual prowess being reflected in "making her pass out" and summed up his feelings on the subject by adding "you have to be willing to do things in a nontraditional way."

Alex's most profound rejection of a dominant ideal is with that of the importance of fathering, in its strictest sense of the man as impregnator:

> There's no reason why we [his fiancé and himself] couldn't use artificial insemination or adoption. Parenting doesn't necessarily involve being the male sire. It involves being a good parent. . . Parenting doesn't mean that it's your physical child. It involves responsibility and an emotional role as well. I don't think the link between parenthood is the primary link with sexuality. Maybe in terms of evolutionary purposes, but not in terms of a relationship.

469

Thus, Alex rejects the procreation imperative encouraged in hegemonic masculinity.

However, while Alex takes pride at overtly rejecting prevailing masculinity as superficial and silly, even he relies on it at times. Alex says he needs to support himself financially, and wouldn't ever want to be an emotional or economic "burden" in a relationship. On one level, this is a common concern for most people, disabled or not. But on another level, Alex admits that it ties into his sense of masculinity:

> If I was in a relationship and I wasn't working, and my spouse was, what could be the possible reasons for my not working? I could have just been fired. I could be laid off. Who knows what happened. I guess, I can see an element of, but that's definitely an element of masculinity and I guess I am just as influenced by that as, oh, as I guess as other people, or as within my definition of masculinity. What do you know? I have been caught.

A different form of rejection is reflected in Leo, a 58-year-old polio survivor. Leo, who has strived for occupational achievement since his youth, seems to value many hegemonic traits: independence, money-making ability, and recognition by peers. But, If you ask him, he will steadfastly deny masculinity's role in shaping his outlook.

Leo said the most important trait to him is his mental capacity and intelligence, since that is what has allowed him to achieve his occupational goals. Yet, he claims this is not related to the prevailing standard. Rather, it ties into his ambitions from before his disability and his willingness to do most anything to achieve his goals.

Before we label him "a rejector," however, note that Leo is a believer in adaptive technology and personal assistance, and he does not see a contradiction between using personal care assistants and being independent. This seems to be a reformulation, just as with Damon and Harold, but asking Leo about this relation to masculinity brings flat denial of any connection.

Leo explained his renunciation of masculinity by saying, "it dosen't mean a great deal . . . it's not how I think (of things)". He said that many of the qualities on our list of hegemonic traits were important to him on an individual level, but did not matter to his sense of manhood. Leo maintained that there were "external" and "internal" reasons for this.

The external factors Leo identified were the Women's and Disability Rights Movements. Both provide support and alternatives that allow a person with a disability the freedom to be a person, and not (to use Leo' words) a "strange bird." Indeed, Leo echoed the call of the Disability Rights Movement when be described himself as a "person first." In this way, his humanity takes precedence and his gender and his disability become less significant.

Also, Leo identified his background as a contributing factor to his outlook. Since childhood, he has held a group of friends that valued intellectual achievement over physical performance. In his youth, Leo said he was in with a group "on the college route." He remains in academia today.

Internally, his view of masculinity comes from maturity. He has dealt with masculinity and related issues for almost 60 years and has reached a point at which he is comfortable with his gender. According to him, his gender conceptions have ranged across all three patterns. This is particularly evident in his sexuality. When younger, he relied on a culturally-valued, genital sexuality and was concerned with his potency. He wanted to "be on top," despite the physical difficulties this presented him. Now, he has a reformulated sexuality. The Women's Movement has allowed him to remain sexually active without worrying about "being on top." He even rejects the idea (but not necessarily the physical condition) of potency, noting that it is "even a funny word—potent—that's power."

Further, his age has allowed Leo to let go of many of the expectations he had for himself when younger. For instance, he used to overcompensate with great physical activity to prove his manhood and to be "a good daddy." But, he said, he gradually learned that such overcompensation just is not necessary.

The practice of "letting go," as Leo and many of our other informants have done is much like that described by essayist Leonard Kriegel (1991), who in a series of autobiographical essays discusses the metaphor of "falling into life" as a way of coping with a disability and masculinity. Kriegel describes a common reaction to coping with disability, that is, attempting to "overcome" it, in his case, by building his upper body strength through endless hours of exercise. In the end, he experienced premature arthritis in his shoulders and arms. The metaphor of giving up or letting go of behavioral expectations and gender practices as a way to gain greater strength and control over one's life is prevalent among men who primarily reject dominant masculinity. As Hahn (1989) notes, this requires a cognitive shift as well as a change in reference group and a source of social support:

> I think, ironically, that men with disabilities can acquire strength by acknowledging weakness. Instead of attempting to construct a fragile and ultimately phony identity only as males, they might have more to gain, and little to lose, both individually and collectively by forging a self-concept about the concept of disability. Certainly this approach requires the exposure of a vulnerability that has been a primary reason for the elaborate defense mechanisms that disabled men have commonly employed to protect themselves. (p. 3)

Thus, men with disabilities who reject or renounce masculinity do so as a process of deviance disavowal. They realize that it is societal conceptions of masculinity, rather than themselves, that are problematic. They have been able to create alternative gender practices. The role of the Disability Rights Movement in this pattern is discussed below.

471

SUMMARY AND CONCLUSION

Our intent in this article is to elucidate the patterns and processes through which men with physical disabilities adjust to the double bind associated with the demands of hegemonic masculinity and the stigmatization of being disabled. Men with physical disabilities depend on at least three different patterns that arise through the active process of coming to terms with societal expectations and definitions. While some men use one pattern more than another, no man depends entirely on any one of the three, and, hence, there are no "reformulators," "reliers," or "rejectors." Exploring these different responses indicates the power of dominant conceptions of masculinity and structural constraints embedded in the social environment while elucidating the struggles and possibilities for altered gender roles.

To judge the patterns and practices associated with any form of masculinity, it is necessary to explore the implications for both the personal life of the individual and the effect on the reproduction of the societal gender order

(Connell, 1990a). Different patterns will challenge, comply, or actively support gendered arrangements.

The reliance paradigm is reflected by an emphasis on control, independence, strength, and concern for appearances. Men who rely on dominant conceptions of masculinity are much more likely to internalize their feelings of inadequacy and seek to compensate or overcompensate for them. Because the problem is perceived to be located within oneself, rather than within the social structure, this model does not challenge, but rather perpetuates the current gender order.

A certain distancing from dominant ideals occurs in the reformulation pattern. But reformulation tends to be an independent project and class-based resources play an important role. As such, it does not present a formidable challenge to the gender order. Connell (1990a) argues that this response may even modernize partiarchy (p. 474).

The rejection model, the least well represented in this article offers the most hope for change. Linked closely to a sociopolitical approach that defines disability as a product of interactions between individuals and their environment, disability is understood as socially constructed.

Members of the Disability Rights Movement, as a result, seek to reconstruct masculinity through a three-prong strategy (see Figure 1). First, they focus on changing the frame of reference regarding who defines disability and masculinity, thereby changing the dynamics of the social construction of both. Second, they endeavor to help people with disabilities be more self-referent when defining their identities. In order to do that, a third component must be implemented: support structures, such as alternative subcultures, must exist.

If the Disability Rights Movement is successful in elevating this struggle to the level of collective practice, it will challenge the legitimacy of the institutional arrangements of the current gender order.

To draw this section of the article to a close before turning to a discussion of suggestions for future research, let us share the observation of two disability researchers, Skord and Schumacher (1982): masculinity is, as currently practiced, a handicapping condition.

SUGGESTIONS FOR FUTURE RESEARCH

There is much fruitful work to be done in the area of masculinity and disability. For instance, one of the limitations of our work is that most of our informants are professionally employed. As discussed earlier, unemployment is very high among men with physical disabilities. Societal factors such as inaccessibility of jobs and the double blind of Medicaid reliance contribute to this fact, and one should not assume that people with disabilities are passive and do not seek employment. Additionally, most of those employed are underemployed in regards to number of hours worked and/or their skill level.[2] Apart from the issue of being able to pay for PCAS, as mentioned above, class differences in masculinity among the able bodied have been documented and we should expect similar differences among men with physical disabilities (see, for example, LeMasters, 1975; Messner, 1992; Rubin, 1976). Additionally, we should expect differences linked to other factors such as sexual orientation, race, and ethnicity.

We can only speculate about what accounts for the different responses of men to the dual demands associated with disability and masculinity. One's reference group is probably a key factor. We also believe that the age of onset of disability affects the process of gender formation and practice. If a boy's disability occurs at a very young age, he may be sheltered from many of the expectations associated with dominant masculinity. However, if it occurs later, we hypothesize that his relationship to his gender will be made more difficult. For instance, if the disability occurs during the 30s and 40s, a man may have more responsibilities and pressures associated with a family and/or a career. At an even later stage in life, however, there may be fewer expectations of a man. Finally, the length of time that a man has lived with his disability may also be a determining factor in how he responds to hegemonic masculinity.

In closing, we hope that this work serves as an impetus for others to take up issues such as these. Until then, we believe that we have provided some insight and understanding into, not only the difficulties that men with physical disabilities face in constructing their identities and masculinities, but also their adaptations, their strengths, and their ability to come to terms with their condition.

473

METHODLOGICAL APPENDIX

This research is based on in-depth interviews with ten men.[3] Informants were located through a snowball sample, utilizing friends and connections within the community of people with disabilities.[4] The age range of respondents varied from 16 to 72. Eight of our respondents were white, two were African-American. All were "mobility impaired" and most were para- or quadriplegics.[5] Given the small sample size and the modicum of diversity within it, this work must necessarily be understood as exploratory.

Due to issues of shared identities, Adam S. Miller did all the interviews. Interviews were semistructured and tape recorded. Initial interviews averaged approximately an hour in length. Additionally, we contacted all of our informants at least once with clarifying questions and, in some cases, to test ideas that we had. These follow-up lasted approximately 30 minutes. Each informant received a copy of his interview transcript to ensure that we had captured his perspective accurately. We also shared draft copies of this article with them a and incorporated their insights into the current version.

The reasons for the thorough follow-up were several. First, from a methodological standpoint, it was important for us to capture the experience of our informants as fully as possible. Secondly, we felt that we had an obligation to allow them to control, to a large extent, the representation of their experience.

Interviews were analyzed utilizing an analytic induction approach (for a description of this approach, see Denzin, 1989; Emerson, 1988; Katz, 1988). In determining major and minor patterns of masculine practice, we utilized the responses to a series of questions including: What is the most important aspect of masculinity to you? What would you say makes you feel most manly or masculine? Do you think your conception of masculinity is different from that of able-bodied men as a result of your disability? If so, how? If so, why? If not, why not? Additionally, we presented our informants with a list of characteristics associated with prevailing masculinity based upon the work of R. W. Connell (1987, 1990a, 1990b, 1991) and asked them to rate their importance to their conception of self. Both positive and negative responses to this portion of our questionnaire guided our insight into how each man viewed his masculinity. To further support our discussion, we turned to the limited academic literature in this area. Much more helpful were the wide-range of biographical and autobiographical accounts of men who have physical disabilities (see, for instance, Murphy, 1990; Callahan, 1989; Kriegel, 1991; Hahn, 1989; and Zola, 1982).

Finally, in analyzing the data we were sensitive to making judgements about our informants when grouping them into categories. People with disabilities are "shoehorned" into categories too much as it is. We sought to discover what was common among their responses and to highlight what we perceive to be the essence of their views. In doing so, we endeavored to provide a conceptual framework for understanding the responses of men with physical disabilities, while trying to be sensitive to their personal struggles.

NOTES

1. Connell (1991, cf. 161-164), writing on working class men, found three similar masculine trajectories. He labeled these protest masculinity, complicit masculinity, and negation of masculinity. Space limitations prevent us from elaborating the similarities and differences in our conceptions. However, our framework is different enough to merit different labels.

2. The difficulty of finding basic statistics, such as unemployment rates, for people with disabilities powerfully demonstrates their marginalized status.

3. The problem of identity management in interviews is acknowledged. Nonetheless, we utilized this method because we were most interested in the subjective perceptions and experience of our informants. To mitigate this dynamic, we relied on probing questions and reinterviews.

4. All the names of informants have been charged. Additionally, some nonrelevant characterstics have been altered to protect their identities.

5. We interviewed men with physical disabilities for three primary reasons. First given the diversity of disabilities and our modest resources, we had to bound the sam-

ple. Second, mobility disabilities tend to be more apparent than other disabilities, such as blindness or hearing loss, and people respond to these men using visual clues. Third, although the literature in this area is scant, much of it focuses on men with physicl disabilities.

REFERENCES

Callahan, J. (1989). *Don't worry, he won't get far on foot*. New York: Vintage.

Connel, R.W. (1987). *Gender and power: Society, one person, and sexual politics*. Stanford, CA: Stanford Univ. Press.

Connell, R.W. (1990a). A whole new world: Remaking masculinity in the context of the environmental movement. *Gender & Society, 4*(4), 452–478.

Connell, R.W. (1990b). An iron man: The body and some contradictions of hegemonic masculinity. In M. Messner and D. Sabo (Eds), *Sport, men, and the gender of order* (pp. 83–96). Champaign, IL: Human Kinetics.

Connell, R.W. (1991). Live fast and die young: The construction of masculinity and young working-class men on the margin of the labor market. *The Australian and New Zealand Journal of Sociology, 27*(2), 141-171.

Denzin, N. (1989). *The research act: A theoretical introduction to sociological methods*. Englewood Cliffs, NJ: Prentice-Hall.

Emerson, R. (1988). Introduction. In E.R. Emerson (Ed.), *Contemporary field research: A collection of readings* (pp. 93–107). Prospect Heights, IL: Waveland.

Hann, H. (1989). Masculinity and disability. *Disability Studies Quarterly, 9*(3), 1–3.

Janeway, E. (1980). *Powers of the weak*. New York: Knopf.

Katz, J. (1988). A Theory of qualitative methodology: The social system of analytic fieldwork. In R. Emerson (Ed.), *Contemporary field research: A collection of readings* (pp. 127–148). Prospect Heights, IL: Waveland.

Kriegel, L. (1991). *Falling into life*. San Francisco: North Point.

LeMasters, E.E. (1975). *Blue collar aristocrats*. Madison, WI: University of Wisconsin Press.

Messner, M.A. (1992). *Power at play: Sports and the problem of masculinity*. Boston: Beacon Press.

Murphy, R.F. (1990). *The body silent*. New York: Norton.

Rubin, L. (1976). *Worlds of pain: Life in the working class family*. New York: Basic Books.

Scott, J.C. (1985). *Weapons of the weak: Everyday forms of peasant resistance*. New Haven: Yale University Press.

Skord, K., & Schumacher, B. (1982). Masculinity as a handicapping condition. *Rehabilitation Literature, 439*(10), 284–288.

West, C., & Zimmerman, D.H. (1987). Doing gender. *Gender and Society, 1*(2), 125–151.

Zola, Irving. (1982). *Missing pieces: A chronicle of living with a disability*. Philadelphia: Temple University Press.

PART VIII

POWER
Multiply Messaged

WOMEN, AIDS, AND POWER IN HETEROSEXUAL SEX
A Discourse Analysis

Lesley Miles

GENDER, POWER, and sexuality are issues initimately connected with one another. This article is based on an exploratory study which set out to examine how the social construction of sexuality, and gendered discourses of sexuality, through inevitably influencing negotiation in sexual relationships, impact on practices of safer sex at this time of the AIDS epidemic. The study focussed on two groups of heterosexual women in South Africa, one black and one white. The methodology used was based on Hollway's (1984, 1989) interpretative discourse analysis, a qualitative methodology grounded in feminist post-structuralism. The study suggested that the unequal relations of gender make it particularly difficult for women to initiate or negotiate safer sex practices, because of the negative consequences they incur from men when they do so.

The author wishes to thank the National AIDS Programme of the South African Medical Research Council (MRC) for financial assistance in the preparation of this article.

THE SOCIAL CONSTRUCTION OF SEXUALITY

As Richardson notes "[i]n our society, it is impossible to talk about sex without also talking about power" (1990, p. 170). The unequal social relations of gender in modern society have to do with the ways in which the society differentially reproduces gendered subjectivities of masculinity and femininity, which perpetuate existing power structures. In South Africa, inequalities based on gender pervade the society, although they may be lived in different ways within the stratifications of the social matrix.[1]

Although gender and sexuality cannot be conflated, they are connected (Rubin, 1984). In the sexual arena, gender inequality is lived through a set of sexual attitudes and practices derived from the social constructions of masculinity and femininity with sexual behaviours other than monogamous heterosexuality seen to be deviant (Rubin, 1984). The dominant construction of sexual practice is masculinist and heterosexist, with heterosexuality viewed as the only normal expression of sexual intimacy, "real" sex being seen as penetrative vaginal intercourse, and alternative sexual practices within heterosexual relationships negatively characterised as "foreplay" (Schneider & Gould, 1987). The intractability of these constructions (and the consequent difficult of changing people's sexual behaviour) must be seen historically, first, in the light of the Christian tradition of sex as a dangerous, inherently negative force (Rubin, 1984), and then in terms of the complex discursive networks of regulation and control of sexuality which, as Foucault (1981) notes, have developed over the last few hundred years in western culture.

The social construction of sexuality inevitably affects the negotiation of safer sex within the sexual practice of individuals. In a society in which the dominant image of sexual practice is ineluctably defined by penetration and ejaculation, other forms of erotic pleasure (such as mutual masturbation, massage, etc) as strategies for safer sex are either not seen as the "real thing" or might pose a threat to male self-esteem (Richardson, 1990). In South Africa, forms of sexual expression alternative to conventional heterosexuality are highly stigmatised (Retief, 1992), and there might be particular difficulties in these becoming accepted as forms of safer sex.

Then, in terms of the unequal power relations of gender, women, no matter how motivated they are, might have difficulty in implementing safer sex practices with partners who are resistant to using condoms or to forms of sexual expression other than penetrative genital sex (Richardson, 1990). Further, a contradiction exists relating to the idea that men are less able to exercise self-control than women in sex, thus women are often assumed to be the more responsible partner. Ironically, if they do assume responsibility for safer sex by carrying condoms, they may be stigmatised as an "easy lay" (Richardson, 1990, p. 172), as "good" women are not supposed to initiate sex. And whereas gay men can organise as a community (and have done so), women, because of social arrangements, have to struggle for safer sex in a privatised

480

MILES

domain (Patton, 1989). Gay men become allies in the fight against AIDS, whereas heterosexual gender relations tend to be oppositional. The way the constructions of sexuality and sexual practice interact with the social construction of AIDS renders the negotiation of safer sex within heterosexual relationships especially problematic.

THE SOCIAL CONSTRUCTION OF AIDS AND THE "OTHER"

AIDS is not just a biomedical phenomenon but a syndrome with a set of social meanings. As Plummer (1988) comments "[a]t the start of the 1980s, 'AIDS' had not been invented" (p. 20). In agreement, Sontag (1988) states that "[l]ike syphilis . . . AIDS is a clinical construction" (p. 20). The construction of AIDS as a syndrome has a particular history, in which its early association with homosexuality is important, but because AIDS is seen as a sexually transmitted disease, it has accrued through a genealogy connected with diseases such as syphilis, a whole number of connected association of contamination and pollution (Gilman, 1988; Sontag, 1988). Gilman suggests that AIDS is linked to a set of images of a "morally repugnant disease" already present in the culture (p. 258). The metaphors of AIDS contribute to the stigmatisation of the disease and the consequent construction of a putative social division between those who are seen to be "at risk" and the general community, which is not. Notions of "risk group" confirm an identity for AIDS sufferers which is essentially blame-worthy, deviant, and delinquent (Sontag, 1988). This stigmatisation has manifested in discourses of AIDS in South Africa, where in early representations (mainly appearing in the media), AIDS was constructed as a demonic killer, and homophobia, racism, and sexism were the prevalent subtexts. For example, distinctions were made between "African AIDS" and "White AIDS" (*The Star*, 13 September 1987, p. 9), and the South African government represented foreign migrant workers as "reservoirs" of the disease (*The Citizen*, 4 September 1987, p. 2). In the same period, there was a spate of newspaper articles representing prostitutes as rampant sources of HIV infection.[2]

In his analysis Gilman shows that people with AIDS are socially constructed as "Other," thus associated with groups which are seen to be Other within a society. These are usually marginalised groups with less power. The primary Other in patriarchy is woman. Gilman's analysis demonstrates the slippage in AIDS discourses of the Other from white male homosexual to black male homosexual, to the deviant female Other—the prostitute. As black women are usually the group with least power in society, they will tend to carry this image of the stigmatised Other. A newspaper report in Durhan headlined "Domestics by day, prostitutes by night: HIV positive all the time" suggests that this may well be the case in South Africa (*Sunday Tribune*, 20 January 1991). In this report police claim that domestic workers (in South Africa, invariably black women) who, according to them, are prostitutes, are either

481

MILES

HIV positive or have AIDS. South Africa is fertile ground for the displacement of AIDS onto the Other, as the legacy of apartheid provides an endless-
ly proliferating Other in the society. This issue of the stigmatised Other (as has
emerged in this study) is an important factor in negotiating safer sex.

DATA AND METHODS: PARTICIPANTS

I obtained my data from two informal group discussions of an hour each
about AIDS and the question of safer sex with currently heterosexually active
women, one a group of four black women (Group 1) and the other a group
of three white women (Group 2), ranging in age from 21 to 25, all university
students. The research participants were recruited informally either directly or
through acquaintances. The discussions were stimulated by a vignette, followed by orienting questions, which focussed on what the problems were
that might come up if the women were to suggest safer sex to sexual partners,
either through the use of condoms, or through sexual practices other than
penetrative genital sex. The material thus obtained was transcribed and
analysed.

The combination of groups (one of black women and one of white) arose
partly from my sense that in the deeply socially divided South African society,
sociological and linguistic differences do inform differences in the experiences of women. Black women, subject to the oppressions of gender, race,
and class, in South Africa are the group with structurally the least power in
the society. I hoped to see the extent to which differential access to power
might influence the practices of safer sex. In the end I felt that, although there
were overlaps, there were also differences between the two groups, but that
these were expressed mainly through difference in access to certain discourses such as feminism and a greater number of options for negotiation for
women in Group 2 (the white women). However, it seemed that the roots of
these differences would be difficult to tease out partly because the black
women in my study were (as university students) middle-class women with a
western-based education. They would have been influenced through their
education by the hegemonic discourses of western society, although their
economic backgrounds may have differed.[3] The white women were, likewise,
middle-class women in the sense outlined above.[4] The discussions were run
in English for practical reasons, although not all the women were English
first-language speakers.[5] (None of the black women were.)

It is appropriate to outline my own position here. I am a middle-class
white woman with a theoretical background in feminism and a commitment
to gender equity and social justice. These commitments inevitably affected
the analysis of the data, and quite possibly what was said, especially in Group
2, as the women in this group were feminist in orientation as well; thus there
were a number of shared assumptions. The discussion with Group 1 (the
black women) was probably affected by my being white, older, and in the po-

482

MILES

sition of researcher; thus structurally I was in a position of greater power. With Group 2 there was perhaps a greater degree of homogeneity between myself and them, and structurally less of a power imbalance; however, because a similar age difference was present, I do not inhabit the same social space as they do. Also because there were fewer women in the group and they were acquaintances (while I had met the black women only once before) greater intimacy may have resulted. These differences in structural positioning and familiarity between myself and each of the two groups may have affected the level of disclosure within each group, and thus the range of discourses exhibited.

I suggest that the discourses which emerged in the groups are illustrative of quandaries facing many young women who are confronted with the issue of AIDS in a context of the sexism, racism, and homophobia of South African society, and that the study has implications for approaches to AIDS preventative strategies.

ANALYSIS

Discursive framework

The male/female split. Gender categorisation in western culture is extraordinarily powerful. The fundamental discursive split is the binary opposition between masculinity and femininity in which masculinity is the positive term. A connected set of qualities and attributes fall on different sides of the line dividing these two. Some metaphoric correlates of the basic male/female dichotomy are active/passive; aggressive/submissive; light/darkness; spirit/matter; culture/nature. Positioning in these gendered splits confers differential social power, with masculinity being structurally dominant and femininity subordinate. Different cultural contexts offer women different levels and forms of power. The discussions analysed here operate in terms of this polarisation, the gendered discourses drawing from discourses of masculinity and femininity available in western culture. There may be influences in Group 1 from discursive practices drawn from African culture, but these would be difficult for me to specify.

Hollway (1984, 1989) identified in her research three discourses centring around sexuality. Although one of the tenets of this approach is that any discourse will be historically and culturally specific, thus discourses delineated in one context cannot simply be applied elsewhere, the three which Hollway identifies are frameworks for the dominant construction of sexuality in western society. She called these the "male sexual drive discourse," the "have/hold" discourse, and the "permissive discourse." Hollway suggests that all of these discourses have as a central notion the idea that sexuality is an unmediated, biologically based drive in the individual. The male sexual drive discourse presupposes that a central feature of masculinity is the desire/need for sex, and that men's sexual impulses are basically animal and difficult to

483

MILES

control. Women are seen as the boundary keepers for these impulses. This idea is ratified by rape laws, marriage laws, and propounded ad lib in the popular media. It includes the idea that men have sexual rights over women. Both men and women are interpellated by the have/hold discourse, although women are more strongly subjects of the desire to procure a man in a committed (marriage) relationship for life. The permissive discourse is one in which the ideal is the free expression of sexual impulses, for both men and women. Versions of these discourses ran through the discussions of both groups.

Discourses of sexuality

Sexual drive discourse (Groups 1 and 2): "You can't control it." This discourse, which emerged in both groups, operates as a framework for the others. It expresses a universally held view of sexuality in western society. It encodes the social construction of sexuality as a biological, asocial given, which propels people into powerful, uncontrollable, and irrational feelings — a passionate arousal which is irresistible once you are in its power. This construction in itself will tend to impede the practice of safer sex, as safer sex inevitably requires some degree of prior thought and decision-making. The condom has to be bought and carried; the use of the condom, or alternative ways of lovemaking have to be suggested etc. All of these suggest a self-consciousness which goes against the loss of control implied by the idea of sexuality as an irresistible drive. For example, from Group 1 (black women):

> Some of the boys you can't control them . . . we'd end up making love without using precautions. [laughter]
> Yes, you're definitely going to do that.
> And you'll regret it after. [laughter] Enjoy now and . . . [loud laughter]
> [L]: Do you go along with that?
> Mmm because you won't even trust the other means of stimulating because you'll end up having sex or you'll end up being highly aroused and you can't . . . you can't . . . do it. You can't hide whilst you are aroused. So you'll end up having sex.
> [L]: So what you're saying is that those feelings are very powerful.
> Yes, sure.
> It's very hard to fight [inaudible].

Although the sexual drive discourse primarily interpellates men, here both men and women are subject to it. This is possibly linked to the permissive discourse. As Hollway points out, in principle women are equal subjects in this discourse. However, social structures and other discourses of sexuality in practice preclude equality within it.

The sexual drive discourse also emerged in Group 2. Here it drew strongly on the notion of irrationality in sexuality—the central comment was that

484

"the logical side isn't there" thus it cannot be relied upon as a motive for action in circumstances of sexual arousal, because "you don't think very practically." The consequence of this for safer sex is clear. However, the appeal of the idea of overwhelming passion and loss of control in a culture which is dominated by an ideology of rational control is understandable. This idea also probably draws on romance fiction.

This split between rationality and irrational feelings which was expressed by Group 2 is deeply part of western binary thinking. It assumes that *either* rationality (control) or irrationality (lack of control) must be dominant. Thus if one is in an "irrational" space it appears impossible to bring in a "conscious," "rational," decision-making faculty. Conversely, if one is using rationality, passion and irrationality must (seemingly) disappear. Feminist theories and poststructuralist theory, however, suggest that subjectivities are multiple. From this perspective, a diversity of coexisting responses such as rationality and passion can co-exist without their being mutually exclusive.

Discourses of stigma (Group 1): "I couldn't possibly be bad, so you must be." The polarisation of gendered discourses constitutes men as subjects of a sexual drive that makes it difficult for them to be "controlled" when they are sexually aroused, thus negotiation of safer sex is rendered problematic. However, there are other aspects to this. The women in Group 1 said it would be difficult for them to suggest the use of condoms to their lovers because there would be a number of negative consequences not obviously related to the male sexual drive discourse, but connected primarily to the negative connotations of AIDS, as discussed earlier. AIDS is still characterised popularly in South Africa as a gay disease, and as such, in terms of the connotations of Other, is powerfully stigmatised. Therefore, if a woman asks a man to use a condom as a means of self-protection, he may think she is suggesting that he has AIDS, which, because of these connotations is highly insulting and imputes a range of negative attributes, the most unwanted possibly being that of homosexuality.

What follows from this putative suggestion is that the man is not trustworthy, which, in the canons of masculinity, is unacceptable. Trustworthiness, as an attribute of male identity, implies authority and control. Men must be seen to be trusted and trustworthy. Male authority must be taken at face value and not questioned. The consequence of this imputation is that the woman is an "untrusting woman." On the other hand, if she indicates that he should use a condom because she wants to protect him, this inevitably implies that she must be immoral. This is an excruciating double-bind – as a woman, you are bad whatever you do – either you are an *untrusting* woman, or you are an immoral woman. The point is that women tend to be seen to be in the negative position in the discourse no matter what they do. The following utterances are examples. The question (from the vignette) was how the group, as women, deal or have dealth with the issue of AIDS and safer sex in a sexual situation:

485

MILES

I find it is a very difficult issue because some guys don't like to use condoms. They feel you are separated, you see. . . [L: Mmmmm]

. . . and some feel like you don't trust them and they feel like you are trying to imply that they might have AIDS. And it's not a very nice thing to . . . like suspecting someone to have AIDS . . . so they believe you should trust them. And they don't like it if you say they should use condoms. So it's really difficult to suggest it. . .

It becomes difficult if you really love that person you see . . . and then you come with . . . condoms and tell him he must use condoms, and he might end up saying no, I don't want to use them. You just don't know what to say because you love the person and then if he doesn't want to use condoms, and you feel it won't be safe for you to have sex with him without condoms, then you just get caught up in a situation where you really don't know what to do. . .

You end up taking the risk.

. . . If you say to him, use a condom because I'm afraid. . .or, maybe, you might be having AIDS, or I might be having AIDS, it causes a bit of tension . . . because if you say—maybe you don't want him to feel bad by saying he should use a condom because you think he might be having . . . maybe you say . . . I might be having it you know and I'm just trying to protect you—he starts thinking . . . you must have been a very happy person. . .

The comments "you really don't know what to do" and "You end up taking the risk" seem to be an expression of paralysis arising from the contradiction discussed above, which is the double-bind arising from a situation in which women are constructed in society as primary Other in opposition to men. Whatever the woman does or says will be wrong. In the nineteenth century women were seen to be inherently "sick" by virtue of their reproductive organs (Ehrenreich & English, 1973). Other examples of this refusal of responsibility and projection onto the stigmatised Other were comments which directly expressed the idea that women were more at risk of AIDS than men, because of their link (in terms of Other) with homosexuality:

And most of them think that they are only carriers and women are the ones who suffer. [Ja] Most of them think that.

[L]: that's interesting, because our sterotype is that it's the homosexual male–gay men . . .

Ja . . . maybe they think that homosexual men because you know, the method they are using, so the other one who is getting AIDS is the other one who is acting like a lady, you see. So then the other one who is really doing, you know . . . I mean, I've talked to someone who thinks that way. [L: Is that so?] Yes. So they always think that ladies will be the ones who will get AIDS.

In this account, the prejudice against homosexuality by men leads to the disavowal of risk to themselves of HIV infection, and the imputation of risk to women.

The idea of male insistence on control emerged in the discussions not only in terms of sexuality, but also in other areas of decision-making Goffman (1959) suggests that self-presentations are often idealised in conformity with accepted values in a society. As men are supposed to be knowledgeable, trustworthy, and authoritative, suggesting the use of a condom disrupts this, partly because it implies untrustworthiness, but also because it implies the stigma associated with AIDS. Linked to this, men are expected to be the decision makers in the household. In a discussion about negotiation in other contexts it was clearly stated that women (in particular, here, black women) were expected to be subordinate to their husbands. When they step outside of this expected behavior they become vulnerable to a range of consequences, for example anger and rejection. I suggest that women feel a strong fear of retribution from men if they are not "trusted."

Then, the double standard of sexual morality is clearly operating within these discourses: if you ask a man to use a condom in order to protect him, "you must have been a very happy person." This links with the discursive construction of the sexually independent female as immoral. This was explicitly stated when one of the women explained two terms in Zulu – for a woman who has many sexual partners, the terms is "isfebe" which means "whore," while the correlate for a man with many lovers, is "isoka" which means that he is a "real man." This double standard emerged strongly with reference to alternative sexual practices, in which it was indicated that a women suggesting practices such as mutual masturbation and so on would be seen as a whore or prostitute, because she would be seen as "too knowledgeable" about sex in a society in which sexual prowess and knowledge is valued in men.

487

> You know, like some black guys really look down on such things as . . . you know . . . it's funny to them . . . like masturbating or reaching orgasm with mutual masturbation. [laughter] [inaudible]
>
> Ja . . . what type of woman is this? What has she been doing all her life? She's been learning all these things in Hillbrow [laughter] or on the streets.

Another complication coming into this (as expressed above) is a subdominant discourse drawn from romance. This emerged in such comments as "if you really love that person." This links up with Hollway's have/hold discourse. Women talk about being in love, and the difficulties this produces for initiating safer sex. Aside from axieties about rejection, what is suggested by this is the idea from the male sexual drive discourse that men are able to have sex without being "really in love," and that being "really in love" for men does not imply the kind of consideration for the woman's feelings that would be expected of a woman.

Women are socialised in western culture to be "good daughters," in other

MILES

words, to be responsible, mature, and to take care of themselves. As students living away from home (as the black women were), these women may take this injunction very seriously. Further, they are aware of the problem of AIDS and are motivated to practice safer sex. However, it is very difficult for them to carry this out unproblematically. There just does not seem to be the space to openly acknowledge the issue of safer sex in a sexual encounter or relationship without one or the other partner being forced to take up a position of "bad person." This position invariably seems to be projected onto women. It seems very difficult for women to negotiate safer sex without a whole range of defensive emotional responses being engendered in men. This was affirmed in Group 2. In accounts from this group, men responded to requests for condom usage at times with anger and even fury. In this context it is not surprising that women may fear the consequences of suggesting safer sex to men.

Sexual history discourses (Group 2): Familiarity and strangeness. In both groups, an idea emerged connected to the stigmatic construction of AIDS which was that in order to feel safe with someone, one should get to know them. It was seen to be possible to "really know" someone, and knowing someone made them safe to have sex with without protection. In other words, familiarity brings safety. This idea emerged especially strongly in Group 2, with consequences which were extremely clear. In this group, a set of images around sexuality emerged, linked to the representation of sex as dangerous and promiscuity as morally reprehensible. This was expressed in the notion of a person's "sexual history" which came up a number of times. It was also linked to a discursive contradiction. On the one hand, need for knowledge of another was voiced and on the other hand, the impossiblity of such knowledge:

> But what if the person has a really dubious sexual history? Wouldn't you insist they use a condom?
>
> I think I would then. But then . . . if they had a very dubious sexual history, I probably wouldn't be interested in sleeping with that person.
>
> [section left out]
>
> [L]: What do you mean by "dubious sexual history"?
>
> Dubious sexual history, like . . . you'd have loads, and loads, and loads of partners. And you'd also . . . like you know . . . well . . . It's like this one guy I was talking about. He had had really loads of partners and I knew some of the partners and they'd had loads of partners and it was just . . . and one of the girls that he'd slept with had had a relationship with a bisexual.

The suggestion is that people should not have "loads of partners", because that makes their sexual history "dubious." As Aggleton, Homans, Mojsa, Watson, & Watney (1989) suggest, number of sexual partners is not necessarily the primary issue in precautions against HIV transmission. While increasing the number of partners (without practising safer sex) increases the possibility of

488

MILES

becoming infected with HIV, and probably what is being expressed here is a healthy sense of self-preservation, the word "dubious" evidences moral disapprobation. In such a context it is likely that openness and truth in sexual matters will be vitiated. These consequences emerged in an account by one of the respondents describing the negative response by men to the idea that she may have had a number of previous sexual partners. This is informed by the perception of women who express autonomous sexuality as bad. Thus she tended to edit to men details of previous sexual relationships.

These moralising discourses work in opposition to the permissive discourse, in which, theoretically, free and untrammeled expression of an individual's sexual needs is proposed. However, while AIDS makes the issue of another's sexual history more salient than it might have been otherwise, punitive moralising discourses, and discourses which position women as immoral when sexual, work against total honesty. Aggleton et al. (1989) state that it is "essential for individuals to be honest about their sexual histories before beginning a new sexual relationship" (p. 81). Until these discourses shift, this is an unrealistic demand in many contexts. This was acknowledged in the idea that "You actually don't know someone as well as you think you do."

Then, this idea of knowledge of another led to the voicing of a powerful contradiction which links in with AIDS as belonging to the stigmatised other. The idea emerged that if the other is familiar, then he/she is "safe":

> I would be far less inclined just to have a one night stand just for fun if I met someone at a party in a similar situation. [L: Mmm] Far less inclined now because of AIDS.
>
> But then it's still this whole contradiction that I think if I know the person a bit better, I have less chance which is not necessarily so.
>
> Ja . . . the funny thing as soon as you've decided you're going into a relationship with a person, you suddenly think you're fine. [laughter] It's the same person that's out there but now once you've met them three times . . . whereas if you think that from the first time you might have caught AIDS, because you've chosen them to go into a relationship with, they're alright.
>
> [L]: That's the . . . the stranger is maybe not okay but a known person is.
>
> Ja, ja. If it's got a future to it, if it's long term, then safe sex goes out of the window.
>
> [L]: So in other words, you might be careful during fairly transitory encounters, but as soon as this looks like it could be serious, then. . .

489

And even if that person has had a lot of sexual partners.

This links up with discourses around AIDS as Other. Someone with whom one has become familiar (to a greater or lesser degree), becomes a person who could not have AIDS *because* s/he is known. We do not "really know" those with AIDS. This operates on both a literal and a metaphorical level. Only one person in the group knew anyone personally who was HIV posi-

MILES

tive, and everyone acknowledged their sense of distance from AIDS and also an assumption that "they" were somehow safe. However, people with AIDS are culturally represented as Other. The binary logic of western thought makes a familiar person not–Other, therefore not–AIDS.[6] On the other hand, it is likely that if someone did contract HIV infection from a partner in a long-standing relationship, the reinstatement of the dimension of Other in the face of this information may well take place. This was confirmed anecdotally to me by an AIDS education worker from the Community AIDS Centre in Johannesburg.

One woman in the group said that in her most recent relationship although she and her partner had initially used a condom they had decided not to continue using them because both disliked using condoms, thus they agreed that they would take a "negotiated risk." Here there is at least negotiation taking place, and the slippage between Other and not–Other is not as stark as in the other accounts.

Discourses of rationality and assertiveness (Group 1): "You can control yourself if you are really worried"; Women have power "We can stop it." A discourse of rational control emerged in Group 1 which is oppositional to the idea of the lack of control of the sexual drive discourse. This was voiced in particular by one person who had a very confident and assertive style, and who spoke more than anyone else in the group. The impression I got was that the other women were to some extent persuaded by her strong delivery (but also basically agreed with her suggestions). The dominant idea inscribed in this discourse is that it is possible to control desire if you are really concerned about AIDS and or pregnancy. It is couched in a phraseology of denial of momentary gratification for fear of the consequences. The question which gave rise to this was about the appeal of alternative sexual practices. Although the general response was that penetration was either the preferred mode of sex, or the respondents had no experience of other sexual practices, one of the participants (D) seemed to feel that if one was really worried about AIDS then it would be possible to try other methods of lovemaking:

[D]: I think it's a possibility . . . depends on yourself, I mean, how much you fear AIDS.

It also depends on whether you can control yourself . . . or maybe, you can make yourself accept that kind of . . . practices . . . sexual practice.

[D]: Of course you can. I mean, you have to. If you are really serious and you are really, really afraid of getting AIDS, you will try anything . . . your life and your health is the most important thing because relationships they don't normally last. And you know, if you are going to let yourself be messed up by one relationship, and you know you could have prevented it . . . I mean, if there's a way and you feel strongly that you don't want to see yourself in that situation, then use it. It's just like if you know that you're not having your contraceptive pills

MILES

with you and you know that you are at a period where you can conceive, then
you just tell yourself that I don't have my condoms, and I don't have my contraceptive pills, . . . you know very well that you don't want to see yourself pregnant . . . then you don't do it.

This powerful assertion of possibility draws on a discourse of individual
choice and rationality and the construction of the individual as serious and
concerned about her future. From this perspective it is possible to cut across
desire and do what is required for self-protection. As a counter to the positioning of women as passive these ideas are very important, and the more
strongly they are voiced the greater influence they will have on social practice. A short-term problem with this for individuals, however, is the potential
negative consequences of the assertion, as discussed earlier. While men and
women are not on an equal footing, and men are not ready to take equal responsibility for safer sex, an individual woman may engender a negative response to such assertiveness.

Another woman in the group at this point agreed with D's remarks, and
later this idea was extended to the idea that, although assertion in relationships might lead to rejection by lowers, it was necessary for women to stand
up for themselves in relationships and protect themselves, in contrast to their
mothers, who, they felt, were subordinate and passive with relation to their
husbands:

> So . . . I don't think . . . it's supposed to continue that way. And we can only stop
> it.
>   We are the only ones. I mean, if they think we can't do without them, we
> must also present an idea or picture that they can't do without us. . .
>   If he doesn't want to understand you and appreciate your way of thinking and
> respect it, then he's no good . . . I don't see why I should mess up my life for
> him.
>   I still believe he's not the only guy who will love me. I mean there are plenty
> out there . . . We don't stand against them and show them that this must come
> to an end. So they get away with it every time.
>   [L]: So what you're saying is that we've got to say "I'm worthwhile enough to
> say what I want and to have it respected"?
>   Yes. At least we have to talk about it. He must convince me that he is right
> and he must be open-minded and listen to what I'm saying and try to under-
> stand my point of view and then we come to a conclusion. But he shouldn't be
> like, "No, it's bullshit. My idea is the right one. You take it or you forget about
> me". Then I would rather forget about him than be suppressed and oppressed
> and. . .

This is a clear statement of the desire for negotiation with equal power, and a
statement of self-worth. The amount of laughter and overlapping talk that this
turn of talk engendered in the group is testimony to the emotional energy

MILES

connected with this issue. When I questioned the group, they all said that they agreed with D and that they should say to men "condoms or no thanks." This was again connected to the issue of contraception, which is important, as what is at issue here is self-protection, both against pregnancy and against HIV infection. However, a problem is that women are often economically and socially dependent on men, and they are also emotionally positioned within a discourse of dependency on men. If the situation in which men are unwilling to negotiate with women in terms of a mutual desire for protection from the possibility of AIDS does hold, while women are caught in these dependencies, the desire for assertiveness may be difficult to carry out.

So although these assertions are crucial in that they suggest a potential shift towards autonomy for women, implementing these injunctions may be more difficult than imagined, precisely because there are emotional needs and defences on both sides, male and female. Towards the end of the discussion, one of the women claimed that when she went back home to her boyfriend, she would in fact not feel able to ask him to use condoms, even though she suspected that he had been having other lovers: "I'm not going to get them. I want to be honest, and I won't . . . it will cause a big thing. I won't do it." This comment highlighted the intractability of the situation, and the difficulty for women to act autonomously in individual relationships, in a context in which (it appears) that men cannot/will not acknowledge that AIDS may impact on their lives. As Richardson (1990) attests, "many heterosexual men ... either do not see AIDS as affecting them, or, if they do, deny it because they are afraid that by acknowledging their concerns they might be thought of as gay or bisexual" (p. 174). Further, in all of these situations discussed, the expectation is that the woman will take responsibility for the sex, whether to do with contraception, AIDS, or being more powerful in the relationship. This is expressed in such phrases as "We ladies . . . " "we must do something about these men . . . " and others similar in tone. This evidences the positioning of women as responsible for relationships and emotional work.

Discourses of the body (Group 2): Intimacy and vulnerability. I turn now to discourses of the body and sexual intimacy which came up together. These were again linked to gender differentiation and revolved around the question of alternative sexual practices. The construction of sexuality as primarily penetrative intercourse has been discussed. This construction was evident, although the comments made indicated both more experience of alternative practices and more immediate openness to them in Group 2 than in Group 1. Primarily, the idea was that other practices were part of penetrative sex, but that restriction to one or the other type would be constraining and that ideally one should be able to "do what you feel like at the time." This idea probably draws

MILES

both from the permissive discourse and from the long-standing feminist critique of the Freudian idea that female passivity and the vaginal orgasm are
signs of mature female sexuality.

Men were seen to be more bound to penetrative sex than the women
were, and it was felt that negotiation of safer sex through these practices
would be difficult: "But it would be very difficult to say 'I don't want penetration' to a man. If one [the man] didn't enjoy it, how would you negotiate
that"? In this part of the discussion, men were characterised in general as being able to get pleasure from penetration, therefore they would tend not to
develop expertise at other forms of sexual pleasure. They were also seen as
generally egocentric in sexuality, uncaring about their partner's pleasure, linking sexual success with performance, and socialised to have sex with as many
women as possible. The latter feature is one of the major tenets of the male
sexual drive discourse. However, some interesting views emerged on the
question of alternative sexual practices. One was the idea that non-intromis-
sion techniques are in fact more intimate than penetrative intercourse, and
that this would make them more difficult to put into practice especially in casual sexual encounters:

> That's why it's a difficult thing to practice this as safe sex. Because it's not the
> type of thing you are going to be doing with one night stands where maybe you
> will need to. . .
>
> It requires that you might need to make yourself more vulnerable as well. Be-
> cause if you take a one night stand of penetrative sex you actually don't have to
> make . . . you're making yourself vulnerable, but you're not making yourself as
> vulnerable. Having someone massage your back is an incredibly . . . I mean, it's a
> much more intimate thing. It comes with caring. The whole thing of negotiat-
> ing intimacy is difficult anyway.

This view was confirmed in anecdotal conversations with friends, both men
and women. And although this is voiced here by women, my feeling is that
many men do not learn a range of skills of sensual pleasure nor are they comfortable in opening themselves to areas of pleasure in which they do not feel
in control–which these kinds of techniques would imply. Of course this may
also be an issue of age–younger men may be more caught up in the dominant
masculinist mode of sexuality.

Leading from this was a discussion which revolved around women's responsibility in the sexual situation. This links in with the idea that women are
the emotional workers in a society and tend to take responsibility for relationships (Eichenbaum & Orbach, 1982; Lerner 1985). This cuts across the
male sexual drive discourse, in which women are positioned as objects in the
sexual context. Although it may be informed by feminist ideals of autonomy
and assertiveness, it also possibly draws from discourses of assertiveness from

493

MILES

human relations, and from the popular psychology of women's magazine advice on sexuality:

> . . . I think it's largely the woman's fault if she doesn't enjoy it enough because it's up to her to tell the man what he must do and what she likes in bed and ... how he must touch her or whatever. But then you have to be quite confident.
>   And quite trusting.

Here, the responsibility for the woman's sexual pleasure is her own. While the opposite—the situation which was espoused in the earlier years of this century, especially by Marie Stopes (Bland, 1983), in which a man (in the context of monogamy) is totally responsible for his wife's sexual pleasure—is not desirable either, a climate of mutual enquiry and openness to the other's desires and needs would provide the ground for genuine negotiation, which would also make negotiation of safer sex easier. However, in the view of this group:

> There are not so many men who stop to say: "What do you like?"
>   There are very few who stop to say what do you like.

Another set of ideas that emerged from this part of the discussion was (in terms of the discursive split between masculinity and femininity), the situation in which in sexuality, men felt entitled to criticise women's bodies, while women felt obliged to protect men from criticism and to affirm their (the men's) attractiveness. This is connected with a long-standing gendered division between the construction of women as the passive objects of the male gaze, and men as subjects of the gaze and the initiators of action (Berger, 1972). Further, it is connected to the intricate prescriptions of the culturally ideal female sexual body, propagated in countless ways, but especially, in post-industrial western society, through the media. Thinness, as Coward (1984) notes, is absolutely central—women should be "without a spare inch of flesh" (p. 40). A comment was made in the group about a newspaper report on a study in which it was claimed that 80% of women feel uncomfortable with their bodies, thus prefer to have sex with the lights off:

> . . . with other sexual techniques, it's exposing your whole body. And I think that might come into it. That some women might feel uncomfortable, they might have a round tummy or fat legs ... or dimples on their back ... that would hold back any other kind of intimacy. And I don't think men feel that. That's the funny thing. A man who's not incredibly physically attractive often doesn't seem to show that. . .

These comments drew agreement from everyone in the group, who were all able to relate this to their own experience of relationships, as I was myself.

494

Women internalise the prescriptions of the ideal female body; men judge women in terms of the ideal, and (this is a suggestion which I do not have the space to explore here), use perceive inadequacies to indirectly express aggression or to blame women for problems in sex or the relationship:

> They actually did a study with people making comments about problems with their sex lives and attractiveness and men tend to blame the female partner and say she's unresponsive and this. And female partners tended to criticise their own attractiveness. And it's just quite interesting. Men would say 'she's not interested . . . ' [in sex]. Men rarely say 'I'm insensitive', or 'I've got a fat belly'. If there was a problem it was normally with a partner.

Accounts followed this of particular incidents of male comments on physical (and other) shortcomings of women in the group. The difficulty, however, of rationally refusing the internalisation of criticism was acknowledged:

> But our society reinforces that we must be attractive to people. It's quite difficult even though from a feminist perspective I would like to break away from that, I can't. I really can't. When it comes down to it, I really still do feel that, I don't want to be seen as unattractive to men.

Clearly here, although subdominant discourses such as feminism do inform a critique of the above situation, still it is extremely difficult for women not to be affected by societal prescriptions of ideal beauty. This has been confirmed for me countless times in conversations with strongly feminist, highly self-conscious women. Moreover, the body is thought of as in intrinsic aspect of identity:

495

> I think criticism of intimate things are more difficult to take.
>   Things you can't change.
>   Also it's not like saying 'What you've done here is a screw up and it's something you can change'. If someone says to you: 'you've got a revolting face, or you're a bitch.' Then you suddenly think 'Well, I'm stuck with it. I'm terrible!' You just don't know what to do about it. It's quite destructive to say that to someone.

Linking in with discourses which position women as responsible for relationship, the women in the group tended to affirm their partner's attractiveness and acceptability to them:

> . . . an example . . . he lost about 20 kgs very rapidly and he had stretch marks on his back and he said to me once: 'Don't you find my stretch marks ugly'? and I looked at him and I said 'Ja, but they're you and you come as a package and yes, of course you've got some imperfections on you but so what?'. And I just thought if I had wanted to, I could have actually really been totally . . . totally

MILES

cruel. And I thought even if I don't like them, do I want to hurt this person. But lots of men don't seem to find that a problem.

Discourse of woman's responsibility. As is evident from much of the foregoing, the discourse of "woman's responsibility" was one which repeatedly emerged at different points in both discussions. This appeared in various forms. In the first group, it emerged in the proposal for assertiveness made by D, and was taken up in the group as "we women have to do something," "we can do something," etc. In the second group it emerged in the context of sexual pleasure. The women is expected to be responsible both for her own pleasure in making requests, and communicating her needs, yet at the same time must be conscious of the man's needs for affirmation, his likes and dislikes in sexuality, and so on. This poses enormous problems for safer sex in its fraught contradictoriness. Responsibility implies power. Yet the responsibility taken by women is "behind the scenes." The division of labour between being unemotional, authoritative and in control (male), and being emotional, labile, and sensitive to relationship needs (female) is not openly acknowledged nor accepted, yet it operates nonetheless. The power in this position is not acknowledged. And because structurally power is given to men, the power of women operates on an unconscious level for men and produces feelings of being threatened (Hollway, 1983).

DISCUSSION AND CONCLUSION

This analysis set out to find out something about how power relations operate within heterosexual sexual relationships, with the aim of examining the potential for the negotiation of safer sex within these relationships. The results suggest that safer sex is not easily negotiated within heterosexual relationships, for a variety of reasons. Although the group discussions consisted of women, the results clearly have implications for men as well. Heterosexual men in particular are subject to the need to disavow the threat of AIDS because of the association of AIDS with deviance in general, and homosexuality in particular. Women who wish to practice safer sex may not be able to suggest it, for fear of (at the least) a negative response, and worse, reprisals in the form of anger and rejection.

Subdominant discourses such as feminist discourses are sites of resistance to dominant ideologies (Levett, 1988). However, while it is clear that resistances are voiced in both groups, it is less easy to distinguish the sources of these resistances. In Group 1, although a powerful strain of assertiveness and the power of women to effect change is present, this is not explicitly drawn from feminist ideas. While feminist discourses are beginning to infiltrate society, the black women seemed to have had less direct access to these discourses than the white women, (or perhaps they found them less useful) and may have

496

MILES

been drawing more on discourses linked to resistance to apartheid. The extent of such influences in this context is speculative, however.

Participants in Group 2 placed themselves explicitly within feminist discourses, and some of the assertions that were made stressed the high value placed on independence and autonomy espoused by feminism. The permissive discourse also informed the valuing of erotic freedom. For these women, there is clearly a consciousness of the contradictions between the feminist and liberationist ideas they espouse and some of the difficulties they have in negotiating not only sexuality but also other relationship issues. However, they seem to have more options than the black women, and in some cases were able to negotiate the issue of safer sex with their lovers. In particular the woman who talked about taking a "negotiated risk," has arrived at a kind of resolution. Her resolution may not be the best one for the prevention of HIV transmission, but at least the space for negotiation is there. This confirms the suggestion made by Kippax, Crawford, Waldby, and Benton (1990) that space for negotiation for women is more easily provided from within the permissive discourse, especially where a women is positioned as "lover" rather than wife–mother, virgin, or whore, the three positions defined by Irigaray (1985, in Kippax et al., 1990) as available to women in western society. The women in Group 1 seemed more bound by both their own feelings of resistance to safer sex (as informed by the sexual drive discourse) and also by the potential negative responses of sexual partners, although all agreed that they should become more assertive in their relationships.

One of the central problems for AIDS preventative strategies is simply the question of gender difference. Men and women do not perceive their needs as similar, but rather as oppositional. There is a sexual and emotional economy in which people are positioned more as antagonists than comrades, with the division of labour not only material but also emotional. The breakdown of the bonds of marriage into the open warfare that often accompanies divorce is testimony to this construction. Women are the emotional workers in the society and tend to take responsibility for relationships. This is not the place to elucidate the complex psychodynamic roots of this situation. However, feminist writers such as Nancy Chodorow (1978) and Dorothy Dinnerstein (1977) suggest that if men were more involved in nurturing and child–care this would help to break down the structural division of qualities between men and women.

But gender arrangements are deeply entrenched in our society. The result of this extreme sense of difference is that there is a lack of common goals for men and women. The kinship felt by gays and lesbians as marginalised groups can be materialised in organisational activities. The organisation around AIDS in North America and the United Kingdom is testimony to such possibilities. Although women's organisations do exist in South Africa, organisations such

497

MILES

as the United Women's Congress (UWCO–now subsumed under the ANC Women's League) have historically concentrated more on the national liberation struggle than on gender issues. The structural arrangements of heterosexuality sexuality still keep women to a great extent separate within couples or nuclear families, thus the difficulties of organising as women on such issues are great.

Another factor informing AIDS issues in South Africa is the question of who the Other is in South African society, which does and will influence who is seen to be most "at risk" of AIDS. The Other, from the perspective of the dominant culture (white, male, middleclass) are those from marginalised groups in the society. In South Africa the Other is black, homosexual, woman. Black women and white women, however, will be constructed as Other in different ways by different people. My analysis clearly suggests that the women in the study–both black and white–are constructed as Other by their male partners.

Another issue which, as an aspect of the larger ideological superstructure of patriarchal societies feeds into the difficulties of negotiating sexuality is the idea of men as the norm–"people, humanity, mankind" (Coward, 1990, p. 132) and women as Other to men. Men, to begin to take responsibility as emotional beings, need to recognise themselves as gendered.

Coward states that

> [w]e see one of the major political problems confronting feminism to be the need to force men to recognize themselves as men. The discursive formation which allows men to represent themselves as non-gendered and to define women constantly according to their sexual status is one with very definite effects. It allows men to deny the effect of their gendered subjectivity on women . . . . Our understanding of the effects of discursive practices leads us to suggest that men can never be displaced from the centre until they can be forced to recognize themselves as men and to take responsibility for this. (p. 132)

Bowen (1985) suggests that men need to explore the historical discourses that have produced their masculinities. From this perspective, new masculinities, different from the present received and rigid forms of masculinity, may be possible. If men began to explore discourses of masculinity, and to develop new ones, perhaps homophobia would give way to acceptance of a range of sexualities: "It is time for heterosexuality and homosexuality to begin to be thought together in all their complex relations, and the centrality of both homo-eroticism and homo-phobia to straight culture to be recognised" (Bowen, 1985, p. 44). This might lead to AIDS being perceived as a threat by both men and women (black and white), and both becoming willing to take responsibility for their own bodies.

ENDNOTES

1. Bozzoli (1983) has referred to a "patchwork quilt of patriarchies" in South Africa, rooted historically in differing social and economic processes. This gives rise to complex hierarchies of privilege and oppression based on race and class between women in South Africa.

2. In the mid- to late 1980s, much of the public information about AIDS and HIV came through the media, that is, largely newspapers, and to a lesser extent radio and TV. The South African state has been notoriously slow to respond to the epidemic. State AIDS education campaigns have until recently been confined to pamphlets, posters, media advertisements, and education videos, and these have tended to reinforce gender stereotyping and been grounded in a conservative, familial heterosexist sexual morality with a prescrptive emphasis on an "abstinence and then marriage" approach (Retief, 1992). This has begun to change in the last few years with the establishment of government-funded AIDS Training, Information and Counselling Centres (ATICC), which operate regionally and are autonomous as far as their programmes are concerned. AIDS education programmes have also been carried out by non-governmental organisations, such as the Gay Association of South Africa (GASA) and the National Primary Health Care Network (NPHCN) and these are usually more progressive.

3. In South Africa, forms of schooling and tertiary education were imported with colonialism, and the universities were primary areas for the propagation of western discourses. Although the University of Cape Town, which is a traditionally white, English university, has over the last decade or so increased is enrollment of black students, it still broadly retains the cultural patterns of its formative period. Present educational institutions are also rooted in apartheid ideology and policies, with concomitant glaring racial and gendered inequalities. However, anyone who goes through formal education in South Africa will be subjected to a basically western-style education.

4. It is axiomatic to say that whites are generally economically more privileged than blacks in South Africa. I did not, however, specifically enquire into the economic backgrounds of the women in the study. These may have differed considerably.

5. I have not considered the question of "culture" in this study, as in the South African context, this is a highly complex and confusing question. It is a term with a number of contested definitions and meanings, which have a range of implications in terms of who uses it and to whom it is applied. Thus, given these complexities, any kind of "cross-cultural" analysis is beyond the scope of this study.

6. As discussed above, the phenomenon of Other will tend to take particular forms in South Africa because of the legacy of apartheid, and specifically the Population Registration Act which assigned people into certain "groups" based on "race." Many people, for example, may literally not "know" individuals classified differently from them, or if they do, will "know" them only in contexts which reinforce their Otherness, which may be then linked to the Otherness of Aids. Thus white women take their black domestic workers to have HIV testing done, but will not ask for testing for themselves. The issue of the Other and AIDS in the South African context is one which I hope to explore further.

499

MILES

REFERENCES

Aggleton, Peter, Homans, Hilary, Mojsa, Jan, Watson, Stuart, & Watney, Simon. (1989). *Aids: Scientific and social issues.* Edinburgh: Churchill Livingstone.

Berger, John. (1972). *Ways of seeing.* Harmondsworth: BBC and Penguin.

Bland, Lucy. (1983). Purity, motherhood, pleasure or threat? Definitions of female sexuality 1900-1970s. In Sue Cartledge & Joanna Ryan (Eds.), *Sex and love: New thoughts on old contradictions* (pp. 8–29). London: The Women's Press.

Bowen, John. (1985). Masculinity and the practice of teaching. Unpublished paper in Helen Taylor (Ed.), *Literature teaching politics 6: Conference papers* (pp. 42–48). Bristol: Bristol Polytechnic.

Bozzoli, Belinda. (1983). Marxism, feminism and South African studies. *Journal of Southern African Studies, 9*(2) 139–171.

Chodorow, Nancy. (1978). *The reproduction of mothering: Psychoanalysis and the sociology of gender.* Berkeley: University of California Press.

Coward, Rosalind, (1984). *Female desire: Women's sexuality today.* London: Paladin.

Coward, Rosalind, (1990). Linguistic, social and sexual relations: A review of Dale Spender's *Man made language.* In Deborah Cameron (Ed.), *The feminist critique of language: A reader* (pp. 111–133). London: Routledge.

Dinnerstein, Dorothy, (1977). *The mermaid and the minotaur: Sexual arrangements and human malaise.* New York: Harper Colophon Books.

Eichenbaum, Louise, & Orbach, Susie. (1982). *Outside in . . . inside out: Women's psychology: A feminist psychoanalytic approach.* Harmondsworth: Penguin.

Ehrenreich, Barbara, & English, Deidre, (1973). *Complaints and disorders: The sexual politics of sickness.* London: Writers and Readers Publishing Cooperative.

Foucault, Michel. (1981). *The history of sexuality. Vol. 1. An introduction.* Harmondsworth: Penguin.

Gilman, Sander, (1988). *Disease and representation: Images of illness from madness to AIDS.* Ithaca: Cornell University Press.

Goffman, Erving, (1959). *The presentation of self in everyday life.* Harmondsworth: Penguin.

Hollway, Wendy, (1983). Heterosexual sex: Power and desire for the other. In Sue Cartledge & Joanna Ryan (Eds.), *Sex and love: New thoughts on old contradictions* (pp. 124–140). London: The Women's Press.

Hollway, Wendy, (1984). Gender difference and the production of subjectivity. In Julian Henriques, Wendy Hollway, Cathy Urwin, Couze Venn, & Valerie Walkerdine, *Changing the subject: Psychology, social regulation and subjectivity* (pp. 227–263). London: Methuen.

Hollway, Wendy, (1989). *Subjectivity and method in psychology: Gender, meaning and science.* London: Sage Publications.

Irigaray, Luce, (1985). *This sex which is not one.* New York: Cornell University Press.

Kippax, Susan, Crawford, June, Waldby, Cathy, & Benton, Pam, (1990). Women negotiating heterosex: Implications for AIDS prevention. *Women's Studies International Forum, 13*(6), 533,–542.

Lerner, Harriet Goldhor, (1985). *The dance of anger: A woman's guide to changing the patterns of intimate relationships.* New York: Harper and Rowe.

Levett, Ann, (1988). Psychological trauma: Discourses of childhood sexual abuse. Un-

500

published PhD Thesis, Department of Psychology, University of Cape Town, South Africa.

Patton, Cindy, (1989). Resistance and the erotic. In Peter Aggleton, Graham Hart, & Peter Davies (Eds.), *AIDS: Social representations, social practices* (pp. 237–251). London: Falmer Press.

Plummer, Ken, (1988). Organizing AIDS. In Peter Aggleton & Hilary Homans (Eds.), *The social aspects of AIDS* (pp. 20–49). London: Falmer Press.

Richardson, Diane, (1990). AIDS education and women: Sexual and reproductive issues. In Peter Aggleton, Peter Davies, & Graham Hart (Eds.), *AIDS: Individual, cultural and policy dimensions* (pp. 169–179). London: Falmer Press.

Retief, Glen. (1992). Sexual stigma and AIDS education. Occasional Paper, Department of Criminology, University of Cape Town.

Rubin, Gayle, (1984). Thinking sex: Notes for a radical theory of the politics of sexuality. In Carole S. Vance (Ed.), *Pleasure and danger: Exploring female sexuality* (pp. 267–319). Boston: Routledge and Kegan Paul.

Schneider, Beth E., & Gould, Meredith, (1987). Female sexuality: Looking back into the future. In Myra Marx Ferree & Beth B. Hess (Eds.), *Analyzing gender: A handbook of social science research* (pp.: 20–153). Newbury Park: Sage Publications.

Sontag, Susan, (1988). *AIDS and its metaphors.* London: Penguin.

501

MILES

GENDER DISPLAYS AND MEN'S POWER
The "New Man" and the Mexican Immigrant Man

Pierrette Hondagneu-Sotelo
Michael A. Messner

IN OUR discussions about masculinity with our students (most of whom are white and upper-middle class), talk invariably turns to critical descriptions of the "macho" behavior of "traditional men." Consistently, these men are portrayed as "out there", not in the classroom with us. Although it usually remains an unspoken subtext, at times a student will actually speak it: Those men who are still stuck in "traditional, sexist, and macho" styles of masculinity are black men, Latino men, immigrant men, and working-class men. They are not us; we are the New Men, the Modern, Educated, and Enlightened Men. The belief that poor, working-class, and ethnic minority men are stuck in an atavistic, sexist "traditional male role," while white, educated middle-class men are forging a more sensitive egalitarian "New," or "Modern male

The authors thank Harry Brod, Scott Coltrane, and Michael Kaufman for helpful comments on earlier versions of this chapter.

role," is not uncommon. Social scientific theory and research on men and masculinity, as well as the "men's movement," too often collude with this belief by defining masculinity almost entirely in terms of gender display (i.e., styles of talk, dress, and bodily comportment), while ignoring men's structural positions of power and privilege over women and the subordination of certain groups of men to other men (Brod, 1983-1984). Our task in this chapter is to explore and explicate some links between contemporary men's gender displays and men's various positions in a social structure of power. Scott Coltrane's (1992) comparative analysis of gender display and power in 93 nonindustrial societies provides us with an important starting point. Coltrane found that men's "fierce public displays and denigration of women . . . competitive physical contests, vociferous oratory, ceremonies related to warfare, exclusive men's houses and rituals, and sexual violence against women" are common features in societies where men control property and have distant relations with young children (Coltrane, 1992, p. 87). By contrast, "in societies in which women exercise significant control over property and men have close relationships with children, men infrequently affirm their manliness through boastful demonstrations of strength, aggressiveness, and sexual potency" (p. 86). This research suggests that men's public gender displays are not grounded in some essential "need" for men to dominate others but, instead, tend to vary according to the extent of power and privilege that men hold vis-a-vis women. Put another way, the micropolitics of men's and women's daily gender displays and interactions both reflect and reconstruct the macropolitical relations between the sexes (Henley, 1977).

But in modern industrial societies, the politics of gender are far more complex than in nonindustrial societies. Some men publicly display verbal and physical aggression, misogyny, and violence. There are public institutions such as sport, the military, fraternities, and the street where these forms of gender display are valorized (Connell, 1991a, 1992b; Lyman, 1987; Martin & Hummer, 1989; Messner, 1992; Sabo, 1985). Other men, though, display more "softness" and "sensitivity," and this form of gender display has been recently lauded as an emergent "New Masculinity."

In this chapter, we will contrast the gender display and structural positions of power (in both public and domestic spheres of life) of two groups of men: class-privileged white men and Mexican immigrant men. We will argue that utilizing the concepts of Modern (or New) and Traditional men to describe these two groups oversimplifies a complex reality, smuggles in racist and classist biases about Mexican immigrant men, and obscures the real class, race, and gender privileges that New Men still enjoy. We will argue that the theoretical concepts of hegemonic, marginalized, and subordinated masculinities best capture the dynamic and shifting constellation of contemporary men's gender displays and power (Brod, 1987; Connell, 1987; Kaufman, 1987; Segal, 1990). We will conclude by arguing that a critical/feminist sociology of men and masculinity should decenter and problematize hegemonic masculinity by proceeding from the standpoint of marginalized and subordinated masculinities.

THE "NEW MAN" AS IDEOLOGICAL CLASS ICON

Today there is a shared cultural image of what the New Man looks like: He is a white, college-educated professional who is a highly involved and nurturant father, "in touch with" and expressive of his feelings, and egalitarian in his dealings with women. We will briefly examine two fragments of the emergent cultural image of the contemporary New Man: the participant in the mythopoetic men's movement and the New Father.[1] We will discuss these contemporary images of men both in terms of their larger cultural meanings and in terms of the extent to which they represent any real shift in the ways men live their lives vis-a-vis women and other men. Most important, we will ask if apparent shifts in the gender displays of some white, middle-class men represent any real transformations in their structural positions of power and privilege.

ZEUS POWER AND THE MYTHOPOETIC MEN'S MOVEMENT

A recently emergent fragment of the cultural image of the New Man is the man who attends the weekend "gatherings of men" that are at the heart of Robert Bly's mythopoetic men's movement. Bly's curious interpretations of mythology and his highly selective use of history, psychology, and anthropology have been soundly criticized as "bad social science" (e.g., Connell, 1992a; Kimmel, 1992; Pelka, 1991). But perhaps more important than a critique of Bly's ideas is a sociological interpretation of why the mythopoetic men's movement has been so attractive to so many predominantly white, college-educated, middle-class, middle-aged men in the United States over the past decade. (Thousands of men have attended Bly's gatherings, and his book was a national best-seller.) We speculate that Bly's movement attracts these men *not* because it represents any sort of radical break from "traditional masculinity" but precisely because it is so congruent with shifts that are already taking place within current constructions of hegemonic masculinity. Many of the men who attend Bly's gatherings are already aware of some of the problems and limits of narrow conceptions of masculinity. A major preoccupation of the gatherings is the poverty of these men's relationships with their fathers and with other men in workplaces. These concerns are based on very real and often very painful experiences. Indeed, industrial capitalism undermined much of the structural basis of middle-class men's emotional bonds with each other as wage labor, market competition, and instrumental rationality largely supplanted primogeniture, craft brotherhood, and intergenerational mentorhood (Clawson, 1989; Tolson, 1977). Bly's "male initiation" rituals are intended to heal and reconstruct these masculine bonds, and they are thus, at least

505

HONDAGNEU-SOTELO/MESSNER

on the surface, probably experienced as largely irrelevant to men's relationship with women.

But in focusing on how myth and ritual can reconnect men with each other and ultimately with their own "deep masculine" essences, Bly manages to sidestep the central point of the feminist critique—that men, as a group, benefit from a structure of power that oppresses women as a group. In ignoring the social structure of power, Bly manages to convey a false symmetry between the feminist women's movement and his men's movement. He assumes a natural dichotomization of "male values" and "female values" and states that feminism has been good for women in allowing them to reassert "the feminine voice" that had been suppressed. But Bly states (and he carefully avoids directly blaming feminism for this), "the masculine voice" has now been muted—men have become "passive . . . tamed . . . domesticated." Men thus need a movement to reconnect with the "Zeus energy" that they have lost. "Zeus energy is male authority accepted for the good of the community" (Bly, 1990, p. 61).

The notion that men need to be empowered as men echoes the naivete of some 1970s men's liberation activists who saw men and women as "equally oppressed" by sexism (e.g., Farrell, 1975). The view that everyone is oppressed by sexism strips the concept of oppression of its political meaning and thus obscures the social relations of domination and subordination. Oppression is a concept that describes a relationship between social groups; for one group to be oppressed, there must be an oppressor group (Freire, 1970). This is not to imply that an oppressive relationship between groups is absolute or static. To the contrary, oppression is characterized by a constant and complex state of play: Oppressed groups both actively participate in their own domination and actively resist that domination. The state of play of the contemporary gender order is characterized by men's individual and collective oppression of women (Connell, 1987). Men continue to benefit from this oppression of women, but, significantly, in the past 20 years, women's compliance with masculine hegemony has been counterbalanced by active feminist resistance.

Men do tend to pay a price for their power: They are often emotionally limited and commonly suffer poor health and a life expectancy lower than that of women. But these problems are best viewed not as "gender oppression," but rather as the "costs of being on top" (Kann, 1986). In fact, the shifts in masculine styles that we see among some relatively privileged men may be interpreted as a sign that these men would like to stop paying these costs, but it does not necessarily signal a desire to cease being "on top." For example, it has become commonplace to see powerful and successful men weeping in public—Ronald Reagan shedding a tear at the funeral of slain U.S. soliders, basketball player Michael Jordan openly crying after winning the NBA championship. Most recent, the easy manner in which the media lauded U.S. General Schwartzkopf as a New Man for shedding a public tear for the U.S.

506

casualties in the Gulf War is indicative of the importance placed on *styles of masculine gender display rather than the institutional position of power* that men such as Schwartzkopf still enjoy.

This emphasis on the significance of public displays of crying indicates, in part, a naive belief that if boys and men can learn to "express their feelings," they will no longer feel a need to dominate others. In fact, there is no necessary link between men's "emotional inexpressivity" and their tendency to dominate others (Sattel, 1976). The idea that men's "need" to dominate others is the result of an emotional deficit overly psychologizes a reality that is largely structural. It does seem that the specific type of masculinity that was ascendent (hegemonic) during the rise of entrepreneurial capitalism was extremely instrumental, stoic, and emotionally inexpressive (Winter & Robert, 1980). But there is growing evidence (e.g., Schwartzkopf) that today there is no longer a neat link between class-privileged men's emotional inexpressivity and their willingness and ability to dominate others (Connell, 1991b). We speculate that a situationally appropriate public display of sensitivity such as crying, rather than signaling weakness, has instead become a legitimizing sign of the New Man's power.[2]

Thus relatively privileged men may be attracted to the mythopoetic men's movement because, on the one hand, it acknowledges and validates their painful "wounds," while guiding them to connect with other men in ways that are both nurturing and mutually empowering.[3] On the other hand, and unlike feminism, it does not confront men with the reality of how their own privileges are based on the continued subordination of women and other men. In short, the mythopoetic men's movement may be seen as facilitating the reconstruction of a new form of hegemonic masculinity—a masculinity that is less self-destructive, that has revalued and reconstructed men's emotional bonds with each other, and that has learned to feel good about its own Zeus power.

507

The New Father

In recent years Western culture has been bombarded with another fragment of the popular image of the New Man: the involved, nurturant father. Research has indicated that many young heterosexual men do appear to be more inclined than were their fathers to "help out" with housework and child care, but most of them still see these tasks as belonging to their wives or their future wives (Machung, 1989; Sidel, 1990). Despite the cultural image of the "new fatherhood" and some modest increases in participation by men, the vast majority of child care, especially of infants, is still performed by women (Hochschild, 1989; La Rossa, 1988; Lewis, 1986; Russell, 1983).

Why does men's stated desire to participate in parenting so rarely translate into substantially increased involvement? Lynn Segal (1990) argues that the fact that men's apparent attitudinal changes have not translated into wide-

HONDAGNEU-SOTELO/MESSNER

spread behavioral changes may be largely due to the fact men that may (correctly) fear that increased parental involvement will translate into a loss of their power over women. But she also argues that increased paternal involvement in child care will not become a widespread reality unless and until the structural preconditions—especially economic equality for women—exist. Indeed, Rosanna Hertz (1986) found in her study of upper-middle class "dual career families" that a more egalitarian division of family labor sometimes developed as a rational (and constantly negotiated) response to a need to maintain his career, her career, and the family. In other words, career and pay equality for women was a structural precondition for the development of equality between husbands and wives in the family.

However, Hertz notes two reasons why this is a very limited and flawed equality. First, Hertz's sample of dual-career families in which the women and the men made roughly the same amount of money is still extremely atypical. In two-income families, the husband is far more likely to have the higher income. Women are far more likely than men to work part-time jobs, and among full-time workers, women still earn about 65 cents to the male dollar and are commonly segregated in lower paid, lower status, dead-end jobs (Blum, 1991; Reskin & Roos, 1990). As a result, most women are not in the structural position to be able to bargain with their husbands for more egalitarian divisions of labor in the home. As Hochschild's (1989) research demonstrates, middle-class women's struggles for equity in the home are often met by their husbands' "quiet resistance," which sometimes lasts for years. Women are left with the choice of either leaving the relationship (and suffering not only the emotional upheaval, but also the downward mobility, often into poverty, that commonly follows divorce) or capitulating to the man and quietly working her "second shift" of family labor.

Second, Hertz observes that the roughly egalitarian family division of labor among some upper-middle class dual-career couples is severely shaken when a child is born into the family. Initially, new mothers are more likely than fathers to put their careers on hold. But eventually many resume their careers, as the child care and much of the home labor is performed by low-paid employees, almost always women, and often immigrant women and/or women of color. The construction of the dual-career couple's "gender equality" is thus premised on the family's privileged position within a larger structure of social inequality. In other words, some of the upper-middle class women's gender oppression is, in effect, bought off with her class privilege, while the man is let off the hook from his obligation to fully participate in child care and housework. The upper-middle class father is likely to be more involved with his children today than his father was with him, and this will likely enrich his life. But given the fact that the day-to-day and moment-to-moment care and nurturance of his children is still likely to be performed by women (either his wife and/or a hired, lower-class woman), "the contemporary reval-

508

HONDAGNEU-SOTELO/MESSNER

orisation of fatherhood has enabled many men to have the best of both worlds" (Segal, 1990, p. 58). The cultural image of the New Father has given the middle-class father license to choose to enjoy the emotional fruits of parenting, but his position of class and gender privilege allow him the resources with which he can buy or negotiate his way out of the majority of second shift labor.

In sum, as a widespread empirical reality, the emotionally expressive, nurturant, egalitarian New Man does not actually exist; he is an ideological construct, made up of disparate popular images that are saturated with meanings that express the anxieties, fears, and interests of relatively privileged men. But this is not to say that some changes are not occurring among certain groups of privileged men (Segal, 1990). Some men are expressing certain feelings that were, in the past, considered outside the definition of hegemonic masculinity. Some men are reexamining and changing their relationships with other men. Some men are participating more—very equitably in some cases, but marginally in many others—in the care and nurturance of children. But the key point is that when examined within the context of these men's positions in the overall structure of power in society, these changes do not appear to challenge or undermine this power. To the contrary, the cultural image of the New Man and the partial and fragmentary empirical changes that this image represents serve to file off some of the rough edges of hegemonic masculinity in such a way that the possibility of a happier and healthier life for men is created, while deflecting or resisting feminist challenges to men's institutional power and privilege. But because at least verbal acceptance of the "New Woman" is an important aspect of this reconstructed hegemonic masculinity, the ideological image of the New Man requires a counterimage against which to stand in opposition. Those aspects of traditional hegemonic masculinity that the New Man has rejected—overt physical and verbal displays of domination, stoicism and emotional inexpressivity, overt misogyny in the workplace and at home—are now increasingly projected onto less privileged groups of men: working-class men, gay body-builders, black athletes, Latinos, and immigrant men.

509

MEXICAN IMMIGRANT MEN

According to the dominant cultural stereotype, Latino men's "machismo" is supposedly characterized by extreme verbal and bodily expressions of aggression toward other men, frequent drunkenness, and sexual aggression and dominance expressed toward normally "submissive" Latinas. Manuel Peña's (1991) research on the workplace culture of male undocumented Mexican immigrant agricultural workers suggests that there is a great deal of truth to this stereotype. Pena examined the Mexican immigrant male's participation in *charritas coloradas* (red jokes) that characterize the basis of the workplace culture. The most common basis of humor in the *charritas* is sexualized "sadism toward women and symbolic threats of sodomy toward other males" (Paredes, 1966, p. 121).

On the surface, Peña argues. the constant "half-serious, half playful duels" among the men, as well as the images of sexually debased "perverted wenches" and "treacherous women" in the *charritas*, appear to support the stereotype of the Mexican immigrant male group as being characterized by a high level of aggressive masculine posturing and shared antagonisms and hatred directed toward women. But rather than signifying a fundamental hatred of women, Peña argues that these men's public displays of machismo should be viewed as a defensive reaction to their oppressed class status:

> As an expression of working-class culture, the folklore of machismo can be considered a realized signifying system [that] points to, but simultaneously displaces, a class relationship and its attendant conflict. At the same time, it introduces a third element, the gender relationship, which acts as a mediator between the signifier (the folklore) and the signified (the class relationship). (Peña, 1991, p. 40)

Undocumented Mexican immigrant men are unable to directly confront their class oppressors, so instead, Peña argues, they symbolically displace their class antagonism into the arena of gender relations. Similar arguments have been made about other groups of men. For instance, David Collinson (1988) argues that Australian male blue-collar workers commonly engage in sexually aggressive and misogynist humor, as an (ultimately flawed) means of bonding together to resist the control of management males (who are viewed, disparagingly, as feminized). Majors and Billson (1992) argue that young black males tend to embody and publicly display a "cool pose," an expressive and often sexually aggressive style of masculinity that acts as a form of resistance to racism. These studies make important strides toward building an understanding of how subordinated and marginalized groups of men tend to embody and publicly display styles of masculinity that at least symbolically resist the various forms of oppression that they face within hierarchies of intermale dominance. These studies all share the insight that the public faces of subordinated groups of men are *personally and collectively constructed performances of masculine gender display*. By contrast, the public face of the New Man (his "sensitivity," etc.) is often assumed to be one-and-the-same with who he "is," rather than being seen as a situationally constructed public gender display.

Yet in foregrounding the oppression of men by men, these studies risk portraying aggressive, even misogynist, gender displays primarily as liberatory forms of resistance against class and racial oppression (e.g., Mirandé, 1982). Though these studies view microlevel gender display as constructed within a context of structured power relations, macrolevel gender relations are rarely viewed as a constituting dynamic within this structure. Rather gender is commonly viewed as an epiphenomenon, an effect of the dominant class and/or race relations. What is obscured, or even drops out of sight, is the feminist observation that masculinity itself is a form of domination over women. As a result, women's actual experiences of oppression and victimization by men's violence are conspicuously absent from these analyses, thus leaving the impression that misogyny is merely a symbolic displacement of class (or race) antagonism. What is needed, then, is an examination of masculine gender display and power within the context of intersecting systems of class, race, and gender relations (Baca Zinn, Cannon, Higgenbotham, & Dill, 1986; Collins, 1990). In the following section we will consider recent ethnographic research on Mexican immigrant communities that suggests that gender dynamics help to constitute the immigration process and, in turn, are reconstituted during and following the immigrant settlement process.

THE RHETORIC OF RETURN MIGRATION AS GENDER DISPLAY

Mexican immigrant men who have lived in the United States for long periods of time frequently engage in the rhetoric of return migration. These stated preferences are not necessarily indicative of what they will do, but they provide some telling clues to these men's feelings and perceptions about their lives as marginalized men in the United States. Consider the following statements:[4]

> I've passed more of my life here than in Mexico. I've been here for thirty-one years. I'm not putting down or rejecting this country, but my intentions have always been to return to Mexico . . . I'd like to retire there, perhaps open a little business. Maybe I could buy and sell animals, or open a restaurant. Here I work for a big company, like a slave, always watching the clock. Well I'm bored with that.

> I don't want to stay in the U.S. anymore. [Why not?] Because here I can no longer find a good job. Here, even if one is sick, you must report for work. They don't care. I'm fed up with it. I'm tired of working here too. Here one must work daily, and over there with my mother, I'll work for four, maybe five months, and then I'll have a four or five month break without working. My mother is old and I want to be with the family. I need to take care of the rancho. Here I have nothing, I don't have my own house, I even share the rent! What am I doing here?

> I would like to return, but as my sons are born here, well that is what detains me here. Otherwise, I would go back to Mexico . . . Mexico is now in a very inflationary situation. People come here not because they like it, but because the situation causes them to do so, and it makes them stay here for years and years. As the song says, this is a cage made of gold, but it is still a cage.

These statements point to disappointments with migration. In recent years, U.S.-bound migration has become institutionalized in many areas of Mexico, representing a rite of passage for many young, single men (Davis, 1990; Escobar, Gonzalez de la Rocha, & Roberts, 1987). But once in the United States the accomplishment of masculinity and maturity hinges on living up to the image of a financially successful migrant. If a man returns homes penniless, he risks being seen as a failure or a fool. As one man explained: "One cannot go back without anything, because people will talk. They'll say 'oh look at this guy, he sacrificed and suffered to go north and he has nothing to show for it.'"

Although most of these men enjoyed a higher standard of living in the United States than in Mexico, working and settling in the United States significantly diminished their patriarchal privileges. Although the men compensated by verbally demonstrating their lack of commitment to staying in the United States, most of these men realized that their lives remained firmly anchored in the United States and that they lacked the ability to return. They could not acquire sufficient savings in the public sphere to fund return migration, and in the domestic sphere, they did not command enough authority over their wives or children, who generally wished to remain in the United States, to coerce the return migration of their families. Although Mexican immigrant men blamed the terms of U.S. production as their reason for wanting to return to Mexico, we believe that their diminished patriarchal privileges significantly fueled this desire to return.[5] Here, we examine the diminution of patriarchy in three arenas: spatial mobility, authority in family decision-making processes, and household labor.

Mexican immigrant men, especially those who were undocumented and lacked legal status privileges, experienced limited spatial mobility in their daily lives and this compromised their sense of masculinity (Rouse, 1990). As undocumented immigrants, these men remained fearful of apprehension by the Immigration Naturalization Service and by the police.[6] In informal conversations, the men often shared experiences with police harassment and racial discrimination. Merely "looking Mexican," the men agreed, was often cause for suspicion. The jobs Mexican immigrant men commonly took also restricted their spatial mobility. As poor men who worked long hours at jobs as gardeners, dishwashers, or day laborers, they had very little discretionary income to afford leisure activities. As one man offered, "Here my life is just from work to the home, from work to the home."

Although the men, together with their families, visited parks, shops, and church, the public spaces open to the men alone were typically limited to street corners and to a few neighborhood bars, pool halls, and doughnut shops. As Rouse (1990) has argued, Mexican immigrant men, especially those from rural areas, resent these constrictions on their public space and mobility and attempt to reproduce public spaces that they knew in Mexico in the context of U.S. bars and pool halls. In a California immigrant community Rouse observed that "men do not come to drink alone or to meet with a couple of friends . . . they move from table to table, broadening the circuits of information in which they participate and modulating social relationships across the widest possible range." Although these men tried to create new spaces where they might recapture a public sense of self, the goal was not so readily achieved. For many men, the loss of free and easy mobility signified their loss of publicly accorded status and recognition. One man, a junkyard assembler who had worked in Mexico as a rural *campesino* (peasant), recalled that in his Mexican village he enjoyed a modicum of public recognition: "I would enter the bars, the dances, and when I entered everyone would stand to shake my hand as though I were somebody—not a rich man, true, but I was famous. Wherever you like, I was always mentioned. Wherever you like, everyone knew me back there." In metropolitan areas of California, anonymity replaced public status and recognition.

In Mexico many of these men had acted as the undisputed patriarchs in major family decision-making processes, but in the United States they no longer retained their monopoly on these processes. When families were faced with major decisions—such as whom to seek for legal help, whether or not to move to another town, or the decision to lend money or make a major purchase—spousal negotiation replaced patriarchal exertions of authority. These processes did not go uncontested, and some of the decision-making discussions were more conflictual than harmonious, but collaboration, not domination, characterized them.

This trend toward more egalitarian patterns of shared authority often began with migration. In some families, men initially migrated north alone, and during their absences, the women acted decisively and autonomously as they performed a range of tasks necessary to secure family sustenance. Commentators have referred to this situation as one in which "thousands of wives in the absence of their husbands must 'take the reins'" (Mummert, 1988, p. 283) and as one in which the wives of veteran migrants experience "a freedom where woman command" *(una libertad donde mujeres mandan)* (Baca & Bryan, 1985). This trend toward more shared decision making continued after the women's migration and was also promoted by migration experiences as well as the relative increase in women's and the decrease in men's economic contributions to the family (Hondagneu-Sotelo, 1992). As the balance of relative resources and contributions shifted, the women assumed more active roles in key decision-making processes. Similar shifts occurred with the older children, who were now often reluctant to subordinate their earnings and their autonomy to a patriarchal family hierarchy. As one man somewhat reluctantly, but resignedly, acknowledged: "Well, each person orders one's self here, something like that . . . Back there [Mexico], no. It was still whatever I said. I decided matters."

The household division of labor is another arena that in some cases reflected the renegotiation of patriarchal relations. Although most families continued to organize their daily household chores along fairly orthodox, patriarchal norms, in some families—notably those where the men had lived for

513

HONDAGNEU-SOTELO/MESSNER

many years in "bachelor communities" where they learned to cook, iron, and make tortillas—men took responsibility for some of the housework. In these cases, men did part of the cooking and housework, they unself-consciously assumed the role of host in offering guests food and beverages, and in some instances, the men continued to make tortillas on weekends and special occasions. These changes, of course, are modest if judged by ideal standards of feminist egalitarianism, but they are significant when compared to patriarchal family organization that was normative before immigration.

This movement toward more egalitarian divisions of labor in some Mexican immigrant households cannot be fully explained by the men's acquisition of household skills in bachelor communities. (We are reminded, for instance, of several middle-class male friends of ours who lived in "bachelor" apartments during college, and after later marrying, conveniently "forgot" how to cook, wash clothes, and do other household chores.) The acquisition of skills appears to be a necessary, but not a sufficient, condition for men's greater household labor participation in reunited families.

A key to the movement toward greater equality within immigrant families was the change in the women's and men's relative positions of power and status in the larger social structure of power. Mexican immigrant men's public status in the United States is very low, due to racism, insecure and low-paying jobs, and (often) illegal status. For those families that underwent long periods of spousal separation, women often engaged in formal- or informal-sector paid labor for the first time, developed more economic skills and autonomy, and assumed control over household affairs. In the United States nearly all of the women sought employment, so women made significant economic contributions to the family. All of these factors tend to erode men's patriarchal authority in the family and empower women to either directly challenge that authority or at least renegotiate "patriarchal bargains" (Kandiyoti, 1988) that are more palatable to themselves and their children.

Although it is too hasty to proclaim that gender egalitarianism prevails in interpersonal relations among undocumented Mexican immigrants, there is a significant trend in that direction. This is indicated by the emergence of a more egalitarian household division of labor, by shared decision-making processes, and by the constraints on men's and expansion of women's spatial mobility. Women still have less power than men, but they generally enjoy more than they previously did in Mexico. The stereotypical image of dominant macho males and submissive females in Mexican immigrant families is thus contradicted by actual research with these families.

MASCULINE DISPLAYS AND RELATIVE POWER

We have suggested that men's overt public displays of masculine bravado, interpersonal dominance, misogyny, embodied strength, and so forth are often a sign of a lack of institutional power and privilege, vis-à-vis other men.

514

Table 1 Comparison of Public and Domestic Gender Displays of White, Class–Privileged Men and Mexican Immigrant Men

	Public		Domestic	
	Power/Status	Gender Display	Power/Status	Gender Display
White, class–privilleged men	High, built into position	"Sensitive," little overt misogyny	High, based on public status/ high income	"Quiet control"
Mexican immigrant men	Low (job status, pay, control of work, legal rights, public status)	"Hombre": verbal misogyny, embodied toughness in work/ peer culture	Contested, becoming more egalitarian	Exaggerated symbols of power and authority in family

Though it would be a mistake to conclude that Mexican immigrant men are not misogynist (or, following Peña, that their misogyny is merely a response to class oppression), there is considerable evidence that their actual relations with women in families—at least when measured by family divisions of labor and decision-making processes—are becoming more egalitarian than they were in Mexico. We have also argued that for more privileged men, public displays of sensitivity might be read as signs of class/race/gender privilege and power over women and (especially) over other men (see Table 1 for a summary comparison of these two groups).

Coltrane (1992) argues that in nonindustrial societies, "men's displays of dominance confirm and reinforce existing property relations rather than compensate for a lack of control over valued resources" (pp. 102-103). His claim that men's *control* (rather than lack of control) of resources is correlated with more extreme microdisplays of masculinity seems, at first, to contradict findings by Penña, Colliston, and Billson and Majors, who claim that in industrial societies, *lack* of access to property and other material resources by Mexican immigrant, working-class, and black males peer culture are correlated with more overt outward displays of aggressive, misogynist masculinity. The key to understanding this apparent contradiction is that Coltrane is discussing societies where women enjoy high social status, where men are highly involved in child care, and where women have a great deal of control over property and other material resources. In these types of societies, men do not "need" to display dominance and masculine bravado. But in complex, stratified societies where the standards of hegemonic masculinity are that a man should control resources (and other people), men who do not have access to these standards of masculinity thus tend to react with displays of toughness, bravado, "cool pose," or "hombre" (Baca Zinn, 1982).

Marginalized and subordinated men, then, tend to overtly display exaggerated embodiments and verbalizations of masculinity that can be read as a desire to express power over others within a context of relative powerlessness. By contrast, many of the contemporary New Man's highly celebrated public displays of sensitivity can be read as a desire to project an image of egalitarianism within a context where he actually enjoys considerable power and privilege over women and other men. Both groups of men are "displaying gender," but the specific forms that their masculine displays take tend to vary according to their relative positions in (a) the social structure of men's overall power relationship to women and (b) the social structure of some men's power relationships with other men.

CONCLUSION

We have argued for the importance of viewing microlevel gender displays of different groups of men within the context of their positions in a larger social structure of power. Too often critical discussions of masculinity tend to project atavistic hypermasculine, aggressive, misogynist masculinity onto relatively powerless men. By comparison, the masculine gender displays of educated, privileged New Men are too often uncritically applauded, rather than skeptically and critically examined. We have suggested that when analyzed within a structure of power, the gender displays of the New Man might best be seen as strategies to reconstruct hegemonic masculinity by projecting aggression, domination, and misogyny onto subordinate groups of men. Does this mean that all of men's changes today are merely symbolic and ultimately do not contribute to the types of changes in gender relations that feminists have called for? It may appear so, especially if social scientists continue to collude with this reality by theoretically framing shifts in styles of hegemonic masculinity as indicative of the arrival of a New Man, while framing marginalized men as Other—as atavistic, traditional men. Instead, a critical/feminist analysis of changing masculinities in the United States might begin with a focus on the ways that marginalized and subordinated masculinities are changing.

This shift in focus would likely accomplish three things: First, it would remove hegemonic masculinity from center stage, thus taking the standpoints of oppressed groups of men as central points of departure. Second, it would require the deployment of theoretical frameworks that examine the ways that the politics of social class, race, ethnicity, and sexuality interact with those of gender (Baca Zinn, Cannon, Higgenbotham, & Dill, 1986; Collins, 1990; Harding, 1986; Hondagneu-Sotelo, 1992; Messner, 1990). Third, a sociology of masculinities that starts from the experience of marginalized and subordinated men would be far more likely to have power and politics—rather than personal styles or lifestyles—at its center. This is because men of color, poor and working-class men, immigrant men, and gay men are often in very con-

516

tradictory positions at the nexus of intersecting systems of domination and subordination. In short, although they are oppressed by class, race, and/or sexual systems of power, they also commonly construct and display forms of masculinity as ways of resisting other men's power over them, as well as asserting power and privilege over women. Thus, to avoid reverting to the tendency to view masculinity simply as a defensive reaction to other forms of oppression, it is crucial in such studies to keep women's experience of gender oppression as close to the center of analysis as possible. This sort of analysis might inform the type of progressive coalition building that is necessary if today's changing masculinities are to contribute to the building of a more egalitarian and democratic world.

NOTES

1. This section of the chapter is adapted from Messner (1993).

2. It is significant, we suspect, that the examples cited of Reagan, Jordan, and Schwartzkopf publicly weeping occurred at moments of *victory* over other men in war and sport.

3. Our speculation on the class and racial bias of the mythopoetic men's movement and on the appeal of the movement to participants is supported, in part, by ongoing (but as yet unpublished) research by sociologist Michael Schwalbe. Schwalbe observes that the "wounds" of these men are very real, because a very high proportion of them are children of alcoholic parents and/or were victims of childhood sexual abuse or other forms of violence. Many are involved in recovery programs.

4. Material in this section is drawn from Hondagneu–Sotelo's study of long–term undocumented immigrant settlers, based on 18 months of field research in a Mexican undocumented immigrant community. See Hondagneu–Sotelo, (1994). *Gendered Transitions: Mexican Experiences of Immigrants*. Berkeley: University of California Press.

5. For a similar finding and analysis in the context of Dominican immigrants in New York City, see Pessar (1986).

6. This constraint was exacerbated by passage of the Immigration Reform and Control Act of 1986, which imposed employer sanctions and doubly criminalized undocumented immigrants' presence at the workplace.

517

REFERENCES

Baca, R., & Bryan, D. (1985). Mexican women, migration and sex roles. *Migration Today, 13*, 14–18.

Baca Zinn, M. (1982). Chicano men and masculinity. *Journal of Ethnic Studies, 10*, 29–44.

Baca Zinn, M., Cannon, L. W., Higgenbotham, E., & Dill, B. T. (1986). The costs of exclusionary practices in women's studies. *Signs: Journal of Women in Culture and Society, 11*, 290–303.

Blum, L. M. (1991). *Between feminism and labor: The significance of the comparable worth movement*. Berkeley: University of California Press.

Bly, R. (1990). *Iron John: A book about men*. Reading, MA: Addison-Wesley.

Brod, H. (1983–1984). Work clothes and leisure suits: The class basis and bias of the men's movement. *Changing Men, 11*, 10–12, 38–40 (Winter)

Brod, H. (Ed.). *The making of masculinities: The new men's studies*. Boston: Allen & Unwin.

Clawson, M. A. (1989). *Constructing brotherhood: Class, gender, and fraternalism*. Princeton, NJ: Princeton University Press.

Collins, P. H. (1990). *Black feminist thought: Knowledge, consciousness, and the politics of empowerment*. Boston: Unwin Hyman.

Collinson, D. L. (1988). "Engineering humor": Masculinity, joking and conflict in shop-floor relations. *Organization Studies, 9*, 181–199.

Coltrane, S. (1992). The micropolitics of gender in nonindustrial societies. *Gender & Society, 6*, 86–107.

Connell, R. W. (1987). *Gender and power*. Stanford, CA: Stanford University Press.

Connell, R. W. (1991a). Live fast and die young: The construction of masculinity among young working-class men on the margin of the labour market. *Australian & New Zealand Journal of Sociology, 27*, 141–171.

Connell, R. W. (1991b). *Men of reason: Themes of rationality and change in the lives of men in the new professions*. Unpublished paper.

Connell, R. W. (1992a). Drumming up the wrong tree. *Tikkun, 7*, 517–530.

Connell, R. W. (1992b). Masculinity, violence, and war. In M. S. Kimmel & M. A. Messner (Eds.), *Men's lives* (2nd ed., pp. 176–182). New York: Macmillan.

Davis, M. (1990). *Mexican voices, American dreams: An oral history of Mexican immigration to the United States*. New York: Henry Holt.

Escobar, A. L., Gonzalez de la Rocha, M., & Roberts, B. (1987). Migration, labor markets, and the international economy: Jalisco, Mexico and the United States. In J. Eades (Ed.), *Migrants, workers, and the social order* (pp. 42–64). London: Tavistock.

Farrell, W. (1975). *The liberated man*. New York: Bantam.

Freire, P. (1970). *Pedagogy of the oppressed*. New York: Herder & Herden.

Harding, S. (1986). *The science question in feminism*. Ithaca, NY: Cornell University Press.

Henley, N. M. (1977). *Body politics: Power, sex, and nonverbal communication*. Englewood Cliffs, NJ: Prentice Hall.

Hertz, R. (1986). *More equal than others: Women and men in dual career marriages*. Berkeley: University of California.

Hochschild, A. (1989). *The second shift: Working parents and the revolution at home*. New York: Viking.

Hondagneu-Sotelo, P. (1992). Overcoming patriarchal constraints: The reconstruction of gender relations among Mexican immigrant women and men. *Gender & Society, 6*, 393–415.

Kandiyoti, D. (1988). Bargaining with patriarchy. *Gender & Society, 2*, 274–290.

Kann, M. E. (1986). The costs of being on top. *Journal of the National Association for Women Deans, Administrators, & Counselors, 49*, 29–37.

Kaufman, M. (Ed.). (1987). *Beyond patriarchy: Essays by men on pleasure, power, and change*. Toronto: Oxford University Press.

Kimmel, M. S. (1992). Reading men: Men, masculinity, and publishing. *Contemporary Sociology, 21*, 162–171.

La Rossa, R. (1988). Fatherhood and social change. *Family Relations, 37*, 451–457.

Lewis, C. (1986). *Becoming a father*. Milton Keynes, UK: Open University Press.

Lyman, P. (1987). The fraternal bond as a joking relation: A case study of the role of sexist jokes in male group bonding. In M. Kimmel (Ed.), *Changing men: New directions in research on men and masculinities* (pp. 148–163). Newbury Park, CA: Sage.

Machung, A. (1989). Talking career, thinking job: Gender differences in career and family expectations of Berkeley seniors. *Feminist Studies, 15*.

Majors, R., & Billson, J. M. (1992). *Cool pose: The dilemmas of black manhood in America*. New York: Lexington.

Martin, P.Y., & Hummer, R.A. (1989). Fraternities and rape on campus. *Gender & Society, 3*, 457–473.

Messner, M.A. (1990). Men studying masculinity: Some epistemological questions in sport sociology. *Sociology of Sport Journal, 7*, 136–153.

Messner, M.A. (1992). *Power at play: Sports and the problem of masculinity*. Boston: Beacon.

Messner, M.A. (1993). "Changing men" and feminist politics in the U.S. *Theory & Society, 22*, 723–737.

Mirandé, A. (1982). Machismo: Rucas, chingasos y chagaderas. *De Colores: Journal of Chicano Expression and Thought, 6*(1/2), 17–31.

Mummert, G. (1988). Mujeres de migrantes y mujeres migrantes de Michoacán: Nuevo papeles para las que se quedan y para las que se van. In T. Calvo & G. Lopez (Eds.), *Movimientos de población en el occident de Mexico* (pp. 281–295). Mexico, DF: Centre de'etudes mexicaines et centroamericaines and El colegio de Mexico.

Paredes, A. (1966). The Anglo–American in Mexican folklore. In R. B. Browne & D. H.Wenkelman (Eds.), *New voices in American studies*. Lafayette, IN: Purdue University Press.

Pelka, F. (1991). Robert Bly and Iron John: Bly romanticizes history, trivializes sexist oppression and lays the blame for men's "grief" on women. *On the Issues, 19*, 17–19, 39.

Peña, M. (1991). Class, gender and machismo: The "treacherous woman" folklore of Mexican male workers. *Gender & Society, 5*, 30–46.

Pessar, P. (1986). The role of gender in Dominican settlement in the United States. In J. Nash & H. Safa (Eds.), *Women and change in Latin America* (pp. 273–294). South Hadley, MA: Bergin & Garvey.

Reskin, B. F., & Roos, P.A. (1990). *Job queues, gender queues: Explaining women's inroads into male occupations*. Philadelphia: Temple University Press.

Rouse, R. (1990, March 14). *Men in space: Power and the appropriation of urban form among Mexican migrants in the United States*. Paper presented at the Residential College, University of Michigan, Ann Arbor.

Russell, G. (1983). *The changing role of fathers*. London: University of Queensland.

Sabo, D. F. (1985). Sport, patriarchy, and male identity: New questions about men and sport. *Arena Review, 9*, 1–30.

Sattel, J. W. (1976). The inexpressive male: Tragedy or sexual politics? *Social Problems, 23*, 469–477.

Segal, L. (1990). *Slow motion: Changing masculinities, changing men*. New Brunswick, NJ: Rutgers University.

Sidel, R. (1990). *On her own: Growing up in the shadow of the American dream.* New York: Penguin.

Tolson, A. (1977). *The limits of masculinity: Male identity and women's liberation.* New York: Harper & Row.

Winter, M. F., & Robert, E. R. (1980). Male dominance, late capitalism, and the growth of instrumental reason. *Berkeley Journal of Sociology, 25,* 249–280.

ESSENTIALISM, WOMEN, AND WAR
Protesting Too Much, Protesting Too Little

Susan Oyama

RECENTLY SOME biological theorists and feminists have converged on "essentialist" accounts of war that are strangely similar in certain ways. At first glance it seems to be an unlikely development, given the frequency with which we have seen antifeminists and feminists line up on opposite sides of the nature-nurture rift. At second glance, though, perhaps the association is not so surprising after all. We seem to be in the midst of a pendulum swing "back to nature" and away from environmentalism. This movement, in turn, is probably part of a more general trend in this country toward conservatism and a certain brand of romanticism, though the issue is a good deal more complex than one might think. Apart from the current emphasis on so-called traditional values, though, the convergence on "biological" views reflects some very common and pervasive beliefs about genes and environment, biology and learning, that are as evident in environmentalist approaches as they are in biological ones.

By essentialist, I mean an assumption that human beings have an underlying universal nature, one that is more fundamental than any variations that may exist among us and that is in some sense always present—perhaps as "genetic propensity"—even if it is not discernible. People frequently define this preexisting nature in biological terms, and they believe it will tend to express itself even though it might be somwhat modified by learning and thus might be partially obscured by a sort of cultural veneer. (For a good discussion of this theme in feminism, see Alison Jaggar (1983, chap. 5). Janet Sayers (1982, 148) criticizes essentialist feminism, and Anne Fausto-Sterling (1985, 195) refers to human sociobiology as a "theory of essences"; Ruth Bleier [1984, chap. 1] criticizes both. Of these authors, Jaggar is perhaps most successful in transcending the biology-culture opposition, but all are aware of the mischief it has caused for scientists and nonscientists alike.

When I say that environmentalist and biological approaches share many assumptions about nature and nurture, I mean that they have often argued about which and how many traits were genetic and which were learned, but, in doing so, they have accepted the premise that genes and learning were properly treated as alternative explanations for human characteristics and actions. They also tended to agree that the possibility of change was somehow illuminated by their disputes.

In a metaphor that is revealing in more than one way, sociobiologist David Barash compares the relationship of nature and nurture to two people wrestling. As they tumble about, their limbs entwine so that it is hard to tell which is which. However entangled they may become, the combatants do not merge; they are separate persons in competition, and our imperfect powers of observation do not change that fact (1981, 12).

Though they routinely declare that the nature-nurture dichotomy is meaningless and that the effects of biology and culture cannot be clearly distinguished, scholars of all stripes (including not only sociobiologists like Barash but many of sociobiology's critics as well—see discussion and references in Oyama 1981, 1982) continue to treat them as separate sources of living form and behavior: some things are (mostly) programmed by our genes, others are (mostly) programmed by our environments. We will return to this conceptual problem later.

Let's look first, however, at some examples of essentialist accounts of women and war. The first several examples come from scholars who have offered us their biological views of human behavior and society, while the last two come from a recent collection of feminist writings.

THE ARGUMENT

Lionel Tiger and Robin Fox say that war "is not a human action but a male action; war is not a human problem but a male problem." If nuclear weapons could be curbed for a year and women could be put into "all the menial and mighty military posts in the world," these authors declare, there would be no war. They immediately concede that this proposition is but a fantasy, and a totally unrealistic one at that, because the human "biogrammar" (a term they use more or less the way others use "genetic program") ensures that such a thing could never happen. Men, they say, have evolved as hunters who band into groups and turn their aggressiveness out against common enemies or prey (1971, 212–13). Political structures in modern societies are formed on this primeval hunting model, and, naturally, men dominate these structures as well. Tiger speculates that women, who do not bond and cooperate as effectively as men, could be given positions in government by special mandate. He feels, however, that it might be quite unwise to expect that even this effort could effect much change (1970, 270–72); presumably, attempts to subvert biologically natural tendencies are not likely to succeed.

Barash accepts the idea that males bond and exclude women from political power (1981, 187–89), though he emphasizes the grounding of male aggression in the competition for reproductive opportunities and reproductively relevant resources (174, for example). He argues that women are only allowed political power if they are in some sense "desexed," by age and/or physical unattractiveness. Otherwise, men refuse to recognize a woman's authority, even when she manages to gain admittance to the male "club" (189–90).

Another writer on biological topics, Melvin Konner, also suggests that, because they are less aggressive than men, women should be placed in authority in order to "buffer" or "dampen" violent conflict between nations (1982, xviii, 126, 420). He seems to reject hunting bands as the evolutionary explanation for human aggression, though he does cite Tiger's work and allows that "something happens when men get together in groups; it is not well understood, but it is natural, and it is altogether not very nice" (203–206). Like Barash, Konner is more impressed with the notion that male aggression is explained by competition for the reproductive resources provided by females: eggs and parental care.

The suggestion that women might be more peaceful than men in positions of power is thus immediately and quite effectively undone by the theorists' other assumptions about natural differences. It is women and men, and the social consequences of these differences. It is a rather neat irony—that the qualities that might save the world are kept out of the public sphere by the very biological order that produces them. (Konner does not say women must always be excluded from power, though he says that it is pointless to use violent female rulers of the past as models for the future because they "have invariably been embedded in and bound by an almost totally masculine power structure, and have gotten where they were by being unrepresentative of their gender" [1982, 126]. He does not say how to implement his suggestion that "average" women be allowed to control the world's arsenals.)

The argument that women are inevitably excluded from political life also

OYAMA

appears, of course, in past and present antifeminist writings on the necessity of patriarchy (see Sayers 1982, for discussion; and Goldberg 1973, for a relatively recent example). Partly because biological arguments have often been associated with reactionary politics, it is now common for theorists to declare their liberal values, deny that biological treatments are necessarily either deterministic or conservative, and emphasize that biological explanation is not the same as moral approval. Then the theorists typically call on us to know our natures in order to transcend them. Barash, for example, asks whether we can use our understanding to overrule the biological "whisperings from within" (1982, 198). At the same time, they often warn against trying to challenge the boundaries and constraints our genes set for us. Charles Lumsden and E. O. Wilson warn that trying to escape these constraints risks the "very essence of humanness." They advise us to learn what the limits are and to set our goals within them (1981, 359-60), while Barash declares that denying natural sex differences is "likely to generate discontent" (1981, 116; for a critique of the language of constraints and limits, see Oyama 1985).

The relationship between politics and science is a complex one, and, though I think it can be argued that at any particular time some scientific approaches tend to be associated with and/or imply certain attitudes toward the moral and political worlds, there is no direct link between reactionary values and an interest in, for example, sociobiological analysis. Biologists become quite as annoyed at having their politics misrepresented as anyone else, and to assume that someone who emphasizes biological bases of human behavior is automatically a "crypto-nazi" is to engage in just the sort of reductionist thinking I am criticizing in this paper. A crucial link between one's scientific and political views is one's conception of will and possibility, and this notion is rarely made explicit. Just because the relationships are so complicated, however, it becomes very important to make assumptions explicit whenever possible, for it is these hidden assumptions that structure the arguments and invite the conclusions.

Examples of feminist essentialism are found in Pam McAllister's collection, *Reweaving the Web of Life* (1982). In "The Prevalence of the Natural Law within Women," Connie Salamone describes women's roles in protecting both the species' young and the natural law that governs the world. This role, if it is not subverted by male values, endows females with a special affinity to other animals and tends to give rise to concern over animal rights and vegetarianism. Salamone contrasts the female "aesthetic of untampered biological law" with "the artificial aesthetic of male science" (1982, 365–66). In "Patriarchy: A State of War," Barbara Zanotti invokes Mary Daly's concept of women's *biophilia* (love for life) and describes the history of patriarchy as the history of war. She asserts that, in making war, patriarchy attacks not the opposing military force but women, who represent life. Soldiers, she suggests, are encour-

524

OYAMA

aged to identify military aggression with sexual aggression, so that "the language of war is the language of gynocide" (1982, 17).

Here I have addressed some versions of the argument: that women are inherently less aggressive than men, war is caused by male aggression, and women are thus somehow more capable than men of bringing about peace—or, at least, if they were in power, women would be less destructive than men. It is a skeletal argument, of course, abstracted from very different sorts of writings.

The transition from individual to international conflict is not necessarily direct; for Tiger and Fox (1971), Barash (1981), and Zanotti (1982), for example, war is specifically the aggression of male-bonded men in groups, and Tiger (1970, 219) distinguishes between individual and group violence. Furthermore, the connection between aggression and peacemaking is not clear. Especially in the work of the male scientists cited above, it is *lack* of aggressiveness, rather than any positive quality, that is emphasized. Even in a world in which women are traditionally defined by their deficits, I'm not sure that peacemaking and peacekeeping should be seen as merely passive (to invoke another loaded dichotomy) results of low levels of aggression. Recent radical feminists are more likely to point out positive female qualities of nurturance, sensitivity to connections, and peacefulness. (I follow Jaggar 1983, and Sayers 1982, in using the term *radical* here. For the purposes of this essay, it entails a tendency to speak of essential feminine qualities in a positive, even celebratory way, rather than insisting on women's basic similarities to men.)

525

LUMPING: HOW TO IGNORE IMPORTANT DISTINCTIONS

The arguments all require that aggression be somehow unitary. They depend on, and encourage, certain kinds of illegitimate "lumping." One sort of lumping is definitional; that is, all sorts of behavior, feelings, intentions, and effects of actions are grouped together as aggressive. Tiger's definition, for example, is so broad that it embraces all "effective action which is part of a process of mastery of the environment"; violence is one outcome of such aggressive activity, but not the only one (1970, 203). That women do not bond in agressive groups implies, then, that they are less capable of "effective action" in the service of "mastery of the environment"—a sweeping statement indeed, and one that bodes ill for any political action on the part of women.

Another approach that allows us to treat aggression as a uniform quantity is cross-species lumping. Very different phenomena often are equated so that, for example, mounting or fighting in rodents, territoriality in fish or birds, and hunting, murder, or political competition in humans are all "aggressive" behaviors. Then there is the lumping of levels of analysis. The activity of nations and institutions is reductively collapsed to the level of individuals or even of hormones or genes. Finally, there is developmental lumping. Activity levels in new-

OYAMA

born babies, rough-and-tumble play in young children, fighting or delinquen-
cy in teenagers, and decisions of national leaders in wars are viewed as somehow developmentally continuous, or "the same." Sex differences in these behaviors are then seen as manifestations of basic sex differences in aggressiveness
(see Money and Erhardt 1972 for a flawed but highly influential treatment of
some sex differences; see also critiques by Bleier 1984; Fausto-Sterling 1985;
and volumes in the Genes and Gender series; also see Klama 1988 for treatment
of more general issues in aggression studies).

Much of this lumping depends on very common modern-day versions of
preformationism and essentialism. Today we think of preformationism as an
archaic relic of outmoded thought, and we snicker about the absurd idea that
there could be little people curled up in sperm or egg cells. But replacing
curled-up people with curled-up blueprints or programs for people is not so
different. That is, whether we speak of aggression in the genes or coded instructions for aggression in genes, we haven't made much conceptual
progress. What is central to preformationist thought is not the literal presence
of fully formed creatures in germ cells but, rather, a way of thinking about
development–development as revelation of preformed nature or essence, as
expression of preexisting program or plan, rather than as contingent series of
constructive interactions, transformations, and emergences. It is a view that
makes real development irrelevant, since the basic "information," or form, is
there from the beginning, a legacy from our evolutionary ancestors (see Oyama 1985, for fuller treatment of these issues).

Nor is the basic reasoning much changed by the less-deterministic-sound-
ing language of biological predispositions, propensities, or limits to flexibility;
the assumptions underlying these apparently more moderate formulations are
not substantially different from the more dichotomous ones that people
ridicule these days. Similarly, saying that, of course, nature combines with, or
interacts with, nurture shows continued reliance on a biological nature defined by genes before development begins and moderated or deflected by an
external, environmental nurture. Even though no one claims our natures to
be absolutely uniform and immutable, the somewhat softer language of genetic predispositions and tendencies shares the logical weaknesses of strict determinism, even if it seems to give us more possibilities for change. One problem is that, in this more moderate sort of account, the genes still define the
boundaries within which action is possible, and they still constitute the ultimate source of control. (Barash likens us to horses being ridden by genetic
riders who give us considerable freedom but who remain in firm command
[1981, 200]). A puzzle for those who hold this view is how to conceptualize a
"we" that is pitted against our genes in a struggle for control over "our" behavior. Another puzzle, for feminists who embrace the argument for inherent
male aggression and dominance, is how to mobilize for change in a world
populated by inherently aggressive and dominant males.

OYAMA

WHAT IS THE POINT OF THIS CRITIQUE?

It is important to be clear about what I am not doing when I critize the nature-nurture opposition or the lumping of different definitions, species, levels of analysis, and developmental phenomena that often accompanies it. I am not saying that aggression, however it is defined, is unimportant. I am not denying that nations are composed of individuals and that individuals are composed of cells, chemicals, and so on. I am not denying that understanding these parts might help us to understand the wholes of which our world is composed. I am not, therefore, rejecting research on individuals, hormones, neurons, and genes, including those of other species. I am not making an environmentalist argument—that biology is irrelevant, that genes don't count, and that everything about our behaviors can be changed (these three are not the same argument, and one of our problems is that we tend to lump them at the same time that we lump biological arguments). I am not even denying certain constancies or similarities among individuals within and across societies, though often we are rather cavalier with our methods of demonstrating these likenesses.

What I am saying is that analysis should be conducted in the interests of the eventual synthesis of a complex, multilevelled reality (just as temporary lumping—of diverse essentialist treatments of aggression, for example—can serve the elaboration of a more complex argument). The levels I have in mind here are not like onion skins that can be stripped away to reveal a more basic reality. After all, when you take away enough of an onion's layers, there's nothing left to reveal. Rather, they are levels of analysis whose interrelationships must never be assumed, but discovered. We will never understand the role of genes and hormones in individual lives or of individuals in society unless we move beyond traditional oppositions. We will never gain insight into the possibilities of different developmental pathways if we assume them to be fixed on the basis of an inappropriate argument. This is the point at which the environmental and biological determinists, as well as the more moderate "in-betweenists" are unwitting allies: they usually agree on what it would mean for something to be biological or cultural even as they argue about relative contributions of genes and learning.

If we want to use scientific analysis to answer questions, we must know what questions we are asking, or we'll never know what evidence could help us answer them. And if we want to fight the good fight, we must know what the enemy is, or we will waste precious time and energy that may not be ours to waste. (Note; I have said what the enemy is, not who, because in this case I am concerned with ways of thinking, not people, that make our task harder.)

QUESTIONS, CONCERNS, AND ANSWERS

We reveal a great deal of confusion when we ask if something is biological. We might be asking about the chemical processes associated with some be-

527

OYAMA

havior, for instance–this is a matter of the level of analysis, and such questions can be asked about any behavior, learned or unlearned, common or uncommon, fixed or labile. We might be asking about development: Does a given behavior, for example, seem to be learned? Is it present at birth? (These questions are not the same thing, since learning can be prenatal.) We might be asking about evolutionary history, which in turn, resolves into several kinds of questions: Is the behavior present in phylogenetic relatives? When did it appear in our own evolutionary line, and why? We might be asking what role, if any, a character now plays in enhancing survival and reproduction. We might be asking whether variation in a character is heritable in a given population (whether differences in the character are correlated with genetic differences). This last question has to do with population genetics, which are useful if one wants to know about the possibility of artificial or natural selection in the population.

These are very different questions for which different evidence is relevant, and they do not exhaust the catalog of biological queries.

None has any automatic bearing on any other, and lumping them together as genetic or biological simply creates confusion and faulty inferences. Often, however, a person asking whether some trait is biological is not interested in these particular questions at all but has something else in mind. She or he is concerned about the inevitability of a trait, or its unchangeability in the individuals evincing it, or its goodness, justifiability, or naturalness, or perhaps the consequences of trying to change or prevent it (will it come bursting out as soon as we drop our guard? Will intervention do more harm than good?). Scientists frequently share these concerns and the confusions that link them to biology.

None of the scientific questions listed earlier–about evolution, developmental timing, or process or level of analysis–is relevant to these underlying concerns. Our misguided but deeply embedded beliefs about genes and biology, however, cloud the issue. *Genetic* and *biological*, in fact, are often effective synonyms for *inevitability, unchangeability*, and *normality*. The common concept of genetic control and guidance of development implies that fate, or at least the range of potential fates, is set before birth. But persons must develop, and development is the result of a whole system; there is no clear way to see the role of genes as more basic, formative, directive, controlling, or limiting than other aspects of system, and the role of any particular factor depends on its interrelations among the others.

Concerns about inevitability are really about possible developmental pathways, not about past or present ones. (Even wondering whether a present state of affairs is immutable implies wanting to know *what would happen if . . .*, and wondering whether it was inevitable implies wanting to know *what would have happened if. . .*) When Barash speculates that male parenting in humans, as in other mammals, is "not nearly as innate as modern sexual egalitarians" think, he seems to be saying something about the probability of reaching certain personal and political goals, and he certainly seems to believe that "innateness" (a concept he never defines satisfactorily) has something to do with the difficulties that he thinks "sexual egalitarians" will encounter (1981, 88).

Because any pathway is the function of an entire developmental system, which includes much more than genes, its qualities are not predictable from genes alone. We would have to understand development extremely well to know whether the necessary conditions for constancy or change in patterns of aggressive behavior would be present in any particular alternative world. To say anything intelligible about possible relationships among nations, we would need to know a great deal about issues that are not in any simple way related to particular sorts of individual aggressiveness.

Inevitability is not predictable from observations at the morphological or biochemical levels of analysis. It is not predictable from the role of learning in the development of a behavior or from its time of appearance. It is not predictable from phylogenetic history, a pattern of heritability in some population, prevalence in certain environments, or even universality. That is, none of these traditional scientific biological questions is relevant to the concerns that most often motivate the questions. To ask biology to address concerns about desirability, furthermore, is to ask science to do our moral work for us.

We must decide what kind of world we want, and why. We won't necessarily succeed in bringing it about, but we shouldn't be deterred prematurely from trying because of biological evidence of whatever variety, either because we believe the biological, in any of its senses, is fixed or because we believe it is dangerous to tamper with what we think of as natural. Similarly, we shouldn't be complacent about natural features we might value (virtues that are thought basically feminine in this world won't necessarily persist in the one that's coming). There is a tendency to view the biological as static, but it is, in fact, historical at all levels. When I say "history," I am referring to contingency, interaction, possibility, and change. (The habit of asking whether some feature of our world is the result of biology or history is thus deeply mistaken). When we ask about biology, though, our concerns tend to be mythological, not historical. Here I do not mean myth as wrong, or "bad," science (though it might be) but as a way of thinking that reveals ultimate truth, eternal necessity, and legitimacy.

Lionel Tiger, chronicler of male bonding and aggression, refers to *Lord of the Flies*, the widely read story of a group of English schoolboys. Marooned on an island, the lads rapidly degenerate into a horde of savage little creatures. Apparently, the author of the book, William Golding, has said he wanted to construct a myth, a tale that would give the key to the whole of life and experience (cited in Tiger 1970, 207). The feminist Zanotti, too, accepts the centrality of male bonding to individual and social life in her claim that, in making war, men are eternally attacking and destroying women (1982, 17).

529

OYAMA

Both theorists invoke unchanging essence to explain gender, relations between men and women, and, thus, the world. But it is a static world in which ancient tragedies are played out again and again according to primal necessity, not a historical world in which necessity and nature arise by process and then give way to other necessities and natures. Nature, then, should not be seen as one term in the traditional nature-nurture. genes-environment, biology-culture pair. It is not a cause of development but rather an emerging product of development.

PLAYING THE GAME

It should be clear by now how I feel about several common strategies for dealing with biological arguments. When someone says, "It's biological," we reply "No, it's not, it's cultural," when instead we should be asking why the cultural and the biological are treated as alternatives in the first place and just what we (and they) really mean by either explanation. I call this the Protesting Too Much Syndrome, because we are often afraid the trait in question is biological in one or more of the mistaken senses described above. Or someone says that we are innately inferior, and we counter, "No, we're not, you are," rather than rejecting the assumption of essential nature that allows *any* pronouncements of this sort. This second strategy I have dubbed the Protesting Too Little Syndrome. It entails agreeing that differences are biological, but reversing the evaluative polarity. Male nature is bad; female nature is good. While it offers the momentary satisfaction of turning the tables, it is based on all the mistaken ideas about nature and nuture that, I think, get us all into so much difficulty—too great a price to pay for Mother Nature's favor. The solution is not to protest precisely the correct amount nor to find the degree of biological determination that is "just right," like some Goldilocks trying to find comfort in a house that is not her own. Rather, it is to protest a whole lot about the *very rules of the discourse*. We mustn't allow the argument to be defined for us. Instead, we must be reflective enough to rethink it.

I am not saying that we ought to throw out everything and start from the ground up. We couldn't do it if we wanted to. But when there are ample grounds for doubting the validity of a conceptual framework or a set of issues, as is the case with the nature-nuture complex, we do ourselves no favor by blindly accepting the terms of the game. Some of our gravest problems come, after all, from letting others set terms for us. The burden of clarification certainly does not rest entirely with women, but, if we shirk our part, how can we do justice to the struggle?

Instead of pitting one mythical account against another, instead of searching for a morally or emotionally resonant evolutionary past to explain the present and then projecting it into the future, we must focus on real historical processes whose courses are not foreseeable on the basis of any account of nature as manifested in hunter-gatherers, baboons or chimps, hormones, brain centers, or DNA strands. I speak here of individual developmental history as well as historical change on the societal level, for it is within these processes that nature and possibility are defined.

ARE WOMEN LESS AGGRESSIVE AND, HENCE, LESS WARLIKE?

I could say much about aggression and about women and maybe even a little about war, but, in this essay I haven't said much about any of them. Perhaps the reason is that the essentialist theories I have been discussing don't say much about these topics either. Instead, I have focused on the ways we think about these topics. War is about politics, diplomacy, economics, and historical continuity and change in relations among people, not about brain centers, testosterone, or rough-and-tumble play. It is like a fight between individuals only by analogy, just as certain encounters between groups of ants is war only by analogy. Perhaps it is significant that when sociobiologist David Barash coauthors a book on preventing nuclear war (Barash and Lipton 1982), it contains nothing about different capacities and contributions of males and females but instead gives lists of very pragmatic suggestions for effective action. Obviously, I would never claim that women have no role in national and international politics, but neither can I make sense of the notion that we ought to be somehow inserted into public life because of some mythic direct line to life, peace, and love. Men are not a plague, and women are not a cure.

REFERENCES

Barash, D. P. 1981. *The whisperings within*. New York: Harper and Row.

531

Barash, D.P., and J. E. Lipton. 1982.*Stop nuclear war!* New York: Grove Press.

Bleier, R. 1984. *Science and gender: A critique of biology and its theories on women*. New York: Pergamon Press.

Fausto-Sterling, A. 1985. *Myths of gender: Biological theories about women and men*. New York: Basic Books.

Goldberg, S. 1973. *The inevitability of patriarchy*, New York: Morrow.

Jaggar, A.M. 1983. *Feminist politics and human nature: Reprint*, Totowa, N.J.: Rowman and Allanheld.

Klama, J. 1988. *Aggression: The myth of the beast within*. New York: Wiley.

Konner, M. 1982. *The tangled wing: Biological constraints on the human spirit*. New York: Holt, Rinehart and Winston.

Lumsden, C. J., and E. O. Wilson. 1981. *Genes, mind, and culture*, Cambridge, Mass.: Harvard University Press.

McAllister, P., ed. 1982. *Reweaving the web of life*. Philadelphia: New Society Publishers.

Money, J., and A. A. Ehrhardt. 1972. *Man and woman, boy and girl*. Baltimore: Johns Hopkins University Press.

Oyama, S. 1981.What does the phenocopy copy? *Psychological Reports* 48:571–81.

———.1982.A reformulation of the concept of maturation. In *Perspectives in ethology*, vol. 5. edited by P.P.G. Bateson and P. H. Klopfer, 101–31. New York: Plenum.

———.1985. *The ontogeny of information: Developmental systems and evolution*. Cambridge: Cambridge University Press.

OYAMA

Salamone, C. 1982. The prevalence of the natural law within women: Women and animal rights. In *Reweaving the web of life: Feminism and nonviolence*, edited by P. McAllister, 364–75. Philadelphia: New Society Publishers.

Sayers, J. 1982. *Biological politics*. London: Tavistock.

Tiger, L. 1970. *Men in groups*. New York: Vintage Books.

Tiger, L., and R. Fox. 1971. *The imperial animal*. New York: Holt, Rinehart and Winston.

Zanotti, B. 1982. *Patriarchy: A state of war*. In *Reweaving the web of life*, edited by P. McAllister, 16-19. Philadelphia: New Society Publishers.

FEMINIST POLITICIZATION
A Comment

bell hooks

ALWAYS A part of my inner listening self closes down when I hear the words "the personal is political." Yes, I understand them. I understand that aspect of early feminist consciousness-raising that urged every listening woman to see her problems, especially problems she experienced as the outcome of sexism and sexist oppression, as political issues. To begin on the inside and move outside. To begin with the self as starting point, then to move beyond self-reflection to an awareness of collective reality. This was the promise these words held. But that promise was all too easily unfulfilled, broken. A culture of domination is necessarily narcissistic. To take woman to the self as starting point for politicization, woman who, in white-supremacist, capitalist patriarchy, is particularly made, socially constructed, to think only me—my body—I constitute a universe—all that truly matters. To take her—this woman—to the self as starting point for politicization is necessarily risky.

We see now the danger in "the personal is political." The personal most known as private, as that space where there is no intervention from the outside, as that which can be kept to the self, as that which does not extend beyond. Knowing the way this culture conceives the personal, the promise was to transform the meaning by linking it with the political, a word so associated in the minds of even small school children with government, with a world of affairs outside the body, the private, the self. We see now the danger. "The personal is political." No sense of connection between one's person and a larger material reality—no sense of what the political is. In this phrase, what most resonates is the word personal—not the word political. Unsure of the political, each female presumes knowledge of the person—the personal. No need then to search for the meaning of political, simpler to stay with the personal, to make synonymous the personal and the political. Then the self does not become that which one moves into to move beyond, or to connect with. It stays in place, the starting point from which one need never move. If the personal and the political are one and the same, then there is no politicization, no way to become the radical feminist subject.

Perhaps these words are too strong. Perhaps some of you remember the poignancy, the depth, the way this slogan reached into your life, grasped hold of your experience—and you did move. You did understand better the link between personal experience and political reality. The ways individual women were able to concretely find the deep structure of this slogan, use it to radicalize consciousness, need not be denied. Still, to name the danger, the ways it led feminist politics into identity politics, is crucial for the construction of a social space, a radical front wherein politicization of consciousness, of the self, can become real in everyday life.

This slogan had such power because it insisted on the primacy of the personal, not in a narcissistic way, but in its implied naming of the self as a site for politicization, which was in this society a very radical challenge to notions of self and identity. The challenging meaning behind the slogan, however, was not consistently conveyed. While stating "the personal is political" did highlight feminist concern with self, it did not insist on a connection between politicization and transformation of consciousness. It spoke most immediately to the concerns women had about self and identity. Again, the radical insistence on the primary of a politicized self was submerged, subsumed within a larger cultural framework wherein focus on identity was already legitimized within structures of domination. Obsessive, narcissistic concern with "finding an identity" was already a popular cultural preoccupation, one that deflected attention away from radical politics. Feminist focus on self was then easily linked not to a process of radical politicization, but to a process of de-politicization. Popularly, the important quest was not to radically change our relationship to self and identity, to educate for critical consciousness, to become politically engaged and committed, but to explore one's identity, to affirm and assert the primacy of the self as it already existed. Such a focus was strengthened by an emphasis within feminist movement on lifestyle, on being politically correct in one's representation of self rather than being political.

Exasperated with identity politics, Jenny Bourne begins her essay, "Homelands of the Mind: Jewish Feminism and Identity Politics," with the assertion:

> Identity Politics is all the rage. Exploitation is out (it is extrinsically determinist). Oppression is in (it is intrinsically personal). What is to be done has been replaced by who am I. Political culture has ceded to cultural politics. The material world has passed into the metaphysical. The Blacks, the Women, the Gays have all searched for themselves. And now combining all their quests, has arrived the quest for Jewish feminist identity.

Bourne's essay speaks to the crisis of political commitment and engagement engendered by relentless focus on identity. I wholeheartedly affirm her effort to expose the ways identity politics has led to the construction of a notion of feminist movement that is, as she sees it, "separatist individualistic, and inward-looking." She asserts: "The organic relationship we tried to forge between the personal and the political has been so degraded that now the only area of politics deemed legitimate is the personal." However, I think it essential not to mock or ridicule the metaphysical but to find a constructive point of connection between material struggle and metaphysical concerns. We cannot oppose the emphasis on identity politics by inverting the logic and devaluing the personal. It does not further feminist movement to ignore issues of identity or to critique concern with self without posing alternative approaches, without addressing in a dialectical manner the issue of feminist politicization—the link between efforts to socially construct self, identity in an oppositional framework, one that resists domination, and allows for the greatest degree of well-being.

To challenge identity politics we must offer strategies of politicization that enlarge our conception of who we are, that intensify our sense of intersubjectivity, our relation to a collective reality. We do this by reemphasizing how history, political science, psychoanalysis, and diverse ways of knowing can be used to inform our ideas of self and identity. Politicization of the self can have its starting point in an exploration of the personal wherein what is first revolutionized is the way we think about the self. To begin revisioning, we must acknowledge the need to examine the self from a new, critical standpoint. Such a perspective, while it would insist on the self as a site for politicization, would equally insist that simply describing one's experience of exploitation or oppression is not to become politicized. It is not sufficient to know the personal but to know—to speak it in a different way. Knowing the personal might mean naming spaces of ignorance, gaps in knowledge, ones that render us unable to link the personal with the political.

In *Ain't I a Woman*, I pointed to the distinction between experiencing a form of exploitation and understanding the particular structure of domina-

535

HOOKS

tion that is the cause. The opening paragraph of the chapter on "Racism and Feminism: The Issue of Accountability" begins:

> American women of all races are socialized to think of racism solely in the context of race hatred. Specifically in the case of black and white people. For most women, the first knowledge of racism as institutionalized oppression is engendered either by direct personal experience or through information gleaned from conversations, books, television, or movies. Consequently, the American woman's understanding of racism as a political tool of colonialism and imperialism is severely limited. To experience the pain of race hatred or to witness that pain is not to understand its origin, evolution, or impact on world history.

Many women engaged in feminist movement assumed that describing one's personal experience of exploitation by men was to be politicized. Politicization necessarily combines this process (the naming of one's experience) with critical understanding of the concrete material reality that lays the groundwork for that personal experience. The work of understanding that groundwork and what must be done to transform it is quite different from the effort to raise one's consciousness about personal experience even as they are linked.

Feminist critiques of identity politics which call attention to the way it undermines feminist movement should not deny the importance of naming and giving voice to one's experience. It must be continually stressed that this is only part of the process of politicization, one which must be linked to education for critical consciousness that teaches about structures of domination and how they function. It is understanding the latter that enables us to imagine new possibilities, strategies for change and transformation. The extent to which we are able to link radical self-awareness to collective struggle to change and transform self and society will determine the fate of feminist revolution.

Focus on self in feminist movement has not been solely the province of privileged white women. Women of color, many of whom were struggling to articulate and name our experience for the first time, also began to focus attention on identity in static and non-productive ways. Jenny Bourne focusses on individual black women who promoted identity politics, calling attention to a statement by the Combahee River Collective which reads: "The most profound and potentially the most radical politics come directly out of our own identity as opposed to working to end somebody else's oppression." This statement asserts the primacy of identity politics. Coming from radical black women, it served to legitimize the emphasis in feminist movement on identity—that to know one's needs as an individual is to be political. It is in many ways a very problematic statement. If one's identity is constructed from a base of power and privilege gained from participation in and acceptance of structures of domination, it is not a given that focus on naming that identity will

536

lead to a radicalized consciousness, a questioning of that privilege, or to active resistance. It is possible to name one's personal experience without committing oneself to transforming or changing that experience.

To imply, as this statement does, that individuals cannot successfully radicalize their consciousness and their actions as much by working in resistance struggles that do not directly effect their lives is to underestimate the power of solidarity. It is only as allies with those who are exploited and oppressed, working in struggles for liberation, that individuals who are not victimized demonstrate their allegiance, their political commitment, their determination to resist, to break with the structures of domination that offer them personal privilege. This holds true for individuals from oppressed and exploited groups as well. Our consciousness can be radicalized by acting to eradicate forms of domination that do not have direct correspondence with our identities and experiences. Bourne states:

> Identity politics regards the discovery of identity as its supreme goal. Feminists even assert that discovering an identity is an act of resistance. The mistake is to view identity as an end rather than a means… Identity is not merely a precursor to action, it is also created through action.

Indeed, for many exploited and oppressed peoples the struggle to create an identity, to name one's reality is an act of resistance because the process of domination—whether it be imperialist colonization, racism, or sexist oppression—has stripped us of our identity, devalued language, culture, appearance. Again, this is only a stage in the process of revolution (one Bourne seems to deny has any value), but it must not be denigrated, even if people of privilege repeat this gesture so often that it has no radical implications. For example: the slogan "black is beautiful" was an important popular expression of resistance to white supremacy (of course that expression loses meaning and power if it is not linked to a process of politicization where black people learn to see ourselves as subjects rather than as objects, where as an expression of being subjects we act to transform the world we live in so that our skin no longer signifies that we will be degraded, exploited). It would be a grave mistake to suggest that politicization of self is not part of the process by which we prepare ourselves to act most effectively for radical social change. Only when it becomes narcissistic or when, as Bourne states, it naively suggests that "structural, material issues of race, class, and power, would first be resolved in terms of personal consciousness" does it diminish liberatory struggle.

When I chart a map of feminist politicization, of how we become more politically self-aware, I begin with the insistence on commitment to education for critical consciousness. Much of that education does start with examining the self from a new, critical perspective. To this end, confession and memory can be used constructively to illuminate past experiences, particularly when such experience is theorized. Using confession and memory as ways

537

HOOKS

of naming reality enables women and men to talk about personal experience as part of a process of politicization which places such talk in a dialectical context. This allows us to discuss personal experience in a different way, in a way that politicizes not just the telling, but the tale. Theorizing experience as we tell personal narrative, we have a sharper, keener sense of the end that is desired by the telling. An interesting and constructive use of memory and confession is narrated in the book, *Female Sexualization: A Collective Work of Memory*, edited by Frigga Haug. Collectively, the women who speak work not just to name their experience but to place that experience in a theoretical context. They use confession and memory as tools of intervention which allow them to unite scientific knowledge with everyday experience. So as not to place undue emphasis on the individual, they consistently link individual experience to collective reality. Story-telling becomes a process of historicization. It does not remove women from history but enables us to see ourselves as part of history. The act of writing autobiographical stories enabled the women in the Haug book to see themselves form a different perspective, one which they describe as a "politically necessary form of cultural labor." They comment, "It makes us live our lives more consciously." Used constructively, confession and memory are tools that heighten self-awareness; they need not make us solely inward-looking.

Feminist thinkers in the United States use confession and memory primarily as a way to narrate tales of victimization, which are rarely rendered dialectically. This focus means that we do not have various and diverse accountings of all aspects of female experience. As we struggle to learn more about how women relate to one another, to men, and to children in everyday life, how we construct strategies of resistance and survival, it is useful to rely on confession and memory as documentary sources. We must, however, be careful not to promote the construction of narratives of female experience that become so normative that all experience that does not fit the model is deemed illegitimate or unworthy of investigation.

Rethinking ways to constructively use confession and memory shifts the focus away from mere naming of one's experience. It enables feminist thinkers to talk about identity in relation to culture, history, politics, whatever and to challenge the notion of identity as static and unchanging. To explore identity in relation to strategies of politicization, feminist thinkers must be willing to see the female self anew, to examine how we are gendered critically and analytically from various standpoints. In early feminist consciousness-raising, confession was often the way to share negative traumas, the experience of male violence for example. Yet there remain many unexplored areas of female experience that need to be fully examined, thereby widening the scope of our understanding of what is to be female in this society. Imagine a group of black women working to educate ourselves for critical consciousness, exploring our relation to radical politics, to left politics. We might better understand our collective reluctance to commit ourselves to feminist struggle, to revolutionary politics or we might also chart those experiences that prepare and enable us to make such commitments.

There is much exciting work to be done when we use confession and memory as a way to theorize experience, to deepen our awareness, as part of the process of radical politicization. Often we experience pleasure and joy when we share personal stories, closeness, intimacy. This is why the personal has had such a place in feminist discourse. To reaffirm the power of the personal while simultaneously not getting trapped in identity politics, we must work to link personal narratives with knowledge of how we must act politically to change and transform the world.

PART IX

BREAKING OUT
Diagnosis and Therapy After Modernity

DISAPPEARANCES, SILENCES, AND ANXIOUS RHETORIC
Gender in Abnormal Psychology Textbooks

Jeanne Marecek

chapter 29

THE FIELD of abnormal psychology has intrinsically to do with definitions of the good life, and judgements about proper and improper forms of behavior and social relations. Thus, when students study abnormal psychology, they learn about historically-contingent, socially-situated moralities, disguised as medico-scientific verities. In addition to performing this cultural function, courses serve a disciplinary function: They convey to students an account of the operations of the discipline, its rightful place in the culture, and the status of psychologist.

In spite of the large number ot textbooks in abnormal psychology, the genre is characterized by remarkable uniformity. Books are typically 600–700 pages in length, and they are accompanied by a standard assortment of resource manuals, "test banks," and lecture outlines for instructors, along with study guides and other items for students. Uniformity is most apparent, however, in the table of contents. There, individuality, creativity, innovation, even distinctiveness seem to be out of the question. This conformity might be an indication of high consensus, but it seems more likely to be market-driven conservatism.

This project began with what seemed to be a simple question: How have textbooks in abnormal psychology incorporated the knowledge produced during the past 25 years by feminist psychologists? The question quickly led to other questions: Why the resistance to feminist thought? What would be put at risk were women, gender, and feminist thought to enter the text?

Feminism, gender, and abnormal psychology. While it might have seemed easy to define feminism in the early 1970s, feminist thought in the 1990s forms a rich tapestry of interlocking, though not always compatible, ideas. Many varieties of feminism, allied with different strains of social and political thought, and with a variety of other critical practices, have emerged. A definitive statement on feminism is beside the point here. Instead, I will describe in brief some feminist critiques of clinical psychology, and some directions in scholarship and activism.

Viewed from a feminist perspective, the history of the field reveals a troubled—and troubling—relationship to women. Diagnoses such as nymphomania, hysteria, neurasthenia, erotomania, kleptomania, and masochism have served to enforce conformity to norms of female domesticity, subordination, and subservience to men's sexual needs: at times diagnoses have reaffirmed class distinctions as well (cf., Camhi, 1993; Groneman, 1993; King, 1990; Showalter, 1985). Sexist uses of diagnosis are not confined to the past, however. Consider the recent proliferation of diagnostic categories for premenstrual difficulties: Premenstrual Syndrome, Late Luteal Dysphoric Disorder, Premenstrual Dysphoric Disorder. The categories would seem to reinstate once again the idea that the female psyche is governed by the (often unruly) female reproductive tract, an idea that has occurred over and over in the history of Western medicine, since at least the time of Hippocrates (Vieth, 1965). Moreover, if women's anger, depression, and discontent come to be interpreted as medical or psychiatric symptoms, difficult and distressing life experiences may be disregarded.

At times, treatments devised for women have served to victimize them further. In the late 19th century, Dr. S. Weir Mitchell of Philadelphia garnered high praise for his treatment of female neurasthenia, a treatment based on compulsory bedrest, over-feeding, and coerced deprivation of intellectual and social stimulation.[1] In England, Dr. Isaac Baker Brown advocated and practiced clitoridectomy as a cure for the "disease" of female masturbation. Brown asserted that although the sturdy women of the servant classes could survive masturbation, the fragile women of the upper classes could not, and would succumb to idiocy, mania, and death. Among those on whom he performed his surgical cure were wayward adolescent daughters and wives who threatened divorce. Questions about therapeutic practices are not confined to the

544

past. We might ask, for instance, about the complex of cultural forces and psychiatric wisdom that lay behind the widespread prescribing of Librium and Valium during the 1960s and 1970s as an anodyne for women's dissatisfaction and lack of fulfillment. We might also ask what role gender plays in negotiations about hospitalizing and discharging women and girls in psychiatric facilities (Holstein, 1987).

The last hundred years are peppered with repeated episodes in which mental health authorities have minimized or denied the sexual abuse of women and children, whether by disbelieving women's reports of childhood sexual abuse, by shifting blame from male perpetrators to victims and their mothers, or by trivializing the effects of victimization (e.g., James & MacKinnon, 1990). Moreover, uncomfortable parallels in both the abuse itself and the response of the mental health professions can be observed in cases in which women have been sexually victimized by their therapists (cf., Noel, 1992).

Protest and challenge have not been the only feminist responses to this history. Indeed, for the duration of the present feminist movement, clinical psychology has been a site for the production of new knowledge about disorders and treatments (Marecek & Hare-Mustin, 1991). Moreover, feminist practitioners have devised and documented new approaches to therapy, assessment, inpatient treatment, and supervision, as well as new forms of crisis intervention based on feminist principles (cf., Enns, 1993; Kravetz & Jones, 1991; Worell & Remer, 1992). Thousands of scholarly works have been published, and there are three journals *(Women and Therapy, Journal of Feminist Family Therapy,* and *Affilia)* devoted exclusively to these issues.

545

THE DISAPPEARING WOMAN

How do textbooks address the complicated and turbulent relationship of women and the clinical professions? How do they incorporate feminists' many contributions to knowledge? The answer is simple and disheartening: They do not. Not only is feminist knowledge virtually absent from the text, women themselves are more or less invisible. To be more precise, gender—as a social fact, as a category of human experience, and as a principle of social hierarchy—is rendered invisible. Key concepts in the study of women and gender—women, gender, sex differences, sex role, and gender role—do not even appear in the indexes of several leading abnormal psychology textbooks; nor do the indexes include entries pertaining to other categories of difference and hierarchy: race, African-Americans, socio-economic status, poverty, and unemployment.

Why these omissions? Once I would have answered that sexism was to blame, and accused the authors of either disavowing the importance of women and gender as objects of study, or of discrediting the intellectual contributions of women scholars. Now I think that answer is too simple (though not necessarily false). Feminist thought is excluded less because it is feminist

MARECEK

than because it flies in the face of psychology's presuppositions about what counts as legitimate knowledge and what are suitable objects and methods of study. The self-identity and aspirations of mainstream psychology, as well as the public image it carefully cultivates, cannot accommodate feminist questions, let alone feminist answers.

Let us return to abnormal psychology courses. Judging from the textbooks, the main pedagogical agenda is teaching a list of disorders gleaned from the most current version of the *Diagnostic and Statistical Manual of the American Psychiatric Association (DSM)*. One by one, chapter by chapter, the *DSM* categories are taken up; this textual strategy implicitly defines the student's goal as distinguishing one disorder from another. This goal can be questioned: Sharp boundaries between diagnostic categories are imposed, not found; in real life, distinctions are blurry and so-called textbook cases are seldom seen (cf., Nurcombe & Gallagher, 1986).

With the *DSM* as their frame of reference, the textbooks are organized around a disease model of psychopathology. In the disease model, disorders are considered real entities that, as Kessler puts it, "have an existence independent of the patient" (1990, p. 141). Not only do women disappear, but also the everyday identities and social categories—such as gender, race/ethnicity, and social class—that shape experience and life chances. Disorders are represented as abstracted entities, as if they existed outside history, and apart from the social, material, and cultural context. Lest the adoption of the disease model seem like a stylistic choice of no great import, let us remember that many of the most common and most debilitating disorders—schizophrenia, depression, anorexia, alcoholism, drug abuse, and suicide—vary dramatically in prevalence from one culture to another, and from one historical period to another. In our own time and place, different social groups vary widely in the risk for these disorders.

SILENCES: THE POLITICS OF DIAGNOSIS

The ebb and flow, fads and fashions, in the history of disorder suggests that diagnoses are inventions, not discoveries. Saying this does not deny that distressing, incapacitating, and destructive forms of behavior exist, or that some of these behaviors may have physiological antecedents or components. Instead, it points to a set of questions about the construct of "disorder." How does this construct figure in our accounts of otherwise unaccountable behavior? How is the boundary drawn between disorders on the one hand and crime, eccentricity, or alternative lifestyles on the other? Who is party to the negotiations that fix the boundaries, and who polices them? What kinds of claims-making activities surround the birth of new categories of disorders and the death of exhausted ones?

As feminist critiques have pointed out, pathologizing certain emotions and practices has served as a means of social control over women and members of other social groups such as immigrants, poor people, and ethnic minorities. Medico-scientific language and diagnostic labels are used in a variety of other persuasive appeals as well. For instance, some opponents of abortion have claimed the existence of Post-Abortion Trauma Syndrome, a psychological disorder that afflicts women after abortion. Some feminists have claimed the existence of Battered Woman Syndrome; this putative psychological disorder has been entered into the law by psychologists giving expert testimony on behalf of women who have assaulted or killed their batterers. A third example is the claim of a False Memory Syndrome, a condition in which individuals come to recall incidents of sexual abuse and other childhood traumas that never occurred.

What is at issue here is not whether some women regret choosing abortions, whether battered women suffer, or whether some people mistakenly recall events that did not occur. Certainly all these things happen, at least some of the time. Rather the issue is what purposes are served by rhetorically transforming the experiences into "syndromes" or "disorders," a transformation that lends the weight of scientific authority to activists' claims. And this opens the further question of the rhetorical uses of more conventional forms of medico-scientific language and of accepted diagnoses.

The prolonged debate over the medical and psychiatric status of premenstrual problems illustrates how diagnoses can be intertwined with economic power as well as social power. As documented by Mary Parlee (1989; 1993) and other participant-observers, corporate interests bankrolled the transformation of premenstrual problems into Premenstrual Syndrome (PMS). Pharmaceutical companies captured the scientific agenda by sponsoring consensus-building conferences that also served as media events. The American Psychiatric Association entered the picture in hopes of wresting jurisdiction over PMS away from gynecologists. The outcome of the latter struggle is the newly-minted DSM category of disorder, Premenstrual Dysphoric Disorder—and a guaranteed supply of psychiatry's long-time favorite patients, middle-class young women.

Why is it that textbooks in abnormal psychology skirt around such stories? Their discussions of categories of disorders portray them as if they were forged in the scientific laboratory, not in the fray of human relations and cultural contestation. Some will no doubt argue that political, ethical, and moral questions should be kept apart from scientific ones. I do not believe that such a separation is desirable, or even possible. But that is not the matter at hand. Whether separate from science or inextricably intertwined with it, political and moral questions deserve discussion by concerned and informed laypersons. What better place to find such a group of individuals than in an abnormal psychology classroom?

Concerns about the rhetorical power of diagnostic language and the possible scientific authority it confers are also pertinent in a local, immediate

547

MARECEK

way. Courses in abnormal psychology indoctrinate students into the specialized language of the mental health professions, and implicitly license them to speak it. Where will students learn about the ethical and moral responsibilities entailed by use of this powerful tool? Like knowledge itself, diagnostic language confers power, but that power is not necessarily benign.

THE ANXIOUS RHETORIC OF SCIENCE

From its beginning, feminism has challenged received truths about women's psychology. As evidence of bias in psychological research mounted, the focus of criticism expanded to the methods of inquiry themselves. In addition, the experiences of women who were working psychologists countered the image of the discipline as a democratic community of ideas. Thus one strain of feminist psychology is deeply skeptical of the values, assumptions, and normative practices of the discipline. This skepticism connects up with other critical intellectual movements, such as social constructionism and postmodern thought (cf., Bohan, 1992; Hare-Mustin & Marecek, 1990; Marecek, 19_ _.)

By and large, textbooks in abnormal psychology side-step the debates now raging in most disciplines about the nature of knowledge, and the processes by which it is produced and warranted. Consider this description of the field of abnormal psychology, paraphrased from the opening passage of a best-selling text:

> As in other sciences, workers gather information systematically in order to describe, predict, explain, and control the phenomena they study. This knowledge . . . is then used by clinical practitioners to detect, assess, and treat abnormal patterns of functioning.

This passage is a fiction, an idealization. It substitutes an orderly, reasoned, deliberate progression from knowledge to application in the place of an account of the actual operations of the discipline, which would invoke tentativeness, uncertainty, serendipity, and clinical guesswork. Moreover, the passage conceals the fact that psychological researchers have ignored many of the people most in need of practitioners' services—poor people, women, nonwhites; the unemployed (Graham, 1992; Osipow & Fitzgerald, 1993; Reid, 1993). Furthermore, the text does not even hint that many practitioners find much or even most research irrelevant, unilluminating, or even derisory (Kaye, 1990; Strupp, 1981).

Two additional myths about the field of psychology are given a prominent place in most textbooks; both call upon conventional, but dubious, ideologies of science. One is the idea that psychology, because it is a science, is necessarily benign, progressive, and humane. Textbook histories of abnormality are told in such a way that a deep divide appears between the so-called modern era and other eras. This divide is elaborated with a set of dichotomies: scien-

MARECEK

tific-superstitious; advanced-primitive; humane-brutal. The discontinuity between present and past is reinforced further by illustrations depicting the inhumane practices of "Other" eras: lunatics in chains in the asylums of the 1800s; colonists dunking witches; primitives engaged in gruesome ritual exorcisms. But showing that (some) pre-scientific practices were inhumane leaves unaddressed the question of whether science-based practices are necessarily humane. Viewed from the perspective of women and other disadvantaged groups, the modern era of abnormal psychology too often falls short of its humane aspirations. Furthermore, technological advances do not necessarily result in advances in human welfare. Consider, for example, the invention of nuclear weapons, or the degradation of the environment by industrial pollutants. Moreover, most observers agree that the advent of high-technology medicine has brought about a regrettable dehumanizing of its patients.

The second myth is that, as a science, psychology stands apart from the culture in which it is embedded. This myth denies that the selection of problems for study, as well as the theories, methods, and practices endorsed by the discipline, are influenced by moral values and political interests. This myth also denies that scientific definitions of abnormality and mental health reflect and reaffirm cultural standards. To what extent do such definitions also reflect the class- and gender-based experiences and interests of mental health professionals? Critical studies offer abundant evidence of the embeddedness of clinical psychology in twentieth-century American culture (cf, Cushman, 1993; Hare-Mustin & Marecek, 1986; Humphreys & Rappoport, 1993). We can ask, therefore, why textbooks seem so preoccupied with asserting the scientific status of psychology, and its detachment from the culture. What ideological ends are served by misrepresenting the actual operations of the discipline? To what extent are claims of scientific objectivity marshalled for the purpose of legitimizing the expertise of psychologists and bolstering the status of the discipline?

CHANGING THE SUBJECT

Whether by intention or not, textbooks perform functions beyond their stated goal of conveying up-to-date information to naive readers. The subject matter of abnormal psychology, whether or not it is cloaked in medico-scientific language, engages authors, instructors, and students in a moral discourse. In addition, abnormal psychology courses, like all courses, serve disciplinary functions, advocating a particular image of the discipline, one grounded more in aspiration than actuality.

The slow trickle of feminist thought into mainstream psychology (and its virtual exclusion from abnormal psychology texts) presents a striking contrast to its prominence in other disciplines such as literary studies, history, anthropology, and sociology. To understand these exclusions, I have argued, we must

MARECEK

549

analyze the cultural and disciplinary functions that textbooks perform. The public image of psychology so carefully cultivated by texts would be undermined if it stood alongside the record of its treatment of women. At the same time the public stance of scientific detachment that the mental health professions assume would give way in the face of evidence of the embeddedness of the professions in their cultural, historical, and social circumstances.

Up until now, the discipline of psychology has not been especially amenable to self-reflection. Instructional practices can serve to promote reflexivity, thus they are an important means of reworking disciplinary commitments and practices. Below I offer a few examples of such practices.

Changing the subject. One way to change the subject is to include what has been excluded. This means not only adding women and other under-represented groups to the discussion, but including the new issues that emerge when those groups become the center of inquiry. Another means of changing the subject is to cross the conventional boundaries of abnormal psychology by bringing in scholars outside the field (e.g., historians of science, critical theorists, cultural historians). Working from a different vantage point, such writers provide a different picture of the field, often raising the moral and political issues that textbooks skirt.

Breaking the DSM habit. The disease model of disorder of the DSM has been a useful device for organizing knowledge of clinical phenomena. But, like any conceptual tool, it privileges certain kinds of knowledge at the expense of others. Foucault says of the disease model that insanity has become "confined within mental illness." The "experience of madness remains silent in the composure of a knowledge which, knowing too much, forgets it" (1965, p. xii).

Breaking the textbook habit. Textbooks impose uniformity, coherence, structure, and closure on a body knowledge. An alternative syllabus of an eclectic combination of materials would mirror more closely the multiplicity of approaches and points of view in the field, its multifocality, and the honest differences among working psychologists.

Cultivating evaluative promiscuity. The so-called scientific standards adopted by psychology offer only one way of evaluating knowledge, a way that has been challenged by some psychologists and by critical theorists outside the field. Evaluated in accord with the standards of other disciplines, the knowledge base of psychology is frequently found wanting—its depictions of psychic life mechanistic, lifeless, piecemeal, reductionist, thin, even implausible.

The "test banks" that accompany textbooks too often seem based on standards similar to scientific ones. By favoring multiple-choice questions, they privilege discrete bits of "correct" information, rather than discursive knowledge, synthesis, and argumentation. They also imply the existence of a single true answer, rather than the multiplicity of perspectives and interpretations that flourish in the field.

CONCLUSION

Critical theorists and historians have begun to construct fuller accounts of the actual operations and the social relations of psychology, focusing on what is left out of the canonical histories of the field and the formal descriptions of its methods of producing knowledge. These accounts further our understanding of how the discipline of psychology disciplines us. Acknowledging the politics of textbooks expands this inquiry into another set of disciplinary practices and social relations, shedding light on the face that psychology shows to the public, its anxieties about status and image, and its rhetorical defenses against those anxieties. Textbooks do more than shape students' knowledge of the discipline. They restrain instructors' pedagogical imaginations. They regulate psychological knowledge by drawing the boundaries of the field. And they play a crucial role in codifying knowledge in the field, by selecting from all that is known that subset to be disseminated as fact.

NOTES

1. Charlotte Perkins Gilman's novella, *The Yellow Wallpaper* (1973/1982), which recounts the suicide of a young wife and mother, is based on her experiences as Mitchell's patient.

REFERENCES

Bohan, J. (1992). *Seldom seen, rarely heard: Women's place in psychology.* Boulder, CO: Westview Press.

Camhi, L. (1993). Stealing femininity: Department store kleptomainia as sexual disorder. *Differences, 5,* 26–50.

Cushman, P. (1993). Psychotherapy as moral discourse. *Journal of Theoretical and Philosophical Psychology, 13.*

Enns, C. Z. (1993). Twenty years of feminist counseling and therapy: From naming biases to implementing multifaceted practice. *The Counseling Psychologist, 21,* (1), 3–87.

Foucault, M. (1965). *Madness and civilization.* NY: Vintage.

Gilman, C. P. (1973/1892). *The Yellow Wallpaper.* New York: Feminist Press.

Graham, S. (1992). Most of the subjects were White and middle class: Trends in published research on African Americans in selected APA journals, 1970–1989. *American Psychologist, 47,* 629–639.

Groneman, C. (1993, June). *Nymphomania and the 20th-century construction of female sexuality.* Paper presented at the Berkshire Conference on the History of Women, Poughkeepsie, NY.

Hare-Mustin, R. T. & Marecek, J. (1986). Autonomy and gender: Some questions for therapists. *Psychotherapy: Theory, Practice and Research, 23,* 205–212.

Hare-Mustin, R. T., & Marecek, J. (1990). *Making a difference: Psychology and the construction of gender.* New Haven, CT: Yale University Press.

Holstein, J. A. (1987). Producing gender effects on involuntary mental hospitalization. *Social Problems, 34,* (2), 141–155.

MARECEK

Humphreys, K. & Rappoport, J. (1993). From the Community Mental Health Center movement to the War on Drugs: A study in the definition of social problems. *American Psychologist, 48,* 892–901.

James, K. & MacKinnon, L. K. (1990). The "incestuous" family revisited: A critical analysis of family therapy myths. *Journal of Marital and Family Therapy. 16,* 71–88.

Kaye, J. (1990). Toward meaningful research in psychotherapy. *Dulwich Centre Newsletter, 2,* 27–38.

Kessler, R. J. (1990). Models of disease and the diagnosis of schizophrenia. *Psychiatry, 53,* 140–147.

King, C. A. (1990). Parallels between neurasthenia and premenstrual syndrome. *Women and Health, 15,* (4), 1–23.

Kravetz, D. & Jones, L. E. (1991). Supporting practice in feminist service agencies. In M. Bricker-Jenkins, N. Hooyman, and N. Gottlieb (Eds.), *Feminist Social Work Practice in Clinical Settings* (pp. 233–249). Newbury Park, CA: Sage.

Marecek, J. (___). Feminism and psychology: Can this relationship be saved? In D. Stanton & A. Stewart (Eds.), *Feminisms in the Academy: Rethinking the disciplines.* Ann Arbor, MI: University of Michigan Press.

Marecek, J. & Hare-Mustin, R. T. (1991). A short history of the future: Feminism and clinical psychology. *Psycholgy of Women Quarterly, 15,* 521–536.

Noel, B. (1992). *You must be dreaming.* New York: Poseidon Press.

Nurcombe, B. & Gallagher, R. (1986). *The clinical process in psychiatry.* NY: Cambridge University Press.

Osipow, S. & Fitzgerald, L. (1993). Unemployment and mental health: A neglected relationship. *Applied and Preventive Psychology, 2,* 59–63.

Parlee, M. B. (1989, March). *The science and politics of PMS research.* Paper presented at the meeting of the Association for Women in Psychology, Newport, RI.

Parlee, M. B. (1993, June). *Contestation and consolidation in scientific discourse about premenstrual syndrome.* Paper presented at the Berkshire Conference on the History of Women, Poughkeepsie, NY.

Reid, P. T. (1993). Poor women in psychology research: Shut up and shut out. *Psychology of Women Quarterly, 17,* 133–150.

Showalter, E. (1985). *The female malady.* New York: Viking Penguin.

Strupp, H. H. (1991). Clinical research, practice, and the crisis of confidence. *Journal of Consulting and Clinical Psychology, 49,* 216–219.

Vieth, I. (1965). *Hysteria: The history of a disease.* Chicago: University of Chicago Press.

Worell, J. & Remer, P. (1992). *Feminist perspectives in therapy: An empowerment model for women.* New York: Wiley.

MARECEK

DISCOURSE IN THE MIRRORED ROOM
A Postmodern Analysis of Therapy

Rachel T. Hare-Mustin

A TEENAGE girl says that her father's friend has made sexual advances to her. No one believes her. Her father takes her to a therapist and tells him to bring her to her senses (Freud, 1905/1963).

A therapist learns that a former patient is having an affair with her current therapist. He intervenes to try to stop the affair, but he does not report the therapist to the licensing board (Hare-Mustin, 1992a).

A father has been sexually abusing his daughter. The mother feels guilty. The father regards his wife's submissiveness as agreement in a fifty-fifty marriage (James & McKinnon, 1990).

Based in part on an address presented at the International Conference on "Narrative and Psycho-therapy: New Directions in Theory and Practice for the 21st Century," Houston TX, May 1991.

A husband and wife have a bitter, long-running dispute. She claims he was having sex with another woman. He says she is crazy. So they argue in therapy (Smith, 1991).

A wife runs off with her lover. The husband calls the therapist. He cannot understand how she could abandon him and their three children (Walters, Carter, Papp, & Silverstein, 1988).

A wife is exhausted by her job and all the housework and childcare. The husband does not see why he should change his life because his wife has a demanding job. Every night there is a struggle with their 4-year-old to get him to go to bed, so he ends up in their bed (Hochschild, 1989).

What do these cases have in common? Although apparently different, they all reflect the dominant discourses in society. By discourse, I mean a system of statements, practices, and institutional structures that share common values. A discourse includes both linguistic and nonlinguistic aspects; it is the medium that provides the words and ideas for thought and speech, as well as the cultural practices involving related concepts and behaviors (see Best & Kellner, 1991). By a restrictive and expressive set of codes and conventions, discourses sustain a certain world view (Clifford, 1986). Thus, as Parker (1992) has pointed out, discourses do not simply describe the social world; they also categorize it. In so doing, discourses bring certain phenomena into sight and obscure other phenomena. The ways most people in a society hold, talk about, and act on a common, shared viewpoint are part of and sustain the prevailing discourses.

554

Discourse theory is one of an array of postmodern approaches to knowledge that ask how meaning is constructed. Postmodernists see numerous competing view-points of the world rather than one true view. Instead of the master narratives and universalizing claims that have characterized knowledge since the Enlightenment, knowledge is conceived of as multiple, fragmentary, context-dependent, and local (Foucault, 1980; Lyotard, 1984). Knowledge has been described as an edifying conversation of varied voices rather than an accurate representation of what is "out there."

Discourse theory is only one of a number of postmodern approaches that could be applied to the analysis of relationships between people and the analysis of therapies. Rather than a full exegesis of the extensive debates and developments in postmodern thought, my purpose here is the more limited one of demonstrating how ideas from discourse theory can illuminate some contemporary issues in therapy.

THE DOMINANT DISCOURSE

"Discourse" comes from the Latin root *discurrere*, which means "to run around," and different and competing discourses circulate in the culture. However, not all circulating discourses are of equal importance; some have a privileged and dominant influence on language, thought, and action. The dominant discourses both produce and are produced by social interaction, a particular language community, and the socioeconomic context. Once designations in language become accepted, a speaker using the language is constrained by such designations in communication with others and in the generation of ideas as well (Bloom, 1981). In this way, language structures one's own experience of "reality" as well as the experiences of those with whom one communicates. When a group of people talk and relate among themselves in familiar ways, much of their talk reflects and reinstates dominant discourses. Moreover, because dominant discourses are so familiar, they are taken for granted and even recede from view. It is hard to question them. They are part of the identity of most members of any society, and they influence attitudes and behaviors, as I illustrate in the discussion that follows.

Therapy as part of the mental health system both depends upon and upholds the dominant discourses. Although many family therapists might regard themselves as mavericks, relatively few in our field are guided by marginalized discourses. The efforts of most therapists represent the interests and moral standards of the dominant groups in society. Therapy is typically well-regarded by elite groups for the goodness of its principles and practices. Thus, an examination of the goals of most family therapies (for example, maintain the family, avoid divorce, keep the children in school, differentiate) reveals that we as therapists are engaged in social control more than social change. Therapy is a normalizing activity; it serves to stabilize "the family." As Madigan and Law (1992) point out, family therapy is not separate from sociopolitical discourses. Indeed, therapy has been described as inflicting on patients the same dominant discourses by which they have previously been harmed (Cushman, 1990).

Subordinate discourses, on the other hand, are the ones that are marginalized, and even co-opted by the dominant discourses, so that they lose their oppositional force. Discourses associated with groups on the margins of society are excluded from influence. They are not spoken with author-ity. They arouse discomfort. An example of co-optation is seen in the way the peace symbol, which originally signified commitment to nuclear disarmament, was reduced to a common item of jewelry, benefit of its original meaning, and even worn by soldiers fighting in Vietnam. Another example of co-optation would be how women's independence became subsumed by and ironically emblematic of the sale of cigarettes to "emancipated" women.

The ideas of many feminist theorists converge with those of postmodern thinkers who have drawn attention to the relation of meaning and power (Benhabib & Cornell, 1987; Diamond & Quinby, 1988; Foucault, 1973, 1980; Jameson, 1981). The inquiry into meaning has focused especially on language as the medium of cognitive life and communication. Meaning-making and control over language are important resources held by those in power. Indeed, Barthes (1972) has called language a sign system used by the powerful

555

HARE-MUSTIN

to label, define, and rank. Moreover, Foucault (1980) has suggested that "correct" representations do not arise from chance twists in conversation, but are shaped by the dominant and specific historical, cultural, and political practices that constitute them. Power is thought of as a network of practices, institutions, and technologies that sustain dominance and subordination. Throughout history, dominant groups have asserted their authority over language through control of the production of knowledge, of the media and publications, and of access to education and to institutions of learning (Hare-Mustin & Marecek, 1990). Among family therapists, Michael White has stood out for his application of Foucauldian postmodernism to therapy (White, 1993; White & Epston, 1990). He has drawn attention both to the ways power is invisible to those who experience it and to how individuals are led to embrace their own subjugation through the influence of certain presumed truths.

There are multiple discourses that speak to the oppression of marginal groups by the structures of power, but I refer to gender because the feminist critique has been one of the most articulated analyses. Postmodernism has been seen by some feminists as a way to open up space for alternative views to those that prevail. Feminist postmodernists have focused on the way dominant discourses produce and sustain the status of those who have power against the competing discourses of those on the margins of society, like women, ethnic minorities, old people, and poor people. These marginalized discourses contest the privileged positions of dominant groups and speak for those who have less control over their lives and who are often regarded as inferior. For example, feminists have drawn attention to women's virtual exclusion from positions of power in public and political life. Discourse about women's participation is systematically trivialized, subsumed, or excluded from issues and debates on public policy and community life; for example, in 1992 when women asked for more representation in government, they were ridiculed as "bean counters." On the other hand, some marginalized discourses, such as those of wife abuse and child abuse, have been brought, through feminist efforts, out of the private realm of the family and into increasing public awareness. One way to assess the relative dominance or marginalization of a discourse is to ask what institutions and ways of being are supported by the discourse.

Dominant discourses reflect and are part of the prevailing ideology. A classic example is the view that women and men are inherently different, with men constituting the norm. At various times in our era, this view has been renewed and reemphasized. After men returned from World War II, the prevailing view of the popular culture no longer regarded women as fitted for the industrial production they had engaged in during the war. Instead, women's unique capacities for caretaking and their home and family responsibilities were emphasized. The family of the 1950s that embodied this model became the basis for the new field of family therapy. More recently, the Reagan era of the 1980s promoted a conservative, pro-family ideology that saw women defined by their crucial role in the family, and this at a time when competing discourses centered on women's independence and choice. The dominant discourse of masculine and feminine differences views women as essentially caring, close to nature, and oriented to meet the needs of others, whereas men are essentially independent and achieving. Considerable effort in the biological and social sciences goes into supporting this prevailing view and trying to identify miniscule differences between men and women. Empirical research that finds differences gets published in scientific journals and touted in the popular media; empirical research that finds no differences rarely gets published in scientific journals or even mentioned in the popular media (Mednick, 1989; Tavris, 1992).

Let me emphasize that both men and women participate in the dominant discourses, including the discourses concerning gender. We share the common view-points and ideas of our particular time and place. Through recurrent, day-to-day practices and meanings, the discourses of gender differences are maintained. Thus, patriachal relations cannot be explained solely by the intentions, good or bad, of individual women and men. They exist in the social institutions and practices of society (Baber & Allen, 1992). As Hanne Haavind (1984) has observed, female subordination and male domination are concealed rather than revealed in gender relations by both men and women. Male domination in the family is often not labeled as such because we do not regard the husband's power as stemming from a desire on his part to dominate. Acceptable masculinity involves domination, but a domination that appears reasonable and not striven for. Similarly, ideal femininity does not have to be completely passive. Femininity can involve aggression and initiative as long as they are not used to dominate men.

557

THE MIRRORED ROOM

The therapy room is like a room lined with mirrors. It reflects back only what is voiced within it. When there is a one-way mirror and reflecting team, they too reflect back what has been provided. If the therapist and family are unaware of marginalized discourses, such as those associated with members of subordinate gender, race, and class groups, those discourses remain outside the mirrored room.

The idea that meaning emerges in social interaction is widely accepted in family therapy and has been prominent since the work of Gregory Bateson and his colleagues. However, the complexity of naming and meaning-making seems to have been reduced in family therapy to a simple view of therapy as a meaning-generating system separated from the social context and wider culture. Although this interactional view goes beyond the idea that an individual can simply generate any meaning he or she might wish, it still disregards the

HARE-MUSTIN

way language and concepts have evolved, been selected, and given prominence by the language community. We do not only use language; it uses us. Language is recursive: it provides the categories in which we think. As Bruner (1986) points out, language "imposes a point of view not only about the world to which it refers but toward the use of the mind in respect to this world" (p. 121). Discourse theory suggests that we do not develop meaning out of a void, but out of a preexisting, shared language, and through discursive practices that reflect and reenact the traditions, power relations, and institutions of the society.

Some therapists seem to regard meaning as newly created in the therapeutic conversation, which allows them to disregard the meanings associated with the positions individuals occupy in the society (see, for example, Anderson & Goolishian, 1988). One result of such context-stripping is that participants come to be viewed as equal despite their different positions in various social hierarchies. However, regardless of the therapist's intention or desire to be no more than an equal co-author of a new narrative, the meanings embedded and enacted in the shared language accord different author-ity to different participants. Structural inequalities influence the therapeutic conversation; what can be spoken about and who can speak it are issues of power. Thus, a therapist is accorded greater authority and expertise by the society than the person(s) seeking a therapist's help in resolving problems. This is reflected in the clients paying the therapist rather than the therapist paying the clients for sessions.

In the therapy session, the conversation of the family and therapist arises from and is determined by the prevailing concepts and ideologies of the language community. As Anderson and Goolishian (1988) have noted, "psychotherapy cannot ignore the categories used by people" (p. 373). Drawing on Rorty's (1972) metaphor of the mirror, they go on to say that the therapist is not simply a mirror reflecting more accurate representations of reality. This is an important point with which I agree. But, I am concerned that it overlooks what is reflected—not reality but, rather, the dominant discourses circulating in the therapy room and the familiar concepts and categories that prevail. It is this construction of reality that determines the therapeutic story of the re-collected past and the pro-jected future (Crites. 1986).

DISCOURSE ANALYSIS

The view that meaning is generated in the mirrored room independently of the prevailing ideologies can be contrasted with an approach to discourse that is self-reflexive and examines both prevailing ideologies and marginalized discourses. As the opening sketches forecast. I will draw examples from the discourses of male-female relationships. What such discourses have in common is that they disguise inequality. Explanations based on essential differences and complementary sex roles, a focus on separate spheres for men and women,

558

HARE-MUSTIN

and quid pro quo solutions to family problems are part of the dominant discourses. These can be appealing to therapists and families alike because they seem to support the ideal of equal relations between the sexes and disguise differences in power and choice (Goodrich, 1991). For example, caring—a presumed, essential female quality—can be understood in relationship terms as a way of negotiating from a position of low power. People in positions of weakness usually have been found to rely on weak-influence tactics (Sagrestano, 1992). Furthermore, because of their higher status roles, white men generally elicit weak strategies from others. Often, when a woman argues with her husband, she appeals for caring, while he evokes principles. But in a relationship where she has more power, as in dealing with her children, she now emphasizes rules while it is the children who appeal for caring. The presumption of essential gender characteristics masks the relations of power.

Many discourses intersect and interact to create the cultural narratives we are familiar with. At any point in time, there co-exist several different discourses that define what is expected of men and women in relation to each other, and that produce feminine and masculine identities (Hollway, 1984, 1989). These identities then become part of an individual's "nature" and constrain and impel an individual's choices. Let us examine, in turn, the male sexual drive discourse, the permissive discourse, and the marriage-between-equals discourse and see how they fare in the mirrored room. In each case, the dominant discourse favors masculine interests and needs. There are, of course, other discourses. For example, our society privileges a discourse of heterosexual relations, obscures a discourse of female desire, and promotes a discourse of female victimization (Fine, 1988).

The cases and illustrations have been selected to highlight aspects of the dominant discourses. Of course, understanding how some discourses are more influential than others does not preclude a therapist's providing a context of listening, openness, caring, and respect, or determine what a therapist will focus on (see Griffith & Griffith, 1992). Some of the cases illustrate how a therapist can give salience to parts of a client's story in order to bring in alternative discourses. In a previous article, I analyzed some of these cases from the perspective of power issues (Hare-Mustin, 1991). Here I focus on discourse analysis and clarifying how a therapist may sustain or challenge dominant discourses.

THE MALE SEXUAL DRIVE DISCOURSE

The dominant discourse in the production of meanings concerning sexuality has been identified by Hollway (1984) as the male sexual drive discourse. It needs little introduction because it is so familiar, both affirmed by experts and typically regarded as common sense. The woman is seen as the object that arouses and precipitates men's sexual urges. Men's sexual urges are assumed to be natural and compelling; thus, the male is expected to be pushy and aggressive in seeking to satisfy them. Whereas men's sexuality is seen as direct and primitive, women are seen as the object of men's sexual drive. Often, women are also viewed as inflaming men's natural sexual urges.

We see evidence of the male sexual drive discourse about men's need and women's compliance not only in the home but also in the day-to-day practices of men toward women who venture into public space. Women are open targets on public streets, and young women particularly, unless accompanied by a child or a man, are subjected to free and evaluative commentary and also to expressions by men of "what I'd like to do" (Bartky, 1988). Women in this way are reminded of their subordination and vulnerability.

Bring Her to Her Senses

A teenage girl with a cough and headaches was brought by her father to see his therapist. He told the therapist to bring her to her senses. The daughter had been accompanying her father on his frequent visits to another family. She complained that the head of the family made sexual advances to her, but no one believed her, including the therapist. Yes, the therapist was Freud, and the patient, Dora (Freud, 1905/1963). This is a classic case of sex, lies, and headaches, storied and restoried (Hare-Mustin, 1991). Donald Spence (1987) has called it a landmark of persuasion unsurpassed in the clinical literature. It is useful to re-examine in terms of the dominant discourses because it is easier to see the possible meanings of behaviors situated in another time and place than to recognize the meanings embedded in one's own social context.

Dora's father often took her along to the K household where he was having an affair with Frau K. The husband, Herr K, had been making sexual advances to Dora since she was age 14, apparently encouraged by Dora's father. Freud never met Dora's mother, but diagnosed her as having a "housewife's psychosis," based on reports of her by Dora's father.

Freud's view of Dora was embedded in the male sex drive discourse, the patriarchal discourse of his era. He assumed that a man had a right to have his sexual needs met, and any young woman would appreicate the attentions of a man like Herr K, be flattered by them, and accede to them. Freud regarded Dora's symptoms as signs of hysteria that he saw resulting from her aroused and disguised sexual desire. When he tried to press his views on Dora, she quit analysis, leading to her being labeled as not only disturbed, but also disagreeable, untruthful, and vengeful. The involved adults denied her allegations; however, some time later, those involved acknowledged that her claims about Herr K were true.

Freud's understanding of the case was compatible with the dominant discourses of his day; he did not recognize that his work arose within a specific social and political context. He gave no credence to Dora's story. Freud was unable to shift from his theory that a seduced girl was the seducer of the man she aroused, and that she in turn was aroused and flattered by the man's ad-

HARE-MUSTIN

vances: a female's story that contested this discourse was regarded as untruthful. As Foucault (1979) has argued, psychoanalysis is a potent discourse through which we construct a particular kind of self, rather than a neutral tool or an instrument of self-discovery and liberation.

A Sissy Male

Masculinity is defined largely by the male sexual drive discourse, a set of prescribed personality and behavioral characteristics associated with heterosexual men. The male sexual drive discourse is a discourse of patriarchal heterosexuality whereby male domination is expected and endorsed. Men who are not conventionally masculine are not regarded as real men, as Stoltenberg (1989) has pointed out. Stereotyped notions of gay men depict them as not masculine in personality and behavior, just as stereotyped notions of lesbians depict them as not feminine.

But what about the sissy male? Allan Hunter (1992) examines this question and describes his experience as, what he calls, a "sissy male," noting that the term "sissy" is entymologically derived from "sister" and connotes the sense of being like a girl or woman. The man with little or no interest in trying to dominate women or compete with other men challenges the male sexual drive discourse. In recounting his experience, Hunter reports he was attracted to women, but he feared that unless he acted like men were supposed to he would never have the close relations and sexual experiences he wanted with women.

Domination and power conflicts are eroticized by the male sexual drive discourse. Hunter admits being concerned that sex would lose its sexiness if it lacked elements of the hunt, the chase, and the seduction. As for the woman, love makes the woman who is loved feel singled out as special and different from the general run of women who are not perceived as equal or interesting people.

The sissy does not have a sense of identity dependent on how different he is from women. For Allan Hunter, the hard part was finding women who were also outside the dominant discourse, for women are not used to playing with men who do not embody masculinity, and who expect women to be seductive teases or passive subordinates. He observed that being outside the dominant discourse can be rather risky and frightening for both men and women.

Cries and Whispers: A Case of Therapist Sexual Abuse

The Boston beauty and prize-winning poet Anne Sexton was in therapy for many years. She was glamorous, talented, troubled, depressed, often suicidal, and frequently hospitalized. Sexton's early therapist provided 300 tapes of therapy sessions to the author of a recent biography (Middlebrook, 1991), with the approval of Sexton's daughter who is the executor of Sexton's estate.

561

HARE-MUSTIN

The release of the tapes drew enormous criticism and provoked an outcry among psychiatrists and psychotherapists over the issue of confidentiality. Alarmed letters and comments appeared in *The New York Times* from leaders in the field who said that this use of tapes, even if Sexton might have approved, would destroy the trust of patients. The noted historian of psychoanalysis, Peter Gay, proclaimed "I would despise any analyst willing to do this" (quoted by Stanley, 1991).

But something else was overlooked. How can we understand the silence of the profession on the sexual abuse of Anne Sexton by her second therapist, who had an affair with her? The destructive consequences that sex with a therapist can have for a patient are devastating and well-documented, including boundary disturbance, inability to trust, feelings of guilt and suppressed rage, severe depression, and serious suicide risk (Hare-Mustin, 1992a). The dominant discourse of the male sexual drive apparently overrode the ethical standards of the profession regarding sex between therapist and patient. The explanations for sex between therapist and patient reflect the male sexual drive discourse: that men's sexual desires are compelling, and that women arouse them by being provocative and seductive. Thus, when the prior therapist learned of the affair, he tried informally to intervene but stopped short of reporting it to the medical review board. The persistence of the view of the woman as seducer was evident in *The Psychiatric Times* where psychiatrist Peter Kramer (1991), in apparent disregard for the therapist's responsibility for what takes place in the therapy session, recently proclaimed, "*She* soon seduced *him*" (p. 5; emphasis added).

An alternative view was presented by Pollitt (1991) in her review, "The Death Is Not the Life." She noted that anyone who suspected that psychotherapy had been bad for women would find plenty of confirmation in the Anne Sexton case. I see the focus on confidentiality as a smoke screen that served to cover up the sexual abuse by the therapist. The dominant discourse supported an outcry over confidentiality and hardly a whisper about sexual abuse.

Father-Daughter Incest

Let us see how the dominant male sex drive discourse provided a network of interpretations and assumptions within which a case of father–daughter incest was understood (James & MacKinnon, 1990). The dominant discourse regards women's lack of interest in sexual relationships with their husbands as abnormal or dysfunctional. In contrast, men's "need" for sex is seen as normal and functional. In this family, the father had been entering the room of his 16-year old daughter at night and fondling her genitals when she appeared asleep. Distraught and uncertain, the daughter disclosed what was happening to her mother.

The wife's submissiveness pervaded her marriage. She was intimidated by

HARE-MUSTIN

her verbally abusive husband. He took charge of the family in numerous ways, from maintaining strict control of family finances to regulating and restricting the children's social activities. The problem of inequality in the marriage was not addressed. Because the wife was afraid to disagree with her husband, he perceived her submission as agreement. Thus, he regarded them as equal and the decisions they made as "fifty-fifty."

The discourse of male sexual drive involves the belief that men must have a sexual outlet in the person of a woman if they are to feel like "real men." The accepted implication is that a man is owed sexual rights by his marriage contract. The mother who has withdrawn from her husband is often seen as the cause of the incest. Thus, it is seen as "natural" for a father who feels unsatisfied or inadequate to exploit sexually his less powerful children. Because of the presumption that a man's sex drive is urgent and must be satisfied, the failure of a mother to protect her children is often treated as more reprehensible than the sexual abuse perpetrated by the father. We see that the male sex drive discourse includes the idea that women are responsible for the moral conduct of men. But when this case was viewed in the context of a patriarchal social structure, the therapists saw it through the lens of the discourse that allows men to attempt to control through intimidation and women to submit.

Another aspect of the male sexual drive discourse was revealed in the case of Rick, a man who was found guilty of sexually abusing his 13-year-old stepdaughter, and served time in prison. Only after a period in therapy did Rick later reveal that he had been abused as a child by an adult male relative. In describing the case, Miller (1993) drew attention to the problem of the abuser's secrets and shame: "One of the most problematic aspects of disclosure for male victims of sexual abuse is that it puts the male in a 'female' position. If he has been sexually victimized, he is 'like a woman' as a sex object" (p. 190).

Male victims of sexual abuse, according to Miller, often do not disclose their own experience, maintaining either a detached air of indifference or a coldly angry stance. They would rather be identified as perpetrators than seen as victims, however more compassionate the view of them as victims might be. This further illustrates how the dominant discourse of the male sexual drive defines acceptable masculine behavior.

THE PERMISSIVE DISCOURSE

The permissive discourse is one that seems to challenge monogamy. It gives both sexes the right to express freely their sexuality. However, permissiveness has different effects for men and women because of their different positions in society. For men, permissiveness can mean open sexual access; for women, permissiveness can mean pressure to accede to men's urging for sexual activity. In combination with the male sex drive discourse, the permissive discourse serves further to coerce women to meet men's needs by labeling reluctant women as up-tight and teases, or as frigid. Many women report they often give in to men's pleading for sexual activity because it seems so important to men (Hollway, 1984). As Gavey (1992) points out, "to say that women often engage in unwanted sex with men is paradoxically both to state the obvious and to speak the unspeakable" (p. 325). The dominant discourse prescribed compliance to male initiatives. Consequently, there is no space for unwanted sex; it remains largely unrecognized or even condoned.

Within the dominant permissive discourse, women are often made to feel they have no right to be hurt or betrayed by male infidelity because women are theoretically allowed the same liberties. Thus, women may not feel justified to complain about men's exercise of sexual rights to which they are presumably also entitled. The permissive discourse justifies men's sexual freedom while punishing women who object to it by denying the validity of their objections.

Sexual Freedom or Plain Truth?

In this case, arguments over the husband's alleged sexual encounter with another woman led to a couple's deteriorating relationship over several years (Smith, 1991). Arriving home unexpectedly from work, the wife found the front door uncharacteristically locked. Her husband answered the door, undressed except for a pair of jeans. His brother's woman friend emerged from the bathroom partially dressed and straightening her clothes. The bed sheets were rumpled and stained with semen. The husband was vehement in his denial that anything improper had taken place, saying that he had had an erotic dream, ejaculated, and then his brother's woman friend had stopped by on an errand.

A therapist could readily take a neutral stance with this couple, not supporting either story while the wife became more agitated in the face of her husband's denials. This would provide the customary evidence that women are emotionally overreactive and give distorted versions of the truth while men deal with facts. Or a therapist could reaffirm the permissive discourse of sexual freedom for each of them. However, what I found interesting in this case was the therapist's response to a woman's different place in the permissive discourse.

The therapeutic approach involved reframing the entire dispute as a comparison of good and bad storytellers, rather than a debate over sexual freedom and truthfulness. The therapist asked both members of the couple to tell their stories about the event. The therapist remarked on the vagueness of the husband's story, in contrast to the detail and vividness of the wife's story. The therapist suggested that they both work on their stories: the husband should try to add more drama and detail as his wife had, since hers was a better story.

564

HARE-MUSTIN

After several sessions the therapist asked the husband to tell the wife's story, but the husband argued that he could not do so because her story was not true and his was the "plain truth."

The therapist finally persuaded him to do so. The husband told the wife's story, and she was much relieved. After a hastily contrived ritual of burning their stories, the couple went home and subsequently reported that their relationship was much improved.

This case could be seen as one where, for several years, the wife had been told that what she saw was not "true." In the face of male authority, a wife is often expected to give way, just as Dora was expected to give way to Freud's meaning. When the wife did not accept her husband's account, she was told that she had a problem, that she was crazy. What the therapist identified as the crucial issue was that this woman's experience was being denied. Without addressing the issue of truth, a task was arranged that confirmed rather than denied the woman's experience. The issue was dealt with, not as one of trying to settle an argument about truth-telling or sexual freedom, but as recognizing the meaning of the wife's experience, however much the experience might be at variance with the dominant discourses of permissive sexuality.

Breaking Up a Marriage

The way the permissive discourse can have different consequences for men and women, particularly married men and women, is illustrated in another case. A husband's infidelity may be implicitly tolerated by the permissive discourse, but a wife who is unfaithful is often regarded as devious and irresponsible. This is particularly so if she is a mother who gives up her "natural" role as nurturing caretaker and wifely helpmate.

In this case, a therapist received an agitated telephone call from a husband who complained that his wife of 12 years had run off with the delivery man, and someone should bring her to her senses (Walters, et al., 1988). When the therapist saw the couple together, the husband directed a tirade against his wife for humiliating him and abandoning their three children. The wife remained silent and downcast. Alone with the therapist, Olga Silverstein, the wife recounted how she had become pregnant when dating him and had given way to her parents' and his insistence that they marry. Now, 12 years later, she was unhappy in the marriage and felt trapped. Since her husband handled all the money, the house and car were in his name and she had no financial resources of her own. But most of all, she could not find a legitimate reason to break up the family. How did the wife choose between her husband and the lover who carried her off?

The therapist did not view this wife's choice as being which of the two men she wanted and should respond to, that is, in terms of the male sex drive discourse. Rather, the therapist saw her choice as one between her desire for independence and her desire to be secure in the submissive pattern in her marriage. On its surface, the case appeared to reflect the permissive discourse of sexual freedom and choice.

However, the therapist suspected that the attraction to the lover might not be the issue. She realized that a woman's leaving one man to go to another, as way out of a marriage, would be more acceptable to society than a woman's choosing to leave a man because she was unhappy. The delivery man was the wife's way of leaving the marriage. The dominant discourses of sexuality do not admit of nonsexual preferences. Thus a woman is allowed to do for "love" what she could not do for herself.

Three years later the couple had divorced, but the lover was no longer in the picture. The husband was remarried. The wife was finishing a degree, working part-time, and caring for the children.

THE DISCOURSE OF EQUALITY

Another dominant discourse is the marriage-between-equals discourse, which allows marriage to conceal the extent of male dominant and female subordination. As Weedon (1987) has pointed out, power is only tolerable in the liberal-humanist tradition if it masks a substantial part of itself. Marriage in the United States reflects the problem of how to manage inequality in a society whose ideal is equality. Inequalities related to gender are traditionally considered unintentional and incidental. The dominant discourse regards men and women as "naturally" so different that they cannot be compared. Thus, the husband is unable to help with household chores because he needs to recover from the stresses of work, or the wife does the cleaning because she is compulsive about the way the house appears. Recall that it was the reputed concern of Dora's mother with maintaining the household that led Freud (1905/1963) to label her as having a "housewife's psychosis." As I pointed out earlier, both men and women participate in this discourse and cooperate in concealing women's subordination and men's domination, and in reframing differences as equality.

Sustaining the Myth of Equality

Let us examine the marriage-between-equals discourse in what Arlie Hochschild (1989) describes as the myth of upstairs/downstairs. When the wife, Nancy, arrives home from her job as a social worker, she scurries between stove, sink, and washing machine, her 4-year-old Joey dogging her footsteps. Meanwhile her husband, Evan, gets irritated if she even asks him to set the table. After dinner, it is Nancy's responsibility to get Joey to bed. "Joey's problem" emerged as a prolonged series of bedtime demands, ending up with Nancy exhausted and Joey in his parents' bed at 11 p.m.

Evan did not see why he should accomodate his life and activities to his wife's choice of a demanding career. Nancy was exhausted. She could no longer feel any interest in sexual relations with Evan; however, it troubled her to seem to be "holding out" on him. Notice that Nancy accepted the male sexual drive discourse, that it was the man's right to have his sexual desires met.

Ultimately, the crisis in the marriage was resolved by Nancy doing the "second shift" at home. The mythic solution Hochschild described was the elevating of the garage to the full moral and practical equivalent of the rest of the house. The "upstairs" was defined as Nancy's responsibility—meals, child-care, shopping, laundry, housecleaning. The "downstairs" was Evan's responsi-bility—the garage and his basement workshop, as well as the dog. This arrangement resulted in Nancy's cutting back her career work to half-time.

In order to maintain the marriage-between-equals discourse, the couple rezoned the territory. The perception of the marriage as fair required that disparities between Nancy's hours of leisure and Evan's be transformed into differences in their personalities. Evan desired himself as laid-back and easy-going, while Nancy was compulsive and well-organized. This explanation fit the dominant discourse, that men and women are "naturally" so different, have such different talents and interests, different traits and ways of being and knowing, that they cannot be compared. Such essentialist ideas have been called "ruses" by Michael White because they disguise what is taking place; they obscure operations of power (see Tomm, 1993). One problem with essentialist views about men and women is that they have become reified and support the very inequities they were meant to undermine (Hare-Mustin & Marecek, 1988; Riger, 1992).

567

Many therapists in the mirrored room would have focused on solving "Joey's problem" and getting him out of his parents bed. Such an approach would likely be oblivious to the issue of equality. The myth of upstairs/down-stairs satisfied both Nancy and Evan, and probably would have satisfied many therapists, too.

A Woman Artist

The discourse of marital equality is violated when one partner pursues his or her interests with such clarity and focus that the label "selfish" is readily ap-plicable. This violation is more apparent in a woman than a man because, as Bepko and Krestan (1993) note: "Not just the marital structure but the pre-ferred form of all heterosexual relationships [is one] in which man is the per-former, the woman his audience, he the important one, she the support sys-tem" (p. 107).

Katherine Bradford is a highly respected abstract painter whose experience is described by Bepko and Krestan. She was in her early thirties, married, and had two children just starting school when she decided she wanted to be a se-rious artist and commit a great deal of time to painting, and not just be a hobbyist who did watercolors in her spare time. In her marriage, Katherine had tried to bury her wishes and see herself as the wife of an important person, but her marriage consumed the energy she wanted to put into her painting. She could not handle both. Katherine observed that male artist friends took themselves seriously, spent money on lots of paint, and had a sense of entitlement. Looking for models, she saw Georgia O'Keefe as an artist who had a real sense of herself, of her own worth.

The marriage-between-equals discourse does not allow the kind of independence that Katherine asserted in choosing to commit herself to painting. She realized she could have stayed busy in the marriage, perhaps buying art or doing something related, and denied her deepest wishes. She might have reframed her marriage around a myth, as in "upstairs/downstairs," and never recognized why she was unhappy or depressed. The traditional discourse of marriage for Katherine would have expected her to be fully involved in the relationship and the little daily tasks that supported it, and not in herself. As Bepko and Krestan observe, women lead interrupted lives, interrupted by the needs of others or their own awareness of inattention to those needs.

In the traditional discourse of marriage, love equals taking care of. Men are expected to do this by economic provision, women by personal services and putting the other ahead of one's self. Men are expected to disregard their needs for relatedness because it will weaken their masculinity—their confidence and dominant position. Women are expected to give of themselves to men and children. What is unequal about these seemingly balanced expectations is that the woman is expected to be an enabler, to make a partner happy at the expense of her "self." For a woman, love equals self-lessness. The discourse of equality makes a woman uneasy if she focuses on herself, her interests, her needs. Instead, as Bepko and Krestan point out, she measures herself by her commitment to others, hoping that this will make her loved and respected.

DISCOURSES AND VALUES

What happens in the mirrored room if questions about dominant discourses such as the male sex drive discourse, the permissive discourse, and the marriage-between-equals discourse are not brought into the conversation? As Waldegrave (1990) has observed, therapy enshrines patriarchal meanings, supporting rather than challenging hierarchies of gender, race, and class. The possibility of reorganizing families is limited by the discourses that the therapist and family bring into the room. Dominant discourses that influence how men and women think and behave serve an important function: they disguise inequality. Too often, the discourses that provide alternative meanings for subordinate groups circulate only outside the mirrored room. In looking for the "unsaid," therapists still may not look beyond the dominant discourses. Thus, the therapeutic conversation, which has been described as "an open conversation," must still take place, like other day-to-day practices, within the prevail-

HARE-MUSTIN

ing discourses. I have suggested through case examples and illustrations that alternative meanings can be brought into the therapy room.

How do we decide which discourses we should support, which alternative meanings should be brought into therapy, which changes we are interested in? One might ask, for example, what privileges feminist understandings over bigoted misogyny, or pluralism over racist practices? Theorists vary on the question of who is to define the criteria for making ethical choices. Many traditional theorists privilege those who are disadvantaged. Thus, John Rawls, a leading theorist of social justice, regards justice as seeing things from the perspective of others. In his second principle, he proposes a method for selecting among competing interests: those individuals who are the most disadvantaged should be accorded the greatest benefit (Okin, 1989). Similarly, a postmodern view, such as Foucault (1979, 1980) puts forth, takes an orientation opposing totalizing regimes.

Postmodern theories, such as social constructionism, have been criticized as being relativistic, as saying that one opinion is as good as another, or that it is all just a matter of semantics (Minnich, 1990). But the postmodern view of knowledge is that values infuse all knowing; postmodernism typically values diversity, plurality, and choice.

Another observation is made by some feminist philosophers who have argued that "the concern with relativism is an artifact of precisely the polarized thought that feminist epistemologists have criticized" (Bohan, 1993, p. 14). For example, Harding (1987) has pointed out that the traditional absolutist-relativist dualism, with its warning about the quagmire of relativism, is the fearful reaction of the dominant group whose position of according truth-value to certain things and not others is under attack. The notion that relativism is an evil to be avoided is itself a culturally embedded claim, shaped by political ends.

From a postmodern stance, all views are relative. The ultimate truth-value of any observation cannot be determined; what we have thought to be objective is not objective (Hare-Mustin, 1992b). This should propel us into dialogue about values and ethics, about what is good in human life and important in public philosophy. Values infuse all knowing, leading postmodernists to ask not only what is concealed by dominant discourses but also why it is concealed. What is the utility of a statement; what ends does it serve?

Because discourses are constituted by shared understandings, they involve the values and mores of everyday life and everyday practices that construct those values. As Cushman (1991) observes: "Far from being a radically relativist or amoral philosophy, social construction is rooted in the moral. But it is not a moral code that receives its authority because it is removed from, transcends, and is superior to the particulars of everyday living. The everyday is real and moral, it is just not transcendently real and moral" (p. 207). This view contrasts with the way decontextualized theories legitimize, justify, and perpetuate current arrangements of privilege and power.

Other postmodern thinkers (for example, Stigliano, 1993) see the possibility for a nonrelativistic ethics as resting on the uncertainty of human existence rather than on an essential moral order unchanged through time and space. To live in a social setting requires cooperation, a network of involvements between people, a network created by and dependent upon their promises. It is out of the interactions and conversations in such settings that ethical traditions emerge. Thus, for postmodernists, judgments about discursive practices are based not on their truth-value but on their function and ethical implications.

CONCLUSION

The postmodern moment has been called politics at its most intense (Shotter, 1991). Competing discourses and multiple views circulate in the society. However, while some discourses constitute the prevailing ways of thinking and acting, others are obscured from the mainstream view, on the fringe. Postmodern thinkers regard knowledge as partial and ambiguous, and they challenge dominant discourses by calling attention to marginalized and subjugated discourses. They see so-called correct representations as arising not from chance twists in conversation, but as shaped by the specific practices that constitute them in that time and place. The taken-for-granted cultural framework that emerges serves a set of power relations. Beliefs that come to be regarded as natural do so only because they reflect the most powerful interest groups in society.

The therapeutic conversation is also not idiosyncratic. Both the process and content in the mirrored room are limited by the discourses that are brought into the room. Thus, there is a "predetermined content" to therapy—that provided by dominant discourses. Conversation can be oppressive, not so much by what it includes as by what it excludes. Therapists who do not recognize this will fail to do more than render existing norms a little less onerous for those most disadvantaged by them. When the range of discourses in the therapy room is too limited and ignores the points of view of those subordinated by race, gender, class, age, sexual preference, ability, and the like, therapy becomes the pursuit of self-replicating images. These images provide the illusory glitter of truth in the mirrored room.

How is the therapist to escape the mirrored room where dominant discourses prevail? How can one step outside one's nonconscious ideology and question it? Of course, one is never entirely free of the ways of thought in one's time and place. Nevertheless, those who work in this area can develop self-reflexivity (Morawski, 1990). This means trying to provide a special vision that can challenge the assumptions of dominant discourses rather than merely going along with them. It also means that the therapist's own influence, the therapist's authority, must be acknowledged rather than denied.

Some therapists are moving in this direction, questioning their own views and questioning why those are the questions they are asking (Madigan, 1993).

What tends to be overlooked in a conversational approach is that whenever therapists speak or refrain from speaking they are taking a stance (Real, 1990). As a critic of constructivism has observed, the influence of the therapist does not disappear by failing to acknowledge it or by renaming it something else (Minuchin, 1991). When therapists are unaware of the embeddedness of their views and how they participate in discursive practices, they are unlikely to be open to alternatives that are being obscured. I have drawn on postmodern ideas to suggest ways of increasing therapists' awareness of the often unacknowledged but prevailing discourses concerning the relations of men and women.

What shimmers and bounces off the mirrored walls of the therapy room are reflections of dominant discourses that are as pervasive as the air we breathe. They can blind us to the marginalized discourses in the world beyond the mirrored room. A postmodern orientation reminds us that all realities are constructions, and some are more influential than others. By opening up the possibility of alternatives, a postmodern view moves beyond existing practices to their transformation.

REFERENCES

Anderson, H., & Goolishian, H.A. (1988). Human systems as linguistic systems: Preliminary and evolving ideas about the implications for clinical theory. *Family Process* 27: 371–393.

Baber, K.M., & Allen, K.R. (1992). *Women and families: Feminist reconstructions.* New York: Guilford Press.

Bartky, S.L. (1988). Foucault, femininity, and the modernization of patriarchal power (pp. 61–86). In I. Diamond & L. Quinby (eds.), *Feminism & Foucault: Reflections on resistance.* Boston: Northeastern University Press.

Barthes, R. (1972). *Mythologies* (translated by A. Lavaers). New York: Hill & Wang. [Original work published 1957.]

Benhabib, S., & Cornell, D. (eds.). (1987). *Feminism as critique: On the politics of gender.* Minneapolis: University of Minnesota Press.

Bepko, C., & Krestan, J. (1993). *Singing at the top of our lungs: Women, love, and creativity.* New York: HarperCollins.

Best, S., & Kellner, D. (1991). *Postmodern theory.* New York: Guilford Press.

Bloom, A.H. (1981). *The linguistic shaping of thought.* Hillsdale NJ: Lawrence Erlbaum Associates.

Bohan, J.S. (1993). *Every answer is a question: Feminist psychology on the brink.* Unpublished manuscript, Metropolitian State College of Denver, Denver CO.

Bruner, J. (1986). *Actual minds, possible worlds.* Cambridge: Harvard University Press.

Clifford, J. (1986). Introduction: Partial truths (pp. 1-26). In J. Clifford & G.E. Marcus (eds.), *Writing culture: The poetics and politics of ethnography. Berkeley*: University of California Press.

Crites, S. (1986). *Storytime: Recollecting the past and projecting the future* (pp. 152–173). In T.R. Sarbin (ed.), Narrative psychology. New York: Praeger Press.

Cushman, P. (1990). Why the self is empty: Toward a historically situated psychology. *American Psychologist 45*:599–611.

———. (1991). Ideology obscured. *American Psychologist 46*:206–219.

Diamond, I., & Quinby, L. (1988). *Feminism and Foucault: Reflections on resistance.* Boston: Northeastern University Press.

Fine, M. (1988). Sexuality, schooling, and adolescent females: The missing discourse of desire. *Harvard Educational Review 58*: 29–53.

Foucault, M. (1973). *The order of things.* New York: Vintage Press.

———. (1979). *Discipline and punish.* Harmondsworth, England: Penguin Books, Ltd.

———. (1980). *Power/knowledge* (C. Gordon, ed.). New York: Pantheon Books.

Freud, S. (1963). *Dora: An analysis of a case of hysteria.* New York: Collier Books. [Original work published 1905]

Gavey, N. (1992). Technologies and effects of heterosexual coercion. *Feminism & Psychology 2*:325–351.

Goodrich, T.J. (ed.). (1991). *Women and power: Perspectives for family therapy.* New York: W.W. Norton.

Griffith, J., & Griffith, M. (1992). Owning one's epistemological stance in therapy. *Dulwich Centre Newsletter 1*:5–11.

Haavind, H. (1984). Love and power in marriage (pp. 136–167). In H. Holter (ed.), *Patriarchy in a welfare society. Oslo, Norway: Universitetsforlaget.* [Distribution in the United States, New York: Columbia University Press.]

Harding, S. (1987). *Feminism and methodology: Social science issues.* Bloomington: Indiana University Press.

Hare-Mustin, R.T. (1991). *Sex, lies, and headaches: The problem is power* (pp. 63–85). In T.J. Goodrich (ed.), *Women and power: Perspectives for therapy.* New York: W.W. Norton.

———. (1992a). Cries and whispers: The psychotherapy of Anne Sexton. *Psychotherapy 29*:406–409.

———. (1992b), November). On the need for second-order change in family therapy research. Paper presented at the Clinical/Research Conference of the American Family Therapy Academy, Captiva Island FL.

———, & Marecek, J. (1988). The meaning of difference: Gender theory, postmodernism, and psychology. *American Psychologist 43*: 455–464.

———, & Marecek, J. (1990). *Making a difference: Psychology and the construction of gender.* New Haven: Yale University Press.

Hochschild, A., with A. Machung (1989). *The second shift: Working parents and the revolution at home.* New York: Viking Press.

Hollway, W. (1984). Gender difference and the production of subjectivity (pp. 227–263). In J. Henriques, W. Hollway, C. Urwin, C. Venn, & V. Walkerdine (eds.), *Changing the subject: Psychology, social regulation, and subjectivity.* New York: Methuen.

———, (1989). *Subjectivity and method in psychology: Gender, meaning and science.*

Hunter, A. (1992). Same door, different closet: A heterosexual sissy's coming-out party. *Feminism & Psychology 2*: 367–385.

572

HARE-MUSTIN

James, K., & MacKinnon, L. (1990). The "incestuous family" revisited: A critical analysis of family therapy myths. *Journal of Marital and Family Therapy 16*: 71–88.

Jameson, F. (1981). *The political unconscious: Narrative as a socially symbolic act.* Ithaca NY: Cornell University Press.

Kramer, D. (1991, October). Said the poet to the analyst. *The Psychiatric Times.*

Lyotard, J. (1984). *The postmodern condition.* Minneapolis: University of Minnesota Press.

Madigan, S.P. (1993). *Questions about questions: Situating the therapist's curiosity in front of the family* (pp. 219–236). In S. Gilligan & R. Price (eds), *Therapeutic conversations.* New York: W.W. Norton.

———, & Law, I. (1992). Discourse not language. *Dulwich Centre Newsletter 1*: 31–36.

Mednick, M.T. (1989). On the politics of psychological constructs: Stop the bandwagon, I want to get off, *American Psychologist 44*: 1118–1123.

Middlebrook, D.W. (1991). *Anne Sexton.* Boston: Houghton Mifflin.

Miller, D. (1993). Incest: The heart of darkness (pp. 181–195). In E. Imber-Black (ed.), *Secrets in families and family therapy.* New York: W.W. Norton.

Minnich, E.K. (1990). *Transforming knowledge.* Philadelphia PA: Temple University Press.

Minuchin, S. (1991). The seductions of constructivism. *The Family Therapy Networker 15*(5): 47–50.

Morawski, J.G. (1990). Toward the unimagined: Feminism and epistemology in psychology (pp. 150–183). In R.T. Hare-Mustin & J. Marecek (eds), *Making a difference: Psychology and the construction of gender.* New Haven: Yale University Press.

Okin, S.M. (1989). *Justice, gender, and the family.* New York: Basic Books.

Parker, I. (1992). *Discourse dynamics.* London: Routedge & Kegan Poul.

Pollitt, K. (1991). The death is not the life. *The New York Times Book Review* (August 18): 1, 21–22.

Real, T. (1990). The therapeutic use of self in constructionist/systemic therapy. *Family Process 29*: 255–272.

Riger, S. (1992). Epistemological debates, feminist voices: Science, social values, and the study of women. *American Psychologist 47*: 730–740.

Rorty, R. (1979). *Philosphy and the mirror of nature.* Princeton NJ: Princeton University Press.

Sagrestano, L.M. (1992). The use of power and influence in a gendered world. *Psychology of Women Quarterly 16*: 439–447.

Shotter, J. (1991). *Power on the margins: A new place for intellectuals to be.* Unpublished manuscript, Swarthmore College, Swarthmore PA.

Smith, T.E. (1991). Lie to me no more: Believable stories and marital affairs. *Family Process 30*: 215–225.

Spence, D.P. (1987). *The Freudian metaphor: Toward a paradigm change in psychoanalysis.* New York: W.W. Norton.

Stanley, A. (1991). Poet told all: Therapist provides record. *The New York Times* (July 15): Al, C13.

Stigliano, T. (1993). The moral construction of the self. *Journal of Theoretical and Philosophical Psychology, 13*: 48–61.

Stoltenberg, J. (1989). *Refusing to be a man: Essays on sex and justice.* Portland OR: Breitenbush Books.

HARE-MUSTIN

Tavris, C. (1992). *The mismeasure of woman*. New York: Simon & Schuster.

Tomm, K. (1993). The courage to protest: A commentary on Michael White's work (pp. 62–80). In S. Gilligan & R. Price (eds.), *Therapeutic conversations*. New York: W. W. Norton.

Waldegrave, C. (1990). Just therapy. *Dulwich Centre Newsletter 1*: 6–46.

Walters, M., Carter, B., Papp, P., & Silverstein, O. (1988). *The invisible web: Gender patterns in family relationships*. New York: Guilford Press.

Weedon, C. (1987). *Feminist practice and poststructuralist theory*. New York: Basil Blackwell.

White, M. (1993). Deconstruction and therapy (pp. 22–61). In S. Gilligan & R. Price (eds.), *Therapeutic conversations*. New York: W. W. Norton

————, & Epston, D. (1990). *Narrative means to therapeutic ends*. New York: W. W. Norton.

HARE-MUSTIN

LOVE AND VIOLENCE
Gender Paradoxes in Volatile Attachments*

Virginia Goldner
Peggy Penn
Marcia Sheinberg
Gillian Walker

AS FAMILY has widened its scope by bringing social problems like battering, child abuse, and incest into the consulting room, the violent aspects of intimate life have become more visible. This has led to intense debate about how to think about and conduct clinical work with these populations (4, 6, 8, 10, 11, 14, 20, 21, 25, 28, 30–32, 34).

In an attempt to engage with these issues and, more generally, to make a contribution to the metatheoretical project of incorporating gender into the basic premises of family therapy (16), we began the Gender and Violence Project at the Ackerman Institute 4 years ago, and decided to focus on battering. Since we considered this a pilot project in which we would learn about these

The authors, listed above in alphabetical order, have contributed equally to the ideas presented in this article and to writing drafts of the original sections. Virginia Goldner synthesized this material and wrote the final draft. Partial funding for this project has been made possible by Jean Stein, through a grant from the Doris Jones Stein Foundation.

kinds of relationships through the process of treatment, we worked primarily (but not exclusively) with couples who sought treatment voluntarily, and we intentionally kept the project small so that we could work slowly, carefully, and in depth with each couple. As a result, we consider the ideas in this essay to be the outcome of a truly collaborative process between the four of us and the men and women who have participated in this study.

OUR METAPERSPECTIVIST STANCE

In our thinking about these matters, we have assumed a doubled vision: gender and violence, men and women; and a double stance: feminist and systemic. This layering of perspectives has inclined us toward the view, supported by earlier research (6, 14), that relationships in which women are abused are not unique but, rather, exemplify in extremis the stereotypical gender arrangements that structure intimacy between men and women generally. Our hope has been that if we could "unpack" the unworkable premises about gender and power that underlie these dangerous relationships, we could interrupt the cycle of violence, and thus make love safer for women and less threatening to men. Insofar as we have been successful in this effort, we hope we have made a contribution that extends beyond the bleak confines of battering relationships by illuminating something more universal about the structure of male-female attachments.

In our project, we were looking for a description that was consistent with our beliefs as feminists, and simultaneously consistent with our beliefs as systems thinkers and therapists. We tried to get beyond the reductionistic view of men as simply abusing their power, and of women as colluding in their own victimization by not leaving. This description casts men as tyrants and women as masochists, which deprives both of their humanity while simultaneously capturing a piece of the truth.

In order to think more complexly, we decided to test ourselves, to see if it was possible to maintain a "both-and" position when treating couples with this problem. Could we see the problem through both lenses? Would that be helpful in stopping the violence? How would this doubled vision translate clinically? Is conjoin therapy philosophically consistent with our feminist position about battering? Could we make it consistent and still maintain our systemic perspective? Could it be made consistent and still be clinically contraindicated? For which couples would conjoint treatment be helpful, and when?

We knew we would be pulled by the "either/or," either implicitly "blaming the victim" because, in seeing how the woman was implicated in her victimization, we would be inevitably implying that she was responsible for it, or, reciprocally, we were at risk of "constructing a villain" because, in not looking beyond the man's abuse of his power, we would not be making contact with the totality of his subjective experience.

By selecting couples who wanted to stay together, and treating them in conjoint therapy, we knew the risks. Both professionally and politically, there are many cogent arguments that the use of battering groups for men and support groups for women is the most appropriate treatment strategy (4, 10, 25, 32, 34). This position makes sense. First, conjoint therapy, by definition, implies that there is a mutual problem to be solved, and this almost inevitably slides into the implication of mutual responsibility for it. This construction of the situation denies and obscures the social reality that the man is more powerful than the woman, and this distortion then falsifies the therapy. If the woman were to act as if she were equal, expressing her opinions and emotions freely, she would put herself in danger after the session. If she protects herself and the fragile relationship that she, for whatever reasons, wishes to maintain, the therapy is inauthentic. On the other hand, there were no well-conceived batterers groups for us to connect with, and the couples who came to us explicitly wanted to be seen conjointly.

These men and women occupied every segment of American society, for example, architects, professors, artists, corporate executives, social workers, small business men and women, chronically unemployed "mental patients" and others with severe social and psychiatric handicaps, and families on welfare. For some clients, this was their first therapy experience generally (or the first for this problem); others had been "through the system," including shelters, groups for batterers, the courts, and so on. In some cases, substance abuse was present and implicated in the violence; in others, drugs and alcohol were not used, or their moderate use did not seem to play a significant role in the problem.

Although these differences obviously shaped our thinking, and our interventive stance and strategy, we found more commonalities than differences with regard to the psychic infrastructure of violence. It is these common themes that we emphasize in this essay.

It was thus, in the context of these kinds of clients and of these ideas and questions, that we began our project 4 years ago. While we continue to question our thinking and modify our approach, we have clarified and refined many of these early questions and dilemmas. Our working assumptions are summarized below:

1. We begin with the recognition that gender inequality is a social reality and that women who are beaten by men are their victims. At the same time, we believe that reciprocities and complementary patterns in the couple's relationship are implicated in the cycle of violence.

2. At an ethical level, we hold the batterer responsible for the violence and intimidation, and we hold the woman responsible for protecting herself, to the extent that this is possible.

3. We believe that social control is sometimes necessary to stop the violence, and that violence is a criminal act for which legal sanctions are appro-

577

priate. However, since we are interested in the psychological dimensions of violence, including the psychological rationalizations for it, our work, whenever possible, is separated from activities of social control.

We also posed for ourselves a moral question: To maintain that violent acts and violent relationships have a psychology, did this once again let batterers "off the hook"? In putting both partners on the same level, since each one has a psychological interior, weren't we making them equal parties to a dangerous relationship we believed was not equal? We decided not.

We decided to maintain a position of "both–and," arguing that one level of description or explanation does not exclude another. To say that violence, domination, subordination, and victimization are psychological, does not mean they are not also material, moral, or legal. In other words, to develop a psychological explanation of violence is not to explain it away.

Thus, our attempt to discern and construct meaning in acts of violence does not overrule or substitute for our clear moral position regarding the acts themselves. Violence may be "explainable," but it is not excusable, and it may or may not be forgivable. That is up to the victim. For us, as therapists, what is important is to make sense of the confusing *circumstance* of violence so that the parties caught in its grip can begin to stop it.

One description we find useful, and useful clinically, is to understand male violence as simultaneously an instrumental and an expressive act. Its instrumentality rests on the fact that it is a powerful method of social control. A man can enforce his will and extend his areas of privilege in a relationship by hitting or merely threatening to hit his wife. Eventually he can get his way merely by a shift in his tone of voice or facial expression. In this sense, violence is a strategy of intimidation in the service of male domination, a strategy that a man consciously "chooses." At another level, violence can be understood as an impulsive, expressive act. It is often felt by men to be a regressive experience, the feeling of "losing it." We believe that both are true: that male violence is both willful and impulse ridden, that it represents a conscious strategy of control, and a frightening, disorienting loss of control.

These two ways of seeing are part of a matrix of explanations we rely on as we try to make sense of the quixotic juxtapositions of love and hate, control and dependency, remorse and cynicism, and change and no change in these dangerous relationships.

In the discussion to follow, we will be weaving ideas across four levels of description and explanation: psychodynamic, social learning, sociopolitical, and systemic. The psychoanalytic aspect of our work involves inquiry about ideas, beliefs, and, more deeply, internal representations of self and other, which are sometimes out of awareness but, when elucidated, often seem to constitute the organizing and unworkable premises underlying these couples' fierce attachments. The social learning dimension focuses on how these particular men and women were socialized into their gendered positions in these relationships. At the sociopolitical level, we include all of the external power differentials between men and women, including men's subjective sense of entitlement, privilege, and permission to rule women, and women's subjective belief that they must serve men. Finally, at the systemic level, we are interested in the transactional sequences, especially positive feedback loops, which are the immediate "cause" of the escalations that lead to violence, as well as all the double-binding processes between the couple, the extended families, and the treatment and social-service contexts that constitute the problem-maintaining system.

It is important to clarify the tension between these different stances in our work. As these remarks indicate, we are working within a "both-and" framework, which means we repudiate the stance of the forced choice. It also means that we repudiate the false dichotomies that forced choices dictate. Indeed, what we are trying to do is to push against the boundary definitions of a variety of philosophical stances in order to see how they stretch, what they disallow, and what it means to shift from frame to frame in order to describe most fully the human and therapeutic dilemmas that these couples present to us.

Although a full discussion of these matters lies well beyond the scope of these introductory remarks, we do want to make one point about our process of making distinctions. We have not found too many hard edges. The moves from a constructivist to a feminist stance, or from a systemic to a psychodynamic perspective, do not appear to require the paradigm shifts that the history of these ideas in family therapy would have led us to expect. We feel considerable freedom of movement. This is because we track the clinical process closely, and because, in whatever frame we occupy, we remain sensitive to the same set of issues: the place of language in constructing reality, the position of the observer or observing group that inevitably frames the problem and defines the terms of the problem-maintaining system, the moral limits of relativism, and the attempt to operate with the belief in an "observer-independent world-out-there" without succumbing to a naive, simple construction of "truth." We remain skeptical about essences, universals, and stable meanings, and we believe the layering of these intellectual perspectives is necessary if we are to capture the nuanced complexity of the issues at hand.

In our clinical work, we have borrowed what we liked from other methods and created new strategies as we went along. If there are distinctive elements to this mixture, they include the following: emphasizing the volitional aspects of violence; clarifying the relationship between violence, therapy, and social control in each case; elucidating the contradictory messages each partner may have already received about how to proceed (strong warnings against conjoint therapy from the shelter movement, family pressure to "stay together" or to separate, and so on); deconstructing the psychological interior of the violent episode for both partners; positively describing and then "unpacking" the attachment the couple feels for each other despite the violence; including (when indicated) the family of origin in the treatment to loosen the grip of negative injunctions and loyalty conflicts; seeing each member of the couple separately when we are concerned about the woman's safety and whenever we believe it will further the treatment; and always understanding the dilemmas of both partners in terms of the gendered premises and paradoxes that bind them.

In this essay, the first of a series, we will emphasize the theoretical aspects of our work, and therefore we make reference to these clinical techniques only insofar as they serve to illustrate the ideas we are developing. Moreover, in our attempt to highlight the overdetermined, gender-specific dilemmas that each partner brings to the couple relationship, we have had to shift our written focus from couple transactions to individual narratives. This does not mean that we consider an individual's history or psyche more pertinent than a couple's present relational pattern. Rather, we have chosen here to elaborate on those aspects of our thinking that are less familiar than the systemic formulations which do remain central to our work. In subsequent publications, we will describe in more detail the clinical approach summarized above.

A FEMINIST RELATIONAL VIEW OF BATTERING

Using the lens of feminist theory, we have been examining the gender assumptions that inform relationships in which women are physically abused. In analyzing men's violence against their female partners, and women's lack of commitment to their own safety, we hope to make a contribution that illuminates something more universal about the structure of male–female relationships under current social conditions.

We begin our analysis, leaning on 20 years of feminist scholarship, with the formulation that gender is a basic metaphysical category which, in every culture, prescribes an artificial division of the world into masculine and feminine. Most languages are elaborately gendered; all the significant elements of the social, natural, and spiritual world are linguistically differentiated by gender; and the mythologies of most cultures rely heavily on gender symbols. Thus, the construction of gender and of gender difference is not merely a psychological process or a social role; it is also a universal principle of cultural life that manifests itself in the individual psyche, the metaphysical framework, and the ideologies of a society (33).

In a now classic article, feminist anthropologist Gayle Rubin (26) observed: "The division of labor by sex can be seen as a taboo against the sameness of men and women which divides the sexes into two mutually exclusive categories and thereby *creates* gender. . . Far from an expression of natural difference, exclusive gender identity is suppression of natural similarities" (p. 180).

This taboo against similarity, and the dread of the collapse of gender difference operates silently and powerfully in all relations between men and women (13). The patriarchal structure of power and privilege in society positions men to experience humiliation when gender divisions blur, and positions women for punishment if they claim male prerogatives. *Indeed we have come to think about battering as a man's attempt to reassert gender difference and gender dominance, when his terror of not being different enough from "his" woman threatens to overtake him.*

While such fears are clearly extreme in these men, they are, according to many current theories of gender-identity formation, normatively central to the development of masculinity (3, 5, 7, 9, 15, 23, 29). Thus, in order to make sense of this kind of male violence, it is necessary to develop an analysis and critique of "masculinity" generally. Although a full discussion of these matters lies well beyond the scope of this essay, the following synopsis of the relevant theorizing is intended to provide a frame-work for understanding our particular way of formulating the issues.

The contemporary theories of gender-identity development that are compatible with our thinking conceive of "gender" as a deeply internalized psychic structure. They presume that gender acquisition is a process of social learning rather than an expression of natural givens. Moreover, now that researchers have shown that gender identity gets established and consolidated between 12 and 36 months (3), much earlier than had previously been thought, it is becoming clear that the development of the self and the acquisition of gender become fatefully intertwined in early life. In other words, personhood and gender identity develop together, co-evolving and co-determining each other. In this sense, gender is not merely "acquired" by the child but, rather, *creates* the conflict-laden layering of internalized self-representations that *become* the child. As a result, one could no more become "degendered" than "deselfed" (17).

The social context of this psychological process is conceptualized by gender identity theorists (most notably, Nancy Chodorow) in terms of the phenomenon of "asymmetrical parenting". Since women are the primary caretakers of children, both boys and girls must begin the project of becoming a person by defining themselves within the context of their relationship to a single, psychologically gendered woman. This lopsided social arrangement, in which men have traditionally played a marginal role, is considered to have decisive consequences for the creation of gendered personalities.

While the girl's psychic structure develops in relation to someone "just like her," the boy constructs his identity via an experience of difference. Because of the primacy of the mother in early life, and the absence of an equivalently substantial relationship with the father, learning to be masculine comes to mean learning to be "not-feminine." Indeed, as Greenson (15) and others have argued, for boys, this gender difference becomes the vehicle for separating from, and dis-identifying with their mothers. In other words, the boy constructs his sense of himself out of a negative: "I am not like my Mother; I

581

am not female." In the view of most gender-identity theorists, this childhood negation creates problems for the psychological foundation of masculinity, so that when the boy becomes a man, this gender structure is potentially threatened whenever experience calls up echoes of that early maternal bond, that early identification, that early separation. The thinking is that since mother, and later all women, exist as continual reminders of what must be given up to be male, it is not surprising that researchers have found that boys maintain more sharply dichotomous gender divisions than girls (5), and that fathers have been shown to enforce gender stereotyping much more rigidly than mothers (18).

By contrast, a woman's identity is forged *within* a feminine relational context and, in a sense, the girl remains part of the mother's psychological space. Gender theorists have argued that this formative female bonding creates the conditions for a woman's empathic orientation, and also for her difficulties in *separating* herself from relationships. Moreover, insofar as the daughter experiences herself as likened to, bonded with, and sometimes virtually *part of* a person of subordinate social rank, she must struggle to claim for herself what her mother was denied: a voice of her own, a mind of her own, a life of her own. Thus, it is not her gender identity that is at risk in her identificatory bond with mother, but her sense of personal power and agency.

Since the girl cannot receive the mantle of power from one who does not have it, she must sometimes settle for "the power behind the throne." This means that the work of becoming female is shaped by the necessity of learning how to become, what Jessica Benjamin (3) has called, an "object of (male) desire," which inevitably must conflict with the task of becoming a subject in one's own right. Instead of being a subject in search of herself, a woman must often transform herself into a "subject-as-object" (7). Not surprisingly, this process of self-betrayal can create its own rebellion.

Given this analysis, men and women under the best of circumstances form attachments in which they must seek in one another the capacities each has lost. This search often results in the problematic complementarities that family therapists encounter in treating couples, and which are often so difficult to change. In our view, it is only when both partners become committed to transcending the rigid categories of gender difference, and can begin to tolerate their disowned similarities, that real change is possible. This would involve, for the woman, reclaiming a sense of her independent subjectivity and establishing or re-establishing her capacity for agency in the world. For the man, the task requires recognition and acceptance of his own dependency needs, and simultaneously learning how to empathize with his mate's subjective experience, with her needs and desires as they exist for her, and not as he defines them.

While such a transformation asks a lot of both partners in ordinarily troubled relationships, it puts a special burden on the man who is violent and the woman whom he abuses. In these circumstances, such a man must tolerate a sense of weakness for perhaps the first time. Since his sense of personal power and psychic autonomy is an illusion that is sustained by denying his illusion that is sustained by denying his dependency needs through controlling his partner, he can become deeply threatened if he begins to see his mate as a person in her own right (who might leave, or disagree, or compete with him). Thus, he may fight against her attempts at independence despite the best of intentions. Indeed, for many of these men, the fear of disintegration, if they sense that the woman may leave them *in any way*, is so great that they will frantically try to regain control by any means necessary (25).

If the woman is to retain a sense of her entitlement in the face of such intimidation, she must silence the voices from within her and the messages from the culture at large. Everywhere she turns she will hear that she is transgressive if she fails to please him. When she does assert her right to her own experience, her own sexuality, her right to be cared for, he may term her hysterical, extravagant, or insatiable. He may threaten to leave her, thus signaling his social and economic superiority, or he may become violent, thus asserting his physical superiority. She may be confused by his rage because her experience of herself and his view of her are disparate; but she too has been raised in a culture that elevates the male perspective, so she may silence her own mind and submit to his construction of reality even if that means being hit (1).

Given these temptations, the conjoint therapy of battering must provide a framework for dismantling the powerful gender injunctions that set the terms for such relationships, terms that virtually prescribe male domination and female subjugation.

GENDER PREMISES/GENDER PARADOXES

In order to challenge the gender assumptions that we believe provide the legitimation for battering, we have had to refine our thinking about the gendering process. Our theorizing presumes that gender is simultaneously rooted in the biological difference between the sexes, and that the other crucial determinants of gender identity are psychological, cultural, and political. Thus, not only do we take as a given the social learning, sociopolitical and psychoanalytic explanations of gender formation that were articulated earlier in this essay, but we also make a bridge between the psychological and social levels by interpolating a family-systems formulation of the gendering process.

We would argue that not only is gender deeply embedded in the psyche, as the psychoanalysts maintain, but it is also *deeply embedded in the politics of family relations*. Similarly, we believe that ideas about how to be male or female are not simply transmitted from parent to child, as the social learning theorists suggest, but that *these premises become part of the family drama*. Elaborating on the earlier work of Penn (24) and Sheinberg (27) that developed the construct of the family or relationship "premise," we now argue that gender

583

premises, like other passionately held beliefs, create relationship binds and paradoxes across the generations, which are then internalized within the psyche and create for each generation a legacy of insoluble contradictions.

The men and women we see in relationships in which there is battering frequently grew up in families in which these gender dichotomies were rigidly prescribed and exaggerated. Because these gender injunctions were writ large, it has been easier to see the inherent paradoxes that are embedded in the gendering process. For example, one woman's story reads, "Mom doesn't stand up to dad and she seems always silently angry and depressed. But, whenever I get argumentative, she says that I'm 'too masculine' and no man will want me." Or, from a man's story we distill the message he felt *his* mother was sending: "Be strong like your father so that you will be able to protect women like me from men like him." And, from a powerful father to his daughter, "The reason I have to beat your mother is that she 'makes me do it.' If only I were married to someone understanding [like you] we could have a happy home." And from father to son: "You must never be a wimp or feel afraid, but watch out for women. They can do you in. For every Sampson there is a Delilah with scissors."

The contradictions inherent in the conflicting logic of these gender constructions generate paradoxes at all levels of psychic and familial organization. The child not only absorbs these mystifying presentations of filial gender arrangements, but is also enlisted in participating in impossible relationship binds as a function of his or her sex. In other words, the child's sex becomes implicated in the political force field of the family drama.

Thus, the gendered relationship maps that organize both family and psychic life tend to generate untenable coalitions, rivalries, and hierarchies, as well as profound internal confusion. It is, we believe, these overdetermined, internally contradictory, deeply embedded relationship premises, which are always at risk of collapsing under their own weight, that infuse the episodes of violence in the lives of these couples.

In the sections to follow, we will attempt to "unpack" the generational premises and paradoxes about gender identity and gender relations that are implicated in the violence/redemption cycle that characterizes these dangerous relationships.

THE MAN'S SIDE

Gendered premises about masculinity are rigidly adhered to in the families of the men we have been seeing who are violent toward women. These premises, for example, that men must be stronger than women, and that they must not be sad or afraid, are in direct conflict with psychological reality. Men, like women and children, often feel dependent, scared, sad, and in need of protection. Since the prohibitions against such "feminized" feelings include the man's private sense of himself, and not only his public persona, the psychological task of denial is constant. This is why intimacy can be so dangerous. When the man's terror of not being different enough from "his" woman overtakes him, violence becomes one means of reasserting gender difference and male power.

The injunction against having "unmasculine" feelings is sent to all men through all the channels of the culture. In our clinical work with violent men, we have been tracking the generational transmission of this prohibition and the ways in which it fatefully compromised both the father/son and mother/son relationship.

Looking first at the fathers, we hypothesize that, in these families, the son developed the conviction that his father's love was contingent on his fulfilling a particular definition of masculinity. In one case, for example, the son's connection to his father was predicted on never showing fear, in another it was a readiness to fight back against a perceived insult to the family, in another, never to listen to a woman's opinion, in another, always to use physical force when threatened. The fact that many of the fathers of these men were abusive underlined that father's love was conditional, and that it could be easily transformed into its opposite: some form of brutality. This set the stage for a lifetime of trying to become the man father would at last love and respect.

Because these men grew up believing that they had to be a "man" in order to be worthy of a man's love, they hid their vulnerabilities even from themselves. Their childhood experience with their fathers was so limited and so conditional that it created an intense but deeply buried longing for male connection. However, since cultural prohibitions and particular family dynamics made having an openly declared, mutually affirming relationship with father impossible, these men had to make a bond with father symbolically. In other words, instead of "being with" father, they settled for "being like" father. In place of a paternal relationship, they could only substitute a paternal identification (5).

This solution is itself part of the problem. Ironically, the only way the "fatherless boy" can maintain some sense of being close to his father is by making himself into the kind of "macho man" who disavows his yearning for closeness and denies any need for others. In one couple, Raymond, for example, described his father in what seemed to be an admiring tone, as "a tough guy, tough emotionally and tough physically." Yet, when the therapist asked, "Did you respect that toughness?", he paused and slowly added, "No, I don't think so. . . . I had very little respect for my father, at least outwardly. At least I used to say all the time that I had no respect for him. I'd even tell *him* that. But now I don't know if that's true. . . . These days I wonder, since I'm very much the same style, if I wasn't really, secretly, thinking it was a good thing. However, I *hated* it at the time."

Given a childhood marked by these extreme demands for gender conformity, men like Raymond enter adult relationships with impossible prohibitions ("I must never feel fear, know need, respect a woman's point of view"). Not surprisingly, such premises prove unworkable since, just as when he was a boy, this man still has yearnings and anxieties, and, despite himself, he is quite capable of being deeply "hooked in" to a woman's experience and to see the world through a woman's eyes. Moreover, he is now in a relationship with a woman, and the temptations to let his guard down are everywhere.

One solution to this quandary seems to involve arranging for an emotional division of labor in which the woman "carries" the unacceptable feminine feelings for both of them. That way, the needs get met and the feelings expressed, but the man does not experience them as coming from within (2). Indeed, it is when he is most close to recognizing the feeling as his own that, we believe, he is most tempted to be violent.

Raymond, for example, repeatedly proclaims he will never be a wimp. This premise has resulted in his alienating virtually everyone around him. He is a man without friends, without a job, and with an extremely troubled relationship with his wife and children. He came to marriage therapy after hitting his wife. He was motivated by her threat to leave him if he didn't change.

In the course of therapy, we observed that anytime Raymond risked listening to his wife, or being persuaded by her point of view, he argued ferociously. We speculated that it was when he was almost convinced by her opinion, or at the moment that he appeared closest to his "wimp" feelings, that he fought against his wife the hardest.

John developed a different strategy for denying his vulnerabilities in order to maintain some kind of attachment with his harsh father. A young wrestler, he was terrified of the city, but denied his fear by converting it into worry over his wife's safety. This "concern" provided the justification for his not allowing her to go anywhere without him. In time, his preoccupation with her safety resulted in his physically restraining her when she tried to go to work. Thus, the man who had been terrified by the city vanished, replaced by a fearless husband who was protecting his wife from the dangers outside their home.

Because John's parents, especially his father, raised him with the strong injunction never to feel fear, let alone to voice it, we speculated that he feels at risk of losing his psychological connection to his father, which for him is fused with his masculine identity, if he acknowledges feeling frightened. To feel fear raises the feared question, "Am I still a man, a man that father would respect?"

Unfortunately, the mothers of these sons were unable to help them work out a viable relationship with their fathers. In fact, we have observed that it was often one son who was selected to be beaten, and this same son was enlisted by his mother in a coalition against his father's brutality. Ironically, the terms of this coalition reinforced the very values and behavior they were intended to resist. For instance, one son describes the source of pride his mother felt at his being a fighter; another son shares that he knows he was his mother's favorite son because he was more "macho" than his brother; another describes how his mother always protected his brother while encouraging him to fight back.

Thus, in many of our cases, the bond between mother and son existed as a covert coalition in the shadow of the father. To the extent that this was a bond organized around a common experience of subjugation, the boy and his mother had become peers, and occupied the same level of the domestic power hierarchy. Yet, this definition of their relationship is contradictory. The mother, because she is a parent, maintains a senior position in the generational hierarchy while the boy, by virtue of being male in a patriarchal household, is somehow elevated above her.

This paradoxical arrangement put many of these boys in an impossible bind. While still needing their mother's care and protection, they often felt they had to behave as her "little man" in order to lend some kind of credibility to her struggles with father. However, if they bonded too openly with mother, they risked becoming "feminized" in father's eyes, and therefore not "man enough" to win father's approval.

This Gordian knot is tied in many ways, as told by the men in our study. But the common thread is that, as children, these boys felt aligned with their mothers, while wishing they could be close to their fathers. They saw the injustice that mother suffered, and felt, in varying degrees, sympathetically loyal to her, but they craved, nonetheless, to be paired with the powerful, critical father. Thus, these men formed deeply ambivalent, covert attachments to both parents, which they themselves could not fully acknowledge.

587

Our effort has been to understand if and how these contradictory parental loyalties are implicated in the violence/redemption cycle these men enacted with their mates. To this end, we have developed a line of questioning that separates the strands of meaning, memory, and feeling packed into the explosive moment and its denouement. Although each man and each fight is unique, a paradigmatic relational pattern has suggested itself to us.

The constant oscillation between "feminized" devotion and "macho" domination, which characterizes the stance of these men toward their mates, and which has been so often observed both in the literature and by their confused wives, can be viewed as a conflict of divided loyalty. When they are "protecting" their women, it is as though they re-enact their fateful bond with their one-down mothers, which then must be renounced whenever their mates act independently. This is because, when the woman wants to be separate, she experiences her partner's "protectiveness" as controlling and intrusive. At such moments, the mutually comforting, gendered arrangement of knight and damsel shatters, and a control struggle ensures. The man, momentarily "unhooked" from the romantic bond, now reasserts the "manhood" that symbolically bonds father to son. He goes "on the attack," with the goal of subduing "womanhood" by any means necessary. Thus, Dr. Jeckyll becomes Mr. Hyde, and back again, as the dynamics of these volatile relationships move through their infernal circle.

DECONSTRUCTING THE VIOLENT MOMENT

In order to loosen the grip of these dangerous sequences, we have developed an interventive strategy that "deconstructs" the psychological interior of the violence/redemption cycle. Through this process we have found that the violent escalation within each man has many highly condensed, former triggers. When, for example, you see a boy running, you see the simple act of running. However, if you were to draw the act of running, it would be a multipositional rendering of the many and discrete moves packed into the act of running—but it would not be the run. Similarly, there are former and discrete relationship conflicts packed into the violent escalation. When a man says, "I just saw black," or "I felt a fire in my veins," the specific conflicts packed into that sentence are unavailable to him because he is "in the run."

Deconstructing the violent moment, or putting into slow motion this high-speed enactment, means fine-graining its precursors. Repetitious questions yield many descriptions that allow the experience of the violent moment to be differently described, thus bringing new meaning to the experience. These new descriptions or language constructions fit themselves around the man's needs, and we hear fragments of old and new relationship conflicts, jumbled ideas, accusing voices, and painful memories, all acting like explosive flack that surrounds a plane on a war mission when any bump may produce an explosion. Repetitiously inquiring about the man's story and carefully separating all its strands encourages him toward a new story, one in which all his feelings may be included.

We have discussed the violent act as a pseudo-solution to a contradiction these men experience when they have feelings they deem unmanly: dependency, fear, sadness, and so on. These are unacceptable feelings in that they do not fit socialized gender premises about masculinity. Indeed, in remembering the escalation that precedes the violent moment, the men often describe an internal struggle between unmanly feelings and macho feelings, which are described as occurring in rapid-fire alternations.

The following example is one in which the therapist deconstructs the moments leading up to a violent explosion. The questions are asked slowly and repetitiously, separating all the man's descriptions, past and present. It is the case of a young wrestler who finds himself far from home, married, estranged from his wife's family, out of work, and dependent on his wife's menial job. His wife has threatened to leave him if he cannot control his violent rages. This particular session follows a 24-hour fight between them. He arrives saying he must have valium "because my head is coming off and I feel like shit!" His wife reports that he held her down, threatened her, and refused to allow her to go to work. Talking with him alone for the first part of the session, he said his anger started the night before when his wife was on the phone with her father.

Th: You overheard that or. . .

John: No, he said it to me on the phone. . . . .At the time I didn't say anything because . . .To myself I said, "That's the biggest mistake you'd ever make."

Th: Your father-in-law's voice stayed in your head till the next morning when you prevented L [wife] from leaving? Did you say anything to him that night?

John: I said, "Listen Mr. B., I would never harm your daughter. She's my wife and I love her." He said, "I want you to know if you ever do, I'd make that one phone call." He made me sick when he said that. He shouldn't have said that. If he was going to take a hit on me, he should have never said it because now he's. . .

Th: Was that a big mix of anger and fear you went to bed with that night before you prevented L. . . .

John: I'll tell you this, her father is seventy years old. The man is in tremendous condition, healthy as a horse, good-looking, and he's got a lot going for him. If he were fifty, I'd have gone down there and hammered the piss out of him so bad he'd never walk again. I'd have gone down there and wiped the floor with him for threatening my life. Yeah, I was angry.

Th: Do you still have some of the feelings from that phone call?

John: I could run my head through that wall right there, I'm so pissed off at the feelings I have right now, for the way . . .I mean, I just feel . . .Take his two sons! They've never done shit in their life. They walked into their father's business and made it. Me, I was cut for twenty-six stitches; they told me I'd die if I went into the fight. I couldn't breathe through my nose. I got hit for twenty-six stitches in the second round and fought for ten rounds in one-hundred hundred degree heat. I fought for my life, broke both my hands. I mean, I've been fighting for my life. I've been fighting to help my family to have everything and then. . .

His story now includes two families, his wife's and his own. The story of his wife's family torments him because he can't measure up to their social status and his father-in-law has terrified him with his threats of a contract killing. (The family is not to our knowledge in any way connected to "organized crime." Thus, the threat represents, in our view, an empty, intimidating gesture that reflects the father-in-law's own feeling of helplessness and need to appear powerful.) His own story includes desperately trying to fight for his family and not succeeding.

Th: So, before you prevented your wife from leaving for work, were all these ideas mixed up in your head? Feeling rejected by her family and feeling you hadn't done what you wanted to for your own family?

John: (howls)

589

GOLDNER/PENN/SHEINBERG/WAL

Th: So, that morning when you got up you were beginning to feel the "fire in your veins"—Is that "fire" a fire about fighting for your life, for your own family and to be a real husband to L and her family?

John: I'm fighting now! I fought all my life to try to help my parents to get a nice home for them, and I have not accomplished that yet. That bothers me. Even though I'm a highly recognized professional, I couldn't turn around and buy bubble gum right now. (howls again)

Th: So, that morning when you got up and you were thinking about these ideas of fighting for your family and against her family's opinion of you, she said she was going to work. And what happened?

John: I said, "Oh no, you're not going to work. You're not going out there when they can shit on you!"

Th: If she has a demeaning job, do you feel you are both brought down? What did she say first?

John: "Oh yes, I'm going." She challenged me! But it wasn't like L challenging me, it was her parents. It was them.

Th: So, although the challenge comes through L, it's really her parents. Are they saying you failed since she has to go to work?

John: I'm twenty-five years old, I'm not thirty-five. Once the challenge is on, I don't care who you are or how many there are. I'll go down. She gets a certain tone in her voice. When I hear it, I hear her old man.

Th: How would you describe it? That tone?

John: It's something that cuts through me like a knife. Her father will not I mean, you can't have a discussion with him because he's right! You're wrong, Jack, you're out like a light. See, this is the way I'm brought up, when you can't handle things, it's that! (leaps up slapping his clenched fist into the palm of his hand) You're not right, Jack, you're out like a light. I don't want to be like that, but the pressure is so strong right now because I'm fighting to turn things around and make things better. And I can't succeed. Its like I'm fighting a losing battle and it's killing me.

Th: So, that morning when you got up feeling scared and angry, you heard her father's voice and felt it was saying that you were disappointing both families. Is that the challenge?

In this conversation, we can hear John struggling with his confusion between his wish to make both families proud of him, and the feeling that they are, in fact, hurting, frightening, and humiliating him. "I try so hard" is a statement of his best image of himself, and also an idea that leaves room for new meanings. He tries so hard to be a proud person who is available to these families, not "the failure" they reject or abuse.

In the course of this deconstruction, we have hardly spoken about his anger toward his wife; the incident involving her is quickly superseded by other voices that seem to be packed like triggers into the escalation. Three prominent voices are involved: his wife's voice, his father-in-law's voice, and his father's voice. These voices embody ideas and issues that John, like many men, are preoccupied with: to bring distinction to one's family, to carve a significant place in the public world, to be recognized by powerful men as powerful, and not to show fear. In sum, they describe his struggle, his fear of failing, and his wish to succeed.

The repetitious listening and tracking of his story allows him to integrate these ideas, all of which had been disconnected from one another and from the overwhelming affects that too often overtake him. By going through the episode in slow motion and "unpacking" his globalized experience of rage, John can begin to confront both the specific issues and the larger themes that ignite his helpless. Once he can see the pieces, he can start picking them up, one by one, and, if he chooses, he can begin to take charge of his reactivity and his life, piece by piece. He can still choose to be violent when these issues arise, but he can also see that he has a choice, which may then make it easier for him to choose differently, and for his wife to demand that he make a different choice.

THE WOMAN'S SIDE

One of the issues that has preoccupied our thinking has been how to construct an explanation of women's participation in violent relationships. As systems thinkers, we could not be satisfied with a description that cast women as hapless victims, and yet we were opposed to lazily constructed narratives of circularity or, worse, of "function of the symptom" notions in which, by some stretch-of-the imagination reframe, the woman was construed to derive some benefit from her victimization.

In order to include the women in the problem definition, but not to "blame the victim," we have attempted to co-construct with our women clients an explanation of how they were "caught" in the battering situation. More specifically, we wanted to understand why these women did not leave these relationships even when they had the material means to do so, and why they did not seem able to resist the pull of an argument, and often chose to cast the first verbal stone, even when they knew that they were putting their safety at risk.

These questions were not only ours. Often it was the women themselves who urgently asked for help in understanding why they stayed embroiled in these dangerous relationships. Andrea, for example, says, "I guess basically I would like to find out what the hell it is that makes me stay. I really don't know. I keep thinking maybe there's something wrong with me." Wanda puts it this way, "Dick says I blame everything on him, and that I'm really the crazy one. I mean, I will admit I'm crazy to stay, but I don't think I'm the crazy one. I might be, but I don't see it."

The mysterious "stickness" of these relationships was all the more intriguing when we discovered that these women, contrary to what we had imagined, were not timid, self-deprecating, fragile victims. They were victims, but they were, in nearly every case, women of substance who had strong opinions

591

and conveyed a sense of personal power. Over the past 4 years, through our process of interviewing, we have begun to understand this fierce commitment to a man and to a relationship that seems so destructive.

Our thinking owes much to the revisionist theories of female development and psychology that have become increasingly influential in recent years. (3, 5, 7, 12, 19, 22, 31). The central insight in all the new work about women is the idea that women form a sense of self, of self-worth, and of feminine identity through their ability to build and maintain relationships with others. This imperative is passed to daughters from mothers whose view of feminine obligation has been to preserve both family relationships and the family as a whole, no matter what the personal cost. Thus, the daughter, like her mother, eventually comes to measure her self-esteem by the success or failure of her attempts to connect, form relationships, provide care, "reach" the other person.

Sarah, who as a child was beaten (as was her mother) by an alcoholic father, and who now is being battered by her husband Mike, put it like this: "From the time that Mike and I got involved, I got the sense that he was like a hurt child. I felt the best way of working on our relationship was to try to build him up and make him feel better about himself." Thus, even in the context of her own victimization, Sarah, against her own best interests, can humanize her abuser and devote herself to his care.

With this idea alone we have the beginning of a positive re-description of the meanings of staying in a bad relationship. For Sarah or women like her, staying put is not about weak character, morbid dependency, or masochism, but is better understood as an affirmation of the feminine ideal: to hold connections together, to heal and care for another, no matter what the personal cost. As another woman client put it, "I stayed for twenty years, even though I knew after a week that it was a mistake, because 'girls make it work.'" In these terms, staying is what gender pride and self-respect demand.

Put another way, staying protects the woman against the guilt engendered by giving up her caretaking role. More specifically, since women learn to be acutely attuned to the needs of others, their gendered capacity for empathy gives them a subliminal knowledge of the batterer's fragile dependency. Often this means they cannot escape the feeling that in leaving they betrayed the terms of the relationship.

As Sophia puts it, "I become confused. I know he's good. I know he can be really bad. But when he's good, he's good. I'm scared if I leave him he'll start thinking 'She's not worth it anyway. Look what she did to me.'" Thus, a woman who walks out must contend with the meanings and consequences of having claimed the male prerogative of putting herself first.

Given that gender prohibitions in the culture at large create a pressure for women to deny their own agency, we were interested in tracking the generational transmission of these injunctions through the stories and memories of the women in our study. It appears that just as battering men tend to come from families in which there was violence, abuse, or exaggerated patriarchal norms, so many of the abused women with whom we have spoken came from families with an excessive patriarchal structure. In many cases, the mothers played extremely subordinate roles to their husbands; in some cases, the gender hierarchy was reversed and the mother appeared to be in the "up" position. But whether the gender hierarchy was conventional or incongruous, the family belief structure held that men should be stronger than and in charge of women. Thus, whether mother's status was elevated or subjugated, these daughters suffered a kind of existential neglect from growing up in families in which women were undervalued, either by a climate of intimidation or by the belief that men *should* subdue women, even if they were unable to do so.

Common to these women's stories is a description of a family that could not abide the daughter making a claim for herself.

Daughters grew up with the belief that being loved was contingent upon some kind of self-abnegation. Even though most women, in reconstructing their past, can remember some ways in which their families supported, or at least tolerated, their independent strivings, the women we have interviewed do not seem to regard their past as including such spaces. They describe feeling that they did not count unless they were tending to the needs of others. Indeed, many remember their parents as having been critical of them for not being "giving" enough. They believed the family viewed their independent aspirations as an aberration, and some women recounted stories in which their attempts at differentiation or separation were labeled as destructive or even crazy.

593

As we explored the relational politics in which these gender prohibitions were enacted, we came to understand better how problematic and contradictory "femininity" had become for the women in our study. Looking first at the mother/daughter relationship, we speculated that the daughters of mothers who were severely subjugated in their marriages were caught in a painful dilemma. They had to construct a feminine identity out of intensely contradictory feelings toward mother: rage and sympathy, contempt and longing, and so on. The problem for such daughters is that, in order to maintain a positive connection to their mothers, they had to become like their mothers, and thus accept the very premises about being female that made their mothers victims in the first place, and, in many cases, left them feeling maternally abandoned. This is because the primacy of mother's relationship with her verbally or physically abusive husband meant that her daughter frequently experienced her as powerless, devalued, and depressed. Moreover, mother's preoccupation with father rendered her unable fully to nurture, protect, or value her daughter.

The generational transmission and repetition of this pattern is reflected, once again, by Sarah who, at age 32, has been in three abusive marriages and borne seven children, all but one of whom were left to live with their fathers. Looking back at ther life and her choices Sarah remarked, "I'm beginning to realize that mom was probably very much like me as far as her place in the household and with dad. She would totally close off her family, all of them, not be in communication with them, and cater to him, cater to his every need."

Daughters like Sarah were caught in complex triangles. On the one hand, they identified with, and were "lumped" by their fathers with their mothers, who were in the down position. On the other hand, they wanted access to the world of their fathers, who seemed to have the freedom to speak, to rant, to have a life outside the domestic sphere. Moreover, many of these women felt that they were, in some way, preferred by their fathers over their mothers. This, in some cases, was a blatant or implicit incestuous bond; in others, it was simply that their fathers liked their "spunk", even as they tried to subdue them.

Thus, like the men in our study, these women were caught in an impossible loyalty bind. Being loyal to mother meant enduring some kind of social and personal subjugation, while openly choosing their fathers meant betraying their mothers and, in some sense, betraying themselves.

It is against the background of these dilemmas of how to connect and how to be different from their mothers, as well as how to claim male entitlements, that we have come to understand the seemingly crazy behavior of these battered women. In their inability to leave these men, we see the loyal daughter re-enacting mother's stance of submission and upholding femininity's ideal of sacrificial caring. In their unwillingness to resist fruitless and dangerous confrontation with these volatile men, we see the rebellious daughter asserting that she is both different from her mother and militantly opposed to femininity's credo of silence.

Given this contradictory set of impulses and ideals, we make sense of these women's "misguided" compulsion to stay embroiled in impossible relationships by offering the idea that the very ferocity of their involvement is a measure of the ferocity of their drive to expand the culture's definition of feminine affiliation so as to include their own voice. These were women driven to be heard, though the price might be "being hit." They were seeking an intimate attachment that included the emotions usually reserved for men: strong opinions and the right to make one's own needs primary. In their own way, these women were defying what Jean Baker Miller describes as "subservient affiliations" (22), and were attempting to assert their right to a relationship that included recognition of their own personhood.

Sue puts it this way, "So you ask me why am I in this kind of relationship? John does the same thing that my dad did the whole time I was growing up, which is as soon as I get my own opinion about something, and begin to tell him what that is, he tells me to shut up. John says shut the fuck up; my dad just used to say shut up. As a kid I would keep trying, but dad would scream louder than me, and then I wouldn't bother anymore. With John, I don't care how much he screams, I just keep trying to get my opinion out."

THE ALLIANCE

It has been hard to assume that the irrationality of violence has its reasons and that those reasons are powerful enough to hold a couple together in a sometimes fatal attraction. But to react only to the violent "face" of the behavior without viewing its other face, the face of atonement and redemption, is to deny the power of the bond that fully possesses the couple. In the wake of the irrefutable logic that compels the couple to separate, the next wave of that logic breaks, and they are caught in the powerful tides of reaffiliation. This redemptive moment in the couple's cycle, which we are calling "the alliance," is as complexly structured as the violent tide that produced it. Both parts of this cycle must be deconstructed, their elements unpacked and critiqued, if the violence is to stop.

The alliance is a unique aspect of the couple's relationship because it acts to sustain and preserve reconnection after a violent rupture has occurred. It is experienced by both partners as a bond; but, since it is a bond termed by others as shameful, sick, and regressive, it remains a secret, hidden from the world.

The strength of this bond has the potential to defeat the most persusaive shelter or antibattering program: the more outside forces try to separate the couple, the more the bonds binds them together. Clearly, neither partner is going to talk openly about their attachment, or even admit their depth of feeling to themselves, when the relationship has been so uniformly stigmatized by others. Since the true nature of the attachment is often a mystery, even from the protagonists themselves, they will remain caught in its grip, common-sense injunctions to separate notwithstanding. Thus, unless this powerful bond is given its due, the relationship will not be visible in all its aspects, and the couple's bond will become a secret coalition against all outsiders, including the therapists.

For these reasons, early in our work with these couples, we listen for any positive descriptions of their relationship, and we encourage those commentaries as part of our therapeutic conversation. Making space for this kind of dialogue takes away the binding power of the secret. This holds a particular value for the woman, since women living in violent relationships often feel their explanations have deserted them. They are confused and shamed by their wish to remain in a situation that is so harmful. Without a self-respecting explanation to hold onto, these women are vulnerable to the popular psychological notions of why women stay in "sick" relationships.

These standard, pop clichés always blame the victim, who must accept a definition of herself as masochistic, appallingly weak, or just plain crazy. Generating a different explanation, which offers a more positive description of her participation in the relationship, leaves her with a sense of dignity, which may make it possible for her to choose, eventually, to leave, or to stay on very different terms.

Making the hidden bond our point of entry into the therapy creates a fresh space for discovery, and frees the process from the stereotypical discourse that the couple knows so well and has come to expect from outsiders. While we may include standard behavioral interventions, such as "time out" and safety plans, we invite the couple's curiosity by calling their attention to their confusion about the relationship. We open space for the woman to tell us that she remains with this man not only because she's too frightened to leave, but also because of an oddly compelling love that she does not understand.

Similarly, the man may be confused by the fact that he brutalizes her and needs to control every aspect of her life. Often, he has a double vision of himself as a decent and good person, and simultaneously as a man who needs to behave viciously, even to destroy the people he loves. But like her, he cannot leave despite the fact that he perceives her power over him to be deeply humiliating.

Through the process of getting to know the underside of these destructive attachments, we have begun to understand what makes them so compelling. The process of unpacking this affectively charged bond into its constitutive elements is a central focus of the therapy. For purposes of this analysis, we will schematize the process even though, in actuality, these elements are psychologically inseparable and conceptually overlapping.

The life stories of these men and women, his and hers, are narratives filled with pain and disappointment. Yet, when the couple tell the story of their relationship, especially how it began, the cloud lifts. It is as though an electrical connection had been made between them, a bond that keeps them attached despite the crazy violence.

Initially, and implicity, the couple's bond is positioned against their families origin and against the world at large. Tracing the history of this theme through the reconstructions of both partners led us to speculate that each of them was looking for a magical rescue from the loyalty binds and gender injunctions they experienced in their original families. They were looking for a deus ex machina, and, like many of us, they found it in the extravagant illusions of romantic love. Each partner believed that they had found a perfect match, and together they formed a complementary, reparative bond premised on the fantasy of a yin/yang "fit" between them.

For our purposes, the most intriguing aspect of their initial attraction was the way in which it seemed to represent, at least in part, an attempt to escape the rigid strictures of gender conformity that had been enforced by their families of origin. For the men who had to deny or suppress any sign of need or vulnerability, the relationship represented the chance to reclaim these affects without dishonor. As one man put it, "Alice accepts my weaknesses and my sensitivity. With my mother, I had to be always strong, never weak". And, for the women who were raised to submit and be silent, the relationship gave early dignity to their voice. In Sarah's words, "Mike respects my opinion as no one else has."

This rebellion against oppressive gender codes creates a belief that the relationship is a unique haven from the outside world. The power (and danger) of this illusory escape fantasy is reflected in the observations of Joe and Alice, a couple who have sustained their feeling of specialness despite Alice's two broken ribs.

> *Joe*: Maybe at one level we argue like hell, which is really true, but at another level me and Alice accept each other a hundred percent. She accepts my sensitivity and my weaknesses, unlike my mother, and she's given me free rein to develop according to my own way of developing.
>
> *Alice*: I don't know why there is a bond between him and me, and not between me and anyone else. I don't know why that's true, except he allowed me to see his weaknesses. Therefore, I don't see him as a threat; even if he hits me I don't really see him as a threat. He allows himself to be vulnerable to me, and I never had that role before, ever. That set our relationship. That formed the bond between us, and it's lasted to this day, damaged as it is. That hooked me.

It should be no surprise that this bond, premised on the hope that love can provide reparation for the injuries of the past and freedom from the constraints of the culture, cannot survive the ordinary insults of daily life. A reparative experience is inherently a critique that cannot be sustained. In this case, it is a challenge to family loyalty and to conventional gender dichotomies.

With regard to gender, insofar as the bond is based on an acknowledgement of repressed similarities, the very desire to loosen gender-incongruent prohibitions pushes the man toward an intolerable feeling of similarity to the women. Eventually, this collapse of difference will become too compromising, and he will have to reassert his masculine difference from her by becoming menacing or even violent.

We can see this turnabout in Joe, who apparently can only tolerate Alice's knowlege of his "weakness" if she devotes herself completely to his care. As he puts it, "One thing I notice that I go through every time I hit her is my intense need for her. . . . When things get to the point that I need her a lot and I can't get her, I want her. I want her, that's it. I want her love, I want her attention, and I'll get it. I'll get it no matter what."

Another trigger embedded in the very terms of the couple's bond is the loyalty conflict it engenders with regard to their families of origin. In a sense, they are serving two alliances, one to their family of origin and one to each other. For many couples, the most incendiary situation is when one member of the couple attacks the other's family. At these times, the one whose family

597

is under attack forfeits his or her alliance with the mate, and rallies toward the family of origin. Now the spouse/ ally appears as a representative of the outside world, an enemy of the original family.

This seems to be especially true of the men. Many of them describe feeling that they always had to stand up for their families, protecting them from the rest of the world. When the families of these men are compared to other families, it is clear that the family felt itself to "suffer by comparison," that other families had more money, status, background, and education. Several men in our group grew up with family slogans that embody this loyalty mandate: "Don't fool with Kuhl," or "The fighting Fagins"! They describe violent fights on behalf of their families when the family endured insults from outsiders, or when they believed they were perceived by others as inferior, incompetent, or deficient. Yet, while violently defending their families from the slings and arrows of outsiders, they were often the sons most beaten and abused within the family.

The following sequence from an interview with Sue and John illustrates how quickly discussion of these issues can get dangerous.

John: Mother is very quiet and timid.
Sue: His mother never says a damn word about anything.
Th: Is she afraid?
John: Of my father? No, she was just. . .
Sue: Tell her about the times you used to call out to her. You're being beaten up, you're under the bed, being smacked around with a belt, you're calling for your mom who sat and listened to it.
John: I guess she was afraid, obviously she was afraid. Listen, I'd get off this if I were you, because I'm starting to get a little upset.

Given the unworkable premises that underlie the bond that binds these couples, the sudden switch from ally to enemy is understandable. As long as all the blame is placed on mother and father, the adult-child victim can feel rescued by a similarly injured fellow traveler. But this stance is inherently unstable because it is too polarized. The axiom "my partner is good, my family is bad," holds until the partner disappoints or (less likely) the family comes through. Given the either/or structure of this paradigm, the alliances are defined as mutually exclusive, and require a Hobson's choice that can lead to violence.

Our goal is to shift the terms of these competing relationships from "either/or" to "both–and" so that one kind of love does not preclude another. To this end, we challenge the fixity of the negatively described family of origin by exploring alternative, more positive explanations for parental failures, and by opening space for good memories to co-exist with the bad. We also use coaching to change the current parent-child relationship patterns, and, when indicated, we include the family of origin in the therapy sessions.

This work is not only useful in reducing the risk of violence; it also plays a part in freeing the woman from her "addictive" inability to give up the abusive relationship. This is because it addresses the power of the redemptive aspects of the abusive cycle, which keep the woman hypnotized. In the powerful bid for forgiveness that follows a violent episode, the man engages in a dramatic act of reparation, which recaptures the woman's loyalty by implicitly addressing the injuries of childhood as well as the current circumstance.

Irma, for example, reported that her husband's violent physical abuse reminded her, oddly enough, of her mother's verbal and emotional style. Since she had been unable to find a way toward her mother that did not include accepting a disturbingly negative view of herself, she had cut off relations with her entirely. Now, in her relationship with her husband, a man who had hospitalized her twice because of his violent beatings, her most positive image of herself is summoned up when he begs her forgiveness for what he has done, begs her acceptance of his need for her, begs her recognition of his divided nature, and begs her largesse in the face of his remorse. At this moment, as the reaffiliation tide of their alliance is summoned, she feels a profound sense of reparation. As she explored the meaning of this experience and the way it kept her bonded to him against her better judgment, she said, "My mother never changed, never understood how deeply she hurt me, never apologized to me!" Over the course of therapy, which included coaching her to change her relationship (and her beliefs) about her mother, Irma became less vulnerable to her partner's desperate apologies, and eventually left him.

In another case, we were able to loosen the romantic grip of the man's remorse by connecting it to his experience with his father. Through careful questioning, we learned that Kent would drive himself into violence because of a need to "hit rock bottom," after which he could feel truly close to his wife. In pulling apart the strands of this odd paradigm, we learned that the only time he could feel bonded to his father was when he confessed to some major inadequacy or transgression. Then, "Because I was more vulnerable than my father, he would be wonderful. He would make everything feel all right and be like a rock for me." Hearing this, his wife said, "For the first time I understand why he has to push things all the way to physical violence. That's the only way he can feel so completely disgusted with himself that he can take some comfort from me."

CONCLUSION

In this project we have attempted to penetrate the infrastructure of relationships in which men are violent toward women. We have found that, for these couples, abuse and coercion co-exist with understanding and friendship in a unique and painful way. When the paradoxical terms of this gendered bond are clarified and critiqued, the freedom to change the terms of the relationship or to leave it behind becomes possible.

599

REFERENCES

1. Anonymous. A battered woman's story: My seduction into abuse. *Journal of Feminist Family Therapy 1* (2): 63-79, 1989.

2. Bayes, M. Wife battering and the maintenance of gender roles: A sociopsychological perspective. In E. Howell & M. Bayes (eds.), *Women and mental health.* New York: Basic Books, 1981.

3. Benjamin, J. *The bonds of love: Psychoanalysis, feminism and the problem of domination.* New York: Pantheon Books, 1988.

4. Bograd, M. Family systems approaches to wife battering: A feminist critique. *American Journal of Orthopsychiatry 54:* 558-568, 1984.

5. Chodorow, N. *The reproduction of mothering.* Berkeley: University of California Press, 1978.

6. Coleman, K.H. Conjugal Violence: What 33 Men Report. *Journal of Marital and Family Therapy 6:* 207–213, 1980.

7. Dimen, M. *Sexual contradictions.* New York: Macmillan, 1986.

8. Sinkelhor, D., Gelles, R.J., Hotaling, G.T., & Straus, N.A. (eds.), *The dark side of families: Current family violence research.* Beverly Hills CA: Sage Publications, 1983.

9. Fogel, G. Being a Man. In G. Fogel, F. Lane, & R. Liebert (eds.), *The psychology of men.* New York: Basic Books, 1986.

10. Geffner, R. *Family violence bulletin.* Tyler TX: Family Violence Research and Treatment Program, University of Texas at Tyler, see all issues.

11. Giles-Sims, J. *Wife battering: A systems theory approach.* New York: Guilford Press, 1983.

12. Gilligan, C. *In a different voice.* Cambridge: Harvard University Press, 1982.

13. Girard, R. *Violence and the sacred.* Baltimore: John's Hopkins University Press, 1986.

14. Gondolf, E. Fighting for control: A clinical assessment of men who batter. *Social Casework 66:* 48–54, 1985.

15. Greenson, R. Dis–identifying from mother: Its special importance to the boy. *International Journal of Psychoanalysis 49:* 370–374, 1968.

16. Goldner, V. Feminism and family therapy. *Family Process 24:* 31–47, 1985.

17. ———. Warning: Family therapy may be hazardous to your health. *Family Therapy Networker 9*(6): 18–23, 1985.

18. Johnson, M. Fathers, mothers and sextyping. *Sociological Inquiry 45:* 15–26, 1975.

19. Jordan, J., & Surrey, J. The self-in-relation: Empathy and the mother daughter relationship. In T. Bernay & D. Cantor (eds.), *The psychology of today's woman.* Hillsdale NJ: The Analytic Press, 1986.

20. Lane, G., & Russel, T. Second-order systemic work with violent couples. In L. Ceasar & K. Hamberger (eds.), *Treating men who batter: Theory, practice, and programs.* New York: Springer, 1989.

21. Men Stopping Violence. *Confronting male privilege, ensuring woman's survival/safety/rights.* Atlanta GA, 1989.

22. Miller, J. *Toward a new psychology of women.* Boston: Beacon Press, 1976.

23. Osherson, S. *Finding our fathers.* New York: The Free Press, 1986.

24. Penn, P. Feed forward: Future questions, future maps. *Family Process 24:* 299–310, 1985.

25. Pressman, B. Wife abused couples: The need for comprehensive theoretical per-

spectives and integrated treatment models. *Journal of Feminist Family Therapy* 1(1): 23–45, 1989.

26. Rubin, G. The traffic in women: Notes on the political economy of sex. In R. Reiter (ed.), *Toward an anthropology of women*. New York: Monthly Review Press, 1978.

27. Sheinberg, M. Obsessions/counter-obsessions: A construction/reconstruction of meaning. *Family Process 27:* 305–316, 1988.

28. Simon, R. (ed.). Special feature: Family violence (several articles). *Family Therapy Networker 10*(3): 20–69, 1986.

29. Stoller, R. *Sexual excitement*. New York: Pantheon Books, 1979.

30. Strauss, M. Sexuality, inequality, cultural norms and wife beating. *Victimology 1:* 54–69, 1976.

31. Swift, C. Women and violence: Breaking the connection. *Stone Center for Developmental Services and Studies* (Wellesley MA), No. 27, 1987.

32. Walker, L. *The battered woman*. New York: Harper & Row, 1979.

33. Young, I. Is male gender identity the cause of male domination? In J. Treblicot (ed.), *Mothering: Essays in feminist theory*. Totowa NJ: Rowman and Allanheld, 1984.

34. Yllo, K., & Bograd, M. *Feminist perspectives on wife abuse*. Beverly Hills CA: Sage Publications, 1989.

PART X

POSTSCRIPT
A Postmodern Moment

SKIPPING STONE
Circles in the Pond

Mary Gergen

JULIA KRISTEVA: "EVERY ... TEXT IS THE ABSORPTION AND TRANSFORMATION OF OTHER TEXTS."[1]

Every voice is the absorption and transformation of other voices. No one speaks alone. One speaks as many, but not all. I then am and are, and are not. I, then, am many, in this finishing touch, the epilogue.

The flow of discourse swirls among us. How do we enter the stream? Some profess as if knowledge flows from pitchers into cups, conveyed from one server to the next. Others say it travels in circles, simultaneously, mutually, giving sensations of sound and motion reverberating, to create more than one experience. Some say it is a symphony of sound, others say its a damn racket!

This text is as a skipping stone, flung along a pond, and as it skips and sinks, it makes circles that ripple to the shores. Where do all these ripplings go? Meanings fragmented and made whole. Sounds—harmonious and dissident—echo and collide in ripples, foam-up and blend into chambers far from home.

The Circles: Intersecting the Social onstructionist Moment with the Feminist Forever.

We are intersecting: inter-*sex*-ion . . . a mutabil-ing of differences, sexual and otherwise, a blending, converging, and complexifying—a conundrum of possibilities, losing clear identity and stable purpose in the converging traffic; becoming, all together, and going out beyond, where we have not dared to go before: it is a risky business, and pleasure.

Postmodern feminist, circle merging with circle, traveling as one on a Mobius strip, with more twist than a Philadelphia pretzel—an endless turning of possible divines. What future can we share?

It is fast company; our reputations are at risk. French philosophers, Lacanian lounge lizards, Foucaultian for(a)gers, Queer choirs, and Straight compatriots, High theory culties, Lionized leftists, Night-marching matriarchs, Political polly-technicians—all barreling down the road at outrageous speeds.

Oh, the good ol' days, when we could see forever, high above this motley crew, where "hot air" kept our balloons aloft. Eternity and the world below us. Wasn't that grand? We've had to leave that Godtrick, as Donna Haraway said, to those who claim a "vision from everywhere and nowhere, equally and fully."[2] We're just stuck staring through glasses spattered with the mud and minutia of the millennia. Forever's fogged up. The rose colored glasses have lost their tint.

606

As a postmodern post-ette, Ellen Rosenau has said: "Postmodernism questions, causality, determinism, egalitarianism, humanism, liberal democracy, necessity, objectivity, rationality, responsibility, and truth."[3] How can a feminist deal with that? What more could one despise, or wish for?

What have these feminists traded for, in this interchange? As modernists, in the limelight, we stood with the beacons of Enlightenment, illuminated in our quest. Our cow ELECTRIC. In this trade we've pulled our own plug, and now embrace the darkness, empty, vast, and full of strange sounds.

Some think its a Jack and the Beanstalk deal. A handful of beans, for a living, breathing neonic cow. How Now, Brown Cow? What do you have to say for yourself?

And what about this new stairway to the stars? The Constructionist Causeway. We're offered a spiraling, spindly kitetale on which to balance our act, to situate ourselves firmly in midair, on a swinging bean stalk. Is this worth giving up the promises of impartial truth and law, foundational methods, and accumulations of facts? Can we accept, as Jane Flax has declared, that "Ultimately nothing justifies our claims, beyond each person's desire and the discursive practices in which these are developed, embedded, and legitimated."?[4]

Yet, some of us are spellbound too. Words bind us in their spell? Starry-

GERGEN

eyed, wanting to throw over the dull and straight and narrow paths set down before us, can we not grab for the ring?

Brass-filled knuckles—they have a certain grip on us as well.

Lets say yes, but its a High Anxiety situation. There is much to criticize, And we've all done our share.

Craig Owens added to the drama: "Few women have engaged in the modernism postmodernism debate . . . postmodernism may be another masculine invention engineered to exclude women."[5]

But we could fix that.

The pm framework is so bare . . . skeletons on parade. It is too lean for our tastes. Feminist social constructionists offer some meat for those bones. Something to hang on it, . . . but we simply won't be "hangers on."

Do we talk in circles? Is that all we can do? Can we even do that? Enveloped within language communities, our words skittering by one another. Words may sound the same, but can they ever be heard as such? Words swing and sway to new makings in each separate clime.

How do we talk aloud ? Can we speak for others? Can others speak for us? What are we saying? Can we keep track? What track can we keep? If we tear up the tracks can we still find a way?

Pastiche personality Beryl C. Curt has said: "Language which flows naturally and easily must always in a 'climate of problematization,' arouse suspicion. Its very ease and fluidity helps to beguile the reader into believing the text is merely mirroring the world 'as it really is,' and obscures its ability to glamour that reality into being." (14)[6]

Turning about, searching for my tale, I plead guilty as well, I wish to glamour a reality into being, spreading glitter, mascara, and rouge, preening these words into worlds. And yet, PAUSE, I am roughing up the language, sandpapering the sense, as well. You may well step with caution.

Trouble can be good. As Jane Flax argues: "The single most important advance in feminist theory is that the existence of gender relations has been problematized."[7]

So the conversation continues. But in a world of surging circles, isn't that our salvation? Not everyone agrees.

There's a Stop sign in the Traffic Circle— someone wants to know if we have a license to **practice** these words. What happened to practice? We can't sit around all day talking. Things happen, don't they? Talk is cheap, they say Actions speak louder than words. In a word. . . .

WHERE HAVE ALL THE POLITICS GONE?

Have they vanished? Suspicion looms: How can we sue in the name of justice, on the basis of our sex, when sex is only someone's construction any more, and justice just a name? How can deconstruction be our friend? With friends like that, who needs enemies? Some whisper, "even if everything is only socially constructed, why not just keep it our little secret? What good would it be to tell the world." How many of us are closet constructionists? When are we going to have an outing?

Jane Flax, from the backseat: "We need to learn ways of making claims about and acting upon injustice without transcendental guarantees or illusions of innocence."[8]

We agree with Jane.

We could give up modernist versions of truth, objectivity and a single knowable reality. We could learn to love RELATIVITY—perhaps.

All conversation stops when this trick is pulled . . . is she the devil in drag? Horns a-plenty or plenty horny. What is to be done with her?

Everybody knows that a "relativist" believes the most outlandish things- Every explanation is as good as another; all things are equal. The moon is made of cheese. The Earth is flat. Man comes from monkeys. . . . World War II did not occur.

But where, the enemy asks, does the equal sign come from? Smuggled in from the contraband caravan?? A Rhetorical Trick . . . who would survive the toll of that blast?

Reject the sign. Nothing is equal. There are many stories and many contexts; How shall I compare them? . . . again, many stories and many contexts.

If you didn't have foundations, relativism could not exist. No attack without foundations.

Who ever wonders about the costs of a foundationalist metatheory? Why is it evil to doubt one's own world view? Is it possible that Certainty is the real devil around here? Is not the God's eye view the enemy?

Do we know who was right, for sure, in Vietnam, or Nagasaki, or Berlin? Is it always a good question to ask? How have those in power used Absolute truth and goodness to tie their nation's youth up in tourniquet knots?

Perhaps we need a new entry into the DSM IV—DAS—Descartes' Anxiety Syndrome. The symptoms include existential angst, fear of chaos, and melancholia for the loss of foundational principles.

Are there cures for this dis-ease? Consider:

Patti Lather, "Relativity has been put forth as the great bugbear against which we must commit to some foundational absolute if anarchy and chaos are not to descend upon us . . . such claims are cultural dominants which masquerade as natural, rational, necessary, but which are less a fact of nature than of human production. They are, in spite of their denial, embedded in... the power/knowledge nexus which provides the constraints and possibilities of discourse."[9]

Feminists may not jive to relativism, but they do not blanch at uncertainty. We can live without all this security. Foundations have never been much protection to the dis-staffed.

Lets lighten up. Get practical, move into circles of action.

Where are the roads taking us?

A new breed of scholar has recently arrived on the scene. Called the Empiricist Social Constructionist, they have evolved by taking "the best" from both worlds—the empirical and the social constructionist. By winnowing the wheat of social constructionist theory from the chaff of the metaphysical, they take social constructionist theory and prove it with data. Here are: "13 ways of looking at an ESC."[10] Where do you see your shadow?

1. All things are socially constructed, except history
2. All things are socially constructed, except my emotions and personal experiences.
3. All social things are social constructions, but "material conditions" are not.
4. All social things are social constructions, but "spiritual reality" is not.
5. All societal things are social constructions, but natural things like rocks are not. (here toe stubbing is mentioned quite often, or sometimes running into walls)
6. Gender roles are socially constructed, but biological categories, like males and females, are not.
7. Objects are socially constructed, but facts are not.
8. Everything is socially constructed, but social constructionism is not.
9. Some things are socially constructed and somethings aren't. You don't know until you do an experiment on them.
10. Scientists using empirical methods can prove whether or not social constructionist theories are true.
11. There's a grain of truth in the notion, but they just go too far.
12. Some of my best friends are social constructionists.
13. I like what I hear, if only I could read that weird stuff.

609

We cannot stop our journey here. Rather, we must follow the path of the untried and untrue. Entering this new zone, things are a bit strange. Some might say bizarre. Yet, colors on the rim of the world are glowing. They beckon and invite. Lets follow the trail a bit further.

What if we take all the challenges together?

GERGEN

that language is not a transparent representation of the world

that realities are cultural constructions

the polarities do not exist in nature, but in language

that facts are neither true nor false, except by the ordination of the social groups involved.

that we must apply values via a leap of faith alone

that political actions are deeds of faith

that identity and knowledge are critically dependent upon interaction to be created, and are partial, fragmented, and temporary

What does this bode for future feminist inquiry?

We can

Critique: de-mystifying old knowledge, destabilizing old systems, undermining foundational assumptions and a priori statements,

Re-spect: nothing valued from the past must be jettisoned. Not experiments, statistics, or observational designs, as long as we do not mistake their evidence for trails to truth.

Invent: Possibilities for new conversations, new interchanges, new interpretations, new actions.

Commit: the Big C word finds its resting place again. This time, it's a dangerous enterprise. One commits without the consolations of certainty. One dares commitment; one accepts the risks. If we value equality, or nurturing, or assertiveness, or any other stance, we must stand up and be counted, even as we accept that there are no foundations to defend us, except the willingness of others to share our visions and our dreams.

Play: with the notion of the relational as the core of the enterprise. If we are created and create through engagement in the world around us, and within us, then our identities and subjectivities, our values and preferences are linked to these interactions. "I am you" or "I am via you" or "we are, together." Feminist/social constructionism alters ways of living, working, loving life and each other in the tenor of each day.

Diana Whitney describes the social constructionist in the realm of spirituality: "A social constructionist view claims relatedness as the organizing principle for life. . . . This shift implies a movement from the view of spiritual development as a possession of the individual, to a view of spiritual development as a quality of relationship: first, one's relationship with spirit, . . . and then with a web of other relationships, . . . people, plants, and animals."[11]

Patti Lather: " The issue is not so much where poststructuralism comes from, but what it will be."[12]

Let's all be there together.

NOTES

1. Semiotike.

2. Haraway, Donna (1 988). Situated knowledges: The science question in feminism and the privilege of partial perspective. *Feminist Studies, 14*, 575.

3. Rosenau, Ellen (1 992). *Postmodernism and the social sciences*. Princeton, NJ,. Princeton University Press. (5). I

4. Flax, Jane (1990). *Thinking Fragments* (127).

5. Owens, Craig (1983) The discourse of others, feminists and postmodernism. In

Hal Foster (Ed.) *The anti-aesthetic, essays on postmodern culture.* Port Townsend, WA: Bay Press. (61)

6. *Textuality and tectonics. Troubling social and psychological science.* Open University Press collective author: Beryl C. Curt (no relation to Cyril Burt of course).

7. Flax, Jane (1990). *Thinking Fragments* (27).

8. Flax, Jane (1993). *Disputed Subjects.* (141).

9. Lather, Patti (1991). *Getting smart. Feminist research and pedagogy with/in the post-modern.* York: Routledge. (117).

10. with a tip of the hat to Wallace Stevens for "13 ways of looking at a blackbird."

11. Whitney, Diana (1995). Social constructionism and spirituality. Presented at Global Leadership, A Conference on Social Constructionism and Mangament. Taos Institute. Taos, NM. October, 1995.

12. Lather, Patti (1995). The validity of angels: Intepretive and textual strategies in researching the lives of women with HIV/AIDS. *Qualitative Inquiry, 1,* 41–68.

CONTRIBUTORS

JANIS BOHAN is Professor of Psychology at Metropolitan State College of Denver. Her presentations and publications reflect her interest in women's place in the history of psychology and feminist psychology. She has edited two books, *Re-placing women in psychology: Readings toward a more inclusive history* (2nd ed.; Kendall/Hunt, 1995), and *Seldom seen, rarely heard: Women's place in psychology* (Westview, 1992). She is presently working on a third book to be published by Routledge, *Coming to terms: Psychology, constructionism, and sexual orientation*.

Susan Bordo is Otis A. Singletary Chair in the Humanities and Professor of Philosophy at the University of Kentucky. She is the author of *Unbearable weight: Feminism, Western culture and the body* (1993), *The flight to objectivity: Essays on Cartesianism & culture* (1987), and numerous other writings on gender, culture, philosophy, and the body.

Laura S. Brown is a feminist clinical and forensic psychologist in private practice in Seattle WA, and Clinical Professor of Psychology at the U. of Washington. She has written and taught extensively on topics of feminist therapy theory, ethics, and practice, and on psychotherapy with lesbians. She has been active in organized psychology as a feminist voice since 1973, and was the 1995 recipient of the APA award for Distinguished Professional Contributions to Public Service and the 1995 winner of Distinguished Publication Award of the Association for Women in Psychology for her most recent book, *Subversive dialogues: Theory in feminist therapy.*

Patricia Hill Collins is a professor in the Department of African-American Studies and Sociology at the University of Cincinnati. Her first book, *Black feminist thought: Knowledge, consciousness, and the politics of empowerment,* published in 1990, has won many awards. Her second book, *Race, class, and gender: An anthology* (edited with Margaret Andersen), originally published in 1992 with a second edition in 1995, is widely used in undergraduate classrooms throughout the United States. She is currently completing her third book, tentatively entitled *Fighting words: Knowledge, power and the challenge of black feminist thought,* to be published by the University of Minnesota Press in 1996.

Mary Crawford is Professor of Psychology and Women's Studies at West Chester University, Pennsylvania, and former Director of Women's Studies at the University of South Carolina. She is the co-author of *Women and gender,* (McGraw-Hill), a textbook in the psychology of gender, now in its second edition. Most recently she published *Talking difference: On gender and language* (Sage, 1995). She is currently research director of the Women's College Coalition.

614

Nancy Datan was Professor of Human Development, University of Wisconsin-Green Bay at the time of her death in 1987 from breast cancer. Prior to that, she spent twelve years on the faculty in the Department of Psychology at West Virginia University, where she was instrumental in organizing several conferences on life span developmental psychology and on aging. Her research (With Aaron Antonovsky and Benjamin Maoz) on responses to menopause among five subcultures in Israel was reported in the book *A time to reap.* She perhaps most liked being thought of as an essayist: Her work included published and unpublished personal and professional essays on love, work, and adult development.

Sara N. Davis is an assistant professor in the psychology department at Rosemont College and an active participant in the Women's Studies Program. Her research in the areas of reader response theory and creativity have appeared in a number of books and journals. "Creativity as purposeful work: The evolving systems approach" will appear in *Creativity research handbook* (Hampton Press, 1996). She is a member of the Philadelphia Women's Studies Consortium.

Michelle Fine is Professor of Psychology at the City University of New York Graduate Center and the Senior Consultant at the Philadelphia Schools Collaborative. Her recent publications include *Chartering urban school reform: Reflections on public high schools in the midst of change* (1994), *Beyond silenced voices: Class, race and gender in American schools* (1992), *Disruptive voices: The transgressive possibilities of feminist research* (1992), and *Framing dropouts: Notes on the politics of an urban high school* (1991).

Jane Flax is Professor of Political Science at Howard University and a psychotherapist in Chevy Chase, Maryland. Her papers on feminism, psychoanalysis, philosophy and political theory have appeared in a number of books and journals. She is the author of *Thinking fragments: Psychoanalysis, feminism, and postmodernism in the contemporary west* (University of California Press, 1990) and *Disputed subject* (Routledge, 1993).

Margery Franklin is Roy E. Larsen Professor of Psychology at Sarah Lawrence College, and a past president of Division 10, Psychology and the Arts, of the American Psychological Association. She co-edited *Development and the arts: Critical perspectives,* with Bernard Kaplan in 1994, to which she contributed a chapter, "Narratives of change and continuity: Women artist reflect on their work." She also co-edited *Developmental processes: Selected writings of Heinz Werner,* and *Child language: A reader,* both with Sybil Barten. Her current work centers on two projects: A collaborative study of baby biographies of the 19th and early 20th century; and an extension of her study of women artists' work.

615

Nicola Gavey is a Lecturer in Clinical Psychology at the University of Auckland, New Zealand. Her research interests center on feminist poststructuralist analyses of rape and sexual coercion within heterosexual relationships.

Mary Gergen is an associate professor in the Department of Psychology at Pennsylvania State University, the Delaware County Campus, and an affiliate of the Women's Studies program. Author of several textbooks, and journal articles on feminist topics in psychology, and editor of *Feminist thought and the structure of knowledge* (New York University Press, 1988), her interests also include studies of personal life narratives. She is a member of the editorial board of *Feminism & Psychology,* and a founding member of the Taos Institute, a consulting group involved with applying social constructionist ideas to family therapy, organizational behavior and other professional practices.

Tom Gerschick is a sociologist at Illinois State University. He does research and publishes in the areas of masculinity, multicultural teaching, and industrial relations. When he is not busy being an academic, he enjoys battling the misguided policies and practices of the 104th U.S. Congress.

Virginia Goldner is· on the senior faculty of the American Institute for

Family Therapy where she is co-director of the gender and violence project. She has published widely and presented around the world on issues of gender and power in intimate life. She was recently appointed to the Board of Directors of the premier journal of family therapy, *Family Process,* where she was described as "one of our field's most widely cited authors and a leading voice for an approach that incorporates systematic, feminist and psychoanalytic thinking with a post-modern social constructionist perspective."

Rachel T. Hare-Mustin is a feminist theorist and clinical psychologist who has taught at Harvard, University of Pennsylvania, and Villanova. Her articles on feminism, post-modern theory, psychotherapy, and professional ethics have appeared in a number of books and journals. She is co-editor with Jeanne Marecek of *Making a difference: Psychology and the construction of gender* (Yale, 1990).

Pierrette Hondagneu-Sotelo is assistant professor of sociology at the University of Southern California, where she also teaches in the Program for the Study of Women and Men in Society, and in the American studies and Chicano/Latino Studies program. She is the author of *Gendered transitions: Mexican experiences of immigration* (University of California Press, 1994). She is currently interviewing employers of domestic workers in Los Angeles.

bell hooks is the pen name for Gloria Watkins, a writer, teacher, and film critic, who speaks widely on issues of race, class, and gender. Her previous books are *Ain't I a woman: Black women and feminism; Feminist theory from margin to center; Talking back: Thinking feminist thinking black;* and *Yearning: Race, gender, and cultural politics,* all published by South End Press of Boston.

Dafna N. Izraeli is Professor of Sociology at Bar-Ilan University, Israel. Her recent books included *Dual-earner families: International perspectives* (with Susan Lewis and Helen Hootsmans, Sage, 1992); *Sociological studies of women in Israel* (with Yael Axmon, Transaction Press, 1993) and *Competitive frontiers: A global perspective on women in management* (with Nancy Adler, Blackwell, 1994).

Michael S. Kimmel is Professor of Sociology at SUNY at Stony Brook. His books include *Men confront pornography* (Crown, 1990), (Beacon, 1992), *Changing men* (Sage, 1987), *Men's lives* (3rd edition, Allyn and Bacon, 1995), *The politics of manhood* (Temple University Press, 1995), and *Burdens of proof: A history of manhood in America* (Free Press, 1995). He is editor of a book series on men and masculinity at University of California Press, a research annual at Sage Publications, and the scholarly journal *masculinities.* He is also spokesperson for the National Organization for Men against Sexism (NOMAS).

Celia Kitzinger is director of Women's studies in the Department of Social Sciences, Loughborough University, England. She is an Associate Editor of the international journal, *Feminism and Psychology,* and has written widely on feminist issues. Her books include: *The social construction of lesbianism* (Sage, 1987); *Changing our minds: Lesbian feminism and psychology* (with Rachel Perkins, New York University Press, 1993); and *Heterosexuality* (with Sue Wilkinson, Sage, 1993). Her most recent book (co-edited with Sue Wilkinson) is *Feminism and discourse: Psychological perspectives* (Sage, in press).

M. Brinton Lykes is Associate Professor of Psychology at the School of Education of Boston College. For the past ten years she has worked with rural Guatemalan health promoters in action research projects with child and youth survivors of state-sponsored violence and war. Her research on human rights and mental health and cultural constructions of women's notions of self have appeared in a number of books and journals. Her most recent co-edited volume is *Unmasking social inequalities; Victim, voices and change* (Temple University Press).

Jeanne Marecek is Professor of Psychology at Swarthmore College, where she teaches courses concerning abnormal psychology, feminist theory, and the psychology of gender. She has published papers on feminism, postmodern theory, and gender in a number of books and journals. Her current work focuses on how popular and "scientific" narratives of suicide and other distressed behavior serve to reinstate and subvert normative gender, age, class, and ethnic relations in Sri Lanka. She is co-editor, with Rachel Hare-Mustin, of *Making a difference: Psychology and the construction of gender* (Yale University Press, 1990).

617

Michael A. Messner is Associate professor in the Department of Sociology and the Program for the Study of Women and Men in Society at the University of Southern California. He is co-editor of *Men's lives* (Allyn & Bacon, 1995) and *Sport, men, and the gender order: Critical feminist perspectives* (Human Kinetics, 1990). He has authored *Power at play: Sports and the problem of masculinity* (Beacon Press, 1992), and co-authored *Sex, violence, and the power in sports; Rethinking masculinity* (The Crossing Press, 1994).

Lesley Miles is engaged in a Masters degree in clinical psychology at the University of Cape Town. This is in the context of a career change from English literature/teaching to psychology. Her current research is on the topic of masculinity, sexual negotiation and HIV. She has published articles, poetry and short fiction in various books and journals. She is at present enjoying the late mothering of a daughter, Julia.

Adam Stephen Miller is a graduate student in journalism at the University of Michigan. His research focuses on people with disabilities, including the persistence of media stereotypes of them and how actual people with disabilities handle the ideological demands of contemporary American society.

Lama Abu Odeh received her doctoral degree in Juridical Sciences at Harvard Law School. She has also studied at the Universities of Jordan, Bristol and York. She is a feminist activist and a founding member of a Women's Studies Center in Jordan.

Susan Oyama is Professor of Psychology at John Jay College and Graduate School of the City University of New York. She wrote *The Ontogeny of Information* and co-authored (and co-edited, under the collective pen name John Klama) *Aggression: The myth of the beast within.* Her work on development, evolution and the nature-nurture problem is multidisciplinary in character and has been published in journals and edited volumes in a wide range of fields, including biology, psychology, philosophy, anthropology, and women's studies. She is particularly interested in ethical and political aspects of scientific work.

Mary Brown Parlee is currently a Visiting Professor at the Women's Studies Program of the Massachusetts Institute of Technology, and was formerly a Professor of Psychology at the Graduate School and University Center of the City University of New York. She has written extensively about women's health issues within the social constructionist realm, and in particular about the menstrual cycle and PMS. Parlee is a Past President of the Division of the Psychology of Women, American Psychological Association.

Peggy Penn, the Director of Training and Education at the Ackerman Institute for Family Therapy from 1985 to 1992, now teaches throughout the USA and Europe. Currently she supervises at the Ackerman Institute in New York City. She has co-authored, *"Milan systemic therapy; Conversations in theory and practice,"* with Luigi Boscolo, Gian Franco Cecchin, and Lynn Hoffman. She has written on chronic illness, consultation, the use of the future as a therapeutic modality, circular questioning, and recently, with Marilyn Frankfurt, on the use of writing in family therapy: "Creating a participant text: Writing, multiple voices and narrative multiplicity." She is also a poet. Her most recent publication was in the *Paris Review,* July, 1994.

Marcia Sheinberg is the Director of Training at the Ackerman Institute. She has studied and contributed to the practice and theory of family centered therapy in the areas of chronic illness, violence and incest. The author of numerous articles, Ms. Sheinberg is very interested in the relationship between social constructionism and feminism as it relates to clinical practice and organizational development. She is particularly drawn by the existing tensions between seemingly contradictory ideas and the potential they offer for generating novel therapeutic and community involvement approaches.

Anthropologist Carol Stack does research on rural and urban poverty, migration, family policy, and the social construction of identity, work, and community. She teaches in the Department of Women's Studies and the Graduate

School of Education at the University of California, Berkeley. She is currently completing a book at the Russell Sage Foundation, *Why work?, The meaning
and dignity of work in the lives of minority youth* (with K. Newman). She has also
written *Call to home: African-Americans reclaim the rural south (1996)* and *All our
kin: Strategies for survival in a black community* (1974).

A New York City native, Leonore Tiefer (Ph.D., 1969) studied physiological psychology at University of California, Berkeley, later respecializing in
clinical psychology. She became a feminist voice in sexology, articulating how
sexuality is determined by sociocultural forces. In the '80's and '90's, as researcher and sex therapist (currently Associate Professor of Urology at Mon-
tefiore Medical Center, Bronx, New York), she witnessed the medicalization
of men's sexuality and understood further how social location constructs the
meaning and experience of sexuality. She recently published *Sex is not a natural act and other essays* (Westview Press).

Barrie Thorne, Professor of Sociology and Women's Studies at the University of California, Berkeley, is the author of *Gender play; Girls and boys in school*
(Rutgers, 1993) and co-editor of *Rethinking the family: Some feminist questions*
(1992) and *Language, gender and society* (1983). As a member of an interdisci-
nary research network funded by the MacArthur Foundation, she is currently
working on a comparative study of urban childhoods, focusing on issues of
social class, ethnicity, and gender.

Gillian Walker is co-director with Virginia Goldner of Ackerman's Gender
and Violence Project. As director of Ackerman's Families, Attention Disorders
and Learning Disabilities Project, she is interested in the interface between
neurobiology and human behavior. Her clinical interests and published articles and books are in the areas of violence, single parenting, learning disabilities, gay and lesbian issues, AIDS and chronic illness.

619

Valerie Walkerdine is Professor of the Psychology of Communication in
the Department of Media and Communication, Goldsmiths College, University of London. Her research and writings on gender, development and psychology have been widely published. Her last book, *Schoolgirl fictions* was published by Verso and her next volume *Young girls and popular culture* was published by Macmillan.

Margaret Wetherell is a Senior Lecturer in Psychology in the Social Sciences Facility, Open University, United Kingdom. She is the author (with
Jonathan Potter) of *Discourse and social psychology* (London: Sage) and *Mapping
the language of racism* (London: Harvester Wheatsheaf). Her research interests
involve the application of discourse theory and method to issues of 'race' and
gender and she is currently working on a project on discourses of masculinity
(with Nigel Edley). Their book *Men in perspective: Practice, power and identity*

was published by Prentice-Hall, 1995. She was a founding member of the editorial group for the journal *Feminism and Psychology*.

Sue Wilkinson teaches Social Psychology and Women's Studies at Loughborough University, U.K. She is the founding and current editor of *Feminism & Psychology: An International Journal,* and the book series *Gender and Psychology: Feminist and Critical Perspectives* (Both Sage Publications Ltd.). Her most recent books include *Heterosexuality: A feminism & psychology reader* (1993) and *Feminism and discourse: Psychological perspectives* (1995)—both co-edited with Celia Kitzinger, and published by Sage. Her current research interests include challenges to heterosexual identities and women's experiences of breast cancer.

COPYRIGHT PERMISSIONS

Michelle Fine. (1988). Sexuality, schooling, and adolescent females: The missing discourse of desire. *Harvard Educational Review, 58*, 29–53.

Jane Flax. (1993). Forgotten forms of close combat: Mothers and daughters revisited. *Disputed Subjects*, 59–71. New York: Routledge.

Nicola Gavey. (1989). Feminist poststructuralism and discourse analysis: Contributions to feminist psychology. *Psychology of Women Quarterly, 13*, 459–475.

Mary M. Gergen. (1992). Life stories: Pieces of a dream. In George Rosenwald & Richard Ochberg (Eds.). *Storied lives*, 127–144. New Haven: Yale University Press.

Thomas J. Gerschick & Adam Stephen Miller. (1994). Gender identities at the crossroads of masculinity and physical disability. *Masculinities, 2*, 34–55.

Virginia Goldner, Peggy Penn, Marcia Sheinberg, & Gillian Walker. (1990). Love and violence: Gender paradoxes in volatile attachments. *Family Process, 29*, 343–364.

Rachel Hare-Mustin. (1994). Discourse in the mirrored room: A postmodern analysis of therapy. *Family Process, 33*, 199–236.

bell hooks. (1989). feminist politicization: a comment. *Talking back*, 105–112, Boston: South End Press.

Pierrette Hondagneu-Sotelo & Michael Messner. (1994). Gender displays and men's power: The "New Man" and the Mexican immigrant man. In Harry Brod & Michael Kaufman (Eds.) *Theorizing masculinities*, 200–219. London: Sage.

Dafna Izraeli. (1993). They have eyes and see not. Gender politics in the Diaspora Museum. *Psychology of Women Quarterly, 17*, 515–523.

Michael S. Kimmel. (1994). Masculinity as homophobia. In Harry Brod & Michael Kaufman (Eds.). *Theorizing masculinities*, 119–141. London: Sage Press.

Celia Kitzinger & Sue Wilkinson. (1994). Virgins and queers: Rehabilitating heterosexuality. *Gender & Society, 8*, 444–463.

M. Brinton Lykes. (1989). Dialogue with Guatemalan Indian women: Critical perspectives on constructing collaborative research. In Rhoda Unger (Ed.) *Representations: Social constructions of gender*, 167–185. Amityville, New York: Baywood Publishing Company.

Jeanne Marecek. (1993). Disappearances, silences, and anxious rhetoric: Gender in abnormal psychology textbooks. *Journal of Theoretical and Philosophical Psychology, 13*, 114–124.

Michael A. Messner. (1992). Like family: Power, intimacy, and sexuality in male athletes' friendships. In Peter M. Nardi (Ed.) *Men's friendships*, 215–237. Newbury Park, CA: Sage.

Lesley Miles. (1993). Women, AIDS, and power in heterosexual sex. A discourse analysis. *Women's International Forum, 16*, 497–511.

622

Lama Abu Odeh. (1993). Post-colonial feminism and the veil. Thinking the difference. *Feminist Review*. No. 43, 26–37.

Susan Oyama. (1991). Essentialism, women and war: Protesting too much, protesting too little. In A. E. Hunter (Ed.), *Genes and Gender VI. On Peace, War, and Gender: A Challenge to Genetic Explanation*, 64–76. New York: Feminist Press.

Mary Brown Parlee. (1992). Feminism and psychology. In Sue Rosenberg & Janice Gordon-Kelter (Eds.). *Revolutions in knowledge: Feminism in the social sciences*, 33–56. Boulder, CO: Westview Press.

Barrie Thorne. (1990). Children and gender: Constructions of difference. In Deborah Rhode (Ed.) *Theoretical perspectives in sexual difference*, 100–113. New Haven: Yale University Press.

Valerie Walkerdine. (1989). Femininity as performance. *Oxford Review of Education, 15*, no. 3.

Margaret Wetherell. (1986). Linguistic repertoires and literary criticism: New directions for a social psychology of gender. In Sue Wilkinson (Ed.). *Feminist social psychology*, 77–95. London: Sage.

623

INDEX